We Shall Suffer There

We Shall Suffer There
Hong Kong's Defenders Imprisoned, 1942–45

Tony Banham

Hong Kong University Press
The University of Hong Kong
Pok Fu Lam Road
Hong Kong
https://hkupress.hku.hk

© 2009 Tony Banham

ISBN 978-962-209-960-9 (*Hardback*)

All rights reserved. No portion of this publication may be reproduced or transmitted in any form or by any means, electronic or mechanical, including photocopy, recording, or any information storage or retrieval system, without prior permission in writing from the publisher.

British Library Cataloguing-in-Publication Data
A catalogue record for this book is available from the British Library.

Digitally printed

Contents

Illustrations	vii
Preface	ix
Acknowledgements	xi
Abbreviations	xv
Notes on the Rolls of Honour	xix
Introduction	1
Capture	3
1942	21
1943	107
1944	153
1945	187
Release	243
Appendices	245
Notes	285
Bibliography and Sources	327
Index	333

Illustrations

Plate section, after p. 19

1. Barbara Redwood on 25 December 1941 near Government House
2. British and Indian POWs captured at Shing Mun
3. Captured Indian Soldiers being disarmed at Argyle Street
4. Official notice to John Idwal Morris's family
5. Interior of Bowen Road Hospital
6. Interior of Tweed Bay Hospital
7. Shamshuipo POW Camp
8. Montage of some of those lost as POWs
9. Posthumous notice of awards to Robert Douglas
10. Carving by Sergeant John Payne
11. US civilian repatriates on the *Gripsholm*
12. Montage of those who survived
13. All POW camps in Japan known to have held ex-HK POWs
14. The mine entrance at Omine
15. Sketch of Oeyama
16. Concert programme from Omori
17. Yoshima coal mine
18. Innoshima
19. James Rogers' pass, from Narumi
20. POWs at Sumidagawa
21. Canadian POWs at Sendai
22. The ashes of the twenty-seven POWs killed by the bombardment of *Kamaishi*
23. Portuguese POWs at Sendai
24. Fushiki/Nomachi (Nagoya #10B) at Liberation
25. The lost B24s: *Ginny* and *Les Miserables*
26. Shamshuipo Camp "N" officers receive their injections at liberation
27. Amputees drink to their health at Liberation
28. Osaka POW Repatriation team
29. Captain H. G. Camp, RA, suffering from severe malnutrition
30. Hangar deck ready for RAPWIs on HMS *Colossus*

31. USS *Goodhue*
32. HMS *Implacable*
33. Eric Bromley and Arthur Deadman (HKDDC) in Victoria, BC, Canada
34. Welcome home from the King, sent to John Idwal Morris
35. A work party from Kobe
36. North Point POW Camp
37. Shamshuipo POW Camp
38. Ma Tau Chung POW Camp
39. Argyle Street POW Camp
40. Stanley Internment Camp

Preface

Following the publication of *Not the Slightest Chance* — a work that studied the Battle of Hong Kong in great detail, and the deaths of all those lost in the fighting — a number of organizations and individuals suggested that I might like to produce a companion volume covering the Hong Kong garrison's experience in the remaining years before liberation.

Initially I hesitated. My worry was that the four main themes of such a work — hunger, boredom, disease, and death — would hardly be conducive to a good read. Worse, the story itself, covering at least sixty different POW camps and the deaths of some 2,500 men and women, would be distractingly fragmented.

The story of the *Lisbon Maru* stuck out as being a classic three-act tale, so I tackled that first. Hong Kong University Press published the resulting work, *The Sinking of the Lisbon Maru*, in 2006. With that out of the way, the picture became clearer. With further thought, I realized that if I reserved for a future volume the story of Hong Kong's irregular units (BAAG, the Hong Kong column of the Chindits, Force 136, and so forth), and the escapees and evaders who formed them, then the story of the camps and the internees could be tackled reasonably cohesively.*

This book, therefore, sets out to describe — in their own words as far as possible — the fates of Hong Kong's POWs and Internees from the moment of capture through, for those who survived, to the moments of liberation and homecoming. Space, of course, precludes telling every individual's story, but by covering every camp, every draft to Japan, and every hospital, some idea of each individual's experience should be conveyed; hopefully, the sample documented here can speak for all. As in the first book, each death is examined and reported.

---

* Escapees are mentioned in this book, but the stories related here end at the moment when those involved left the camp (unless they were subsequently recaptured).

For this is not a clinical history of numbered armies and faceless regiments, but of named individuals struggling with starvation and dysentery. This is history drawn from raw human endurance; an intertwining of personal experiences leading to a fuller picture of the movements of this small group — the Hong Kong POWs and Internees — through the confined worlds they perforce inhabited from the surrender to liberation. Hence the title which, as with *Not the Slightest Chance* before, comes from the 1941 statement of Prime Minister Winston Churchill:

> If Japan goes to war there is *not the slightest chance* of holding Hong Kong or relieving it. It is most unwise to increase the loss *we shall suffer there*. (author's emphasis)

Acknowledgements

While the focus of this work is exclusively the fate of Hong Kong's 1941 garrison, it should be noted that a multitude of others: American, Australian, British, Dutch, New Zealand and more, shared the experiences of many of the camps described here. Their suffering was no less, and their contribution to the final victory at least equally valuable.

The following individuals and institutions were kind enough to provide assistance in the creation of this work:

Ex-POWs and Internees

Barbara Anslow, Civilian; Edith Badger (née Mason), Civilian; Dee Dee Bak, Civilian; Solomon Bard, HKVDC; Norman Broadbridge, HKVDC; 'Bunny' Browne, General List; Phil Doddridge, Royal Rifles of Canada; Luba Estes, Civilian; Jack Etiemble, Royal Artillery; Tom 'Taffy' Evans, Middlesex; Gordon Fairclough, Royal Artillery; James Ford, MC, Royal Scots; Ian Forsyth, Punjabis; Major Hancock, Hong Kong Mule Company; James Hart, RASC; Wallace Hastings, Royal Navy; Graham Hill, Middlesex; Rodney Giddins, Royal Artillery; Sir Michael Kadoorie, Civilian; Ross Lynneberg, RNZNVR; George MacDonnel, Royal Rifles of Canada; Thomas Middleton, Royal Navy; Dennis Morley, Royal Scots; Wally Scragg, Hong Kong Police; Edward Shayler, Winnipeg Grenadiers; Grant Shepherd, Royal Navy; Herbert Slaytor, Royal Scots; Ray Smith, Royal Rifles of Canada; Nick Spoov, Civilian; Tony Weller, HKVDC; Peter White, Civilian.

Descendants and Relatives of POWs and Internees

Brian Bromley, son of Ernest Bromley, HKDDC; Sue Butler, daughter of Cyril Mace, Royal Artillery; Isabella Cooper daughter of James Miller, Royal Scots; Suzie Coxhead, daughter of Geoffrey Coxhead, HKVDC; Elizabeth Doery, daughter of Jean Gittins, Civilian; Steve Favell, great nephew of Albert (Bill) Oxley, Middlesex; Michael Ferrier, son of Vivian Ferrier, HKRNVR; Mark Fielding-Smith, grandson of Arthur Betts, Middlesex; Morley Forsyth, son of Tom Forsyth, Winnipeg Grenadiers; Carol Hadley, daughter of Borge Agerbak, Winnipeg Grenadiers; Max Holroyd, son of Maxie Holroyd, RN; Susie Hunter, granddaughter of Arthur Taylor, RN; Richard Goldsbrough, cousin of J. Munro, Royal Artillery; Colin Gordon, son of Vyner Gordon, Royal Scots; Alan Gray, nephew of Hector Gray, RAF; Archie Hart, son of James Hart, RASC; Hilary Hamilton, daughter of Geoffrey Hamilton, Royal Scots; Nicholas James, grandson of Bevan Field, HKVDC; Michael Longyear, nephew of Alec Howard, HKVDC; Vic Marsh, son of Tom Marsh, Winnipeg Grenadiers; Tom Middleton, son of Thomas Middleton, Royal Navy; Rob Milner, grandson of Noel Hammond, HKVDC; Rosemary Mitchell, daughter of Jack Mitchell, HKVDC; Michael Morris, son of John Morris, Royal Engineers; Michael Palmer, grandson of George Palmer, Royal Rifles of Canada; Ron Parker, son of Maurice Parker, Royal Rifles of Canada; Kathleen Porter, sister of John McFerran Cassidy, Royal Navy; Robbie Poulter, son of William Poulter, Middlesex; Faye Powell, daughter of Robert Bede Moore, Royal Naval Dockyard Police; Kamal Prasad, son of Kamta Prasad, 2/14th Punjabis; Jo Price, granddaughter of Sister Joan Whiteley, Queen Alexandra's Imperial Nursing Service; Roger Proulx, son of Benny Proulx, HKVDC; Ron Rakusen, son of Manassah 'Nat' Rakusen, HKVDC; Anna Rozario, daughter of Cicero Rozario, HKVDC; Jonathan Searle, son of Lancelot Searle, HK Police; Ken Skelton, son of Sydney Skelton, Royal Rifles of Canada; Jim Trick, son of Charles Trick, Winnipeg Grenadiers; Carol Waite, daughter of Norman Briggs, American civilian; Mark Weedon, son of Martin Weedon, Middlesex; Sue Wilkinson, daughter of Bill Spooner, Royal Scots; Richard and Bill Wiseman Jnr., sons of Bill Wiseman, RASC; Barbara Wrighting, daughter of David Davidson, RASC; and Jeni Zuber, daughter of Bill Lowe, HKVDC.

Fellow Researchers and Enthusiasts

Firstly, thanks to four people who kindly contributed a great deal of time and effort into furthering the research upon which this book is based: Keith Andrews, Wes Injerd, Roger Mansell, and Elizabeth Ride. Without their assistance, this work would not have had the required depth of coverage on the POW Index Cards (and other items) at Kew, the various relevant records at the National Archives and Records

Administration (NARA), and the Ride Papers at the University of Hong Kong Libraries.

Among many other individuals who kindly assisted were: Paul Banham, Stuart Braga, Ron Bridges, Tony Bushell, Geoff Emerson, Toru Fukubayashi, Michael Hurst MBE, Jacky Kingsley, Tim Ko, Vince Lopata, Ian Quinn, Dr Charles Roland, Nina Staehle, Wal Storer, Ron Taylor (Hong Kong), Ron Taylor (UK), Andy Thomson, Stephen Wall, Rob Weir, and Jason Wordie. Two friends in Hong Kong also gave considerable help with translations and other matters, but declined a mention here.

Institutions

The University of Hong Kong Libraries, Special Collections
The Imperial War Museum (Rodderick Suddaby)
National Archives and Records Administration (NARA)
The National Archives, Kew
The Commonwealth War Graves Commission
Hong Kong Public Records Office
Canadian National Archives
The Royal Scots Regimental Museum, Edinburgh (David Murphy)

Lastly, to Colin Day and Hong Kong University Press for backing yet another project of such deep interest to so few!

Every effort has been made to trace the copyright holders of works quoted in this book. If anyone has information concerning any author or document for whom I have been unable to trace ownership, I would always be happy to hear from the copyright holder and thank them by name in future editions.

Abbreviations

Units

AEC	Army Educational Corps
CADC	Canadian Army Dental Corps
CCPR	Chinese Company Police Reserve
CMP	Corps of Military Police
CPC	Canadian Provost Corps
CV	Civilian
HKCR	Hong Kong Chinese Regiment
HKDDC	Hong Kong Dockyard Defence Corps
HKMC	Hong Kong Mule Corps, RIASC
HKPF	Hong Kong Police Force
HKRNVR	Hong Kong Royal Naval Volunteer Reserve
HKSRA	Hong Kong and Singapore Royal Artillery
HKVDC	Hong Kong Volunteer Defence Corps
HQ	Headquarters, China Command
ICPR	Indian Company Police Reserve
IHC	Indian Hospital Corps
MN	Merchant Navy
MPSC	Military Provost Staff Corps
MX	Middlesex (1st Battalion the Middlesex Regiment)
PJ	Punjab (2/14th Punjabi Regiment)
QAINS	Queen Alexandra's Imperial Nursing Service
RA	Royal Artillery
RADC	Royal Army Dental Corps
RAF	Royal Air Force
RAMC	Royal Army Medical Corps*
RAOC	Royal Army Ordnance Corps
RAPC	Royal Army Pay Corps
RASC	Royal Army Service Corps
RAVC	Royal Army Veterinary Corps

---

* Note that almost all military acronyms had slang versions. RAMC, for example, was popularly known as "Rob All My Comrades." RASC was "Rob And Squeeze Corps," and, later, RAPWI would be "Remain As Prisoners of War Indefinitely."

RCAMC	Royal Canadian Army Medical Corps	
RCAPC	Royal Canadian Army Pay Corps	
RCASC	Royal Canadian Army Service Corps	
RCCS	Royal Canadian Corps of Signals	
RCOC	Royal Canadian Ordnance Corps	
RCS	Royal Corps of Signals	
RE	Royal Engineers	
RIASC	Royal Indian Army Service Corps	
RM	Royal Marines	
RN	Royal Navy	
RNR	Royal Naval Reserve	
RNVR	Royal Naval Volunteer Reserve	
RP	Rajput (5/7th Rajput Regiment)	
RRoC	Royal Rifles of Canada	
RS	Royal Scots (2nd Battalion the Royal Scots Regiment)	
SJA	St John's Ambulance	
WG	Winnipeg Grenadiers	

Causes of Death

Aa	Anaemia		DOW	Died of wounds
Al	Alcohol poisoning		Ea	Emphysema
An	Angina pectoris		Es	Enteritis
Ap	Appendicitis		EX	Executed
As	Avitaminosis		Ff	Friendly fire
Ax	Accident		Gl	Glycol poisoning
Az	Azotemia		GSW	Gun shot wound
BC	Building collapse		Gu	Gastric ulcer
Bi	Beri-beri		He	Haemorrhage
Bs	Bronchitis		Hs	Hepatitis
Cbi	Cardiac beri-beri		Je	Jaundice
Ce	Cerebroaemia		Ls	Lympharynitis
Cf	Cardiac failure		Ma	Malaria
Ci	Cirrhosis of liver		Mn	Malnutrition
Cs	Colitis		Ms	Meningitis
Da	Diphtheria		Mu	Murdered
De	Debility		My	Myocarditis
Dm	Dementia*		Ns	Neuritis
Di	Diarrhoea		Pa	Pneumonia
Dr	Drowned		PC	Plane crash
Dy	Dysentery		Pe	Pellagra

* Note that dementia is typically the third stage of pellagra.

Ph	Pharingytis	Ss	Sclerosis
Pi	Peritonitis	TB	Tuberculosis
Ps	Polyneuritis	Td	Typhoid
Pu	Pulmonary infiltration	Ts	Tonsillitis
Rm	Rheumatism	Ty	Typhus
Sa	Septicaemia	Ul	Ulcer

Places of Hospitalization, Death and Burial

dhh	Died at Hiroshima Military Hospital
diw	Died at Ichioka Ward
dkh	Died at Kokura Military Hospital
dkoh	Died at Kobe Hospital
doh	Died at Osaka Military Hospital
dsh	Died at Sagamihara Military Hospital
dsgh	Died at Shinagawa Hospital
dt2	Died at Tokyo #2 Military Hospital
oba	Originally buried Argyle Street Cemetery
obq	Originally buried Queen Mary's Hospital (QMH)
obr	Originally buried Royal Naval Hospital (RNH)
obs	Originally buried Shamshuipo rifle ranges
twb	At Tweed Bay Hospital
BRH	Bowen Road Hospital
CSUC	Chinese School University Compound
HKH	Hong Kong Hotel Relief Hospital
IGH	Indian General Hospital
QMH	Queen Mary's Hospital
RNH	Royal Naval Hospital
SAH	St Albert's Convent Relief Hospital
SSH	St Stephen's College Relief Hospital
STH	St Teresa's Hospital
UH	University Hospital
WMH	War Memorial Hospital
K	Known grave (at Stanley or Sai Wan military cemeteries in Hong Kong unless otherwise stated)
U	Unknown grave. Commemorated in Hong Kong unless otherwise stated.
UP	Unknown grave. Commemorated in Plymouth.
UPO	Unknown grave. Commemorated in Portsmouth.
UC	Unknown grave. Commemorated in Chatham.
UT	Unknown grave. Commemorated at Tower Hill.

UCWD	Unknown grave. Commemorated in the list of Civilian War Dead.
UX	Unknown grave. Not in CWGC records.
HKJ	Hong Kong Jewish Cemetery
CCC	Cape Collinson Roman Catholic Cemetery
HKM	Hong Kong Muslim Cemetery
HKC	Hong Kong Cemetery
HKR	Hong Kong Roman Catholic Cemetery
Y	Yokohama Cemetery

Awards

CGM	Conspicuous Gallantry Medal
DSO	Distinguished Service Order
GC	George Cross
KCfBC	King's Commendation for Brave Conduct
MBE	Member of the British Empire
MC	Military Cross
MiD	Mentioned in Dispatches
MM	Military Medal
OBE	Officer of the British Empire

General

ADMS	Assistant Director of Medical Services
AHQ	Advanced headquarters
APA	Auxiliary Personnel Attack
BAAG	British Army Aid Group
BMH	British Military Hospital
CWGC	Commonwealth War Graves Commission
DMS	Director of Medical Services (Selwyn-Clarke)
FEPOW	Far Eastern Prisoner of War
FIGs	Field Intelligence Groups
FOGs	Field Operation Groups
IORs	Indian Other Ranks
KWIS	Kweilin (Guilin) Intelligence Summary
ORs	Other Ranks
POW	Prisoner of War
RAPWI	Recovered Allied Prisoners of War and Internees
VCO	Viceroy Commissioned Officer
WIS	Waichow Intelligence Summary

Notes on the Rolls of Honour

The Rolls of Honour in this book are presented by camp, in chronological order of death. When more than one death occurred on the same day in the same camp, names are presented alphabetically without distinguishing between ranks. For some of the earlier deaths after surrender, such as those at the Queen Mary Hospital, the deaths are listed at the hospitals where they occurred. However, deaths that occurred after men were in POW camps are listed by camp, even if the deceased actually passed away in a hospital (for example, Shamshuipo POWs may have died in the camp, in St Teresa's Hospital, or at Bowen Road. All are listed under Shamshuipo).

Although hospital records for the period of fighting were largely preserved — with the exception of St Stephen's — such records are only quoted here if it is believed that wounds received then were responsible for the victims' later demise.

Those entries followed by a date in bold indicate that the date ascribed to the death in this book is derived from my researches, and contradicts the records of the CWGC. The date ascribed by the CWGC is that in bold. Occasionally, if the date of death is uncertain, the CWGC may have originally ascribed a range of possibilities, such as 1–2.10.42; unfortunately, in the online system at least, these have now been converted to the earliest date in the range (i.e. the 1st in this example). It was not uncommon for the date of death to be recorded as the date of burial. Typically, these events were only a day apart, thus these have not been corrected in this work.

It is hoped that a future work will cover ex-Hong Kong POWs (evaders, escapees or released local Chinese) who lost their lives later in the war on a variety of battlefields, and these deaths have not been recorded here.

Unfortunately, for reasons of space, it has been necessary to encodify much of the detail presented in these rolls. The codes used are explained in the abbreviations section above.

Introduction

> I hopes that somebody who likes us, that's Eli and Willy, will keep this book and pass it on to Eli's and Willy's G. G. Grandchildren, whatever century they're in, whatever colour they are, whatever they believe in, if they are of Eli's and Willy's stock they'll be good 'uns, darn good 'uns.[1]

This book is no *King Rat*-like epic narrative, nor a heroic tale in the style of *The Bridge over the River Kwai*. Instead, it is a simple chronological account of what happened to thousands of ordinary people caught up in the Japanese invasion and occupation of Hong Kong.

It is told not in my words, but in theirs. My role is as a journalist, or even an editor, responsible for the structure of the work — and for conducting 'interviews' (whether through direct correspondence, or finding primary sources elsewhere) — but preserving objectivity through my own silence.

Here I have observed that the behaviour epitomised in King Rat was rare, and perhaps the occasional flashes of kindness and compassion are truly a more remarkable story. And heroism, where it existed, typically occurred in dark situations where it was invisible to all but those suffering.

Of course, this must by definition be a patchy work, dependent very much on my ability, or lack of it, in tracing sources. In some cases it has worked well, with quotes that echo each other and build great depth, but in other areas — and the Indian POW's experience is the prime example — a lack of easily available source material has resulted in less coverage than is appropriate.

Readers who wish to know what it was *like* to be in a POW or Internment Camp for years on end should look elsewhere, perhaps at books such as William Allister's *Where Life and Death Hold Hands* or Jean Gittins' *Stanley: Behind Barbed Wire*. But for serious students of the history of Hong Kong's garrison, seeking to understand what happened to them from 1941 to 1945, the answers will hopefully be found in the following text.

Capture

'When the Japs come here,' [Lieutenant Colonel 'Monkey' Stewart] said, 'after we have laid down our arms and are defenceless, they will massacre us.' He was desperately tired and sad. I fetched him a mug of tea. He thanked me and said, 'You are very young and fit. There is no obligation for you to stay. Find a boat and get away.'

— Captain Anthony Hewitt, Adjutant,
1st Battalion the Middlesex Regiment[1]

Hong Kong, when it was attacked by Japan on Monday, 8 December 1941, was garrisoned by approximately 11,000 regular soldiers, backed up by some 2,000 members of the Hong Kong Volunteer Defence Corps, and 1,000 members of other disciplined services. Although — theoretically — all the families of the British garrison had been evacuated to Australia in 1940, several thousand non-Chinese civilians were also present.

Some 1,550 of the defenders had lost their lives[2] by the time the Governor, Sir Mark Young, surrendered the Colony on the afternoon of Christmas Day. Stunned by their change in circumstances, those who survived took stock. Many ethnically Chinese defenders, acting by themselves or with explicit encouragement from officers, slipped off their uniforms and merged into the crowds. Few Caucasians could follow suit, though a handful of enterprising souls claimed 'friendly' nationalities such as Irish or Scandinavian.

The remainder, British, Indian, Canadian, Hong Kong, and others, laid down their arms and entered the uncertain and dangerous world of prisoners of war. They would have mixed and unpredictable fortunes; several hundred would escape,[3] nearly 2,500 would die, and the remainder would spend three years and eight months in conditions from which few would ever fully recover. Local Chinese civilians would mainly be starved out of the Colony — even the POWs felt lucky to avoid their fate. A handful of foreign civilians would escape, a fortunate few hundred (primarily Americans, and later Canadians) would be repatriated, and some — though seldom in as brutal conditions as their military counterparts — would die. The remainder would suffer the hunger, lack of medical facilities, and lack of privacy, of internment.

Most people imagine that, at surrender, the garrison was taken prisoner en masse. In fact, prisoners were taken from the very start of the fighting, with Graham Heywood and Leonard Starbuck of the Observatory being first, apprehended while they were checking instruments on the border as the Japanese crossed into the Colony on 8 December.[4]

Escapes and evasions started in those early days too, with the destroyers HMS *Scout* and HMS *Thanet* leaving port only hours after Hong Kong was attacked, and with aircraft escaping from Kai Tak almost up to the time when Kowloon was evacuated.[5]

As the Japanese pushed south from the border, they soon attacked and captured the defensive line that had been placed in their way — and in particular, the Shing Mun Redoubt. Heywood and Starbuck's fate was there followed by a number of Royal Scots, primarily from A Company, and personnel of the HKSRA's co-located Observation Post.

As the military evacuated the Mainland, following the loss of the Redoubt and the breach in the Gin Drinkers Line which resulted, those civilians who could, escaped with them.

Ted Ross was with the Ministry of Information: "That night (Dec. 11–12) was an ugly one for Kowloon dwellers. The fifth column was well organised, and they did all in their power to create disturbances. Automobile barricades were thrown across the streets, and gangs of hoodlums, many of them armed, roamed the streets, looting shops, smashing windows. One chap I met later on the Hong Kong side described his own little getaway. He and his wife jumped in their car in an attempt to get down to the Star Ferry. (The ferries, both passenger and vehicular, were plying back and forth full blast). They spotted another foreigner walking in that direction and picked him up, and a few minutes later came up against a barricade of cars thrown right across Nathan Road. Slowing down, they suddenly climbed over the sidewalk and got around the end, but a number of hoodlums sprang onto the running boards. While the man driving was trying to fight them off and keep the car going at the same time, the chap they had picked up produced a pistol and short four in quick succession, the rest scrambling for safety. It was a lucky thing for them they had delayed their dash just long enough to pick up that fellow."[6]

Few, if any, further men of the garrison were captured on the mainland. One Winnipeg Grenadier, Private John Gray, disappeared, but whether he was captured and killed or set upon by looters has not yet been ascertained.[7]

These early prisoners were taken to Fan Ling, and did not rejoin their comrades until mid January. However, the Japanese had also captured several hospitals on the mainland (and the nurses who had stayed with their charges), and a number of enemy civilians who had not managed to cross to the island. For the moment, they were left where they were.

Then, following Kowloon's evacuation, came a pause. From 13 December until the evening of 18 December, Hong Kong Island was under siege. All military facilities came under concerted attack from artillery and bombs.

On the night of 18 December, the Japanese launched their invasion of the island. Initially they blasted their way through the beach defences of the 5th/7th Rajputs between Shau Kei Wan and North Point. The fighting there was fierce, and few if any records of POWs captured in the beachhead exist.[8]

Stopped by a strong defence at the North Point Power Station and a strengthening resistance running south from there, the Japanese turned south too and advanced in parallel with this nascent defensive line, heading into Wong Nai Chung Gap. The next defenders to be captured were rounded up during and after the heavy fighting on Jardine's Lookout and in Wong Nai Chung Gap on 19 December. Some one hundred or more of them were locked in a building there overnight.

Tom Marsh, Winnipeg Grenadiers: "The building was a low roof shed about sixty feet long by thirty feet wide with a concrete floor. There was some heavy trestle tables down the center. The shed had probably been used as a mess hall by the garrison. It was now crammed with prisoners of the Japs; Whites, Chinese and Indians. Most of them were in some sort of uniform. Many, like myself, were wounded and some appeared to be dead. The floor literally ran with blood. There was not enough room in which to lie down, so closely were we packed. Most sat huddled in attitudes of despair with their knees drawn up. The only clear space was around the guard by the door and he kept it this way by the swing of his rifle butt. Here was gathered all the misery of military defeat. There was no food and worst, no water. Thirst, doubly prevalent when one is wounded, was an acute torture. I saw no Red Cross or any attempt on the part of the Jap to minister to the wounded. Many collapsed and died where they fell. A few of the prisoners tried to help a comrade or an immediate neighbour but most of us stayed huddled, awaiting we knew not what. It was now high noon and the sun was hot in the sky. The place was thick with flies pestering the wounded. Although I did not recognize them all, there were several Grenadiers from A

Company in the hut, among them the Mitchell brothers, both Lieutenants, also Sergeant Pugsley, Cpl. Hiscox, and Pte. Matte. The guns of battle were still booming towards Hong Kong. The Japs had planted one right beside our hut and its discharge shook the building. I heard the sound of a nearby mortar shell exploding and knew that our own mortars were seeking the range on the Jap gun position. Then it came. Two mortar shells, almost simultaneously, one landed squarely on the roof of the building. There was a blinding flash, shrieks and moans all was confusion. Instinctively I had thrown myself under the only available shelter, the trestle table, on top of what I later discovered to be a dead Imperial with half his head blown off. Under him was a live Chinaman who was bleating piteously. Miraculously I was not hit. From my vantage place under the table I saw that the place was a shambles. There was a gaping hole in the roof and beneath it a pile of bodies. The only reason that many escaped death or further injury was the fact that we were so closely packed our companion's bodies protected us. Most of the survivors were splattered with fresh blood over bandages and previously caked and dry wounds. The Guard by the door was killed outright. Moans and groans could be heard on all sides. The door was flung open and excited Japs pulled out the body of the sentry but forced all others back into the shed with their bayonets. The door was then closed and it must have been an hour before it was again opened. We quite expected there would be another direct hit. With apprehension we awaited the explosion but it never came. We heard the jabbering of Japanese voices and the doors were thrown wide open. They had reached a decision about us. A dozen or more guards entered and began sorting the living from the dead, the seriously wounded from those who were able to walk. Those able to walk were crowded to the door and out onto the road, where their hands were tied behind them with wire."[9]

These men were marched through the Taitam Valley, and north along Mount Parker Road until they reached King's Road. They were led to the North Point Refugee camp, where they found some civilians already interned. Dee Dee Bak was one, having just been marched down to the camp with her family from Braemar: "We were not fed that day, just given a tin of tea (the tin we had to supply ourselves, which we found on the beach) boiled in sea water, oil from sunken vessels floating on the top. Undrinkable of course except for a few sips. We were very cold as we were not allowed to take anything with us and left with only the clothes we were wearing. It was a very long hut crammed with other people. We slept on the floor huddled together for warmth and lack of room. There was no toilet except a small bucket overflowing in a small section cordoned off with a curtain(?). This we avoided as long as we could."

Bevan Field had also been captured at Wong Nai Chung Gap and had been on the same march: "In the hut across the five or six yards in between I could see some civilian prisoners, looking very forlorn and lost. One young woman appeared to be tragically white and strained as if she had quite recently been through terrible experiences. I went out intending to enquire from them how they were managing, and was quickly shoved in again by a Japanese sentry."[10]

Dee Dee Bak, although she did not know the man's name, had been shocked by the site of a badly wounded Canadian, Lieutenant McKillop: "I recall on entering, the sight of a soldier lying on a table still in his overcoat, his abdomen covered in blood and I am sure it was his guts exposed. He was moaning in pain and this went on most of the night. In the morning he was no longer there so I can only assume he had died."

In fact, after they had spent the night at North Point Camp, the soldiers had been ferried to Kowloon. After a further night at the Maryknoll School, they were marched out again.

Marsh, who had arrived in Hong Kong — with the rest of the Canadians — amid much fanfare only a month earlier, continued: "This day we marched again along the streets of Kowloon. What a change from the time we marched with bands playing and warm meals and good billets awaiting us. Now we hobbled along on sticks and makeshift crutches, many supported by stronger comrades. Others were carried on wooden stretchers. Finally we entered the compound of Argyle Camp, lately used as a Chinese refugee interment camp.[11] Our group was halted and I collapsed upon the ground where I stood. I had made it this far but I could not go a step further. I desired nothing so much as to sink down to the ground, to be left alone, and to make no further effort. All of the group were allotted to certain dilapidated huts that surrounded the compound, the badly wounded to two huts designated as hospitals. When all were gone I was left alone lying on the square. An Englishman, a medical Corps Orderly, came over and knelt beside me. Placing his arm beneath my head he raised me to a sitting position, 'Come on chum!' he said encouragingly, 'You can make it!' They told me later that they had all thought me dead but he, noticing a movement, had come back to make sure. The Englishman half carried me to one of the hospital huts and turned me over to a friend of his, a big Scotsman who had been badly wounded in the thigh while fighting in the streets of Hong Kong with the Volunteers. He was a marine engineer but his ship had been scuttled and lay at the bottom of the bay. Scotty lay on three boards raised about a foot from the ground on the framework of an old wooden bunk. He helped place [me] on the boards next to himself, groaning as he moved over to make additional room. He took my blanket and as he had none, wrapped it around the both of us. He then made himself my personal nurse and physician."

Winnipeg Grenadier Charles Trick was on the same march: "I was with Lt McKillop, who was a funeral director from Portage. He was badly wounded but he was smart enough that he didn't let on so he got out of there but he only lasted another day or two. They took us out of there that morning, that would be the 21st I suppose, and they marched us back to North Point and kept us there and then they took us across to the mainland at Kowloon. They made us parade in from [sic] of all the Chinese with all the wounded and sick. We had a door, four of us, and we were carrying Lt McKillop who couldn't walk anymore, he was bleeding to death. The blood was running off the door and running down our arms and there was nothing they would do for anybody who was wounded, the hell with them. So we paraded around Kowloon for a day or two. Some of the guys died and we still kept parading. They (Japanese) were showing off to the Chinese their power and their might. There was an old refugee camp on Argyle Street full of Chinese, or had been. It was full of straw and there was a bunch of Indians that were already there when we got there."[12]

Other men were captured in skirmishes between then and the surrender, and in the main were taken to North Point refugee camp, which then started its short career as a POW camp.[13]

One of the first captures of enemy civilians on the Island took place at the Repulse Bay Hotel. At one time, as many as 250 military personnel were involved in the Hotel's defence, but they were evacuated by night so that the occupants could surrender peacefully. Just before Japanese troops entered, two uniformed defenders were found still on the premises and were hurried out. Then a Canadian Rifleman, Riley, was discovered where he had been sleeping upstairs. There was no choice but to disguise him as a civilian.[14] Later, the hotel's residents were marched through Wong Nai Chung Gap to the Duro paint factory in North Point.

Some men were captured and killed, and some were captured then escaped again. James Hart was one of the latter. He had been Lieutenant Colonel Fredericks' driver during the whole of the campaign, and on the 19th had been taking Fredericks to Stanley Fort via Pokfulam, Aberdeen, and Repulse Bay. After an ambush between Deep Water Bay and Repulse Bay, Fredericks was instructed to go to The Ridge south of Wong Nai Chung Gap, where they stayed until Sunday evening.

Sunday, 21 December. Hart: "On the Sunday, just after it got dark, we left the Ridge. Our object was to try to recapture the road junction, between the two bays, but it proved unsuccessful, the group [of] 60-100 scattering in all directions. Myself and quite a few others got over a wire fence, past some houses, and down to the water's edge. I made my way to Repulse Bay in the company of another soldier. Halfway towards the Repulse Bay we climbed up towards the road, crossed it, and went into some dense undergrowth for the rest of the day (Monday). After it got dark, there was quite a bit of noise, people rushing past us, in the direction of the Repulse Bay Hotel, we heard English being spoken, so we joined the group, as we joined them, word got out of another ambush. I take it, that it was everyone for himself, and we were all hiding in the undergrowth. All day on the Tuesday everything was very quiet, then just as it was beginning to get dark, I became aware of some activity behind us, a Jap soldier was standing over me with his rifle prodding me to get up. I was taken to Eucliff House and tied up, and made to kneel down. After a while a Jap soldier came towards us and started to bayonet a 2nd Lt. of the R.A.O.C.,[15] he then started on me, and his first thrust was towards my abdomen, but as I had a leather belt as well as my web belt, this did not do any real damage to me, but his second thrust did. It penetrated my side, near my armpit, and I thought, my lung, and with this thrust it knocked me down a slope onto a ledge. Looking up I could see the Jap having another go at the Officer, who eventually rolled down the slope and stopped on top of me. Our barbaric friend had not finished with us yet, as we lay on the ledge, he came down to make sure we were dead. He started on the Officer once more, then I got two bayonet thrusts on my back, and two on the head, and rolled to the bottom of the lawn. When it got dark, and I found I could use my arms and legs, I somehow was able to rub my arms and sever the ropes on the rocks, then got over the barbed wire and down to the water's edge. After a struggle, and almost naked, I swam across Repulse Bay in the direction of Stanley. When I was leaving the water, I was guided up the sands by a Capt of the Middlesex Regt, who was hiding in a drain nearby. After giving the Officer the best way to Stanley Fort, I made my way via the water's edge to Chung Hom Kok where I met up with the Canadian Regt, who were in that area. Whilst we were hiding in the rocks, near Stanley Village, on Xmas day we were eyewitness to the deaths of hundreds of Japs, trying to reach Stanley Fort; we witnessed three assaults, but the defenders held firm. Around 4 pm we saw three or four cars headlights ablaze, going up to the Fort, we did not know that was a party going into the Fort, to let them know that the Governor of Hong Kong had surrendered."[16]

Staff Sergeant James O'Toole was with the same group initially. Tied up between the road and Deep Water Bay Golf Course, they were then marched off by their captors: "We came at last to the path that runs around the range to Violet Hill above Repulse Bay . . . There they took Captain Bonney away and we never saw him again, he had up to then been quite fit and helped us along when ever possible. We were then marched along the track toward Wong Nei Chong Gap.[17] Collecting prisoners on the way, mostly Indians, some Volunteers. Arriving at the gap we stood for about four hours all huddled together whilst it rained and blew like merry hell. Never felt so miserable and down hearted as at this time, if they had started shooting us, I for one wouldn't have cared much; it was Bloody. We numbered about 80 and some of us had managed to work our hands free."[18] Marched to Tai Koo, they were then taken by barge to Kowloon and ended up — via Mary Knoll — at Argyle Street Camp.

Marsh at Argyle Street, on Christmas Eve: "The day before Christmas some of the survivors of D Company of the Winnipeg Grenadiers, who had made such a heroic stand at Wong Nei Chong Gap, arrived. The survivors of this Company surrendered only after their ammunition was exhausted. They had held up the Japanese advance in their section for five days. Among the survivors who I knew were Sergeant Bob Manchester of D Company and Sergeant Pugsley of A Company. They both visited me as I lay beside Scotty."

But the fighting was still continuing. Early on Christmas day, the Japanese reached the St Stephen's College Relief Hospital on the front line at Stanley. They captured the building, but killed many of the patients in the process. Later, mass rapes were carried out with eight nurses (three British and five Chinese) being murdered, as were, later, the two senior medical officers and two further Canadian soldiers.[19]

On the same day, the front line on the Island's north coast was also giving way, and the Japanese reached the Jockey Club Relief Hospital. Miss Amy Williams was the Matron in charge.

Amy Williams: "At about 0.800 hours on December 25th, Mrs Barron and I were clearing up our rooms when I heard Dr Selby talking in a loud voice on the floor below, and on looking over found he was in conversation with a Japanese officer who was accompanied by two soldiers . . . [on arrival at the ground floor] I was informed by a soldier that two of the British girls, one a sister had been taken away from the dining room by the Japanese soldiers. I was on my way upstairs again to see if this was true, when I met both girls coming down, one of them broke down and cried on my shoulder and both said they had been raped . . . I was told that two Chinese nurses had been taken away, but they had both returned by the time I was informed. Both had been raped and I gave them treatment. This occurred three times that morning at 1030 — 1130 and 1230 hours, on each occasion two girls, on the last occasion one of them was an Indian."[20]

This continued with European nurses (including Portuguese and Russian) all night.

On Friday, 26 December, Amy Williams noted: "The staff by this time were in a terrible state, most of the Chinese had managed to get away and the remainder begged me to give them some morphia or poison. I talked to them for a while and it was decided to wait until 1400 hours and we would again discuss what we would do. At 1330 hours a motor car drew up to the gate and when I went to see who it contained I saw Dr Selwyn-Clarke standing on the door way."

Now that Hong Kong had surrendered, some semblance of order was being restored. Tom Forsyth of the Winnipeg Grenadiers noted: "POWs at Mount Austin Barracks on Dec 25th 1941, moved to Peak Mansions 9.30 pm, Dec 26th. Moved to H.K. University Dec 27th. Moved to Victoria Barracks Dec 28th."[21]

The capture of some men was delayed. Corporal David Davidson, RASC, who had been at The Ridge with Hart and others, had found a small boat with his sergeant Danny Gunstone: "It was evident that we would not now get out of sight of the main island during darkness so we made off towards a beached destroyer [HMS *Thracian*] on the rocks between Chung am Kok and Repulse Bay. After struggling all night through we arrived just before dawn. As we were attempting to board the destroyer, we were challenged by someone aboard; as the challenge was in English we had no fears and were soon hauled aboard. Our raft was made safe and we were conducted below only to find the party of mixed stragglers who had left the beach before us. They had made the same decision as we had thinking it best to have a whole night of darkness to get clear of the island. It was now Christmas Day, but there was not much to feast on. Rummaging around, the chaps in advance of us had found a tin of peas, some jam and the remains of a loaf of bread which was speckled with green mould. This was shared out and between about thirty of us the portions were far from generous. We spent the daylight hours camped below deck, it was hot and stuffy and the fumes rising from the engine room (where the crew of the destroyer had broken all the ships rum bottles) were almost overpowering. As soon as it was dark we sallied forth and assembled our boats which ranged from the large rowing boat to smaller boats and our raft. We set off line ahead, each boat roped to the next. We headed out to sea, our destination Lamma Island. Shortly before dawn we arrived at a rocky shore on Lamma Island, the waves were breaking on the rocks with such force that we had to look for a sandy beach on which to land. We decided to go eastwards, and navigated round a rocky peninsular and arrived at dawn on the sandy shore right across from where we had first struck land. There was a village not far away from here and we bought eggs, tea and sugar, so we had boiled eggs and sweet black tea for breakfast. A small brook rippled over the rocks into the sea and here we washed and attended to the wounded. We had run out of field dressing and as CQMS Hamlen was in need of a clean dressing, I washed out my singlet and that was used as a dressing for his now very inflamed gaping wound. During our last voyage we had passed through an oil slick and as my legs were dangling in the sea, the service dress trousers I was wearing were stiff with oil. Danny Gunstone was in the same plight, so we conferred together and decided that nothing less than amputation would cure the state of our trousers, so with the aid of a jack knife, we cut off the legs just below the knees. From the villagers we were informed that a few miles away there was a larger village where Junks operated from. It seemed a good thing for us to move off in that direction in order to get on a Junk and escape to the Chinese mainland."

The 'stragglers' Davidson had fallen in with were primarily Canadians of A Company Royal Rifles who had escaped from The Ridge under Major Young: "I had 34 men in my party, and was lucky enough to venture upon a chance to obtain an old motor boat anchored 500 yards off shore. I swam out and brought it ashore . . . We altered our course for the beached *Thracian*, a small destroyer which was about 3/4 mile from Stanley Peninsular. We stayed there all that night and the next day . . . We left that night on three of the *Thracian's* Carley floats . . ."[22]

After they landed on Lamma island, Davidson continued: "With the major in the lead the Canadians set off at a hot pace. Our small party consisting of CQMS Hamlen, Sgt Shaw, CQMS Meyer and myself followed on at a more leisurely pace. The main party were soon out of sight but taking it in turn we assisted Happy Hamlen along the narrow path which led to the next village. The path was overgrown with spiny prickles from both sides. Its normal usage was for single file but to make our way and assist our wounded comrade we had to walk three abreast. We now came to regret being so hasty in cutting off our trouser legs as we were getting badly scratched. When we arrived at the village the haggling was over and we were hastily conducted on the junk and stowed away below deck. As a place of refuge it was ideal but beyond that there was little to be said that was good about the junk. It was ill ventilated and reeked of previous occupants that ranged from chicken, pigs, etc to the Chinese themselves, whose education in respect of hygiene was truly lacking. Whilst cooped up below deck on the junk the plight of the severely wounded amongst us became evident to all. It was clear that they needed care and attention that could only be provided by a hospital. To take them away into the unknown depths of China proper would have been signing their death warrant. In the light of the prospect of taking comrades to their certain doom, we reviewed our plans and after much persuasion we managed to get the junk master to take us to Telegraph Bay so that we might walk from there to Queen Mary Hospital. As we had no idea of the situation on the island of Hong Kong, we only knew that things must be quite desperate. The fact that the garrison had already capitulated was unknown to us. As we landed in Telegraph Bay[23] the junk master was frightened for his life and property, as soon as we stepped ashore, he was gone with the wind. So there was no turning back. We had not taken many steps when we were surrounded by Chinese armed with British arms. At the point of the bayonet we were roughly marched off and handed over to the Japanese. Despite the sorry state of our wounded it took us a whole day to get our captors to agree to us taking the wounded to the hospital a few hundred yards away. In the end they suddenly changed their mind and we staggered to the hospital entrance, handed over the wounded and then returned to join the rest of the party."[24]

On Hong Kong Island's south coast, Aberdeen was surrendered late on 25 December by Lieutenant Bush and Commander Pears, to a Lieutenant Suzuki. On the 26th, the naval contingent there was ordered to march to Murray Barracks.[25]

Lewis Bush: "They [the corporal and private first class who first arrived] seemed doubtful about the wisdom of approaching too close and so I went to meet them and spoke in Japanese. The corporal smiled as if greatly relieved and pointing to his bandaged neck said that he'd been wounded by one of our bullets, that his company commander [Suzuki] would arrive shortly, and asked if there was anything he could do for us."[26] (p. 143)

Bush, having lived in Japan pre-war, and having a Japanese wife, Kaneko,[27] spoke the language fluently.

Bush: "There seemed to be a fixed idea in the minds of some that the Japanese were killing all our men found in the hills who had not reported after the surrender, and [Maltby] was particularly anxious about a large number known to have been at the magazines at Shouson Hill, near

Aberdeen, and accused the Japanese of having shot them all. The Japanese colonel said he knew nothing about them, but Suzuki hastened to explain that there was indeed a number of men in the magazines who refused to come out, who threatened to blow up the whole area, and said his men had been fired on whenever they approached. A senior naval officer asked me if I could get the Japanese to agree to promise these men safe conduct and not punish them if I could get them to come out of the magazines. This was readily forthcoming and I was instructed to convey [Maltby's] orders to them to surrender immediately. I was warned that I might have difficulty as the officer in charge was a particularly stubborn Australian of the Royal Engineers who might choose to blow up the thousands of tones of munitions and explosives rather than surrender. [Maltby] thanked Suzuki for his assistance in obtaining food for the troops in Murray Barracks, Kaneko was given all manner of messages for the wives of officers, and she promised to try and find the Scottish terrier of [Maltby's] aide-de-camp, and after leaving her at Marina House, we returned to Aberdeen with two trucks for our attempt to get the Australian and his comrades out of the magazines. It was almost 2 a.m. when we set out with Suzuki and he agreed that the less Japanese we took with us the more chance we stood of success. The route was through man-made cuts in the mountains, and we drove onto an open space, off both sides of which were barred doors leading into the magazines. Francis and I both shouted that we had come from [Maltby] and wished to speak with the senior officer. I heard someone say: 'Tell them to bugger off!' There seemed to be an argument going on inside and then Manning, a naval officer, appeared, astounded to see us, and was soon joined by several others, and then a well-built, imposing officer made his was forward.[28] This was the reputedly tough Australian. He looked it. I repeated the order from [Maltby] and told him that safe conduct had been guaranteed and that I would stake my own life on their being escorted to Murray Barracks. Suzuki now came forward. 'Who's he?' I was asked. I told them how we had been treated by Suzuki's unit, and the Australian said, 'Well, I still think it would be better to blow up the whole bloody dump, and believe me that is what was going to happen as soon as we ran our of grub, about the day after tomorrow. All right chaps, this is it. Open up!' There were about twenty officers and men. We passed around the rum. Suzuki seemed greatly relieved and confessed that his unit had pondered for days over the problem of how to remove the inmates without bringing down half the mountain in the event of an explosion. They had made themselves very comfortable, but had been on short rations, except for chocolate of which they had an abundance, but were almost out of water.

Soon, twenty or thirty Japanese officers and men arrived who treated the Australian and his pals like heroes, and when we got down to Aberdeen a Japanese officer arrived with beer and whisky in plenty. The magazine heroes certainly did themselves well and we all shared in the liquid refreshment provided by the Imperial Japanese Army from our captured stores. The next morning we took them into Murray Barracks, each weighed down with more than he could reasonably carry. Whether the idea was popular or not with his comrades, I am sure that had we not gone out to them, the Australian would have provided Hong Kong with the nearest thing to an atomic blast; for he had prepared everything for the big event. He told Suzuki that if he survived the war he'd return the whisky and beer in his favourite pub in George Street, Sydney." (p. 147)

Civilians away from the fighting were awaiting developments.

Norman H. Briggs was an American civilian living on the Peak: "Mac, the Suters, and I were billeted in the Company house, 459 the Peak, which was called Altadena: The first visit at the house we had from the Japanese was on December 26th. They came in sometime during the afternoon. All 23 of us were in the house when they arrived, plus 15 Chinese servants. Around eight Japanese came in . . . The officer asked who we were, British or American? We replied both, then gave them a list showing our names, ages, sex, and nationality as requested."[29]

Saturday, 27 December. The majority of the Royal Naval prisoners were concentrated at the Seaman's Institute, next to the China Fleet Club in Wanchai. Canadian Benny Proulx, HKRNVR, observed: "As we stood waiting in the dark, we noticed the Chinese servants from the Institute quietly sneaking out of the building with all sorts of foodstuffs in their arms. They were doing an efficient job of looting, a job of which we heartily approved since their families were starving and the Japs, who would otherwise get the food, were not."[30] (p. 127)

The Japanese started moving the non-Chinese civilians to areas of concentration, primarily hotels, though some had already congregated in hospitals and certain office buildings.

Some, both military men and civilians, decided not to become POWs. Cedric Salter, Royal Scots, declared himself to be a Norwegian called Hans Thorsen, and thus stayed out of camp. Civilian Phyllis Harrop conveniently remembered her earlier marriage to a German, and claimed his nationality, while American Emily Hahn did the same with her marriage to a Chinese national. Osler Thomas of the Field Ambulance — having been badly wounded in the face at the Salesian Mission massacre early in the fighting, simply evaded capture and, as many others would do, made his way into China.

Sunday, 28 December. One of the first civilians to be re-housed in 'short-time' hotels was Barbara Redwood: "I was with the ARP outfit and I think our group was the first to be sent to the Chinese 'hotels' by the Japs. During the battle, we were billeted in Dina House, Duddell Street, off Queen's Road Central. After the surrender, a Jap officer came and told us we must leave Dina House. One of our number knew of an empty office just around the corner from Dina House, so we just picked up our bags and went there, and started clearing out the rubbish there, when some one came in and said we must return to Dina House and go where we were sent. Back we went, but only for about an hour, when a lorry came to take the females in our group to the Tai Koon Hotel on Queen's Road; the men had to follow on foot. All this happened on 28th December. The ladies were sent to the second floor cubicles, the men to the 4th floor, two to a cubicle but only one big bed."[31] In later notes, she added: "The cubicles were all in a line, along which ran a wide verandah looking out on to Des Voeux Road where the trams run; wooden and glass partitions in between. Each cubicle had a large bed which took up most of the width; then a washbasin. Another line of cubicles backed on to the front row, so you could talk through the flimsy partitions to 5 immediate neighbours".[32]

Over the next few days, most British and enemy civilians found themselves in similar accommodation.

Monday, 29 December. Slightly over 2,000 men who had been trapped with East Brigade in Stanley (and largely left to their own devices since) were finally marched over Wong Nai Chung Gap, to North Point. Middlesex, Volunteers, Royal Rifles, Royal Artillery and others, stepped through the debris of the earlier battles, and the bodies that had accumulated then and in the aftermath of forced marches since.

By this time, members of the garrison who had been in the western side of the island at the time of the surrender, had been concentrated in barracks. On the following day, between the Naval Dockyard and the Cecil Hotel, these POWs were put on board Star Ferries to Kowloon. Arriving Kowloon side at 9 a.m. they were marched along Nathan Road and Argyle Street to Shamshuipo camp.

Tuesday, 30 December. Forsyth: "Had an early breakfast of 1/2 cup of tea and a large spoonful of beans, left Victoria Barracks about 7, moved by slow stages down to the ferry where we saw a large number of bodies floating in the water, ferried across and had a long roundabout march to Sham Shui Po barracks where we found everything in a state of ruin and desolation. After we left, the Chinese had systematically looted and destroyed . . . the biscuits we slept on had been torn to pieces and the coir stuffing scattered everywhere. Not a window remained in a hut or a door, even the brass faucets were gone, while the pipes had been torn out of the washrooms, and every scrap of wood that could be torn away from anything was gone, even the seats of the toilets. A scene of utter chaos such as I never thought to see."

Tuesday, 30 December. Donald Hill, RAF: "At dawn we prepare to move off. Frank and I sling our kitbags on a pole coollie style. We sling blankets round our neck. We are determined to bear our humiliation without a murmur, our day will surely come. We form into units and after two hours waiting move off, over six thousand strong. Arrive at the ferry and, after another long wait, are ferried across to Kowloon where we form into units again. Off again but where, no one knows. After a mile or so we come back into Nathan Road. By this time we begin to feel the strain and have to rest frequently. Each unit has its own guard. Thousands of Chinese line the streets, a few jeering, but mostly quiet, and some are in tears. It would appear that we are going to Sham Shui Po, several miles away. Our guard is a decent fellow and, seeing we are having a tough time, allows coollies to carry our kit. Eventually reach SSP barracks eight hours after leaving China Command. A battle for billets commences. The whole camp has been stripped of every useful article by looters and had also been bombed. All doors, windows, furniture, and fittings had been taken leaving just hulks of buildings. Even in peace time it was an awful dump, but now it looked as if a typhoon had hit it. We found a small hut and then a tremendous hunt started for anything resembling a bed. Found some horse hair and wrapped it into one of my blankets. Several men had been here for days, being captured earlier on. Two WO's had been tied up with wire, stripped of everything, and left for three days without food or water after having seen several of their comrades bayoneted."[33]

All those involved remembered their initial impressions of the camp. Jim Hart: "Everyone rushed to get a space. There wasn't a window left in the place. Everything had been ransacked except the Jubilee Buildings — they still had windows. No one would climb up the walls just to take the blinking windows out!"

Frank Evans: "After about thirty of us had been allocated to each hut there was a scramble for anything we could find that would be of use in captivity. Empty tins, pieces of timber, broken beds, ragged clothing and bedclothes, broken crockery — yes, anything of use."[34] (p. 22)

Whitehead, arriving at Shamshuipo: "I recognised 'Buck' Harding [who], a fellow member of the AA Regiment, had been imprisoned for more than a week after being captured near Wong Nei Chong soon after the assault on the island. His unit continued firing until they ran out of ammunition, when Captain Plummer ordered a desperate but vain bayonet charge. Buck was lucky. Those of his mates badly wounded were bayoneted and shot by the Japanese, and the rest, tethered together with telephone cable, were marched to North Point and then shipped to the mainland. His news of conditions in Sham Shui Po were not good."[35] (p. 41)

North Point was equally unappealing, but as it had been a refugee camp pre-war — rather than a barracks — it was rather more 'porous'.

Sergeant Les Fisher at North Point: "I was placed in charge of twelve Chinese St John's Ambulance Brigade and I told them that if I looked half as much like a Chinese as they did I should be away. Within three days only seven remained."[36] (p. 33)

Others were also thinking of escape and evasion, though it could never be an easy proposition for the Caucasians. Moreover, after the shock of eighteen days of battle, and the exhaustion that followed, few had the stamina to try.

Anthony Hewitt: "It was vital to evade capture, for it would be much more difficult to escape from imprisonment, yet immediate evacuation by sea seemed hopeless. Indeed everything seemed hopeless. My world was an empty void. We had surrendered. It was not terror, but a ghastly feeling of utter hopelessness that overcame me." (p. 1)

On the same day, 30 December, at Argyle Street, the new POWs were attempting to restore some order. O'Toole: "Major Paterson of Jardines (a Vol) was the senior in camp and therefore became Camp Commandant with Lieut Barnet (Vol) as adjutant (he had a typewriter). They did all possible to run the camp as per King's Regs but didn't know too much . . . Our strength was now 1000 of which 700 were Indians, they squabbled and argued over everything especially over the splitting up of the rations."

Wednesday, 31 December. Forsyth: "Spent a restless night though bone tired. An Imperial staff sergt lay outside dying of an internal haemorrhage and calling for help. Some of his friends knelt beside him; they said he could not be moved. They carried him away in the morning, when he was dead. Inside our hut big Tiny kept us all awake with a terrific cough. Each man got 3 hard tack crackers for breakfast, the same for dinner. We are cleaning up the huts, and the grounds, sweeping up the broken glass and the shattered mortar and dirt and refuse of every description, the same as we did at Murray barracks and the University and Victoria barracks.'

Wednesday, 31 December. Baugh of the RAF: "We met several people who had been captured in action, including L.A.C. Palmer who was one of my equipment assistants. He had been captured in the vicinity of Shouson Hill after being wounded by machine gun fire, but fortunately not seriously."[37]

Wednesday, 31 December. Hill, a colleague of Baugh: "Moved to a slightly bigger hut, the Wing moving in with us, the men are in another hut close by. There are over six thousand men in the camp with no sanitation and rotten food. We have no lights and go to bed soon after dusk. We have one meal at nine and another at five consisting of soggy rice and are permanently hungry. And so ended nineteen forty one."

ROLL OF HONOUR FOR 1941

Those who lost their lives from 8 December 1941 to 31 December 1941 are listed in the work *Not the Slightest Chance*.[38] However, research for *We Shall Suffer There* has added the following names:

Ryan, Kerry Gill	Corporal	7586999	RAOC	22.12.44	MiD	U 22.12.41[39]
Stacey, Alfred Ernest	Private	7635541	RAOC	22–23.12.44		U 22–23.12.41[40]
Young, William	Petty Officer	P/KX 79038	RN			U 24.21.14[41]

Barbara Redwood on 25 December 1941 near Government House, just before capture. From left to right: Viv Garton, Barbara Redwood, Wally Skinner. Courtesy of Barbara Anslow (née Redwood).

British and Indian POWs captured at Shing Mun (10 December 1941). "Potato" Jones is bottom left. In the greatcoat is Sergeant Summers; next to Summers is Laird. The man with the eye-patch is Thompson; holding him, in the dark jacket, is Willcox. Courtesy of *Mainichi Shimbun*.

Captured Indian soldiers being disarmed at Argyle Street (30 December 1941). Courtesy of *Mainichi Shimbun*.

Official notice to John Idwal Morris's family upon his capture. Courtesy of Michael Morris.

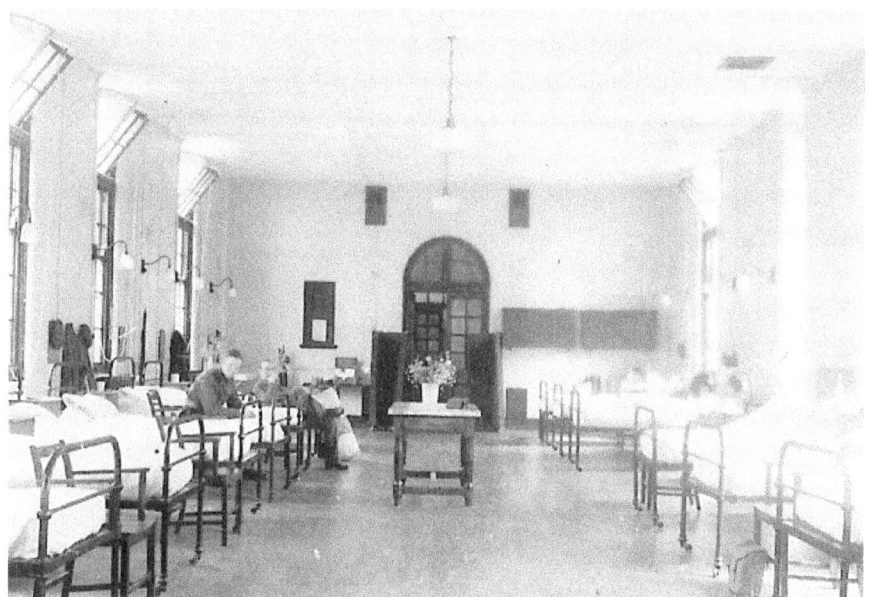

Interior of Bowen Road Hospital (taken shortly before the war). Photo by John Idwal Morris. Courtesy of Michael Morris.

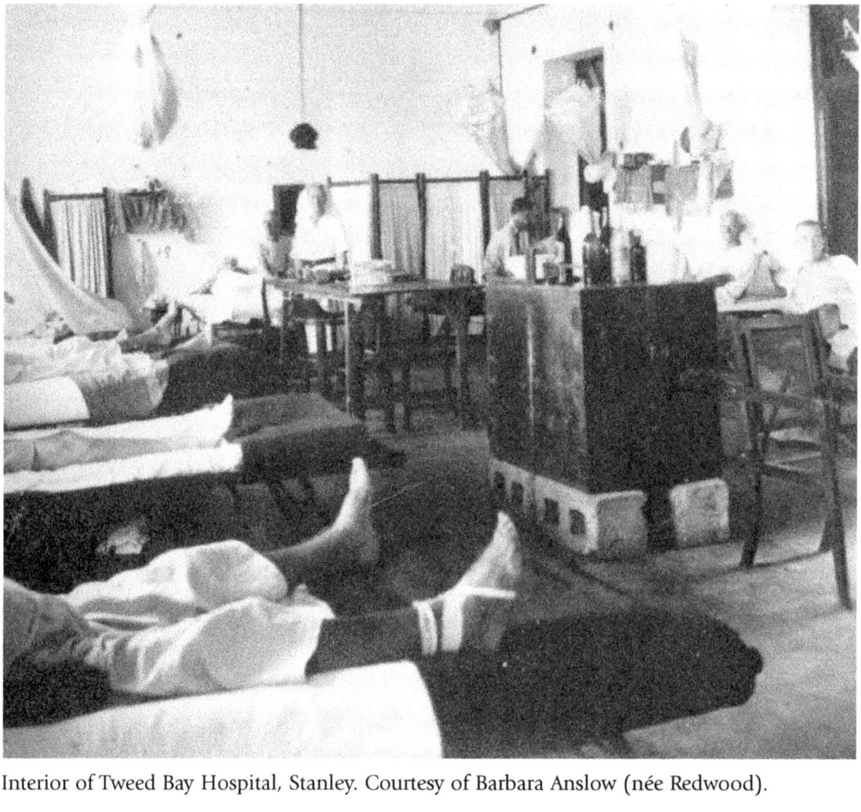

Interior of Tweed Bay Hospital, Stanley. Courtesy of Barbara Anslow (née Redwood).

Shamshuipo POW Camp by Cicero Rozario. Courtesy of Anna Rozario.

Montage of some of those lost as POWs. Top row, from left to right: William Organ, Paul Connolly, Reginald Guppy, Frank Ferrington, Glen Paul; bottom row, from left to right: Gerard Attwell, William Mair, Charles Goodwin, Cecil Freeman, Hubert Bujold.

Posthumous notice of awards to Robert Douglas, Royal Scots, one of many who passed away in the infamous diphtheria epidemic. Courtesy of Mark Sellar.

The Under-Secretary of State for War presents his compliments and by Command of the Army Council has the honour to transmit the enclosed Awards granted for service in the war of 1939-45. The Council share your sorrow that 3053715 R Douglas in respect of whose service these Awards are granted did not live to receive them.

Carving by Sergeant John Payne, given to Sergeant Tom Marsh (both Winnipeg Grenadiers). Courtesy of Vic Marsh.

US civilian repatriates on the *Gripsholm*. Courtesy of Cathy Thomas (daughter of Ray Pidcock). Front row, from left to right: 1. Folts 2. Bill Costen 3. ? 4. Mal Southwick 5. Ray Pidcock 6. Chic Sprague 7. Mills 8. Erwin Kock 9 Pete Kipp. Middle row: 1. Jack Sindlinger 2. Henry Durschmidt 3. Mac Ulrick 4. Elmer Nelson 5. ? 6. Jack Richmond 7. Jones 8. Dick Sanger 9. Chief Meyers. Back row: 1. Keemaham 2. ? 3. ? Myer 4. Frank MacCorkle 5. Charles Larson 6. Fred Twogood 7. Al Bourne 8. (obscured) 9. Herb Rea 10. Teitys 11. Norman Briggs 12. ? 13. Austin Glass 14. Frank Peters 15. ? 16. King Paget 17. ?

Montage of those who survived. Top row, from left to right: Joan Whitely, Kay Christie, Kamta Prasad, James O'Toole, Manassah "Nat" Rakusen; bottom row, from left to right: Vladimir Alec Itenson, Gordon Joynson, Henry Merlock, Kenneth Hogarth, Maurice Parker.

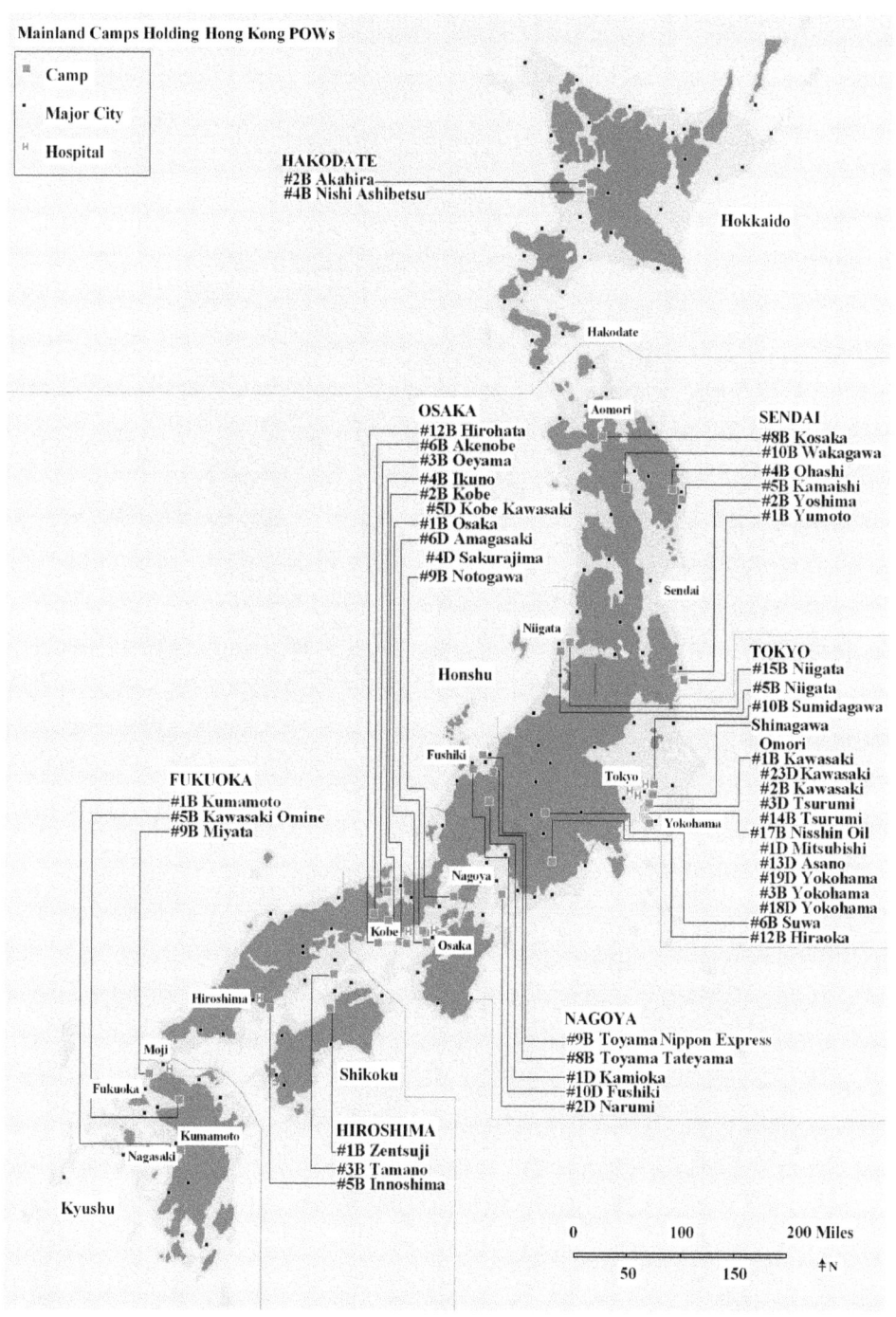

All POW camps in Japan known to have held ex-HK POWs. Illustration by Tony Banham.

The Mine Entrance at Omine (Fukuoka #5B). NARA.

Sketch of Oeyama (Osaka #3B), by Marcel Van Damme, Winnipeg Grenadiers. Courtesy of Helen Chinske (daughter of Marcel Van Damme).

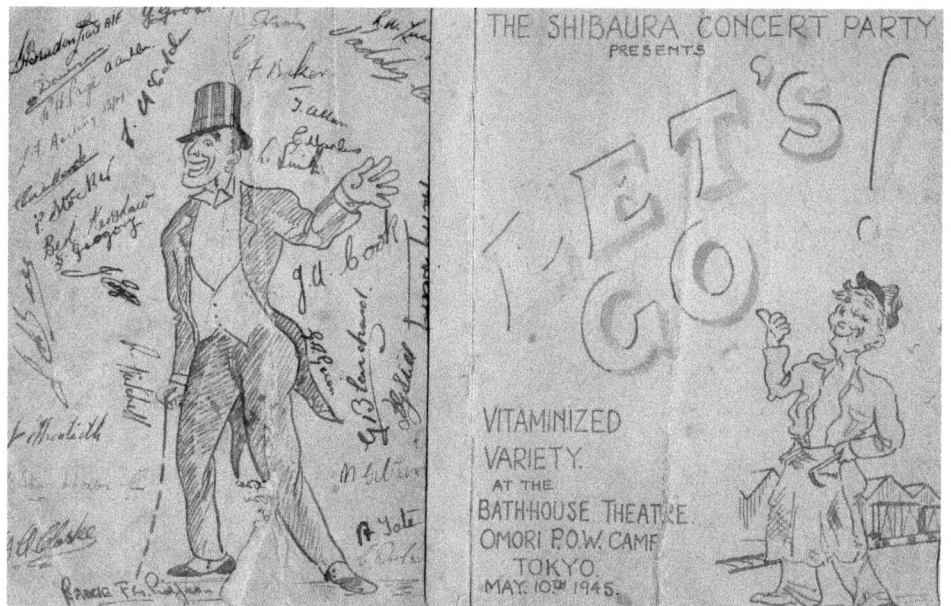

Concert program from Omori. Courtesy of Susan Simmonds.

Yoshima coal mine, by Cicero Rozario. Courtesy of Anna Rozario (daughter of Cicero Rozario).

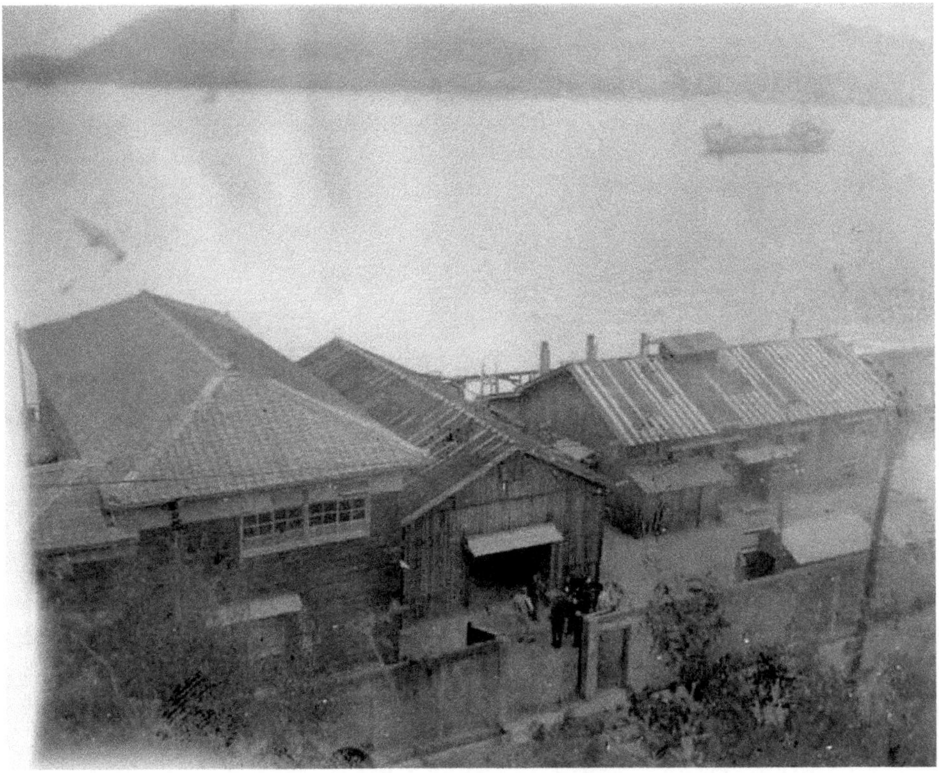

Innoshima (Hiroshima #5B).

Royal Naval Yard, H.K.

F.P.R.O. No. T 420

Ticket No.

Name J. ROGERS.

Occupation WARRANT OFFICER

Dept. H.K. R.N.V.R

H.M.S. CORNFLOWER

Thumb Print.

PHOTOGRAPH.

T 420

Full Face

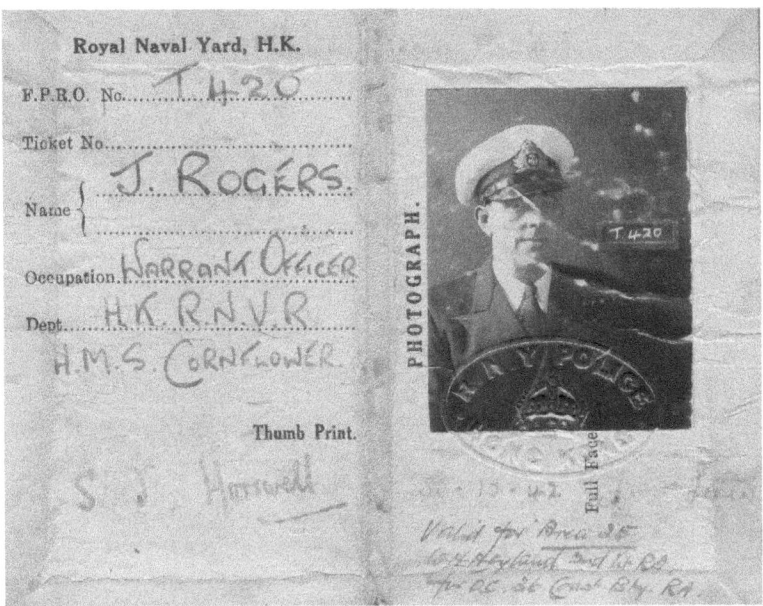

James Rogers' pass, from Narumi (Nagoya #2B). NARA.

POWs at Sumidagawa (Tokyo #10B). Courtesy of Jenny Watts, daughter of Charlie Alexander (via Tony Hyman).

Canadian POWs at Sendai #2B. Courtesy of Ed Shayler. Back row, from left to right: Morris Peterson, Dick Wilson, John Polluck, George Peterson, Fred English, Tom Mulvaney, Jim Furey, Chuck Bradshaw, Frank Drier, Derek Rix, Al MacTier, Sid Vale. Middle row: Walter Slovinsky, Soren Paulson, Ed Shayler, Thomas St. Germain. Front row: "Dolly" Davis, John Beaton (?), George "Sailor" Morgan, George Temple, Fred Poitras, Tom Hoskayne.

The ashes of the twenty-seven POWs killed by the bombardment of *Kamaishi*.

Portuguese POWs at Sendai #2B. Back row, from left to right: A. P. "Chunky" Xavier, H. A. "Ariri" Noronha, E.A. "Dicky" Noronha, Arthur Basto, Robert A. Souza, L. A. Souza, A. J. M. Prata, E. J. "Turibio" Cruz, Jesus (food control), George Ablong. Fourth row: Marciano Silva, Benny Marcal, F. W. Reis, Tonin Sequeira, T. M. Castilho, Caetano Azedo, J. F. D. Ribeiro, D. C. Alves, J. A. Marques, Pepe Baleros. Third row: Carlos "Sluggo" Soares, David Leonard, E. A. V. Remedios, Norman Leonard, Henrique Ribeiro, Richard Silva, Harry Mathias, A. F. Noronha, Freddy Rocha, Robbie Rocha, C. A. Roza, Garcia, E. J. Figuereido, Gussy Sequieira. Second row: L. R. Campos, C. A. J. Ribeiro (standing), Luiz Xavier, A. C. Neves, Zinho Gosano, C. F. dos Remedios, Dr A. M. Baptista (US Army), J. C. Remedios, Reggie Reed, R. J. "Bob" Barnes, A. Cruz (Macau), Luzito Remedios. Front row: M. A. Larcina, Roberto Silva, G. S. Edwards, "Alichey" Ribeiro, E. S. Marques, Rocque Silva, A. "Archilles" Jorge, Hugo Ribeiro, Henry Souza, Cicero Rozario, A. B. "Tony" Carvalho, Billy Wilkinson, A. M. "Smokey" Xavier.

Fushiki/Nomachi (Nagoya #10B) at Liberation. Courtesy of Dennis Morley.

The lost B24s: *Ginny* and *Les Miserables*.

Shamshuipo Camp "N" officers receive their injections at Liberation. Courtesy of Ian Forsyth. Left to right: Laurence Purves (RASC), Robert Geer (HKVDC), Ernest Toull (RA), Kamta Prasad (Punjabis), George Farrington (RM), Alan Guinness (RA). Injector, Osmond Skinner (HKVDC).

Amputees drink to their health at Liberation (Dave Wanstall far left). Courtesy of Andy Wanstall.

Osaka POW Repatriation team. Courtesy of Charles Jordan.

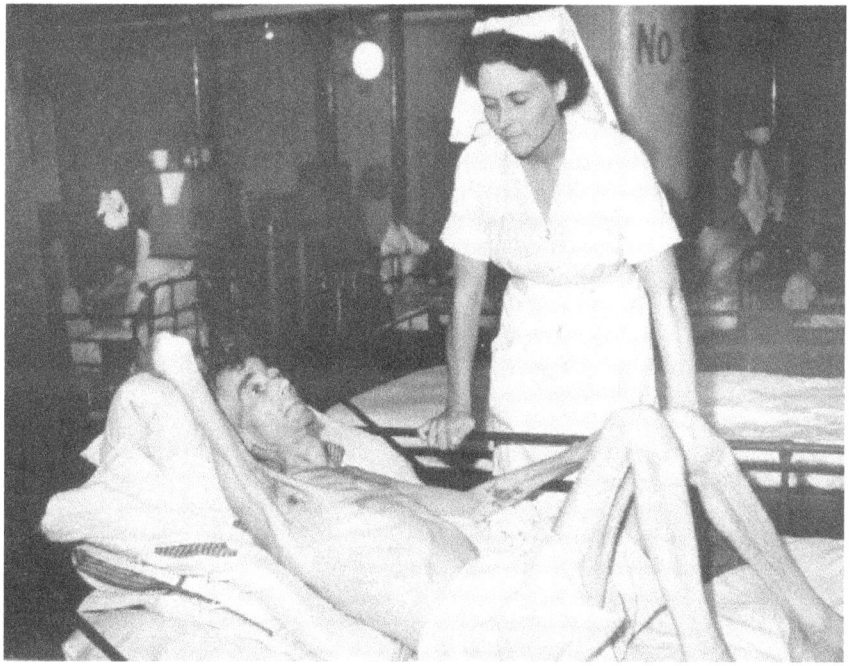

Captain H. G. Camp, RA, suffering from severe malnutrition. He was taken from Central British School hospital to HMS *Oxfordshire*, where he is seen attended by Sister S. M. Augustus. September 1945. IWM: A 30523.

Hangar deck ready for RAPWIs on HMS *Colossus*.

USS *Goodhue*. Courtesy of Faye Hamilton (whose husband served aboard).

HMS *Implacable*.

Eric Bromley and Arthur Deadman (HKDDC) in Victoria, BC, Canada. Courtesy of Brian Bromley.

BUCKINGHAM PALACE

The Queen and I bid you a very warm welcome home.

Through all the great trials and sufferings which you have undergone at the hands of the Japanese, you and your comrades have been constantly in our thoughts. We know from the accounts we have already received how heavy those sufferings have been. We know also that these have been endured by you with the highest courage.

We mourn with you the deaths of so many of your gallant comrades.

With all our hearts, we hope that your return from captivity will bring you and your families a full measure of happiness, which you may long enjoy together.

George R.I.

September 1945.

Welcome home from the King. Sent to John Idwal Morris. Courtesy of Michael Morris.

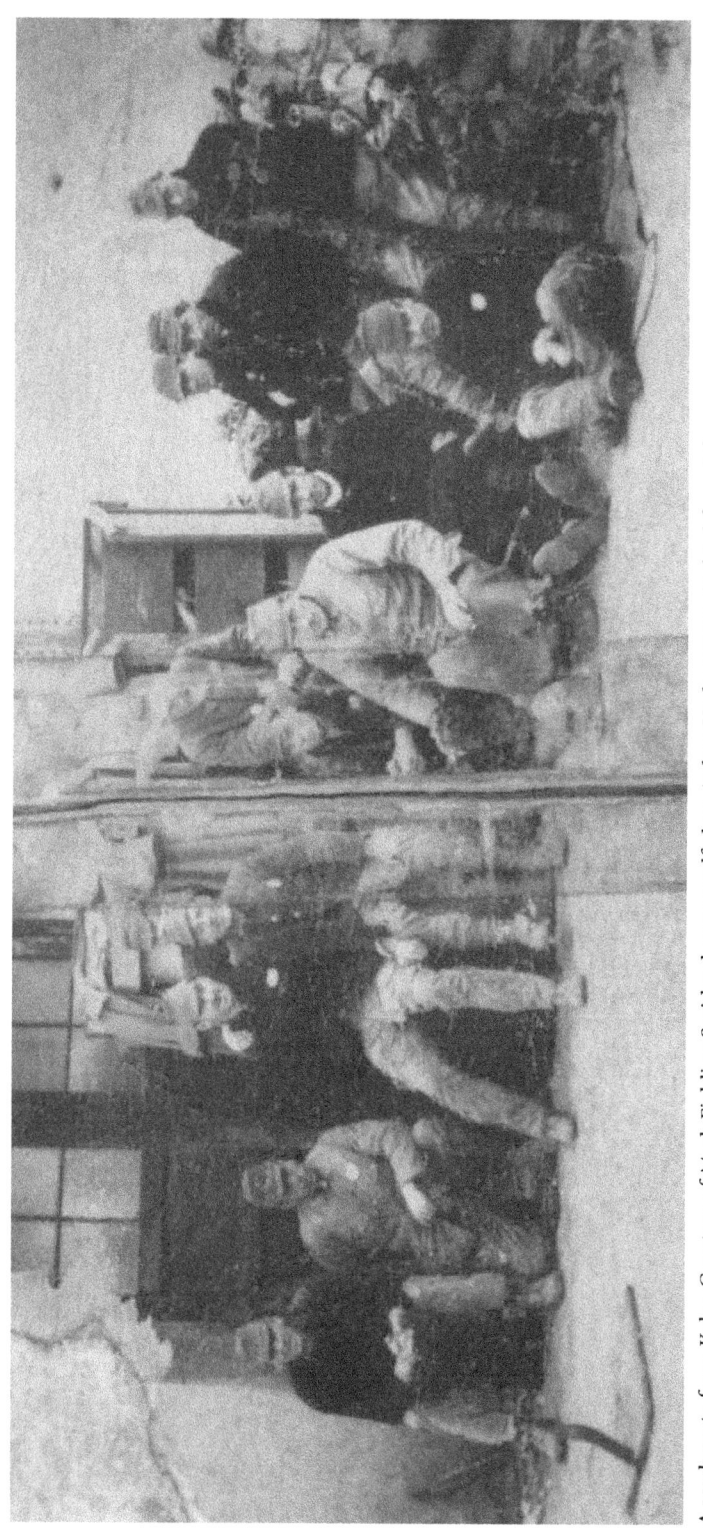

A work party from Kobe. Courtesy of Mark Fielding-Smith whose grandfather, Arthur Herbert Betts, is third from left.

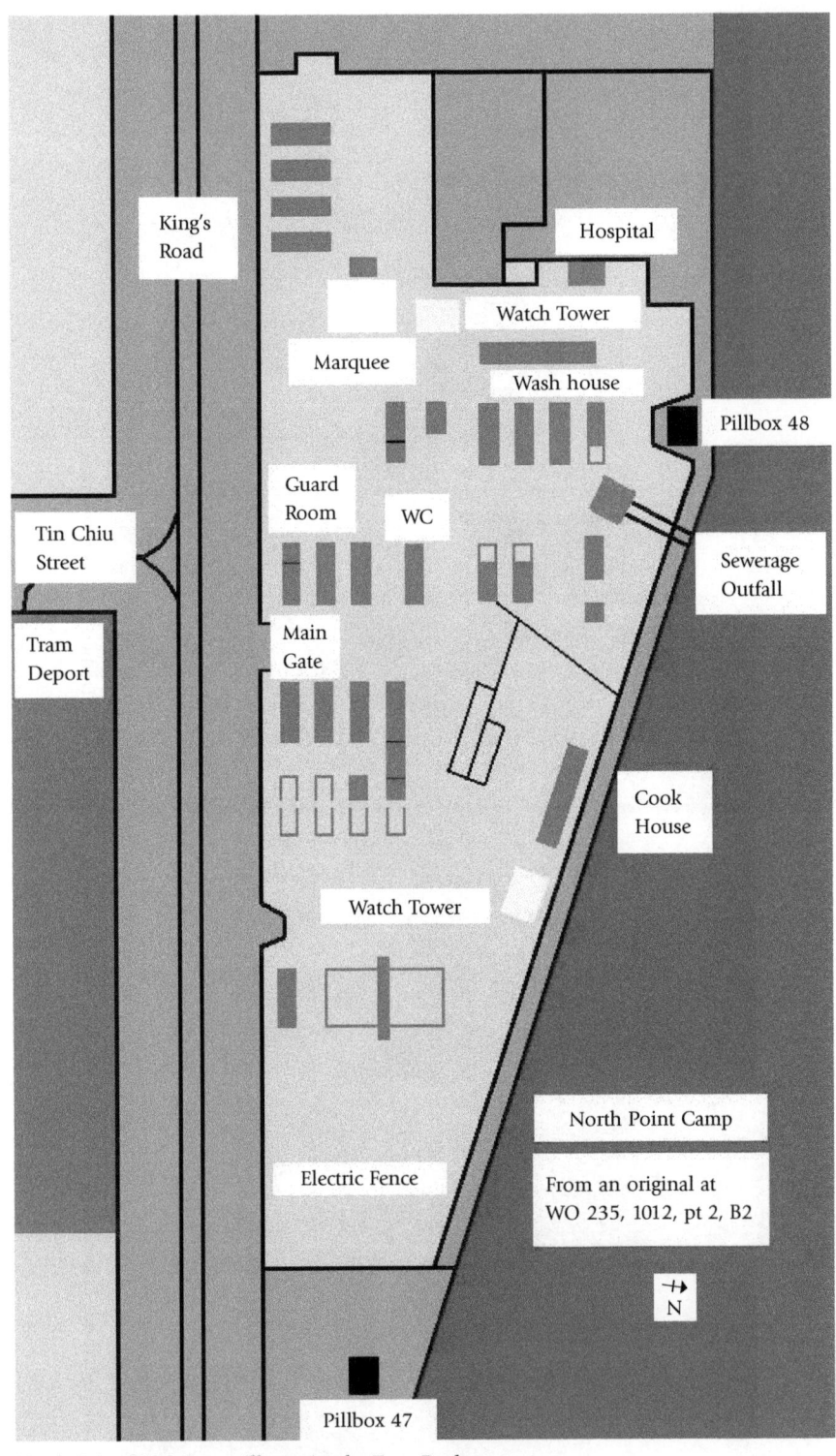

North Point POW Camp. Illustration by Tony Banham.

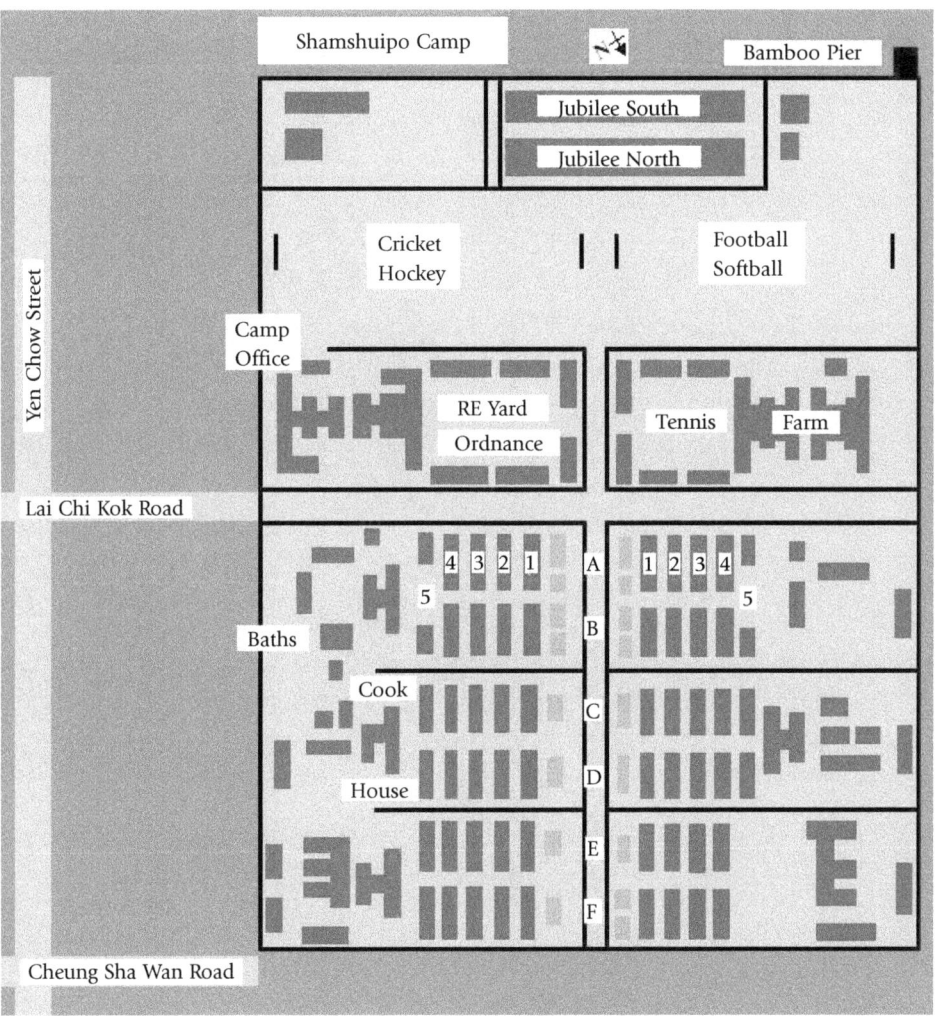

Shamshuipo POW Camp. Illustration by Tony Banham, from an original sketch by Cicero Rozario.

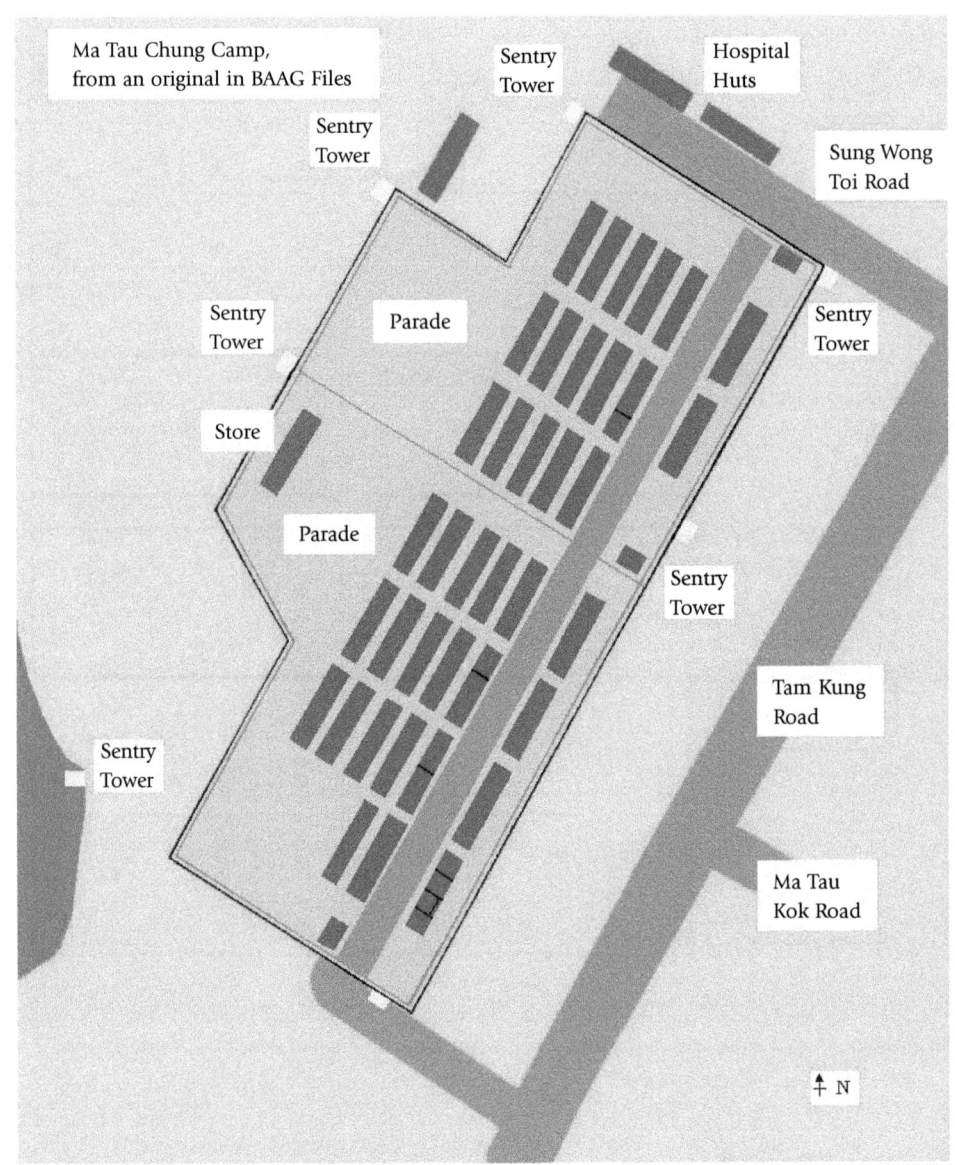

Ma Tau Chung POW Camp. Illustration by Tony Banham.

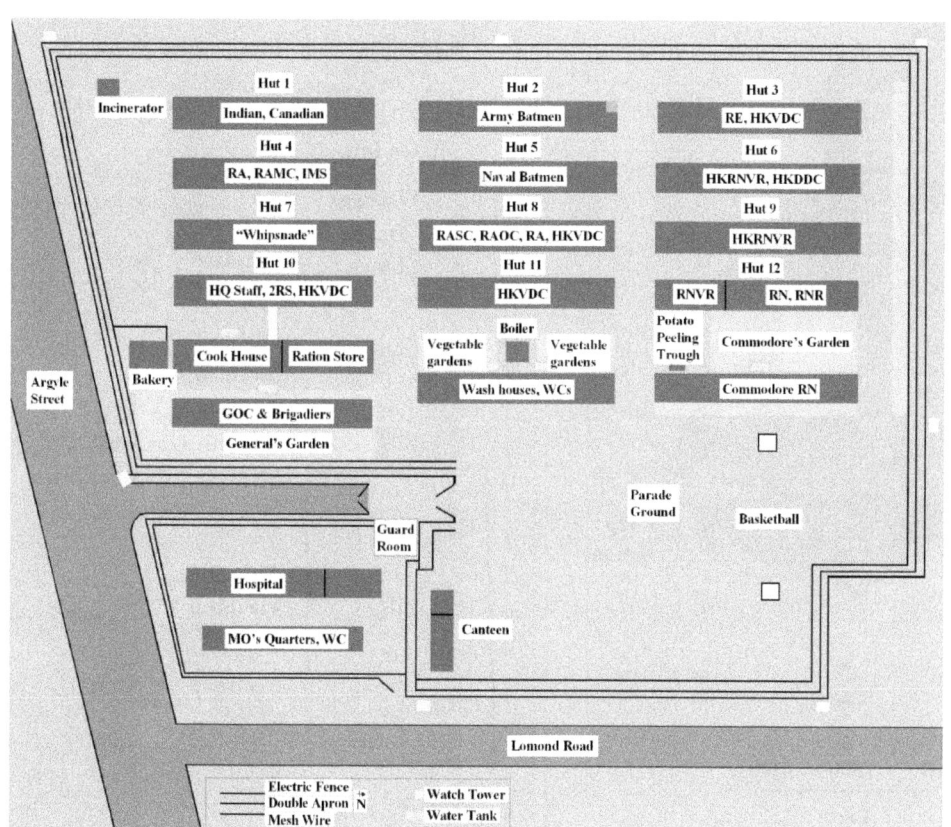

Argyle Street POW Camp. Illustration by Tony Banham, from an original sketch by Ian Forsyth, 2/14th Punjabis.

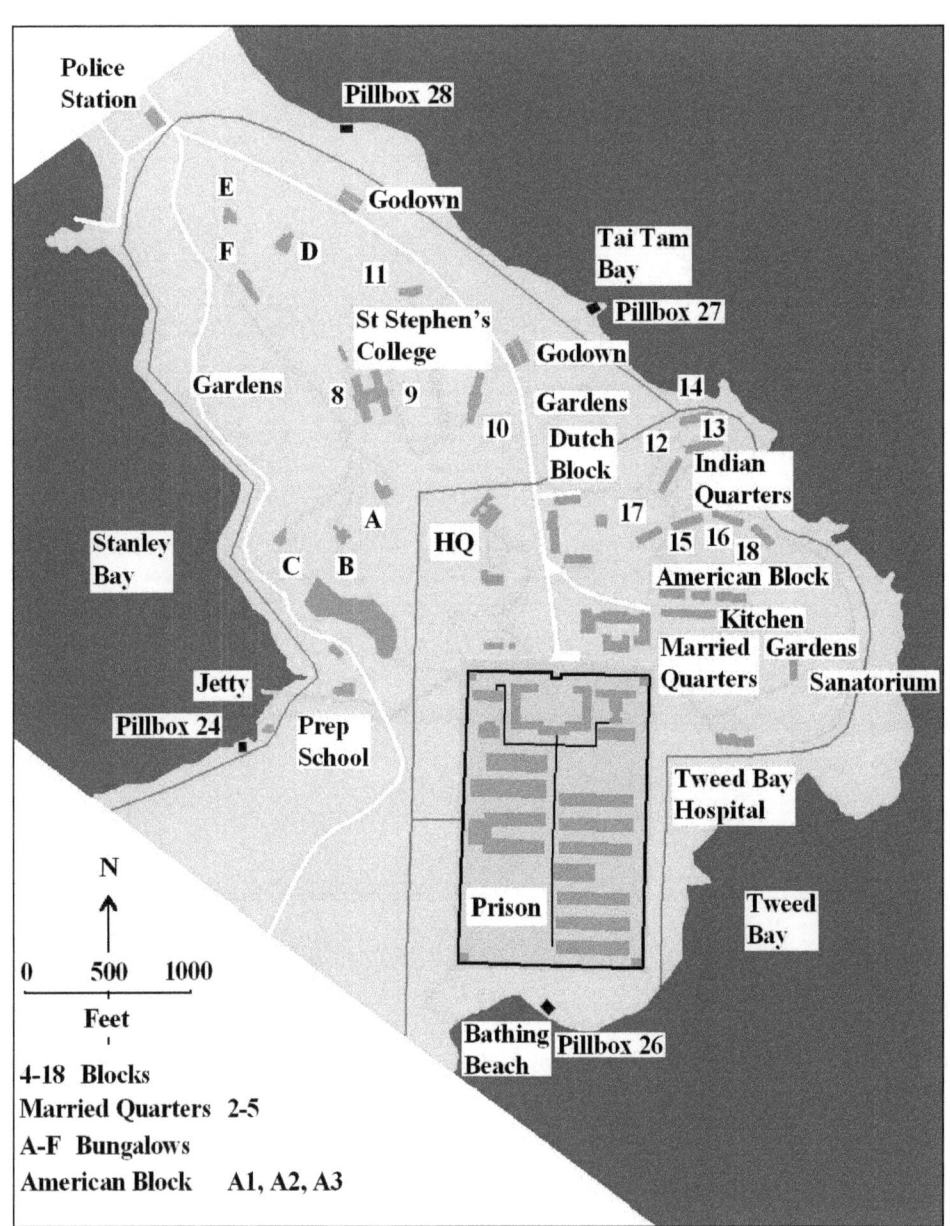

Stanley Internment Camp. Illustration by Tony Banham.

1942

> They say a man is his true self when drunk, well you should see 'em go back to the raw in here. Very few are the same men after six months, and that goes for all classes, what they are really made of just comes out. The first thing they get into their heads was that rank didn't count any more we are all equal now. Therefore discipline is out. The big majority just want to lay on their beds all day, read, play cards, get up to eat & watch the next chap to see that he hasn't got a bit extra, this state of mind is awful and applies to most of us unless you get something to do. You get sick & tired of the same faces around all the time, the same fool arguments rage over nothing.
>
> — Staff Sergeant James O'Toole, RAOC

As 1942 began, just seven days after the surrender, the Japanese occupying forces were still attempting to gain control of their new conquest. Initially, POWs were spread arbitrarily between Shamshuipo, Argyle Street, and North Point, with many still in other locations and the hospitals. While efforts at concentration had begun, the majority of non-Chinese civilians were still at large, and many local Chinese members of the garrison had shed their uniforms and merged with the population at large.[1]

The initial Japanese focus, therefore, lay in rationalizing the camps and hospitals, and taking a census of the 'European' civilians. In consultation with the Director of Medical Services, Selwyn Selwyn-Clarke, the area between Stanley Village and Stanley Gaol was selected as the main civilian internment camp; it offered the isolation that the occupying forces required, together with clean sea breezes that Selwyn-Clarke thought beneficial to health. The internees would arrive there in late January.[2]

By the end of the same month, Shamshuipo had been established as the POW Camp for British regular soldiers, HKVDC, and RAF; North Point was holding the Canadians and the Royal Navy; Ma Tau Chung was opened as the British Indian Army camp, and all 'enemy' civilians had been sent to Stanley Internment Camp.[3]

In the early months, a few of those with the necessary spirit and determination would escape, but the lack of food soon sapped the energy of the majority. As the year wore on, epidemics and instances of malnutrition diseases started to appear in ever growing numbers. Dysentery and diphtheria soon made their mark as the biggest killers; the 'peace' of 1942 would kill almost as many men as died in the fighting.

In the spring, following a number of escapes, the Japanese decided to separate the officers from the men, and a special camp for the former was established at Argyle Street.

By September the Japanese had realized that shipping POWs to work in Japan's mines, factories, and docks would free up Japanese men to join the services. Almost 2,500 men would be shipped out by the end of the year, though over 800 would die when the second vessel to depart, the *Lisbon Maru*, was torpedoed off Shanghai.

The end of the year would find the surviving POWs spread across South China, Shanghai, and a number of new POW camps in Japan itself.

DIARY FOR 1942

January 1942

Thursday, 1 January. Forsyth, Shamshuipo: "Quite cold in our windowless, doorless hut, very windy. Dust and ashes are swirling around from the rubbish fires which are burning all day yesterday around our huts. Men are grouped around little cooking fires trying to boil water to make tea. A chill cheerlessness pervades the camp."

As part of the rationalization of camps, the Royal Naval Hospital was closed down. Convalescents were sent to St Albert's Convent, and the seriously wounded to Bowen Road.

Ralph Goodwin was lying wounded at the RNH: "Patients on the road to recovery, which included me, were sent to St Albert's Convent at Rosary Hill, while the more seriously hurt went to Bowen Road Hospital. By that time it was possible for me to walk with the aid of one crutch, and we soon settled down to life in our new surroundings. The Japanese gave orders that no one was to leave the hospital compound, but they put no guards round the area and we had a great deal of freedom. Cloud frequently settled down almost as low as the hospital, and under cover of their thick folds those patients who were fit enough went foraging on the battlefields along the top ridge. Large quantities of clothing and equipment were gathered, and a certain amount of canned goods to augment the rations for the lucky finders."[4] (p. 21)

Having now decided what to do with the enemy civilians, the Japanese took action early in the New Year.

Sunday, 4 January.   Policeman George Wright-Nooth: "The Gendarmerie issued a proclamation ordering all Europeans, except third nationals and the police, to assemble at the Murray Road Parade Ground. They were to bring only what they could carry. They were divided into groups and moved under guard into various waterfront hotels."[5] (p. 79)

Barbara Redwood: "On the 5th January 1942, we, the ARP people, were sent by the Japanese to Murray Parade Ground where little tables and paper and pens had been put; we were told that other civilian prisoners would be coming and line up and our job was to register each one. However, this job had hardly got under way when the Japs for some reason changed their minds about it, and we were sent back to the [Tai Koon Hotel]. From then on, civilians could be seen (from our verandah facing Queen's Road) being led along; a large contingent was directed into our hotel. One day I saw my elder sister Olive walking by with her Food Control colleagues. They ended up in a hotel beyond ours called the Nanking."[6]

Wright-Nooth continued: "I saw them go past the Gloucester Hotel, herded together under their guards. There were old men and women struggling with what they had managed to save from the wreck. There were women with children in their arms. Some carried blankets strapped across their backs with suitcase in hand, other had packs, others still used Chinese carrying poles or had bundles wrapped in blankets. The rich and the poor were alike. It was a pathetic sight." (p. 79)

The majority of enemy civilians were soon concentrated at a large number of hotels, hospitals, and places of work.[7]

Monday, 5 January.   John Stericker,[8] approaching Room 132, Tung Fong Hotel, noted: "As we marched up the stairs we were counted and deflected to either floor, four to a room, men and women, just as they came. In my room I had a bulky colleague in my own firm, while I touched the six-feet mark myself. With us was an elderly cripple and his wife. This was 5th January, and here we remained until 21st January. In other words we had sixteen nights and for those sixteen nights, in each cubicle, four people slept on one bed seventy-two inches by thirty-six. We could only do this by resting our buttocks on the bed, as on a seat, with our heads against any soft article of clothing we could spare, and our feet resting on our suitcases. Take the sum of any four average adult shoulder-widths and see how they fit into seventy-two inches." (p. 141)

In Stericker's hotel, there were just two toilets for 150 people. And still they kept coming. Not surprisingly, some British and American civilians had decided to stay put.

Briggs was one of those on the Peak: "We had a month's supply of food at the house, and we did not know what would happen if we reported to the Parade Ground. If they asked us later why we didn't go, we could plead ignorance. We decided to stay, even though we knew we were running a risk by not reporting. It turned out we made the right decision."

However, Selwyn-Clarke's suggestion had been good. The Stanley Camp was allocated the grounds of St Stephen's College, the old cemetery, and the Stanley Prison warders' buildings (though not the prison itself). While too small for the number of people interned, it was a relatively pleasant environment.[9]

But the non-enemy civilians were even less lucky. Amongst their number were many who fell somewhere in between the two groups. Although not considered 'enemy aliens', neither were they Chinese. They lacked both the formal protection given to the former by the rules of war, and — in some cases — the latter's informal family support. Their social network had been destroyed by the invasion, and they were left to fend for themselves.

Luba Estes was one of these people: "In the row of apartments where we were staying, the house at the far end, was also full of people . . . they suffered terribly. I don't think we ever found out why they were punished. The families in that house were all ordered outside. All the men were made to line up on one side, the women and children on the other. And in front of the women and children, the Japanese soldiers proceeded to execute all the men. In the same compound, in front of the house we were in, one day, I heard dreadful agonizing screams. I was nearest to the front window on the ground floor and I looked out through the curtains — about 25 feet away, I saw three Chinese men piled one on top of the other, being systematically bayoneted by three Japanese soldiers. They stabbed their bodies in unison with a fierce shout each time . . . over and over again. An adult pulled me away because I was staring frozen in horror. The three men did not die right away. These poor men took all day dragging themselves on their stomachs, spreading out in different directions and none of us dared to help. No one. Nothing. By morning they were dead."[10]

Stericker, before being taken to the Tung Fong Hotel had noted: "In many places, too, one found the bodies of Chinese who had been shot or bayoneted for looting. An even more ghastly sight was the Chinese who were tied together, alive, to the trees by the lower Peak tram terminus. Day after day, in three large groups, these unfortunates could be seen, strung together, with ropes around their necks and hands. As one fell through sheer exhaustion, he would drag the next man down with him, slowly throttling him. There was nothing any of us could do about them except pray and hate." (p. 138)

For many Chinese families the only hope of survival was to escape north, back to their family roots. Major Kenneth Baird, of the Winnipeg Grenadiers was moved by what he saw.[11] From Shamshuipo he reported: "For the past week we have seen thousands of Chinese refugees going back to where they came from. It was said that over 500,000 flocked into Hong Kong and Kowloon; with them leaving it will mean that many less to feed, and perhaps better conditions. To see them in an endless chain wending their way slowly up through the hills makes one admire their hardiness. They are slight in build and so thin, and yet they carry incredible loads slung on the ends of a bamboo pole. They start sometime before daylight and go in one long stream until afternoon, about 12,000 to 15,000 each day. We can see the road for a distance of about two miles and it is one mass of people." (p. 41)

Wednesday, 7 January. Tom Forsyth of the same regiment added: "Their plight is pitiful. All on foot, women and little children and babes in arms, climbing the steep rocky road over the mountains, their worldly goods in a bundle on their backs, retracing the same road down which they had fled not so long before, hoping for safety and protection from a brutal conqueror. What possible hope would they ever have of reaching Chinese occupied territory?"[12]

Benny Proulx, a fellow Canadian serving with the HKRNVR, added: "Each dawn those who had died still lay beside the winding road." (p. 160)

Thursday, 8 January. Redwood noted: "300 more internees crammed into our hotel."

Thursday, 8 January. As part of a plan master-minded by Lieutenant-Colonel Ride of the Combined Field Ambulance, Lance Corporal Francis Lee Yiu Piu of the Hong Kong Field Ambulance[13] escaped onto a sampan by jumping from a poorly-guarded jetty at the western corner of Shamshuipo.[14]

Friday, 9 January. Clearly Lee's escape had gone unnoticed. Donald Hill at Shamshuipo: "Jap General arrives with an escort of twelve cars and troops manning machine guns in lorries. He drives to the gods [*sic*] hut, steps out, has his photograph taken, and drives off without a word. What a farce. Many wild rumours but as usual no truth in them."

Friday, 9 January. As pre-arranged, Lee brought the sampan back to Shamshuipo at 20.30. After clearing the area of unwanted spectators, Lt. Col. Lindsay Ride, HKVDC, Lts. D. Davies and D. Morley, HKRNVR, boarded the boat with their escape equipment and departed.[15]

Saturday, 10 January. O'Toole at Argyle Street: "We had no clothes, soap, razors, and most of the poor devils who had not been to the Mary Knoll had no blanket. Just slept fully clothed as the nights were very cold. I managed to get a note to Alan Barwell who was at La Salle College just across the way, he sent me in a blanket, some shorts, socks, & half a cake of soap, a great help especially the soap and blanket. Unfortunately soon after this he was moved to Stanley with the internees, so could write no more. Chinese used to come to the wire and sell fags at high prices 10 for a dollar. Often you got an empty packet. If they were caught a good beating up was the punishment."

Nevertheless, people were willing to risk beatings or financial loss for food. Already the poor diet was having an effect.

Tuesday, January 13. Hill: "Many sick with tummy trouble. One feels fairly fit but completely lacking in energy. Twenty Scots arrive from Fan Ling, amongst them being Potato Jones,[16] who commanded the company at the Shing Mun Redoubt, and Lieut Thompson, who was hit by a grenade and is practically blind. Japs refuse to take him to hospital[17] which will probably cost him his sight."

Saturday, 17 January. Frank Evans: "There is extra fencing around the camp and it is impossible for anyone to come near. Two persons, a boy and a girl, were shot for trying to sell food to us.[18] Andy Stevenson and Eric Earnshaw are quite depressed tonight." (p. 26)

Stevenson and Earnshaw were not the only ones. Almost every POW in Shamshuipo remembered the shooting and although each diary entry differs, the essential shock of the incident remains the same. Baird recalled: "The Japs are shooting the Chinese that bring things to the fence for sale. [They shot two girls], just youngsters about 12 years old, killing them both." (p. 55)

With trading through the wire becoming more dangerous, and the number of POWs still increasing, both rations and morale were suffering.

Monday, 19 January. Hill: "Now get three meals of rice a day but quantity the same. Rice by itself is awful muck, but we save our small stock of milk and sugar for our evening tea. Over hundred men arrive from Queen Mary's hospital."

Tuesday, 20 January. Hill: "More men arrive in lorries, some unable to walk, and dressed only in pyjamas and socks. Troops give a concert including dance band. Cigarettes very scarce."

Wednesday, 21 January. Hill again: "Fight between Middlesex and Indians. Rice ration very short."

Outside the camp, to their relief (at least initially) the civilians were finally on the move.

Wednesday, 21 January. Redwood: "In the morning, we were given a quarter of an hour in which to pack and get out of the hotel. Were marched down Des Voeux Road." Gwen Priestwood was in the same group: "Then we were all lined up in columns of four abreast and made to march along the Praya to a small jetty where the Jardine Matheson boats used to tie up. A small boy of five or six, with blue eyes and fair hair, walked along in front of me. He wore a blue overcoat, and from its belt hung everything his mother thought he would need: an enamel mug, a spoon, knife, and fork, a small chamber, scissors, an enamel saucepan, and other things. His mother walked beside him, a light curtain pole over her shoulder, with an assortment of bundles hanging on it — probably her few remaining belongings."[19] Redwood continued: "Then boarded top-heavy Macau steamer and set out for Stanley. The boat was too big to go right up to the jetty at Stanley, so we had to transfer to a junk. From the jetty there was a path across the beach which led up a steep bank, near St Stephen's preparatory School."

The POWs were also being reorganized. The Indian soldiers were about to be concentrated at the Ma Tau Chung refugee camp, the Canadians (and Royal Navy) at North Point, and the HKVDC and British army regulars at Shamshuipo.

Wednesday, 21 January. The Indians in North Point Camp were moved to Ma Tau Chung Camp on Argyle Street. On the following day, the Indians in Shamshuipo would follow, and then the HKVDC and British army regulars started to move out of North Point. Allister, at North Point, recorded their leaving. "The Volunteers were moved to Sham Shui Po, and with them went a large slice of richness and colour. Classes ended. Free time disappeared. Malnutrition diseases increased everywhere and diphtheria showed up. The Canadians sank into a bog of gloom and monotony." (p. 72)

Friday, 23 January. Those Canadians still at Shamshuipo moved to North Point. Forsyth: "After counting and recounting by the Japs we start at 10, march in fours thru Kowloon, cross to Island on the ferry, see many sunken boats on the way over with parts of their funnels or smoke stacks showing. Reach North Point camp; wait while some Imperials and Chinese Volunteers march out to make room for us. What is left of Royal Rifles are here."

On the same day, Fisher of the HKVDC was passing Forsyth mid-harbour, making the reverse journey to Shamshuipo: "We were marched along King's Road and embarked on a ferry . . . Steaming down the harbour we saw many sunken ships with only their funnels and masts showing."[20]

Friday, 23 January. The last British and American civilians on the Peak were also about to be relocated. Briggs noted: "We did get word from the Representative that we were all to be downtown at Queen's Pier at 10:00 AM on Saturday when we would go to Stanley."

As Wright-Nooth recorded on arriving at Stanley: "Our Bungalow, which was called Bungalow 'C', was in an awful condition. Aside from the graves the vicinity had live small arms ammunition strewn around like so much confetti; many unexploded grenades (mostly Japanese), mortar bombs and rifle grenades had been left precisely as they had been abandoned. The building itself had a shell hole through the roof, all windows were smashed and the walls scarred by bullets or shrapnel. The water pipes had burst, the drains were blocked and overflowing, blood was spattered everywhere."[21] (p. 87)

Briggs at the American Block: "As far as housing goes, the Americans were far better off than anyone else. The quarters we were in were designed to hold around 400 people. We were smaller in numbers than the British, and the Dutch did not have enough to have a separate building by themselves. The group of buildings that the Japanese assigned to us were in a unit by themselves. We were lucky that our number adequately filled them. Where we would have five or six people in a room, the British would have from eight to ten in the same size room. We were very fortunate in this and it may have been done purposely by the Japanese, but in the main I think it was just good luck. If there were any advantages that could be given, I think the Americans were favored."

However, fellow American Wenzell Brown of the University of Hong Kong added, about the leader of the American group: "Primary among his accomplishments was that he had secured a more than fair allotment of space for us and also more than a fair proportion of the food that came into camp. This was accomplished through misrepresentation of our numbers."[22]

Jean Gittins' experience agreed with Briggs: "The Americans, on the other hand, stood out as the most favoured nation: throughout their short internment they enjoyed many privileges in food and accommodation which were denied the rest of the camp. Whether they had the money to bribe the Japanese authorities, or they were merely given these privileges to arouse dissension among internees, I am unable to say, but I remember the envy we felt towards them even though there was nothing we could do about it."[23] (p. 117)

Briggs continued: "I arrived at Stanley on Saturday afternoon January 24, 1942. I was assigned to room with three other men, Henry Durrschmidt, Erwin Kock, and F. X. Lee. I did not take long to get settled, as I had only the two suitcases. As soon as they arrived, the Americans were taken care of. If they did not get a room assignment immediately, they at least had a temporary one before nightfall. Unfortunately, the British were not as organized. When they arrived, they had absolutely no idea of where to go."

By this stage, almost all enemy civilians had been interned at Stanley. The exceptions were a large number of bankers and their families who remained in the Sun Wah Hotel and continued to work at their banks. This work, however, was limited to resolving debts and signing bank notes for the Japanese.[24]

Now it was the turn of the POWs at Argyle Street Camp to be redistributed.

Saturday, 24 January. Deloughery at North Point: "British Naval personnel and a few Canadians moved in from Argyle St. Camp. We were very pleased to see this group as many of them including Major C. Young and Capt. M. Banfill of R.R.C. were reported as dead up until this time."[25]

Saturday, 24 January. O'Toole: "Break up of Argyle St camp. The Indians went to a camp of their own thank God, the Canadians to North Point, HK civilians if any to Stanley. All volunteers and regulars marched off to Sham Shui Po camp. Here we met all the old hands and were very glad to be together again. Bill N had plenty of cigarettes and some tinned food that they had bought over the wire, but also had plenty of clothing & their watches as they had not been captured but surrendered when the colony gave up under General Maltby's orders. Lucky chaps, had never had the pleasure of thinking they were going to be shot. Sham Shui Po camp had been the barracks of the Middlesex Regt pre war. It consisted of Hankow and Nankin barracks".

James Bertram, on arrival at Shamshuipo: "The camp lay between the hills and the sea, on a reclaimed harbour flat scored by deep typhoon drains. The whole area had formerly been used as a British military barracks. There was room for several thousand men; and the general design of the camp was not too bad — two large gravel parade grounds at either end, and two broad surfaced avenues shaped in cruciform. Everything reflected the sort of military mind that delights in chessboard uniformity — the barrack huts, spaced as rigidly as tent lines, were long low affairs with concrete floors. A freak amid all this severity was a fantastic four-storey block of flats [Jubilee Buildings] that rose like a mirage along the water front."[26] (p. 109)

Saturday, 24 January. A Dutch submarine crew arrived in North Point.[27] Proulx: "Three officers and thirty men, survivors of a submarine crew from the Royal Netherlands Navy, were brought into the camp. Their sub had been sunk by shellfire off Khota Baru on the first day of the war, when the Japs landed two hundred miles north of Singapore."

Tuesday, 27 January. But as some men entered, others departed. Four men escaped from North Point: Lieutenants J. Douglas, J. W. Hurst, B. Thompson (all RNR) and P. O. Telegraphist Maxwell Holroyd, RN. As Lieutenant Douglas, Commanding Officer, HMS *Tern* reported: "On 27th January I organised small escape party consisting of four, we crossed the Harbour in a stolen boat, hid five days in Kowloon Hills, walked for 20 days into China travelled by truck, train and San Pan to Lashio where we left for Calcutta by plane. Two of our escape party remained in Siu Kwan the other two of us came to Calcutta."[28]

Wednesday, 28 January. In the early morning, Benny Proulx together with two of the newly-arrived Dutch officers (Hordyke and Idema) also escaped from North Point. Proulx: "At twelve-fifteen, I and the two Dutchmen stood at the wall of our hut and through the open slits in the wooden walls we watched the guard start for the far end of camp. At the main gate he would pause for three to four minutes, before continuing to the water-front. Three of four minutes would be time enough. We slid through the door and ran towards the sea wall at a crouch." (p. 117) Jumping over the sea wall into the mud, they entered a sewer pipe, climbing up it in darkness and unpleasant conditions until they emerged in the hills.

Just a day later, the Japanese government clarified their position vis-à-vis the Geneva Convention which they had signed though not ratified:

> Gaimusho
> Tokyo
> 29th January 1942
>
> The Imperial Government has not yet ratified the Convention relative to the treatment of prisoners of war of 27th July 1929. It is, therefore, not bound by the said Convention. However, it will apply mutatis mutandis the provisions of the said Convention to English, Canadian, Australian and New Zealand prisoners of war in its hands.[29]

Saturday, 31 January. Anthony Hewitt, adjutant of the 1st Middlesex, had chosen that night to escape with Douglas Scriven and Eddie 'Junior' Crossley RNZAF: "That evening, Sunday, 31 January 1942, the three of us were invited to a 'last supper' in the RAF mess in Jubilee Buildings. They provided us with lots of extra bits of food to make the rice more edible. They were obviously very fond of Eddy, and determined to give him a good send off." (p. 21)

Three more men, Major Munro, RA, Flying Officer N. L. Baugh, RAF, and Captain I. B. Trevor, HKVDC were planning an escape the same night. Baugh: "We prepared a small raft of firewood to take our packs, which contained clothing and food supply, we intended to push the raft to the breakwater and swim to the shore some distance away from the camp where we thought there would not be any sentries, and so into the Kowloon hills along the stream bed . . . On the night of the 31st January we attempted to leave but the raft was unsuitable and we abandoned the attempt rather than risk losing our equipment."[30]

February 1942

In February 1942, the Japanese noted that the following numbers of Hong Kong POWs were in their hands: British: 5,072, Canadian: 1,689, Indian: 3,829, Others: 357, giving a total of 10,947.[31]

Sunday, 1 February. Hewitt, Scriven, and Crossley tried to escape at about 01.00, but found their way to the sampan blocked by other POWs claiming that 'their' boat was bringing food into the camp. Like the Munro party before them, they abandoned the attempt. However, others were to be more successful. That night, John Whitehead, Danny Parrott, Reg Lewis (all RA), and Mike Jacobs RAMC escaped from Shamshuipo via a drain.

Whitehead: "Danny slipped into the drain, followed by me, then Mike, with Reg bringing up the rear . . . in the dark it was a nightmare crawling among the rubble and fighting our way through the tangled mass of barbed wire . . . Eventually we reached the exit, a wide cylindrical pipe exuding its filth into the junk yard." (p. 77) Reg was separated from the others when the sentries started firing, and a bullet hit his mess tin and was deflected through his collar bone. Lying in the drain's effluent, he was saved by two Royal Scots who broke out of camp and dragged him back. He was brought into the sick bay and the Japanese never knew he had escaped. The other three men reached British lines.[32]

Sunday, 1 February. Hill was aware of both air force officers' escape plans: "Feb first. Japs stop all food coming into the camp. Whimpey and Junior due to try again tonight. Four of us get up at two to wait for the trading junks. Several hundred in queue. Sampan arrives at four and we buy sugar, milk, and sardines. Whimpey goes just before midnight, it being very light. Shortly after, we hear rifle fire and we pray that he made it. Bullets fly past our verandah. Junior gets off at two am in one of the trading junks."

Major Munro, RA, Flying Officer N. L. 'Whimpey' Baugh, RAF, and Captain I. B. Trevor, HKVDC had finally escaped from Shamshuipo. Baugh: "On the night of the 1st–2nd February at 2320 hours we left the camp and swam to the shore where we landed 0020 hours. We were all exhausted, but after a short rest we proceeded on our course roughly north over Golden Hill and Smuggler's Reach where we passed many unburied dead bodies."

Monday, 2 February. Anthony Hewitt, Crossley, and Scriven, also escaped, some twenty-four hours after their initial attempt, using the sea route at about 01.00. By this time, the guards were at last awake to all the escape activity. Hewitt: "A shot rang out, followed by three more. The clouds had shifted and the moon shone brilliantly on the stationary sampan. The bullets hit the water, ricocheting over our heads. Crowding down in the bottom of the sampan, we swore in Cantonese and English at the boatman, to make him go on paddling, but the shooting had been enough to force him to take the oar in his thin bony hands and paddle again, guiding the vessel along and close to the seaward side of the breakwater, giving us some cover from view. In a few seconds the moon clouded over again, but the sentries had got their machine gun into action and opened up with bursts of fire. Bullets sprayed all over the place, some bouncing off the water, some hitting the stone and concrete with an awesome crack, often a little too close for comfort. Eddie, lying full length in the bottom of the boat, kept up a steady flow of Anzac oaths, stronger at each near miss. But the shooting was wild, the pale moon and the breakwater protected us." (p. 28)

Monday, 2 February. That night, Lieutenant Gordon Fairclough, of the 17th Heavy AA Battery HKSRA, with Lieutenants Phillip A. L. 'Jumbo' Passmore, and 'Jock' Wedderburn RA, in yet another escape from Shamshuipo, took an almost identical route to the Hewitt party. Fairclough: "Dougie Clague cut the wire, enough for us to squeeze through, and we dropped into the sampan."[33]

In just seven days, seventeen of the Hong Kong garrison's officers and men, and two of their Dutch allies, had escaped.

Meanwhile, relatives of the POWs still tried to visit Shamshuipo camp to bring food or just to see loved ones. Jean Gittins: "We reached the appointed spot at 5.30 in the morning. [My husband Billy] and others were behind the barbed wire fence, staring into the semi-darkness, waiting. A small group of relatives who had obviously been given a similar message were standing on the other side of the wide road. Some of the girls sobbed quietly — the guards, they told us, had been anything but friendly, having shouted abuse at them and threatened to shoot if they moved any closer to the camp. In the murky light of early morning we were barely able to recognise the prisoners who were dressed alike in khaki. Billy waved his forage cap incessantly. It was bitterly cold."[34] (p. 34)

Friday, 6 February. Following the escapes, all RAF officers other than Hill were moved from Shamshuipo to Saigon. Hill: "Wake up to find the others busy dressing and packing. They have been ordered to be ready to move at short notice but I am not included. No one knows what it's all about. Just time for brief farewells and they are gone, driven off in a car and what luggage they follows [sic] in a lorry. I am now the only RAF officer left."

Wing Commander Alf Bennett was one of those taken by boat to Canton, and by plane from there (via Hainan) to Saigon. He described the Saigon camp thus: "[We were taken to a] military prison and put in a cell, say 14 feet by 20, 12ft high, one end was barred with wooden bars, the lower right half was the door so you had to bend double to get in. At the other end there was a small window high up in the wall through which you could see the blue sky and the glorious frangipani — there were no beds or bedding we had to sit, — squat, on the floor all day, not permitted to lie down by guards. Lights on all night nothing to read . . . In the far corner was a six gallon can that was widely used in the Far East for petrol with a wire handle — that was our shit bucket".[35]

Saturday, 7 February. Hill continued: "Eight officers move into the flat including a Chinese called Evans. In my room I have Captain Chippywood and Lieut Tressider. Ian Blair and Mathers of the Punjabis bring along some chapatties which go down well with butter and marmalade. Roy Haywood and Glasgow join us and spend a pleasant evening. Ken had been to Kai Tak on a working party and been roughly handled by a sentry but an officer apologised and gave him a tin of plums which he brings along."

The Japanese quickly realized that the POWs were a potential labour force. The first Shamshuipo work parties were to the Taipo Road to clear demolition charges placed there before the invasion by the Royal Engineers. Next, work started on extending Kai Tak airport, and soon other POWs were acting as dockers at Aberdeen, unloading Japanese war materials.[36]

Cicero Rozario: "We were put to work at Kai Tak Airport. We cleaned nullahs. We were also assigned the chore of shovelling down a whole hill to enlarge the airport. Some soldiers died from landslides despite out futile efforts to dig them out. The First Aid Station under a nearby tree was where we would get some rest by feigning illness. But the Japanese sentries caught on to us pretty fast when the sick grew from two or three to ten from one day to the next. They chased us back to work with fixed bayonets. Nonetheless we were able to sneak in some sleep time unnoticed in the tall grasses around Kai Tak. Our other big job was at Aberdeen where we had to take oil and kerosene drums down to the pier and load them onto barges for transport to Lai Chi Kok Socony Installation. There were so many drums that it took us six months to clear the godowns. We would be up at 5am for breakfast and then assembled in the parade ground to be counted. Then we were put on a barge for the hour trip to Aberdeen. Most of us napped on the barge, some chatted while others read books. The Japanese supplied us with quite a good library of books."[37]

Writing about these work parties, Whitehead had noted: "A comical ritual that only the British squaddie could devise was performed by these fatigue parties at the camp's main gate. The returning group, with a wave of the open hand, would shout 'Hi-di-hi!", and those marching out would respond with 'Ho-de-ho!', keeping a deadpan face as they waved with the opposite hand. The camp guards, assuming that this was a British military ceremony, would come to attention and bow. It took all the squaddies' will power to keep a straight face until they were out of sight." (p. 65)

Tuesday, 10 February. Professor Gordon King escaped from the University of Hong Kong via Saikung.[38] Mr Arthur Bentley, Government Pharmacist, would follow on Chinese New Year's Day.[39]

Thursday, 12 February. Hong Kong's Governor, Sir Mark Young, was flown to Woosung (where he would stay until September).[40]

Saturday, 14 February. Frank Evans: "I have heard the sad news that Jack Smart has died and will be buried today. Six lads left camp this morning to dig his grave. Captain Thompson was allowed to go with them and to the funeral at Bowen Road hospital burial ground."[41]

Wednesday, 18 February. Major James Gray, RAMC: "Two prisoners died as a direct result of accidents on working parties. Corporal Piddington, 1st Middlesex Regt. was killed by a landslide on 18 February 1942."[42]

Bill Oxley of the Middlesex: "There was a clause in this Contract when Britain first had Hong Kong that no-one was allowed to touch this sacred hill near Kai Tak, but the Japanese did. The prisoners moved it by hand. We lost one man in this operation, 'Harry X', who was buried alive after a fall of earth."[43]

Tuesday, 24 February. Two Royal Scots, Joe Gallagher and Dan Hodges, on the spur of the moment, decided to escape from Shamshuipo by crawling under the wire. Grimsdale: "The reason why they tried to escape was that a Japanese sentry had told them there was no truth in the story that Canton had recently been retaken by the Chinese. They assumed from this that the contrary was true and that Canton was in fact once again in Chinese hands. They therefore started out with the idea of walking to Canton."[44]

Wednesday, 25 February. St Albert's Convent, which had still been acting as a hospital until this time, was abandoned. Now the only operating hospitals were Bowen Road and St Teresa's. Goodwin: "On the 25th of February we were ordered to vacate St Albert's and the sick were sent to Bowen Road Hospital while those who were almost well were taken by truck to the North Point Camp." (p. 23)

Goodwin continued on his arrival at North Point: "What had happened? Who were these broken, spiritless, dirty, slovenly, unshaven, gaunt-looking spectres who started at us with unfriendly, unwelcoming eyes? Could these be the same officers who had so recently looked so immaculate on the dance floor of the Hongkong Hotel? Two months had passed since the last guns boomed, and that scene of desolation made us wonder with trepidation what conditions in the camp could be. What forces had been at work to bring men so low in so short a time?"

The explanation was simple.

Fisher at North Point: "The wooden army huts were a scene of indescribable filth, with rubbish and excreta, both horse and human, lying in all the huts and odd corners. The hot sun had brought out clouds of flies and we had to set to and clean the place up with no brushes and no water. It was a heartbreaking and filthy job and we had to sleep 170 in each hut . . . Our latrine was the sea wall, a cold place at night, and rather tricky; the idea was to fasten your belt on to the fence and strap-hang over, otherwise you fell off the edge." (p. 33)

Ken Cambon, also at North Point: "There were no facilities of any kind. In the absence of plumbing we squatted on the sea wall, holding on to a wire fence. I was once of the first to get dysentery and spent some of the worst hours of my life hanging onto that fence. Truly this was the lowest ebb. There were still many bodies floating in the bay. I was holding onto the fence, very weak with fever, nauseated and racked with the cramps that only bacillary dysentery can create, when I glanced down in the water to see a bloated face drift by."[45] (p. 35)

Later, latrines were built, plumbing was repaired, and one building was converted into a hospital.

Goodwin: "The dysentery hospital[46] at North Point was a shocking reflection on our captor. That noisome place of healing was situated in a stone stable near the waterfront. The floor was of cobblestones, ventilation and light were provided by two very small windows and a small door. And the interior was always in deep gloom. Two four-gallon cans were the only conveniences provided. Four or five patients were always clustered around each of those inadequate receptacles, needing to use them at the same time, and the place reeked with the stench of ordure which ran among the cobbles and fouled the blankets of those men lying on the ground." (p. 24) However, as Cambon said: "Thank God I had my attack before there was a hospital." (p. 36)

Allister, also at North Point: "Every hut had its fill of bizarre histories, of tragedies, of minds hovering on the brink. Some had already passed over the edge. Morgan, a young Royal Rifle, tall, heavy-set, raised in luxury, was one of these. He wandered over the camp, digging out small clumps of earth and grass to eat. I watched him with pity, horror, and envy. He would not survive, but he had escaped." (p. 55)

Friday, 27 February. Four Medical Officers, twenty RAMC orderlies, and thirty nurses were sent to St Teresa's (80 beds) to set up a POW hospital for Kowloon.

In the week ending 29 February, Donald Hill noted: "Two Scots who escaped have been shot."[47] And from Shamshuipo, Bertram recorded: "I saw one shoot a Chinese girl who came too near the camp, searching for shell fish along the beach; she lay twitching in the mud for nearly half an hour before he put another bullet through her head. These guards were fond of catching the small boys who played in the streets near the camp wire. They would line the youngsters up against the wall of their billet and torture them for an afternoon, before finally bayonetting them." (p. 111)

March 1942

Sunday, 1 March. Frank Evans: "It is St David's day and my mother's birthday, and I wonder how she is."[48] (p. 31)

For most prisoners, two months of starvation had stilled all thoughts of escape. But not for all.

Thursday, 19 March. In Stanley Camp, Gwen Priestwood had teamed up with British policeman Walter Thompson.[49] On the 18th they had arranged to go to the hospital so that their room-mates would not be implicated in their escape. Having left them, Priestwood described: "I walked round to a hiding-place where we had concealed our clothes and our food store. I changed into my 'escape outfit'. Over my lingerie I wore two pairs of woollen pants, three woollen vests, one pink sweater, one green sweater, one yellow sweater — all of wool — and one blue cotton sweater. That's not all. I also had on a navy blue woollen cardigan, a green cardigan, and . . ." (p. 60) She went on to list a further six items of clothing.

"Finally we started. My pack weighed about thirty pounds. [Thompson's] between thirty-five and forty. We had biscuits, bully beef, a few extra clothes, first-aid equipment, an extra pair of shoes. It had been raining, and in the darkness, pack-laden, I slithered and slid down the path. We shot down a bank to the road, hardly breathing. We lay there a minute, listening for sentries. Then we crawled to the barbed wire — and wriggled through. Our packs got tangled and caught in the barbs. We struggled frantically, expecting every moment to hear the grunting challenge of a sentry. I thought, as I struggled, of the stories I'd heard about what happened to people caught trying to escape from the military camps. One man had been brought back and beheaded in full view of the camp![50] . . . And then, at last, we unbarbed ourselves, rolled into a ditch, got up, brushed off the mud, and, slipping across and down the bank, found ourselves on a beach in the blackness. We were free!"

That same night an Anglo/American party of Frank Wright, Parker Van Ness, Raymond O'Neill, Israel Epstein and Elsie Fairfax-Cholmeley also managed to escape from Stanley. F. W. Wright recounted: "During my stay in Stanley I was always on the lookout for a possible way to get out . . . Then on the 16th March Miss Cholmeley who was living in the same quarters asked me whether I was still thinking of making a break. I told her I would if there was a chance. She then introduced me to Epstein and Van Nes. After having a chat, I was informed that they were preparing for a get-away and that they had found a small boat near the beach and had made an oar from one of the doors, and that they already had a rudder and paddle, so were more or less ready . . . Then on the 18th afternoon Mr. Epstein informed me that he had heard on the quiet that there were two planning to escape that night which meant that we had to move and move fast, so we decided to get away that night and be ready at 9 p.m." After waiting quietly on the beach for an hour, Van Nes cut the wire and they dragged the boat to the water. Despite it taking on water far quicker than expected, they made it to Cheung Chau in about fifteen hours, and from there to Macau and eventual freedom.[51]

However, Hong Kong residents had little hope of escape.

Luba Estes: "Eventually, we were able to return home to our house in Kowloon on the mainland. Another sight that I shall never forget was on the return trip on the ferry crossing the harbor. We sailed past numerous floating and very bloated bodies. Undoubtedly there were too many dead to be picked up around the colony, so the ones in the harbor had to wait. As we approached our house on Kadoorie Avenue, we walked by Chinese men, probably looters, strung up and tied to chain link fences with their feet just a foot or so above ground. They had been beaten, and were either dying or already dead. This became a common sight. Our home had been totally looted of everything and there was nothing in the pantry. My mother had little cash on her and the banks were closed. I suppose the banks were frozen, in fact, the city came to a complete stop. For us, this was the beginning of real hunger. Eventually food and clothing could be bought in the streets from vendors sitting in rows on the sidewalks. The currency my mother used was her jewellery . . . two or three cans of something, for a gold ring. We spotted some of our looted belongings for sale, but we could not afford them."

April 1942

Wednesday, 1 April. Cedric Salter, Royal Scots, having passed himself off as a Norwegian since surrender, was arrested in Nathan Road. He escaped.[52]

Sunday, 5 April. Anna Waters: "Col. Sutcliffe, OC of the Winnipeg Grenadiers, was admitted to Bowen Rd. about the 2nd of April, 1942. He was in a dreadful state — malnutrition, beri-beri, dysentery and was very anemic. Everything that could be done was done but it was too late then. He died the evening of April 5th, Easter Sunday. The Japanese seemed very sorry. They allowed 25 of our officers to come in from camp for the funeral on Mon. afternoon. They allowed us to get several wreaths and they had their own too. Our three padres conducted the service. All our own patients that could go were there and also many of the British. The burial took place in the little hospital cemetery just outside the gate." From "Report by Miss Anna May Waters, Nurse with the Canadian Forces at HONG KONG", as given on board, the MS *Gripsholm*, November 1943. (Interestingly, the hospital diary gives the date of death as 23 March.)

Wednesday, 8 April.   Kenneth Bidmead, Brian Fay, George Morrison, and Vic Randall escaped from Stanley, but security had tightened. In the first escape to fail completely, they did not get far. On that same day, "four Englishmen, supposed to be policemen, were imprisoned at St Margaret's School, Happy Valley where CHIA was also a prisoner. Their names were BIDMEAD, MORRISON, FAYE and RENDELL WEAKES (?). BIDMEAD, FAYE and WEAKES were placed in separate cells, while MORRISON occupied the same cell as CHIA did. The four men were questioned two or three times, and were badly treated. BIDMEAD was obstinate and so was handcuffed. He was also kicked about. WEAKES was ill due to his inability to eat rice".[53] They were to spend the next two years in Stanley prison.[54]

Friday, 10 April.   John Pearce, Douglas Clague, Lynton White and David Bosanquet escaped, though without the blessing of certain senior officers who feared reprisals. Having found a manhole cover in a weed-covered corner of Shamshuipo, they had attempted escape in March but were disturbed. By early April, the tide and moon suited their purposes again, and aided by various diversions they escaped through a sewer to the sea. Bosanquet looked back from the water: "What a sight! We see the whole western perimeter of the camp ablaze with light and the monkey-like figures as if upon a stage standing in from of the footlights while we wallow in the water. Then the bugle sounds 'lights out'. Immediately a Japanese patrol appears from the direction of the hospital area. We watch the changing of the sentries. Voices from the parade ground die away. The prisoners return to their quarters for the night. The concertina blares out the final chords of 'Happy Days Are Here Again'. Then silence."[55] (p. 88)

Fisher: "Sleeping next to Pierce and Boussanquet [*sic*] in the same hut had been Lofty Lloyd, who I knew, a nice quiet fellow and a member of the Kowloon Cricket Club. After Pierce and Boussanquet escaped a waterproof sheet was found on the barbed wire fence, and on it were the initials of Lloyd. He was taken out for interrogation by the Kampetai (secret police), and we never saw him again." (p. 38) Lloyd did not survive interrogation.

Friday, 10 April.   In Stanley, they heard that the four escapees had been recaptured. The news was bad for morale, which was already far from high. As Wright-Nooth noted, two days later: "I am learning lots of things in this camp about human nature and people's characters which in normal times would have taken me years to learn. Above all I have learned that people should be happy if they enjoy good health, a good bed and three square meals a day." (p. 84)

Meanwhile, the Japanese had decided to send the Royal Naval contingent at North Point to rejoin their countrymen at Shamshuipo. The few Canadians held outside North Point would be brought in, making it an exclusively Canadian camp.

Friday, 17 April.   Padre Uriah Laite: "On Friday evening the naval men were ordered to be ready to move to Sham Shui Po Camp on Saturday morning at 9:30 o'clock. Every man was very busy packing until 'Lights Out' at 2300 hrs. As some were leaving mattresses etc., I was fortunate in having one given to me. I was also given a blanket, a sheet, a pillow, and a pair of long rubbers. I shall be able to fix my bed properly now and get better rest."[56]

Saturday, 18 April.   Forsyth: "A heavy sky, a drizzle with a gusty windy drive behind it. Miserable day for the navy to move out. They are bustling about. Some staggering under huge packs, guards posted on vacated huts to prevent looting. The navy spent an hour on the parade square in the rain while their packs were being searched . . . This afternoon 80 Canadians came in from Argyle and Sham Shui Po, 20 of them Grenadiers. Dick Wilson, Alex Colvin, McCauley and Sgt. Marsh among the bunch."

On arrival, Marsh himself noted: "This camp was cleaner than the one we had just left, although in a terribly dilapidated condition by our standards. Rags and sacks covered the doors and windows and we slept on sacking and old floor boards tied or lay on the frameworks of the previous bunks."

Laite: "A number of our men, who had been taken prisoners with me at Wan-Nai-Chong, and sent to Argyle Street prison, and later to Sham Shui Po, came back to camp. Most of them had been wounded and I was glad to see them. We shall compare notes during the coming week. Lt Blackwood who was the last officer to be wounded, and whom I fixed up before our surrender, was welcomed by us and we shall get our story of Wan-Nai-Chong fight again from him and we shall be able more fully to compare notes and get the story complete." Baird also reported the move: "Two officers and 20-odd men came back to us. All the navy moved out of this camp; they seem to be concentrating all the Canadians in one camp. I felt sorry for the naval men moving, it simply poured. Everyone was soaked and cold. They had to stand on the parade square for hours in the rain; all their kits were opened and got soaking wet. There will no doubt be a lot of sickness among them as there were a lot of them over 60 years of age and had come off the retired list when the war started." (p. 90)

Saturday, 18 April. As the Royal Naval Officers and other ranks left North Point for Argyle Street — which was being opened as a dedicated officers' camp — and Shamshuipo respectively, Goodwin noted: "A small steamer took the party to Shamshuipo, and when we were all assembled at the camp, Colonel Tokunaga, Commandant of all POW camps, Hongkong, gave an exhibition of his swaggering arrogance which we were to come to know only too well. Combined with is natural obesity his manner earned for him the sobriquet of 'The White Pig'. Spray flew from his mouth as he stamped and shouted, and he took particular pleasure in venting his foul temper on Commodore Collinson, RN, who was repeatedly pushed in the chest during the harangue. When it was all over the officers were sent to Argyle Street". (p. 26) The Argyle Street Camp (known as POW Camp 'N') accepted the majority of officers, who were accompanied by one hundred Other Ranks who primarily acted as cooks and batmen.[57]

Fisher in Shamshuipo: "In April the Japs suddenly decided that the officers should be in a camp of their own so all except a nucleus was packed off to Argyle Street camp. Our officer commanding was now a Staff Major Boon, probably picked out by the Japs for his weakness. It was said that an early beating up he got made him collaborate for he never seemed to plead anything on our behalf." (p. 40)

Going to Argyle street, Frank Evans recorded: "When we started on our walk through the streets of Kowloon that afternoon in April, we did not know where we were going, but after covering about three miles we arrived at Argyle Street camp, near Kai Tak . . . There was no sign of life on the streets, and shop windows were shattered and everywhere appeared to have been looted. We arrived in the new camp about 4.30 pm." (p. 35)

Evans continued: "In my hut, No. 2, under the control of C. Barman, Q.M.S.[58] and Sgt. Tupper, there were men from all walks of life, and their good nature and humour kept me going. John Moulton, R.A.F., nicknamed 'the mighty atom' (if I remember correctly) could be very funny, causing fits of laughter. Ken Sawyer, RAOC, who made a drawing of the hut for me, was a good artist, and W. Sprague HKVDC was quite musical and managed to assemble a small harp from all sorts of bits and pieces."

Friday, 24 April. Second Lieutenant Silva and a Royal Artillery batman were taken out of Argyle Street, with others taken from Shamshuipo.

Nevertheless, amidst these changes, ordinary life continued.

Monday, 27 April. Barbara Redwood at Stanley: "Mum had her womb removed." Dr Kirk and Professor Digby had performed the two-and-a-half-hour operation.

Tuesday, 28 April. Frank Evans: "This morning I attended a lecture on the 'English Legal System' given by Major The Lord Merthyr, and it was considered excellent by all present." (p. 42)

May 1942

Friday, 1 May. Redwood in Stanley: "Kennard and D. Deakin married."

Saturday, 2 May. Laite: "Yesterday the road next to our compound was closed to traffic for a while as a Japanese Prince was to pass along the route. All prisoners of war were ordered to remain indoors, so only from our windows could we see the advance guard on motor cycles, the cars containing His Highness and party, and the rear guard of armed soldiers, in trucks, pass."[59]

Tuesday, 5 May. In the first of three repatriations to Shanghai, a large number of third-national sailors stranded in Hong Kong, plus some Hong Kong residents and a handful of Stanley internees departed for the voyage on the *Tainan Maru* via Taiwan.

Sir Michael Kadoorie was only eight months old at the time, but remembers the family lore: "My grandfather together with my parents and my sister and I were transported on a ship from Hong Kong to Shanghai, a journey which took 6.5 days because the ship had to zig zag to avoid American submarines. The majority of the passengers were all congregated in the hold in poor conditions and the hatches were opened at night with warnings from the guards that we were in American submarine infested waters. Incidentally, the ship had already been sunk but it was refloated and repaired. Another story which my father told me was that he did not know which was sorer, my behind or his hands from washing nappies in salt water!"

Nick Spoov:[60] "As things were getting less and less bearable in Hong Kong under the Japanese occupation, more and more non-belligerents were trying to get away from a rather bleak Hong Kong, to Shanghai, where life had remained much as it was before the outbreak of the war, with its large foreign population, a goodly proportion of whom were us Russian émigrés. Thus, there were on board: the Kadoories in strength, including a several-weeks [sic] old Michael, the Belgian Consul to HK plus family, being repatriated under diplomatic privileges, an assortment of stranded Scandinavian and other seamen, a contingent of Russian émigrés and members of the crew of Soviet cargo ship which somehow got disabled during the fighting in HK. The latter circumstance made for some rather amusing episodes between the two sides, including a couple of budding romances, until the ever present watchful eye of the KGB, or rather, the NKVD as it was known then, put an end to any developing fraternization. The trip lasted some ten days, instead of the usual three, as we were hugging the coast, and with good reason: during that ten day interval, the first major naval encounter, The Coral Sea Battle (unless I am mistaken) took place, and all sorts of rumours were floating about, in addition to the triumphant Japanese version we were given on board. And yes, I was miserably sick with jaundice at the time, and was the butt of many half-way sympathizing jokes."

Friday, 15 May. The four Stanley recaptured escapers were seen again. Wright-Nooth: "They were seen by Lance, Henry and Colin, who at forty yards did not recognise them because they had changed so much. However, on looking again they recognised [Bidmead]. How can people be so inhuman? They were just a mass of skin and bones with long unkempt hair and beards. They were hardly able to walk. They must have been starved and badly questioned. Lance and Co. came back to the bungalow very much upset . . . an unpleasant sight that of men reduced to animals." (p. 113)

Saturday, 16 May. Frank Evans: "An exciting day in the camp today. Five officers and one other rank returned after torture. They are in bad condition physically and their friends could hardly recognise them." (p. 43) These were the men who had been taken away after the last escapes from Shamshuipo in April. They included John Barron, Alec Pearce, Shrigley and Silva.

Now that the POWs had all but exhausted their spirit for escape, the Japanese demanded that each man sign a form promising that he would not try.

Friday, 22 May. Lowe: "We have been told that we must sign re escapes — if not we are 'for it'. Petchy, Macanally & other Middies were 'grilled' by the Japs, but refused to sign."[61]

Saturday, 23 May. Lowe continued: "Our Wedding Day. 7 yrs ago. After a lot of arguing all except 106 signed the non-Escape — led by General & officers. 106 taken out."

Saturday, 23 May. James Gray, RAMC: "On 23 May 1942 all prisoners were ordered to sign a so-called affidavit swearing that they would not attempt to escape while prisoners of the Imperial Japanese Army. A hundred and seventeen refused and were made to sit in an open field with a loaded machine gun pointing at them, and were given neither food nor drink until they signed. Eighteen still refused to sign, some of whom were removed to Stanley Gaol, where after a week they were made to sign a statement that they had been guilty of mutinous conduct. An officer who was treated this way is Captain Badger of the Middlesex."

Saturday, 30 May. Meanwhile, in the main islands of Japan, the question of what to do with POWs was being addressed. War Minister Tojo's instructions were delivered to the commander of the Zentsuji Division, on his visit of inspection there.

> To this Division is attached a prisoner of war camp. Prisoners of war must be placed under strict discipline as far as it does not contravene the law of humanity. It is necessary to take care not to be obsessed with a mistaken idea of humanitarianism or swayed by personal feelings towards those prisoners of war which may grow in the long time of their imprisonment. The present situation does not permit anyone to lie idle doing nothing but eating freely. With that in view, in dealing with the prisoners of war, too, I hope you will see that they may be usefully employed.[62]

And on the same day, at Stanley, a tiger — having presumably swum across from the Mainland — was shot by Indian policemen.

June 1942

Wednesday, 3 June.   Redwood: "D.M.S. came in yesterday and wanted nursing sisters for Kowloon."

Wednesday, 3 June.   Forsyth: "Five Rifles and Five Grenadiers, including Brigadier Holmes and Major Bailie and myself took a trip by bus to the dock, ferried over to the Kowloon side, took another bus and rode 4 or 5 miles to Jap HQ on the Kowloon side at Argyle Street near St Teresa's hospital". There they made recordings for broadcast.

Wednesday, 3 June.   'Bill' Wiseman, RASC, who had been at the British Military Hospital on Bowen Road, was transferred to Stanley Gaol: "I realised that there must be about a dozen other prisoners, four British civilians, probably police, and up to eight VCOs, both PMs and Sikhs, the latter including Rissaldar Major Mahinder Singh."[63] (p. 29)

Friday, 12 June.   Forsyth: "Two men very sick with dysentery were finally granted permission by the Japs to go to the Bowen Road hospital, loaded on the back of a truck, one died on the way, the other just after arriving."[64]

But in Stanley, for the American internees at least, events were taking a happier turn.

Briggs at Stanley: "Rumors and facts kept increasing, repatriation, repatriation. It was just like a mirage, something in the distance, but you could not touch it. The Japanese told us the *Asama Maru* would arrive on June 15th and would sail on the 16th. About the 12th they informed us there had been a delay, and we would sail on the 23rd. On June 19th we were informed that the delay would be indefinite, that we would not sail on the 23rd."

Saturday, 13 June.   Redwood: "Tonight was a concert given to the Americans because they are due to leave soon. Carol Bateman[65] arranged it, and the costumes, etc. were grand. Graceful dancing; piano duet by Elizabeth Drown and Mrs Barton, chorus with good lines about how 'we do like to be beside the seaside', and the joys of the Stanley prom, but the lack of 'to and from'."

Wednesday, 17 June.   Redwood's sister Mabel arrived from BRH. Redwood: "have been hearing about 'Bickley' who was so brave though blind,[66] and how she wept buckets when she fed him; and about the first time someone asked for a bottle; and how she was always breaking thermometers."

Thursday, 18 June. Forsyth: "Had some very interesting discussions with old Cole from Swan River, and Bill Adams who used to work for Skinner at Dropmore. Both are good gardeners." From North Point, the Grenadiers and the Rifles alternated daily in sending two hundred men to work on Kai Tak airfield.

Tuesday, 23 June. Briggs at Stanley: "We read in the paper that the *Asama Maru* had left Yokohama on Thursday for Hong Kong, and the *Conte Verde* had sailed from Shanghai for Singapore. The *Asama Maru* would arrive on Monday, June 29, the date on which we would embark, and sail on June 30th. We really believed it now. This was the first definite announcement, and the dates confirmed in the paper. The Japanese told us that our baggage would be picked up and inspected on Sunday, then put on the ship on Monday. We could keep one small over night bag to carry ourselves, but all other baggage would be put on for us."

Wednesday, 24 June. Redwood: "We have heard guns these past few days. It was suggested that the Nips are re-enacting the capture of Hong Kong."[67]

Saturday, 27 June. Driver Thomas McMaster died. He was the first recorded casualty from the diphtheria epidemic which would sweep through the camps.

Monday, 29 June. Briggs: "We were all up early on Monday with the excitement of leaving . . . The British were all lined up to bid us farewell. I never have seen, I never again want to see, and I never expect to see a sadder or more depressing sight than that departure from Stanley. There were quite a few British women who had married American men. They were permitted to go. However, they were leaving behind brothers, sisters, and parents . . . My cabin was on D deck, number 367. There were fifteen of us in it. However, we were fortunate, as we had a porthole. Although it was just above the water line, we did have it open most of the time. There were one or two rough days when we had to close it, but for all practical purposes, it remained open. The boys down on E deck did not even have a porthole."

Tuesday, 30 June. The American internees finally left Stanley.[68] Briggs: "At 6:00 PM there were three long blasts on the whistle, we heard the propellers turning over, and we were finally moving. We were off! Everyone was on the port side, waving towards Stanley. We were too far out to see anyone, but we were all waving. Suddenly from St Stephen's came a flash. Someone had gotten a mirror and was signaling us goodbye. The last signal was a V for Victory. I have often wondered if anyone got into trouble over that. Signaling from an internment camp would certainly be a military offense."

Some fourteen Americans elected to remain in Stanley: priests, those with Chinese wives, and those with businesses that they hoped to salvage at war's end. Stericker noted: "We were sorry to see our American friends go, although it afforded us much-needed space. Many were able to carry messages to our families, and it was good to think that we had some reliable contact with the outside world. However, as our real troubles did not start until several months after the Americans left, the reports they made hardly gave a true picture."

July 1942

Sunday, 5 July. 'Reports' from Stanley were also reaching Shamshuipo. Lowe: "Stanley reported to be overcrowded & 'much free love being practised'."

However, the truth was less exotic.

Thursday, 9 July. Redwood: "Mrs Barrow's baby Oriana died this morning, of water on the brain."

Thursday, 23 July. In the camps, despite the regular deaths, a way of life was being established. Forsyth: "Some fellows with a few tools are doing some fancy woodcarving, McBride and Brezensky very good at it." Allister, also at North Point: "Gradually the period of shock, gestation, was drawing to a close and new shoots of vitality began to appear here and there. The instinct for survival asserted itself. Rolly Damours, who spoke Chinese, was a language freak and gathered a few cohorts to study Japanese. George Grant and Jack Rose joined him, taking lessons from Rance, the Eurasian interpreter." (p. 58)

Thursday, 23 July. Briggs: "The pier at Lourenco Marques was modern and up-to-date with traveling cranes and railroad tracks on the pier. The Portuguese ran in some empty freight cars, and the exchange started. We went off the stern of the *Asama*, passed along on the inside of the freight cars, and went aboard the stern of the *Gripsholm*. The Japanese got off the bow of the *Gripsholm*, passed along the outside of the freight cars, and went aboard the bow of the *Asama* . . . You should have seen the difference in the procession of these two groups of people. It was very easy to tell the treatment each group had received by just looking at them and seeing the personal belongings attached to each. Here we were with our clothes ragged and torn, our suitcases, cardboard boxes, straw baskets, and any container that we could get to hold our few personal belongings, tied up with rope, string, wire and anything that we could find. We were thin, drawn, and looked as though we had been through the mill, which we had. No doubt about that. In contrast to us, the Japanese got off with snappy new American clothes, nice matched leather luggage. They looked well fed and happy. The women particularly looked very stylish with new hats and matched outfits. They surely presented a far different sight than we did."

Sunday, 26 July. About fifty Stanley internees normally resident in Shanghai were sent home. Stericker noted: "Some of the more senior were lucky, as from Shanghai they were able to get on to a repatriation ship, the *Kamakura Maru*, which was repatriating Allied consular officials. Amongst the fortunate ones was my stable companion, Roger Heyworth. The Allied nationals in Shanghai were not yet interned."[69]

Thoughts of others were also turning towards escapes again.

Tuesday, 28 July. Tse Dickuan, a Chinese clerk working for the Japanese administration at Shamshuipo noted: "About the same time a number of prisoners attempted, by tunnelling, to escape from Sham Shui Po Camp."

Eight POWs — Sergeant Plumber, LSBA Harrington, Lance Corporal Hills, Lance Corporal Dunne, RAOC, Lance Corporal Byrne, Middlesex, Private Connolly, HKDDC, Private Branson, Middlesex, and Private Stopforth, RAOC — were caught trying to escape.[70]

Sergeant G. E. Plumber 6199228, Middlesex: "[I was in barracks] from 25 Dec 41 until 29 Dec. On 29 Dec all British ranks were moved to Sham Shui Po Camp at Kowloon. I remained in this camp until July 28, 1942. I attempted to escape but somehow information was forwarded to the Japanese and we were handed over to the Japanese authorities. That was on 28 July 1942. Myself and seven others were placed in Kowloon Magistry Jail to await a court martial by the Japanese."[71]

They would be there for 29 days.

Friday, 31 July.   News travelled rapidly. Lowe: "Discovery of hole dug in one of empty flats in Jubilee, given away by sentry. Connolly's brother in the gang."[72] Frank Evans: "There was an attempt to escape on August 1st 1942, when six men were caught tunnelling, and later on two men from the Royal Engineers managed to escape but were later caught and killed." (p. 37)

August 1942

Sometimes the Stanley internees received unwelcome reminders that they were living on a battlefield.

Saturday, 1 August.   Redwood: "Little boy McLeod blew himself up — he's alright so far."

Sunday, 2 August.   Lowe of the discovered escapees: "Chaps still in hole, but allowed food."

Tuesday, 4 August.   Jim Hart: "Our first RASC casualty was a clerk. First he was given a spoonful of sugar today, then of butter tomorrow, and jam the next day. But when he was dying it had to stop — they had to save it for men who had a chance. Within two weeks he was dead."[73]

Tuesday, 4 August.   The first diphtheria death was recorded in North Point Camp.[74]

Tuesday, 4 August.   Lowe: "Moved into top flat of Jubilee, lovely lovely Horace the corpse still floating round & now got a pal who 'ums even higher than 'orace 'imself. [Wish] he'd pop and sink."

Friday, 7 August.   Lt. Colonel Bowie, RAMC: "Boxer gave me a message from the Japanese that on the following day Simson the A.D.M.S., Shackleton the commanding officer, a named number of officers and other ranks of the staff and 40 patients were to leave Bowen Road and all women staff were to be transferred away from the hospital 48 hours later. At the time we considered that only 12 patients were fit enough to go to POW camp. All except two of the women staff were to be transferred to the Civilian Internment Camp on the Stanley Peninsula".[75]

Monday, 10 August. Redwood noted that the VADs arrived in Stanley. Bowie took stock at Bowen Road: "I found myself in charge of 211 patients including 25 officers with a staff of 6 medical officers including myself, one dental officer, a quartermaster, a Church of England chaplain, 55 other ranks RAMC and RADC and six Royal Engineers plus one civilian engineer."

Tuesday, 11 August. St Teresa's hospital was closed. The patients were sent to BRH or Shamshuipo. From then on, Bowen Road Hospital was the only hospital available in Hong Kong to the POWs, except for the so-called hospitals in the camps.

Tuesday, 11 August. Briggs: "We arrived in Rio de Janeiro on a delightful day. As we came into the harbor, directly ahead of us was a perfectly huge ship. No one knew definitely, but it was either the *Queen Mary* or the *Queen Elizabeth* as there are only two boats of that size afloat. She was on troop transport duty bound for somewhere. Just as we were edging into the dock, the *Queen* pulled anchor and departed . . . The next morning, Tuesday, August 25, we were called to report on the deck at 5:00 AM for quarantine inspection. Everyone was up, there was no mistake about that. It was a cold, windy morning up on deck, but there was America. We could see the buildings of Lower Manhattan! On one side we could look over to shore and see homes with nicely kept lawns and trees all green and fresh. On the other side was the city of New York."

Friday, 14 August. Redwood: "Stott (Bok) at French Hospital escaped". Stott had been a Volunteer. Suffering after the surrender from a ruptured duodenal ulcer he had been taken eventually to Tweed Bay Hospital after the Japanese ordered the evacuation of the medical facilities set up at La Salle College. Stott reported:

> People began to file in with dysentery, Mr Shepherd of the CPR Company dying of it. In my small ward approx. 20' x 20' there were 14 patients on camp beds, 9 of whom were suffering from dysentery . . . At this period an effort was made to send elderly patients and those whose condition required more and better food, to hasten recovery, to the St Paul's Hospital, Causeway Bay. My name was included as I was still too weak to walk unsupported and was almost bloodless.
>
> . . . I was sent with a party of others to that Hospital on February 20th, 1942 . . . I discussed my idea of escaping with Dr Selwyn-Clarke. Had I been able to do so I would have endeavoured to pass as Eurasian, but unfortunately was too well known by local enemy agents to succeed,

Dr Selwyn-Clarke listened intently but made no suggestions to help neither did he request me not to escape . . . [A relation from Chungking] brought me a black Chinese jacket and trousers and warned me to prepare for Tuesday evening 11th August, 1942. I had made a survey of the rear wall into the deserted land behind just as dusk fell when people's eyes had not quite got used to the dark. Against this wall had been built a gardeners' tool shed which facilitated getting over the wall though I would have to jump to avoid the broken glass . . . landing on both heels I knew that I had sprained them. Resting for a while I crawled along the nullah running past hospital and found rope secreted by friends. I crawled through barbed wire and looping rope round support lowered myself into nullah drawing rope on landing at bottom. With feet so painful I had to sit and drag myself inch by inch along the slimy slippery bottom towards the typhoon shelter into which the nullah emptied . . . The tide was low and I had to hobble as best I could to the waiting sampan which in turn took me to a slightly larger shrimp boat with a sail. Here I lay until 4 o'clock a.m. when we set off. We dropped anchor for a while to east of Kellet Island, then set off in direction of Stonecutters Island, passing between that and Shamshuipo Camp; beating back and forth we eventually passed through Capsicum Pass and then on to a point opposite Castle Peak. Here we anchored for the night and set off at dawn for Macau.[76]

Wednesday, 19 August. Just days after Stott's successful venture, four Winnipeg Grenadiers, Payne, Berzenski, Adams and Ellis escaped from North Point.[77]

Maurice Parker: "at about nine o'clock in the evening, there was a hurry-up call ordering everyone to fall in and be counted. It was raining and cold. Nights in the winter season are always cold but the days are warm. This particular night was especially cold, which fact coupled with the rain made it a most miserable night to be about. As there were not enough ground sheets or great coats to cover every one, the Japs would not allow any of us to wear the ones we had, so they made us all turn out clothed as we were, in shorts and many of us did not even have shirts on. Usually the sick did not turn out for a count but would be counted where they lay. This time in spite of the cold and the rain, they were ordered to be brought out as well. The whole thing seemed very unusual. All the big Jap brass-hats were on hand and we wondered what was going on. They made us all stand- not sit lounge or recline-sick as well as those not sick. Soon we were all soaking wet and chilled to the marrow. Jap Officers together with escort guards were running all over the place, bayonets drawn and fixed. Hours passed and we were counted time and time again. At about two o'clock, in the morning a Jap Navy Motor Launch came close to the camp sea wall, its search light scanned here and there, its motor purred as it slid through the dark waters. It suddenly dawned on us that someone had escaped — who?" At about this time, in the confusion, two British sappers, Ferguson and Howarth, also made their escape from Shamshuipo.[78]

Thursday, 20 August. Forsyth: "The Jap officers are giving Nick, George's brother a hard time, beating and cross examining him. They think he ought to know something about his brother's escape."

Friday, 21 August. Laite: "There has been great excitement around camp during the past two days. Yesterday morning Sgt Bayne [sic], L/Cpl Herzinski [sic], Pte Ellis and Pte Adams, were reported missing. We immediately knew that they had escaped. Our companies had special roll call, but nothing could be found of them. It was then reported to our O.C. who in turn reported it to the Brigadier. We all hoped that it would be withheld from the Japs for a few more hours in order to give the fellows a better chance to get away. However, the camp commandant was notified and we were all out for a muster parade. A ban which had been placed on the camp for fear of the spread of infectious diseases was immediately lifted and everything was astir. We learn now that the fellows had been planning this for a long time and had maps, money, binoculars, and a compass with them, as well as enough food for about ten days. I know the boys and believe that they have brains and ability, and given a fair chance, should get through the Jap lines and on to Chinese territory. We wish them luck. Some of the men were later questioned by the camp commandant, and asked why the boys left. He was told frankly but honestly that they felt what many feel. First, that it is the duty of any soldier to plan for and try to escape, and again, that it is better to stop a bullet in an attempt to escape than it is to slowly starve in this camp. The officers are fed a bit better than the men and we are poorly fed but most of the men will certainly show bad signs of malnutrition. Already many of them are showing them. Others must follow. Following are the names and addresses of the four men who escaped.
- Sgt John Bayne, 125 Harroppy Ave., St. Vital, Manitoba (24)
- L/Cpl George Berzenski, 457 Macdermott Ave., Winnipeg (26)
- Pte Percy J. Ellis, Wawanesa, Manitoba (25)
- Pte John H. Adams, 609 Balmoral St., Winnipeg (25)"

Recaptured, the four Canadians were brought into Kowloon Gaol on or about 23 August 1942. Lance Corporal W. L. 'Bumpy' Hills, 6700507,

Middlesex, was one of the previously recaptured British escapees already in the Gaol when the Canadians were brought in. They were thrown into the same cell and started to talk. Hills: "They escaped from Hong Kong, managed to acquire a row boat and attempted to row across the bay to the mainland to a place called Kaitak aerodrome. When they got halfway across they found that the boat was leaking, they tried to bail it out but the boat submerged and the current being very strong it took them out to sea. Japanese junks were passing but refused to pick them up as they were British soldiers. After they had drifted out of the bay, practically to the open sea, a small man of war picked them up. I believe the sergeant told us that he threw his map and compass away before the Japanese picked them up. They were brought to Kowloon Police Court prison and were put into the cell with us. They were like drowned rats when they came in and still had all their rations and packs. They were dressed in Canadian battledress, ammunition boots, and gaiters."[79]

Plumber was in the same gaol: "They had broke out of the Canadian camp at North Point at 2 a.m. They helped themselves to a Chinese rowing boat at 3 a.m. and attempted to row across the harbour to the mainland. During the journey across the harbour the boat sprung a leak and became water logged. Seeing as three of the party could not swim they remained near the boat until picked up by the Chinese 13 hours afterwards. They were handed over to the Japanese by the Chinese and put into the same cell as I. I remember Sergeant Payne because I spent most of my time discussing Payne's plans. Berzenski[80] I remembered because he was always riding the Japanese sentry, and Ellis because he had a touch of malaria and I was assisting in caring for him. The fourth man I do not remember, probably because he was so quiet and in the background."

In North Point, men waited for news and tried to pass the time.

Tuesday, 25 August.   Forsyth: "In the evening, Dick Trick, Milt Dann, Jack Hay, and myself sit around and talk farming from every conceivable angle."

Wednesday, 26 August.   Forsyth added: "Some men came back from Bowen Rd. They brought the news of the death of Lucas and Jim Chapman. The latter died on the 14th and was buried on the 15th. One of the saddest things that has happened. He had quinsy and dysentery, was a married man with four children, Chapman had always been so optimistic, so enthusiastic, his booming voice and his hearty laugh were known all over the camp."

On that same day, the four Winnipeg Grenadiers — Sergeant John Payne, Private John Adams, Lance Corporal George Berzenski, and Private Percy Ellis — were executed.[81]

But this failed escape marked a watershed. The POW camps in Hong Kong had continued largely undisturbed for several months. However, all was to change when the first shipment of POWs to Japan took place.

Having decided that it made more sense to turn the POWs into slave labourers — to populate the mines, the factories, and the dockyards of the homeland so that more Japanese might be freed up for the armed forces — a series of transportations ('drafts' as they would come to be known) to the Japanese homeland was about to begin.

Thursday, 27 August.   Lowe: "Rumour that Japan has asked for a truce. 600 men — so called 'bad characters' weeded out — rumour hath it that they are going to Japan!"

The POWs had mixed feelings. Some — especially those who had put down roots in Hong Kong — saw no possible advantage in going to the enemy heartland. Others felt that the situation there could not be worse than that in Hong Kong, and might even be better. There would be no chance of escape, but at least it would be a break from the monotony of their day to day existence.

Sunday, 30 August.   Lowe: "Draft now isolated & placed in barbed wire enclosure. Lt Hill & Ford also Capt Badger going."[82]

September 1942

Friday, 4 September.   Redwood at Stanley: "Baby Ogley born today, and baby Cautherley yesterday".

The First Draft: *Maru Shi*

The first draft of prisoners of war to Japan, on the *Maru Shi*, boarded on 3 September 1942 and left Hong Kong the following day with 618[83] POWs aboard.[84] These were the 'hard men', many of whom had refused to sign the 'no escape' chit. The majority came from the Royal Scots, the Middlesex, and the Royal Artillery, with a handful from the Royal Navy and other units.

James Ford, MC, Royal Scots: "The Japanese listed all the men who had been in their prisons outside the wire — all the men who had been in conflict with them including those who would not sign the declaration saying that they would not escape. As I remember there were about 100 odd on that list. The Japanese then asked us to make this up to 600 people. My brother and I, who were responsible for the Royal Scots, listed all the tough guys and all those suspected of forcing food from fellow, weaker prisoners. We soon had a quotation up to 100 Royal Scots."[85]

The Fords — and the officers responsible for the other units — chose well. These men would have the best survival rates of any draft in Japan, though they would be there longest.

Ford, who travelled with his men: "The conditions on the boat were cramped but reasonable. The troops were in the forward hold and so crowded that they could not all lie down at once. The officers were held in a small room off the funnel. We were wakened every night when the cinders were brought up to be scattered in the sea."

These prisoners were originally sent to three camps:
- Tokyo #3 Branch Camp (Yokohama Stadium)
- Tokyo Main Camp (Shinagawa)
- Tokyo #1 Branch Camp (Kawasaki)

Ford: "When we arrived at Yokohama Docks we were split into two groups — one for Yokohama, the other for Tokyo. The Yokohama men all went to the Stadium Camp. The Tokyo men went up to a camp between Tokyo and Yokohama, I can't remember the name of it, but from there they built the Omori Camp."

But in fact there was a third camp. One hundred men (four from the Royal Navy, and the remainder from the army) were sent to Tokyo #1B (Kawasaki).

Blomfield, a sailor who had been captured by the Germans and handed over to the Japanese, was already at Kawasaki and witnessed the arrival of the Hong Kong POWs: "[They] were in a deplorable condition when they arrived, suffering from beri-beri, pellagra, scabies, ringworm, pediculosis, lice, acne, malaria, haemorrhoids, and ear diseases. They had had many deaths from dysentery and diphtheria, and as medical supplies were so short they had cut cards for who should have anti-diphtheria serum."[86]

The Tokyo Main Camp was Shinagawa. The POWs there would spend the next ten months building a new Tokyo Main Camp (Omori).[87] But James Ford and the other half of the draft had been sent to 'the Stadium Camp', Tokyo #3 Branch Camp.

James Ford: "September 15: Disembarked Yokohama. Capt. Otway, R.E., Lieut. Price, R.A.M.C.,[88] myself and some 200 men posted to Stadium Camp (originally Camp 2, later Camp 3B, Tokyo Area) in which we found Squadron Leader Birchall[89] and W.O. Onyette, both of the R.C.A.F., and about half-a-dozen men, all of whom had come from Ofuna that same day. About a month later, Capt. Kauffman, U.S.M.C., and 72 Americans arrived from the P. I."

Leonard Birchall recalled: "Then, suddenly, in came this great big influx of these guys who had been on these hell ships coming up from Hong Kong, and starved and beaten and what-not as well. But just full of hate. Not just [towards] the officers, but the Japanese, everybody — they were still fighting. God! These officers — Cecil Otway from the Royal Engineers and Jimmy Ford from the Royal Scots — they got me on the side and said, they told me, they said, 'If you go out there, if you say the wrong thing, you'll be out behind the sheds and dead inside of 5 minutes. We tell you now.' And they meant it. I knew, after I met them, after I stood up in front of these guys, that it was true. I said [to myself], 'You're going to have to fight like a hawk to get these guys to have any respect for anything. There's no way of enforcing discipline — you're in real trouble.' So I had to go out, and we had the food dished out. It was the first food they'd had in I don't know how long. It was just a bowl of rice and some soup. We said, 'All right, you guys dish the soup and the rice out. Here are the officers' bowls.' There were six of us. I said, 'Here are six bowls. You guys put the food in, divy it out as you can, and we're not going to touch it; you go ahead and do it -- our bowls are there. Now, anybody thinks that we got more than you did, you change it. We're not going to touch ours until everybody has been served and is happy. We're going to do this *every* meal from here on out.'"[90]

Ford noted that at Yokohama: "We lived in relatively good quarters under a baseball stadium. The officers had a separate room. Latrines, cookhouse, washstand and bathhouse were situated in a yard outside. Primitive, but comparatively good." As for health: "[Captain Kauffman USMC] and British orderlies did their best with inferior and inadequate materials. Serious cases were removed to Shinagawa of which you will doubtless have heard. Our comparatively low death rate (7 or 8 men) was due to

Kauffman's work and to the fact that the officers of this camp were able to buy medicines secretly through venal or friendly camp officials."[91]

These were the first Japanese Homeland camps that the HK POWs would experience. Luckily, they were not the worst. Ford continued: "The few prisoners not on outside working parties were usually allowed to exercise in the pitch. We had a small library and some musical instruments . . . All 'fit' men, (the arbitration was Japanese) required to work. A proportion of the officers also compelled to work. Generally 10 hours a day, with 2 rest days per month. Manual labour in brickyard, shipyard, sawmill, railway siding, etc. . . . Stadium Jap officials: Camp Commandant: Lieut. J. Hayashi, Interpreter: Mr Minamoto. The only other name I can recall is Otaki. He was in charge of the kitchen and pilfered our rations."[92]

September 1942: Continued

Tuesday, 8 September. Over one hundred Chinese POWs (97 from the HKVDC) were released from Shamshuipo. Private Wong Yin Khoon, 5055, reported: "In the first week of September, all Chinese totalling 137 were taken to St Teresa's Hospital where they were well fed for two weeks. Throat swabs and anus swabs were taken. They were required to give the name and address of a guarantor. Most of the Malayan students have no parents or relatives in H.K. hence they decided to take the consequences of being sent back to Shamshuipo camp by giving May Hall as the address and naming no guarantor. But they were told that the name and address of a guarantor was only required as a matter of normality, and that they could even name persons among themselves or persons whom they think may have left Hong Kong. On the 15th the C in C of Prisoners of War Camp made a speech. About half the number were released. The remainder was taken to Hong Kong on the 17th where they were taken even [sic] by the various departments."

Wong Yin Khoon continued: "There were four of us in the China Light and Power Company, Wong Yin Khoon (F.Amb.) Seah Tin Toon (F. Amb.), Chan Peng Seng (R.E.) and Wong Yen Tou (St John's Amb.) Seah and myself having no home was put by the Japs into Chan's house to sleep on the balcony. Chan was told to keep an eye on us. Our work was carrying electric lamp posts that were taken down near Kai Tak in the Airfield enlargement scheme. We got one Sunday off in two weeks. On my first day off I went over to see my cousin. I was told of the possibility of getting relief at Waichow. I told Chan the news on my return. A fortnight later my cousin came over to see me. We discussed the plan of escape with Chan . . . It was then that the 5 May Hall students were caught."[93]

Wednesday, 9 September. Forsyth: "Tonight we heard that L. Cpl Whillier died at Bowen Rd with ulcers in mouth and throat. He was a very fine fellow, was in the artillery with Victor Hart in the last war."

Saturday, 12 September. Laite: "This morning at 0700 hrs Pte John ['Rocky'] Spicula Smith of B Co died in our camp hospital of Dysentery. We bury him today at noon. The Japs have sent in five very lovely wreaths for the grave. The funeral was conducted at 1245. The party of fifteen men, besides eight bandsmen with Capt Pendregast in charge. Lt Col Holm, Lt Col Trist, Major Atkinson and Capt Golden also attended. He was given full military honours."

Saturday, 12 September. The Maryknoll missionaries were released from Stanley Camp and moved to Bethany.[94]

Monday, 14 September. Five of the recaptured British escapees — Private James Stopforth (RAOC), Private Paul Connolly (HKDDC), Private Maurice Dunne (RAOC), Private Victor Branson (Middlesex), and Lance Corporal William Byrne (Middlesex) — were executed. Dickuan: "They were made to dig their own graves. After which they were bayoneted." Hills' family note that the men were forced to pick straws. The five with the short straws were executed, the remaining three were sent back to Shamshuipo.

Hills and the two other men involved in this escape lived to tell the tale. This had been Connolly's second escape attempt, he had made an earlier attempt with Royal Scots friend Dennis Morley (who later would survive the *Lisbon Maru*).[95]

Friday, 18 September. Meanwhile work parties continued. Lowe: "Up at 4 am fall in 5.15 then buggered about until 6.30 embark on ferry — 700 of us. Arrive Kowloon City 8.15 march to Kai Tak. Numbered and renumbered. Start work 9.15 Work in parties of 100 carrying stones. Darned hot. Break 10.15–10.30. Tiffin 12.30–1.30. Second break 3.30–4 pm. when we received 2 cigarettes! Work until 5.30 pm. Then back to camp about 7. Muster again at 9 Chow 10 & lights out 12!"

And then a second draft to Japan was arranged. As before, men were segregated and inoculated, but this time — following the success of the earlier voyage to Yokohama — the Japanese were more confident. This time they demanded 2,000 of the fit POWs to be loaded. In fact 2,000 'fit' men no longer existed, but nearly 1,900 would be readied for the voyage.[96]

Friday, 25 September. Sergeant Bill Poulter: "On the morning of September 25th 1942 we were paraded and counted, sorted into groups and then into sections and then recounted, and then the whole rigmarole was done again until they were satisfied. At mid-day we were marched to the Bamboo Pier and then embarked on one of the ferryboats and taken out to one of the ships at anchor in the harbour. As we came round the bows of the ship we saw that her name was the 'Lisbon Maru'."[97]

The Second Draft: *Lisbon Maru*

The second draft, the *Lisbon Maru*, was boarded on 25 September and sailed with some 1,834 POWs on 27 September.[98]

Poulter: "We are a bit of a tight fit with 1800 men on board but at least the food we've had is a little better than we have had in the camp. I have my brother with me, so at least I know that he is OK. We occupy three holds. No 1 Forward hold is mainly Royal Navy and Royal Marines with a few soldiers. No 2 hold, the one that I'm in, is in two sections. The bottom section is occupied by The Royal Scots and Royal Corps of Signals. The upper section by the Royal Engineers, The Middlesex Regiment and some Royal Artillery. Others are placed in the third hold towards the stern of the ship. All went well until just after roll call on October the 1st. The mess orderlies had just gone up on deck to draw rice ration for breakfast when there is a hell of a commotion, topside. The orderlies are hustled back down below, and one of them says that there is a submarine knocking about. He is right. Not only is there one about but he has fired a 'tin fish' at us. I feel sure that I heard the one that missed us and I'm positive about the second because I felt and heard it hit us."

Tracked by the American submarine USS *Grouper*, the *Lisbon Maru* was torpedoed on 1 October, and after the POWs had been left in the holds of the listing vessel for 24 hours, sank on the morning of the second. Although there was a successful breakout from the holds, over 800 men drowned as they were swept out to sea or dashed against the rocky outcrops of the Zhoushan Archipelago. It was the biggest loss of life from a single event that the Hong Kong garrison would ever experience.

The survivors were pulled from the sea, or rounded up from the islands they had swum to, and taken to Shanghai.

Poulter was one of those picked up by Japanese vessels: "All that day October 2nd 1942 until the 5th we cruise around the islands picking up men, until there is scarcely enough room to move. We are all kept on the top deck and are not allowed to go below. To add to our discomfort it rained and was bitterly cold. This helped to finish off many of the men and they are buried at sea, or to be more exact they are just dumped overboard. We have had nothing to eat or drink from September 30th until October 3rd when they gave us two small biscuits and a cigarette tin of luke-warm milk. We landed at Woosung on the 5th and out of eighteen hundred men that embarked on the 'Lisbon Maru' only about half are left. Of that about two hundred of my own regiment, including all ranks, survived I never heard any man complain of the submarine that sank us, in fact they all agreed it was the right thing to do."

Taffy Evans at Woosung, Shanghai: "A few days later we were put on a boat called the *Shinsei Maru*, and at long last I could get a rest. The hold they put us in, about 200 of us, it was full of old cars, trucks, etc. I got into the cabin of a truck, and at long last began to feel warm. On the way we were only given two meals of old stoney rice."[99]

The *Shinsei Maru*, also known as the *Washington Maru*, took these men to Moji where a train met them. Some sick POWs never even made it onto the train, but were hospitalized at Moji. The train stopped at Kokura to let more sick men off, then again at Hiroshima, before arriving at the first camp: Kobe. Although a trail of sick and dying men were left at every stop, eventually the majority arrived at Osaka No. 1 and Osaka No. 2 (Kobe) camps (minus a handful who were left in Shanghai after the sinking and who would eventually end up in the Hakodate camps in Japan).

The *Lisbon Maru* prisoners were initially sent to:
- Osaka #1 Branch Camp (Minato-ku, Osaka)
- Osaka #2 Branch Camp (Kobe, or 'Kobe House')

In the Hong Kong POWs' experience, Osaka #1 Branch Camp (Minato-ku, Osaka) and Osaka #2 Branch Camp (Kobe) would be the deadliest of the Japanese Mainland camps. With 214 deaths between them, they had an ugly reputation. However, the vast majority of these deaths were due to the shock, exposure, exhaustion, and infections experienced before and during the sinking of the *Lisbon Maru*, rather than anything exceptional about these camps themselves.

Poulter: "Arrived at Kobe on October 12th at about 12.50 pm. We were hustled off the train and formed up outside the station. We had an escort of our own, the sentries that have travelled with us on the train, plus some Mounted Military Policemen. Those of us that are unable to march are put on a lorry; the remainder is marched through the streets for about a mile and a half. We passed quite a few people on the [sic] as we marched through the streets but they only stopped and looked at us, their faces were pretty expressionless, but nobody laughed at us. I have not washed or shaved or even combed my hair since September 27th, so along with the rest of the men, we must look a pretty picture."

Robert Wright on his first glance at 'Kobe House': "The new camp was made up of two red-brick warehouses with iron bars and shutters, and wooden slats across the windows. A grim looking place, it turned out, ironically, to have belonged, before the war, to a British shipping company."[100] (p. 94)

The train continued, and finally let a similar party off at Osaka.

Geoffrey Hamilton at Osaka: "We were a pretty sorry lot on arrival at Osaka. There were about 350 of us, including seven officers. There were three Royal Navy officers, of whom Lieutenant Pollock was our senior officer. Of the four Army officers one had been Distribution Manager of the *Daily Mail*, and one was Ginger Howell who had opened the hatch for our escape."[101]

Interestingly, though, three men who escaped the *Lisbon Maru* also escaped recapture. Arthur 'Bill' Evans, William Johnstone, and Jim Fallace — all Old China Hands nominally belonging to the HKRNVR — were hidden by the islanders, and three months later escaped to British lines in China. Stericker was a close friend of Bill Evans as both worked for British American Tobacco: "Arriving on a beach he was greeted by a few Chinese villagers who had been spectators of the scene. One of the villagers gave him a helping hand ashore, then offered him a cigarette. It so happened that the cigarette was of a popular brand made by my firm, and Bill knew just enough Chinese words to indicate that he had more or less made that cigarette with his own hands. The villager, being an opportunist and having a certain amount of faith in the Allied cause, thought to himself that if he could rescue this Englishman he might be able to claim a fair reward at the end of the war. He therefore hid Bill Evans in the village and, that night, he was joined by two more compatriots."

September 1942: Continued

Between them, these first two drafts had removed nearly 2,500 men — primarily from Shamshuipo. This opened enough space for the remaining POWs in North Point to be moved to Shamshuipo on the 26th. North Point Camp was then closed.

But the men left in Hong Kong had their own worries. Disease was still taking its toll, and it would still get worse.

Wednesday, 30 September. Forsyth: "Cpl Iverach of D Coy died last night with Diphtheria."

Allister, at Shamshuipo: "[Jan Solecki and George Yaholkovsky approached] the head doctor, Colonel Ashton-Rose, a physician in the Indian army, and volunteered to help in the dysentery ward with no pay. The colonel snorted with surprised approval, accustomed as he was to haranguing lazy RAMC orderlies. He himself was a colourful, abrasive character who made enemies by stepping on toes and who tackled the Japanese fearlessly . . . They came to the dysentery ward each day, pushed their way through the thick stench, selected the worst-looking patient and set to work. First they carried him outside in the warm sun, stripped away his fouled clothes and tossed them into boiling water. Then they scrubbed the crusted shit and corruption from head to toe — ears, armpits, feet, hair, under the testicles where the shot was glued in layers — scrubbed and scraped with rags and fingers . . . Then they washed all the bedclothes, the filthy sheet and blanket, and took out the black iron bed with no mattress and attacked the bedbugs with disinfectant. They laid the patient in the sun to dry, gently placing towels over him to avoid sunburn, pampering him and handling him like a porcelain doll. Needless to say, he must have felt he was dreaming, after so much brutal disinterest. Then, while he rested, they went in to get the next patient."[102] (p. 75)

Some men reacted this way, and others in the opposite. Dora Chambers, widow of ERA James Wilfred Chambers: "Tug [Wilson] had been blinded during the bombardment of Hong Kong. He was also unable to get out of bed. Tug was so thin that Wilf could put one hand, middle finger and thumb touching, around his thigh. Some of his previous POW carers would eat their share of rice and sometimes Tug's too, telling him that there was no food. Some men are driven to do terrible things when they are hungry. The doctor knew that Wilf would 'play the game' and Wilf did . . . Using scraps of paper, Wilf made a pack of cards, shaping the paper so that Tug could tell by the feel of them which 'cards' were which. They passed a lot of time playing cards together."[103]

October 1942

Sunday, 4 October.   Redwood: "This evening I was close to the pianos when Mrs Drown and Heath played. Mary was sitting opposite on the front row of chairs, and the shadows showed the lines of her face; I felt like weeping all the evening, partly with looking at her and thinking of how near she and Doug were to being together when this war started, and partly for her health. It left me with the feeling that I used to have about her — before I left CSO — protecting towards her. Mrs Grant's face full of worries past and present, was also in the row behind. And sitting on a nearby window sill was Sheila Bruce, looking so wistful, about her mother, I thought [who died the week before the Japanese attack]. And Peggy Taylor — looking amazingly like Mary — her sister-in-law, was sitting beside her . . . All these people missing their men, and humming softly to Schubert's 'Ave Maria' and 'Today I Feel so Happy', and 'Cheek to Cheek,' and roaring out 'Sail Away'; then a quick 'I Want to be Happy' and 'Rule Britannia' worked into it, every one yelling out that Britons never would be slaves."

Within days the story of the sinking of the *Lisbon Maru* got back to the Hong Kong camps, and caused a great deal of worry. Ian Forsyth: "We all wondered when our turn might come. Some POWs made life jackets, four press-tight tin lids sewn into a sandbag."[104]

Thursday, 8 October.   Lowe: "Tommy Barton (RROC) came up for a yarn. Bread ration down to 1 loaf daily. Heard today that LISBON MARU torpedoed & sunk & 1000 of draft drowned. This draft included Pegg, Huggett, Robinson, Macanelly, Sniper Dixon, Hughes, Dodger Green."

Sunday, 11 October.   Deaths in Shamshuipo peaked at six in a single day, all from diphtheria and related diseases.

Monday, 12 October.   Laite: "Oct. 12. During the past week we have had many deaths from Diphtheria and dysentery. Yesterday — Sunday — four Canadians and one English soldier[105] were buried. The four Protestants were taken to the church hall where a brief service was held by Capt Strong of the Navy, and myself. The father of the English chap is in camp and attended the service. The mother and sister are at Stanley prison camp at Hong Kong and do not know of the soldier's passing. It was pathetic to see the old father kiss the boy's coffin three times, once for mother, once for sister, and once for himself."

A few days later, Henry Budden (the father) wrote this letter to his friend Wanstall who had lost a leg in the Japanese attack:

Henry E. Budden
Hong Kong Prisoner-of-War

Dear Mr Wanstall,

I am only now able to get a few lines to you at last although I only have a short time to do so. I have been thinking of you and wondered how you got on after that terrible night of December 15th when after stopping your bleeding with my shirt I obtained a stretcher but had to assist in getting Mr Birekit to the gate, when I hoped to come back for you but owing to the severe bombing, the Police and others would not allow me to come over to you which worried me very much. After the bombing had subsided I returned to find you had been shifted. I then went to the Industrial School Surgery and found that they had made you comfortable and sent you to the RNH. I have heard since that you were getting on O.K. and hope you will continue to do so. I think myself your actions should be brought before the Admiralty for consideration as when the planes came over all the other Service people ran for the shelter leaving only you and I only in charge of the pumps and boiler. At the same time as you got injured I had a lucky escape. My right trouser leg and also my pants got a long cut for 10 inches round at the top of the thigh without even scratching me. But this is nothing to some of the other shocks I had.

I'm sorry to say that my only son died here on the 11th and I have now to look forward to being reunited with my wife and daughter at Stanley.

Will you please let me have your names in full along with your service No and home address. So that I might write you when again we are home and well.

Not to hurry as at [illegible]

Wishing you all the best.

          I am your,
          Henry E. Budden
          28.10.42[106]

Thursday, 15 October. In common with other groups of POWs, survivors from the *Lisbon Maru* were required to broadcast radio messages. This example will suffice: "This is Signalman Charles Pooley, Royal Navy, of . . . Ambleside Avenue, Peacehaven, Sussex, speaking from the prisoner of war camp in Osaka, Japan, to all of my family and relatives in England. Well, all, I have now been in Japan three or four days. Arrived after a very arduous journey in which the ship I was travelling on was torpedoed by a submarine, a lot of us being lost or missing, but I was lucky enough to be picked up by the Japanese Navy after several hours in the water, but please do not worry about me, because I am feeling very well and am happy. I had a long train journey after arriving in Japan in which I had time to admire the countryside. It was very much like an English countryside. The authorities in charge of this camp have been fine and the treatment has been quite good. Don't forget to keep your chins up and I am always thinking about you all and I send my love to Pauline Francis. Please tell her that I still think about her and hope that she and all of Frank's family are safe and well. And here is a chance to wish you all a Merry Christmas. I would like to inform Mr and Mrs Cassidy of 1 Picardy Avenue, Belfast, Ireland, that John Cassidy, Signalman, is here with me and is quite well at present. Anyone hearing this message, please inform my family. I hope you are all listening in at home, Goodbye and especially mother, and God bless you all until we meet again."[107]

Saturday, 17 October. Back in Hong Kong, deaths through disease and injuries on working parties continued. Major James Gray, RAMC: "Private E. A. Roberts, Hong Kong Volunteer Defence Corps, and five other prisoners were injured on the 17 October 1942."

Saturday, 17 October. Baird: "I took the funeral party out today. We buried five more Canadians, three Royal Rifles and two Grenadiers. One was Eric Eastholm from my company. He had been with me since the war started. Just recently we have been able to buy — buy, mind you — some anti-toxin for the Dip. cases, but not one-tenth enough. The camp have [sic] spent hundreds of yen, put up by all the officers to buy this anti-toxin." (p. 129)

Sunday, 18 October. T. J. J. Fenwick and J. A. D. Morrison, of the Hong Kong and Shanghai Banking Corporation, escaped from the Sun Wah Hotel with the assistance of BAAG agent Lo Hung Sui (who had been sent to help them so that BAAG could learn the Japanese intentions for Hong Kong's economy).

Monday, 19 October.   Redwood: "Norah Witchell's 20th birthday."[108]

Tuesday, 20 October.   Forsyth, who was seriously ill in Shamshuipo Camp hospital: "Freeman was in the hut. He had been dying by inches for a month, the orderly said, because he couldn't force down the rice and greens any more. He passed away the fourth day I was in the hospital."

James Bertram, in the same camp, was luckier: "In October I got diphtheria. I was lucky, however, in being one of the latecomers. By this time our doctors had antitoxin, so I spent the winter in 'hospital' in Jubilee Buildings [it] was fairly primitive; but at least we had iron beds and medical attention from our own doctors. I was in a room with three other patients. One was an Ulsterman RA who had got diphtheria in the leg; his private passion was sailing, and he spent most of his time making model boats. His neighbour was a young Welsh stoker who had been in the Cicala . . . The fourth patient was an English militiaman, the worst case of the lot. Paddy was crippled and Taff was paralyzed, but Sid had everything wrong with him that a man could have." (p. 113)

Tuesday, 20 October.   Poulter was in an equally bad way at Kobe: "It is rumoured that we shall be moved to a proper hospital in Osaka . . . We were put into open lorries and the trip took two and half-hours with no stops on the way. This was fatal to the men suffering from very bad diarrhoea and consequently there were very many messy pairs of pants on arrival. I was lucky, but only just. I can't say that I saw much of the journey, as my thoughts were concentrated elsewhere! Hospital? It is under the stands or terraces of the Osaka Stadium or Ochinioka. It is a trifle better than we have left in two respects. One is that we have a real Doctor and it is much lighter and a bit more room. The Doctor is Surgeon Lieutenant Jackson. So far he has no medical supplies, but we are living in hopes."

The first dedicated POW hospital in Japan, Ichioka Ward, had been established under Surgeon Lieutenant Jackson. Wallace Hastings was one of the medics allocated to serve in this hospital: "Dispersion to various camps followed and I and several others were sent to Osaka Stadium Hospital for POWs under the supervision of Surgeon Lieutenant Jackson RNVR . . . The hospital was an area beneath a sports stadium the outside of which we never saw. It consisted of straight walkway of somewhere between sixty and one hundred yards in length."[109] Ichioka was to be the death of many POWs, though all remembered Jackson and his staff with great affection and respect.

Hastings continued: "Patients were brought from nearby British occupied POW camps in Osaka and Kobe and the hospital rapidly filled and remained so until we left. With limited facilities and medical supplies it was difficult to provide adequate treatment to them. Most were suffering from deficiency diseases together with various illnesses and the poor diet severely retarded recovery. Meals consisted of rice gruel for breakfast, three small slightly sweet bread rolls for lunch and for supper, boiled rice and a watery soup made from a swede-like vegetable called daikon. Occasionally there was an issue of pickled seaweed and more rarely a portion of salted fish. A further extra on a rota basis was a portion of the burnt rice which adheres to the sides of the cauldron in which it is cooked. Treatment given was very basic; dressing of wounds from injury; bedsores which were an inevitable complication and general nursing care for those with other illnesses. Wet and dry beri-beri was suffered by all including staff."[110]

Sunday, 25 October. In an enormous boost to the morale of POWs and civilians alike, the first American air raid attacked Hong Kong. Redwood: "Great excitement today — many planes about, very high, and in the blue blue sky there was smoke as if from a gun high on the Peak. Some people saw anti-ac puffs at them later."

Baird: "Twelve of our planes came over and dropped a few bombs on the docks. Oh! Molly, they sounded great; it means we haven't been forgotten after all these long months. A cheer went up from all our camp." (p. 130)

From now on, such attacks would be regular occurrences. Although men would occasionally be injured by shrapnel or bullets, none of them yet realized how dangerous these raids would become — especially to the prisoners in Japan.

Wednesday, 28 October. Lowe: "At about 11.30 am <u>They Came</u> and we saw some lovely dive bombing. Hash Anderson hit by shrapnel."

Thursday, 29 October. Major James Gray, RAMC: "On 29 October 1942 Corporal Woodward RASC died from multiple injuries caused by the fall of a tree the day before."

Saturday, 31 October. The first 'true' Stanley baby (i.e. conceived in Stanley Camp itself) was born to Mrs Mitchell.[111]

In the same month, BAAG established contact with the prisoners in Shamshuipo, and in the camp they formed a team of Ford, Gray, Routledge, and Hardy. Over the next two months, Ford was able to pass a message to Newnham in Argyle Street saying that they were in contact with BAAG, and Newnham in turn involved Ma Tau Chung — recruiting Captain Ansari as the main contact. The first seeds of a plan for a mass escape were being sown.

November 1942

Sunday, 1 November. Laite: "Sunday, Nov. 1. One of the Imperials was killed at Kai Tak airport during the week."

Sunday, 8 November. A BAAG report noted the disposition of Indian POWs:

> Four soldiers all HKSRA and one policeman were brought out of Hong Kong successfully by F.I.G.s. An organisation has been laid on for further contact with reliable soldiers and, provided POWs from the Camp are used as guard, we should have easy means of contact. Their names and numbers are as follows:-[112]
>
> 3640, Hav. MEHNCA SINGH, 20th Bty. 12th Coast Regiment, RA
> He was first interned in SHAM SHUI PO and later in MA TAU CHUNG. He left the latter Camp in September 1942 together with some 200 other Sikhs and was quartered at Gun Club Hill. He was ordered by Subedar MAXIM KHAN to work in the Indian Independence Affairs Inquiry Office in Union Building. (MEHNCA SINGH was referred to in X.I.S.No.6 dated 14.9.42, Sub-Division No. 1 last Para.)
>
> 4877 L/Nk LASHKAR SINGH, 2nd Mtn. Bty., RA
> He was taken prisoner at SHINGMUN on the 11th of December along with Captain JONES, Royal Scots, and Lieut. WILCOX, R.A. whilst doing F.O.O. work He was taken to North Point Camp and was then posted to the Independence League as a clerk.
>
> 7751, L/Nk SANTOKH SINGH, 35th Coast Bty. RA
> Surrendered at Stanley on 25th December, taken to North Point Camp and thence to MA TAU CHUNG. He was taken out of MA TAU CHUNG with 200 other Sikhs and sent to Gun Club Hill. He likewise was taken out and sent to the Independence League as a typist.

5496, L/Nk DALIP SINGH, 1st Mtn. Bty. RA
In TAITAM area on 18th December. Reported sick — given medical attention and four days off duty, and was taken to a separate shelter to sleep. Battery retired on the 20th without informing him. He was still lying in fever when discovered by Japanese Officer. He saw several atrocities involving POWs both in the hills and later in the hospital.

Both L/Nk LASHKAR SINH and L/Nk DALIP SINGH attempted to obtain third national passes with a view to escape into China via KWANGCHOWAN, but met with difficulty,

799, Policeman NARVANT SINGH
Enlisted in 1937, Hongkong Police Force. Retired from Kowloon and reported to Gloucester Hotel and remained till the end of the war. He was then sent to Stanley and was given 'Two Stars' rank and was on guard duty round Stanley Camp. Before leaving Hongkong, he consulted Supt. of Police LUSCOMBE who encouraged him to go and told him he would find THOMPSON, former Hongkong police inspector.

They state that the following Indians are out. Details of their sections and places where they are believed to be serving are appended.

HINDUS

PLACE	P.M's	Rajputs	Dogras	Sikhs	Tot.
Canton	1,200	–	–	100	1,300
Hainan	80	–	–	220	300
University Hall	50	–	–	–	50
Aberdeen	70	–	–	–	70
Stanley Barracks	20	–	–	–	20
Stanley Village	40	–	–	–	40
Shouson Hill	30	–	–	–	30
Lyemun Barracks	30	–	–	–	30
Murray Barracks	50	–	–	–	50
Kowloon D.Y.P.	–	–	–	50	50
H.K.P & Watchmen, Dockyard Police, Sikh near SSP	))50)	–	–	30	80
P.M.s near West Pnt Near west point	)		100		100
Near BlackHead Ft. in Direction of North.	)12)	200	–	28	240

On the road between Prince Edward Road and Argyle Street	))100)	–	–	–	100
On Jordan Road near Gun Club Hill	))50	–	–	–	50
Fanling	30	–	–	–	30
Taipo	40	–	–	–	40
Near Tai Lam	50	–	–	–	50
Kowloon Tong	28	–	–	–	28
Austin Road	2	–	–	2	4
Subedar Mhas Khan Party, place unknown	))50	–	–	–	50
TOTAL	1,982	200	100	450	2,712

Clearly the idea of Indian POWs being in Canton at this time was a surprise to Clague, who noted: "An agent has been sent to Canton immediately to re-check whether there are in fact any Indians in Canton. He is armed with letters in English and Punjabi."

The report went on to state that the number remaining in Ma Tau Chung Camp was approximately 1,065, and that SUBADAR INMAR KHAN 5/7th Rajput was now Camp Commandant.

> The Camp is now being run as a normal army camp with daily programme, involving parades, rifle drill, marching drill, musketry, and P.T., and school (Japanese is taught).
>
> It is stated that 500 rifles are kept in the Camp for training and manning purposes !!!
>
> The following posts are manned from the Camp daily:-
> 1. 11 men to Japanese HQ (2 NCOs and 9 soldiers) near ARGYLE STREET   11
> 2. 1 Indian and 10 men   11
> 3. 2 NCOs, 9 men — Railway Station   11
> 4. Star Ferry — 1 NCO and 9 men   10
> 5. Whitfield Barracks — 6 soldiers   6
> 6. Oil Company — 3 men   3
> *7. Gun Club Hill — 3 NCOs and 12 soldiers   15
> *8. House Guard — 3 soldiers   3
>   TOTAL: 70[113]
>
> * post now demolished

> The guards leave MA TAU CHUNG at 0900 hours and proceed by truck to various posts. They remained on duty till 0900 hours the next morning when they are relieved and then proceed back to the Camp. Small quantities of ammunition are said to be held secretly on the Camp, but there is no definite proof of this.
>
> Food in the Camp is inadequate and, if there is trouble of any description, the Japanese reduce rations. There appears to exist much anti-Japanese feeling in the Camp. Fuller details may be had from the men themselves. Maps are being brought up to date.

Sunday, 22 November. Redwood: "Went to tea at C Bungalow. Tony's birthday is tomorrow really. It is the lowest bungalow, built on the edge of the hill. Tea in the garden — delightful setting; smooth grass, blue and silver sea; blue, blue, sky; hills green and smooth in the distance, and planes droning high up all the afternoon. Mr and Mrs Hyde Lay and Bailey were the other guests. Mrs Hyde Lay very sweet and nice and kind and attractive and homely — 'Betty'."

Sunday, 29 November. Laite: "This has been a very happy day in the life of our camp. Red Cross parcels, which came to Hong Kong at the end of July, have at last been distributed and today each man in camp received one. They were more or less standard packages. Mine was packed at Bermondsey, England, and contained 1 tin Galantine (Jellied meat), 1 tin tomatoes, 2 oz Maypole tea, 2 packets sugar (4 oz), 1 tin margarine, 1 tin cheese (4 oz), 1 apple pudding (16 oz), 8 oz golden syrup, 1/2 lb bacon, 1 lb minced beef and vegetables, 1 tin condensed milk, 1 creamed rice, 1 tin biscuits, 1 soap, 4 oz chocolate."[114]

December 1942

In early December, Woosung Camp, Shanghai, was closed down and the entire POW population (mainly US Marines, but including those survivors of the *Lisbon Maru* who had been too sick for further travel), were moved to the nearby camp of Kiangwan (now Jiangwan).

Monday, 7 December. Bill Oxley in Shamshuipo: "It was about this time that we all had 'Electric Feet' (Malnutrition). I was now in a sorry state; I had septicaemia, huge sores on my back; my lips were yellow blisters. I could not speak for fear of my lips sticking together, and had to keep my mouth open. I was near to death. There were a lot worse off than me. I thought I would go to the hospital block to see Philip Nelms. We had soldiered together now over ten years. I forced myself to go and see him. When I did see him, I saw he had wet beri-beri. His poor arms and legs were so swollen, like 'Popeye'. Tears came to my eyes; I said 'Hello, Philip'. He just stared in front of himself, and did not know me. Poor lad, he died that night."[115]

Electric feet were a major problem in all the camps. Medic Wallace Hastings in Ichioka Ward, Japan: "The dry beri-beri causes severe nerve pain in the lower limbs especially the feet and ankles. Some relief can be obtained by cooling, and I can vividly remember one patient who, to achieve this walked outside in the snow. Some days later his toes turned black and gangrene set in necessitating the removal of all of them on both feet. This was done by Dr. Jackson without anaesthetic, the tissue was without sensitivity by now and was, therefore, of no consequence. The rest of his feet were affected and severe sepsis set in. They were cleaned and bandaged. Healing was very slow. Some time later on removal of the bandages for re-dressing his feet were covered with maggots. On seeing this, Dr. Jackson told me to leave them, re-apply a clean bandage and review in a few days time. Later inspection found that the sepsis had completely gone. With further care, the patient recovered sufficiently to walk again albeit with difficulty having no toe joints. His name is lost to me but he was soldier of Scottish origin. There were many deaths. Disposal of bodies was by cremation arranged by the Japanese. Before collection we had to put the body into empty daikon tubs which were like large half barrels, placing them in a sitting position with legs drawn up to the chest and head bowed forward. Following cremation, the ashes were returned to the hospital."

Friday, 11 December. O'Toole in Shamshuipo: "All the invalids who are not quite hospital cases have been moved into Jubilee North. Cooper, Bull, Hillman, Standin, Malekin, Hewitt are all there. S/M Eley is in hospital in a pretty bad way, he is one of the bed-downers right from the start conserving his energy so to speak, used to laugh at us wearing ourselves out on jobs. He'll have to take a good grip to pull through."

Monday, 14 December. O'Toole continued: "Weighed today 10 st 7lb- that's three lbs more than before the war, so I should be alright, no wasting away yet, not much guts though. Allowed to send Christmas cards to Stanley. Sent to Alan Barwell, Joan Whiteley, Peggy Harrison."

Friday, 18 December. O'Toole: "Feet been giving me gyp the last two days and nights; seems to make the old heart pound too. Christensen a Volunteer & Norwegian[116] died today in his hut, has had bad feet for a long time, no other reason known, may have had a weak heart. Just passed away in his sleep."

Tuesday, 22 December. O'Toole: "Sgt Makelin A.E.C. died today of dysentery, his wife and baby are at Stanley they used to live above us in Kennedy Road; always thought him quite a tough egg. But who can say. Japanese send in 2 Christmas trees for the churchs [sic]."

Thursday, 24 December. Redwood: "Some 30 odd people left for Shanghai today — including Bill O'Neill of Reuters."[117]

Monday, 28 December. Wright: "The 28th was darkened for me by the death of my good friend Elliot. I had carried him to hospital the day before, and his loss greatly saddened me. He was so young and so very likeable."

Thursday, 31 December. That night Bill Lowe of the Volunteers Armoured Cars recorded: "Armoured Car Dinner! Corned beef on toast, veg soup & oxo, M & V pie (specially made thro' Ken in Bakehouse) ginger, chocs, pop corn, jam & bread, tea & cocoa, decorated table & hut really was great Valentine came in for a drink. Present Doug Walker, John Lee, Frank Lee, Corneck, Hutch, Tocker, Tate, Lionel, Labrousse, Ed Murphy, Dave, Pat, Knight, Miller (11 starce), Berd, Crawford, Ginger, Connolly, Ingram, Gibby & self & so ends 1942; here's to 1943 & may it bring us Peace."

The New Year would bring no peace, but it would bring a slowing down of the deaths. After 1942, no year would seem quite so bad.

ROLL OF HONOUR FOR 1942

Queen Mary Hospital[118]

Delaney, Morris	Rifleman	E/29123	RRoC	4.1.42	U 2.1.42 obq[119]
Polson, John Alexander C.	CQMS		HKVDC	14.1.42	K 2.1.42[120]
Gillies, Hamilton Oliver	Private		HKVDC	3.1.42	U 5.1.42 DOW obq
Gordon, Vyner Reginald	2nd Lieutenant	294917	RS		K 6.1.42 DOW[121]
Wojnarsky, John R.N.	Private	H/41668	WG	7.1.42	U 6.1.42 DOW
Remer, Louis	Private	6203205	MX	10.1.42	U 12.1.42 DOW[122]
Neve, George Eric	Major	31062	HQ		K 23.1.42 DOW[123]

Royal Naval Hospital

Horvath, James E.	Signalman	H/38902	RCCS			U ?.1.42 DOW obr[124]

Argyle Street

Till, Earl Beverley	Private	H/41855	WG			K 1.1.42 Dy
Sturgeon, James Basindale	Lance Corp.	1454	HKVDC			K 2.1.42 Dy
McKillop, Orville Watson	Lieutenant		WG			K 4.1.42 DOW[125]
Mogra, Jimmy Edulji	Private	DR312	HKVDC			K 4.1.42 DOW[126]
James, John David Leslie	Corporal	550248	RAF			K 14.2.42 DOW GSW
Sorby, Vincent Dare	Private		HKVDC	15.1.42		K 16.1.42 DOW Oba[127]

Sham Shui Po

Lam Kang	Sapper	231	HKVDC			K 1942[128]
Wan Yuk Lung	Sapper	538	HKVDC			U 1942
Kwok Wing	Private	-	HKCR			U 7.1.42
Jafar Khan	Sepoy	15964	RP			K 8.1.42 obs
Mahabir Singh	Sepoy	15145	RP			K 8.1.42 obs
Ram Partap Singh	Sepoy	16236	RP			K 8.1.42 obs
Jagmal Singh	Sepoy	9217	RP			K 9.1.42 obs
Ackerman, Leonard A.	Staff Sergeant	7581855	RAOC	3.1.42		K 13.1.42 obs[129]
Reed, Stephen Arnold	Private	3856	HKVDC		BRH	K 15.1.42 DOW
Walker, C.J.	SQMS	10596702	RAOC			U 18.1.42[130]
Wong Siu Man	Sapper	639	HKVDC			U 21.1.42
Dobson, Herbert	Sergeant	7757240	RAVC	2.2.42	BRH	K 23.1.42
Gullane, Philip Leyden	Private	3063596	RS		BRH	K 28.1.42[131]
Martin, Francis	Private	DR95	HKVDC		BRH	K 30.1.42 DOW[132]
Lam Yung Fok	Sapper	418	HKVDC			U ?.2.42
Clarke, Henry William	Signalman	2350848	RCS	7.2.42		K 6.2.42 obs[133]
Piddington, Reginald A.	Lance Corp.	6201878	MX	18.2.42		K 8.2.42 oba[134]
Smart, Jack	Corporal	7885633	RAPC		STH	K 13.2.42 Dy
Marriott, Henry	Sapper	3869	HKVDC			K 14.2.42
Wallace, Alexander	Corporal	3053686	RS		STH	K 16.2.42 Dy oba
Wosencroft, Stanley R.	Corporal	7261290	RAMC		BRH	K 19.2.42 Al[135]
Harvey, William Albert H.	Private	3054172	RS		STH	K 25.2.42 Dy oba
Chorley, Grosvenor F.	Private	3053721	RS		STH	K 5.3.42 Dy oba
Heggie, Joseph Smith	Private	3054836	RS			K 11.3.42 oba[136]
Li Kwok	Sergeant	338	HKVDC			U ?.4-6.42
McKay, Samuel	Private	3054051	RS			K 2.4.42 oba
Johnson, Ivor George	Signalman	1971	HKVDC			K 5.4.42 Bi
Gilmore, Walter Charles	2nd Lieutenant	EC/16723	PJ		BRH	K 9.4.42 GSW[137]
Thompson, William J.	Lance Corp.	2354	HKVDC			K 9.4.42 Dy/Bi
Law, William Alfred	Private	6201449	MX	12.4.42	BRH	K 10.4.42 DOW[138]
Cunningham, Daniel	Bombardier	850130	RA			K 11.4.42 oba
Basnett, Arthur William	Private	3053763	RS	20.4.42	STH	K 19.4.42 Dy/Pa oba[139]
Lloyd, Norman Duplan	Sergeant	2969	HKVDC			K 25.4.42 Mu[140]

McGill, John	Private	3127337	MX		STH	K 26.4.42 Cbi/Mn/Di oba
Moore, Dennis R.H.	Private	3288	HKVDC		STH	K 30.4.42 Dy[141]
Tong Pui	Sapper	635	HKVDC			U ?.5-6.42
Bristow, Frederick George	Private	6201510	MX		STH	K 6.5.42 Dy oba
Shaw, William	CSM		HKVDC			U 9.5.42 [142]
Stanesby, Sydney John C.	Private	19559	HKVDC Argyle		BRH	K 14.5.42 Ul
Gubbay, Sarah	Nurse	ND47	HKVDC		STH	K 17.5.42 HKJ
Stephens, Ronald V.	Sapper	1874763	RE		BRH	K 17.5.42 GSW[143]
Lacey, Harry	Corporal	4643	HKVDC			K 21.5.42 Dy
Pettingell, Gerald	Private	132	HKDDC		STH	K 23.5.42 Dy[144]
Ferrington, Herbert Frank	Lance Corp.	6201407	MX		STH	K 26.5.42 Mn/Es oba
Lawrence, John Henry	Private	DR88	HKVDC		STH	K 29.5.42 CCC Ma
Jennings, Francis Arthur	Private	111	HKDDC		STH	K 3.6.42 Es/Cf
Rodgers, Joseph	Bombardier	1667726	RA		STH	K 9.6.42 Dy oba
Lemon, Ernest John	Sapper	1873799	RE		STH	K 25.6.42 oba[145]
McMasters, Thomas Y.	Driver	2015964	RE			K 27.6.42 Da oba
Wilson, Frederick T.	Sapper	2013624	RE		STH	K 27.6.42 Da oba
Westwood, Eli	Gunner	860117	RA		STH	K 29.6.42 Ms/Dy oba
Raitt, Raymond	Private	3063221	RS		STH	K 30.6.42 Td oba
Toon, Walter Edward	Corporal	517395	RAF		STH	K 4.7.42 Da
Jack, James	Lance Corp.	2820153	RCS		STH	K 6.7.42 Da oba
Cripps, John Vincent G.	Gunner	872693	RA		STH	K 8.7.42 Dy oba
Mitchell, Donald M.	Sig Bosun		RN		STH	K 8.7.42 Dy[146]
Devine, Cyril Edward	Private	6199806	MX		STH	K 10.7.42 Dy oba
Faughnan, John	Sapper	1877296	RE			K 13.7.42 oba
Lawson, Francis John	Sergeant	922970	RAF	10.7.42	STH	K 13.7.42 Da
Smith, George	Corporal	519737	RAF	13.7.42	STH	K 14.7.42 Da
Forrester, Joseph Neil	Private	3059323	RS			K 15.7.42 Dy oba
Weaver, Berti Richard	Gunner	822885	RA		STH	K 18.7.42 Sa oba
Gibson, Thomas	Private	3059105	RS		STH	K 19.7.42 Da oba
Bevan, Granville Aubrey	Ord. Coder	D/JX216195	RN		STH	K 19.7.42 Da
Lees, John	Signalman	2325743	RCS		STH	K 20.7.42 Da oba
Davies, Kenneth Vernon	Supply Asst.	D/MX82684	RN		STH	K 23.7.42 Da
Grant, William Haddon	Sapper	814028	RE			K 23.7.42 Dy oba
Simmonds, Bertie Thomas	Private	6202632	MX		STH	K 23.7.42 Bs oba[147]
Hailey, Guy	Private	723	HKVDC			K 24.7.42 Es/Cf
Brown, William Edgar	Gunner	1529443	RA		STH	K 25.7.42 Dy oba
Keeble, George Frederick	Gunner	860925	RA		STH	K 25.7.42 Dy
Rodgers, Herbert Henry	Signalman	2353858	RCS		STH	K 25.7.42 Da oba
Guterres, Joaquim J.	Lieutenant		HKVDC	27.7.42	STH	K 26.7.42 Dy
Thomas, Douglas	Gunner	872301	RA	6.7.42	STH	K 26.7.42 Dy oba[148]
Hurn, Alexander Charles	Corporal	S/57124	RASC		STH	K 4.8.42 Dy
Hunt, Leonard Reginald	Corporal	550345	RAF			K 4.8.42 Da
Heffer, Jack	Gunner	843580	RA			K 7.8.42 Sa oba
Guppy, Reginald Albert	Corporal RM	PLY/22197	RM			K 8.8.42 Da
Salisbury, Thomas	Sergeant	833097	RA		STH	K 9.8.42 Da oba
Casey, John S.A.	Bombardier	850462	RA			K 11.8.42 Da oba[149]

Douglas, Robert	Lance Corp.	3053715	RS		K 11.8.42 Da oba
Grinton, Eric George	Gunner	838409	RA		K 12.8.42 Da oba
Baker, Laurence Cecil	Gunner	3542	HKVDC		K 12.8.42 Da
Rapp, Frederick Christian	Private		HKVDC BRH		K 12.8.42 Cf
Skinner, Ernest W.	W.O.II QMS	1059232	RA	18.8.42	K 13.8.42 Da oba
Harrington, George T.	Private	3293	HKVDC		K 14.8.42 Da
Paterson, John Courtney	Private	7608845	RAOC		K 15.8.42 Dy
Dean, Reginald Ernest	A.B.	P/JX149800	RN		K 15.8.42 Da
Anderson, John	Signalman	P/CDX2459	RN		K 16.8.42 Da
Backhurst, Keith Keel	Private	7673629	RAPC		K 16.8.42 Sa
Roberts, Stanley Eric	Private	4420	HKVDC		K 16.8.42 Da
Morley, Frederick	BSM	1051733	RA	16.8.42	K 17.8.42 Es oba
Longfield, Stuart	Private		HKVDC		K 18.8.42 Da
Ainslie, George	Private	2841	HKVDC		K 20.8.42 Da
Porter, Leslie	Gunner	872624	RA		K 21.8.42 Da oba
Sheppard, Alfred Cecil	Gunner	1712256	RA		K 21.8.42 Sa oba
Sinclair, Harold	Sapper	1870487	RE	28.8.42	K 22.8.42 Da oba
Jack, Lawrence	Sergeant	1834	HKVDC		K 22.8.42 Da
Caswell, Charles Alfred	L. Seaman	P/JX164941	RN	22.9.42	K 22.8.42 Pe
Vieira-Ribeiro, Eduardo	Private	4059	HKVDC		K 23.8.42 Da
Petchey, Basil George E.	Gunner	1708134	RA		K 24.8.42 Sa oba
Player, Arthur Howard	Signalman	2323209	RCS		K 26.8.42 Mn oba
Lapworth, Leslie	A.B.	C/JX210031	RN		K 26.8.42 Da
Halstead, Tom Heap	Signalman	2323426	RCS		K 29.8.42 Da oba
Hughes, William Thomas	Gunner	1493028	RA		K 31.8.42 Da oba
Smith, Robert Robinson	SQMS	10714833	RASC		K 31.8.42 Dy
Anyon, Kenneth Ewart	Gunner	1492305	RA		K 2.9.42 Da oba[150]
Merry, William Albert H.	Private	849688	MX		K 2.9.42 Dy oba
Stirling, Thomas S.	Gunner	842905	RA		K 2.9.42 Da oba
Wilkinson, William E.	A.B.	D/JX137073	RN		K 2.9.42 Da
Manning, Arthur David	Sergeant	6201417	MX DCM	2.9.42	K 3.9.42 Da oba
Allam, Arthur Godfrey	Sapper	2039641	RE		K 4.9.42 Da oba
Helson, Wilfred Lorenzo	Corporal	1854436	RE		K 4.9.42 Da oba
Christie, William Stewart	Private	3054154	RS		K 5.9.42 Da oba[151]
Pratt, Walter	Lance Corporal	2818018	CMP		K 5.9.42 Da
Hutchinson, George H.	P.O. Tel	D/J111178	RN		K 5.9.42 Da
Barker, Alfred	Gunner	824789	RA		K 6.9.42 Dy oba
Deakin, Arnold	Gunner	863051	RA		K 8.9.42 Es/Da Oba
Yoong Yew Moy, George	Signalman	5183	HKVDC		UX 8.9.42[152]
Jeffrey, Richard	Marine	PLY/X.2411	RM		K 9.9.42 Dy
Woplin, George C.	A.B.	P/JX164895	RN		K 10.9.42 Pe/Di
Leonard, Albert Edwin	Private	6213528	MX		K 10.9.42 Da oba
Mayzes, Eric Thomas	Private	6202306	MX		K 11.9.42 Es oba
Moores, Henry	Lance Bdr.	838451	RA		K 11.9.42 Es oba
Humphreys, Joseph Jacob	Chief Eng Off		MN SS Ebonol	11.10.42	K 11.9.42 Es/Pe
Pragnell, Charles Fred	Lance Corp.	DR203	HKVDC		K 12.9.42 Es
Govan, Harry Maitland D.	Lance Corp.	3054219	RS		K 13.9.42 Da oba
McCallum, Thomas	Private	3051777	RS		K 13.9.42 Es oba

Turner, Ronald Benjamin	Lance Corp.	6201035	MX		K 13.9.42 Es oba
Branson, Victor	Private	6202767	MX		K 14.9.42 EX
Byrne, William George	Lance Corp.	6202127	MX		K 14.9.42 EX
Dunne, Maurice Trevor	Private	6200791	RAOC		K 14.9.42 EX
Stopforth, James	Private	7608231	RAOC		K 14.9.42 EX
Connolly, Paul	Private		HKDDC		K 14.9.42 EX[153]
Frew, George Alexander	Master		MN SS Anjou		K 14.9.42 Es/Rm
Terran, Charles	S.Sergeant	7256471	RAMC		K 15.9.42 Td
Wright, Charles John F.	Lance Corporal	864687	CMP		K 15.9.42 Es/Da/My
Ware, John Henry	Ch Eng Off		MN		K 16.9.42 Mn/De
Crowe, Joseph George	Lance Corp.	7008733	MX		K 18.9.42 Es oba
Street, Daniel	Private	6214372	MX		K 19.9.42 Es/Mn oba
Buist, James	Lance Corp.	3054437	RS		K 23.9.42 Pa oba[154]
Stewart, James	Lance Corp.	2689317	RE		K 23.9.42 Es/Ma oba
Jennings, Ernest Thomas	Private	6203279	MX		K 24.9.42 Mn oba
Hickman, John Frederick	Lance Corp.	2141	HKVDC		K 26.9.42 Es/Mn
Rose, Stanley Albert	LAC	620400	RAF		K 25.9.42 Dm
Cullum, Harold	P.O.	D/JX96876	RN		K 27.9.42 Mn
Coughlan, Peter Gordon	Rifleman	E/30230	RRoC		K 28.9.42 Dy
Cusson, Paul Marc	Corporal	K/83964	RCOC	BRH	K 28.9.42 Da
Sinclair, Charles	A.B.	C/JX151440	RN		K 28.9.42 Sa/Da/Mn
Feather, James William	Marine	PLY/X 1819	RM		K 29.9.42 Mn/As
Raites, Edward	Private	H/6898	WG	BRH	K 29.9.42 Da/He
Iverach, John Andrew	Corporal	H/6693	WG		K 30.9.42 Da
Redhead, Thomas	Signalman	K/83057	RCCS	BRH	K 30.9.42 Ts[155]
Christensen, Harold	Seaman		MN		UX 1.10.42[156]
Gibbs, Douglas A. Robert	Corporal	E/29961	RRoC		K 1.10.42 Dy/Es
Willey, Ivan Emmerson	Rifleman	E/30306	RRoC 2.10.42		K 1.10.42 Da
Kendall, Donald	Rifleman	E/30187	RRoC	BRH	K 3.10.42 Da
Armstrong, George	Private	H/6239	WG 5.10.42		K 4.10.42 Da/Pn
MacArthur, John Edwin	Rifleman	E/29847	RRoC 3.10.42		K 4.10.42 Da
Jenkins, William B.	Private	HKDDC			K 5.10.42 Pa/Mn
Walsh, James Stanford	Corporal	E/30405	RRoC		K 5.10.42 Da
Pearce, William Richard	CSM	B/81614	RCASC	BRH	K 6.10.42 Sa
Welsh, Delbert William L.	Rifleman	E/30384	RRoC		K 6.10.42 Da
Lock, Ernest Andrew	QMS	1863545	RE		K 6.10.42 Da oba
Barclay, William John	Rifleman	E/30450	RRoC		K 7.10.42 Da
Mabb, Herbert Henry	Private	H/6530	WG		K 7.10.42 Da
Robidoux, Marcel E.J.	Private	H/6597	WG		K 7.10.42 Da
Welsh, Allen Benjamin	Rifleman	E/30395	RRoC		K 7.10.42 Da
Coady, John Alfred	Private	L/13478	WG	BRH	K 9.10.42 Da
Moore, Wilfred Samuel	Private	H/6674	WG		K 9.10.42 Da/Es
Dubois, Leo Peter	Rifleman	E/30057	RRoC		K 10.10.42 Da
Budden, Gilbert Easthope	Corporal	2965	HKVDC		K 11.10.42 Da/Cf/Ss
Danyluck, Nicholas	Rifleman	E/30094	RRoC 12.10.42		K 11.10.42 Da
Huntingdon, Ralph	Rifleman	E/30261	RRoC		K 11.10.42 Da
Iles, Percy John	Private	H/6650	WG		K 11.10.42 Da/Cs

Smith, Laurence	Rifleman	E/30279	RRoC		K 11.10.42 Da
Stevens, Clarence George	Rifleman	E/30497	RRoC		K 11.10.42 Da
Nichol, David Scott	Lance Corp.	H/17410	WG		K 12.10.42 Dy/Cs
Pearson, Douglas Edwin	Private	H/6958	WG		K 12.10.42 Da
Pearson, Montague	Joiner 5/C	D/SR8463	RN		K 12.10.42 Da
Nicholson, William	Rifleman	B/40683	RRoC		K 13.10.42 Dy/Cs
Hinton, George	A.B.	P/J32954	RN		K 14.10.42 Mn/Cf
Sauson, Edward Lewis	Sergeant	E/29904	RRoC		K 14.10.42 Da
Thomasson, Thomas	Private	H/6778	WG		K 14.10.42 Da
Huth, Charles Edwin M.	Private	3052079	RS		K 14.10.42 Tb oba
Turner, Frederick Charles	Signalman	2352608	RCS		K 14.10.42 Mn/Cf oba
Chenell, John Maxwell	Lance Corp.	E/30406	RRoC		K 16.10.42 Da/Cs
Cormier, Leo Abbey	Rifleman	G/18272	RRoC		K 16.10.42 Cs
Eastholm, Eric Elon	Private	H/6160	WG		K 16.10.42 Da
Forbes, James Phillip	Private	H/6272	WG		K 16.10.42 Da
Vermette, Patrick	Corporal	E/30451	RRoC		K 16.10.42 Di/Mn/Cs
Laplante, Romain Joseph	Private	H/75223	WG		K 17.10.42 Es
Mullin, Elmer Owen	Rifleman	E/30663	RRoC		K 17.10.42 Da
Capes, Charles J.	Purser		MN SS Fausang HK		K 18.10.42 Mn[157]
McAra, William Roger	Rifleman	E/30124	RRoC		K 19.10.42
Cheyne, Peter James	Private	3059385	RS		K 19.10.42 oba
Thompson, John Alex	Rifleman	G/22778	RRoC		K 21.10.42 Cs/As[158]
Howard, Harry S.	Private	H/17032	WG		K 22.10.42 Cs
Pike, Alfred Charles S.	Ch Eng Off		MN SS Tung On HK		K 22.10.42
Pettit, Frank Herbert	BQMS	1033593	RA		K 22.10.42 As oba[159]
Patterson, James Richard	Rifleman	E/30580	RRoC		K 23.10.42 Cs
Pelletier, Gerard Joseph	Rifleman	E/30315	RRoC		K 23.10.42 Cs
Buchanan, George	Private		HKVDC		K 25.10.42
Freeman, Edward John	Private	H/6075	WG		K 26.10.42 Aa
Rathmell, Richard	CSM	2231	HKVDC		K 26.10.42 As
Foster, Stanley Percy	Private	H/6533	WG		K 28.10.42 Da
Lapointe, Valmore W.	Lance Corp.	E/30311	RRoC		K 28.10.42 Dy
Whitbread, Sydney G.	Private	L/2871	WG		K 28.10.42 Es
Gallagher, Victor D.	Gunner	850885	RA		K 28.10.42 Pe oba[160]
Woodward, John	Corporal	S/134377	RASC		K 29.10.42
Morphew, Percy L.	Private	DR144	HKVDC		K 29.10.42 Es/As
Barclay, Robert McMillan	Rifleman	E/30417	RRoC		K 30.10.42 Cs
Boutin, Marius	Rifleman	E/29807	RRoC	29.10.42 BRH	K 30.10.42 Dy
Lewis, Joseph Mark	Private	H/20871	WG		K 31.10.42 Cs
Noble, Russell G.	Lance Corp.	E/30196	RRoC		K 31.10.42 Cs
Nicholas, Thomas A.	Chief Off.		MN MV Fook On HK		K 31.10.42
Mannell, John Wesley	Private	H/6757	WG		K 1.11.42 Cs
Lariviere, Ernest	Private	H/6506	WG		K 2.11.42 Cs
Lavoie, Joseph Eugene R.	Lance Corp.	D/115025	CPC		K 2.11.42 Pa[161]
Clarke, Frederick Thomas	Private	6340701	MX		K 3.11.42 Mn oba[162]
Bicknell, Herbert John	Private	67	HKDDC		K 5.11.42 Dy/As
Clapperton, Albert George	Rifleman	E/30266	RRoC		K 5.11.42 Da/Es

Name	Rank	Number	Unit			Death
Coates, Russell D.	Rifleman	E/30154	RRoC			K 5.11.42 Pa/Da[163]
Harper, George Blake	Lieutenant		WG		BRH	K 6.11.42 Da
Forsyth, Robert	Rifleman	B/40795	RRoC			K 9.11.42 Da/Cs[164]
Suits, William Roger	Rifleman	A/23080	RRoC			K 10.11.42 Dy
Chewter, George William	Private	H/6510	WG			K 12.11.42 Da
Terry, Edward Louie	Captain	RCAPC	BRH			K 14.11.42 Da/Aa
Mann, Lindsay Richard	Corporal	E/30014	RRoC		BRH	K 15.11.42 Da/Pa
Cave, Leonard James	Private	2795	HKVDC			K 16.11.42 As/Es
Robinson, Henry	Private	H/6637	WG			K 17.11.42 Cs
Sweetman, Herbert F.	Rifleman	E/30259	RRoC			K 18.11.42 Cf[165]
Whalen, Joseph Michael	Rifleman	C/65092	RRoC			K 20.11.42 Da/Es
Clift, John Henry	Lance Corporal	843639	CMP			K 21.11.42 Es
Whitton, Eric S.	Sergeant	7683619	CMP		BRH	K 22.11.42 Pe
McAllister, Arthur	Rifleman	E/30369	RRoC			K 24.11.42 Dy/Es/As
Ferguson, John Steven	Gunner	3181	HKVDC			K 25.11.42 Pe/Dm
Gemmell, David	Private	H/17304	WG			K 26.11.42 Es
Egan, John	Sergeant	HKDDC	BRH			K 27.11.42 As
Smith, William Alexander	Private	H/41807	WG			K 27.11.42 Da/Cs
Abel, Frederick J.	Sergeant	H/6154	WG			K 28.11.42 Cbi
MacLaughlin, Thomas	Rifleman	F/40988	RRoC			K 28.11.42 Da/Cs
Aitken, Deighton	Rifleman	E/30391	RRoC	2.12.42	BRH	K 30.11.42 Pe/Bi
Easton, Sidney George J.	Sapper	1942548	RE			K 1.12.42 Pe/Da oba
Peckham, Leslie Wilfred	Sergeant	1/10390	HKDDC			K 1.12.42 Da/Pe/Dm
Jones, Evan	Sapper	1880505	RE		BRH	K 2.12.42 TB
Houston, Thomas Jackson	Gunner	3051	HKVDC		BRH	K 4.12.42 As/Ap
Post, John Russell	Rifleman	G/18468	RRoC		BRH	K 4.12.42 TB
Foxall, Reginald	Private	H/6061	WG			K 6.12.42 Da/Es/Bi
Nelms, Philip Albert	Lance Corp.	6201206	MX		BRH	K 7.12.42 Bi
Grinstead, George W.W.	Private	6213497	MX			K 8.12.42 oba
Stevens, Alfred Watson	A.B.	P/J22598	RN			K 9.12.42 Pa
Thomas, Clifford	Private	H/75233	WG			K 9.12.42 Pe
Cross, George Edwin	Private		HKVDC			K 10.12.42 Ce
Grattan, Alexander G.	Seaman Gunner	5G	HKRNVR		BRH	K 10.12.42 Pe/Bi
Pritchard, Clifford V.H.	Private	6202155	MX			K 10.12.42 oba
Le Mesurier, Georges J.	Captain	108057	HQ		BRH	K 11.12.42[166]
Lee, Alfred Reginald	Private		HKDDC			K 12.12.42 Da[167]
Meuross, Montague E.	Private	6202938	MX		BRH	K 12.12.42 Pe/Dy
Way, Ken Theodore	Private		HKDDC			K 12.12.42 Da
Rolfe, William Redvers	A.B.	C/J57713	RN			K 16.12.42 Ty/Da
Kevan, Thomas Crombie	Sergeant	3616	HKDDC			K 17.12.42 Da/Pe/Dm
Mann, Maxwell Alastair	Rifleman	E/30022	RRoC			K 18.12.42 Da
Christensen, Neils Orskov	Lance Bdr.	4354	HKVDC			K 18.12.42 Cf
Macklin, Robert	Sergeant	3446359	AEC			K 22.12.42 Es/Aa
Sayeks, George Walter	Private	L/2562	WG	22.12.43	BRH	K 22.12.42 Pe/Cs
Bone, Adam	Sergeant	3224	HKVDC		BRH	K 24.12.42 Ma[168]
Paling, Alfred Ronald	Sergeant	546125	RAF			K 31.12.42 Pe

1942

North Point

Freeman, Cecil	Lieutenant		RNR		BRH	K 23.1.42[169]
Rodd, Orville Wilson	Private	H/6086	WG			K 29.1.42
Cook, Percy Robert	Coder	P/JX174934	RN		BRH	K 30.1.42
Kingston, Frank Edward	Ch.E.R.A.	P/M18451	RN			K 26.2.42[170]
Coleman, John A.	Sergeant	E/30060	RRoC			K 18.2.42 DOW[171]
Green, Albert Raymond	Corporal	H/6129	WG		BRH	K 24.2.42 DOW[172]
Quinn, James	Ord. Tel	P/JX159300	RN		BRH	K 4.3.42[173]
Rogerson, Thomas John	Lieutenant		RNVR		BRH	K 11.3.42 Ul
Kellaway, Gordon Garnet	Rifleman	B/74350	RRoC			K 18.3.42[174]
Sutcliffe, John Louis R.	Lieutenant-Col.		WG	6.4.42	BRH	K 5.4.42 Bi/Dy
Carter, Albert Edward	Sergeant	B/83222	RCASC		BRH	K 22.4.42 Pa
Blyth, John	Engineer		MN			K 4.5.42
Little, John Samuel	Signalman	K/34073	RCCS	3.6.42	BRH	K 5.6.42 Dy[175]
Bacon, Lerreat	Rifleman	E/30652	RRoC		BRH	K 11.8.42 TB
Lucas, Harold Fred	Private	L/2870	WG		BRH	K 11.8.42[176]
Chapman, James Everett	Private	H/6271	WG		BRH	K 15.8.42 Ts
Adams, John Henry	Private	H/6294	WG	MiD		K 26.8.42 EX
Berzenski, George	Lance Corp.	H/6700	WG	MiD		K 26.8.42 EX
Ellis, Percy John	Private	H/6771	WG	MiD		K 26.8.42 EX
Payne, John Oliver	Sergeant	H/6016	WG	MiD		K 26.8.42 EX
Firth, Malcolm	Rifleman	E/30735	RRoC		BRH	K 28.8.42 Cs
Antila, Leo Sikstus	Rifleman	E/30276	RRoC	20.8.42	BRH	K 30.8.42 Cs
Pomeroy, George Robert	Rifleman	C/65270	RRoC		BRH	K 1.9.42 Ts/Bi
Moffatt, John Austin	Private	H/6599	WG		BRH	K 2.9.42 Cs/Bi
Ross, Cyril Matthew	Rifleman	E/30444	RRoC		BRH	K 6.9.42 Ul
Gunter, Murlin	Rifleman	E/30302	RRoC		BRH	K 9.9.42 Da
Whillier, Walter Clifford	Lance Corp.	H/6901	WG		BRH	K 9.9.42 Ts/Bi
Coffin, Ninian Allan	Rifleman	E/30459	RRoC		BRH	K 12.9.42[177]
Lumb, David William	Sergeant	A/99507	RCAPC		BRH	K 12.9.42 Dy
Smith, John Spikula	Private	H/6110	WG			K 12.9.42 Es/Bi
Moore, Douglas Haig	Private	H/6371	WG		BRH	K 18.9.42 Da/Dy
Hawkes, Douglas	Private	H/6837	WG		BRH	K 20.9.42 Da/Cf
Harkness, William	Private	H/6219	WG		BRH	K 21.9.42 Da[178]
Boudreau, Sylvestre	Rifleman	E/30474	RRoC		BRH	K 25.9.42 Dy/Pa
White, Wesley James	Lance Sergeant	K/34757	RCCS		BRH	K 25.9.42 Da[179]
Pastuk, Nicholas	Private	H/41790	WG		BRH	K 26.9.42 Da

Lisbon Maru[180]

Abel, Clifford Alan	Sick Berth Att.	D/SR 8625	RN		UP 2.10.42 Dr[181]
Adam, George Currie	Lance Corp.	3053623	RS		U 2.10.42 Dr
Adams, William	BSM	798881	RA		U 2.10.42 Dr
Adamson, Charles V.	BQMS	1424392	HKSRA		U 2.10.42 Dr
Aikman, Ronald Edward	Lance Corp.	6201459	MX		U 2.10.42 Dr
Allan, Hugh Hamilton	Private	3063607	RS		U 2.10.42 Dr
Allanson, Kenneth E.	Captain	132900	RA		U 2.10.42 Dr
Alexander, Adam Glen	BSM	821969	RA		U 2.10.42 Dr
Alchin, Milton Carl	PC	HKDDC	RN/DYP		U 2.10.42 Dr

Allen, William Richard	Marine	PLY/X 2196	RM		UP 2.10.42 Dr
Allin, Bernard Lester	Signalman	2589561	RCS		U 2.10.42 Dr
Allison, Patrick Joseph	Private	3055948	RS		U 2.10.42 Dr
Allport, Albert Edward	BSM	1064171	HKSRA		U 2.10.42 Dr
Ambrose, Fred	Corporal	PLY/22402	RM		UP 2.10.42 Dr
Anderson, John	Lance Bdr.	7013283	RA		U 2.10.42 Dr
Anderson, John McLeod	Private	3055011	RS		U 2.10.42 Dr
Anderson, Victor Emanuel	Bombardier	7076955	RA	10.42	U 2.10.42 Dr[182]
Andrew, Matthew Beaton	Private	3055215	RS		U 2.10.42 Dr
Andrews, Leslie William	Private	6210653	MX		U 2.10.42 Dr
Archer, Albert William	Stoker 1st Class	C/KX 105774	RN		UC 2.10.42 Dr
Archibald, Robert Miller	Private	3054433	RS		U 2.10.42 Dr
Archibald, William	Private	3063611	RS		U 2.10.42 Dr
Arndle, Edward	Gunner	872469	RA		U 2.10.42 Dr
Ashford, Ronald Edward	Telegraphist	P/JX 201901	RN		UPO 2.10.42 Dr[183]
Astill, Arthur	Gunner	845230	RA		U 2.10.42 Dr
Atkinson, Edwin	Lance Corp.	2325182	RCS		U 2.10.42 Dr
Atkinson, Robert	Chief P.O.	D/J 108082	RN		UP 2.10.42 Dr
Attwell, Gerald	Able Seaman	D/SSX 20157	RN		UP 2.10.42 Dr
Audsley, Harold	Sapper	1991557	RE		U 2.10.42 Dr
Auld, Alexander	Private	3052678	RS		U 2.10.42 Dr
Austin, William	Bombardier	850939	HKSRA		U 2.10.42 Dr
Bache, Herbert Henry	Private	2570708	RAMC		U 2.10.42 Dr
Backhurst, Alfred Leonard	Private	6212951	MX		U 2.10.42 Dr
Bader, Bernard John	Sergeant	847343	HKSRA		U 2.10.42 Dr
Bailey, Francis Joseph	Gunner	853083	RA		U 2.10.42 Dr
Bailey, Reginald Kenneth	L. Sick Berth Att.	C/MX 52582	RN		UC 2.10.42 Dr
Bain, John Harper	Lance Corp.	3055225	RS		U 2.10.42 Dr
Baker, George Sidney	Private	6202719	MX		U 2.10.42 Dr
Baker, Jack	Eng. Rm. Art. 3	P/MX 48263	RN		UPO 2.10.42 Dr
Baker, John James	Private	6208382	MX		U 2.10.42 Dr
Baker, Thomas Ernest	Private	6202324	MX	U 12.10.42	U 2.10.42 Dr[184]
Balaam, Arthur John	Gunner	872506	RA		U 2.10.42 Dr
Baldwin, William Charles	Gunner	6459432	RA		U 2.10.42 Dr
Banks, Raymond	Lance Bdr.	843622	RA		U 2.10.42 Dr
Barbour, James Munro	Lance Corp.	1872348	RE		U 2.10.42 Dr
Barlow, William Arthur	BSM	816130	RA		U 2.10.42 Dr
Barnes, Cyril	Gunner	1426883	RA		U 2.10.42 Dr
Barnes, John	Private	3054424	RS		U 2.10.42 Dr
Barnes, Walter	Private	6201248	MX		U 2.10.42 Dr
Barratt, Walter Arthur	Private	6213453	MX		U 2.10.42 Dr
Barrett, John Charles	Private	6203704	MX		U 2.10.42 Dr
Baskerville, Albert T.	BSM	1057504	RA		U 2.10.42 Dr
Bath, Ronald Jack	Private	6202182	MX		U 2.10.42 Dr
Baxter, James Philip	Gunner	860125	RA		U 2.10.42 Dr
Barnes, John	Gunner	850757	RA		U 2.10.42 Dr
Bates, Ronald Langley	Clk of Wks	30877	RE		U 2.10.42 Dr
Beaton, James Thom	Gunner	862199	RA		U 2.10.42 Dr
Bedford, George	Corporal	2323921	RCS		U 2.10.42 Dr

Beesley, Norman	Sapper	2131054	RE		U 2.10.42 Dr
Bell, David Bowie	Private	3063614	RS		U 2.10.42 Dr
Bennett, John	Lance Corp.	6203921	MX		U 2.10.42 Dr
Bennett, Leonard Charles	Corporal	5614598	MX		U 2.10.42 Dr
Bennison, William	Gunner	1722934	RA		U 2.10.42 Dr
Benson, Joseph Hugh	L. Supply Ass.	D/MX 102740	RN		UP 2.10.42 Dr
Berry, Ralph	Master Gunner	1061660	RA		U 2.10.42 Dr
Berry, Thomas Malcolm	Private	3054386	RS		U 2.10.42 Dr
Best, Harold Ernest	Able Seaman	D/JX 169805	RN		UP 2.10.42 Dr
Bevis, Herbert Thomas	Chief E.R.A.	P/M 22609	RN		UPO 2.10.42 Bi
Bickmore, Ernest Alfred	Able Seaman	C/JX 174010	RN		UC 2.10.42 Dr
Biggs, Arthur Leonard	W.O. Minewatcher		HKRNVR		U 1.10.42 Dr
Bilton, Arthur	Writer	D/MX 66814	RN		UP 2.10.42 Dr
Birch, Arthur Edward	Leading Seaman	D/SSX 22726	RN		UP 2.10.42 Dr
Black, Andrew Christie	Private	3054080	RS		U 2.10.42 Dr
Black, George	Gunner	3049404	RA		U 2.10.42 Dr
Blackman, Albert Lionel	Sergeant	1869539	RE		U 2.10.42 Dr
Bliss, David Ken	Able Seaman	D/J 53499	RN		UP 2.10.42 Dr
Boag, John Law	Sapper	1896309	RE		U 2.10.42 Dr
Bond, James William	CQMS	6196027	MX		U 2.10.42 Dr
Bond, William Horace	L. Sick Berth Att.	D/M 36415	RN		UP 2.10.42 Dr
Bonfield, Frank	Master at Arms	D/M 39742	RN		UP 2.10.42 Dr
Boothroyd, George H.	Telegraphist	P/SSX 31937	RN		UPO 2.10.42 Dr
Bowditch, Alfred Edward	Gunner	1073423	RA		U 2.10.42 Dr
Bowey, George Henry	Private	6201825	MX		U 2.10.42 Dr
Boyce, Samuel John	Lance Bdr.	1063039	RA		U 2.10.42 Dr
Boyes, William James L.	Chief E.R.A.	D/M 26910	RN		UP 2.10.42 Dr
Boyle, Hugh	Private	3053138	RS		U 2.10.42 Dr
Boyle, Thomas John	Gunner	1426774	RA		U 2.10.42 Dr
Boyne, Martin William A.	P.O. Sick Berth	D/M 36394	RN		UP 2.10.42 Dr
Bradford, Alfred Thomas	Bandsman	6201856	MX		U 2.10.42 Dr
Bremner, William	Gunner	1725305	RA		U 2.10.42 Dr
Brennan, Michael	Corporal	1871620	RE		U 2.10.42 Dr
Bright, Arthur William	Leading Stoker	P/K 20823	RN		UPO 2.10.42 Dr
Brockley, Wilfred	Private	7538255	RADC		U 2.10.42 Dr
Brooks, Charles Frederick	Master Gunner	1410996	RA		U 2.10.42 Dr
Brooks, Sidney	Gunner	856993	RA		U 2.10.42 Dr
Brotherston, Andrew	Sergeant		HKDDC RN/DYP		U 2.10.42 Dr
Brown, David McNeilace	Able Seaman	D/JX 194203	RN		UP 2.10.42 Dr
Brown, Joseph Peter	Sapper	1874475	RE	10.42	U 2.10.42 Dr[185]
Bryant, Willie	Private	6208393	MX		U 2.10.42 Dr
Brydie, Cecil C.	Shipwright	D/MX54814	RN		UP 2.10.42 Dr
Bull, Walter	Private	6196305	MX		U 2.10.42 Dr
Burdett, Kenneth	Gunner	4613293	RA		U 2.10.42 Dr[186]
Burgess, Frederick	Gunner	3528355	RA		U 2.10.42 Dr
Burnell, Robert James	Lance Sergeant	1501972	HKSRA		U 2.10.42 Dr
Burnett, Alexander B.	Private	3052803	RS		U 2.10.42 Dr

Burnett, Peter	Lance Corp.	3054976	RS	U 2.10.42 Dr
Burnley, Fred	Bombardier	1424508	RA	U 2.10.42 Dr
Burns, Evan Owen	Gunner	1492323	RA	U 2.10.42 Dr
Burns, Thomas McDermid	Lance Corp.	3055018	RS	U 2.10.42 Dr
Burrows, Edgar George	Stoker P.O.	C/KX75164	RN	UC 2.10.42 Dr[187]
Burrows, Frank	Lance Bdr.	851337	RA	U 2.10.42 Dr
Burrows, Vernon Howard	Gunner	872712	RA	U 2.10.42 Dr
Butler, Thomas	Gunner	872746	RA	U 2.10.42 Dr
Butler, Walter William	Gunner	800932	RA	U 2.10.42 Dr
Cadle, Edward Terence	Gunner	1492325	RA	U 2.10.42 Dr
Calvert, Hans	Signalman	D/JX 229549	RN	UP 2.10.42 Dr
Campbell, Clifford H. H.	Private	6213470	MX	U 2.10.42 Dr
Campbell, James	Private	3055253	RS	U 2.10.42 Dr
Campbell, William	Sick Berth Att.	D/MX 80127	RN	UP 2.10.42 Dr
Campbell, William	Lance Sergeant	LSA/68	HKPF	U 2.10.42 Dr[188]
Carley, John	BSM	1064034	RA	U 2.10.42 Dr
Carpenter, Maurice David	Staff Sergeant	1869997	RE	U 2.10.42 Dr
Carrell, George Thomas	Private	6200773	MX	U 2.10.42 Dr
Carrington, William	Private	3055976	RS	U 2.10.42 Dr
Carter, John Ernest	Lance Corp.	1871950	RE	U 2.10.42 Dr
Carter, Leslie John	Gunner	2037805	RA	U 2.10.42 Dr
Cartwright, Leslie George	Signalman	2325662	RCS	U 2.10.42 Dr
Caseley, Frank	Gunner	1715099	RA	U 2.10.42 Dr
Caslake, Edwin Reginald	Corporal	6198731	MX	U 2.10.42 Dr
Cassin, Francis	Able Seaman	D/JX 153144	RN	UP 2.10.42 Dr
Chalgrave, Frank	Private	6205010	MX	U 2.10.42 Dr
Chalmers, Alexander	Private	2880057	RS	U 2.10.42 Dr
Chapman, Douglas V.	Private	6210065	MX	U 2.10.42 Dr
Charles, Douglas Amos	Corporal	6201537	MX	U 2.10.42 Dr
Charles, Sidney	Sergeant	1862399	RE	U 2.10.42 Dr
Charlton, Rennison	Private	3054558	RS	U 2.10.42 Dr
Cheek, George Henry	Able Seaman	P/J 30260	RN	UPO 2.10.42 Dr
Chick, Henry	Private	6207041	MX	U 2.10.42 Dr
Chilcroft, Robert Albert	Able Seaman	C/JX 198043	RN	UC 2.10.42 Dr
Childs, Thomas Bernard	Gunner	868767	RA	U 2.10.42 Mu[189]
Chown, George Henry	Gunner	1712333	RA	U 2.10.42 Dr
Christian, Charles Harold	Gunner	856067	RA	U 2.10.42 Dr
Christie, George A.	Private	2818250	RS	U 2.10.42 Dr
Clapperton, Robert	Corporal	46786	RS	U 2.10.42 Dr
Clark, James	Private	3187171	RS	U 2.10.42 Dr
Clark, William	Private	6214177	MX	U 2.10.42 Dr
Clarke, Charles Arthur	Private	6201495	MX	U 2.10.42 Dr
Clarke, John Henry	Private	814618	MX	U 2.10.42 Dr
Clarke, Wilfred Allan	L. Telegraphist	D/JX 138843	RN	UP 2.10.42 Dr
Clayton, Samuel	Gunner	868235	HKSRA	U 2.10.42 Dr
Cleggett, Albert Ernest	Signalman	2323569	RCS	U 2.10.42 Dr
Clifford, George Frederick	Private	6201165	MX	U 2.10.42 Dr
Clogg, George Alfred	Gunner	1426788	RA	U 2.10.42 Dr
Cockburn, Richard	Gunner	847145	RA	U 2.10.42 Dr

Cole, Frederick William	Gunner	1438817	RA		U 2.10.42 Dr
Coleman, Patrick	Private	3053270	RS		U 2.10.42 Dr
Coles, Joseph William R.	Sergeant		HKDDC RN/DYP		U 2.10.42 Dr
Colthorpe, Wilfred	Lance Bdr.	860371	RA		U 2.10.42 Dr
Combe, Alexander Hunter	Corporal	2979624	RS		U 2.10.42 Dr
Commerford, John	Lance Corp.	6010413	MX		U 2.10.42 Dr
Coneghan, James	Private	3054426	RS		U 2.10.42 Dr
Connolly, John Patrick G.	Private	6203260	MX		U 2.10.42 Dr
Cook, Henry	Private	3050398	RS		U 2.10.42 Dr
Cook, James	Lance Corp.	3054069	RS		U 2.10.42 Dr
Cook, Peter Harold	Signalman	2324228	RCS		U 2.10.42 Dr
Cooke, James Leslie Cyril	Corporal	1870684	RE		U 2.10.42 Dr
Cooke, John Patrick	Private	6202967	MX		U 2.10.42 Dr
Cooke, Leonard	Gunner	856036	RA		U 2.10.42 Dr
Cooper, Albert Edward	Lance Corp.	6201935	MX		U 2.10.42 Dr
Cooper, George William	Corporal	1871659	RE		U 2.10.42 Dr
Copping, Henry George	Private	6202987	MX		U 2.10.42 Dr
Cornwall, Andrew	Private	3055714	RS		U 2.10.42 Dr
Couch, Henry	Gunner	1426655	RA		U 2.10.42 Dr
Cousins, George John F.	BSM	1421493	RA		U 2.10.42 Dr
Crabtree, Allan	Signalman	D/SSX 30457	RN		UP 2.10.42 Dr
Craddock, Thomas G.	Gunner	1492336	RA		U 2.10.42 Dr
Crangle, John Raphael	Able Seaman	P/UD/X1399	RNVR		UPO 2.10.42 Dr
Crawley, Frederick W.	Signalman	2330255	RCS		U 2.10.42 Dr
Creed, Frederick William	Gunner	853685	RA		U 2.10.42 Dr
Crichton, George	Private	3054865	RS		U 2.10.42 Dr
Crittenden, Albert Stanley	Sapper	1871588	RE		U 2.10.42 Dr
Cross, William Albert	Lance Bdr.	847267	RA		U 2.10.42 Dr
Crossley, Charles William	W.O.	22A	HKRNVR	UP 12.10.42	UP 2.10.42 Dr[190]
Crowley, Patrick Joseph	Sergeant	6198993	MX		U 2.10.42 Dr
Cuell, William Tom	RQMS	1416464	RA		U 2.10.42 Dr
Culpeck, Francis Henry	Lance Corp.	6200956	MX		U 2.10.42 Dr
Curtis, Llewellyn	Gunner	863047	RA		U 2.10.42 Dr
Dainty, George Henry	Gunner	5109685	RA		U 2.10.42 Dr
Dair, Robert Francis	Sergeant	1409461	HKSRA		U 2.10.42 Dr
Daly, Joseph Hunter	Private	3055918	RS		U 2.10.42 Dr
Dannan, Stephen John	Lance Corp.	2323003	RCS		U 2.10.42 Dr
Davis, Donald Edward	Staff Sergeant	1868908	RE		U 2.10.42 Dr
Davis, Harold Raymond	Sapper	2125441	RE		U 2.10.42 Dr
Davis, John Peter Richard	Private	6213434	MX		U 2.10.42 Dr
Davis, Joseph William	Gunner	847243	RA		U 2.10.42 Dr
Dawes, James	Lance Sergeant	6200365	MX		U 2.10.42 Dr
Dawson, George	Staff Sergeant	1869525	RE		U 2.10.42 Dr
Day, Harry	Clark of Works	1862866	RE		U 2.10.42 Dr
Delderfield, George A.	Lieutenant	132905	RA HKSRA		U 2.10.42 Dr
Denyer, George	Staff Sergeant	1869033	RE		U 2.10.42 Dr
Dickson, George Jackson	Private	3055960	RS		U 2.10.42 Dr
Dixon, Norman	Sergeant	847485	RA		U 2.10.42 Dr
Doane, Ernest	Gunner	842328	RA		U 2.10.42 Dr

Dochard, John	Gunner	853687	RA		U 2.10.42 Dr
Dodson, Charles Henry	Yeoman of Sig.	C/230594	RN		UC 2.10.42 Dr
Donnely, John	Lance Corp.	3054473	RS		U 2.10.42 Dr
Dooley, Clifford Vincent	Lance Bdr.	872637	RA		U 2.10.42 Dr
Drew, Wilfred	Bombardier	859572	RA		U 2.10.42 Dr
Ducker, Neville James	Elec. Artificer 1	D/MX 59150	RN		UP 2.10.42 Dr
Duddridge, Richard Henry	PC	PC/35	HKDDC RN/DYP		U 2.10.42 Dr
Dunlop, George	Lance Corp.	3245377	RS		U 2.10.42 Dr
Durie, George Brown	Lance Sergeant	3053692	RS		U 2.10.42 Dr
Durose, Robert James	Master Gunner	1420122	RA		U 2.10.42 Dr
Dutch, Cecil Henry F.	BSM	1425042	RA		U 2.10.42 Dr
Easterbrook, William G.R.	Boatswain Bosun		RN		UP 2.10.42 Dr
Eaton, George	Private	6204419	MX		U 2.10.42 Dr
Edge, Leonard	Lance Corp.	3054374	RS		U 2.10.42 Dr
Edwards, James Thomas	Sergeant	850320	RA		U 2.10.42 Dr
Edwards, John E.D.	Able Seaman	D/JX 132038	RN		UP 2.10.42 Dr
Egan, John	Private	3312481	RS		U 2.10.42 Dr
Ellard, Cecil	Gunner	847363	RA		U 2.10.42 Dr
Elley, Harold Edward	Sergeant	833465	RA		U 2.10.42 Dr
Elliott, Frederick A.	Private	6208210	MX		U 2.10.42 Dr
Ellis, Ernest	Private	3054506	RS		U 2.10.42 Dr
Elms, David Kenneth	Supply Assistant	P/MX 86702	RN		UPO 2.10.42 Dr
Embleton, William	Private	3054566	RS		U 2.10.42 Dr
Embling, James Albert	Sapper	1871734	RE		U 2.10.42 Dr
Evans, Douglas Charles	Gunner	1492741	RA		U 2.10.42 Dr
Everett, Leslie Charles	Gunner	880812	RA		U 2.10.42 Dr
Eves, John Charles	Sergeant	1414266	RA		U 2.10.42 Dr
Fage, Charles Edward	Able Seaman	D/JX168086	RN		UP 2.10.42 Dr
Fairbairn, Alexander D.	Private	3055928	RS		U 2.10.42 Dr
Farrie, John Reid	Writer	D/MX 69160	RN		UP 2.10.42 Dr
Ferrie, Gordon	Signalman	2326553	RCS		U 2.10.42 Dr
Fidler, Edward Dixon	Lance Bdr.	868294	RA		U 2.10.42 Dr
Finch, Harold	P.O. Stoker	P/K 61634	RN		UPO 2.10.42 Dr
Finch, Richard Howell	Leading Seaman	D/JX 153328	RN		UP 2.10.42 Dr
Findlay, Edward	Private	2029542	RS		U 2.10.42 Dr
Fisher, Albert Louis	Yeoman of Sigs.	D/JX 150282	RN		UP 2.10.42 Dr
Fisher, Joseph	Gunner	856824	RA		U 2.10.42 Dr
Fishlock, Ernest Alfred J.	Lance Sergeant	1867802	RE		U 2.10.42 Dr
Flett, Andrew	Chief Skipper		RNR		UP 2.10.42 Dr
Flinter, Edwin Stuart	QMS	1020057	RA		U 2.10.42 Dr
Foley, Andrew	Private	6203401	MX		U 2.10.42 Dr
Ford, George	Private	3054539	RS		U 2.10.42 Dr
Ford, Sidney C.	Gunner	5488266	RA		U 2.10.42 Dr
Forster, Arnold William	Sapper	1890153	RE		U 2.10.42 Dr
Forsyth, James L.W.	Leading Seaman	P/JX 146260	RN		UPO 2.10.42 Dr
Foss, John George	Gunner	872623	RA		U 2.10.42 Dr
Foster, Edward Sinclair	Sapper	1880614	RE		U 2.10.42 Dr
Foster, James Thomas	Private	6208381	MX	**U 11.10.42**	U 2.10.42[191]
Fox, Henry	Signalman	2325079	RCS		U 2.10.42 Dr

Name	Rank	Number	Unit	Fate
Francis, Evan Charles	Leading Seaman	D/JX 156024	RN	UP 2.10.42 Dr
Franklin, John Wilfred	Gunner	845742	RA	U 2.10.42 Dr
French, Walter Leonard	Private	6201176	MX	U 2.10.42 Dr[192]
Frenchum, Frank Ernest	Private	6203000	MX	U 2.10.42 Dr
Fry, William Francis	Sapper	1874912	RE	U 2.10.42 Dr
Fudge, John Alfred	Gunner	1712437	RA	U 2.10.42 Dr
Fulcher, Cecil Eric	Lance Bdr.	860034	RA	U 2.10.42 Dr
Fullagar, Albert Oliver	Gunner	842511	HKSRA	U 2.10.42 Dr
Fullerton, Thomas	Private	3053684	RS	U 2.10.42 Dr
Fyffe, Neil	Private	3053612	RS	U 2.10.42 Dr
Gadd, George Richard	Gunner	2033165	RA	U 2.10.42 Dr
Gailey, Leonard Henry	Gunner	3711645	RA	U 2.10.42 Dr
Gale, Edward George	Signalman	2331384	RCS	U 2.10.42 Dr
Gale, John Frederick T.	Private	6202413	MX	U 2.10.42 Dr
Gallagher, Joseph Brendin	Gunner	847480	RA	U 2.10.42 Dr
Gardiner, George	Private	3054498	RS	U 2.10.42 Dr
Gardner, Andrew Pollock	Private	3055001	RS	U 2.10.42 Dr
Garrett, Arthur Thomas	Petty Officer	P/J 106280	RN	UPO 2.10.42 Dr
Garth, Patrick	Corporal	3055939	RS	U 2.10.42 Dr
Gates, Edwin William	Leading Seaman	C/J 105411	RN	UC 2.10.42 Dr
Gentry, Frederick James	Private	6199070	MX	U 2.10.42 Dr
George, Alfred William	Lance Sergeant	828506	RA	U 2.10.42 Dr
Gibson, Frederick William	Private	6202703	MX	U 2.10.42 Dr
Gibson, Hugh	Lance Corp.	3053728	RS	U 2.10.42 Dr
Gibson, Richard	Lance Corp.	3054008	RS	U 2.10.42 Dr
Gill, Norman Henry	Gunner	1426792	RA	U 2.10.42 Dr
Glister, Montague Henry	Gunner	1712442	RA	U 2.10.42 Dr
Glover, Herbert Edwin	Lance Corp.	6201458	MX	U 2.10.42 Dr
Godfree, Ronald Frank	Leading Stoker	C/KX 88260	RN	UC 2.10.42 Dr
Godfrey, Alfred Trevor	Lieutenant	147712	RA	U 2.10.42 Dr
Godson, Austin	W.O.II	3049334	RS	U 2.10.42 Dr
Goff, James Henry	Sapper	1871771	RE	U 2.10.42 Dr
Goldie, Charles	Private	3053767	RS	U 2.10.42 Dr
Goodman, Albert	Corporal	6201734	MX	U 2.10.42 Dr
Gordon, Ian Francis	Lance Corp.	6201482	MX	U 2.10.42 Dr
Gormon, James Thomas	Sergeant	2319515	RCS	U 2.10.42 Dr
Goudie, Harold	Signalman	2353843	RCS	U 2.10.42 Dr
Gould, Henry Y.J.	RSM	5720230	RA	U 2.10.42 Dr
Gourlay, Ian Douglas	Sapper	1853785	RE	U 2.10.42 Dr
Gracey, Peter Douglas	Captain	64552	RCS	U 2.10.42 Dr[193]
Graham, Duncan	Eng. Rm. Art. 3	D/MX 55900	RN	UP 2.10.42 Dr
Grainger, James	Private	3054844	RS	U 2.10.42 Dr
Grant, Denis	Sapper	1875491	RE	U 2.10.42 Dr
Grant, Edward	Private	3054206	RS	U 2.10.42 Dr
Gray, Christopher F.	Sapper	1874465	RE	U 2.10.42 Dr
Gray, Frederick Bernard	Private	6201219	MX	U 2.10.42 Dr
Green, Albert John	Gunner	872245	RA	U 2.10.42 Dr
Green, Ernest Edward	Sergeant	2317132	RCS	U 2.10.42 Dr
Green, Frederick	Lance Sergeant	6203552	MX	U 2.10.42 Dr

Name	Rank	Service No	Branch	Notes
Green, Herbert	Signalman	P/JX 187137	RN	UPO 2.10.42 Dr
Green, Jack Gardfield	Lance Corp.	5435557	RE	U 2.10.42 Dr
Green, William Henry	Corporal	PO/22388	RM	UPO 2.10.42 Dr
Green, William John	Gunner	853432	RA	U 2.10.42 Dr
Greenwood, Norman T.J.	Commissioned Telegraphist		RN	UP 2.10.42 Dr[194]
Gregory, Thomas Henry	Sapper	1874478	RE	U 2.10.42 Dr
Greig, William	Private	3055409	RS	U 2.10.42 Dr
Grey, William Edward	Petty Officer	D/J 106392	RN	UP 2.10.42 Dr
Grist, Victor Charles	Private	2033091	MX	U 2.10.42 Dr
Gubb, Percy William M.	Private	6213442	MX	U 2.10.42 Dr
Guille, John Robert	Gunner	856673	RA	U 2.10.42 Dr
Haines, Charles Henry	Private	6202150	MX	U 2.10.42 Dr
Hall, Douglas James	Lance Corp.	2324196	RCS	U 2.10.42 Dr
Hall, Geoffrey Nathaniel	Gunner	870143	RA	U 2.10.42 Dr
Hall, Reginald Ernest	Private	6200766	MX	U 2.10.42 Dr
Hall, Samuel	Private	3312015	RS	U 2.10.42 Dr
Hall, Thomas	Sergeant	3051855	RS	U 2.10.42 Dr
Hall, Walter	Gunner	850942	RA	U 2.10.42 Dr
Hall, Walter John	Private	6204496	MX	U 2.10.42 Dr
Hamill, Thomas	Private	3054391	RS	U 2.10.42 Dr
Hamilton, Isaac	Private	3053609	RS	U 2.10.42 Dr
Hammond, Frank	Stoker 1st Class	D/KX 91967	RN	UP 2.10.42 Dr
Handford, John Frederick	Lance Corp.	6203528	MX	U 2.10.42 Dr
Hanley, George	Gunner	851944	RA	U 2.10.42 Dr
Hannan, Thomas Bernard	Lance Bdr.	838575	RA	U 2.10.42 Dr
Hardington, Ronald	Gunner	872514	RA	U 2.10.42 Dr
Hardy, Francis Gordon	Leading Seaman	C/JX 138044	RN	UC 2.10.42 Dr
Hare, Charles	Private	6213445	MX	U 2.10.42 Dr
Harkinson, William John	Signalman	3312404	RCS	U 2.10.42 Dr
Harper, Henry George	Lance Bdr.	851852	RA	U 2.10.42 Dr
Harper, Ronald George	P.O. Stoker	C/KX 79052	RN	UC 2.10.42 Dr
Harrigan, Francis William	Lance Corp.	1874466	RE	U 2.10.42 Dr
Harris, Charles Richard	Private	6203248	MX	U 2.10.42 Dr
Harris, George Arthur	Able Seaman	P/SSX 19802	RN	UPO 2.10.42 Dr
Harrison, Richard Stuart	W.O.	60A	HKRNVR	UP 2.10.42 Dr
Haviland, Charles Stephen	Telegraphist	C/J 53451	RN	UC 2.10.42 Dr
Hart, Robert	Private	3055004	RS	U 2.10.42 Dr
Harvey, Cyril	Gunner	1460537	RA	U 2.10.42 Dr
Harvey, Cyril	Private	6201300	MX	U 2.10.42 Dr
Harvey, James	Private	3054818	RS	U 2.10.42 Dr
Hatchett, Percy John	Private	6194537	MX	U 2.10.42 Dr
Hatfield, Charles Henry	Lance Corp.	6200350	MX	U 2.10.42 Dr[195]
Hatton, Thomas	Gunner	1426632	RA	U 2.10.42 Dr
Havercroft, Samuel	Private	3054791	RS	U 2.10.42 Dr
Haynes, Harold George	Lance Corp.	823461	RE	U 2.10.42 Dr
Hayward, Walter Alfred	Private	6197328	MX	U 2.10.42 Dr
Hawkins, Joseph Edward	Lance Sergeant	1873339	RE	U 2.10.42 Dr
Hawkins, William Henry	Gunner	1680996	RA	U 2.10.42 Dr

Hawksworth, William E.J.	L. Signalman	C/JX 136629	RN		UC 2.10.42 Dr
Headley, William Arthur	Captain	102329	HKSRA	MiD	U 2.10.42 Dr
Healy, Dennis	Able Seaman	C/JX 228518	RN		UC 2.10.42 Dr
Hemmingfield, Arthur	Gunner	1722938	RA		U 2.10.42 Dr
Henderson, David	C/Sergeant	3050476	RS		U 2.10.42 Dr
Henderson, Francis	Drummer	3054418	RS		U 2.10.42 Dr
Henderson, Lancelot	BSM	1055915	RA		U 2.10.42 Dr
Hendy, Norman	P.O. Sick Berth	D/MX 48101	RN		UP 2.10.42 Dr
Heslop, James	Gunner	4271271	RA		U 2.10.42 Dr
Hewer, Edward Henry J.	Signalman	2324099	RCS		U 2.10.42 Dr
Hewitt, Frank	Gunner	2571743	RA		U 2.10.42 Dr
Hewson, Thomas James	Gunner	838991	RA		U 2.10.42 Dr
Hickman, Oscar	Lance Bdr.	851812	RA		U 2.10.42 Dr
Hildred, Reginald John	Gunner	822542	RA		U 2.10.42 Dr
Hill, Ernest	Gunner	863022	RA		U 2.10.42 Dr
Hill, George	Able Seaman	D/JX 194218	RN		UP 2.10.42 Dr
Hinge, Frank Charles	Able Seaman	P/J 97839	RN		UPO 2.10.42 Dr
Hiscock, Albert Roy	Gunner	872629	RA		U 2.10.42 Dr
Hitchin, Henry Alfred	Gunner	841096	RA		U 2.10.42 Dr
Hodge, John Henry	Signalman	2330299	RCS		U 2.10.42 Dr
Hodge, Walter Resolution	Corporal	726718	RCS		U 2.10.42 Dr
Hodgson, Robert	Leading Stoker	P/K 65270	RN		UPO 2.10.42 Dr
Hodkinson, Kenneth T.	Private	3055984	RS		U 2.10.42 Dr
Hogan, William	Gunner	1426776	RA		U 2.10.42 Dr
Holt, James Samuel	Telegraphist	P/JX201158	RN		UPO 2.10.42 Dr
Homburg, John Sydney	Sergeant	1870026	RE		U 2.10.42 Dr
Hooley, Reginald	Gunner	1720618	RA		U 2.10.42 Dr
Hope, Arthur	Private	6283550	MX		U 2.10.42 Dr
Hopkins, Francis Yonge	Signalman	C/J 59399	RN		UC 2.10.42 Dr
Horner, George Borham	Gunner	850600	RA		U 2.10.42 Dr
Horsley, Eric	Marine	PO/X 2159	RM		UP 2.10.42 Dr
Hosford, Robert	P.O. Telegraphist	D/JX 139032	RN		UP 2.10.42 Dr
Houghton, Francis John	Private	2613967	MX		U 2.10.42 Dr
Howarth, John F.	Lance Bdr.	3382511	RA		U 2.10.42 Dr
Howson, Ronald	L. Sick Berth Att.	D/MX 53857	RN		UP 2.10.42 Dr
Hughes, William	Private	3054029	RS		U 2.10.42 Dr
Hull, George James P.	L. Sick Berth Att.	D/MX 55902	RN		UP 2.10.42 Dr
Husband, Edwin	Corporal	2022101	RCS		U 2.10.42 Dr
Hutchinson, George W.	Chief P.O.	C/JX 126731	RN		UC 2.10.42 Dr
Hutchison, William	Private	2750645	RS		U 2.10.42 Dr
Hutton, Edmund Feltham	Leading Writer	D/MX 66831	RN		UP 2.10.42 Dr
Iles, Arthur Henry	Private	6206824	MX		U 2.10.42 Dr
Irving, Malcolm	Private	3054163	RS		U 2.10.42 Dr
Isaac, Harry	Gunner	847279	RA		U 2.10.42 Dr
Iszard, George	Lance Corp.	5335415	MX		U 2.10.42 Dr
Jackson, Albert James	Private	6201824	MX		U 2.10.42 Dr
Jackson, George Allborn	Private	3054098	RS		U 2.10.42 Dr
Jalland, Jack Edward	Able Seaman	C/JX 125501	RN		UC 2.10.42 Dr
James, James Ivor	Private	6201862	MX		U 2.10.42 Dr[196]

Jeffrey, Andrew Buchan	Private	3055283	RS	U 2.10.42 Dr
Jenkins, Charles	Private	3054979	RS	U 2.10.42 Dr
Jenkins, Ernest	Corporal	3054179	RS	U 2.10.42 Dr
Jennings, Albert George	Private	6203943	MX	U 2.10.42 Dr
Jinks, Henry	Gunner	2325377	RA	U 2.10.42 Dr
Johns, Denzil	BQMS	1416983	HKSRA	U 2.10.42 Dr
Johnson, Arthur James	Gunner	880914	RA	U 2.10.42 Dr
Johnson, Frederick W.	C.P.O. Writer	C/MX 53641	RN	UC 2.10.42 Dr
Johnson, Oliver	Gunner	851492	RA	U 2.10.42 Dr
Johnson, Wilfred James	Sapper	2111602	RE	U 2.10.42 Dr
Johnston, James	Private	3054478	RS	U 2.10.42 Dr
Johnston, Robert James	Private	3312573	RS	U 2.10.42 Dr
Jones, Gonville Royce	Petty Officer	D/JX 138348	RN	UP 2.10.42 Dr
Jones, Herbert Cyril	Marine	PLY/X 48	RM	UP 2.10.42 Dr
Jones, James Thomas A.	Signalman	D/JX 232518	RN	UP 2.10.42 Dr
Jones, Thomas David	Private	6213447	MX	U 2.10.42 Dr[197]
Jordan-Bowditch, Horace	Signalman	2333643	RCS	U 2.10.42 Dr
Joslin, Henry John	Lance Corp.	6201201	MX	U 2.10.42 Dr
Kearns, James Bruce	Eng. Rm Art. 1	C/MX 55895	RN	UC 2.10.42 Dr
Kehoe, Edward Michael	Sapper	1868723	RE	U 2.10.42 Dr
Kelly, Maurice	Private	3055718	RS	U 2.10.42 Dr
Kemp, Stanley	Able Seaman	D/JX 167288	RN	UP 2.10.42 Dr
Kennard, Herbert W.G.	Petty Officer	C/J 18821	RN	UC 2.10.42 Dr
Kennedy, Albert	Lance Corp.	4535885	RE	U 2.10.42 Dr
Kennedy, John Alexander	Private	2874298	RS	U 2.10.42 Dr
Kenny, Michael	Gunner	863041	RA	U 2.10.42 Dr
Kerruish, John Alfred	Lance Bdr.	1492450	RA	U 2.10.42 Dr
Kew, Henry Charles	Seaman Gunner	6G	HKRNVR	UP 2.10.42 Dr
Kimber, James	Lance Sergeant	860930	RA	U 2.10.42 Dr
Kimber, Walter William	P.O. Motor Mec.	P/MX 67981	RN	UPO 2.10.42 Dr
Kimpton, William Ernest	Sapper	2078353	RE	U 2.10.42 Dr
King, Ernest Alfred	Telegraphist	P/JX 178899	RN	UPO 2.10.42 Dr
King, John Kenneth	P.O. Supply	C/MX 54645	RN	UC 2.10.42 Dr
Kinnard, William Henry	Gunner	868984	RA	U 2.10.42 Dr
Kirby, Alfred	Private	3061781	RS	U 2.10.42 Dr
Knowles, Roland Ernest	Captain	147496	RA MC	U 2.10.42 Dr
Knox, David	Seaman Gunner	7G	HKRNVR	UP 2.10.42 Dr
Lake, Alexander Sidney	Sapper	5725990	RE	U 2.10.42 Dr
Lamb, Peter McDonald	Private	3054188	RS	U 2.10.42 Dr
Lane, Francis Edward	Gunner	872298	RA	U 2.10.42 Dr
Lane, John Hugh	Gunner	842492	RA	U 2.10.42 Dr
Langdell, Stanley	Private	6213525	MX	U 2.10.42 Dr
Langridge, Walter T.	Gunner	860097	RA	U 2.10.42 Dr
Law, Reginald	Private	6213526	MX	U 2.10.42 Dr
Lawlor, William John	Private	6210537	MX	U 2.10.42 Dr
Lee, Frederick Charles	Private	6213534	MX	U 2.10.42 Dr
Lee, Frederick George	Eng. Rm. Art. 3	D/MX 47790	RN	UP 2.10.42 Dr
Lees, Alexander	Eng. Rm. Art. 3	D/MX 51876	RN	UP 2.10.42 Dr
Leigh, Thomas Richard	Gunner	1426547	RA	U 2.10.42 Dr

Lewis, Arthur	Signalman	419577	RCS	U 2.10.42 Dr
Lewis, Daniel	L. Sick Berth Att.	D/MX 49903	RN	UP 2.10.42 Dr
Lewis, Ernest	Gunner	872538	RA	U 2.10.42 Dr
Lifton, Cyril Alfred B.	Shipwright 1/C	C/M 27929	RN	UC 2.10.42 Bi
Limacher, Frank Oliver	Gunner	855243	RA	U 2.10.42 Dr
Linklater, Arthur	Private	3054084	RS	U 2.10.42 Dr
Linton, James Frederick	Gunner	1438820	RA	U 2.10.42 Dr
Lintott, George	Private	3055000	RS	U 2.10.42 Dr
Little, John Thomas	CQMS	6195113	MX	U 2.10.42 Dr
Littlefield, Frederick	Private	6203592	MX	U 2.10.42 Dr
Livesey, Albert Charles	Gunner	1492461	RA	U 2.10.42 Dr
Lochrie, George S.	Lance Sergeant	3054097	RS	U 2.10.42 Dr
Logan, Sydney	Private	3063125	RS	U 2.10.42 Dr
Loughlin, Peter Harry	Police Sergeant	PSA/45	RN/DYP	U 2.10.42 Dr
Love, Noel John	Gunner	1426793	RA	U 2.10.42 Dr
Ludford, Arthur Herbert	Master at Arms	D/M 39771	RN	UP 2.10.42 Dr
Lyon, George	BSM	819554	RA	U 2.10.42 Dr
McAndrews, George B.	Sapper	2070145	RE	U 2.10.42 Dr
McBride, Alexander D.	Gunner	851575	RA	U 2.10.42 Dr
McCallum, William	Corporal	3055201	RS	U 2.10.42 Dr
McCormack, Bernard	Lance Bdr.	851886	RA	U 2.10.42 Dr
McCulloch, William	Private	3044711	RS	U 2.10.42 Dr
McDermott, Cornelius	Private	3312004	RS	U 2.10.42 Dr
McDermott, James	Gunner	1493080	RA	U 2.10.42 Dr
McDermott, Lawrence	Gunner	1060132	RA	U 2.10.42 Dr
MacDonald, Thomas	Lance Corp.	2321689	RCS	U 2.10.42 Dr
Mace, Frank Edward	Gunner	5181300	RA	U 2.10.42 Dr
Mace, Harry Leslie	Gunner	5498724	RA	U 2.10.42 Dr
Macey, Frank Leslie	Private	6203568	MX	U 2.10.42 Dr
McElroy, John	Gunner	860391	RA	U 2.10.42 Dr
McEneaney, James	Signalman	2323476	RCS	U 2.10.42 Dr
McGhee, James Preston	2nd Lieutenant	180036	RS	U 2.10.42 Dr
McGivney, John	Gunner	1722943	RA	U 2.10.42 Dr
McGillivray, James	Private	3053697	RS	U 2.10.42 Dr
McGrath, William Patrick	Petty Officer	D/J 98250	RN	UP 2.10.42 Dr
McHugh, Bernard	Private	3528442	RS	U 2.10.42 Dr
Mackay, William	Private	2927763	RS	U 2.10.42 Dr[198]
Mackenny, William Henry	L. Sick Berth Att.	D/MX 50095	RN	UP 2.10.42 Dr
McKinlay, Robert	Piper	3054096	RS	U 2.10.42 Dr
McIlwraith, Wilfred A.	Sapper	1873030	RE	U 2.10.42 Dr
McLean, Andrew M.	Private	2980621	RS	U 2.10.42 Dr
McLean, Joseph Henry	Lance Bdr.	1426733	RA	U 2.10.42 Dr
McMeechan, Hugh M.	Private	3055184	RS	U 2.10.42 Dr
McPherson, Charles D.	Private	3063711	RS	U 2.10.42 Dr
McQueen, George M.	Able Seaman	D/JX 169654	RN	UP 2.10.42 Dr
McSherry, Peter	Private	2975315	RS	U 2.10.42 Dr
Mair, William	Skipper		RNR	UC 2.10.42 Dr
Manders, Thomas George	Sapper	1876394	RE	U 2.10.42 Dr
Mann, Charles Henry	Able Seaman	D/JX 137274	RN	UP 2.10.42 Dr

Marriott, William Henry	L. Telegraphist	C/JX 145860	RN	UC 2.10.42 Dr
Marrs, William	Signalman	P/JX 190653	RN	UPO 2.10.42 Dr
Marsh, William Thomas	Sergeant	819817	RA	U 2.10.42 Dr
Marshall, Henry Gibson	Private	7884695	RS	U 2.10.42 Dr
Marshall, Thomas	Private	3051064	RS	U 2.10.42 Dr
Martin, Frank	Warrant Wardmaster		RN	UPO 2.10.42 Dr
Mason, William Alfred	Gunner	863085	RA	U 2.10.42 Dr
Matthew, Alexander M.	Private	6213541	MX	U 2.10.42 Dr
May, Wilfred	Able Seaman	C/JX 219867	RN	UC 2.10.42 Dr
Maynard, James Alfred	Private	6201245	MX	U 2.10.42 Dr
Mead, James Charles E.	CSM	3046672	RS	U 2.10.42 Dr
Medley, Lloyd Charles	Gunner	845448	RA	U 2.10.42 Dr
Melbourne, Frank Edward	Private	6895657	MX	U 2.10.42 Dr
Mellows, Stephen John	C.P.O. Writer	D/MX 47034	RN	UP 2.10.42 Dr
Melton, John William	Petty Officer	P/J 39300	RN	UPO 2.10.42 Dr
Mendelson, Arthur L.	Private	6202787	MX	U 2.10.42 Dr
Metcalfe, Ernest	Marine	PO/215951	RM	UPO 2.10.42 Dr
Metcalfe, Thomas Arthur	Private	3523209	MX	U 2.10.42 Dr
Miller, Donald	Private	3063332	RS	U 2.10.42 Dr
Minchin, Arthur Felix	Gunner	317526	RA	U 2.10.42 Dr
Miners, James	Gunner	4343532	RA	U 2.10.42 Dr
Morgan, Trevor Kenneth	Lance Corp.	2323570	RCS	U 2.10.42 Dr
Morris, Richard	Private	3054809	RS	U 2.10.42 Dr
Morris, William Thomas	Private	6203949	MX	U 2.10.42 Dr
Morrison, Edward	Private	6213567	MX	U 2.10.42 Dr
Morrow, William	Lance Corp.	3054065	RS	U 2.10.42 Dr
Morse, Charles John	P.O. Stoker	D/K 65312	RN	UP 2.10.42 Dr
Mose, George Alfred	BSM	1422598	RA	U 2.10.42 Dr
Moxham, Henry Richard	Lance Corp.	1867732	RE	U 2.10.42 Dr
Murphy, Thomas	Private	6202110	MX	U 2.10.42 Dr
Murray, John Stuart	Private	6201274	MX	U 2.10.42 Dr[199]
Murray, William	Private	3063686	RS	U 2.10.42 Dr
Murrell, Arthur Robert	Private	6210542	MX	U 2.10.42 Dr
Musto, Stanley Arthur	Lance Sergeant	1069779	HKSRA	U 2.10.42 Dr
Nayler, Herbert Edgar	CQMS	6199294	MX	U 2.10.42 Dr
Nellist, James	Gunner	1438807	RA	U 2.10.42 Dr
Newington, Richard T. J.	Lance Sergeant	1870427	RE	U 2.10.42 Dr
Newman, Thomas Harry	Lance Sergeant	1869298	RE	U 2.10.42 Dr
Newnham, Bertram C.	Lance Corp.	837990	RCS	U 2.10.42 Dr
Newton, Percy Alfred	2nd Lieutenant	145629	MX	U 2.10.42 Dr
Norman, Alfred William	Gunner	1712272	RA	U 2.10.42 Dr
North, Albert James	Gunner	5569751	RA	U 2.10.42 Dr
North, Frederick Ernest	Private	5988980	MX	U 2.10.42 Dr
O'Connell, Jeremiah	Gunner	1426783	RA	U 2.10.42 Dr
O'Connor, Michael Oliver	Private	3055943	RS	U 2.10.42 Dr
O'Rourke, Thomas	Private	3055389	RS	U 2.10.42 Dr
O'Sullivan, Bartholomew	Stoker P.O.	P/K59642	RN	UPO 2.10.42 Dr
Oakley, Thomas Ernest	Gunner	1470954	RA	U 2.10.42 Dr
Officer, John Moore	Major	47734	RAMC	U 2.10.42 Dr

Oliver, John Robert	Leading Seaman	C/SSX 21162	RN		UC 2.10.42 Dr
Ormiston, John Mitchell	Lance Corp.	3059298	RS		U 2.10.42 Dr
Orr, Terrance Nolan G.	Gunner	1426795	RA		U 2.10.42 Dr
Osman, Harry James	Petty Officer	P/J 105839	RN		UPO 2.10.42 Dr
Oswald, Ronald George	Private	6201303	MX		U 2.10.42 Dr
Ousgood, Fred	Chief E.R.A.	P/MX 46649	RN		UPO 2.10.42 Dr
Owen, George Thomas R.	Signalman	C/J 80397	RN		UC 2.10.42 Dr
Owen, Glyn	Gunner	1493336	RA		U 2.10.42 Dr
Owen, Gordon John	Lance Sergeant	1066923	RA		U 2.10.42 Dr
Pacey, Arthur	Lance Corp.	6202172	MX		U 2.10.42 Dr
Page, Charles Albert	Sergeant	2316934	RCS	MM	U 2.10.42 Dr
Page, William Cecil	Bombardier	843727	RA		U 2.10.42 Dr
Palmer, Joseph Benjamin	Private	6201414	MX		U 2.10.42 Dr
Panting, Hugh Eric R.	Corporal	5496071	MX		U 2.10.42 Dr
Pape, George William	Private	6201830	MX		U 2.10.42 Dr
Parker, Raymond John	Lance Corp.	6201466	MX		U 2.10.42 Dr
Parkins, George Baden	Signalman	C/J 46941	RN		UC 2.10.42 Dr
Parlette, Reginald George	Supply Assistant	C/MX 86692	RN		UC 2.10.42 Dr
Parsons, Arthur John	Corporal	2323514	RCS		U 2.10.42 Dr
Paterson, Henry	Private	3054793	RS		U 2.10.42 Dr
Payne, Arthur	Gunner	840853	RA		U 2.10.42 Dr
Payne, Terence Robert	Lance Corp.	6207623	MX		U 2.10.42 Dr
Pearce, Raymond John C.	Corporal	6201785	MX	MiD	U 2.10.42 Dr
Pearson, Alfred	Private	6201235	MX		U 2.10.42 Dr
Pearson, Harry	Sergeant	2317200	RCS		U 2.10.42 Dr
Peffers, Adam	Corporal	3051813	RS		U 2.10.42 Dr
Pelham, Harold Alfred G.	Corporal	6201290	MX		U 2.10.42 Dr
Pembroke, William Henry	Gunner	843803	RA		U 2.10.42 Dr
Pennick, Reginald Joseph	Lance Corp.	6201384	MX		U 2.10.42 Dr
Penny, Richard Arthur	Private	6207076	MX		U 2.10.42 Dr
Pepper, Frank Crookes	Sapper	1872831	RE		U 2.10.42 Dr
Perkins, Leslie George	Chief E.R.A.	D/MX 46040	RN		UP 2.10.42 Dr
Perry, Donald Charles	Corporal	1873120	RE		U 2.10.42 Dr
Philipson, John Beaver	Lance Sergeant	853246	RA		U 2.10.42 Dr
Phillips, Edward John	Private	6213577	MX		U 2.10.42 Dr
Phillips, Reginald Ernest	Lance Corp.	3054045	RS		U 2.10.42 Dr
Phillips, Sydney W.E.	P.O. Stoker	D/KX 82081	RN		UP 2.10.42 Dr
Phipps, John	Signalman	2323912	RCS		U 2.10.42 Dr
Pickston, Leslie	Signalman	2353661	RCS		U 2.10.42 Dr
Pike, Horace Henry G.	Chief Stoker	D/KX 75591	RN		UP 2.10.42 Dr
Plummer, William Arthur	Sergeant	5381717	RA		U 2.10.42 Dr
Pollard, Leonard Hugh	L. Telegraphist	P/WRX 622	RNVR		UPO 2.10.42 Dr
Pollock, James	Private	3063734	RS		U 2.10.42 Dr
Pope, Donald Charles	Sapper	1922409	RE		U 2.10.42 Dr
Potter, Alan Stanley	Corps Officer		SJA		U 2.10.42 GSW
Potter, John Henry	Signalman	2325012	RCS		U 2.10.42 Dr
Potter, John Thomas	Gunner	868809	RA		U 2.10.42 Dr
Potter, Robert	Gunner	1712293	RA		U 2.10.42 Dr
Powell, Albert Victor	P.O. Cook (S)	D/MX 46646	RN		UP 2.10.42 Dr

Powell, William John	Lance Corp.	3055656	RS		U 2.10.42 Dr
Pragnell, Charles	Gunner	851835	RA	U 12.9.42	U 2.10.42 Dr[200]
Pressley, Harvey	Gunner	1718185	RA		U 2.10.42 Dr
Priest, Henry Herbert A.	Gunner	1712297	RA		U 2.10.42 Dr
Priest, William James	W.O.	95A	HKRNVR		UP 2.10.42 Dr
Priestley, George	Gunner	1714991	RA		U 2.10.42 Dr
Pring, Mark Edward	Private	6207641	MX		U 2.10.42 Dr
Pritchard, James	Gunner	1071368	RA		U 2.10.42 Dr
Probert, Sidney Charles G.	Private	6213548	MX		U 2.10.42 Dr
Pryke, William Arthur J.	Motor Mechanic	P/MX 68681	RN		UPO 2.10.42 Dr
Pullar, James	Bombardier	836220	RA		U 2.10.42 Dr
Rainey, Eric	Sapper	2017013	RE		U 2.10.42 Dr
Rainsford, Henry Charles	Gunner	1426705	RA		U 2.10.42 Dr
Ramage, Humphrey G.	Sapper	795808	RE		U 2.10.42 Dr
Ramsay, John Fitcher	Private	3055647	RS		U 2.10.42 Dr
Ramsden, John Richard	Able Seaman	C/J 60050	RN		UC 2.10.42 Dr
Ramsey, James Robert	CSM	6196028	MX		U 2.10.42 Dr
Rankin, Thomas	BSM	1061282	RA		U 2.10.42 Dr
Raper, William George	Gunner	805922	RA		U 2.10.42 Dr
Ratcliffe, Norman Ernest	Sapper	1871671	RE		U 2.10.42 Dr
Rawlings, Frank	BSM	2202439	RA		U 2.10.42 Dr
Redfern, George Stanley	Signalman	2353662	RCS		U 2.10.42 Dr
Read, Reginald John	W.O.	107A	HKRNVR		UP 2.10.42 Dr
Reed, George William	Gunner	859682	RA		U 2.10.42 Dr
Rees, Leonard Frederick	Gunner	1715105	RA		U 2.10.42 Dr
Reeve, Sidney Arthur	Sapper	1912172	RE		U 2.10.42 Dr
Reynolds, Alfred John	Stoker 1st Class	P/SS 125467	RN		UPO 2.10.42 Dr
Rice, Thomas	Able Seaman	P/JX 148679	RN		UPO 2.10.42 Dr
Richards, Frederick W.	Sergeant	7258137	RAMC		U 2.10.42 Dr
Richards, Robert William	Sergeant	3051826	RS		U 2.10.42 Dr
Richards, Stanley John	Gunner	1713996	RA		U 2.10.42 Dr
Richardson, Joseph H.	Marine	PO/X 89	RM		UPO 2.10.42 Dr
Riches, Jack Ernest	PSM	6198989	MX		U 2.10.42 Dr[201]
Richmond, Robert Henry	Lance Corp.	1871596	RE		U 2.10.42 Dr
Ricketts, George R.	Gunner	853695	RA		U 2.10.42 Dr
Ridden, Donald	Private	6202704	MX		U 2.10.42 Dr
Ritchie, Robert Hyslop	Private	3054099	RS		U 2.10.42 Dr
Ritchings, Thomas	Gunner	872724	RA		U 2.10.42 Dr
Roberts, Alfred Henry	Bombardier	844989	RA		U 2.10.42 Dr
Roberts, Charles Arthur	Lance Corp.	1871282	RE		U 2.10.42 Dr
Roberts, Leonard	Private	6202331	MX		U 2.10.42 Dr
Robertson, Albert Thomas	Private	839788	MX		U 2.10.42 Dr
Robertson, Mornington	Corporal	2566140	RS		U 2.10.42 Dr [202]
Robertson, Peter Ian N.	Lance Corp.	2333539	RCS		U 2.10.42 Dr
Robinson, Charles	Shipwright 3/C	C/MX 48323	RN		UC 2.10.42 Dr
Robinson, Henry Charles	Motor Mechanic	P/MX 69813	RN		UPO 2.10.42 Dr
Robinson, John	Gunner	872357	RA		U 2.10.42 Dr
Robinson, Joseph	Signalman	2353612	RCS		U 2.10.42 Dr
Robinson, Percy Albert G.	Sapper	1875612	RE		U 2.10.42 Dr

Rodgers, Stephen P.	L. Sick Berth Att.	D/MX 54162	RN		UP 2.10.42 Dr
Rogers, Ernest James W.	Gunner	1491034	RA		U 2.10.42 Dr
Rogers, John Francis	CQMS	6340597	RCS		U 2.10.42 Dr
Rompen, George	Private	4448040	RS		U 2.10.42 Dr
Rooker, Roy Leslie H.	Lance Corp.	6202947	MX		U 2.10.42 Dr
Roos, Victor Edward	Able Seaman	C/JX 141248	RN		UC 2.10.42 Dr
Ross, John Connacher	Private	3055736	RS		U 2.10.42 Dr
Round, Walter Thomas	Gunner	1426753	RA		U 2.10.42 Dr
Rule, Albert	Private	6213551	MX		U 2.10.42 Dr
Rule, Charles Frederick	Lance Corp.	6202369	MX		U 2.10.42 Dr
Rushman, Mervyn Francis	Sergeant	PLY/X 488	RM		UP 2.10.42 Dr
Russell, Alexander	Lance Corp.	3054869	RS		U 2.10.42 Dr
Russell, Reginald Edward	Private	6202948	MX		U 2.10.42 Dr
Russell, Robert	Private	6202362	MX		U 2.10.42 Dr
Russell, Thomas	Sergeant	1046474	RA		U 2.10.42 Dr
Samuels, Christopher	Private	6201438	MX		U 2.10.42 Dr[203]
Sansum, Harry	Private	6198239	MX		U 2.10.42 Dr
Sawyer, William Arthur	Petty Officer	C/J 101193	RN		UC 2.10.42 Dr
Sayce, Thomas	Gunner	2215242	RA		U 2.10.42 Dr
Schorsch, Robert	Private	6210550	MX		U 2.10.42 Dr
Scott, Alexander C.	Private	3053649	RS		U 2.10.42 Dr
Scott, Arthur Reginald G.	Sapper	5725545	RE		U 2.10.42 Dr
Scott, Donald	Private	3128873	RS		U 2.10.42 Dr
Scott, Frank Douglas	Gunner	849557	RA		U 2.10.42 Dr
Scott, Robert Ferrie	Private	3053792	RS		U 2.10.42 Dr
Scully, John Patrick	Corporal	2323331	RCS		U 2.10.42 Dr
Seager, Albert Ernest	Gunner	863185	RA		U 2.10.42 Dr [204]
Searle, Henry George A.	BQMS	1043916	HKSRA		U 2.10.42 Dr
Selwood, George William	Gunner	1712254	RA		U 2.10.42 Dr
Sercombe, William M.	E.R.A. 2/C	D/MX 49610	RN		UP 2.10.42 Dr
Sharp, Duncan	Gunner	900140	RA		U 2.10.42 Dr
Sharp, Henry Thomas	Chief Ord. Art.	C/M 38907	RN		UC 2.10.42 Dr
Sharrock, Harold Maynard	Lance Corp.	3054194	RS		U 2.10.42 Dr
Shepherd, George	Gunner	3381216	RA		U 2.10.42 Dr
Shepherd, Thomas W.	Signalman	2323228	RCS		U 2.10.42 Dr
Sherlaw, George Fitness	Lance Sergeant	1054920	RA		U 2.10.42 Dr
Sherman, Soloman	A.B.	D/JX192821	RN		UP 2.10.42 Dr
Shields, Thomas Perkins	Chief E.R.A.	P/195ED	RNR		UPO 2.10.42 Dr
Shipp, Cecil Edward	Sergeant	1867862	RE		U 2.10.42 Dr
Shirkey, John Dollar	Able Seaman	P/SSX 14017	RN		UPO 2.10.42 Dr
Shirley, Ernest Francis	BSM	751875	RA		U 2.10.42 Dr
Short, Leslie Charles	Bandsman	796168	MX		U 2.10.42 Dr
Simmonds, Harold A.P.	P.O. Telegraphist	P/J 32688	RN		UPO 2.10.42 Dr
Simmons, Edward Walter	Sapper	1874074	RE		U 2.10.42 Dr
Simpson, Matthew Allen	Lance Bdr.	1603474	RA		U 2.10.42 Dr
Simpson, Thomas	Lance Sergeant	6201485	MX		U 2.10.42 Dr
Sinclair, Frederick L.	Private	6201225	MX		U 2.10.42 Dr
Singleton, Thomas	Lance Sergeant	1868579	RE		U 2.10.42 Dr
Skinner, John	Corporal	3054151	RS		U 2.10.42 Dr

Name	Rank	Number	Unit	Status
Smale, Albert Edward	Signalman	C/J 27525	RN	UC 2.10.42 Dr
Smalley, Frank	Bandsman	6201403	MX	U 2.10.42 Dr
Smith, Albert Edward	Gunner	1712260	RA	U 2.10.42 Dr
Smith, Ernest Alexander	Sergeant	2029653	MX	U 2.10.42 Dr
Smith, Frederick William	Gunner	856075	RA	U 2.10.42 Dr
Smith, John Brazier	Gunner	556398	HKSRA	U 2.10.42 Dr
Smith, John Peter	Gunner	847789	RA	U 2.10.42 Dr
Smith, Leslie Frank	Lance Corp.	1871507	RE	U 2.10.42 Dr
Smith, Leslie Ivor	Sergeant	853737	RA	U 2.10.42 Dr
Smith, Matthew	PSM	2977171	RS MiD	U 2.10.42 Dr
Smith, Patrick	Corporal	3048063	RS	U 2.10.42 Dr
Spall, Arthur Ernest	Private	6202929	MX	U 2.10.42 Dr
Spare, Dermot	Corporal	2319390	RCS	U 2.10.42 Dr
Sparkes, John Charles	Gunner	851848	RA	U 2.10.42 Dr
Spence, John Frederick	Lance Sergeant	1871927	RE	U 2.10.42 Dr
Spencer, Geoffrey W.	Lance Corp.	1874667	RE	U 2.10.42 Dr
Spencer, Reginald Charles	Sapper	1873351	RE	U 2.10.42 Dr
Spiers, George Edward	Private	6214370	MX	U 2.10.42 Dr
Stancer, Frank Lewis	Lieutenant	184087	RS	U 2.10.42 Dr
Stanford, Frederick	CSM	6908612	RS	U 2.10.42 Dr
Stanners, Adam Ramsey	Private	3054521	RS	U 2.10.42 Dr
Steed, Thomas	S.B.A.	C/SR59	RN	UC 2.10.42 Dr
Steele, William Ernest	Private	6213589	MX	U 2.10.42 Dr
Stemp, Reginald Stanley	Gunner	1712269	RA	U 2.10.42 Dr
Stewart, Forbes	Piper	3053467	RS	U 2.10.42 Dr
Stewart, William	Private	6202990	MX	U 2.10.42 Dr
Stewart, William G.	Corporal	3211328	RS	U 2.10.42 Dr
Stickley, Thomas	Private	6195813	MX	U 2.10.42 Dr
Stobbart, John Douglas	Gunner	872643	RA	U 2.10.42 Dr
Stocker, James Lawrence	Gunner	856855	RA	U 2.10.42 Dr
Stoker, Ralph William	E.R.A. 1st Class	P/190 ED	RNR	UPO 2.10.42 Dr
Stone, George Frederick	Bombardier	860091	RA	U 2.10.42 Dr
Stone, Thomas John	Leading Stoker	D/KX 94034	RN	UP 2.10.42 Dr
Stott, James Black	Corporal	2323463	RCS MM	U 2.10.42 Dr
Sturdy, Patrick Joseph	Sergeant	6201477	MX	U 2.10.42 Dr
Suggitt, Robert	Signalman	2351049	RCS	U 2.10.42 Dr
Sumner, William	BQMS	818673	RA	U 2.10.42 Dr
Sweeney, Daniel C.	Supply Assistant	P/M 37259	RN	UPO 2.10.42 Dr
Tait, Alexander	Private	6202334	MX	U 2.10.42 Dr
Tait, Robert	Private	3063568	RS	U 2.10.42 Dr
Talks, Vernon	Dvr	2324091	RCS	U 2.10.42 Dr
Tarner, John Norman	Corporal	6200730	MX	U 2.10.42 Dr
Taylor, Alec	Private	6207790	MX	U 2.10.42 Dr
Taylor, Gerald Francis	Sergeant	7536269	RADC	U 2.10.42 Dr
Taylor, Norman	Gunner	881724	RA	U 2.10.42 Dr
Taylor, Sydney George	Master Mariner		MN SS Shrivati (Bombay)	UTH 2.10.42 Dr
Taylor, Sydney John	Signalman	D/SSX 33879	RN	UP 2.10.42 Dr
Thackeray, Samuel Robert	Gunner	850564	RA	U 2.10.42 Dr

Thomas, Alfred Llewellyn	Sapper	1872659	RE		U 2.10.42 Dr
Thomas, Cyril	Private	6202751	MX		U 2.10.42 Dr
Thomas, Edwin	Gunner	872633	RA		U 2.10.42 Dr
Thomas, Jack	Private	6200963	MX		U 2.10.42 Dr
Thomas, Jack Henry	Private	6201172	MX		U 2.10.42 Dr
Thompson, Frederick John	Lance Bdr.	860782	RA		U 2.10.42 Dr
Thompson, William	Corporal	1871390	RE		U 2.10.42 Dr
Thomson, Alexander	Private	2877781	RS		U 2.10.42 Dr
Thomson, Andrew	Private	3055945	RS		U 2.10.42 Dr
Thomson, David Haston	Private	3051845	RS		U 2.10.42 Dr
Thorn, Ronald Alfred	Sapper	1871903	RE		U 2.10.42 Dr
Thrush, James Waters	Gunner	1715110	RA		U 2.10.42 Dr
Tivey, Richard John	Private	6213111	MX		U 2.10.42 Dr
Tomlinson, John Bramley	Corporal	2322410	RCS		U 2.10.42 Dr
Tooley, Michael	Lance Bdr.	1040797	RA		U 2.10.42 Dr
Townsend, George	Gunner	2574607	RA		U 2.10.42 Dr
Tozer, Stanley Herbert	Commissioned Shipwright		RN		UP 2.10.42 Dr
Trinder, George	RQMS	3049838	RS		U 2.10.42 Dr
Tucker, Joseph Henry	Private	6202940	MX		U 2.10.42 Dr
Tunmer, William Arthur	Bandsman	6199244	MX		U 2.10.42 Dr
Turnbull, James	Sapper	1873561	RE		U 2.10.42 Dr
Turner, Frank	Sapper	2040931	RE		U 2.10.42 Dr
Turner, William Arthur	Stoker 1st Class	P/KX 109310	RN		UPO 2.10.42 Dr
Twomey, Wilfred Roy	Sapper	1873830	RE		U 2.10.42 Dr
Upton, Edward George	QMS	1866078	RE		U 2.10.42 Dr
Valentine, George F.W.	Able Seaman	P/J 20240	RN		UPO 2.10.42 Dr
Valentine, Roland Edward	Private	6211128	MX		U 2.10.42 Dr
Vallance, George William	Private	2216490	MX		U 2.10.42 Dr
Viotto, Joseph	Gunner	847011	RA		U 2.10.42 Dr
Waddington, Wilfred G.	Gunner	851194	RA		U 2.10.42 Dr
Wakefield, Joseph W.	Private	4973727	RS		U 2.10.42 Dr
Wakeham, Ernest William			CV		U 2.10.42 Dr[205]
Walker, Frederick Charles	Sergeant	6199899	MX		U 2.10.42 Dr
Walker, Leighton William	Major	38495	RS		U 2.10.42 Dr
Walker, William	Sergeant	2874626	RS		U 2.10.42 Dr
Wallace, Warner	Gunner	856113	RA		U 2.10.42 Dr
Walters, John	Private	3054946	RS		U 2.10.42 Dr
Warburton, John	Gunner	1492565	RA		U 2.10.42 Dr
Ward, Bernard M.J.	Gunner	845291	RA		U 2.10.42 Dr
Warder, Alexander C.	Lance Sergeant	1061893	RA		U 2.10.42 Dr
Warren, Christopher	Signalman	2330321	RCS		U 2.10.42 Dr
Waters, Robert Edward	Private	6213557	MX		U 2.10.42 Dr
Wathen, Walter Norman	Lance Sergeant	2314610	RCS		U 2.10.42 Dr
Watkins, John Patrick	Private	6202797	MX		U 2.10.42 Dr
Watson, Arthur	Seaman Gunner		HKRNVR		UP 2.10.42 Dr
Watson, Thomas	Bombardier	826539	RA		U 2.10.42 Dr
Weaver, John Douglas H.	Lance Corp.	6201811	MX		U 2.10.42 Dr
Webb, Donald	Sick Berth Att.	D/MX 57578	RN		UP 2.10.42 Dr
Webb, Sidney	Able Seaman	C/J 110817	RN		UC 2.10.42 Dr

Webster, Allan	Private	4191829	MX		U 2.10.42 Dr
Webster, George	Gunner	847445	RA		U 2.10.42 Dr
Webster, George	Private	6201463	MX	U 21.3.44	U 2.10.42 Dr[206]
Weeks, Douglas Reginald	Signalman	2324122	RCS		U 2.10.42 Dr
Wellington, Richard H.	BSM	1425771	RA		U 2.10.42 Dr
Wells, William George	Bombardier	1058220	RA		U 2.10.42 Dr
Welsh, James Blaney	Private	3054597	RS		U 2.10.42 Dr
Weston, John William	Lance Sergeant	1863657	RE		U 2.10.42 Dr
Wexham, Robert Martin	Warrant Supply Officer		RN		UC 2.10.42 Dr
Whelan, William	Lance Sergeant	1867404	RE		U 2.10.42 Dr
White, Ralph James	Able Seaman	P/JX 146392	RN		UPO 2.10.42 Dr
White, Robert	Drummer	3054849	RS		U 2.10.42 Dr
Whitefield, Charles A.	Sergeant	2318017	RCS		U 2.10.42 Dr
Whitehead, Arthur F.	Gunner	1866939	RA		U 2.10.42 Dr
Whitehouse, Herbert	Private	6201205	MX		U 2.10.42 Dr
Whitham, James Percival	Lieutenant	221895	MX		U 2.10.42 Dr
Wigzell, Wallace Frank	CSM	2311126	RCS		U 2.10.42 Dr[207]
Williams, Frederick Ivor	Lance Bdr.	1492580	RA		U 2.10.42 Dr
Williams, Harry Edward I.	Ordinary Coder	D/208165	RN		UP 2.10.42 Dr
Williams, Ronald F.	Gunner	1427413	RA		U 2.10.42 Dr
Williams, Thomas Alun	Sapper	1870215	RE		U 2.10.42 Dr
Williamson, James	Private	3054063	RS		U 2.10.42 Dr
Willis, Francis	Lance Corp.	2321824	RCS		U 2.10.42 Dr
Wilson, Arthur Stanley	Gunner	868801	RA		U 2.10.42 Dr
Wilson, Charles Edward	Lance Corp.	3054164	RS		U 2.10.42 Dr[208]
Wilson, John Campbell	L. Telegraphist	P/WRX489	RN		UPO 2.10.42 Dr
Wilson, William Eric	BSM	1424207	RA		U 2.10.42 Dr
Withington, Henry	Bombardier	5245673	RA		U 2.10.42 Dr
Witty, Herbert Charles	Lance Corp.	6202382	MX		U 2.10.42 Dr
Wood, Lawrence Arthur	Lieutenant	149465	MX	MiD	U 2.10.42 Dr
Woollcott, Edgar Joseph	Sapper	1925110	RE		U 2.10.42 Dr
Woolley, Bertram	Private	6200754	MX		U 2.10.42 Dr
Woolridge, Edward	Gunner	843519	RA		U 2.10.42 Dr
Woolwright, Alfred	Lance Sergeant	3054082	RS		U 2.10.42 Dr
Wordley, Ernest George	Private	7519158	RAMC		U 2.10.42 Dr
Wyllie, William	Private	3050493	RS		U 2.10.42 Dr
Yeoman, Herbert George	Gunner	851690	RA		U 2.10.42 Dr

On the way to Shanghai

Siddans, John	Able Seaman	D/J115494	RN		UP 4.10.42[209]

Shensei Maru

Mulcahy, Michael D.	Able Seaman	D/JX 143657	RN		UP 7.10.42[210]
Drake, William Stanley	W.O.	29A	HKRNVR		UP 8.10.42[211]
Young, Kenneth Eldred	Lieutenant	92883	MX	U 2.10.42	U 8.10.42[212]
Stewart, Murdo	Telegraphist	NZV07421	RN		UN 10.10.42[213]
Makel, George Smith	BSM	426254	RA	1-2.10.42	U 10.10.42[214]
Bromley, Robert William	Lance Sergeant	1425948	HKSRA	U 14.10.42	U 10.10.42[215]
Archer, Frederick Wilfred	Supt. E.D.	1861837	RE	U 15.10.42	U 10.10.42[216]

Woosung (Chan Hwo Hin), Shanghai[217]

Bailey, Stanford Arthur	Boom Skipper		RNR		K 7.10.42 Y Dy[218]
Cane, Ronald Arthur H.	Corporal	1869471	RE	2.10.42	K 7.10.42 Y Dy
Williams, George	C.E.R.A. II	D/M.37680	RN		K 7.10.42 Y Dy
Heath, Charles Richard	W.O.I.	1862139	RE	2.10.42	K 8.10.42 Y Dy
Butcher, Eric Robert	W.O.	17A	HKRNVR		K 9.10.42 Y Dy
Stone, Edward Ronald	Sapper	1574428	RE	2.10.42	K 9.10.42 Y Dy
Fergus, John	Sergeant	3052141	RS	2.10.42	K 10.10.42 Y Dy
Todd, James Somerville	CPO	D/JX149160	RN		K 10.10.42 Y Dy
Grant, Donald Joseph	Corporal	1874312	RE		K 11.10.42 Y Dy
Symons, Robert Charles	Yeo of Signals	D/JX147813	RN		K 12.10.42 Y Dy
Reeves, Ronald	Corporal	6201116	MX		K 13.10.42 Y Dy
Thomas, Gwynfor	Sick Berth Att.	P/MX64986	RN	2.10.42	K 15.10.42 Y Dy
Horder, Douglas George	Motor Mech.	P/MX67988	RN		K 16.10.42 Y Dy
Watts, Joseph Henry	Corporal	2321582	RCS	2.10.42	K 20.10.42 Y Dy
Campbell, William S.	Staff Sergeant	1867026	RE	2.10.42	K 23.10.42 Y Dy[219]

Kiangwan, Shanghai

Newbold, William James	Signalman	2324193	RCS		K 26.12.42 Y Dy

Osaka #1 Branch Camp (Minato-ku, Osaka)

Harvey, John Baptiste C.	Private	6200684	MX		(XD2)	K 6.10.42 Y Dy[220] diw[221]
Evenett, Alan George	Signalman	2330259	RCS	20.10.42	(XD2)	K 10.10.42 Y Dy doh
Ayres, Frederick Henry E.	Sergeant	6201876	MX		(XD2)	K 11.10.42 Y dkh
Chiswell, Reginald C. G.	Shipwright	D/M28197	RN		(XD2)	K 11.10.42 Y
Foster, John Arthur	Gunner	872412	RA		(XD2)	K 11.10.42 Y dkh[222]
Goodwin, Edwin John W.	Corporal	1862204	RE		(XD2)	K 11.10.42 Y dkh
Harrison, James Alfred	Sapper	2111363	RE		(XD2)	K 11.10.42 Y Dy dhh
Hewett, Edward Tucker	Marine	CH/X 458	RM		(XD2)	K 11.10.42 Y Dy dhh
Rowlands, Fred Forsyth	Sapper	1860929	RE		(XD2)	K 12.10.42 Y Pa diw
Kilgore, John	Gunner	872531	RA		(XD2)	K 12.10.42 Y Pa diw
Price, Walter	Signalman	D/JX235643	RN		(XD2)	K 12.10.42 Y Dy doh
Dyke, Leslie Edward	ERA 2nd Class	C/M39586	RN		(XD2)	K 13.10.42 Y Cf
Grafton, Ernest Charles	Private	6202775	MX		(XD2)	K 13.10.42 Y Dy diw
Beare, John	Lance Corp.	1871471	RE		(XD2)	K 14.10.42 Y Pa diw
Morgan, John	Lance Corp.	1874158	RE		(XD2)	K 14.10.42 Y Cs diw
Wall, Thomas Mervyn	Sergeant RM	PLY/X22054	RM		(XD2)	K 14.10.42 Y Dy dhh
Mason, James William	Gunner	1715095	RA		(XD2)	K 15.10.42 Y Dy diw
Burford, Frederick James	Tel	P/JX201141	RN		(XD2)	K 16.10.42 Y Dy doh
Griffith, Robert Thomas	Supp. Ass.	D/MX65858	RN		(XD2)	K 16.10.42 Y Dy doh
Mills, James	BSM	1062585	RA		(XD2)	K 17.10.42 Y Dy doh[223]
Morgan, Melville	M. Stoker	C/KX105321	RN		(XD2)	K 17.10.42 Y Dy dhh
Hart, Colin James	Lieutenant	177486	RS		(XD2)	K 18.10.42 Y Dy dhh
Matheson, Donald	Motor Mech.	P/MX64555	RN		(XD2)	K 18.10.42 Y Dy dhh
Thomas, Ivor Edward	A.S.	P/SSX28641	RN		(XD2)	K 18.10.42 Y Dy doh
Matthews, Thomas	Private	6212893	MX		(XD2)	K 18.10.42 Y Dy dhh
Rogers, Joseph Thomas	ERA II	P/MX50729	RN		(XD2)	K 18-19.10.42 Y

Dow, Robert	L Stoker	C/KX90980	RN		(XD2)	K 19.10.42 Y Dy doh
Duffy, John	P.O.	D/JX134983	RN		(XD2)	K 20.10.42 Y Dy dhh
Dowling, Maurice	Stoker 1st Class	P/SS117816	RN		(XD2)	K 21.10.42 Y Dy
Havelock, William	A.S.	C/J80251	RN		(XD2)	K 22.10.42 Y Dy diw
Gilzean, John Atkinson	Sapper	1869008	RE		(XD2)	K 22.10.42 Y Cs diw
Morrow, John Alexander	Lance Corp.	3059290	RS		(XD2)	K 22.10.42 Y Da diw
Allison, John	CPO Sick Berth	D/MX45771	RN		(XD2)	K 23.10.42 Y Dkh
Bundy, Cecil	Sergeant	2319902	RCS	28.10.42	(XD2)	K 23.10.42 Y Dy diw
Payne, Ernest William	A.S.	C/J94361	RN		(XD2)	K 23.10.42 Y Dy diw
Tibble, William Ernest J.	CSM	6194081	MX		(XD2)	K 24.10.42 Y Dy dhh
Castle, Thomas Richard	Sergeant	6197065	MX		(XD2)	K 25.10.42 Y Dy dhh
Jordan, Leonard Arthur	W.O.I.	1859184	RE		(XD2)	K 25.10.42 Y Dy diw
Schofield, Ralph	A.S.	D/SSX19755	RN		(XD2)	K 27.10.42 Y Dy doh
Bairstow, Ronald W.	Private	7538134	RADC		(XD2)	K 28.10.42 Y Dy dhh
Anderson, Thomas Albert	PO Tel.	C/JX144913	RN		(XD2)	K 29.10.42 Y Dy
Clayton, Bernard	Private		HKDDC RN/DYP		(XD2)	K 29.10.42 Y
Mill, William Frederick	Sergeant		HKDDC RN/DYP		(XD2)	K 29.10.42 Y Cf
Adams, Leonard George	Petty Officer	D/JX130985	RN		(XD2)	K 30.10.42 Y Da
Maxted, Richard	L/Tel	C/JX140591	RN		(XD2)	K 31.10.42 Y Dy diw
Milrose, James Alfred	Signalman	2350958	RCS	1-31.12.42	(XD2)	K 11.42 Y doh[224]
Coates, Ernest	Signalman	2330292	RCS	26.11.42	(XD2)	K 2.11.42 Y
Grove, Norman	Lance Corp.	2324059	RCS		(XD2)	K 6.11.42 Y Dy diw
Childs, George M.	P.O.	C/JX147246	RN		(XD2)	K 9.11.42 Y Dy diw
Spong, Harry Charles	Lieutenant	89855	RCS MBE		(XD2)	K 11.11.42 Y Dy diw
Neil, Ernest Robert	A.S.	D/SSX14813	RN MiD		(XD2)	K 16.11.42 Y Dy dhh
Smith, Edwin Leslie G.	A.S.	P/J28740	RN		(XD2)	K 18.11.42 Y diw
Spanner, Harold Albert T.	Chemist	CV			(XD2)	U 24.11.42 doh[225]
Martin, Douglas Herbert	Gunner	6012515	RA		(XD2)	K 27.11.42 Y Ea doh
Welsh, Bertie George	Sergeant	1863567	RE		(XD2)	K 28.11.42 Y Dy diw
Lawton, Albert	Signalman	2324220	RCS		(XD2)	K 30.11.42 Y Dy diw
Burrows, Kenneth George	A.S.	P/J102981	RN		(XD2)	K 5.12.42 Y Dy diw
Lord, Harold H.	Signalman	2353654	RCS	1.12.42	(XD2)	K 7.12.42 Y Dy diw
Preece, Bernard Victor	Signalman	2324242	RCS		(XD2)	K 12.12.42 Y Pa diw
Goldsmith, Frederick E.	Private	6723293	MX		(XD2)	K 15.12.42 Y Dy dhh
Mullett, Leslie Alfred	W.O.		HKRNVR	21.10.42	(XD2)	K 16.12.42Y Dy dkh
Badger, James Spencer	Lieutenant	111255	RE		(XD2)	K 18.12.42 Y dkh[226]
Kennard, Harold Leslie	L/Sergeant	768835	RCS		(XD2)	K 28.12.42 Y Dy diw

Osaka #2 Branch Camp (Kobe)

Jupp, John Edmund	W.O.		HKRNVR	(XD2)	K 12.10.42 Y
Morgan, Wilfred	Sergeant	1049726	RA	(XD2)	K 13.10.42 Y Es/Bi
Phillips, Joseph	Lance Corp.	3054068	HQ.C.C. Det.	(XD2)	K 13.10.42 Y Dy doh
Sinclair, Alexander G.	Private	3063759	RS	(XD2)	K 13.10.42 Y Dy doh
Dixon, Aaron Hedley	Private	6210892		(XD2)	K 16.10.42 Y Dy
Jones, Harry George	Private	6202789	MX	(XD2)	K 16.10.42 Y Dy doh[227]
Cuthbertson, Norman H.	Captain	74594	RS	(XD2)	K 17.10.42 Y Dy doh
Hobbs, Frank William	QMS	1860696	RE	(XD2)	K 17.10.42 Y Dy
McFarlane, John Chapman	Boom Eng.		RNR	(XD2)	K 17.10.42 Y[228]

Taylor, Guy Ralph	Corporal	1874436	RE	(XD2)	K 17.10.42 Y Dy doh
Wilson, George F.E.	Staff Sergeant	1862768	RE	(XD2)	K 17.10.42 Y Dy
Booth, James Dunbar	Sergeant	2874392	RS	(XD2)	K 18.10.42 Y Dy
Ferriss, Stanley Richard	Private	6201181	MX	(XD2)	K 18.10.42 Y Dy doh
Fountain, Alfred Morris	Sapper	2014599	RE	(XD2)	K 18.10.42 Y Dy doh
Gilbert, Donald Arthur	Lance Corp.	2325023	RCS	(XD2)	K 21.10.42 Y Pa[229]
Stewart, Henry William	Lieutenant-Col.	9005	MX OBE MC	(XD2)	K 21.10.42 Y Dy diw
James, Charles Alfred	Corporal	1871324	RE	(XD2)	K 22.10.42 Y Da
Dexter, David Cameron	Sapper	1874684	RE	(XD2)	K 24.10.42 Y Dy
Innis, Leslie Walrond	Major	22631	RE	(XD2)	K 24.10.42 Y Dy doh
Ford, Albert Edward	QMS	1865943	RE	(XD2)	K 25.10.42 Y Dy doh
Bater, Harold Charles	CPO Supply	D/M37318	RN	(XD2)	K 25.10.42 Y Dy diw
Phillips, Eric Gladstone	Lieutenant	146774	RA	(XD2)	K 25.10.42 Y Dy diw
Elliott, Harry George	Private	6213488		(XD2)	K 27.12.42 Y Cbi
Tavendale, Ian Ross	Sergeant	833477	RA	(XD2)	K 27.10.42 Y Dy
Harrison, Edward	Private	6202330	MX	(XD2)	K 28.10.42 Y Cbi
Myles, James	Private	3055407	RS	(XD2)	K 30.10.42 Y Dy
Cohen, Norman	Private	6203958	MX	(XD2)	K 31.10.42 Y Dy
Goodfellow, Isaac	RSM	3050915	RS	(XD2)	K 31.10.42 Y Dy
Sach, George Henry	Private	6198387	MX	(XD2)	K 31.10.42 Y Dy
Butterfield, Edward	Private	3055692	RS	(XD2)	K 7.11.42 Y Dy
Stafford, Arthur John	Lance Bdr.	853211	RA	(XD2)	K 7.11.42 Y Dy doh
Sandell, Alfred Albert	Private	6213002	MX	(XD2)	K 9.11.42 Y Dy
Crabbe, William Gordon	W.O.		HKRNVR	(XD2)	K 10.11.42 Y Da doh
Thompson, Charles C.	Gunner	1438819	RA	(XD2)	K 12.11.42 Y Cs diw
Miller, Charles Alfred	Private	6202863	MX	(XD2)	K 14.11.42 Y Dy doh
Harlow, Harry	Lance Corp.	3059154	RS	(XD2)	K 15.11.42 Y Dy
Searle, Alfred Edward	Private	6214365	MX	(XD2)	K 15.11.42 Y Dy doh
Park, Hamilton White	Corporal	3053694	RS	(XD2)	K 18.11.42 Y Dy
Beament, George Robert	QMS	1865764	RE	(XD2)	K 24.11.42 Y Pa diw
Betts, Charles	Sergeant	5769666	MX	(XD2)	K 28.11.42 Y Dy diw
Watts, Thomas	P.O.	P/J14612	RN	(XD2)	K 30.11.42 Y Dy
Gales, Christopher	CSM	1859679	RE	(XD2)	K 1.12.42 Y Bi/Az
Crichton, Thomas Easton	Corporal	3050013	RS	(XD2)	K 12.12.42 Y Cs
Eddleston, William H.	Gunner	1492736	RA	(XD2)	K 13.12.42 Y Cs doh
Shepherd, George Bernard	Sapper	1877730	RE	(XD2)	K 14.12.42 Y Mn
Bull, Francis Charles	A.S.	D/JX165781	RN	(XD2)	K 17.12.42 Y Dy
Meakin, Frank	Corporal	6207916	MX	(XD2)	K 24.12.42 Y Dy
Eaton, Walter T.	Private	836184	RNH	(XD2)	K 29.12.42 Y Dy doh

Tokyo Main Camp (Shinagawa)

Reid, Fred William	Private	T/7344533	RASC	(XD1)	K 13.9.42 Y Dy dt2
Thorpe, Horace William	Gunner	5879560	RA	(XD1)	K 5.10.42 Y Dy dt2[230]
Bennett, Thomas Wilfred	Private	6203600	MX	(XD1)	K 26.10.42 Y Pa
Clarke, Geoffrey	Private	S/57286	RASC	(XD1)	K 29.10.42 Y[231]
McMenamin, Patrick G.	Gunner	1725327	RA	(XD1)	K 7.11.42 Y Dy/Bi dt2[232]
Stannard, William W.	Private	3063763	RS	(XD1)	K 7.12.42 Y Dy dt2

Taylor, John Stonehouse	Private	S/134370	RASC	(XD1)	K 27.12.42 Y Pa dsh
Smith, Sidney	P.O. Stoker	D/KX75526	RN	(XD1)	K 27.11.42 Y Dy dt2

Tokyo #1 Branch Camp (Oshima-cho, Kawasaki)

Farr, George Harold	Private	6202933	MX	(XD1)	K 14.12.42 Y Es
Davis, Victor Christian	Lance Sergeant	6203244	MX	(XD1)	K 15.12.42 Y Ma[233]

Tokyo #3 Branch Camp (Yokohama Stadium)

Crossan, Harold G.	Sapper	1875331	RE	(XD1)	K 3.10.42 Y Dy dt2
Campbell, Thomas R.	Gunner	872768	RA	(XD1)	K 7.10.42 Y Dy dt2

Ma Tau Chung

Gaj Raj Singh	Lance Naik	11566	RP			U ?
Muni Lal	Sweeper	21G/411	IHC			K 41-45
Muhammad Husain	Jem	2577	HKSRA			U 2.1.42
Muhammad Amir Khan	Havildar-Major	3099	HKSRA			U 2.1.42
Sultan Bakhsh	Subadar-Major	2043	HKSRA			U 2.1.42
Muhammad Shafi	Gunner	4971	HKSRA			U 4.1.42
Bachan Singh	Gunner	7705	HKSRA	19.12.41		U 10.1.42
Haribanu Dutt Sherma	Pundit	-	RP			D 14.1.42
Munshi Khan	Gunner	5382	HKSRA			K 22.1.42
Rahmat Khan	Gunner	8040	HKSRA			K 23.1.42
Amin Chand	Sepoy	11622	PJ			U 8.2.42
Abdul Rahman	Gunner	5317	HKSRA			K 14.2.42
Chhatar Singh	Sepoy	11957	RP			K 14.2.42
Inayat Ullah	Gunner	4198	HKSRA			K 15.2.42
Firoz Khan	Sepoy	19507	PJ			U 15.2.42
Buwa Singh	Gunner	3954	HKSRA			U 15.2.42
Kamikar Singh	Havildar	2729	HKSRA			U 15.2.42
Jagir Singh	Gunner	3660	HKSRA			K 15.2.42
Khalas Khan	Gunner	3643	HKSRA			K 2.3.42
Mahbub Ali	Sepoy	16065	PJ			K 6.3.42
Fazal Ahmad	Sepoy	11158	PJ	23.3.43	BRH	K 23.3.42
Kehri Singh	Sepoy	14787	RP			U 29.3.42
Nur Illahi	Sepoy	11549	RP			U 29.3.42
Ranga Khan	Sepoy	9893	RP			K 8.4.42
Ahmad Khan	Gunner	3353	HKSRA			K 20.4.42
Ram Dhan Singh	Sepoy	21194	RP			K 21.4.42
Hari Bhan Datt Dwivedi	Religious Teacher	-	RP			U 30.4.42
Ram Saran Tiwari	Cook	F/1	RP			K 30.4.42
Pyara Singh	Sepoy	16025	PJ			K 5.5.42
Kartar Singh	Gunner	7642	HKSRA			K 7.5.42
Tirath Ram	Naik	10020	PJ			K 12.5.42
Niranjan Singh	Sepoy	19090	PJ			K 25.5.42
Ram Singh	Sepoy	10710	RP			U 26.5.42
Ram Singh	Sepoy	20482	RP			K 26.5.42
Sri Ram Singh	Sepoy	15890	RP			K 28.5.42
Hem Singh	Sepoy	10723	RP			K 31.5.42

Name	Rank	Number	Unit	Status
Ram Bakhsh Singh	Sepoy	8583	RP	K 19.6.42
Shafi Muhammad	Driver	174689	HKMC	K 6.7.42
Nur Muhammad	Gunner	5092	HKSRA	U 6.7.42
Bans Bahadur Singh	Sepoy	16075	RP	K 9.7.42
Fazl Din	Naik	13295	RP	U 10.7.42
Ghulam Muhammad	Gunner	5280	HKSRA	K 10.7.42
Jafar Ali	Sepoy	10054	RP	U 10.7.42
Jai Singh	Sepoy	14697	RP	K 14.7.42
Barkat Ali	Gunner	7918	HKSRA	U 18.7.42
Shadi Khan	Sepoy	15064	RP	U 23.7.42
Juma Khan	Sepoy	18518	PJ	K 24.7.42
Khushi Muhammad	Gunner	2570	HKSRA	K 24.7.42
Abdul Karim	Sepoy	16011	RP	U 25.7.42
Firoz Khan	Sepoy	13978	RP	K 4.8.42
Yasin Khan	Sepoy	8884	RP	U 4.8.42
Nur Khan	Gunner	5085	HKSRA	K 5.8.42
Ali Khan	Sepoy	15301	PJ	U 8.8.42
Shah Jahan Khan	Gunner	5091	HKSRA	K 8.8.42
Ghulam Muhammad	Gunner	7782	HKSRA	K 8.8.42
Allah Dad	Havildar	3351	HKSRA	U 8.8.42
Janga Singh	Gunner	3701	HKSRA	K 9.8.42
Chiddan Lama	Naik	A5/8507	IHC	K 9.8.42
Udan Singh	Sepoy	11052	RP	K 17.8.42
Ghulam Muhammad	Sepoy	12359	RP	U 19.8.42
Habib Ullah Khan	Sepoy	19493	PJ	K 19.8.42
Amanat Khan	Gunner	5189	HKSRA	U 21.8.42
Din Muhammad	Gunner	5117	HKSRA	K 23.8.42
Shiraz Khan	Sepoy	8090	PJ	K 23.8.42
Dost Muhammad	Sepoy	13761	RP	U 25.8.42
Amir Hussain	Gunner	5149	HKSRA	K 26.8.42
Allah Ditta	Sepoy	20878	RP	U 29.8.42
Banta Singh	Gunner	7695	HKSRA	U 2.9.42
Ahmad Khan	Cook	128	HKSRA	U 5.9.42
Gurdip Singh	Havildar	2869	HKSRA	U 5.9.42
Narotam Singh	Sepoy	13831	RP	K 10.9.42
Arif Husain Khan	Sepoy	174662	HKMC	K 11.9.42
Chhote Singh	Sepoy	20787	RP	K 11.9.42
Allah Dad	Cook	248	PJ	K 12.9.42
Phinjup Lama	Amb. Sepoy	AS/18063	IHC	K 15.9.42
Khunab Gul	Sepoy	15470	PJ	K 1.10.42
Awal Singh	Sepoy	10630	RP	K 9.10.42
Gul Akbar	Sepoy	13864	PJ	K 14.10.42
Firoz Din	Gunner	5241	HKSRA	U 14.10.42
Allah Yar	Gunner	3361	HKSRA	K 16.10.42
Sahpal Singh	Sepoy	20479	RP	K 18.10.42
Muhammad Khan	Gunner	4983	HKSRA	U 19.10.42
Muhammad Din	Gunner	5294	HKSRA	K 20.10.42
Muhammad Khan	Gunner	3737	HKSRA	U 20.10.42
Fazl Khan	Driver	180536	HKMC	K 24.10.42

Karam Khan	Sepoy	11275	PJ	K 24.10.42
Kartar Singh	Cook	151	HKSRA	U 25.10.42
Fazl Haq	Gunner	8143	HKSRA	K 26.10.42
Nizam Din	Gunner	4994	HKSRA	K 26.10.42[234]
Shah Zaman	Gunner	8152	HKSRA	K 29.10.42
Farman Ali	Boy Trumpeter	7526	HKSRA	K 1.11.42
Muhammad Ashraf	Gunner	8047	HKSRA	U 2.11.42
Waryam Singh	Sepoy	9145	PJ	K 2.11.42
Niranjan Singh	Gunner	7649	HKSRA	K 3.11.42
Khushi Muhammad	Gunner	7726	HKSRA	U 4.11.42
Raghu Bir Singh	Sepoy	21052	RP	K 4.11.42
Muhammad Khan	Sepoy	19715	RP	K 7.11.42
Abdul Satar	Gunner	5155	HKSRA	U 8.11.42
Dalip Singh	Sepoy	16235	RP	K 9.11.42
Jora Singh	Gunner	4656	HKSRA	U 10.11.42
Sajawal Khan	Sepoy	19390	PJ	K 11.11.42
Mir Akbar	Sepoy	16202	PJ	K 14.11.42
Ghaus Muhammad	Gunner	2894	HKSRA	U 14.11.42
Sher Muhammad	Lance Naik	2898	HKSRA	K 14.11.42
Nur Illahi	Sepoy	19374	PJ	K 15.11.42
Sher Muhammad	Sepoy	13625	RP	K 17.11.42
Babu Singh	Sepoy	13096	RP	K 19.11.42
Muhammad Akbar	Lance Naik	173329	HKMC	K 23.11.42
Shera But Khan	Sepoy	17847	PJ	K 24.11.42
Muzaffar Khan	Gunner	5447	HKSRA	K 24.11.42
Muzaffar Khan	Sepoy	10625	RP	U 26.11.42
Balu Singh	Sepoy	13939	RP	K 28.11.42
Lakhan Singh	Sepoy	15431	RP	K 30.11.42
Mian Muhammad	Water Carrier	858	PJ	K 30.11.42
Wilayat Khan	Sepoy	19408	PJ	K 2.12.42
Ahmad Khan	Gunner	2897	HKSRA	K 3.12.42
Gian Singh	Sepoy	16209	PJ	K 5.12.42
Wali Muhammad	Gunner	4898	HKSRA	K 6.12.42
Jahan Singh	Lance Naik	10501	RP	K 9.12.42
Bahadur Sher	Havildar	11871	PJ	K 12.12.42[235]
Chhedar Singh	Sepoy	13514	RP	K 14.12.42
Muhammad Sharif	Gunner	7935	HKSRA	U 16.12.42
Muhammad Khan	Sepoy	20275	RP	K 17.12.42
Sultan Khan	Gunner	7860	HKSRA	K 19.12.42
Mir Asghar	L. Hav	11862	PJ	K 24.12.42
Fateh Muhammad	Cook	834	PJ	K 25.12.42
Muhammad Malik	Gunner	5042	HKSRA	U 25.12.42
Mukand Singh	Lance Naik	2564	HKSRA	U 28.12.42
Rakhmat Din	Lance Naik	11405	PJ	K 31.12.42

Stanley

Maranjan Singh	CV		UCWD no date
Phillips	CV	Mrs. Died in hospital	UCWD no date

Scott, M.A.	CV	Miss		UCWD no date
Smith, Mrs. J. S.	CV			UCWD no date
Bond, Charles	CV	69		UCWD 29.1.42
Stevenson, Dudley V.	CV	In French Hospital		UCWD 6.2.42
Sheppard, John Oram	Warrant Off.	117/A	HKRNVR	K 10.2.42[236]
Hutton-Potts, P.O.	CV			UCWD 11.2.42
Lossius, I.J.	CV			UCWD 19.2.42
Jackson, Herbert W.	Lance Sergeant	A/178	HKPF	K 5.4.42[237]
Martin, J.A.	CV			UCWD 6.4.42
Charrington, E.C.	CV			UCWD 12.4.42
Ogilvie, Alexander	CV	66, Piano Tuner, 6 Granville Rd., KL		UCWD 19.4.42
Fancey, John	CV	24, Clerk, 1 Carnarvon Building, KL		UCWD 20.4.42
Henriques, George	CV			UCWD 21.4.42
Simmons, Albert W.J.	CV	61		UCWD 22.4.42
Deacon, Stuart	CV	57, at Tweed Bay Hospital		UCWD 24.4.42
Fogarty, P.C.	CV	Indian Civil Service		UCWD 30.4.42
Groves, Arthur	CV	Aged 12 hours		UCWD 4.5.42
Geske, F.	CV			UCWD 5.5.42
Hall, May	CV			UCWD 15.5.42
Mitchell, Ethel	CV	63		UCWD 16.5.42
Fisher, Frederick A.W.	CV	74 ARP		UCWD 31.5.42
Peuster, P.O.	CV			UCWD 15.6.42
Denton, Camille Tweed	CV	2 months		UCWD 7.6.42
Hall, Minnie	CV			UCWD 22.6.42
Greaves, A.R.G.	CV			UCWD 4.7.42
MacNaught, John Webster	CV	80		UCWD 8.7.42[238]
Barrow, Oriana Elizabeth	CV	Aged 4 months		UCWD 9.7.42
Ross, Christine Miriam	CV	58, Mrs.		UCWD 30.7.42
Williamson, Mary	CV	75		UCWD 2.8.42
Robertson, R.C.	CV			UCWD 4.8.42
Mason, Joseph	CV	42		UCWD 5.8.42
Saunders, John Cornish	CV	74, at St Paul's (French) Hospital		UCWD 9.8.42
Peuster, W.P.	CV			UCWD 10.8.42
Dockrill, Walter Roy	CV	65, Manufacturer, 12 San Chuk Yuen Road		UCWD 11.8.42
Ellis, Leontine	Nurse	ND32	HKVDC	K 17.8.42[239]
McFerran, David Albert	CV	54, of Lamma View, Pokfulam		UCWD 18.8.42
Rapp, A.	CV			UCWD 30.8.42
Shaw, William	CV	58, Victoria Hospital, Barker Road		UCWD 5.9.42
Bush, Albert Edward	CV	48		UCWD 23.9.42
Kershaw, William	CV	45, Medical Storekeeper		UCWD 20.10.42
Burn, George Andrew	CV	65 At St Paul's Hospital		UCWD 27.10.42
Blair, Mabel Evelyn	CV	58, Mrs.		UCWD 30.10.42
Clark, Anthony	CV	Aged 12 days		UCWD 14.12.42
Lillicrap, Samuel	CV	53		UCWD 22.12.42
Macklin, Robert	CV			UCWD 22.12.42

British Army Aid Group

Cheung Po Man	L. Seaman	BAAG Died malaria Aug 42	UX 8.42[240]

1943

> We were crammed into the hold on top of coal, so closely packed together there was never room for everyone to lie down at the same time. There were three hundred men in our hold and for some days only 10 men were allowed on deck to use the latrines at one time. As many had chronic diarrhoea this was a deplorable state of affairs. Red Cross supplies were put on board for us but the Japs used them their selves and what they couldn't use they threw overboard. Our buns we took on board were soon covered with a thick greyish hairy mould. We cut the outside off and ate the rest until the mould progressed thru the buns and made us sick. Then we ate rice and were served a fish stew so rank many could not eat it and those who did were sick. But the worst of all was when heavy planks were put over the hatchways and canvas over that and we sweltered in the terrible heat down below. We tore off every article of clothing we had and fanned ourselves till we were utterly exhausted. I have a good idea now what it must have been like in the Black Hole of Calcutta or in the dark holds of African slave ships.
>
> — Private Tom Forsyth, Winnipeg Grenadiers

The year 1942 had not been kind to Hong Kong's garrison. Some 1,468 of them had died during the year — a number almost equal to the 1,500 or so who had been lost in the December 1941 fighting. Some 822 of these deaths had been immediately caused by the sinking of the *Lisbon Maru*, with others dying shortly after of the effects of the sinking. The remainder — bar those who had died of wounds incurred during the attempted defence of Hong Kong, or who had been executed after failed escape attempts — had largely succumbed to disease. Dysentery had been the biggest single killer, with diphtheria second, and the various malnutrition and avitaminosis diseases (which were a result of the totally inadequate diet of the POW) a distant third.

At the start of 1943, those POWs still in Hong Kong were spread between Argyle Street, Shamshuipo, Ma Tau Chung, and Bowen Road Hospital (where 341 patients were still hospitalized, from the 1,225 POWs who had been admitted during the year).

Ma Tau Chung's population had been greatly reduced, thanks to guard duties outside the camp, and transfers to China, but some 600 POWs were still present.

Argyle Street, holding some 700 officers and batmen/cooks, had settled down into a routine that was generally dull and dreary, though not without the occasional bright spot. Parker: "In between these experiences we would carry on with our daily routine. Wood had to be cut, vegetables cleaned and prepared for cooking, rice had to be sifted and cleaned or ground into rice flour, clothes had to be repaired. Some of the men ran a tailor shop. This crew patched and repaired clothes on an old sewing machine. Shoes had to be mended. The shoe repair shop was run by Major, the Lord Myrthyr. Although a Peer of the Realm at home, he became the best cobbler in camp and would work at his job day in and day out. He never missed a day. Have you ever had your shoes repaired by a Lord; 'Ho', well I have. Myrthyr was very much respected and admired by all. In the evenings we would invite him to talk on personalities he had known in England or on politics as he saw it. These talks were most intellectual and inspiring and we were grateful to him for helping to pass the time away for us so nicely."[1]

Shamshuipo Camp had seen the most change over the year. Reductions of nearly 2,500 men sent on drafts to Japan, and the officers and batmen/cooks to Argyle Street, had been balanced by some degree by the addition of the Canadians, Royal Navy, and others from North Point. Fortunately the diphtheria epidemic of autumn 1942 was now all but over, and mortality from all causes was reduced (for example, there would only be seven deaths from all causes in January). The other big change had resulted from the removal of the majority of the officers: the Japanese left Major Cecil Boon, RASC, in charge, and together with a number of carefully selected NCOs, he ran the camp very much in accordance with Japanese wishes.[2]

Hong Kong's enemy civlians were at Stanley Internment Camp and, for the bankers, the Sun Wah Hotel. The numbers at Stanley had been reduced by the repatriation of the Americans, but even with the American Block now housing others, overcrowding and the concomitant lack of privacy were still the main complaints of internees. In Stanley Jail, some unfortunates (such as the four failed escapees) still languished.

In China, some 30 or more *Lisbon Maru* survivors were at Kiangwan Camp near Shanghai, and over 1,000 Indians captured in Hong Kong were on Hainan Island or in Guangzhou.

And in Japan, some POWs (the majority being ex-*Lisbon Maru*) were in a number of hospitals stretching from Kokura to Osaka, while the remainder were in the camps. Those in Tokyo Main Camp (Shinagawa) were still engaged in building the replacement camp, Omori. Some of their comrades from the first draft were in Tokyo #1 Branch Camp (Oshima-cho, Kawasaki), while far more languished in Tokyo #3 Branch Camp (Yokohama Stadium). For the survivors of the *Lisbon Maru*, in Osaka #1 Branch Camp (Minato-ku, Osaka) and Osaka #2 Branch Camp (Kobe), the situation was deplorable. A further 23 men would die in the first two months of the new year, to be added to the 111 who had died in the last two and a half months of 1942.

Three more transportations to Japan during 1943, plus one to Taiwan, would further reduce the number of POWs in Hong Kong. Diseases, though not as virulent as 1942, would still account for several hundred men in Hong Kong and Japan.

By the end of the year little would have changed in Hong Kong. The civilians would still be at Stanley Internment Camp, with others at Rosary Hill (though the last bankers would have left the Sun Wah Hotel). The military POWs would still be at Shamshuipo, Ma Tau Chung and Argyle Street in Hong Kong, and Kiangwan in China. But in Japan, far more camps would be in operation. Tokyo Main Camp (Omori) would have supplanted Shinagawa (though the latter would still be operational as a POW hospital). Meanwhile, Tokyo #3 Branch Camp (Yokohama Stadium), Tokyo #3 Dispatched Camp (Tsurumi Shipyard), Tokyo #5 Branch Camp (Niigata-Rinko), Osaka #1 Branch Camp (Minato-ku, Osaka), Osaka #2 Branch Camp (Kobe), Osaka #3 Branch Camp (Oeyama), Osaka #4 Dispatched Camp (Sakurajima), Osaka #5 Dispatched Camp (Kawasaki-Juko, Kobe), Osaka #6 Dispatched Camp (Amagasaki), Fukuoka #5 Branch Camp (Omine Coal Mine, Kawasaki-machi), Nagoya #2 Branch Camp, and Hiroshima #5 Branch Camp (Innoshima) (Narumi) would all hold POWs from Hong Kong.

DIARY FOR 1943

January 1943

Saturday, 2 January. Laite: "Jan. 2, 1943. Last night we had a New Year's visit from two of our English friends, Capt. H.G. Caskeed, Chief Officer of H.M.R.F.A. Ebonol, and 2nd Engineer R.H. Nichol, of the same ship. The former is know to us as 'Jaeger', and is a great teller of stories. He has sailed into most worthwhile — and some not so worthwhile — ports of the world, and last night kept us in laughter for a while, telling us stories of Lisbon, South America, and England. He went back to farming for four years but the call of the sea was too persistent and so he went back to sea. His stories about his farming experiences are very amusing. I list a couple of his specials as 'The purchasing of a cow', 'The raising of hogs and chickens', and 'The Christmas Eve with wife away on a buying expedition'. This morning the Captain of his ship — Capt J. Solby — came in to have a game of cribbage with me. I had beaten him a few days ago, and he came to renew the attack. This was his day. Guy Walker, engineer, also visits us."

Friday, 8 January. Baird: "We were awakened at 6.30 this morning by the bugler blowing the fall-in at the 'double'. That means in a h… — of a rush — so we tumbled out of bed and put on all the clothes we possessed, because the past three days have been awfully cold, and finally landed on the big parade square. It seems they are changing the commander of the camp, who happens to be Lt. Wada, the commander we had at North Point camp. He was very decent to us there so I hope he will continue to be the same. He has just returned from Japan, having been away three months."[3] (p. 152)

Saturday, 9 January. Laite: "A number of parcels came to our camp from people in Hong Kong. Most of the 500 parcels were for the British prisoners. A few however, came for Canadians, and one was for me. It contained a 5lb tin of Apricot jam — either Canadian or English, certainly not Chinese, 7lbs beef drippings — fat, 2 lbs rolled oats, 1 tin of beef, or mutton, 1 tin of evaporated milk, and 1 cake of Palmolive soap. The other officers, and especially, Capt Walker, Bardal, and Pendregast — roommates teased me about this new lady friend — Mrs. B. Fox, 29 Pok Fulam Road, Hong Kong."[4]

Monday, 11 January. The Maryknoll missionaries, who had been released from Stanley in 1942, left Hong Kong for China in two groups, the second following on 17 January.

The Third Draft: *Tatsuta Maru*

Monday, 11 January. Laite: "On Monday the 11th we received another surprise. We were called on a special muster parade, when the men were divided into two classes, A and B. About 600 men were placed in the A class, while others were put in the B class. Others are in hospital. Now we feel that since the A group have been tested for dysentery, and inoculated against certain diseases, and separated from the rest of the camp, that it must be for a draft to be taken out of this part of China, to Japan or elsewhere, to work. Another similar group, and number has been taken from the Imperials, and they are with our A group in isolation."

Fisher was one of those in isolation in Shamshuipo: "This time huts were wired off, and the Selectees, as Boon called them, were separated from the rest of the camp. For a week we were inoculated, tested, and generally messed about. . . . The next day the same thing happened but this time the groups of 50 were marched off to the ship. However, when our turn came we found that the Japs were reading selected names only, and after three or four hours 38 of our 50 had been taken and we were not required and had to go back to the huts." (p. 49)

Monday, 11 January. O'Toole: "Monday: — a special parade. All A men told to fall out in front; later B men join them. Then the best of the C men.[5] Told to pack up and be back on parade in an hour. Told to move into Canadian lines, and wire is put around us. Stay out on the square for about three hours first. No Volunteers detailed yet."

Tuesday, 12 January. O'Toole continued: "Fairly comfortable in new temporary billet, managed to get my bed across. Bill Nichol and Bashford stay as C men: Way, Saddington, Read, Meeking, Hildersley, Bloefield and me together in No 1 party A draft. Have our throat swabbed and glass rod up the rectum to search for dysentery etc. Not very pleasant."

Wednesday, 13 January. O'Toole: "Inspection T.A.B & C combined. Still really don't know what we are on, can't be anything else but a boat. 180 volunteers put on and all those in dip segregation awaiting swabs, including Peters, this rather surprised them as some had just got over dip."

Thursday, 14 January. O'Toole: "Swab result back, would you believe it I'm positive, so off the draft, 10 of us altogether. Moved into Jubilee South & isolated. Boocock, Jeffery & myself in R.A.O.C. Can't say it worried me much, didn't really want to go. The draft were vaccinated today. I missed this of course. Feet still tiresome at night."

Friday, 15 January. Bill Lowe had tested negative: "More Arse tickling & swabbing today & we are now completely wired in — a prison in a prison. Special times (1 hr) set for communication with rest of camp. More news of advance by Russians & N. Africa. Haven't written Elah; if any silly rumours get our re our sinking en route & she knew I was on boat, then she'd worry. On other hand if I write when I get 'there', altho' it'll be a bit of a shock, she'll know I'm O.K. So will wait & see. We're all very happy, altho' wish I wasn't leaving Elah & HongKong — altho' as Ma always used to say — 'its all for the best'. So here's good health & good luck to us all & may the Devil take the rest!"

The *Tatsuta Maru* (16,975 tons and 584 feet long) had sailed on her maiden voyage between Yokohama and San Francisco in April 1930, but the transliteration of her name was changed to *Tatuta Maru* in 1938. She became a troop transport for the Japanese Navy in 1941, and would end her days two years later when sunk by a US submarine. Her sister-ship the *Asama Maru* was almost identical.

This was not a dirty old freighter like the *Lisbon Maru*; in fact, this was one of NYK's flagships. The *Asama Maru* and the *Tatsuta Maru* were two of the finest and most luxurious ocean liners ever to sail the Pacific. Japanese-designed, built in 1929, they hailed from the renowned Mitsubishi shipyard. They were multi-class ships, and had provision for cargo as well as the all-important mail. For this voyage, some lucky POWs would be allocated to cabins, but many others would be in the holds.

This third transportation departed Hong Kong on 19 January 1943, and comprised some 1,176 men. This was also the first draft that included Canadians, although only one Canadian officer (Captain John Reid, RCAMC) accompanied the men.[6]

Laite: "Yesterday morning at six o'clock they paraded out of the camp and onto the ship at Kowloon docks. Special treatment and favours had been given the men by the authorities and before leaving the camp, each man was given 10 yen in Japanese currency, a pair of socks, and a pair of woollen gloves. On their arrival at the ship they were also given candy and cigarettes, for the voyage."

Allister was one of the Canadians aboard the *Tatsuta Maru*: "All the men streamed down into the hold, it seemed to shrink. How in the world could this area, the size of a large room, hold 700 bodies? The answer was simple: it couldn't. These four airless steel walls with a bare steel floor became a giant sardine tin packed with living, squirming human creatures. There was nothing to do but take turns lying down and standing or sleeping in a sitting position. The heat rose. The air was soon foul. The food was pitifully meagre. Tommy Marsh said this was what the slave ships out of Africa must have been like." (p. 90)

Tom Marsh himself recounted: "We were poured down the hatch and into the hold like so much coal. There were no bunks, nothing but steel walls and stanchions. We were packed so tight that there was no room to lie down. I sat on the metal stairs that went up to the hatch for three days it took to get to Nagasaki. Guards were mounted above and kept a constant watch over us. We thought of submarines but worried little. We were a miserable bunch. I thought of my boyhood and the stories I had read of the old slavers that sped through the night with their cargo of slaves battened down in filthy and stifling holds. I never thought then that I should live to experience something very similar."

Friday, 22 January. Lowe was one of the Volunteers who, like the Canadians, were in the holds: "Spent 2 uneventful days on board. Sleeping is pretty rotten in the hold & it's damned crowded, big arc light shining on us all night. Not too bad, queue for chow, washing & bogs. Arrived Nagasaki at noon, ashore at 6 pm."

Sydney Skelton of the Royal Rifles of Canada: "Landed at Nagasaki, disembarked at dark. Japs presented us with six of the nicest scones we've tasted since leaving Canada."[7]

Upon arrival, these men would be divided into separate parties and taken by train from Nagasaki to five different camps:
- Fukuoka #5 Branch Camp (Omine Coal Mine, Kawasaki-machi)
- Hiroshima #5 Branch Camp (Innoshima)
- Osaka #4 Dispatched Camp (Sakurajima)
- Osaka #6 Dispatched Camp (Amagasaki)
- Tokyo #3 Dispatched Camp (Tsurumi Shipyard, Kawasaki 3D)

Skelton himself was sent to Fukuoka #5B, Omine. On 24 January he noted: "Then marched to station and boarded a train for interior. Trip was a tough one, everyone who had 'hot feet' had to keep same out of windows all the way. Breakfast on train was a small 'Bento' (worker's box) containing rice, fish and different sorts of Japanese greens with a set of chop sticks each. Changed trains at 'Orio' and 'Ita' and finally detrained at Kawasaki. Marched through drab, filthy looking streets, couple of men weak from trip dropped to side of road and were kicked and prodded-on by the slant eyed monkeys. I was all in myself but as we all know to stop only meant a hammering and being kicked about. Finally we reached what looked to be a school ground (presence of children made me come to this conclusion) and lined up, numbered and about 10 Japs rambled off some bloody speech on how we should conduct our selves. (Could see slag heaps not far off, so it looks like mine work.) Looking on hill above us, I could see the camp fence, 9 foot high running right around, barbed on top. Order to move was given and I was in one of first groups to enter Prison Yard. We were taken into a two storied building: shoes were removed and placed in lockers. From here, we were shown our rooms: 8 men to a room, blankets and mattresses, mat flooring to sleep on. The place was clean and looked very comfortable after the filth we had been living in for a year. I was very tired and about to try and catch a nap when someone said 'there's a hot bath that will hold about 60 men'. So away we went and what a grand feeling to bath in hot water again. Relieved and tired, sat down for smoke and then fell sound asleep for some time. Next I was awakened and told we were to go to have dinner. We came into clean mess hall, long tables all ready set with soup made of meat, potatoes and carrots. Butter and scones. We thoroughly enjoyed this after which was another roll call, then to bed and oh how I am tired."

Bill Lowe of the HKVDC was on the train to Hiroshima #5B, Innoshima: "Got tea & cakes on shore, left by train at 11.30 for a 'place where they make parts of ships'! There are 100 of us (85 volunteers) in charge of W.O. Fable. Good train journey & good chow, together with Ken. Japs quite decent to us. Arrived at Onomichei about 3 & walked thro' town to ferry. Got to Mitshinosho at 5 pm. Walked a short distance & got to camp where we found RAF chaps (100). Don't seem a bad crowd, but look funny dressed in Jap uniforms. Had a bath (hot) & loaf of bread (small) fish, soup, rice & so to bed. Weight 70 kilos."[8]

In charge at Sakurajima was Warrant Officer I James Eugene Fryer, 7th Heavy Anti Aircraft Regiment, Royal Artillery. Robert Bede Moore of the Dockyard Police was in the group sent here: "I was put to work in a ship yard, the 'Osaka Iron Works' building oil tankers and landing barges."[9]

James Hart, RASC, was one of those sent to Amagasaki: "Of the 200 of us who went to Amagasaki we were made up of Royal Navy, RAF, Royal Scots, RAOC, RASC, RC of S. Surgeon Commander J A Page RN who was in charge of our group. WOI Grace RAOC was the Senior NCO. We docked in Nagasaki. All of the POWs as far as I know left in trains to various destinations. Our party left the day we docked at night time, getting to Amagasaki the next evening. We had two stops on the journey where we collected food rations. Our last stop before Amagasaki was Kobe. Our party all worked at the Atana factory doing various jobs, unloading barges that had coal, iron ore, and other items for the furnaces. Some on lathe machines or other types of machinery. We had our midday meal in the factory. Amagasaki, what we could see of it, was not too large, but one building about three or four storeys high was made of stone. 95% of the houses were made of timber."[10]

Marsh was in the party of Canadians dispatched to Tokyo #3D: "The following afternoon we reached Tokyo and pulled into the huge modern station. We were detrained and marched a short distance to another train, passing through a subway in doing so. It must have been suppertime for the station platforms were crowded with Japanese commuters, each almost an exact replica of the other. Cheap fedora hat with feather in brim, dirty white collar, black string tie, black morning coat, baggy gray pants, white dirty socks and Oxfords or rubber canvas shoes. Here we had the white-collar brigade, each a caricature of a London banker. They swarmed about the platform like beetles. They pushed and swayed. Some were eager to see the prisoners while others were more concerned in keeping their feet and position. I saw several fall off the platforms onto the tracks and scurry to get back before the trains came. I saw few women."

Marsh continued: "Finally we came to a small station on the outskirts of Yokohama. Here we detrained and were told to get our bags. All was confusion. The guards gave us no time to find our own bags and cuffed us around. At least our luggage was put on a couple of trucks, and with a Jap officer on horse back in the lead, we marched two miles to our new camp. The district was a poor one and given over to industry. Everything looked dirty and dilapidated. There were bits of rusty machinery scattered around and evidently a lot of small sheds were used to house machines that did subcontract work for the shipyard nearby. We saw few people. Our camp was in a factory yard enclosed on one side by a steel works and the other by a refinery. In this yard had been recently built two large buildings 120 ft. long by 35 ft. wide. Each of these housed 250 men. There was a five foot passage down the middle of each bay that ran crossways to the hut. These huts were built of flimsy material, mostly bamboo and laminated wood. The roof was of gray clay tile and was so heavy that after a few weeks the building sagged. Few of the windows opened. The beds were wooden platforms covered with a grass mat and divided by strips of wood. The floor was dirt mixed with lime but it had already crumbled in many places."

Leo Berard arrived at the same camp: "The buildings of Kawasaki 3D were built of boards of rough lumber. There was no floor; the aisles were dirt. The sleeping areas were raised approximately sixteen inches and made of rough lumber and covered with straw matting. Each man's space was separated by a wooden lath giving each man a two-foot-wide by seven-foot-long area. There was one wooden shelf above each spot where you could put your personal things." (p. 116)

Berard continued: "The left wing housed the Grenadiers and the right wing housed the Royal Rifles. RSM Oscar Keenan WG, and RSM Leslie Shore Royal Rifles each had a small private area from where they were responsible for supervising the men. Captain Reid was the doctor."[11]

Lionel Speller: "[Reid] was the only Canadian officer that was sent to Japan. And if you can imagine with nothing to work with, and I mean nothing, and to look after 500 men and be the Camp Commandant, the liaison between the Japs and us, nobody, but nobody, could have done better. Dr. Reid was another Birchall as far as I'm concerned. Although he wasn't the man that would stick up his fists and fight, he wasn't that type. He tried to do it with diplomacy and words. But if there was ever a man that should have got their DSO or their DCM it was Dr. Reid because, I don't care, you'd have to be something out of this world to do the job he did after we went to Japan."[12]

January 1943: Continued

More than 3,500 POWs had now been shipped to Japan, or had perished on the way.

Monday, 25 January. Lowe was at Innoshima: "Had photographs taken, the camp is well situated right on sea shore on an island. Hills all round, well wooded & a small village near by. No signs whatever of war. Chow good. Fish, Orange trees."

From Innoshima, the main working parties would be: Karoto Foundry, Habu Docks, and Mitsumosho. While the Canadians at Tokyo #3D had been lucky enough to have been accompanied by Captain Reid, those at Innoshima were glad to have Corporal 'Dai' Mogford, RAMC. As Lowe said: "We were extraordinarily fortunate in having Mogford with us for he was a man of outstanding quality." RAMC professionals, and their naval equivalents, were in much demand in Japan.

At Kobe House, the work parties for the ex-*Lisbon Maru* POWs continued: Minatagowa (known as *Iron Ore*); Toya Steel (an iron foundry); Showa Denki (known as *Graphite* — "it's a dirty job but there is a nice little train ride to it. All I did all day was to unravel rope"); Kamigumi's ("we were unloading two hundred pound sacks of Copra");[13] Mitsubishi Takehome (known as *Tacky's*); Dai Ichi Shinko (known as *Rice Ball Rubber*); Higashinada (known as the *Coal Job*); Itsumigumi's (known as *Sweets*); Ohamigumi's ("ten men and myself are sent to unload a barge of half burned flax"); Senpakoo (unloading ships); Jam (warehouse); Bran, Kobeco, Sumitomo's, and others.

However, at Fukuoka #5B, for example, the work was mining. Dockyard work, for those with the nerve, offered sometimes huge opportunities for the pilfering of vital food stuffs; factories might at least present some chances; but mines offered none.

February 1943

Tuesday, 2 February. Martin Weedon[14] at Kobe House: "Out with working party for first time. Five officers out daily. By electric train to Osaka where we marched to Yoshihara oil refinery. Through narrow little streets — all the houses made of wood, quite picturesque, but God help them if ever bombed with incendiaries." (p. 36)

Saturday, 13 February. Lavarie died at Tokyo #3D. Marsh: "Gradually the number in our section declined. One at a time they sickened and were removed to the hospital, never to return. We were down to four. A chap named Roy Robinson, who was a particular friend as he came from my home district. Another named Lavarie and one other made up our group. We four discussed the demise of the others and one day, feeling miserable, I predicted that I would be the next to go. Roy would not have it and urged hanging on although he was actually weaker then myself. Lavarie said very little and soon after sickened and was taken away and died. This left only three in our bay."

Tuesday, 23 February. BAAG's Waichow Intelligence Summary No. 20[15] noted that three further parties of Indians had been successfully brought out:

No. 2910 Havildar MEHDI KHAN[16]
No. 4830 Gunner ATTA SINGH
No. 7620 Gunner KARKAIL SINGH

"These men met 21 at KWANTI Race Course and were escorted to safety. Judgement on Hav. MEHDI KHAN should be suspended pending a further report from this H.Q. as I doubt if he has carried out his orders correctly concerning the passing of information from this Office to other Indians, because he was afraid. There is nothing to indicate that he is anyway pro-Japanese, but I would not say that rightly or wrongly he would not trust many of his fellow Indians in Hong Kong."

No. 2338 Jemadar (A/Subadar) DADAN KHAN. 4th Medium Battery R.A., H.K.S.R.A. 1st H.K. Regt. R.A.
No. 2769 Jemadar SADARA SINGH, 36th Coast Battery R.A. 8th Coast Regt. R.A.
No. 4902 Havildar NAIMAT ALI, 2nd Mountain Battery R.A. 1st H.K. Regt. R.A.
No. 3934 Naik JAGAT SINGH, 17th A.A., 5th A.A. Regt.
No. 3708 Naik CHANGAHL SINGH, 36th Coast Battery, 8th Coast Regt. R.A.
No. 3680 Naik ABDUL RASHID 25th Battery, 1st H.K. Regt

"These men were met by 61 at SHATIN PASS and came via the sea route."

No. 3896 Gunner MADHO SINGH 12th Coast Bty., 8th Coast Regt. R.A.
BASAT SINGH

The latter was: "a civilian from LIN MA HANG Mine who came out against orders, they have been in touch with one of our Agents for some time and it was intended to use them as contacts and a promise was given that they would be brought out in due course. However, the other two Indian soldiers at LIN MA HANG (names and numbers will be forwarded) said they did not want to come as they were having too good a time and it is therefore unreasonable to expect men willing to come to risk their chances by staying with men who have every reason to inform the Japanese. Apart from the refusal of the above soldiers to leave enemy territory, there is reason to believe that these men have given the Japanese a description of 21 and 12 and the names of their villages, which the Japanese raided but found that the families of both had left for WAICHOW some months ago. Further reports will be obtained from the remaining escapees, if time permits, before transport and passes are arranged; failing this, may we please be given a copy of their statements which will be checked."

This report also noted that BAAG Agent "89 reports that most Indians in CANTON area have been transferred to LAU FAN KIU, a bridge on the Northern outskirts of CANTON City", and gave the following list of the locations of Indian POWs at this date:

The following is a list of the positions of Indian Soldiers Prisoners of War, who were captured on the fall of Hongkong, as supplied by escaped Indian P.O.Ws. It will be noted that they give the number of men in MA TAU CHING as 500. INT/H.Q./215b dated 4.Feb.43, gives a figure of between 200 and 300. However, I consider, in the absence of any authoritative information, our figure of 400 given in W.I.S. No.16 dated 14 Jan.43, is more likely to be the most reliable figure.

(1) 150 men (50 R.A. and 100 men of the 2/14th) in ARGYLE STREET, HOMANTIN. KOWLOON. Officers: Jemadar SARSA KHAN (R.A.) Jemadar KHAN SHERIN (?) (2/14th Punjab).
(2) 200 men of the 5/7th Rajputs in CARNARVON ROAD and CHATHAM ROAD. Officer: Subedar Major NAIN SINGH
(3) 120 men of the R.A. in a house between AUSTIN ROAD and AUSTIN AVENUE, opposite H.K.S.R.A. Orderly room, with Jemadar SADHU SINGH.
(4) 50 men of the R.A. in a house South of ST. MARY'S Church School in CHATHAM ROAD, with Havildar FARMAN ALI.
(5) 30 men of the 5/7th Rajputs in KAI TAK Aerodrome, Kowloon City.
(6) 70 men of the 2/14th Punjabis in FANLING area. Officers: Subedar KHAWAS KHAN. Jemadar HASHAM KHAN.
(7) 30 men of the R.A. and 2/14th in SHEUNG SHUI, under charge of Havildar NUR KHAN.
(8) 40 men of the R.A. and 2/14th in Murray Barracks, Hongkong. Officer: Jemadar MUNSHI KHAN
(9) 40 men of the R.A. in Lye Mun Barracks with Jemadar FARZAND ALI.
(10) 5 men in Rubber Factory in MA TAU WEI ROAD, Kowloon City District.
(11) 40 men of the R.A. in Aberdeen Industrial School.
(12) 20 men in Au Tau Government School under charge of Havildar GHULAM MOH'D.
(13) 30 men in UN LONG Market.
(14) 44 men of the 2/14th Rajputs[17] at Tsun Wan Humes Pipe Coy. Officer: Jemadar MUCHUL HAZ.
(15) 10 men of the R.A. in GREEN ISLAND Cement Coy., KOWLOON
(16) 10 men of the R.A. in PAKTAI STREET in a Storehouse.
(17) 200 men of the 2/14th and Royal Naval Yard Police in KENNEDY TOWN, under Jemadar SHAMBU RAM.
(18) 40 men in Stanley Church.
(19) 25 men of the R.A. in New Magazine in ABERDEEN.
(20) 47 men of the R.A. in Hong Kong University under Havildar MOHAMED ANWER.

(21) 22 men of the R.A. near Mong Kok Ferry Wharf.
(22) 23 men of the R.A. in Yaumati Public Dispensary.
(23) 3 men of the 2/14th in Gas Company's Drum Yard in TOKWA WAN ROAD, HUNG HOM.
(24) 40 men of the 2/14th in Kowloon Docks, HUNG HOM.
(25) 3 men of the R.A. at the Taikoo Sugar Refinery Coy., Hongkong.
(26) 5 men of the R.A. at the British & American Tobacco Factory, HONGKONG.
(27) 2 men of the R.A. at Hongkong Hotel's Garage in MAGAZINE GAP ROAD.
(28) 5 men of the R.A. in the Rope Factory, KENNEDY TOWN, HONGKONG.
(29) 10 men of the 2/14th at TYTAM Water Works, HONGKONG.
(30) 5 men of the R.A. at LIN MA HANG Mines in New Territories.
(31) 3 men of the 2/14th in Telephone Building in NATHAN ROAD, KOWLOON.
(32) 5 men of the 2/14th Punjab in Old Kowloon Magistracy in SHANGHAI STREET, YAUMATI, KOWLOON.
(33) 5 men (4 of the 5/7th and 1 of the R.A.) at Gas Works in JORDAN ROAD, KOWLOON.
(34) 4 men of the R.A. at Dairy Farm and Cold Storage, WANCHAI.
(35) 15 men of the 2/14th Punjab in Officers Mess Jubilee Fort.
(36) 215 men of the R.A. sent to HAINAN ISLAND.
(37) 500 men in MA TAU CHUNG Camps, KOWLOON.
(38) 1,300 men in CANTON.

The above information received from the Indian P.O.W.s escaped from Hong Kong on 22 Feb. 43. The total number of Indian Soldiers P.O.W.s as given above is 3,368.

Sunday, 28 February. Lowe at Innoshima: "Had snow during the month & has been cold. The Hong Kong lads saw snow & ice for the first time in their lives & were very excited about it. We get rice & soup & occasionally a little bread. For 185 men we get 56 kilos rice a meal, which is about 9–10 oz per man. Also get fish (quite good salmon) & vegetables."

Sunday, 28 February. Weedon at Kobe: "Ninety-six of sick, including most of hospital and RAMC, taken away to new camp, reputed to be housed in hills above Kobe. Ewan Graham and Bowles both taken." (p. 41)

Sunday, 28 February. Poulter at Kobe: "Spent all day spring-cleaning. Our hospital is going to move up into the hills to a place called Kawasaki.

Evidently these little horrors are getting a shake on over this proposed visit by the Red Cross People."[18] This new camp was Osaka #5D (Kobe Kawasaki).

March 1943

Ian Macgregor in Argyle Street: "When Neville Thursby asked me to provide a book of Cocktail Recipes as a prize in his lottery, my directions for his immediate future were as frank as they were explicit.

'Why,' I asked him, 'must you pick on me? I despise Cocktails. What self-respecting Wine Merchant doesn't? And even if I liked them, why should I add yet another Reference Book to the World's overburdened supply?'

'Balloons,' said Neville. 'You're a Wine and Spirit Merchant — an utterly unscrupulous one too. And besides, one cannot have too much of a good thing.'

'You're telling me,' said I, 'but you can have too little, and I've been a teetotaller under compulsion for over two years. I can hardly rely on a 'rice memory' for more than one or two recipes.'

'Well, do the best you can then,' was his unhelpful reply. And that is exactly what I have done.' "[19]

Friday, 5 March. Forsyth at Shamshuipo: "Rumor has it that the Japs asked the Indian troops to volunteer for service with them, and when they refused they starved them for a week till they finally gave in. Then 150 of them were put to guard an airfield in the New Territories and one night they all disappeared."

Wednesday, 17 March: At Stanley camp, Sir Vandeleur Grayburn and Edmonston of the Bank were arrested.[20]

Saturday, 20 March. Forsyth: "Garnet Stodgell died early this morning of dysentery, pellagra and malnutrition."

Sunday, 21 March. Lance Naik Raja Khan: "On 29.12.41 the Japanese moved us to North Point Camp, and on 24.1.42 we were taken to Ma Tau Chung Camp where all the Indian POW were interned. The Japanese treatment of everyone in this camp was very bad. On 4.7.42 I was sent to Canton and attached to the 1st Bty. which was doing fatigue duties for a Japanese air unit. We were continually being pressed to take up arms for the Japanese and conditions were quite intolerable. I was therefore very glad when Hav. Mohd. Akbar asked me if I wished to join him in escaping. He made all the plans and on 21.3.43 he told us he was ready and that evening we made a successful get-away."[21]

The escaped were:

Iftikhar Ali	C.H. Major	9361	5/7th Rajput
Karam Bux	Havildar	3085	1st HK Regt HKSRA
Mohamed Akbar	Havildar	3181	1st HK Regt HKSRA
Raja Khan	Lance Naik	5336	8th Coastal Regt R.A.
Bahadur Ali	Lance Naik	179769	HK Mule Corps
Said Umran	Driver	180694	HK Mule Corps
Mohamed Amir	Sepoy	16231	5/7th Rajput
Nasir Ahmed	Gunner	5348	8th Coastal Regt RA
Sultan Ali	Gunner	5351	8th Coastal Regt RA

April 1943

Thursday, 1 April. Forsyth: "Old J.J. Davis died of heart failure. Went to a lecture tonight entitled 'God in Education'. While it was in progress we could hear strains of music and wild cries from a nearby hut where a square dance was in full swing."

Thursday, 1 April. BAAG received Message F/5 from Douglas Ford in Shamshuipo, dated 1 April 1943.[22]

Herewith Camp strengths etc. with comparative figures:

UNIT	FIT	SICK B.	SICK C.	HOSP.	
HKVDC	232	139	204	69	644
DOC	2	–	47	16	65
RASC	15	2	26	11	54
12 (C) RA	–	–	6	5	11
8 (C) RA	6	–	7	5	18
R. Navy	8	10	26	11	55
AEC	–	–	3	1	4
MIDD'X	14	7	14	14	49
CMP	–	–	6	–	6
5th AA	6	–	39	17	62
RE	9	7	5	8	29
MER. SER.	1	1	7	1	10

RAF	4	3	15	7	29
RAOC	5	4	11	6	26
RAPC	–	–	8	5	13
CIVILIANS	5	2	4	5	16
R.SCOTS	12	6	13	14	45
RC of S	2	5	4	–	11
RNYP	7	–	2	3	12
RAMC	33	–	2	3	38
CANADIANS	235	80	120	270	705
TOTAL	596	266	574	471	1902
1-3-43	507	325	654	396	1882
25.1.43	340	240	767	525	1872

These figures are exclusive of officers:-
Imperials — 13 combatants, 10 Medical and 50 Merchant Service and Army Corps.
Canadians — 59 combatants, 5 Medical, and 4 Padres and Entertainment Officers.
(Total Camp strength — 2048)
Cheerio and Good Luck.

Sunday, 11 April. Bob Moore's postcard from Sakurajima read: "Dear Mother, I am interned in the Camp mentioned overleaf, and am in good health. I am working daily for pay — this helps to pass the time away. Take good care of yourself. Remember me to all the family and friends. Goodbye for now and may God Bless you till we meet again. Hoping to hear from you soon. Your Loving Son, BOB."

Monday, 12 April. BAAG Agent 60 (George Kotwall, ex-3 Coy HKVDC), engaged in trying to organize the escape of Captain Ansari[23] from Ma Tau Chung Camp, attended a meeting of the Indian Independence League, but was betrayed. He was arrested by the Japanese on the 21st, and taken to Central Police Station. There he would be tortured and executed, but the Japanese now knew about his contacts in Ma Tau Chung.[24]

Tuesday, 13 April. O'Toole at Shamshuipo: "81 in from Bowen Road most of the crippled, Sgt Nunn R.E. who lost a leg was with them, have been fitting up a couple of huts in the hospital compound for them to live in. Had my first hot bath in the Japanese type wash house which they have built for us . . . The half hut I am in now has 19 people. Roussel (dockyard), Morosov (RE) in bunk. Bill Nichol, Bashford (bunk),

Moores, Napalof, O'Toole, Hogart Sgt, Graff, Nicols, Tilison, Bonney (The Rev), Webb, Crabb, Pugh, Mr Haynes, Hall (dockyard), Felix Love, Hill R.E., and Buckley just in from Bowen Road."

Friday, 16 April: BAAG received a message from Ma Tau Chung:

> The following message from Capt. ANSARI 5/7 Rajputs who is a prisoner in [Ma Tau Chung], was received at this A.H.Q. through NARANJAN SINGH and 19 on 16 Apr. 43:
>
> INKY CUSTODIAN OVERHAULED ALIVE AND KICKING. STOPPED TWO FROM LYEMUN RIGHT WING. ALWAYS READY TO RUSH OUT OF THE RING TO STOP A LONG ONE.[25]

Sunday, 25 April.   Laite: "Today I received a gift from Dr. P. S. Selwyn-Clark, 2 Naka, Meizi Dori, Hong Kong, consisting of 1 large tin Marmalade, 1 tin Beef Dripping, 1 tin Rolled Oats, 1 tin Chocolates, and 1 tin Hot Cross Buns. I shared the chocolates with the officers of our unit. Then I passed the tin to Lt Blackwood, he said, 'No! Padre, it can't be. It is just a mirage I see and not the real thing'."

But Selwyn-Clarke's opportunities for doing good would shortly be curtailed. In parallel, following the arrest of Agent 60, the whole carefully assembled BAAG communication network was about to crumble.

May 1943

Sunday, 2 May.   Selwyn-Clarke was arrested at St Paul's Hospital. Selwyn-Clarke: "I was told that I was under arrest as the head of the British espionage in Hong Kong, that I had been sending messages to the British Army Aid Group in Free China and to Mr. John Reeves, the British Consul in Macao, and that these messages concerned the damage caused to Japanese ships by the U.S. Pacific Fleet, the movement of Japanese troops, and other such matters."[26] (p. 83) He was taken to nineteen months solitary confinement, the first ten being in a cell under the Supreme Court, undergoing regular 'interrogation'.

Ansari was also arrested.

Saturday, 8 May.   To most POWs, unaware of the events going on around them, life continued on as normal. Baird: "Your letter of May 10 arrived today, also one from Mother, just one year after you wrote it.[27] You have no idea how wonderful it was to receive it, also Mother's. I got Jack Norris to read them to me and I wore my dark glasses so the old tears wouldn't be too evident. This scrawl may not be legible. However, I must try and express my feelings of happiness at hearing from you. I am sorry to hear of your Uncle Jim's death and Harvey Sanderson at Pearl Harbor."[28] (p. 168)

June 1943

Tuesday, 1 June. Poulter at Kobe: "The first day of June and reveille is now at 5am. It won't be long now before it's not necessary to go to bed in order to be up in time for work! Great excitement on the job today several of the men found some bottles that look as though they may contain wine. They sampled them and had a reasonable drink, all except Titch Coomer, he got really stinko. We got him back to camp OK and when the Jap sentry asked what was wrong with him I told him that he had Malaria!"

Sunday, 6 June. Forsyth: "Old Dave Johnston (a veteran of world War 1. He had a silver plate in his head from the Battle of Vimy Ridge) went into camp hospital, has lost a lot of weight." He died the following evening.

The Sun Wah Hotel was finally closed, and the last bankers moved to Stanley Internment Camp.[29]

Monday, 7 June. BAAG received information that there had been 173 arrests in total in Hong Kong, of POWs and civilians, both Chinese and 'enemy aliens' still outside the camps. "At the time of the recent arrests the French Hospital was surrounded for one week. Drs. SELWYN-CLARKE, BUNJEE, NICOLSON and other of their associates were all detained and interrogated. The first 3 were taken to Gendarmerie H.Q. BUNJEE was manhandled and fainted. In addition, Dr. Arthur WOO, K.C. YEO, Dr. WAH (?) and 'other doctors', GEORGE SHEE, B. RANDALL. HELEN HO, and DOROTHY LEE were all detained on suspicion of being involved in recent escapes and having contacts with us. Dr. ARTHUR WOO is said to have been charged with having concealed some RADIUM from the Japanese authorities and later to have been released. Our informant also reports the arrest of D.C. EDMONSTON, FATHER P.JOY and 3 other

Jesuits, T.C. MONAGHAN, CHESTER BENNET, M.A. DA SILVA, G. VANBERGEN, RUDY CHOA, and TYNDALL and adds that TYNDALL and HYDE have been tortured."[30] (p. 56)

Friday, 11 June. Fisher at Shamshuipo: "We have just learned that the Indian volunteers[31] imprisoned in Ma Tau Kok have been released (there were only nine of them). Of course, we wondered if this is a prelude to the Portuguese getting their freedom and this camp being finally disintegrated."

Sunday, 27 June. From Kobe, Bill Poulter wrote home: "Dear Doffa, I am alive and well, in fact everything is O.K. Don't worry, tell Robin to be a good boy. So long my love, I'll be seeing you soon. All my love to you both. WILLIAM POULTER."

Monday, 28 June. Arrests began in Stanley, connected to the discovery of secret radios. Stanley Rees, William John Anderson, James L. Anderson, W.R. Scott, John Fraser and others were taken into Stanley Gaol.[32]

July 1943

Thursday, 1 July. Fisher at Shamshuipo: "A typical trick was pulled off so that Colonel Price, officer commanding Canadians, and Captain Valentine, officer commanding Hong Kong VDC could not contact Kindell.[33] Just before Kindell arrived the two commanding officers were sent for by Boon. He was not in his office so they had to wait, and while they waited the party of about eight Japanese and Boon with Kindell in the middle went round the camp." (p. 59)

On the same day, the BAAG group in Shamshuipo was arrested: Gray, Routledge and Hardy; and at Argyle Street, Lt. Haddock and Manuel Prata.

Saturday, 10 July. Douglas Ford at Shamshuipo, and Newnham at Argyle Street, were arrested.[34]

Sunday, 11 July. Fisher at Shamshuipo: "A popular Royal Scots officer has suddenly been taken out of camp and we don't know why — maybe a diary has been found." (p. 61)

Monday, 12 July. Weedon at Kobe: "News leaked out that all officers but eight being moved to separate camp at the end of month. Don't like idea of separating from O.R.s at this stage, especially as no Mx. Officers included in eight remaining behind." (p. 58) In fact the rumours were incorrect — though non-*Lisbon Maru* officers were sent to Zentsuji (Hiroshima #1B) — and six ex-*Lisbon Maru* officers appear to have been sent from Osaka to Zentsuji at this time.

Wednesday, 14 July. Laite: "On Wednesday Staff Sgt McNaughton had a birthday. He is about 55 but says he is 21 — or rather this is his 21st birthday, so he, with Sgt Pugsley, challenged Barnett and I, to a game of cribbage, and we beat them in two rubbers, three out of five games, and two out of three. What fun we had. I told him that I didn't have the heart to tell him how sorry I was, but that I would later write him a letter of sympathy. However since we had a few eggs on hand, we saved a few slices of our day's ration of bun, and give him egg sandwiches, to celebrate his natal day, and our victory. Before leaving, I put a black band around his arm, by which he could announce to the other sgts, his defeat."

Friday, 16 July. In Hong Kong, twenty-three men, including fifteen senior officers with Maltby amongst them, were separated from the other prisoners, under suspicion of being involved in the BAAG affair.

Tuesday, 20 July. Laite: "I had a very interesting evening with Pte Marsh of Middlesex Regt, who was with his regiment in France as a truck driver. He was through the whole show until after the evacuation from Dunkirk. High tribute was paid by him to the Guards' Brigade which held up the German Army at Abbeville, three miles from Dunkirk, and so made the evacuation possible. He later spent three months in London, during the awful raids. He later came here, and was through the show with us. We did have a laugh when he told me that on the tip — $1.00 Canadian, or $3.25 H.K. — which I gave him on the day of our landing from Canada, for taking our grips, and us along to the Peninsula Hotel, he got drunk."

On the same day, in Japan, the new Tokyo Main Camp at Omori was finished, and the POWs at Shinagawa — who had arrived on the first draft from Hong Kong — were moved into their new accommodation:

Bertram described the new camp thus:[35] "The barrack huts at Omori were of a standard Japanese military pattern. They were wooden sheds about thirty yards long, with small 'bunks' at either end occupied by officers, barrack commanders, and the like. The barrack itself had a length of perhaps twenty yards over all, with double decks of sleeping space on either side of a narrow central aisle made of damp packed earth. Boots were discarded on a shelf at ground level, and the occupants then scrambled into the lower deck, or climbed perpendicular wooden ladders to the upper deck some four feet beneath the roof."

The main work parties from Omori were: Mitsubishi (warehouse); Shiodome (railway, with the hancho being Peter Paul, RN, of HMS *Thracian*); Shibaura (railway, with the hancho being Topper Brown); Onagi (railway); the beach (construction at local naval depot); Tokyo Sempaku (unloading boats); Sumidagawa 'the coconut job' (railway, which would later become a separate camp).

But these first POWs from Hong Kong maintained their unique survival rate. Bertram: "Omori at all times presented the amazing spectacle of a prison camp under the strictest discipline — and often, for months at a time when Watanabe was on the rampage, under a genuine reign of terror — in which the prisoners as a matter of course cheerfully condescended to their captors, and never for a moment left them in any doubt as to who were the better men. Welsh miners and London cockneys and Irish seamen, half-starved and sweated like coolies on the docks and railways of Tokyo, they were somehow on top of the Japanese throughout the piece. They stayed on top, too, though they were knocked silly for their pains."[36] (p. 146)

About the same time, Lieutenant Hill was moved from Shinagawa to Hiroshima #1B. There he was grouped with other Hong Kong officers who had come over on the *Lisbon Maru*. After this, the Shinagawa site would become the well-known POW hospital for the Tokyo area.

August 1943

Goodwin: "Plans of escape were constantly under review. Sometimes alliances were half formed, but those were always finally discarded because of my belief that a solo effort was the only one that had a reasonable chance of success. Only once was a partnership almost completed, when Brigadier Wallis of the headquarters staff suggested that we join forces. Our place and method of departure had been agreed, and our attempt was waiting upon suitable weather when the Japanese again interfered. It was decreed that all officers of the rank of colonel and above should be sent to Formosa, and my partner was included in the draft."[37] (p. 27)

The 'Special' Draft

Wednesday, 4 August. There was a 'special' draft of fourteen senior officers (previously implicated in the BAAG affair) and their batmen, twenty-one in all, to Taiwan. On board were:

Keble Andrews-Levinge	Lt.-Col.	Commanding RASC
Leveson G.B. Campbell	Captain	DSO
Esmond H.M. Clifford	Colonel	Command RE
Alfred C. Collinson	Commander	Commanding RN
Charles Eric Earnshaw	Private	RAPC
William Fairburn	Stoker	RN
Noel Forde	Colonel	Commanding RAPC
John Hastings	Private	RASC
Gilbert Rivers Hopkin	Colonel	OBE Commanding RAOC
Hugh J. Kilpatrick	Colonel	Financial Advisor General List
Christopher Maltby	Major General	MC
Torquil McCleod	Brigadier	CBE Commanding RA
Frank Burt Minhinnick	Eng. Captain	OBE
Andrew Peffers	Brigadier	CBE Admin.
George Henry Ropers	Marine	RN
Henry Barron Rose[38]	Colonel	MC Commanding HKVDC
John Thomas Simpson	Colonel	Commanding RAMC
Fred Wright Smith	Private	RASC
Graham Fred Tanner	Private	RASC
Cedric Wallis	Brigadier	MC
Harry G. Winkworth[39]	Private	Middlesex

Maltby's party of twenty-one arrived at Shirakawa Camp on 9 August, but that of Governor Sir Mark Young and his batman Waller would not arrive until 12 September. From there, they would be flown to Japan in October 1944, then to Shenyang, China.

August 1943: Continued

Sunday, 8 August. O'Toole at Shamshuipo: "Another draft about 546 men. GMP. AA. RAF. Re's, and Canadians, no fuss at all just paraded & segregated. 24 yen now certain but must wait until draft goes. Hope I don't have to leave here couldn't stick cold weather, quite happy here with plenty to do. Strange that I never get a letter, hope they know at home I am a POW. Balls rather sore itch like hell, scratch them at night & gets skin off & they weep. Tiger Balm might fix up when money comes."

Saturday, 14 August. Forsyth: "I am one of 430 warned of a draft to Japan, 330 Canadians, 25 Dutch Navy, remainder are Imperials."

They embarked on Sunday, the 15th.

The Fourth Draft: *Manryu Maru*

The fourth draft left Hong Kong on 15 August 1943 with 470 men.

Initially it was to include a Canadian Chaplain, a doctor, Captain Howard Bush, RCASC, one company officer each from the Royal Rifles of Canada and the Winnipeg Grenadiers, plus Lewis Bush of the HKRNVR. In the end, the only officer to be sent was Lewis Bush. Lewis Bush had been kept at Stanley as a 'dangerous spy' until moving to Shamshuipo Camp in March 1943 where he was put in charge of the Naval Unit.

Bush: "Just after dawn on August 15th, 1943, we assembled on the parade ground for our march to the pier at Kowloon Docks . . . We formed into units, myself at the head of the column, and at 7 o'clock marched through the gate out in to the main road. Two trucks brought up the rear with our kit and these were soon filled with those unable to walk."[40]

Not surprisingly, Bush was unknown to the Canadians in the draft. Forsyth: "The mystery man on board was Sub. Lieut. Bush of the British Navy. He was said to have married a Japanese girl before the war, spoke the language like a native, still wore his uniform and cap and was allowed extra-ordinary privileges, on deck all the time. He wasn't allowed to do much for us but he did what he could."

Manryu Maru was a cargo ship of about 1,000 tons, recently salvaged from the bottom of Hong Kong harbour, and designed as a river steamer for the run between Hong Kong and Guangzhou. It had just two holds, and they were half full of coal.

Lewis Bush, Arthur Rance (a Japanese-speaking Canadian of the HKVDC),[41] and an RAF medic called Joe Edmunds shared a cabin which also became the first-aid post. An RAF WO was in charge of the forward hold, and a Canadian Sergeant Major[42] was in charge of the rear. Bush appointed a WO of the RAOC as his second in command.

Canadian Ken Cambon: "Food and fresh water were [lowered into the holds] in big tubs. Since many were seasick, and unable to eat, the rest of us were better fed than we had been for a long time. The lighting was very dim and there was no room to stretch out, but still some managed to play cards." (p. 51)

Bush visited the lower hold: "The foul, hot air struck me like the blast from an open furnace. Many had been sick and the stench was shocking. Few could lie down full length. Some were playing cards, one man was playing a mouth organ, the others just squatted and lolled about jesting, grumbling, cursing or just staring up at the deckhead." (p. 177)

Bush noted that conditions in the forward hold were a little better, thanks to the efforts of the NCOs of the Royal Rifles of Canada. But many men were also sick.

Bush: "Edmunds and the Canadian medical orderly were soon in demand and in no time we had some fifty men prostrate on deck. Some were seriously ill, especially three or four who had just been released from hospital to catch the draft. 'Joe' saw Captain Ito to request that all be allowed to stay on deck. He would not agree, but said that twenty of the most seriously sick could remain."[43] (p. 176)

The ship sailed to Osaka via Keelung, Taiwan.

Cambon: "We did have one submarine scare shortly after leaving Taipei. All the hatches were battened down and we were warned to be very quiet by the guards. It was a tense time as we were indeed like rats in a trap. Some planes flew over and the emergency ended." (p. 52)

Forsyth: "I saw E. C. Harrison of Bury, Quebec, while he himself was sick on the voyage give up his blankets and bed space to another sick man who for lack of space was clinging to a ladder. Harrison then perched on the ladder himself for three days. He was one of the most self-sacrificing men I ever saw."[44]

On arrival at Osaka, the men from this ship were sent by train to two camps:[45]
- Tokyo #5 Branch Camp (Niigata-Rinko)
- Osaka #3 Branch Camp (Oeyama)

Although they did not yet know it, these would be two of the deadliest camps in Japan. The POWs walked from Chiko dock in Osaka, through the town to a tram station, then took a tram to the railway station, and finally boarded trains. Two hundred and seventy-six Winnipeg Grenadiers and Royal Rifles went to Niigata.

Tom Forsyth was one of that Niigata party: "We finally docked near Osaka late afternoon of September first. Marched a short distance then climbed aboard streetcars, then changed to a train. The railway was laid along the coastline for miles and miles and we had a constant view of the open sea on our left as we sped north and of the mountains on our right. We passed thru many tunnels. When mealtime arrived each man was given a square wooden box (about 6 inches square and one inch deep) full of rice with a little seaweed and pickle in it. We travelled roughly 180 miles north before we reached camp 5B on the outskirts of the City of Niigata."

Niigata working parties varied. Rinko was the coal dock, Shintetsu was an iron foundry, and Marutsu was a cargo dock.

To Oeyama went 13 Royal Engineers, 7 Military Police, 1 RAMC (John Harvey), 60 Royal Artillery, 17 RAF, and 100 Canadians. I. J. Bevan was one of the Artillerymen in this group: "On the 15th August we left Sham Shui Po and arrived here on the 1st Sept."[46]

August 1943: Continued

Monday, 16 August. Leo Berard at Tokyo #3D: "In the summer of 1943, Pte. Michael Panco, a native of Dauphin, Manitoba, was so sick that we had to take him to one of the Tokyo hospitals.[47] Panco only weighed sixty-seven and a half pounds and was obviously in very serious condition. When this had to be done, our doctor (Captain Reid) chose the prisoners who were in better condition to help the Jap escort take the sick man to hospital by train. I was selected for this one. We had to move quickly to get on the train because it didn't stop for very long and we were carrying the sick man and being pushed by our escorts at the same time. The Japanese population stared at us with mixed attitude; some couldn't care less and some with a pitiful glance that showed they were thinking how awful to see someone suffer this way. Private Panco died on August 16, 1943, three weeks after he was admitted to hospital."

Thursday, 26 August. Fisher at Shamshuipo: "One of our choir died suddenly from malaria. His name was Woods, aged 54. He had a family in Australia and was very pleased to have just heard that they had received news that he was safe and well. He proudly showed me a photograph of his 18-year-old daughter who had got her first job down there. As we followed the rough coffin to the church I felt terribly sorry." (p. 71)

Thursday, 26 August. The *Hong Kong News* of 26 August 1943 announced that: "the Hong Kong Branch of the International Red Cross will stop cash allowances to dependents of PW and civilian internees, and establish a centre for them at St ALBERT'S HALL CONVENT, ROSARY HILL, No. 43 STUBBS ROAD."[48]

Peter White: "As we were among the first to arrive at Rosary Hill, my mother volunteered for the position of Chief Cook, but because her written English was lacking, she was refused this position, but offered the job as Cook, which she accepted. Part of my duties consisted of cleaning out the stoves and ovens and hauling the ashes outside to be recycled (sifted and unburned coals made into brickettes, to be reused). Pretty hard work for an 11-year-old boy, so I was re-assigned to general duties such as garbage collection of all floors. I also helped with sawing and chopping wood for the kitchen. I later was asked to help out in the Hospital Kitchen which was located on the top floor. Duties consisted of fetching the daily rations for the patients and staff from the main kitchen, three flights of stairs down and up! Those who were able to supplement their rations with extras, did this by selling their possessions and purchasing goods on the black market. Our medical staff consisted of a husband and wife team of Hungarian doctors, holding British Passports. They were quite concerned with the health of everyone, in particular children, so they ordered regular purchases of cow bones which were burned in the kitchen ovens, pulverized into smaller pieces and ground down to a consistency of grains of sand. This was mixed with shark liver oil, rendered from sharks' livers in our kitchen. All children up to the age of 15 were made to take a spoonful of this concoction once a week. UGH! Hygiene was good, although it took a lot of courage to take a daily shower in ice-cold water, especially in winter! Our main complaint was Bed Bugs! Nothing we could do would get rid of them."[49]

The daily menu at Rosary Hill consisted of:
Breakfast: One ladle of cooked bran sometimes salted to make it more palatable. Once a week it might be sweetened with raw brown sugar.
Lunch: One bowl of rice and one ladle of boiled soya beans.
Dinner: One bowl of rice with a ladle of mixed vegetables and beef, if one could find a bit of beef, as it was rationed to 30 lbs per 1,000 persons (the population was just over 1,000). People on working parties (making brickettes, etc.) were allowed 1/2 bowl of rice extra.

Friday, 27 August. Gunner Mathieu of the HKVDC was killed on the wire at Shamshuipo. A popular man, his passing was noted by many. Laite: "One of the French internees was accidentally killed while doing fatigue duties. It was his wedding anniversary, and before going to work he was able to speak to his wife across the wire."

Saturday, 28 August. Fisher at Shamshuipo: "A disastrous day yesterday. Matthieu, our erstwhile French teacher was killed in camp . . . We are all very upset by this because Matthieu was a very popular man. His wife is outside and saw him only the day before on the way to Kai Tak." (p. 71)

Fisher continued on the same day: "We had another death too in the Hong Kong VDC. A fellow called Stimson, formerly of the KCR. He had been failing for some time and a number of us, including Charles and myself, offered blood for transfusion. It was not required, although he had anaemia."

Tuesday, 31 August. BAAG reported that the 'latest party' of Indians to arrive at A.H.Q. included: "Jemadar LAL Khan was on the Committee of the J.I.F.C. (Military) in HONGKONG and his 'escape' should not only throw a spanner into the works of the 'League', but he should be able to give us valuable information on the workings of the 'League'. PC ALIM DIN is our Agent No. 45, who I considered it desirable to bring out at this stage of the game (together with the Indian Party for whom I have been 'angling' for some time) on account of his very close association with 68 and my desire to divorce 68 entirely from Indian activities (I now have other separate Indian contacts inside) and let him concentrate on his main job — i.e. the CAMPS."

September 1943

By September 1943, only 600 Indian POWs remained at Ma Tau Chung.

Thursday, 2 September. O'Toole "A.R.P. — 1.45PM. SACONIY oil installation at Lai Chi Kok. Quite heavily bombed, a great cloud of heavy black smoke went up & darkened the sky. Fire lasted over a week. We had to take precautions in camp against fire as it is only just across the bay. This is certainly the most damage to date. Buses & motor traffic were stopped in colony due to lack of fuel, only military and taxi continue. Admitted large loss to Hong Kong but of no consequence to war effort." The conflagration was noted by everyone in Shamshuipo.

Rozario: "The other big job was at Aberdeen. We had to take oil and kerosene drums down to the pier and then later load them on to a barge to be taken to Lai Chi Kok Socony Installation. There were so many drums that it took us six months to clear the godowns. We got up at 5:00 a.m., had breakfast and waited on the parade ground to be counted. Then we were put on a barge which took over an hour to reach Aberdeen. Most of us slept on the barge and others chatted and read books. The Japanese brought in a lot of books and we had quite a good library.

While we were working on the drums, an Allied spotter plane flew over us every morning.[50] The air-raid siren went and the Japanese guards ran up the hills, far away from the drums. We sat on the drums as we had our own spies and we knew the same spotter plane came over every morning. The American bombers never bombed the prison camp and they seemed to know where we worked. When all the drums were taken to Lai Chi Kok, the spotter plane still came around as usual, and the siren went and everyone looked towards Lai Chi Kok. One fine day, there was a heavy droning sound and we told ourselves, 'This was it.' The huge tanks went up in black mushroom smoke and we could see the drums going up through the smoke, and a lot of fighter planes strafed the godowns until there was nothing left. The fire in Lai Chi Kok burnt for a week. Every day, we took our bowl of rice at dinnertime to the field and watched the huge fire, singing 'Over there, everywhere, the Yanks are coming'. By the third day, the Japanese guards were also singing with us. If they found out what we were singing they would have set on us with fixed bayonets."

Bill Oxley: "They swooped low over their target, the gas-converters. Petrol was stored there. They unleashed their bombs; the noise was terrifying, but terrific. We stood as one man cheering, almost going mad — 'Well done, Yanks!' 'Hit the bastards hard!' . . . The raid lasted twenty minutes, then they were gone. They were not intercepted. Petrol landed in our camp, fires were started; we laughed and cried. We were not forgotten. WE WERE WINNING!"

The fire was finally reported out on the 10th.

Saturday, 4 September.   Bush arrived at Omori where he would share accommodation with Badger of the Middlesex, Harry Parker RN, Quilliam, RN, and PO Mitchell of MTB08.

Monday, 6 September.   BAAG reported: "The following information has been obtained from Jemadar LAL KHAN, HKSRA, Gunner HADAYAT KHAN, HKSRA, P.C. ALIM DIN, and PC HUSSAIN DIN, Indian S.K.Ps who arrived at A.H.Q. on the evening of 31 August. About 600 internees still in [Ma Tau Chung]. The camp commander is Sub. MEHER KHAN,

5/7 Rajputs, who is pro-Japanese (neither pro-Indian nor pro-British) ... an average of one or 2 die each week in the camp, due mostly to dysentery and weakness."[51]

Tuesday, 14 September. Manuel Prata, arrested at Argyle Street on 1 July together with Lt. Haddock, died under interrogation.[52]

Tuesday, 21 September. At Argyle Street, Commander Young, Commander Craven, and Lieutenant Dixon were arrested on suspicion of running an illegal radio. A further six officers, including Lt. Col. Field, and with Major Boxer being the last, would be arrested by the 27th.[53]

Parker: "They began to question this man and that man and the funny thing about it was that each man questioned was one of those in the know. The pressure was being applied; nerves were becoming jumpy, rations had been greatly reduced as a warning that they knew and that the situation would become worse if they were not told. Days during which they were questioned for hours on end broke down two men who, no doubt reluctantly, told all they knew with the result that about twenty prisoners were taken out of camp, innocent and guilty alike, and were thrown into a foul jail."

While these officers were being arrested, Canadian civilians were finally being repatriated from Stanley on a ship coming down from Shanghai.

Wednesday, 22 September. Redwood: "SS *Teia Maru* arrived late in windy, rainy evening. Next morning we watched John Stanton, John and Stuart Valentine and Peter Potts (all schoolboys) arriving (from Shanghai) to join their families here. Watched the Canadian sisters, and all the others leaving — Gladys Collard from the hospital, the Salmons."

Thursday, 23 September. Canadian Nursing Sister Kay Christie: "As far as the Japanese were concerned, May Waters and I were Canadian civilian refugees and we were thus included in the group who left Stanley Camp on September 23, 1943, on the first leg of a ten-week journey home. The first four weeks of this trip was on a dreadful Japanese ship called the *Teia Maru*[54] where the conditions were even worse than at the internment camp. Built for 400 cabin passengers, there were 1,530 of us on board. After our arrival in Goa, four weeks later, the Swedish-American liner *Gripsholm* arrived with 1530 Japanese internees from the U.S. who were to be exchanged for us. Several days later, the Japanese internees were put on board our ship and we went aboard the *Gripsholm* which was like a touch of heaven, clean and well-loaded with good food, such a contrast to what the Japanese had forced us to endure."

On the same day, a fellow Canadian, Skelton, was considering his situation in the mines at Omine. "September 23, 1943. Working in dead-end shaft. Blast fumes terrible, choking, spitting, coughing, ear splitting explosions and dust that makes you choke up and want to drink buckets of water. On top of this you stop work in the dust and a foul smelling hole to eat. Yes, eat a ration of cold bloody rice with a few stinking greens or sometimes two slices of pickled turnip. This in itself was enjoyed for the pangs of unending hunger could never (it seemed) be satisfied. Buntai-Jo's (section bosses), squawking, bellowing lot of bastards giving ridiculous of their mighty nation. And we listening with hate and want revenge, itching to lay your greasy, dirty hands on his brown pudgy neck and squeeze every ounce of bloody life out of the slant eyed yellow parasite. Great tales of suicide planes of 'Hara Kiri' before yielding to mercy of American 'Heutis'. They just go on and on and then think we eat it all up and then all of a sudden it finally dons on them that we've been pumping them for information and that many precious minutes of mining the 'Banzai' shaft had been wasted and with a grinning snarl jumps to his feet and yells the 'Syo Hietchiemai' (start work)."

October 1943

Thursday, 7 October. Fisher at Shamshuipo: "Bad news today. Lance Corporal Farmer of the Hong Kong VDC has died. He has had a bad time in here, having been in Bowen Road Hospital for a period and returned here looking very ill and thin. About two weeks ago he had a call of nature in the night and without thinking struck a match in the latrine. This is contrary to orders and one of the guards ran him into the guardroom for the night. He was released next day after interrogation (I was told he was treated quite decently), but has been in hospital ever since." (p. 81)

Tuesday, 19 October. In a sham trial at Stanley prison, forty-two of those arrested in the radio affair received judgement. Thirty-two were convicted of treason.

Thursday, 21 October. A number of the officers arrested in Argyle Street after the radio affair were returned to the camp. The others were sent to Stanley Jail.

Wiseman: "On 21st October Lt Col Field and four others were brought back to Camp but their haggard appearance and the grim news of Craven, Boxer and Co. did little to improve morale." (p. 36)

Thursday, 21 October. Warrant Engineer Arthur Taylor, RN, at Tokyo #1B noted: "At Kawasaki Station."[55]

Friday, 29 October. The thirty-two convicted prisoners were driven to Stanley beach and decapitated.

November 1943

Tuesday, 2 November. In Stanley, Barbara Redwood and others received notice: "That a number of the men arrested in the middle of the summer had been executed, including F. Hall who had recently married Eileen Bliss (in camp), Mr. J Fraser (Defence Secretary); Mr. Scott (Police) and about 4 others".

An unlikely but more pleasant surprise awaited the POWs in Kobe.

Wednesday, 3 November. Captain Martin Weedon: "Big surprise search when working parties returned. Some sugar and a tin of peaches discovered on one of the men. Did not, however, discover remaining sixteen tins on him! Sounds almost incredible, but true. Total of 186 tins brought into camp by one section alone, of thirty men." (p. 68)

Weedon's account was indeed correct. Sergeant Poulter continues the story: "When we arrived back at camp all the camp staff were out ready to search us. Before the search started, the Jap CSM said, 'If anybody has stolen any thing, step forward now and you will not be punished, but if any thing is found during the search—!' Darkie Hobson said, loud enough for us to hear, 'Stand fast every body.' He then stepped forward and pulled a Two Pound tin of Peaches out of his pocket. Talk about flabbergasted, the Jap staff was knocked flat, and dumb! When they recovered from the shock, the Japs dismissed the rest of us; consequently we all got our stuff in. We all got unloaded as quickly as possible, then Drummy and myself went down to see if we could help Darkie, as he still had about thirty tins of sardines on him. They had kept Darkie outside the Guardroom and when he saw us, he tumbled what we were after and asked the guard if he could go to the latrine. This was granted and as soon as he got inside we unloaded him as quickly as possible and got the stuff away. After his visit to the latrine the Japs came back into the yard and slapped him but not very much. Then they decided to search him, but they were too bloody late! They kept him standing outside the guardroom for three hours and then let him go. By his action he made it possible for our section to get into camp over two hundred and eighty tins of fish, which was quite a good haul. When we decide to pinch anything now, we take the whole case. It's quicker and safer, as strangely enough, a whole box missing is not so conspicuous as a half-empty case. We burn the boxes to help cook our rice; at least I burn the boxes because I usually do the cooking."

Tuesday, 9 November. Forsyth in Niigata: "Reid of Rifles died today. Makes eleven dead since we arrived here. At least they will never be hungry or cold anymore." Ken Cambon at Niigata hospital commented: "The small room set aside as a hospital was filled with cases of pneumonia and dysentery. The lack of a doctor and adequately trained personnel was compounded by the absence of any modern medications. We were given injections of camphor to use for pneumonia. This was understandably ineffective, in fact I sometimes wondered if it made things worse. The dysentery was treated with bismuth subnitrate, but we had no way of coping with the dehydration that was the killer." (p. 62)

December 1943

Wednesday, 1 December. The senior officers from Shamshuipo and Argyle Street, arrested during the radio affairs, were given a sham trail at the Supreme Court. Newnham, Ford, and Gray were sentenced to death, the other three to fifteen years imprisonment.

Wednesday, 1 December. Eighteen Indian soldiers died at Ma Tau Chung.[56]

Monday, 6 December. Forsyth in Niigata: "Heard Archie Rutherford had just died. Hard, very hard . . . no C Coy men will ever forget him."

Thursday, 9 December. In Shamshuipo, O'Toole discovered that another draft was in the offing: "Personnel selected & segregated to new huts. About 200 crips the rest volunteers. Very orderly and no fuss RAOC have now only about 15 here the following are on: Parker, Mitchell, Jefferys, Standen, Smith, Wright, Bocock, Eley, Malekin, Whitmore, Hewitt, Buckley, Pickles."[57]

Thursday, 9 December. Fisher at Shamshuipo: "I was out at Aberdeen yesterday and on returning found that momentous things were taking place. Eight disused huts have been wired off, and 50 officers' batmen from Argyle Street are ensconced within; there is to be another draft . . . After morning muster various names were read out in groups of 50. Charles and I were in group 3, and Tommy and Jimmy Dalzeil in Group 5. Five hundred were called altogether and the rest dismissed. We were then told to pack our kits and go over to eight huts which were wired off for us 'selectees'. There were 66 in our hut, all sleeping packed in heaps of blankets and kits. We lived like this for six days, but were in the highest of spirits." (p. 92)

Saturday, 11 December. Almost exactly a year after the first news of Indian POWs having been transferred to Canton, a BAAG report noted:

> On 13th October, a Chinese woman[58] reported to Colonel HOOPER in WAICHOW and stated that her brother who was working for the Japanese at TIEN HO A/d, CANTON, had come into contact with several Indian POW who wished to escape.
>
> Honourable British, Chinese and
Indian Officers
> This is a humble request from the Indian War Prisoners at Canton.
>
> In spite of undergoing extreme hardship and troubles since last two years still the cruel and barbarous treatment towards us continues. In addition no rejoicing news of any sort reaches us which can at any time please and strengthen our minds.
>
> The bearer of this, a Chinese named in the margin, says that he is one of your favourites. As we have to take some very important work from him can you please verify him to be true. Can any British or Indian officer reply as follows:
>
> (a) The name of the former GOC at Hong Kong
> (b) The name of the prisoner GOC in Hong Kong
> (c) The name of the prisoner CRA
> (d) The name of the prisoner infantry brigadier
> (e) Numbers of artillery units and names of their commanding officers if of artillery or same for infantry if of infantry or Chinese officers any other information which can prove that the statement of the bearer is true.
> 6/10/43 at Canton

The Fifth Draft: *Soong Cheong*

Frank Evans: "There was a good Samaritan in my hut, namely Len Price of the Royal Engineers, who handed me and D. T. Blazey, R.A., ten yen each to buy some tinned beans and tuna in the canteen for use on the voyage. I considered it a very fine gesture on his part when he himself could well do with the food." (p. 69)

The fifth draft to Japan would be on 15 December 1943 and included 496 POWs. Lieutenant John Abbott of the Middlesex was in command.

Wednesday, 15 December. Laite: "Our draft of over 500 left on the 15th. Before leaving, Barnett and I arranged for a fellow, Humphreys (R.N.), to celebrate his 25th wedding anniversary with us. Sgt Ian Lyle of 11 Alderbank Place, Edinburgh, came with him, and we enjoyed our meal together."[59]

Wednesday, 15 December. Fisher at Shamshuipo: "The morning of the 15th dawned and we were lined up on the roadway in our fifties. Along came Boon with typed lists which contained names which were read out. To my amazement my name was not read out, but when I saw others too standing alone I realised that some of us had been removed from the draft." (p. 94)

Bertram, however, was on the draft: "The camp gave us a magnificent send-off. Ever since the episode of the *Lisbon Maru*, it had been customary to farewell any draft for Japan as though they were sacrificial victims on the way to the minotaur. We feasted on fried bully and fruit tart — the best that remained from the Red Cross rations — and the Entertainment Bureau ran a special farewell concert." (p. 125)

Wednesday, 15 December. Frank Evans: "Today at 12.30 pm we are on board a Japanese ship and we moved off at 4 pm. There are 150 of us in a hold but I have had the chance of going up on deck to see Hong Kong for the last time. Down the hold it's very stuffy and we are packed like sardines. Cliff, Reg, Len and I are together in a corner and we are terribly hungry, even after some baked beans! Captain Abbott of the Middlesex Regiment is in charge of all of us and Sergeant Sutherland of the Royal Scots is the leader of our party of ten or twelve. Danny Fowler, RCS, is nearby and we are a good company and, considering everything, quite cheerful. The Argyle Street Camp Commandant and a few of the guards are with us on board." (p. 69)

Bertram: "[*Soong Cheong*] was, in fact, a veteran China coaster of a little more than a thousand ton's burden; and for eighteen months she had been resting on the bottom of Hong Kong harbour. This was her first trip since her salvage and refitting. She was well and truly laden with a bulk cargo of iron ore, so that we stepped directly from the lighter into her wells. The prisoners were to go on top of the cargo, in the 'tween decks for and aft. By a spin of the coin the Canadians — rather less than half the draft — went forward, and we moved into the double hatches aft. We were no sooner into the holds than the guards slammed the single steel door that led to a companion, and boarded up the hatches. There were no portholes, for we were below the waterline. There were no lights. In indescribable confusion and an atmosphere rapidly rivalling the Black Hole of Calcutta, we strove to sort ourselves out." (p. 127)

Thursday, 16 December. Frank Evans: "Many chaps are sick this morning and rushing up on deck as fast as they can. I am very sick myself — very weak and rather depressed. I could not sleep last night, hardly any air down here and it is like a dungeon with no room to turn around — sleeping head to toe." (pp. 69-72)

The ship spent most of the following day at anchor with the engines out of order, but when the men woke on the 18th, they were told that they were on the coast of Formosa, at the Techow docks.[60]

Monday, 20 December. Frank Evans: "We've received orders to get ready to be transhipped to a Japanese troopship tomorrow morning because this ship is out of action again and we are not moving. There will be troops on board the other one — whatever it is it cannot be worse than this one." (pp. 69-72) The waiting troopship was the *Toyama Maru*.

Tuesday, 21 December. Frank Evans: "Carried our kits up on deck in readiness and waited and waited without any food. A barge came for some stores and Captain Abbott with a few lads went across to the trooper. We had waited there for hours and at last a small boat came for some of us . . . The troopship appeared like a castle in front of us, with a rope ladder down its side. The sea was choppy and stepping from the barge to that ladder carrying my haversack and kitbag was quite frightening. As soon as we arrived on deck, we were ordered down the hold. In order to get to our bed spaces we had to crawl on our hands and knees to the lower tier. The headroom was about three feet, no hope of standing up, and we managed to drag in our kits into a space of fifteen square feet for the three of us. After some rice we tried to go to sleep but we were disturbed by rats and cockroaches." (pp. 69–72)

Wednesday, 22 December. Frank Evans: "No sign of us moving from here. It's worse here than in the other ship."

On Christmas Eve the complement of the ship were issued with soap, socks and vests, and on Christmas Day tea with sugar, meat and vegetable stew, a tin of sardines between three, two bananas each, a slice of melon, with a slice of pork and vegetable stew for dinner. Frank Evans: "Had a singsong before going to bed, and Captain Abbott read a short story to us!" At 14.00 on 26 December, the ship started moving at last — into a storm.

Monday, 27 December. Frank Evans: "One Japanese soldier has a broken leg. The sea is getting rougher, and the ship rocks and rolls." (p. 73) The *Toyama Maru* sailed north to anchor for New Year in the islands off which the *Lisbon Maru* had been lost a year before.

December 1943: Continued

Friday, 17 December. Forsyth: "Little Waterhouse of the Royal Rifles, one of the gamest kids I ever saw. Too small for the heavy work, sick and underweight, he toiled uncomplainingly, sheer willpower sustained him to the end, when a veritable walking skeleton, he tottered in from work, between two of us. Death came as a merciful release."

Saturday, 18 December. Newnham, Ford, and Gray were taken to Shek-O beach and shot in the back.[61]

Thursday, 23 December. Boxer, Dixon, Craven, and Young (previously arrested in Argyle Street) were tried and sentenced to five years each.

Friday, 24 December. Forsyth at Niigata moved temporarily next door to #15B: "Raining, raw, cold. Moving to another camp about a mile away. Carried our kit over on our back, then returned for the blankets and a load of straw, made a third trip for another huge bundle of straw. New camp only half finished, no doors or windows. Very cold. No kitchen equipment."

Friday, 31 December. 234 patients remained at Bowen Road; 120 had deficiency diseases, 13 dysentery, eight tuberculosis, and 25 with war wounds.

ROLL OF HONOUR FOR 1943

Sham Shui Po / Argyle Street

Name	Rank	Number	Unit			Date
Collins, John	Private		HKDDC			K 5.1.43 Es
Irvine, Glenford	Rifleman	E/30172	RRoC			K 10.1.43 Da[62]
Wilbur, Clarence Joseph	Rifleman	E/30485	RRoC			K 17.1.43 Cbi/Cs
Medhurst, George	Rifleman	C/65164	RRoC			K 22.1.43 Pe
Singleton, Walter Ben	Lance Corp.	H/6256	WG			K 22.1.43 Cs
Sumner, William John	Private	H/6815	WG			K 25.1.43 Pa
Britto, Henry Maria	CSM	1290	HKVDC		BRH	K 31.1.43 Ma/Aa
Chicoine, Gaston	Rifleman	E/30495	RRoC	10.2.43	BRH	K 9.2.43 TB/Pe
McAlpine, Owen	Sergeant	3044401	RS		BRH	K 10.2.43 Ma/Mn
Patterson, Ivan	Private	7536265	RADC			K 10.2.43
Paxton, William	Private	168	HKDDC		BRH	K 11.2.43 As[63]
Legacy, John Fidell	Rifleman	E/30399	RRoC		BRH	K 20.2.43 Pe
Higgins, James Joseph	Bombardier	3111	HKVDC MM + Bar			K 21.2.43 Pa
Chapman, Frank	Lance Corp.	E/29935	RRoC		BRH	K 14.3.43 Ty/Mn
Stodgell, Garnett James	Private	H/6688	WG			K 20.3.43 Cs
Davis, John James	Private	H/6050	WG			K 1.4.43 Cf
Turland, John Charles W.	Gunner	872424	RA		BRH	K 15.4.43 oba
Brannon, Owen Patrick	MQMS	7876205	RE		BRH	K 4.5.43 Dy/Pa
Brown, Walter Joseph	Private	4052	HKVDC		BRH	K 14.5.43 TB
Ryan, Patrick	Sergeant	3771	HKVDC		BRH	K 14.5.43
Brown, Alexander	Private	H/6931	WG		BRH	K 26.5.43 Pe
Murray, Ian Norman	Sergeant	5252	HKVDC	31.5.43	BRH	K 1.6.43[64]
Halfyard, Robert Edward	L. Seaman	D/J105831	RN		BRH	K 2.6.43 Ul
Johnston, David	Private	H/6858	WG			K 7.6.43 Pe
Barros, Luiz Antonio	Private	2437	HKVDC			K 23.8.43 HKR Ma
Wood, Arthur Frank	Sergeant		HKDDC			K 25.8.43 Ma
Mathieu, Pierre Benjamin	Gunner	4681	HKVDC			K 27.8.43 Ax[65]
Stimpson, Cornelius C.	Corporal	3075	HKVDC			K 27.8.43 As/Es
Hunt, Peter Norman	Driver	T/215978	RASC			K 7.9.43[66]
Prata, Manuel Gonzaga	Private	3606	HKVDC			K 14.9.43 HKR Mu[67]
Pope, William Rufus	Sergeant	E/29819	RRoC			K 16.9.43 Aa
Farmer, Clarence L.	Lance Corp.	DR162	HKVDC			K 7.10.43 Pe/Bi
Atkinson, Ronald Edward	Lance Corp.	H/6905	WG MM		BRH	K 8.10.43 Ap
Budden, Henry Easthope	Private		HKDDC			K 9.10.43 Bi/Ma/Cf
Armstrong, Cyril	Lieutenant-Col.	10760	RAMC MBE		BRH	K 19.10.43 Ul
Viner, Wilfred Brinley	Private	T/7876812	RASC		BRH	K 19.10.43 Es
Donaldson, Thomas	Master		MN SS Kau Tung HK			K 22.10.43
Holmstrom, Stuart	Private	H/6940	WG		BRH	K 20.10.43 Es
Haynes, Frank Henry W.	Civilian Mst. Art.		RAOC		BRH	K 27.10.43 Dy
Burns, Robert Kirkwood	Ch. Eng. Off.		MN SS Chengtu HK	10.11.43	BRH	K 1.11.43 Dy[68]
Reason, Harry	Corporal	10596694	RAOC			K 1.11.43 As/Es
Badger, George Charles	Private	L/13725	WG			K 5.11.43 Ma
Sioux, Tony	Private	H/41699	WG			K 16.11.43 Pa[69]
Samson, Albert Joseph	Private	H/6909	WG	12.11.43	BRH	K 17.11.43 Ls

Laplante, David Gabriel	Private	H/41654	WG	25.11.43	BRH	K 22.11.43 Cs
Forsyth, William Ronnie	Private	421	HKVDC			K 23.11.43 Ul
Oige, Joseph Howard	Private	H/41666	WG			K 28.11.43 Da/Cs
Rodger, George Sinclair	Engineer		MN			K 28.11.43
Boswell, Ernest Arthur	Private	H/6063	WG		BRH	K 29.11.43
Whittaker, William Henry	Sergeant	3874	HKVDC			K 7.12.43 HKC Mn/Bs
Baskett, Paul Evelyn	CSM	V1923	HKVDC MBE			K 9.12.43 Pa
Kaye, Ronald	Sapper	1873341	RE			K 9.12.43
Hamelin, Fred Francis	Private	H/41694	WG		BRH	K 10.12.43
Tufail Muhammad		PC 200	HKDDC RN / DYP			K 11.12.43 HKM
Whyte, Samuel Howard	Private		HKDDC		BRH	K 13.12.43[70]
Ford, Douglas	Captain	99752	RS GC			K 18.12.43 EX
Gray, Hector B. 'Dolly'	Flt Lieutenant	44061	RAF AFM GC			K 18.12.43 EX
Irvine, Ronald	Rifleman	E/30033	RRoC			K 18.12.43 Cs
Newnham, Lanceray A.	Colonel		HQ GC MC			K 18.12.43 EX
Jackson, Ronald Charles	LAC	992747	RAF		BRH	K 28.12.43 TB

Fukuoka #5 Branch Camp (Omine Coal Mine, Kawasaki-machi)

Murray, George Wesley	Rifleman	A/23153	RRoC	(XD3)	K 4.5.43 Y Cbi
MacDonald, Lorne	CQMS	E/30439	RRoC	(XD3)	K 5.8.43 Y Pa
Savoy, Edward Joseph	Rifleman	G/32318	RRoC	(XD3)	K 20.8.43 Y Cbi
Wood, Donald Gordon	Lance Corp.	E/30176	RRoC	(XD3)	K 17.9.43 Y Es

Osaka #1 Branch Camp (Minato-ku, Osaka)

Grant, Kenneth	Private		HKDDC RN/DYP	(XD2)	K 1.1.43 Y Cs diw[71]
Lithauer, Ronald Louis	Lance Corp.	2325527	RCS	(XD2)	K 1.1.43 Y Dy diw
Sheehan, Maurice	Private	6202103	MX	(XD2)	K 29.1.43 Y Cbi
Stokes, David	A.S.	P/J34983	RN	(XD2)	K 24.1.43 Y Cs diw
Bennett, Sidney	Signalman	2323504	RCS	(XD2)	K 17.2.43 Y Da diw
Yarwood, Colin	Leading Tel.	P/WRX617	RN	(XD2)	K 18.2.43 Y Cs diw
Curry, William	Staff Sergeant	1861266	RE	(XD2)	K 19.2.43 Y
Ireland, Michael Norman	Writer	P/MX70045	RN	(XD2)	K 24.2.43 Y Cs diw
Fieldhouse, Stanley	Signalman	2353991	RCS	(XD2)	K 4.3.43 Y Pa diw
Dousett, Samuel	P.O.	C/JX156068	RN	(XD2)	K 22.3.43 Y Dy
Ransford, Charles	Signalman	2353860	RCS	(XD2)	K 22.3.43 Y Cs diw
Scally, Dennis Frederick	Writer	P/MX80371	RN	(XD2)	K 11.4.43 Y Es diw
Bell, Norman McCleod	A.S.	D/JX19422	RN	(XD2)	K 27.4.43 Y diw
Dennett, Francis Leslie	BQMS	847065	RA	(XD2)	K 20.5.43 Y
McEwan, Henry	Gunner	845360	RA	(XD2)	K 22.5.43 Y Pu diw
Eldridge, Harry Norman	A.S.	P/J110399	RN	(XD2)	K 25.5.43 Y Es diw
Lawson, Alexander Brown	Private	3053784	RS	(XD2)	K 31.5.43 Y Cf diw
Gay, Harry	Supp. Ass.	C/MX58799	RN	(XD2)	K 2.6.43 Y Cbi diw
Spiller, Frederick John	Gunner	855016	RA	(XD2)	K 3.6.43 Y Es diw
Cassidy, John McFerran	Jnr 4th Class	P/UDX1320	RN	(XD2)	K 29.6.43 Y Cf diw
Farmer, George	Lance Corp.	3059158	RS	(XD2)	K 5.7.43 Y Cbi diw
Edge, Ellis Taylor	COA	P/M6033	RN MiD	(XD2)	K 7.7.43 Y Cbi diw
Varney, Harry	A.S.	PIJ/8390	RN	(XD2)	K 1.10.43 Y Es diw
Ashton, Cyril Richard	L Tel	C/SSX20134	RN	(XD2)	K 1.11.43 Y Cbi diw

Chambers, James Lee	A.S.	C/SSX28512	RN	(XD2)	K 14.11.43 Y Pa diw
Taylor, Alexander	Colour Sergeant	3051885	RS	(XD2)	K 5.12.43 Y Dy dhh

Osaka #2 Branch Camp (Kobe)

Gray, George John	Private	6202108	MX	(XD2)	K 2.1.43 Y Bi
Davis, Frederick James	Corporal	6194972		(XD2)	K 17.1.43 Y Cs
McAlarney, Joseph	Lance Corp.	3054207	RS	(XD2)	K 17.1.43 Y Dy
Hughes, Leonard	Lance Corp.	6207586	MX	(XD2)	K 18.1.43 Y Cf/Mn/Bi/De
Slann, Frederick Allan	Private	6210552	MX	(XD2)	K 23.1.43 Y Mn
Blackie, Arthur Henry	Corporal	3054165	RS	(XD2)	K 24.1.43 Y Bi diw
Woods, Frank	Lance Sergeant	845902	RA	(XD2)	K 26.1.43 Y Dy
Hilton, Frank William	Captain	71817	RA	(XD2)	K 27.1.43 Y Dy diw
Smart, Stanley	P.O. Stoker	D/KX81418	RN	(XD2)	K 1.2.43 Y Bi/Pa
Day, Reuben John	Lance Corp.	1874426	RE	(XD2)	K 5.2.43 Y Bi
Pattullo, David	Private	3053616	RS	(XD2)	K 7.2.43 Y Dy
Gardner, George Albert	Private	6201661	MX	(XD2)	K 8.2.43 Y Pa
Payne, Sidney	Sapper	1991421	RE	(XD2)	K 11.2.43 Y Bi
Matthews, Vivian R.	Lieutenant	146689	RA	(XD2)	K 13.2.43 Y
Root, Alfred Edward	Private	6203948	MX	(XD2)	K 14.2.43 Y Cs/Mn
Cheesewright, Cyril	Lieutenant	149468	MX	(XD2)	K 17.2.43 Y Pa
Edgar, Robert	Private	3054528	RS	(XD2)	K 19.2.43 Y Bi/Mn
Toothill, Robert Ernest	Private	3059144	RS	(XD2)	K 21.2.43 Y Bi/Cs
Walkden, Alan Frank	Lieutenant	221894	RA Att. HKSRA	(XD2)	K 23.2.43 Y Pa
Lamb, Joseph Patrick	Private	6210636	MX	(XD2)	K 28.2.43 Y Cs
Greig, Joseph	Private	3055733	RS	(XD2)	K 2.3.43 Y Pa
Gray, Ian	Private	3055728	RS	(XD2)	K 3.3.43 Y Cbi
Skinner, Sidney Albert	P.O.	C/JX132691	RN	(XD2)	K 3.3.43 Y Bi/Cs
Bowes, George William	Lieutenant	205366	RS	(XD2)	K 4.3.43 Y Cf
Gordon, Robert J.	Private	7518982	RAMC	(XD2)	K 4.3.43 Y Cbi
Wilderspin, Harry Albert	Lance Corp.	6201867	MX	(XD2)	K 4.3.43 Y Pa/Bi
Miller, Alan	Private	3059019	RS	(XD2)	K 6.3.43 Y Pa
Duff, Joseph Parkerson	Private	3054089	RS	(XD2)	K 8.3.43 Y Cbi
Huggett, John	Private	6213513	MX	(XD2)	K 9.3.43 Y Pa
Tyrer, Robert Frederick	Private		HKDDC RN/DYP	(XD2)	K 10.3.43 Y Pa[72]
Fraser, William Noble	Sergeant	3049325	RS	(XD2)	K 12.3.43 Y Cbi
Painting, Robert	Corporal	6200827	MX	(XD2)	K 12.3.43 Y Pa
Maxwell, Andrew	Lieutenant (QM)	3928607	RAMC	(XD2)	K 13.3.43 Y Es
Parker, James Ernest	Private	6202344	MX	(XD2)	K 20.3.43 Y Bi/Pa
Hardy, Cyril Thomas	Corporal	1871443	RE	(XD2)	K 21.3.43 Y Bi/Pa
Tubb, Cecil	Gunner	6394452	RA	(XD2)	K 22.3.43 Y Pa
Sullivan, William	Private	6213591	MX	(XD2)	K 23.3.43 Y Bi/Pa
Bindon, Frank James	Private	6201249	MX	(XD2)	K 24.3.43 Y Pa diw
Moyes, Henry	Bandsman	3054403	RS	(XD2)	K 26.3.43 Y Pa
Jones, John	Private	6198827	MX	(XD2)	K 28.3.43 Y Mn
Dyne, Charles Forbes	Corporal	2075873	RE	(XD2)	K 5.4.43 Y Bi
Fox, William Robert	Sergeant	5989045	MX	(XD2)	K 5.4.43 Y Pa
George, Frederick Charles	Boom Engineer		RNR	(XD2)	K 6.4.43 Y Cbi[73]
Neubronner, Robert	S/Sergeant	1931975	RE	(XD2)	K 8.4.43 Y Dy

Gardiner, Leslie John	Chief Sto.	D/K56461	RN	9.4.42	(XD2)	K 9.4.43 Y Bi[74]
Funnell, John	Private	6202119	MX		(XD2)	K 15.4.43 Y Bi
Jeffs, Sydney Hill	Ch.ERA	C/MX46760	RN		(XD2)	K 21.4.43 Y Pa
Fawcett, John Robert	Sapper	1871744	RE		(XD2)	K 26.4.43 Y Bs
Burnett, Alan Frederick	Sapper	2191935	RE		(XD2)	K 3.5.43 Y Pa
Cox, William Thomas	Corporal	6199136	MX		(XD2)	K 3.5.43 Y Es/Bi
Gunn, Laurence Frederick	Private	6213499	MX		(XD2)	K 11.5.43 Y Pa
Bunker, John Sidney	Private	6207610	MX		(XD2)	K 25.5.43 Y Cbi
Chalmers, Andrew	Corporal	3054504	RS		(XD2)	K 2.6.43 Y Pa
Sturges, Albert	Private	6202743	MX	2.7.42	(XD2)	K 2.7.43 Y Cs[75]
Toombs, Joseph Henry	Lance Corp.	6208218	MX		(XD2)	K 4.7.43 Y Pa
James, William Anderson	Private	3054486	RS		(XD2)	K 22.7.43 Y Es
Harrison, Harold	Sapper	1874428	RE		(XD2)	K 1.8.43 Y Cbi
Gough, Albert Stanley H.	Drummer	3054530	RS		(XD2)	K 5.8.43 Y Es diw
Ranson, Eric	Private	6200793	MX		(XD2)	K 1-5.11.43Y Bi[76]
Pegg, Charles Walter	Private	6212991	MX		(XD2)	K 1.11.43 Y Bi/Es
Horswell, Sydney James	Major		HKDDC RN/DYP		(XD2)	K 15.11.43 Y Dy
Leith, Harry Lauder	Signalman	2319998	RCS	11.10.42	(XD2)	K 12.43 Y Pa[77]
Linton, Victor Joseph F.	Lance Corp.	6200987	MX		(XD2)	K 21.12.43 Y Cbi

Osaka #3 Branch Camp (Oeyama)

Grieve, John	Lance Bdr.	1708010	RA	(XD4)	K 10.10.43 Y Ma
Proulx, Ernest	Private	H/41845	WG	(XD4)	K 11.12.43 Y Ax[78]
Boddy, Frederick George	Sapper	1874283	RE	(XD4)	K 18.12.43 Y Cbi

Osaka #4 Dispatched Camp (Sakurajima)

Franklin, John Henry	Lance Sergeant	863711	RA	(XD3)	K 11.2.43 Y Cs
Wise, Reginald John J.S.	Private		HKDDC	(XD3)	K 26.2.43 Y Pa
Cockley, Alfred Arthur	Gunner	1712337	RA	(XD3)	K 8.3.43 Y An
Blake, David Samuel	Private		HKDDC	(XD3)	K 28.12.43 Y An

Osaka #5 Dispatched Camp (Kawasaki-Juko, Kobe)

Andrews, William Henry	CPO	D/J43976	RN	(XD2)	K 22.3.43 Y Pa

Osaka #6 Dispatched Camp (Amagasaki)

Read, Arthur Ian	A/S.M.	7585756	RAOC	(XD3)	K 12.2.43 Y Pa
Jacques, John	Signalman	P/JX205696	RN	(XD3)	K 2.3.43 Y Pa diw
Davies, Henry	A.S.	D/JX153156	RN	(XD3)	K 10.3.43 Y Bs diw
Evans, Arthur John	Private	S/227164	RASC	(XD3)	K 10.4.43 Y Cs/Bi
Stare, George Christopher	Tel	P/SSX31692	RN	(XD3)	K 10.4.43 Y[79]
Glass, Robert Rutherford	Corporal		RAOC	(XD3)	K 7.8.43 Y Pa diw
Chambers, George Henry	AC 2	1059768	RAF	(XD3)	K 24.12.43 Y[80]

Tokyo Main Camp (Shinagawa)

Pinnock, William Jacks	Private	6201233	MX	(XD1)	K 22.2.43 Y Dy dsh[81]
Merchant, David Johnson	Private	3053641	RS	(XD1)	K 7.3.43 Y Ps dsh
Anderson, Colin Kindness	Private	3053544	RS	(XD1)	K 22.3.43 Y Ps dsh
Thompson, Robert S.	BSM	1068858	RA	(XD1)	K 13.5.43 Y[82]
Harris, Gerald Mark	Sapper	1874487	RE	(XD1)	K 6.6.43 Y Ps dsh

Tokyo Main Camp (Omori)

Hall, Ralph	Private	3054843	RS		(XD1)	K 13.12.43 Y Ns

Tokyo #3 Branch Camp (Yokohama Stadium)

Grint, William Henry	Gunner	4532721	RA		(XD1)	K 8.2.43 Y Cbi
Starck, Charles Roy	Gunner	840312	RA		(XD1)	K 5.3.43 Y Dy dt2
Price, Ernest Thomas	L Stoker	C/KX81053	RN		(XD1)	K 3.2.43 Y Dy dt2

Tokyo #3 Dispatched Camp (Tsurumi Shipyard)

Lawrence, Bert	Rifleman	E/30257	RRoC		(XD3)	U 29.1.43 Cbi[83]
Hendry, David	Private	H/6583	WG		(XD3)	K 13.2.43 Y Bi
Lavarie, Cecil Fox	Private	H/6821	WG		(XD3)	K 13.2.43 Y Pa
Fox, Erwin Albert	Private	L/22223	WG		(XD3)	K 16.2.43 Y Hs
Englehart, Rupert Charles	Lance Corp.	E/29983	RRoC		(XD3)	K 28.2.43 Y Mn/ Pa dsh
Lamb, Patrick William	Rifleman	E/30598	RRoC		(XD3)	K 26.7.43 Y Pa/Es
Panco, Michael (Mikey)	Private	H/20581	WG		(XD3)	K 16.8.43 Y Pu dsgh
Goodenough, Murray T.	Lance Sergeant	E/21892	RRoC MM		(XD3)	K 22.12.43 Y Pa[84]

Tokyo #5 Branch Camp (Niigata-Rinko)

Harrison, Edmond C.	Rifleman	E/29926	RRoC		(XD4)	K 9.9.43 Y Mn
Benwell, Marven	Rifleman	E/30699	RRoC		(XD4)	K 10.9.43 Y Mn
Maloney, Eddie Joseph	Rifleman	E/29882	RRoC		(XD4)	K 14.9.43 Y Mn
Chanell, Albert Ben	Rifleman	E/30392	RRoC		(XD4)	K 26.9.43 Y Mn
Roussel, Leo	Private	H/62833	WG		(XD4)	K 8.10.43 Y Mn
Culleton, Wellington	Rifleman	E/30039	RRoC		(XD4)	K 2.11.43 Y Pa
MacRae, Allan Howard	Corporal	E/30053	RRoC	MiD	(XD4)	K 2.11.43 Y Cbi
Reid, Lloyd George	Rifleman	C/41424	RRoC		(XD4)	K 9.11.43 Y Es
Ray, Irvin	Rifleman	F/29946	RRoC		(XD4)	K 13.11.43 Y Pa
Sarty, Perry	Rifleman	F/40751	RRoC		(XD4)	K 15.11.43 Y Bi/Es
Haley, Reginald	Rifleman	E/29999	RRoC		(XD4)	K 21.11.43 Y Pa
Breen, Frederick	Corporal	E/30299	RRoC		(XD4)	K 22.11.43 Y Es
Knapp, William Arthur	Lance Corp.	E/30545	RRoC		(XD4)	K 22.11.43 Y Pa
Evans, Robert Daniel	Private	H/17707	WG		(XD4)	K 23.11.43 Y Pa
Hunter, Stanley Hamilton	Corporal	H/6569	WG		(XD4)	K 23.11.43 Y Es
Robertson, Gilbert Alan	Private	H/41703	WG		(XD4)	K 29.11.43 Y Pa
Charuk, Nicholas John	Lance Corp.	H/6557	WG		(XD4)	K 30.11.43 Y Es
Danyliuk, William	Private	L/20065	WG		(XD4)	K 1.12.43 Y Pa
Ingalls, Keith Campbell	Corporal	E/29833	RRoC		(XD4)	K 1.12.43 Y Es
Zedan, Michael	Private	H/41718	WG		(XD4)	K 5.12.43 Y Pa
McTaggart, Hugh T.	Corporal	H/6279	WG		(XD4)	K 5.12.43 Y Es/Pa
Rutherford, Archibald R.	Lance Sergeant	H/6057	WG		(XD4)	K 5.12.43 Y Bi/Es
Smith, Norman A.	Rifleman	C/63078	RRoC		(XD4)	K 9.12.43 Y Bi
McLaughlin, George R.	Private	H/6686	WG		(XD4)	K 20.12.43 Y Bi/Pa
Phillips, Edward	Lance Sergeant	E/30244	RRoC		(XD4)	K 21.12.43 Y Ph/Pa
Heuft, Ernest	Private	H/6254	WG		(XD4)	K 23.12.43 Y Es
Taylor, Reginald Samuel	Rifleman	E/29853	RRoC		(XD4)	K 23.12.43 Y Es/Pa

Wallace, Herbert	Rifleman	E/30195	RRoC	(XD4)	K 26.12.43 Y Es
Harding, Robert	Rifleman	E/30713	RRoC	(XD4)	K 27.12.43 Y Ph/Pa

Ma Tau Chung

Kalu Khan	Sepoy	785261	HKMC	U 2.1.43
Muhammad Shafi	Gunner	5472	HKSRA	U 5.1.43
Ram Sewak Singh	Lance Naik	13065	RP	K 8.1.43
Bhuta Khan	Groom	741685	HKMC	K 9.1.43
Gopal Singh	Sepoy	15063	PJ	K 16.1.43
Ram Awad	Cook	F/7	RP	K 17.1.43
Shah Nawaz	Gunner	8034	HKSRA	K 25.1.43
Mehar Singh	Naik	2571	HKSRA	U 17.2.43
Ram Lal Singh	Lance Naik	11718	RP	U 1.3.43
Lal Khan	Gunner	5071	HKSRA	K 9.3.43
Bagh Ali	Gunner	4978	HKSRA	K 9.3.43
Abdul Rakhman	Driver	783393	HKMC	U 19.3.43
Ali Khan	Gunner	4934	HKSRA	U 23.3.43
Khan Zaman	Sepoy	15672	RP	U 8.4.43
Labh Singh	Gunner	7541	HKSRA	U 25.4.43
Khacheru Singh	Sepoy	20456	RP	K 7.5.43
Ahmad Din	Sepoy	6030	RP	U 8.5.43
Amir Hamzar	Sepoy	15810	RP	U 8.5.43
Babu Din	Sepoy	10603	RP	U 8.5.43
Muhammad Nawaz Khan	Gunner	5089	HKSRA	U 8.5.43
Bharat Singh	Sepoy	21192	RP	U 20.5.43
Diwan Chand	Sepoy	16171	PJ	U 27.5.43
Nur Husain	Naik	3064	HKSRA	U 3.6.43
Wais Muhammad	Lance Naik	3073	HKSRA	K 3.6.43
Ram Swarup Singh	Sepoy	21055	RP	K 12.6.43
Muhammad Hanif	Gunner	7532	HKSRA	U 30.6.43
Allah Din	Gunner	4742	HKSRA	U 16.7.43
Muhammad Latif	Gunner	8162	HKSRA	U 17.7.43
Amar Shah	Sepoy	17844	PJ	K 21.7.43
Nur Muhammad	Gunner	5076	HKSRA	U 27.7.43
Ballu	Sweeper	741405	HKMC	K 1.8.43
Malik Singh	Gunner	4879	HKSRA	U 3.8.43
Ram Biswaz Singh	Sepoy	14512	RP	K 10.8.43
Bachan Singh	Sepoy	12977	RP	K 18.8.43
Muhammad Khan	Sepoy	14625	RP	U 20.8.43
Spin Gul	Sepoy	18470	PJ	K 24.8.43
Gujjan Singh	Naik	2941	HKSRA	U 28.8.43
Akbar Ali	Sepoy	8781	RP	U 8.9.43
Idu Beg	Sepoy	12734	RP	U 8.9.43
Barkat Ali	Gunner	5484	HKSRA	U 8.9.43
Dalip Singh	Gunner	3754	HKSRA	U 9.9.43
Munshi Singh	Lance Naik	16220	RP	K 10.9.43
Hukam Singh	Sepoy	12533	RP	K 12.9.43
Onkar Singh	Sepoy	11582	RP	K 13.9.43
Muhammad Hayat	Gunner	5093	HKSRA	U 13.9.43

Mangal Singh	Gunner	4696	HKSRA	U 13.9.43
Pyara Singh	Gunner	7573	HKSRA	U 15.9.43
Jamadar Khan	Gunner	7959	HKSRA	K 17.9.42
Allah Ditta	Sepoy	10290	RP	U 21.9.43
Chhedar Singh	Sepoy	19493	RP	K 24.9.43
Babu Singh	Sepoy	14774	RP	K 30.9.43
Sheo Bihari Tiwari	Cook	F/3	RP	K 1.10.43
Sheo Nath Singh	Lance Naik	12768	RP	K 1.10.43
Yaran Khan	Sepoy	20386	RP	U 6.10.43
Asgar Ali	Naik	3210	HKSRA	U 6.10.43
Muhammad Sadiq	Gunner	5182	HKSRA	U 6.10.43
Rahm Ali	Gunner	8124	HKSRA	K 16.10.43
Paras Ram	Sepoy	15833	PJ	U 17.10.43
Muhammad Khan	Sepoy	8279	PJ	K 25.10.43
Haidar Khan	Gunner	7888	HKSRA	U 26.10.43
Ghulam Nabi	Jemadar	14923/I.O.	RP I.O.M.	U 28.10.43
Ansari, Mateen Ahmed	Captain	1694	RP GC	K 29.10.43 Ex[85]
Kesho Singh	Sepoy	13161	RP	K 31.10.43
Hashmat Ali	Gunner	5193	HKSRA	U 5.11.43
Ali Akbar	Lance Naik	5068	HKSRA	K 13.11.43
Jaga Nath Singh	Sepoy	15163	RP	K 13.11.43
Fateh Bahadur Singh	Sepoy	8507	RP	K 18.11.43
Chandar Singh	Sepoy	15180	RP	K 24.11.43
Chandar Singh	Sepoy	9353	RP	K 25.11.43
Khuda Bakhsh	Saddler	741789	HKMC	K 25.11.43[86]
Rasila Ram	Sepoy	13672	PJ	U 27.11.43
Mul Singh	Sepoy	11045	RP	K 29.11.43
Badlu Singh	Sepoy	20512	RP	K 1.12.43
Bishan Singh	Sepoy	21116	RP	K 1.12.43
Hanuman Singh	Sepoy	15767	RP	K 1.12.43
Jang Bahadur Singh	Sub	3399/I.O.	RP	K 1.12.43
Lalu Singh	Sepoy	11329	RP	K 1.12.43
Mahabal Singh	Sepoy	11461	RP	K 1.12.43
Mansa Singh	Sepoy	14487	RP	K 1.12.43
Pitam Singh	Sepoy	21066	RP	K 1.12.43
Pitambar Singh	Lance Naik	10857	RP	K 1.12.43
Raghu Bir Singh	Sepoy	7002	RP	K 1.12.43
Raj Bahadur Singh	Sepoy	16263	RP	K 1.12.43
Rajpal Singh	Lance Naik	14035	RP	U 1.12.43
Rajpat Singh	Jemadar	8999/I.O.	RP	K 1.12.43
Ram Chandar Singh	Sepoy	8078	RP	K 1.12.43
Ram Singh	Sepoy	15445	RP	K 1.12.43
Sadhu Singh	Sepoy	15721	RP	K 1.12.43
Sarju Singh	Sepoy	20732	RP	K 1.12.43
Muhammad Ali	Gunner	8163	HKSRA	U 1.12.43
Surjan Singh	Gunner	3275	HKSRA	K 2.12.43
Khadim Husain	Gunner	4992	HKSRA	K 2.12.43
Ali Muhammad	Gunner	5296	HKSRA	K 8.12.43
Baldeo Singh	Sepoy	11472	RP	K 10.12.43

Shiraz Gul	Sepoy	15386	PJ		K 11.12.43
Moti Lal	Cook	7540	RP		K 18.12.43
Sher Zaman	Sepoy	9406	RP		U 18.12.43
Gharib Gul	Lance Naik	12643	PJ		U 18.12.43
Jalal Din	Gunner	5191	HKSRA		U 20.12.43
Mir Dad Khan	Sepoy	19475	PJ		K 22.12.43
Falak Sher	Gunner	3919	HKSRA		U 28.12.43
Nahar Singh	Gunner	7868	HKSRA		U 29.12.43

Stanley

Ross, John	CV	69		UCWD 3.1.43
Taylor, Horace Cecil	CV	Store Keeper Attached to RE	BRH	K 4.1.43[87]
Willey, Brian Anthony	CV	2		UCWD 24.1.43
Morrison, Kenneth S.	CV	56, Merchant director		UCWD 15.2.43
Hall, A.	CV			UCWD 16.2.43
Cameron, Christina	CV	45		UCWD 12.3.43
Greenburg, Essie	CV	51, Mrs.		UCWD 12.3.43[88]
Evans, Violet May	CV	40, Ms. Filing Clerk, Jardine		UCWD 6.4.43
Cressall, Paul Ewart MC	CV	50		UCWD 8.4.43
Gordon-White, Kingsley	CV	30, at Mental Hospital		UCWD 2.5.43
Oatway, Louis Hillesden	CV	50		UCWD 4.5.43
Humphreys, Elizabeth A.	CV	54, wife of Alfred David		UCWD 8.5.43 twb
Clark, John Caer	CV	65, husband of M. Clark		UCWD 8.6.43
Nelson, Reginald Trounge	CV	64		UCWD 12.6.43
Forbes, Duncan Douglas	CV	56, Merchant, No 358/9		UCWD 27.6.43
Jaffer, Kolsoom	CV			UCWD 22.7.43
Timm, Marie, Eleanor L.	CV			UCWD 29.7.43
Potter, Marion	CV	82		UCWD 17.8.43
Lenfesty, Frederick P.	CV	57		UCWD 27.8.43
Sells, Sonny	CV	2		UCWD 1-30.9.43
Margal, A.A.	CV			UCWD 3.10.43
Copland, James	CV	45, Marine Eng. Jardine		UCWD 8.10.43
Hayne, Frank Henry W.	CV	57, at Bowen Road Hospital		UCWD 27.10.43
Harmon, Thomas Victor	CV	46, Civil Servant		UCWD 21.11.43
Kirkby-Gomes, Dr. S.G.	CV	76, died at St Paul's Hospital		UCWD 22.11.43
MacGowan, Lilian Mary	CV	47, wife of J. F. MacGowan		UCWD 5.12.43
Younger, Cecil Walter	CV	44		UCWD 7.12.43 twb
Ozoria, Euxico Maria	CV	At Rosary Hill		UCWD 23.12.43

British Army Aid Group[89]

Tsang Tak Hing	Lance Bdr.		BAAG		U 1.43
Grayburn, Sir Vandeleur			BAAG		21.8.43
Hai Mun Lee			BAAG		7.9.43
(Hunt, Peter Norman	Driver		RASC		7.9.43)
So Biu			BAAG		7.9.43
Wu Tak Wing			BAAG		U 7.9.43
(Prata M.G.	HKVDC		BAAG		14.9.43)
(Ansari, M.A.	Captain	5/7th Rajputs	BAAG	GC	29.10.43)

Bashir Ahmed			BAAG		29.10.43
Bennett, Chester			BAAG		29.10.43
Bradley, Frederick William			BAAG		29.10.43
Chan Cho Kit			BAAG		29.10.43
Chang Yit, Cleveland Elroy			BAAG		29.10.43
Chan Ping Fan			BAAG		29.10.43
Chan Sin Chuen			BAAG		29.10.43
Fraser, John Alexander			BAAG	GC	29.10.43
Hall, Frederick Ivan George			BAAG		29.10.43
Hyde, Charles Frederick			BAAG		29.10.43
Kotwall, George			BAAG		29.10.43
Lau Kwok Ping			BAAG		29.10.43
Lau Tak Kwong			BAAG		29.10.43
Lau Tak Oi			BAAG		29.10.43
Lee Kung Hoi			BAAG		29.10.43
Lee Lam			BAAG		29.10.43
Lo Wing			BAAG		29.10.43
Luk Chung Kit			BAAG		29.10.43
Majid Feroz			BAAG		29.10.43
Monaghan, Thomas Christopher			BAAG		29.10.43
Naranjan Singh Grewal			BAAG		29.10.43
Rees, Hubert Stanley			BAAG		29.10.43
Scott, Walter Richardson	Deputy Commissioner		BAAG		29.10.43
Sinton, Alexander Christie			BAAG		29.10.43
Waterton, Douglas William			BAAG		29.10.43
White, William John			BAAG		29.10.43
Wong, Shiu Pun Preston			BAAG		29.10.43
Yan Cheuk Ming			BAAG		29.10.43
Yeung Sau Tak			BAAG		29.10.43
Yung Sham Cheung			BAAG		29.10.43
(Ford, Douglas	Captain	Royal Scots	BAAG	GC	18.12.43)
(Gray, Hector Bertram	F/Lt.	RAF	BAAG	GC	18.12.43)
(Newnham, Lanceray Arthur	Lt. Colonel		BAAG	GC	18.12.43)

1944

The invasion in Europe shouldn't be long now, events should soon start moving in the Balkans. I do hope & trust all is well at home, fancy I may see 'em all next year & the sermons either '45 or '46 — which will it be? Just fancy one of Ma's Sermons Teas once again & being able to sit down in an easy chair in front of a fire with a pipe & a drink. Our existence here wouldn't be so bad if food was more plentiful & if only we could receive letters. Haven't heard from home for more than 2 years. And if only people at the Dock Moru (No 212) & Mori (238) would treat us more reasonably, after all we do a good day's work & they'd get more out of us if they'd treat us more like humans & less like animals. I wonder if they have ever thought that sometime in the future positions will be reversed, then it'll be our turn! However in spite of our threats & lust for vengence on them, few of us will remain here long enough after the end to be able to do anything — even if we wished to & that's doubtful as we all will be glad to shake off the dust of this accursed country from our feet for ever. Gosh I do hope & pray that it is going to end this year. It's starting snowing.

— Private Bill Lowe, HKVDC

By the beginning of 1944, the POWs in Hong Kong occupied the Bowen Road Hospital, Shamshuipo Camp, Argyle Street Camp, and Ma Tau Chung. In China, the stragglers from the *Lisbon Maru* were still at Kiangwan (now Jiangwan), and there were many Indians in Guangzhou and on Hainan Island.

And of the 4,000 men who had been shipped to Japan, nearly 2,750 were still alive and spread across some twelve camps:[1]
- Tokyo Main Camp (Omori)
- Tokyo #3 Branch Camp (Yokohama Stadium)
- Tokyo #3 Dispatched Camp (Tsurumi Shipyard)
- Tokyo #5 Branch Camp (Niigata-Rinko)
- Osaka #1 Branch Camp (Minato-ku, Osaka)
- Osaka #2 Branch Camp (Kobe)
- Osaka #3 Branch Camp (Oeyama)

- Osaka #4 Dispatched Camp (Sakurajima)
- Osaka #5 Dispatched Camp (Kawasaki-Juko, Kobe)
- Osaka #6 Dispatched Camp (Amagasaki)
- Fukuoka #5 Branch Camp (Omine Coal Mine, Kawasaki-machi)
- Nagoya #2 Branch Camp (Narumi)

During 1943, a further 379 of the POWs and internees had died in total. Malnutrition, and its effects on the immune system, had been the biggest killer, though some 40 of this number had been executed for activities linked to BAAG.[2]

The year 1944 would see the last and smallest draft to Japan, and a growing realization that the war was going in the Allies favour. However, what boost this may have given to morale was often offset by a growing desperateness amongst POWs longing for the war's end. At the same time, the increasing strength of the American bombing in Hong Kong, and far more so in Japan, was becoming a threat both directly and — indirectly — through Japanese supply lines being disrupted; the Allies' own success was starving the surviving prisoners.

DIARY FOR 1944

January 1944

Saturday, 1 January. The year began with a hut collapsing at Tokyo #5B Niigata, killing eight Canadians. Forsyth was in that hut: "About 3.30 early this morning when we were all sound asleep from fatigue in the long bunk shed on the sandy hillside, I was awakened by the wrenching, creaking sound of straining timbers. All was in darkness, the hut seemed to be sinking beneath me, then I heard the awful screams of men crushed and trapped beneath the wreckage. The very first thing I thought was 'earthquake!' as I felt the building settling over me. I was in the upper bunk but not all the deaths were in the lower. On my right beneath the beams died Staff Sword and Les [Sauson], on my left Harold Jones was killed, while in the lower bunk little Joe Furey one of the brightest boys that had ever enlisted . . . Seven men died that night, and eight later and 17 men were put in hospital with broken ribs or pelvis'. They were put in casts and when the lice got inside the casts they suffered the tortures of the damned."

Elsewhere, the New Year was celebrated rather more appropriately. That same day, Poulter at Kobe reported: "A convoy has arrived, so our day off was cancelled and we had to go to work. The No 1 of Takahama's, who cannot speak English, gave Challis and myself nearly half a pint of Sake each in which to drink his health. We drank it but what we said in English had no bearing on his *good* health, in fact he should have dropped dead on the spot!"

Monday, 3 January. Fisher at Shamshuipo noted the passing of Alberto Soares. "We had a death in camp today. A young Portuguese fellow was gardening when he collapsed and died of heart failure." (p. 98)

But at least in Hong Kong it was not too cold. For those men still bound for Japan on the *Toyama Maru* (now, thanks to the storms, with only one functioning latrine on deck), the weather was becoming colder and colder, and by 3 January, it was snowing. After anchoring off Moji on the 5th, the ship docked on the 6th.

These prisoners were originally sent to two camps:[3]
- Nagoya #2 Branch Camp (Narumi)
- Osaka #3 Branch Camp (Oeyama)

Alec Howard, HKVDC, was in the Narumi group: "Jan 6th Left Shimonoseki on train 7.30 pm. Jan 7th. Arrived Narumi camp 4.30 pm."

Frank Evans was on the train for Oeyama: "We were freezing cold at the railway station where, with all our baggage, we waited for a train to take a number of us to an unknown destination, whilst the remainder went on different trains to other parts of Japan. We were soon huddled into a rail coach and started on our long train journey to somewhere about 500 miles from Nagasaki. A small box-full of cold rice was handed to each of us as the train left the station. Very soon we were out of the urban area and in the midst of hills and dales covered with a deep layer of snow. When the day was drawing to its close, we arrived at a station in the Oeyama area, near Kaya-cho. We were met there by a number of Japanese together with a group of men who were unshaven and looked badly dressed, thin and haggard. After we assembled together to be counted we were marched to the prison camp, and en route one of them whispered into my ear and said: 'We are Canadians and we are dying here every day. You are coming to a death trap.' That is all he said, and I could see in his eyes how afraid he was of the guards around us . . . that camp was apparently considered the worst one in Japan."[4] (p. 98)

Evans continued: "The prisoners already in the camp, mostly Canadians, were thin, tense and dejected, and suffering badly from malnutrition. They considered their treatment very nearly intolerable, and working daily in the nickel mine placed great strain on men who were almost physical wrecks. Between twenty and thirty of us were soon settled in one of the huts in the centre of a camp consisting of British, Canadian and later American prisoners, a total of about six hundred. Along one side of the hut, covering about three-quarters of the space, there was a raised platform made up of tatamis to lie on. There were wooden framed sliding doors covered with paper separating the sleeping part from the long alleyway, with a narrow table and a form to sit on along the opposite side. We kept our kits at the end of the bed space. Sleeping on the straw pillow and hard tatami with two blankets plus my clothing was far from comfortable!" (p. 98)

Tuesday, 11 January. Lowe at Innoshima: "Big scare on now re beri-beri. Bruce has it & had a heart attack. We've been weighed & all lost weight. Mugford RAMC has done a lot of hard work in bringing to notice of Comm how bad the food is & he deserves great credit for his work."

Saturday, 15 January. Flying Officer (doctor) Walter Riley arrived at Narumi from Osaka (though he had been captured on Java) as the new MO.

Sunday, 16 January. Fisher at Shamshuipo: "A certain Swiss who was in here and went to Bowen Road with TB has been released — good luck Houssamann, you should never have been a prisoner anyway." (p. 103)

Wednesday, 19 January. Stanley became Military Internment Camp, Stanley, but life there continued much as before. Boredom, along with the lack of privacy and insufficient food, remained the major problems. Entertainment of any kind was at a premium. Mabel Redwood: "If one had to select a favourite performer in Stanley, I think most internees would vote for Mrs Betty Drown. Every Sunday evening, she sat down at the piano in the club room and played non-stop. No programme was announced; Betty merely played as the fancy took her, and a more varied selection of music it would have been hard to find. I think she must have known every tune ever written, and if any one could not recall a title when making a request, one had only to hum a bit of it and she would play it."[5]

Entertainment was equally important at Rosary Hill. Peter White: "There was an attempt to provide schooling for the children, organized by Mrs. Betty White (no relation). Entertainment was provided with a couple of concerts organized by Mrs. Ellen Field.[6] The last one was memorable; when she sang 'There'll always be an England' to an appreciative audience, among those in attendance were several Japanese officers. Thank God they obviously didn't understand English, or there might have been serious consequences! They clapped politely at the conclusion. Needless to say, there were no more concerts after that!"

But in Japan, entertainment was not the most pressing issue. As Stenning, at Oeyama, reported the same day: "Death by freezing in bed (Sergeant J. Wilson R.A.)."

Thursday, 20 January. Forsyth at Niigata #5B witnessed the weather being put to cruel use: "I saw Mortimer . . . tied to stakes one evening in mid-winter, snow on the ground, clad only in short and trousers, barefooted, bareheaded, hands behind their backs, about 6 feet of slack rope to let them run around the pole which they did all night to keep from freezing . . . Mortimer was in hospital with frozen feet, gangrene set in, and he died three days later."[7] Cambon also witnessed the incident: "Miraculously the upper part of his body was only superficially frozen, and he could move his arms. However, his lower limbs were past repair and soon became gangrenous. The smell in the small room of the hospital was overpowering."[8]

February 1944

Surgeon Lieutenant Commander Samuel Stenning, Royal Australian Naval Service, who was the senior medical officer at Oeyama from 15 October 1943 to 23 June 1944, kept careful notes.

Tuesday, 1 February. "The main fault in treatment lies in the fact of sending men to work who were unfit. This happened repeatedly, the men responsible being Medical Sergeant Nakayama, Lieutenant Hazami, Sergeant Takahashi, and Corporal Tarodati, in descending order. The deaths of Sapper G. Cund, R.E., Gunner E. King, R.A., and Private J. Bross of the Winnipeg Grenadiers were directly due to this and the above men must be held responsible."[9]

Wednesday, 2 February. At Oeyama, John Friesen, who had been assaulted by Tugby and Harvey for selling half a scone for a cigarette, died. Of this event Stenning noted: "On one occasion — when H/6951 Pte. John Friesen, Winnipeg Grenadiers, a patient on the waiting list became maniacal, Sgt. Harvey, without consulting me and before informing me that Pte Friesen was acutely ill, struck the patient with his fist and rendered him unconscious. Then he informed me of his action. I saw Pte. Friesen immediately. He was moribund and I was unable to do anything. Pte. Friesen died within two hours without regaining consciousness."[10]

Thursday, 3 February. Redwood at Stanley: "Mrs Doris Groves [wife of Sergeant Groves, HKPF] died during childbirth, also the child, Arthur, leaving a husband and a three-year-old daughter Joyce in camp." Wright-Nooth noted: "After a previous baby, also in this camp, which died at birth and for which a caesarean operation was necessary she had been warned not to have another."[11] (p. 200)

Saturday, 12 February. Arthur Taylor: "At Kawasaki Station — breakfast, beans & soup — lunch, rice & soup — tea, rice & soup — Private Fenn[12] & Ted Mynatt[13] left for Shinagawa Hospital — bath night — David Wilson returned from Shinagawa."

March 1944

Saturday, 18 March. Leo Berard at Tokyo #3D: "S/Sgt. Ellis died yesterday at 05.20 hours, a big lad with a lot of good plans for after the war, hadn't been sick hardly except run down with the usual beri-beri and malnutrition." (p. 150)

Monday, 20 March. A number of Tokyo #3B (Yokohama Stadium) POWs were moved to Tokyo#13D (Asano docks).

Friday, 24 March. Fisher at Shamshuipo: "I have just come in from the other ward. I went to see Sergeant Wooley of the Volunteers. He came in with dysentery some time ago and has been losing ground. He looks ghastly with sunken face and eyes, his thighs no thicker than my arm. I found it hard to be able to say much to him, because my expression must have given me away, but he managed to smile for me, but I doubt he will be with us much longer." (p. 114)

Tuesday, 28 March: Taylor: "42nd birthday anniversary — what a day!!! Started raining at 2 a.m. — rained nearly all day — left camp 8.15 a.m. in lorries — lunch arrived 1 hour late — ceased work 5.30 p.m. — waited in rain for half an hour for lorry — lorry broke down, walked to camp, arriving 6.30 p.m. — breakfast, beans & soup — lunch, rice & soup, tea, fried fish, rice & soup. Edge[14] returned from Shinagawa."

Jackson at Ichioka hospital: "From October 1942, to July 1944 I endeavoured, against orders, to maintain clinical notes to cover about 700 admissions and 202 deaths. In March 1944, however, my quarters were raided by Japanese officials who confiscated every scrap of paper and arrested my writer, G.H. Bignal,[15] and myself. We were taken to the guard room of Osaka main hospital, where we were interrogated all next day. As a result the hospital staff was broken up and the hospital was closed four months later. I was dispatched to a 'punishment' camp in Kameoka."[16]

Wallace Hastings also remembered the hospital's end: "Routinely we had snap inspections with no warning and on one such occasion which was in 1944, during the searching of the doctor's office some Japanese newspapers were found, showing maps of the far eastern theatre of war indicating the movements of Allied and Japanese ships. Their discovery caused an uproar among the Japanese officers present. For some reason they believed that the staff were involved in a conspiracy and the result of this we were informed that all staff would be individually dispersed to other camps. We were told to pack our belongings and the following day I was taken in the company of one armed guard by rail to Hirohata Camp near Himeji. I arrived to find that it was peopled by about four hundred American servicemen from the Philippine war zone and one Australian airman."

Wednesday, 29 March. Lowe at Innoshima: "Damn cold month & gosh how I've felt it. Got loot today. Coxhead beaten up for pinching Nip rice ration."[17]

April 1944

Saturday, 1 April. A number of Tokyo Stadium (Yokohama) POWs were transferred to Niishin Oil and Yokohama Stevedores.

Easter Sunday, 9 April. Baird in Hong Kong: "Just 27 years ago today I was in the Vimy Ridge show. I didn't expect to get out of that show alive, let alone being on the other side of the world from my wife and daughter."[18] (p. 187)

Friday, 21 April. Forsyth at Niigata: "Robley of the Rifles died today at 10 o'clock. He had beri-beri, infected leg, and amoebic dysentery."

Friday, 21 April. O'Toole at Shamshuipo: "Draft assembles. At work on new kitchen for officers in F lines at the time, but put on all the same. Kit packed and examined & lodged in Group 2 F2, Arthur in F1."

Sunday, 23 April. O'Toole continued: "Taken off the draft at midday with Alf Pugh have to start work straight away on the kitchen again, since 21/4 we have been working from 7.30 to 5 excused all parades."

On the same day, Fisher at Shamshuipo added: "Last Wednesday, nine officers, all medical officers, and all those previously selected, 200 in all, were given three-quarters of an hour to pack their kit and get into 'F' lines which has been wired off. So the draft is on! . . . Sergeant Groome had a row with [Boon] and told him he was not fit to be called a British officer, and refused to call him 'Sir'. Boon threatened to take him before the Japs but did not do so, but Groome's name is now on the draft. Similarly all those who fell out with the Stooges are also on the draft. It seems that Boon is running the camp very well for his masters." (p. 117)[19]

Saturday, 29 April. Leo Berard at Kawasaki #3D: "[Jim Emo] had especially good qualities to be our brigade Provost Sergeant — Irish personality galore, physical ability in jujitsu, wrestling, and boxing. He didn't have to use his physical attributes; his personality would suffice . . . When he died of double pneumonia on April 29, 1944, our whole camp mourned his death and acknowledged his great fight to live." (p. 142)

The Sixth Draft: *Naura Maru*

Saturday, 29 April.[20] The final transportation from Hong Kong departed carrying just 220 men.

Cicero Rozario noted: "One fine day, we went out on a working party and on returning at 6:00 p.m. the Japanese Camp Commandant and a few dignitaries were waiting for us at the football field. They were there to pick the fitter men to go to Japan. They made us walk around the field, couldn't make up their minds, and finally said 'All go'. We were put on one side of the Camp and separated from the other prisoners by barbed wire. We made a hole in the barbed stuff and came out to chat with our friends and returned at night to sleep. One chap almost got caught by the Japanese sentry. He ran and jumped over the fence. The guard fired and missed. This was Father Zinho Gosano. The Japanese doctors and specialists were there every day to give us injections, swabs and other tests. I think there were about twenty in all and you have to stand in line whether your turn was today or tomorrow. One chap objected to being stuck with a glass rod in the stool test. He let go when they stuck with glass rod into him. The medic got the full blast and showed this chap that he was really mad. It's a wonder he survived the beating."

Sunday, 30 April.   Laite also reported: "A draft of about 200 men left yesterday for parts unknown to us. Amongst them were 148 Canadians."

Rozario continued: "Then we were sent down to the hold where our quarters were. The place was full of flies as the ship was carrying a cargo of Chinese condiments (the likes of 'min-see' and 'tau-see'). Then the shocker came — our sleeping quarters were up against the sides of the ship about four feet from the ground. You had to sleep side-by-side with your knees bent as you only had three feet from your head to your toe. I was sleeping between David and Stanley Leonard and if I moved a little, their fists would automatically fall on my chest. It was torture sleeping in our cramped space but we whiled away the time playing cards for cigarettes when we weren't sleeping."

Bill Oxley was also on board: "Our ship was the *Asama Maru*[21] . . . The voyage was fraught with danger. We were battened down with a green tarpaulin over the battens. We slept on coal; the heat was unbearable. They would not let us go up to the toilet, so we 'went' where we could. Food was given to us at night; the tarpaulin was removed, one batten lifted while six sentries guarded the hold. In the early morning, the batten was put back, also the tarpaulin. Below, we sat naked. The heat and the stench of excreta and urine was almost overpowering, but they would not lift the covers to give us respite."

The ship docked at Moji. Oxley: "We had arrived at our destination. We all came up on deck, shielding our eyes. For fifteen days we had not washed or shaved. We were also lousy and filthy, with excreta all over us. We stank. A crew member of the ship came along with a hose pipe. He ordered us to strip, which we did, and as we stood in line, he walked along hosing us down with ice-cold water, even though there was frost everywhere. I could not believe this was real, and wondered why they didn't shoot us and have done with it. We were in hell."

On arrival, all the POWs on this vessel were sent by train to Sendai #2 Branch Camp (Yoshima Coal Mine).

Rozario: "They put us on a train and we were seated for the next forty-eight hours. We had to put the blinds down whenever we approached the stations. We couldn't lie down and the beri-beri, which plagued half the group, got worse and your ankles grew to double their normal size and it was very tiring when you walked. The toilet was at the back of the last coach. You had to squat and hang on to two handles. You could not go to the lavatory when nearing a station because they braked and you went flying. We learned that the hard way."

When they arrived at the station, Bill Oxley noted: "Another little shit of an officer stood on the station, beaming. He had 12 soldiers with him, with fixed bayonets. He formed us into threes, with sentries at intervals beside us. He screamed 'Smee!' (quick march) and we were away once again. We marched for about twenty minutes between the close-knit mountains. Suddenly, around the next bend, we saw two very high wooden doors, which were open. All around the doors were very high wooden fences — they must have been fifteen feet high."

Saturday, 13 May. Captain Robinson, RAMC, arrived at Sendai #2 (Yoshima) with all but one of the men from this draft (the last had been sent to Shinagawa hospital).

Rozario: "[We] had to walk in an underground route for about five miles, I believe, and we finally came out into the open. We had to climb a hill to get up to the two huts there. The Volunteers from Hong Kong were in one hut and the Canadians and regular soldiers in the other. Later, ten American servicemen joined the Canadians."

Bill Oxley: "Next morning at 4 o'clock we were awakened by the beat of a bass drum, and we arose from the platform where we slept. The 'Ancho' (Corporal) told us only to put on our trousers and shoes, and fall in outside. We stood outside in the compound, were placed twelve men in a line, four men deep. The Corporal said that we were going outside to do exercises. 'Do you know how to row a boat?' One foot forward, grasp the oars, and pull back; do that continually, at the same time shouting 'Hi-Saw' (heave). This exercise was carried on for 15 minutes, then we were told to rub our chests with our knuckles until they were red. After our exercise, we had our rice, and some cooked peanuts, then we were each given a little wooden box with a lid, and two little chopsticks, with rice inside, and one slice of orange. We were told this was our 'binto' when we stopped for a 'yasame' (rest). 'Now you go to work — quick march!' We followed the 'Ancho' around a mountain, and came to a very high scaffold, with a big wheel on the top. One man said, 'My God! It's a coal mine!' We were all stunned and terrified."

Settling down at Sendai #2B, Rozario said: "In the beginning, we went down the mines in the coal trucks, but they were often derailed, causing a lot of minor injuries, so we went down on foot, half-a-mile every day. We would run down the rail tracks and shout 'buraco' when we jumped over a pot-hole, to warn the others behind. After a while, the Japanese were calling 'buraco' too. The usual was five men working on a phase, or more or less, depending on the size of the phase. We drilled the coals down and then shoveled them into small trucks which were towed up and unloaded by Japanese girls up top. Then the empties were sent down and our men picked them up and delivered them back to the phases. In a gang of five, you had a driller (operating a 70 lb pneumatic drill), and the 'shovelers', shoveling the coal to the coal trucks which would be emptied at the other end where the proper transport trucks are. Two men at the other end shoveled the coal into the big trucks — usually four coal truck loads to a transport truck. If it snowed heavily, less of the empty coal trucks came down as the cable house and machinery would be surrounded with snow on those days."

Manassah 'Nat' Rakusen[22] noted: "Each gang of four or five men were given a quota of coal to get out of the mine, usually from 12 to 25 tons, depending on the type or condition of the coal face, but usually it meant about 8 hours solid work. There were other types of work, such as timbering, general maintenance of the track, piping, wiring, etc., which, although arduous enough, was not so 'driving' as on coal. I always tried to get into one of the latter type of gangs, as also, as a rule, their situation was not so hot as on coal. Still, I had in all many months in coal gangs and sometimes it was only by sheer willpower that I was able to carry on until our quota was done. I will say that most of the men made allowances to some degree for my age and marked unsuitability for the work, and if possible or practicable, permitted me to do less than my real share, but this was seldom possible, as when working in pairs (usually the system) one had to 'keep up' with your opposite number.

I had one month off with a crushed finger (a rail dropped on it) but it healed up remarkably well and now there is hardly a sign of the terrible mess it was. Apart from that, I had only about five days off, from August 1944 to the end. Shifts were 10 or 11 days duration, and after a day's rest you switched with the other shift — that is, one was on day shift and the other on nights, and vice versa. The day shift reveille was 4.30 a.m.

(for a couple of months it was 4 a.m.), roll call 4.45; breakfast, and down the mine at 6 a.m. We returned to camp anywhere from 4 to 6 o'clock, as we were kept down until all the gangs had finished their quotas. We were very fortunate in that, by working in a coal mine, we were able to have a hot bath (communal one) every day. Naturally, almost everyone returned dirty and black with coal and it was a great relief to get into the bath after a wash down and soak all the aches and pains away.

I should have mentioned that on day shift, the kitchen sent down a small lunch box for each man, containing cereal and a spoon-full of some vegetable. After bath, the evening meal was served (I should say 'taken') and by the time one had made down one's bed it was practically time for the evening roll-call at 7 p.m. Lights out was 7.30, so you can see one had no time for relaxation of any kind. We managed to keep quite warm at nights, but the place was infested with fleas — I cannot describe how really bad they were, thousands of them in and around one's blankets, and nothing you could do about it. It was scratch, scratch, until one fell asleep exhausted. In the morning you could wake up covered with bites, but you didn't mind, as fortunately, they didn't carry any disease. There also was a certain amount of lice, but I was lucky to keep clear of this pest, as there was nothing you could do about it — just kill as many as you could every day."

May 1944

Monday, 1 May. More Yokohama Stadium POWs were sent out to Tokyo sub-camps. Ford led the #19D party: "Yokohama Stadium camp was disbanded in Spring 44, when we separated into small parties and went to live nearer our respective jobs. I took command of a stevedore party consisting of P/O Hard, R.A.F., and 50 British other ranks. We worked for the Yokohama Stevedore Company and were housed by them at Camp 19 D which opened with our entry on May 1st, 44."

Ford explained: "When Yokohama Stadium Camp was closed we all went to the firms who we worked for. I went to the stevedore camp [#19D]. There was a camp at Asano Dock [#13D] and Nisshinseyu (vegetable oil) [#17B], a camp at the Firebrick Factory [#18D]. I think that was all."

Tuesday, 2 May. Redwood at Stanley: "Robert Mitchell born (parents married in camp, with Rosemary Mitchell born in Oct. 1942) . . . Mrs

R.G. Rose died, leaving husband in other camp, and Dawn aged 12 and Gerald, about 8, in here".[23]

Wednesday, 3 May. O'Toole at Shamshuipo: "150 officers move into F lines very strict rules reference us having no contacts with them, who wants to anyway." Over the next two weeks or so, on 4, 11, and 22 May, the officers moved from Argyle Street to the northern end of Shamshuipo Camp, which was wired off from the remainder of the camp. The two parts of the camp retained the names 'N' and 'S'.

Sunday, 7 May. Laite: "On Friday one of the Japanese soldiers was accidentally crushed by a truck, and died a few hours later."

Tuesday, 9 May. Redwood: "Little Brian Gill drowned in the fresh water pool at the beach. We went to his funeral next day. Father Meyer made him a coffin, and I'll never forget: 'Heaven is the Prize' which the children sang."[24]

Wednesday, 10 May. Arthur Taylor in Tokyo was also hearing bad news: "Received Elsie's letter of 15-8-43 & Ivy's letter of 26-9-43, 10-10-43, & 20-10-43, containing news that Dad died 9th October — Mum not too well."

Saturday, 13 May. Baird reported the closure of Argyle Street: "Here we are, back again at Sham Shui Po. They say three times and out. We were warned on Wednesday evening to be ready to move at 8.30 a.m. Thursday, so we had plenty of time to get our litter all packed . . . we got here about 11.00 a.m." (p. 190)

Tuesday, 16 May. Fisher at Shamshuipo: "Yesterday at 5.20 pm young Michael Dodwell sank peacefully away. No one could help him. One man, Assesero, who was Russian, but worked for Dodwells, sold his watch and bought all kinds of food for him, all to no effect."[25] (p. 120)

Tuesday, 16 May. Poulter at Kobe: "Another Albuhera Day and we had a get together like last year. Those present were. Capts. Man and Weedon, Lt's. King and Graham, RSM Challis, RQMS Hale and Chaplin, CSM Soden, C/Sgts. Poulter and Lomax, Sgts. Jeffree, Quick, Ruck, Hobson, Gilham, Dyson and Drum Major Holdford."

Friday, 19 May. Fisher at Shamshuipo: "Yesterday 25 cases [of Malaria] were taken to Bowen Road. One seaman, who was in hospital when I was only got as far as the bamboo pier because he was so ill. He was taken back to our hospital soaking wet, and died later. His wife died in 1943 in Stanley, but he had never been told officially."

Saturday, 27 May.   Coxhead at Innoshima: "Card from home!! Dated Jan 25th 1944. Straight to Zentsuji No. 2. 'ALL WELL AND HOPEFUL. FRIENDS EVERYWHERE REJOICE TO HEAR OF JAPAN CARDS AND HONG KONG LETTER. NEWS MADE CHRISTMAS HAPPY. GOD BLESS YOU. MUM AND ELIZABETH'."[26]

June 1944

In June, the Indian POWs moved from Ma Tau Chung to the recently vacated Argyle Street. This would make Ma Tau Chung available for later re-opening as a civilian camp, Ma Tau Wai.[27] The POW/Internee situation in Hong Kong would then remain largely unchanged until the end of the war.

In Japan, Captain Eric Marsden, Royal Corps of Signals, was sent from Omori to Yokohama Brickworks Camp.

Thursday, 1 June.   Wright-Nooth at Stanley: "Rice grinding was a tedious and, for the elderly, an exhausting chore. In June 1944, Professor [Byrne] had the ultimate misfortune of dropping dead from a heart attack while grinding rice to make a cake for his sixtieth birthday." (p. 125)

Monday, 5 June.   Botelho and Lieutenant Shrigley were arrested.

Wednesday, 7 June.   Colonel Field, James Smith, and Godfrey Bird were arrested.

Thursday, 8 June.   Coxhead at Innoshima heard a cryptic message at lunch: "We have crossed the moat and breached the western wall."

On the 11th he continued: "Pressing on with second front: Cherbourg, Havre, Caen (latest) F/camp. German claims of 2 battleships & 1800 planes & 6 Divisions 'wiped out'. Still pouring men, tanks in."[28]

Sunday, 18 June.   Fisher at Shamshuipo: "Charlie Hatt of our company is very ill. He is 65, and has never been able to assimilate rice properly, and now he can keep nothing down but slops. He has a numb feeling in the stomach, which usually means he has pellagra in that region." (p. 125)[29]

Wednesday, 28 June.   Shrigley was reported dead.[30]

July 1944

Tuesday, 4 July.   Coxhead at Innoshima: "Arrival of American Red+ clothes; splendid material." Accompanying the clothes was a letter, presumably from the previous July:

> July 29
> 300 Park Avenue
> Freeport
> NY
>
> Hallo there!
>
> Just dropped into say hello for a minute. I've just finished this sweater and though I didn't mind knitting it, I'm really much happier about the whole thing now that it's over. It's not the sweater I mind so much as the sweltering, and I do mean hot, weather that makes me feel that nobody in his right mind would ever wear the thing. However, perhaps it's a slight bit cooler where you are — and please don't think I'm as much of a picklepuss as I sound. Now that I speak of it, I wonder where you are and what sort of a time you are having, where you're from — all that stuff. Please don't think me rude when I say that if you'd like to get letters now and then — well, I'd love to write them and maybe this letter could be an introduction,
> 'Bye now,
>
> (signed) Catherine Eddy
>
> (I'm still a miss and just 21)[31]

Sunday, 16 July.   Goodwin at Shamshuipo: "For weeks there had been electrical storms with constant rains, and Sunday the 16th of July 1944 was just another day of pouring rain, without, however, the usual display of lightning. In fact, when darkness fell, the rains came down with never a flash to break the darkness, a most unusual condition. Never before had there been such an opportunity." (p. 42)

Monday, 17 July. In the early morning, Goodwin escaped through climbing the electric fence, in a rainstorm, taking the greatest care — by climbing on the insulators — not to be electrocuted: "I was off the ground, the insulator had not broken, I was not electrocuted. Now for the next step. It had to be my right foot[32] this time, but the step was not so high. In poising for this step my bare leg pressed hard against the third electric wire. There was no insulator on that one, and it was standing out nine inches from the post. Those were moments of supreme danger. All my weight was concentrated on the small insulator top, little more than an inch in diameter, and my left foot was rapidly tiring. My bare leg was pressed hard against a live wire; my right foot was precariously poised on the top insulator, and my hands were grasping the post between strands of concertina wire. With my leg against the live wire one touch of those invisible strands above would have been fatal." (p. 45)

Later, the two officers who slept either side of him, Lt Chown RNVR and Lt Trapman 12 CRRA, were arrested and interrogated, as were his two friends Lt Glover HKRNVR and Lt Thomson RNR.

Tuesday, 18 July. Baird: "We have had some excitement in camp the past two days. Sometime Sunday evening or night, one of the officers in this camp escaped. I think it a selfish thing to do at this stage of the game as he cannot give any information or be of any use to the army on physical grounds. Then everyone in camp is left holding the sack, and a few will really take it on the chin in the way of punishment the Japs hand out."[33] (p. 197)

Parker added: "He planned the thing alone and went by himself. He slept right opposite me but I never suspected he was going to make a try for it. Thinking back, however, we remembered he did do an awful lot of walking and in his bare feet, too, but bare feet weren't unusual, we all went around that way."

Wednesday, 19 July. Weedon at Kobe, although he did not know it then, was hearing rumours that would lead to the end of the war: "Unconfirmed rumours of fall of Saipan."[34] Every flat space on the islands of Saipan and Tinian would be converted into huge modern airbases, from which B29s would later flatten most Japanese cities, and kill not a few POWs. Eventually, of course, from Tinian they would carry The Bomb.

Marsh at Tokyo #3D was at the wrong end of a B29 raid: "One night in July a large-scale attack with firebombs was made in our district. The ack-ack was terrific. The whole world seemed aflame. In spite of the efforts of our guards to keep us from witnessing the sight we stood and gazed at the conflagration. Only a river running nearby and the fact that our huts had tiled roofs saved our quarters from the fire. Smoke and sparks were all around. I saw a terrible sight that night. I watched a string of American bombers, in line astern formation, following their leader. The lead aircraft made for the very centre of the ack-ack fire and at this point burst into flames. Plane after plane followed to the same point and were shot down. Altogether I counted five. I felt sick. We all prayed for those gallant lads. One of the Jap guards, like quite a few Japanese who prided themselves on their aesthetic qualities, got quite a kick out of seeing his home town destroyed. He stood gazing on the burning city in rapt ecstasy and then raising his arms to the sky he turned to us and said in English, 'Drama! Drama'. He was convinced he had a front seat at a good show, all for nothing. He appeared quite mad and if he had a fiddle like Nero I'm sure he would have played us a tune. For several days following the bombing we saw long files of civilian refugees filing past our camp trekking into the hills. The Japanese Officials had cleared the whole district of its inhabitants. The remaining hovels and dwellings that had survived the firebombing were pulled down to prevent the further spread of the fire but little was left to save."

Sunday, 23 July. Gittins at Tweed Bay Hospital, Stanley: "The church service was to be held in our ward. I was asked to choose the hymn. Without hesitation I suggested my favourite, 'Abide with me'. Immediately after the service, Sister Gordon took me out on the balcony and quietly told me that Bill Faid had slipped from our roof and, having fractured his skull, was dead on arrival at the hospital." (p. 96)

Monday, 24 July. Redwood at Stanley: "Mr A.L. Shields died; his wife had been repatriated with Canadians."

Wednesday, 26 July. Laite at Shamshuipo: "Sgt Major Rose of H.K.V.D.C., whose wife died at Stanley recently, has been notified that his two children, Dawn and Gerald are to be repatriated to Canada, if homes can be provided for them. Naturally, when Barnett and I heard of it, we each offered our homes to them, and today I have written the following card to their guardian at Stanley.

> Miss Gladys MacNider,
> Block 3, Room 17,
> Military Internment Camp Stanley.
>
> This card assures hearty welcome to Dawn and Gerald, from my family at 3677 West 19th Avenue, Vancouver, B.C., Canada. This leaves me well and in good spirits. Know you will be happy together. Best wishes for you and fondest love to my family. Sincerely,
> U. Laite.

Sunday, 30 July. Taylor: "At Kawasaki station — Private Condon, R. Scots died 10.30 p.m."

Monday, 31 July. Taylor: "Jimmy Coils, A.B. died at 3 a.m. — at Kawasaki Station- Condon & Coils cremated — English burial service read by Major Barry."[35]

August 1944

Thursday, 3 August. Laite continued: "Last midnight we were all roused from our slumbers by Ack Ack fire, because our bomber was over dropping bombs near our camp — some say on or near Cosmo docks. The plane was very low, and by the vibrations glass was broken in a nearby hut. Planes were over again at 4 a.m., but it was too cloudy and dark for bombing. All of us heard the midnight visitor, and the siren sounding, but most of us were asleep before the all clear sounded. Are we getting callous or is it just steady nerves?"

Wednesday, 16 August. Fisher at Shamshuipo: "Today in camp a Canadian tried to commit suicide. He gashed his throat, but not fatally, and now has 54 stitches in it; a pretty nasty reminder for the rest of his life, poor devil." (p. 140)

Friday, 18 August. BAAG reported that the Indians at MA TAU CHUNG CAMP were transferred to ARGYLE STREET CAMP. "There are now approximately 500 Indian PWs in the camp, which is divided into two portions. One portion on the NORTH side of the camp consists of a hospital for Indians in and outside the camp. The PW portion if the camp is on the SOUTH side . . . The number of inmates in the hospital on 18th August 1944 comprised 50 PATHANS, 60 PUNJABIS, 30 RAJPUTS and 24 SIKHS. The hospital staff consists of 5 doctors as follows: Jem, MOHAMED OMAR (2/14 PUNJABS), Jem. KARTAR SINGH (Civilian), JEM. DOSHT MOHMED (2/14 PUNJABS, Jem. REIM MULLAH (Civilian), and Jem. ? (DOGRA Civilian). These doctors are only capable of doing minor operations, and any major cases are left to die. There are 5 medical orderlies: Sepoy DILDA KHAN and 4 others taken from the camp but names unknown. There are very few drugs in the camp hospital, — no aspirin and very little quinine. Any drugs wanted have to be bought by the individual outside the camp. The dead are buried on the small hill EAST of the camp next to the vegetable garden."

It noted too that the Indian command structure (for the purpose of discipline the Camp was divided into 4 Coys, A, B, C, and D) there was:

Camp Commander	Sub. MER KHAN	5/7 Rajputs
Platoon Commanders	Sub/Maj ABDERMAN KHAN	2/14 Punjabs
	Sub/Maj MAGAR SINGH	HKSRA
	Sub/Maj MOHAMED ALI	HKSRA
	Sub/Maj PARITAM SINGH	HKSRA
	Jem. NAWABU	2/14 Punjabs
	Jem. RAM SINGH	2/14 Punjabs
	Jem. BAKHTAWAR SINGH	HKSRA
	Jem. AKHIM KHAN	RIASC
Jem. Adjutant	Jem. AMIN KHAN	2/14 Punjabs
Q.M.H.	Hav. JAMROSE KHAN	2/14 Punjabs
Interpreter	L/Nk AZAR KHAN	2/14 Punjabs[36]

Monday, 20 August. Weedon at Kobe: "Concert party taken by lorry to new hospital in outskirts of Kobe in afternoon. Went with them. Concert a great success and very pleasant change to see new surroundings and new faces. Almost a hundred patients and several doctors, in charge of Commander Page, who came up from HK soon after us." (p. 105)

Thursday, 24 August. Arthur Taylor: "2nd Anniversary of Camp opening – at Nisshin – work ceased at noon – back at camp 2.15 – 2.30 bath – 4 p.m. speech by Commandant, very good speech – presentation of cigarettes to joto boys – concert – big tea, white rice, curry and macaroni soup, fried fish, mashed potatoes, silko beans – 2 packets of cigarettes w/ 1 apple per man – letters for people who had not been sick since May, if there were letters here for them."

Saturday, 26 August. Fisher at Shamshuipo: "Yesterday too we had another memorable event, our first successful suicide. He was a Canadian who was in the Hong Kong VDC being chief engineer in Anderson Meyer pre-war. He was about 40 years old, and some say he had bad news from home. This prompted him to climb on to a beam in the latrine and fall off backwards in an endeavour to break his neck. However he failed to do this but fractured his spine and died at 4.00 am today."[37] (p. 140)

Tuesday, 29 August. Redwood at Stanley: "D.C. Edmonston died. This was sad. He had been in gaol and his wife and daughter Mary (who bought Olive's gold manicure set for Mary's birthday in January for Yen 30) were notified that he was dying and allowed to see him, but he didn't know them and died, and his body was allowed to be buried in camp cemetery."

September 1944

Thursday, 7 September. Redwood at Stanley: "Mrs Hyde died, leaving a little boy of six named Michael, whom Lady Grayburn is looking after; Mrs Hyde's husband[38] was among those executed in October 1943."

Saturday, 16 September. BAAG reported:

> The following Indian escapees arrived at A.H.Q. WAICHOW on 16 SEP 44. All these I.O.R.s belong to 2/14 PUNJAB REGT and arrived in two separate parties:
> (a) 1st party from SHATAUKOK (L259833) comprising the whole Indian Garrison:
> 12172 L/Nk SHER ABBAS
> 9099 Sepoy AMIR KHAN
> 1264 Sepoy FAKIR KHAN
> 13912 Sepoy HAKHIM KHAN
> 14770 Sepoy KHAN MIR
> 16848 Sepoy GHULAM HASSAN
> 18331 Sepoy SAIDA KHAN
> 19888 Sepoy RAKHMAT SHAN
> 19470 Sepoy RAKHAM GUL
> (b) 2nd party from SHEUNGSHUI (L155792) being part of the garrison of 60 there:
> 13914 L/Nk RESHAM KHAN
> 9052 Sepoy ZAMIR KHAN

>   2049 Sepoy KHALIL DIN
>   19894 Sepoy ASHAM KHAN
>
> The escapes of the 2 parties were unaided but are a direct result of our maintaining constant touch.
>
> In addition, a party of 4 arrived at WAICHOW on 1 Sep 44 from LINMAHANG lead mine (220839). This party consisted of:
> 3910 Gnr JAGIR SINGH
> 12639 L/Nk KHAN ABAS
> 13571 Sepoy ABDUL HASSAN
> 20266 Sepoy ZARIN GUL.
>
> There are now 17 I.O.R.s waiting to be evacuated and interrogated at Waichow.[39]

On 27 September 1944, Major Herbert Beadnell, RAMC, the senior officer at Oeyama,[40] wrote a four-page closely-typed letter to the camp commandant, listing in great detail his concerns about the POWs in Oeyama. Under the heading "Men who, in my opinion, are not fit for work; or are likely to become so under existing conditions", he listed 49 POW numbers. Under "The following men are, in my opinion, now only fit for light work and, under existing conditions, are likely to become as bad as the above men in time", he listed a further 41 numbers. Finally, under "The following men are deteriorating in health especially rapidly", he listed another 41, predicting a further "at least 60–70 deaths among the English and Canadian during the approaching winter".[41]

Wednesday, 27 September. Even in the better camps, such as Innoshima, luck was running out for some men. Coxhead at Innoshima: "As the working party returns to camp, Ashton Hill dies. He has been ill w' flu for the past few days, but the cause of death is cardiac due to beri-beri, and very swift and unexpected by the medical staff. A service, held by Fabel. A hard and bitter blow, bringing home to us all that Ashton has done for the camp."

Saturday, 30 September. Coxhead continued: "At lights out, Stirling Lee, who was taken ill a few days ago, is in a state of collapse and dies at 9.30. His body is at once taken to the chapel, where Rm. 3 mount guard all night."

October 1944

Thursday, 5 October. Poulter at Kobe: "A rest day to celebrate the opening of Kobe House, October 5th. This is the day that we should have arrived here, but owing to an engagement with a submarine we arrived a few days late. I fail to see what we have to celebrate about, of course I'm thankful to be alive, but I fail to see why I should celebrate because Kobe House was opened."

But celebrate they did. That day Weedon noted: "Whole parade ordered to face east, remove caps, and bow to the Emperor. Remarks of all and sundry best left unrecorded. The Emperor's ears must have been burning! Afterwards presentation to selected workers (cigarettes, and small bottles of saki, in once case wrapped up in yesterday's paper!) and to one of R. Scots who saved a woman from drowning in the harbour recently."[42] (p. 111)

Monday, 9 October. The senior officer party in Taiwan departed for Shenyang.

Friday, 13 October. Wright-Nooth at Stanley: "Monty Johnson DSM, a superintendent in the police reserve, died from TB yesterday . . . Monty was one of my room mates at C Bungalow. There he used to spend most of the day playing piquet with Oscar Eager while Belle, his wife, was the terror of the ladies' room." (p. 201)

Monday, 16 October. Shamshuipo was hit by a heavy air raid. Redwood viewed the attack from Stanley: "There was a terrific air raid. Planes like great silver birds."

Laite added: "At 15.40 hrs today we had a very heavy air raid. About 28 bombers accompanied by fighters came over — a total of 50 or 60. Some of the lighter planes passed over our camp so low that markings could be easily discerned, and did they spit fire as they flew? A large concentration of ships must have received quite a straffing. Ten men in camp were hit — eight of them were Canadians — but none seriously. We understand that two officers from the camp adjoining, were taken to Bowen Rd Hospital. Pieces of shrapnel or shell came through roofs of huts. One shell burst on the roof of our hut and pieces came through, wounding Mr. O'Neill on the elbow. Our only place of shelter is beneath our beds, and canvas, or open spring beds, would not very effectively stop heavy pieces of shell. We do hope that walls don't collapse."

Wiseman was at 'the camp adjoining' referred to by Laite: "There was a lot of flak flying in Sham Shui Po on the 16th, particularly over on the ORs side. Only one of the [Camp 'N'] huts, ours, was hit, 40 mm coming through our roof almost immediately over my bed space. 'Hank' Eardly, a HKRNVR Sub, who was on his bunk within a yard of me, was badly wounded in both legs. His blood fountained out, actually hitting the roof before his mess mate and I could put tourniquets around his thighs." (p. 38)

But however dangerous the situation was becoming in Hong Kong, it was far worse in Japan. Marsh at Shinagawa Hospital, Tokyo: "Going through parts of Tokyo we saw grim evidence of the effectiveness of the American bombing. Whole areas were laid waste, most being burned out. Shinagawa Camp was placed right in the heart of the district and the Japs were using it to protect themselves from American bombs. The camp itself was much the same as the others. A high board fence surrounding a collection of low sheds with tiled roofs and few windows. Here were held most of the medical personal both American and British that the Japanese had captured during the first two years of the war. The Medical Officer in charge under the Japanese Commandant was a Commander Surgeon of the British Navy captured at Hong Kong. He was a tall, elderly, distinguished looking Englishman who always wore full navy regalia, gold braided hat and coat sleeves and ribbons were possibly the only clothes he possessed. He did not wear a monocle but it would have suited his facial expressions perfectly. When questioning the patients his jaw would drop, one eyebrow would come down and he would constantly say, 'Haw'. He was however a very good surgeon and a helpful, honest and well intentioned man. He was often in trouble with the Japs, as they hated his type and what he stood for."

Friday, 20 October: BAAG reported that "[b]etween 13th and 15th August 100 civilians were interned, comprising Eurasians, South Americans, and Overseas-Chinese."[43] As the Indian POWs had been moved out of Ma Tau Chung by that time, presumably these were the first inmates of Ma Tau Wai.

Sunday, 22 October. Redwood at Stanley: "'One Armed' Sutton died." Wright-Nooth: "Sutton died at 10.10 this morning. He went into hospital suffering from beri-beri, a lacerated stomach, and general malnutrition, and seemed to give up all desire to live — a strange thing in a man who has led so successful and adventurous a life." (p. 220)

November 1944

Beadnell wrote: "On the 17th day of November 1944, H1609 Pte. Shayler, H. of the Winnipeg Grenadiers died. In Oeyama Camp from undernutrition and pneumonia. This man had been working fairly regularly, although suffering from undernutrition until his admission to hospital with pneumonia. A few days after his admission to hospital, he died suddenly and unexpectedly. The exact cause of the sudden fatal collapse is not known. It is my belief that his poor general health may have contributed to the fatal results."[44]

Tuesday, 21 November. Redwood at Stanley: "Major C. M. Manners died."

Tuesday, 28 November. Coxhead at Innoshima: "Gerry, Tandy[45] and others go to Buddhist temple where a Buddhist Service takes place & the ashes of Ashton Hill and Stirling Lee are laid on an altar alongside those of the 8 RAF men who died before our arrival here."[46]

At about this time, the POWs in Tokyo #1B wre transferred to Ajinomoto (Tokyo #23 Dispatched Camp).

December 1944

Sunday, 3 December. Stanley William Easter, Royal Engineers, was transferred from Omine to Fukuoka #1B (Kumamoto).

Tuesday, 19 December. Frank Evans at Oeyama: "It was so easy to plunge into the 'slough despond' and I remember a fine pal of mine, Maurice Pickles. Telling me one day, 'we'll never get out of here, Taffy.' He was suffering very badly from beri-beri, had lost hope, and within a week he was dead. I would never have expected him to give up because I considered him a chap with a lot of determination and inward strength. Losing him upset me very much . . . It is impossible for me to convey to the reader the state of our existence in Oeyama during the winter of 1944, and truly one had to be there to realise fully the plight of the prisoners. They were far too sick to work, but parties for the mine and factory had to continue. Men were beaten daily for something or other, for example failing to salute a sentry or for stealing, and during work some would collapse and then be taken back to camp. Our boots were worn out and some were bare footed while others wrapped their feet in pieces of clothing or bits of blanket. Prisoners developed gangrene in their feet and legs, which were also affected by pellagra and beri-beri, causing much pain and severe depression."

Wednesday, 20 December. Arthur Taylor: "Transferred to Nisshin Camp – Ch. Lts. South[47] & S. P. O. Yates[48] joined from Omori – Lt. Sherry, USN, Lt. Perkins, US Army & Doctor Darmore[49] USA – signed non-escape form again – damn cold night."

Friday, 22 December.

> BAAG KWIZ 78/10 (Date: 22.Dec.44)
> MATAUCHUNG Camp (220587) is now an internment camp for 'undesirable' third nationals, Russians, Latin Americans and some old people previously released from STANLEY Camp.
>
> The persons largely responsible for the selection of 'undesirable' third nationals for internment are J.J. RICHARDS, a Eurasian, and O.S. Lam, a Chinese-Indian (Nov 44 — Graded C2).
>
> Kweilin Intelligence Summary
>
> Comment:
> Internment of 'undesirables' reported previously by other sources. RICHARDS is known to have worked for the Japs for a long time. He was one of those interned by the British authorities at the outbreak of hostilities. It has previously been reported that he was entrusted with the examination of documents, alleged to be Consular archives, discovered on the river boat Sai On, seized by the Japs in MACAO in 1943.

Consuelo Delgado y Perez was a typical (and, like others, certainly not deserving the description 'undesirable') Ma Tau Wai internee: "My mother's mother was Spanish and my mother is Eurasian. Being a child at the time, all she remembered was the name Argyle. She thinks the camp was near Kai Tak airport. My mother says it was a blessing to be put in the camp because they were literally starving when they were on the outside. My grandmother was a widow, and as a Caucasian woman in a Chinese populace (with four children) there was very little she could do other than rely on the charity of others. And, as you know, there was very little charity. Everyone had lost everything overnight, including their shirts, and of course, some their heads. The Japanese did not feed the internees in my mother's camp well, but they did feed them. And they were allowed some social and educational programs — including Japanese lessons. I have read of the cruelties and deprivation in Stanley and other camps and wonder why the internees in my mother's camp were 'spared'. My mother remembers an American cook ('Mr. Jingle'), an Australian family (the Peveril-Guests), a British family (the Fergusons), an Indian gentleman ('Mr. Mooney') who would, several times a day, kneel and pray to Mecca, and many other characters. So perhaps Ma Tau Wai became a place to put people who were 'others' — kind of a motley bunch?"[50]

Saturday, 30 December. Redwood at Stanley: "Marie Barton married to Vincent Morrison."

Sunday, 31 December. Lowe at Innoshima: "And so ends 1944. We all hope & pray that 1945 will bring Peace to the World, Freedom to all Horios of whatever nationality or colour. I did hope for Peace this Xmas. I'm sorry I've lost a little faith, damn it. I do want to see them all again at dear old Hayfield. We drank the New Year in, in Tea & wished everybody a Happy New Year."

ROLL OF HONOUR FOR 1944

Sham Shui Po / Argyle Street

Name	Rank	Number	Unit		Date
Soares, Alberto Carlos	Private	2440	HKVDC		K 3.1.44 Cf
Gaunt, John Arthur	Gunner	4664	HKVDC	BRH	K 4.1.44[51]
Eady, Frederick Thomas	Private	7675954	RAPC	BRH	K 6.1.44
Gover, Ronald A.	Rifleman	B/38359	RRoC		K 9.1.44 TB
King, Joseph Victor	2nd Eng Off		MN SS Yat Shing	BRH	K 19.2.44 Aa[52]
Woolley, William John	Sergeant	3898	HKVDC		K 25.3.44 Pe
Davis, Paul	Oiler		MN		UX 28.3.44 Bi[53]
Lewis, Edgar	Captain	221888	HQ 2nd Echelon	BRH	K 4.4.44 Hs
Stevenson, James	2nd Eng Off		MN SS Ben Nevis		K 10.4.44[54]
Paul, Glen Francis	Sergeant	H/3148	CADC		K 21.4.44 Dy/Ma[55]
Weill, Leo	Gunner	3688	HKVDC		K 27.4.44 HKJ
Brooks, Leonard	Lance Bdr.	4970622	RA	BRH	K 29.4.44
Walton, Hugh	Private	3063790	RS	BRH	K 2.5.44 Dy[56]
Dodwell, Michael Carr	Gunner	4856	HKVDC		K 15.5.44 TB
Evans, Harold Alfred	Private		HKDDC	11.5.44	K 18.5.44 Cbi
Sokalski, George	Private	H/6924	WG		K 30.5.44 Ma/Bi
Hunt, Hubert James	Sergeant	1835	HKVDC	BRH	K 31.5.44
Oates, Edward Connors	Third Officer		MN SS Yat Shing HK		K 5.6.44
Shrigley, Ralph James	Lieutenant		HKVDC		K 28.6.44 Mu[57]
Elliott, William	Corporal	3192	HKVDC	BRH	K 30.6.44
Foster, George Bertram	Corporal		HKVDC		K 8.7.44
Kirby, William Edward	Master		MN MV Glenmoor		K 12.7.44[58]
Chalmers, Isaac	Master		MN SS Whithorn		K 15.7.44
MacNamara, Henry C.	Lieutenant	221889	RA		K 16.7.44[59]

Fifer, Roy Valentine	Private	K/92337	WG		BRH	K 17.7.44 Dm
Smith, Sidney George	Captain		HKVDC MBE DCM		BRH	K 20.7.44 Ap
Jones, Thomas	Master		MN SS Tai Min HK		BRH	K 1.8.44
Pritchard, Thomas R.D.	Master		MN SS Taishan HK			K 10.8.44
Hale, Frederick Montague	Sapper	DR139	HKVDC			K 26.8.44
Gunn, William Donald	Surg. Lieutenant-Cdr.		RN		BRH	K 8.9.44
Carter, Reginald	Major	17469	HQ		BRH	K 14.9.44[60]
Broom, John McCullum	2nd Eng. Off.		MN SS Mausang HK			K 17.9.44
Yeung Sing Man	Sapper	575	HKVDC 40 Coy RE			U 25.11.44
Lee Shek Chuen	Sapper	626	HKVDC 22 Coy RE			U 18.12.44
Anderson, Joseph Stewart	Master		MN SS Patricia Moller			K 30.12.44

Fukuoka #5 Branch Camp (Omine Coal Mine, Kawasaki-machi)

McKinley, Sterling W.J.	Rifleman	E/29981	RRoC	(XD3)	K 9.4.44 Y Cbi
Chenell, William Radley	Rifleman	E/30381	RRoC	(XD3)	K 21.4.44 Y Pa
Campbell, Ralph Wesley	Rifleman	E/30471	RRoC	(XD3)	K 14.7.44 Y Ax[61]
Fitzpatrick, Charles Joe	Rifleman	E/30684	RRoC	(XD3)	K 14.7.44 Y Ax[62]

Hiroshima #5 Branch Camp (Innoshima)

Ashton Hill, Robert	Lance Corp.	3893	HKVDC	(XD3)	K 27.9.44 Y Pa
Lee, John Stirling	Lance Corp.	4667	HKVDC	(XD3)	K 1.10.44 Y Pa
MacKinnon, John M.	Lance Corp.	4645	HKVDC	(XD3)	K 28.11.44 Y Bi
Fleming, William	Private	4840	HKVDC	(XD3)	K 5.12.44 Y Ul[63]

Nagoya #2 Branch Camp (Narumi)

Doucett, Peter	Rifleman	G/18332	RRoC	(XD5)	K 5.2.44 Y Cs[64]
Nix, Kenneth Roy	Bandsman	6202380	MX	(XD5)	K 8.2.44 Y Cs/Bi
Shuster, Edward	Corporal	4051	HKVDC	(XD5)	K 1.3.44 Y Gu/Pi
Walker, William Laird	BSM	2691	HKVDC	(XD5)	K 3.3.44 Y Cs
Scott, William	Private	3053613	RS	(XD5)	K 16.3.44 Y Cs/Cf
Rough, Harry Robson	Private	3055925	RS	(XD5)	K 16.3.44 Y Cs
Ward, Thomas Richard	S/Sergeant	2607974	MPSC	(XD5)	K 20.3.44 Y[65]
Hood, John Mair	Corporal	DR294	HKVDC	(XD5)	K 21.3.44 Y Cs/Bi
Gow, David	Sergeant	3375	HKVDC	(XD5)	K 12.4.44 Y Pa
Gibbs, Arthur Henry	Lance Corp.	6202707	MX	(XD5)	K 22.4.44 Y Cbi
Jack, James Mackenzie	RSM	209	HKVDC	(XD5)	K 15.9.44 Y Pi/Bi
Crump, Edwin Herbert	Signalman	5381830	RCS	(XD5)	K 18.10.44 Y Bi/Mn
Bel, H.	Private		HKVDC	(XD5)	K 3.11.44 Y Cbi[66]

Osaka #1 Branch Camp (Minato-ku, Osaka)

Stewart, Donald	A.S.	D/JX146752	RN	(XD2)	K 7.5.44 Y Pa diw

Osaka #2 Branch Camp (Kobe)

Fooks, Frederick John	Sapper	1872958	RE	(XD2)	K 16.1.44 Y Cs doh
Tibbs, John Francis C.	Corporal	2031740	RE	(XD2)	K 28.2.44 Y Cs
Ross, Henry James	S/Sergeant	7262015	RAMC	(XD2)	K 15.5.44 Y Pu
Collocott, Thomas Lionel	Private	6207656	MX	(XD2)	K 11.6.44 Y TB

Osaka # 3 Branch Camp (Oeyama)

Name	Rank	Number	Unit		Date
Wilson, John Bertram M.	Sergeant	809818	HKSRA	(XD4)	K 19.1.44 Y Es
Ling, Kenneth Robert	Gunner	1426671	RA	(XD4)	K 21.1.44 Y[67]
Clarkson, Fred	Sergeant	590664	RAF	(XD4)	K 23.1.44 Y[68]
Banks, William	Lance Sergeant	779082	RA	(XD4)	K 24.1.44 Y Bi
McLellan, Earl	Private	H/6324	WG	(XD4)	K 25.1.44 Y Bi
Cund, Henry George	Sapper	2125462	RE	(XD4)	K 1.2.44 Y Bi/Cs
Blanchard, Arthur Joseph	Private	H/75235	WG	(XD4)	K 2.2.44 Y Bi
Friesen, John Enger	Private	H/6951	WG	(XD4)	K 2.2.44 Y Bi[69]
Rowley, William Thomas	Gunner	1521732	RA	(XD4)	K 5.2.44 Y Bi
Davies, Eli Robert	Bombardier	842976	RA	(XD4)	K 9.2.44 Y Cbi
Hole, William Lenard	Gunner	856082	RA	(XD4)	K 10.2.44 Y Cbi
Pott, Norman Archibald	Private	H/6888	WG	(XD4)	K 11.2.44 Y Cbi
Marsh, Clifford James	Private	H/41672	WG	(XD4)	K 12.2.44 Y Bi/Cs
Hodgson, Edward Cartner	L/Sergeant	3593342	CMP	(XD4)	K 13.2.44 Y Bi/Cs
Webber, George Richard	Flight Sgt.		RAF	(XD4)	K 13.2.44 Y Cbi
Brown, Samuel	Staff Sergeant	822236	RA	(XD4)	K 14.2.44 Y Cbi
McConnell, Thomas J.	Lieutenant	221172	RA	(XD4)	K 14.2.44 Y Cbi
Maynard, John Vernon	Lance Bdr.	872299	RA	(XD4)	K 15.2.44 Y B[70]
Teggarty, William	Corporal	1068381	CMP	(XD4)	K 16.2.44 Y Cbi
Dumaine, Joseph A.G.	Private	H/77288	WG	(XD4)	K 17.2.44 Y Cbi
Day, Isaac John	LAC	157773	RAF	(XD4)	K 19.2.44 Y Cs
Ball, Leonard Walton	Gunner	1490617	RA	(XD4)	K 21.2.44 Y Cbi
Matthews, Norman C.	Private	H/6044	WG MiD	(XD4)	K 22.2.44 Y Cbi
Bross, Carl Joseph	Private	H/6372	WG	(XD4)	K 23.2.44 Y Cbi
Dennison, Norman	Lance Sergeant	833887	RA	(XD4)	K 24.2.44 Y Bi/Cs
Johnson, Edward Thomas	Private	H/6440	WG	(XD4)	K 25.2.44 Y Cbi
Lavallee, Ernest	Private	H/41865	WG	(XD4)	K 27.2.44 Y Bi/Cs
Keelty, John Patrick	Lance Corporal	5618165	CMP	(XD4)	K 28.2.44 Y Bi
Humphry, Bert D'Arcy L.	A.S.	P/J42027	RN	(XD5)	K 29.2.44 Y[71]
Brass, George Wilson	Sergeant	567436	RAF	(XD4)	K 1.3.44 Y Cbi
Reid, Mark Thomas A.	Gunner	1502328	RA	(XD4)	K 1.3.44 Y Bi/Cs
Sargent, William Horace	Sergeant	824892	RA	(XD4)	K 4.3.44 Y Bi/Cs
Paul, Ernest Joseph	Private	H/40700	WG	(XD4)	K 5.3.44 Y Pu
Harrington, Robert	Gunner	1426857	RA	(XD4)	K 23.3.44 Y Cbi
Hull, Herbert John	Private	H/6601	WG	(XD4)	K 15.4.44 Y Bi
McGinnis, William J.	Private	L/2848	WG	(XD4)	K 25.4.44 Y Bi
Shayler, Henry Albert	Private	H/6309	WG	(XD4)	K 17.11.44 Y Pa
Grainger, William Alfred	Corporal	H/6578	WG	(XD4)	K 23.11.44 Y Bi
Townsend, George Harold	Corporal	H/6135	WG	(XD4)	K 25.11.44 Y Bi
Delorme, George Daniel	Private	H/6758	WG	(XD4)	K 4.12.44 Y Pa
Heath, Albert Edward	Sapper	1874413	RE	(XD4)	K 18.12.44 Y Pa
Pickles, Maurice	Private	7610360	RAOC	(XD5)	K 19.12.44 Y Cbi
Birkinshaw, Albert E.	Lance Bdr.	840346	RA	(XD5)	K 20.12.44 Y Pa

Osaka #4 Dispatched Camp (Sakurajima)

Name	Rank	Number	Unit		Date
Buckley, Leslie	Gunner	5498761	RA	(XD3)	K 3.1.44 Y Pa
Curd, William John J.	Sergeant		HKDDC RN/DYP	(XD3)	K 3.1.44 Y Cf

Deacon, George William	Sergeant		HKDDC	(XD3)	K 21.1.44 Y Cbi
Blair, Younger Ralph	Sergeant		HKDDC	(XD3)	K 18.2.44 Y Pe
Lombary, Marcel Philyp	Lance Corp.	6202791	MX	(XD3)	K 20.2.44 Y Bi/Cs
Wheeler, Harry	Lance Bdr.	5569552	RA	(XD3)	K 2.3.44 Y Pa
Harness, Thomas Edward	Gunner	838377	RA	(XD3)	K 5.3.44 Y Cbi
Luckett, William George	Lance Bdr.	828266	RA	(XD3)	K 8.3.44 Y Cbi
Kyle, Hubert	Gunner	833155	RA	(XD3)	K 14.3.44 Y Cs dkoh
Atkins, Arthur	Lance Bdr.	860937	RA	(XD3)	K 15.3.44 Y Cbi
Webster, George Alfred	Private	6201926	MX	(XD3)	K 21.3.44 Y Es[72]
Evans, David Daniel	Lance Bdr.	918830	RA	(XD3)	K 22.3.44 Y Cf
Barraclough, Leslie C.	Bombardier	825468	RA	(XD3)	K 28.3.44 Y Pa
Bearman, George Henry	Private		HKDDC	(XD2)	K 28.3.44 Y Pa[73]
Shaw, Willis B.	Sergeant		HKDDC RN/DYP	(XD3)	K 28.3.44 Y diw[74]
Willson, Donald George	Bandsman	6201222	MX	(XD3)	K 13.4.44 Y Cbi
Mann, Alexander Leonard	Private		HKDDC RN/DYP	(XD3)	K 19.4.44 Y Pa[75]
Owens, Ernest Maldwyn	Lance Bdr.	840444	RA	(XD3)	K 8.6.44 Y TB diw
Lavis, Arthur George	Lance Sergeant	1422526	RA	(XD3)	K 24.7.44 Y TB dkoh
Smith, Harry	Sergeant	36	HKDDC RN/DYP	(XD3)	K 9.8.44 Y Bi dkoh
Allaway, Leonard James	Private	4030955	MX	(XD3)	K 15.9.44 Y Bi
King, Frank Gordan	Gunner	842287	RA	(XD3)	K 1.11.44 Y Cs
Foreman, Herbert George	Private		HKDDC	(XD3)	K 8.11.44 Y Es
Stoneham, William T.	Private		HKDDC	(XD3)	K 16.12.44 Y Cbi

Osaka #6 Dispatched Camp (Amagasaki)

Fieldhouse, John Thomas	P.O. Stoker	P/KX93901	RN	(XD3)	K 3.1.44 Y Cs
Miles, Frank William	Sergeant	2655414	MPSC	(XD3)	K 30.3.44 Y[76]
Worrall, Geoffrey Clare	W.O.		HKRNVR	(XD1)	K 13.12.44 Y Cbi

Sendai #2 Branch Camp (Yoshima Coal Mine)

Fernandes, Eduardo A.	Private	3856[77]	HKVDC	(XD6)	K 18.12.44 Y Ax dsgh[78]

Tokyo #1 Branch Camp (Oshima-cho, Kawasaki)

Coyle, Hugh	Private	3055188	RS	(XD1)	K 7.3.44 Y Pa dsgh
Condon, Alfred	Private	3054947	RS	(XD1)	U 30.7.44 Cf[79]

Tokyo #3 Dispatched Camp (Tsurumi Shipyard)

Allen, William Harold	Corporal	E/29952	RRoC	(XD3)	K 19.1.44 Y Pa
Aitkens, Edward Carlton	Rifleman	E/30383	RRoC	(XD3)	K 1.2.44 Y Pa
Firlotte, James	Rifleman	E/30016	RRoC	(XD3)	K 1.2.44 Y Pa
Hallett, Lawrence Garry	Private	H/6895	WG	(XD3)	K 2.2.44 Y Bi/TB
Lowe, George Albert	Corporal	H/6078	WG	(XD3)	K 18.2.44 Y Pa dsgh
Rowland, Roney	Lance Corp.	A/3625	RRoC	(XD3)	K 23.2.44 Y Pa dsgh
Webster, Robert William	Sergeant	H/6045	WG	(XD3)	K 7.3.44 Y Pa dsgh
Cole, Elmer William	CQMS	E/30215	RRoC	(XD3)	K 16.3.44 Y Pa/Dy dsgh[80]
Ellis, Lyle Leonard	CSM	K/92050	RCAPC	(XD3)	K 17.3.44 Y Pa

Hamilton, Sterling Waldo	Rifleman	E/30113	RRoC	(XD3)	K 23.3.44 Y Pa dsgh
Skene, William James	Private	H/20708	WG	(XD3)	K 15.4.44 Y Pa
Emo, James Thomas	CSM	D/117580	CPC	(XD3)	K 29.4.44 Y Pa
Todd, Earl Crawford	CSM	E/22890	RRoC	(XD3)	K 5.11.44 Y Ax[81]
Wyrwas, Fred Arnold	Rifleman	E/30138	RRoC	(XD3)	K 24.12.44 Y Bi dsgh
Smith, Victor Gordon	Private	H/41690	WG	(XD3)	K 27.12.44 Y Je dsgh

Tokyo #5 Branch Camp (Niigata-Rinko)

Colvin, Frederick James	Private	H/6848	WG	(XD4)	K 1.1.44 Y BC
Furey, Joseph	Private	H/6384	WG	(XD4)	K 1.1.44 Y BC
Jacquard, John Angus	Rifleman	F/42667	RRoC	(XD4)	K 1.1.44 Y BC
Jones, Harold B.	Private	H/6483	WG	(XD4)	K 1.1.44 Y BC
Mazerolle, Emile B.	Rifleman	E/30555	RRoC	(XD4)	K 1.1.44 Y BC[82]
Olafson, Budvar Peter	Private	H/6269	WG	(XD4)	K 1.1.44 Y BC
Sauson, Lester Lawrence	Sergeant	E/29903	RRoC	(XD4)	K 1.1.44 Y BC
Sword, David Laurie	Staff Sergeant	B/95056	RCASC	(XD4)	K 1.1.44 Y BC
Gibbons, Harold Earl	Rifleman	A/44596	RRoC	(XD4)	K 2.1.44 Y Pa
Watson, Richard Henry	Private	L/22333	WG	(XD4)	K 5.1.44 Y Pa
Bottie, Leo Joseph	Rifleman	F/41001	RRoC	(XD3)	K 6.1.44 Y Pa/Es
Boulding, Albert Edward	Private	L/22816	WG	(XD4)	K 7.1.44 Y Pa
Willett, Fred	Rifleman	E/30141	RRoC	(XD4)	K 9.1.44 Y[83]
Caruso, Frank Tony	Private	H/6445	WG	(XD4)	K 13.1.44 Y Cbi
MacNaughton, Alden Lee	Rifleman	E/30027	RRoC	(XD4)	K 25.1.44 Y Es
Syvret, David	Rifleman	E/29879	RRoC	(XD4)	K 30.1.44 Y Bi/Pa
Waterhouse, William E.	Rifleman	E/30759	RRoC	(XD4)	K 31.1.44 Y Cbi
Snear, Thomas W.	Rifleman	E/30461	RRoC	(XD4)	K 1.2.44 Y Pa
Barnes, Kenneth	Rifleman	E/30117	RRoC	(XD4)	K 4.2.44 Y Es
Snedden, Jack Gerald	Rifleman	B/68222	RRoC	(XD4)	K 8.2.44 Y[84]
Bisson, George	Rifleman	E/30281	RRoC	(XD3)	K 13.2.44 Y Bi[85]
Richards, Thomas Medley	Sergeant	E/30185	RRoC	(XD4)	K 13.2.44 Y Pa
Lovell, Thomas Roy	Corporal	H/6654	WG	(XD4)	K 24.2.44 Y Bi
Martin, James	Sergeant	E/17046	RRoC	(XD4)	K 25.2.44 Y Es
Bowes, David William	Private	H/6752	WG	(XD4)	K 27.2.44 Y Pa/Cbi
Pidgeon, Joseph A.E.	Rifleman	E/30487	RRoC	(XD4)	K 27.2.44 Y Ma
Hicks, Frank	Rifleman	A/23006	RRoC	(XD4)	K 28.2.44 Y Es
Guitard, Gabriel	Rifleman	E/30503	RRoC	(XD4)	K 1.3.44 Y Es
Kitteringham, John H.	Private	H/77628	WG	(XD4)	K 3.3.44 Y Es
McLeod, Rodrique (Roy)	Rifleman	B/41357	RRoC	(XD4)	K 3.3.44 Y Bi/Es
Gee, John Moffat	Corporal	G/32406	RRoC	(XD4)	K 7.3.44 Y Bi
Mortimer, James Lake	Rifleman	B/41307	RRoC	(XD4)	K 7.3.44 Y Bi[86]
Pope, 'Shorty' Colin	Sergeant	E/29818	RRoC	(XD4)	K 25.3.44 Y Bi/Es
Welsh, Melvin Burton	Rifleman	E/30396	RRoC	(XD4)	K 31.3.44 Y Bi
Perreault, Arthur	Corporal	E/29906	RRoC	(XD4)	K 10.4.44 Y Es
Young, Lewis Edward	Private	H/41770	WG	(XD4)	K 7.5.44 Y Pu
Woodward, Cyril Sydney	Private	H/6137	WG	(XD4)	K 9.6.44 Y Pu
Hope, Alexander	Sergeant	D/117576	CPC	(XD4)	K 17.6.44 Y Bi/Es
Irwin, Robert Roy	Private	H/6592	WG	(XD4)	K 12.8.44 Y Bi

Tokyo #15 Branch Camp (Niigata Tekko)

Roblee, Lloyd Logan	Rifleman	F/40323	RRoC	MiD	(XD4)	K 21.4.44 Y Pa
Irving, Morton Alex	Rifleman	E/30221	RRoC		(XD4)	K 27.4.44 Y Cbi

Ma Tau Chung

Lam Chun Keung	Gunner	5136	HKSRA	U 1944
Rahmat Ali	Subadar	–	RP MiD	U 13.1.44
Nanku Singh	Jem	8363	RP	K 15.1.44
Ghulam Haidar	Sepoy	18337	PJ	K 23.1.44
Kaur Singh	Gunner	7582	HKSRA	U 23.1.44
Muhammad Afsar	Gunner	5112	HKSRA	K 26.1.44
Wilayat Khan	Havildar	3125	HKSRA	U 31.1.44
Muhammad Arif	Gunner	4629	HKSRA	U 8.2.44
Ram Pal Singh	Lance Naik	13965	RP	K 16.2.44
Gulab Khan	Gunner	5271	HKSRA	U 28.2.44
Man Singh	Sepoy	9352	RP	K 3.3.44
Nazir Ahmad	Gunner	7588	HKSRA	K 5.3.44
Husania	Sweeper	F/203	RP	U 9.3.44
Sagar Singh	Sepoy	16039	RP	K 11.3.44
Muhammad Sadiq	Gunner	8053	HKSRA	K 12.3.44
Wahid Gul	Sepoy	13657	PJ	K 16.3.44
Gaya Bakhsh Singh	Sepoy	10965	RP	K 30.3.44
Nur Muhammad	Gunner	5393	HKSRA	K 17.4.44
Jagar Singh	Gunner	7537	HKSRA	U 12.4.44
Ram Pal Singh	Sepoy	12728	RP	U 21.4.44
Gurdayal Singh	Gunner	7593	HKSRA	U 13.5.44
Shafqat Ali	Gunner	5342	HKSRA	U 16.5.44
Mula Singh	Gunner	7694	HKSRA	U 23.5.44
Sher Ghulam	Naik	12174	PJ	U 26.5.44
Chiragh Ahmad	L/Havildar	14959	RP	U 2.6.44
Hazara Singh	Gunner	7722	HKSRA	U 3.6.44
Lal Khan	Sepoy	11023	RP	U 4.6.44
Hira Singh	Sepoy	7336	RP	U 15.6.44
Aziz Muhammad	Havildar	7449	RP	U 16.6.44
Mir Badshah	Sepoy	12907	PJ	U 21.6.44
Ata Muhammad	Sepoy	9882	RP	U 22.6.44
Murad Khan	Gunner	4672	HKSRA	U 22.6.44
Faqir Khan	Sepoy	19492	PJ	K 27.6.44
Abdullah Khan	Sepoy	7384	RP	K 6.7.44
Jafar Ali	Jem	59560/I.O.	RP	U 9.7.44
Abdul Rahman	Gunner	3360	HKSRA	U 15.7.44
Muhammad Ashraf	Lance Naik	15505	PJ	U 18.7.44
Jangir Singh	Gunner	3850	HKSRA	U 21.7.44
Diwan Singh	Sepoy	11115	PJ	U 23.7.44
Niranjan Singh	Gunner	4665	HKSRA	U 29.7.44
Ram Pal Singh	Sepoy	9370	RP	K 5.8.44
Brij Pal Singh	Sepoy	10890	RP	K 18.8.44
Ghulam Rasul	Gunner	8001	HKSRA	K 8.9.44
Fazl Dad	Gunner	5458	HKSRA	K 8.9.44

Yusuf Khan	Sepoy	13101	PJ		K 10.9.44
Bidhi Singh	Sepoy	19624	PJ		U 15.9.44
Muhammad Karim	Gunner	5116	HKSRA		K 18.9.44
Dilawar Khan	Havildar	9179	RP		U 19.9.44
Adat Shah	Sepoy	16261	PJ		K 20.9.44
Ram Singh	Gunner	5491	HKSRA		U 21.9.44
Bachan Singh	Gunner	5473	HKSRA		U 29.9.44
Taj Din	Gunner	7934	HKSRA		K 1.10.44
Wali Muhammad	Gunner	5370	HKSRA		K 7.10.44
Ghulam Muhammad	Gunner	8076	HKSRA		U 10.10.44
Khan Bahadur	Lance Naik	177578	HKMC		U 10.10.44
Kirpa Ram		871	PJ		U 20.10.44
Parmodh Singh	Sepoy	16356	PJ		U 25.10.44
Mehma Singh	Lance Naik	7763	HKSRA		K 30.10.44
Abdul Hamid	Gunner	5283	HKSRA		U 1.11.44
Daya Ram	Sepoy	16322	PJ		U 6.11.44
Allah Ditta	Barber	-	RP		U 8.11.44
Gula Raz	Sepoy	18200	PJ		K 25.11.44
Gajadhar Singh	Sepoy	18312	RP		K 26.11.44
Munshi	PC		HKDDC	RN / DYP	U 3.12.44
Gul Akbar	Sepoy	9379	PJ		K 8.12.44
Ghulam Nabi	Gunner	4745	HKSRA		U 16.12.44
Gul Muhammad	Gunner	5356	HKSRA		K 17.12.44
Latif Husain Khan	Sepoy	15604	RP		U 19.12.44
Abdul Karim	Sepoy	786614	HKMC		U 20.12.44
Ashraf Khan	Lance Naik	13863	PJ		U 23.12.44
Muhammad Khan	Gunner	8169	HKSRA		U 25.12.44

Stanley

Matthews, Ernest Dudley	CV	68, ARP, Lt. Col. (rtd)	UCWD 6.1.44
Smith, Grace Rose	CV	75	UCWD 14.1.44
Groves, Doris	CV	27, wife of Arthur G. Groves	UCWD 3.2.44
Reading, Edward	CV	61, husband of B. M. Reading	UCWD 6.2.44
Starling, Edwin Leonard	CV	45, at Tweed Bay Hospital	UCWD 11.2.44
Barnes, Francisco H.	CV		UCWD 5.3.44
Hing, Joseph Chee	CV	Died at the French Hospital, hus. Margaret C.	UCWD 10.3.44
Seager, Lucy Jackson	CV	At Rosary Hill	UCWD 21.3.44
Henson, Edith May	CV	65, wife of Joseph E.	UCWD 16.4.44
Rose, Rachel Grace	CV	33, wife of H. H.	UCWD 2.5.44
Gill, Brian Patrick Hirst	CV	3, master	UCWD 9.5.44
Shilton, Cyril Conway	CV	58, at Tweed Bay Hospital	UCWD 11.5.44
Wilmer, Ethel Kate	CV	63	UCWD 22.5.44[87]
Byrne, George Thomas	CV	59	UCWD 1.6.44
Joseph, Sayed, Ala Haiem	CV		UCWD 18.6.44
Hedley, Wallace	CV	Died at the French Hospital	UCWD 25.6.44[88]
Faid, William	CV	51, Professor of Physics at HKU	UCWD 23.7.44
Shields, Andrew Lusk	CV		UCWD 24.7.44
Cunningham, Agnes Mary	CV	67, Mrs.	UCWD 25.7.44
Moss, John	CV	58	UCWD 1.8.44

Pryde, Walter	CV	57		UCWD 12.9.44
Brown, J. M.	CV			UCWD 17.9.44
Dabelstein, Winifred E.	CV	39		UCWD 21.9.44
Johnson, Maurice Alfred	CV	61		UCWD 12.10.44
Maurice, A.J.	CV			UCWD 12.10.44
Duncan, Maria Anne	CV	72		UCWD 13.10.44
Humphreys, Bruna Rose	CV	55		UCWD 15.10.44
Manners, Charles	CV	62, OBE, Major (rtd)		UCWD 22.10.44
Sutton, Francis Arthur	CV	60, MC		UCWD 22.10.44[89]
Hyde, Florence Eileen	CV	40, HK Bank, at Tweed Bay Hospital		UCWD 7.11.44
Lee, Emma Rawlins	CV			UCWD 13.11.44
Warden, Ernest Thomas	CV	44, Revenue Officer		UCWD 22.11.44
Dann, Achilles George	CV	56		UCWD 25.11.44
Hazeland, Ernest Manning	CV	74		UCWD 28.11.44
Knox, Thomas	CV	60, husband of Jessie, at Tweed Bay Hospital		UCWD 13.12.44
May, Rev, George C.	CV	77, died at the Red Cross Home for aged and sick		UCWD 14.12.44[90]

British Army Aid Group

Lui Kar Yin		BAAG		U 1944
Chiang Fong		BAAG		U 30.1.44
Tsang Yiu Sang		BAAG		U 4.2.44
Ki Kam Chan		BAAG		5.44
Edmonston, David Charles		BAAG		29.8.44
Basto, Carlow Henry		BAAG		31.8.44
Kotwall, Jimmy		BAAG		31.8.44
Chan Hung Chiu		BAAG	Diamond Head	31.10.44
Chau For		BAAG	Diamond Head	31.10.44
Ng Han Chuen		BAAG		31.10.44
Ng Yau Hing		BAAG		31.10.44
Yeung Kong		BAAG		31.10.44
Yang Kun Yue		BAAG		U 26.11.44
(Illin V.	Police	BAAG		Dec 44)

1945

> Would we, the men from Hong Kong, be the legion of forgotten men? Think of all the great battles that followed, gobbling up the headlines and broadcasts. Think of the millions bombed and slain around the globe. Think of the women in men's garb on the production lines, making bombs . . . Rosy the riveter. It had all moved on past us. History had run over us like a steamroller, leaving us behind, squashed in the muck.
> — Signalman William Allister, Royal Canadian Corps of Signal

By now, the Hong Kong POWs were reduced to just one hospital — Bowen Road, with just 145 patients at the beginning of the year — and two camps: Shamshuipo for the remaining British and Canadians, and Argyle Street for the Indians. The civilians still languished at Stanley Military Internment Camp, Ma Tau Wai, and Rosary Hill.

Kiangwan (now Jiangwan) in China was still holding Hong Kong POWs at the start of the year.

The Indian POWs were still in a wide variety of locations across Hong Kong and South China.

In Japan, the survivors were now spread across thirteen camps (plus a few more, to which individual medical officers had been sent):
Osaka #1 Branch Camp (Minato-ku, Osaka)
Osaka #2 Branch Camp (Kobe)
Osaka #3 Branch Camp (Oeyama)
Osaka #4 Dispatched Camp (Sakurajima)
Osaka #6 Dispatched Camp (Amagasaki)
Sendai #2 Branch Camp (Yoshima Coal Mine)
Fukuoka #1 Branch Camp (Kumamoto)
Fukuoka #5 Branch Camp (Omine Coal Mine, Kawasaki-machi)
Nagoya #2 Branch Camp (Narumi)
Tokyo #3 Dispatched Camp (Tsurumi Shipyard)
Tokyo #5 Branch Camp (Niigata-Rinko)
Tokyo #15 Branch Camp (Niigata Tekko)
Tokyo #23 Dispatched Camp (Ajinomoto)

Some 315 more of the POWs and Internees had perished in 1944 (of whom fourteen had been working for BAAG). The death rate was decreasing, but this was due to nature's inbuilt mechanisms: those with limited resistance to disease and malnutrition had already passed on; only the toughest were left.

The year 1945 would begin drearily and end deliriously. The ability of the Japanese to protect their prisoners, let alone feed them adequately, had deteriorated rapidly. Those in Japan were constantly being shuffled from place to place, as existing camps were threatened or destroyed by encroaching American air power. It was clear to all that the Allies would be victorious, but when the end finally came it would be a complete surprise to those still expecting an invasion — and all the dangers that such an action would pose for those in Japanese hands. And once they were free, the POWs and Internees would be shocked by the scale, skill, and sheer modernity of the fleets and personnel that rapidly assembled to carry them home. The world had changed.

DIARY FOR 1945

January 1945

Thursday, 4 January. Redwood at Stanley: "Batty-Smith lectured (most interestingly) on experiences in POW camp in Germany for almost 4 years."

Friday, 5 January. KWIZ 80, 5 January 1945 "The internee Commandant of MATAUCHUNG Camp (220586) is TOM BOLT. Comment: BOLT was Senior Overseer in the Public Works Department before the war. He was interned in STANLEY for some months in 1942, but was released upon a friend's guarantee."

Tuesday, 9 January. O'Toole at Shamshuipo: "MacCulloch dies suddenly of brain clot was only taken ill in afternoon, died that night. Old complaint. Was bearer on party went out to cemetery, no coffin, age 34 really 46."[1]

Tuesday, 9 January. Fisher at Shamshuipo: "Our first death of the year occurred last night. Sergeant McCulloch of the RAOC collapsed and died of heart trouble in a few hours." (p. 170)

Sunday, 14 January. Alec Howard at Narumi: "Bombs dropped near camp. Damage to roofs and Nip Anjon killed."

Tuesday, 16 January. A major American air raid developed over Hong Kong. Redwood viewed the build-up from Stanley: "They came in waves — and one of the first times I saw them was when 2 planes crashed; one collided with the other, the first one had flames coming out of the tail, fell pretty quickly. It came down fairly high up on this side of the Peak. The other fell very slowly, and one pilot bailed out; another had his parachute out but couldn't get free of the plane. One piece of wing was slowly turning over and over for a long time".[2]

Tuesday, 16 January. O'Toole at Shamshuipo: "S.M. Williams died, had fever malaria for few days, then heart gave out. Biggest raid to date say 300 planes — lost 14 says paper. Watched it from Cook House, they dived right down on to the ships, certain death with 5 destroyers there blazing pom-poms. They've got guts those lads two planes on fire one parachute also, heart breaking to see them flutter down like Butterflies. They were at it all day, stuff lands in the camp from A.A. no one hurt. I had fine view with Bushy Bowers can see all round from there."

Fisher was at the same camp: "A shell has just burst on the roof over our heads and filled the room with debris, wood, tiles, and dust. I heard the whine a fraction before it struck, and dived under the table. We picked up a small brass nose cap of a shell from my bed, and a dozen pieces of shrapnel from the room." (p. 172)

But the situation at Stanley Camp was far worse. Redwood: "Someone said they thought Jap HQ had been hit — then Watanabe[3] came down and said that two people in Bungalow C had been hurt, one on the point of death. Volunteers went off with stretchers, etc. and about ten minutes later, Owen Evans came tearing down and said that nearly everyone in Bung. C had been killed."[4]

Stericker was nearby and saw a cloud of dust arise from the area of the Bungalow: "Soon afterwards we heard cries for help, and while we ran down the path another wave of planes came over. As we threw ourselves into a ditch more bombs fell and the ground around us was churned up by tracer bullets. Arrival at the bungalow showed that the bombs had dropped in the most vulnerable place possible. They had fallen right into a small compound surrounded by the house itself, the servants' quarters, and the garage. There was a steep hillside both above and below. Had the bombs fallen ten yards farther away in any direction the destruction would have been considerably lessened. As it was, all except the room on the west front was completely blasted. Some ten bodies were found immediately. They had been thrown out on to a lawn, quite unscarred, and appeared to be peacefully asleep. Three bodies had to be dug out from under the fallen roof. One woman died on her way to hospital." (p. 201)

L. A. Collyer[5] commented: "That has put paid to the lot of us, as we have suddenly realised that accidents do happen even in war. Just imagine being a prisoner for 3 years and then killed by one of your own fellows, it certainly is terrible." Collyer went on to mention that on the 18th three people injured in the bungalow incident were still in hospital, together with two others injured in other parts of the camp (Hargreaves with a shrapnel wound, and Blake with a machine gun bullet in the leg).

Wiseman, in Shamshuipo: "According to the Formosans hardly anything in the harbour escaped [the bombers'] attention, certainly a large tanker was sunk a mere 1/4 mile away towards Stonecutters. As before there was plenty of flak, but nobody was seriously hurt though a WO died of heart failure.[6] During these and subsequent raids we were herded into our huts while the sentries took whatever cover they could find but not their Nip NCOs, in particular the Sergeant Major who always stood, leaning on his sword, erect and immobile equally impervious to AA and strafing aircraft. After one raid he got a cheer from us, acknowledging it with a grave nod of the head." (p. 40)

Wednesday, 17 January. Fisher at Shamshuipo: "There had been one fatality, in that Bill Williams, the camp Sergeant Major, had collapsed and died of a heart attack. He had been a popular fellow, often standing between Boon and us, and doing a very difficult go-between job very well." (p. 170)

Edie Badger[7] in Rosary Hill: "Almost every day we would hear the B24s flying over us, sometimes stopping to bomb us and sometimes just flying over us. Food was getting real scarce and the Japanese were going to the markets and gathering up everyone putting them on junks then setting the junks on fire. Scorched bloated bodies were a common sight seen all over the waters of Hong Kong. It was just horrible."

In Japan, 1945 would be the year of the bombers.

Saturday, 20 January. Poulter at Kobe House: "I saw my first B29 today, January 20th, and it was a lovely sight. The Japs threw AA shells at it but they were miles short, or at least, so it appeared to me. No Jap planes went up after it, so it just flew around at leisure. Nice one Yanks. There is also a rumour that we are to have a big POW painted on the roof of our camp. I wonder if the Yanks have got bombs that can read?"

Monday, 29 January.   Fisher at Shamshuipo: "Meanwhile 150 men have left camp for an unknown destination." (p. 170) In fact, they had been sent to dig up Happy Valley racetrack for planting crops.

February 1945

Thursday, 1 February.   Collyer in Stanley: "All of the Civilian, Army & Navy Sisters & The Volunteer Nursing Services have done marvellous work, both during and after the war, & some of them paid heavily. The work the Sisters have done in the Camp Hospital certainly deserves recognition, & this makes me doubt very much that they will get it, more likely it will be ignored. But I don't think there's a man in the Camp who doesn't think the same."[8]

Collyer continued: "Others deserving of some sympathy are some of the Eurasians, they did not have the opportunity of being evacuated, but the Govt. were pleased to make use of their husbands, etc. during the war. It's a frightful mess all round."

Monday, 12 February.   Taylor at Nisshin Camp: "Fenn died at Shinagawa, date unknown."[9]

Wednesday, 14 February.   Collyer again: "Capt. Batty-Smith died yesterday. That sure is tough as he was a prisoner in Germany for 4 years during the last war & had spent 7 years altogether as a prisoner of war. He was previously aide-de-camp to the Governor, but was interned when we surrendered."

Tuesday, 20 February.   Fisher at Shamshuipo: "Yesterday the 150 gardening working party arrived. All of them looked ill and tired, hollow cheeked and dishevelled." (p. 180)

Tuesday, 20 February.   Fisher continued: "In Bowen Road Hospital Leo Weill is dying. He has some unusual disease which requires periodic attention at the hospital. Pre-war he went to Queen Mary, but now he can get no treatment. His mother's appeals have been ignored. His younger brother, Maurice, has just died in Shanghai — a tragic affair."[10] (p. 170)

Monday, 26 February. Redwood: "Jean Lyon married to Chisholm."

March 1945

Saturday, 10 March. Bertram at Omori: "The big bombers, coming in over the fires, were more clearly visible than in the beam of a searchlight. They looked to be no higher than five thousand feet. Every gun in the Japanese capital was banging away at them, so that the barrage was continuous — an immense shattering wall of noise across the night. It was the most daring night raid we had yet seen, and numbers of B–29's were hit as we watched. But steadily the fires were spreading. The two biggest ones had joined, and the wind was taking their golden plumes far out across the bay . . . Occasionally a twist of the great fires sent a wave of heat that smote our faces across miles of water." (p. 192)

Monday, 12 March. Fisher at Shamshuipo: "We had to go out today at a minute's notice. Our job was to take down the barbed wire from around the old Ma Tau Wei internment camp, and then wire off the former Heep Yuen school. Rumour has it that this place, which has been badly looted, is going to replace the Bowen Road Hospital." (p. 185)

Tuesday, 13 March. The bombing of Japan was having effect. Tokyo #13D was closed with the POWs being transferred to Sendai #5B. Tokyo #3D was also closed, with the Canadian POWs there being dispersed to Tokyo #10B (Sumidagawa), Tokyo #6B (Suwa), Sendai #4B (Ohashi), and Sendai #1B.

Allister was in the group of fifty bound for Sumidagawa: "We knew nothing of the Japanese plans, only that fifty men were given orders to pack for a move. I was on the list. We prepared in a state of anxious dread. After all, this had been a sort of home for two years. These men had surrounded me since we left Canada. Now it was all going to change drastically. George Grant was the only other signalman going . . . We were loaded into two open trucks where we sat on our kits, waiting to leave 3D. At last we stopped at our new home: Sumidagawa, decrepit, small, uninviting, in a coal yard on the outskirts of Tokyo beside a rail ramp. There was a rail and canal junction; long rail platforms ran parallel to canals, where beans, rice, coal and pig iron were loaded from rail car to barge. In the coal yard trains brought coal to be unloaded and shovelled into trucks. Since most civilians had been evacuated because of the bombs, prisoners — expendable — were brought in to replace them. The hut was a small run-down, two-tier affair, half the size of 3D, with a tiny square in front and a narrow space on one side. It sat squeezed between dark mountains of coal. It housed 250 furyos." (p. 174) Those included British POWs, shipped from Hong Kong on the first draft.

Charles Trick was in the group bound for Sendai #4B: "In March we moved up to a place called Ohafti, which was a mining area. They had a big smelter right on the coast called Komitchi. We were in about 12 miles in this mine. We worked underground in the mine. That was the worst part; that was far worse than . . . The fact that you're working underground and had five miles to walk and five to come back all uphill. The rations were getting worse as the war went on. If they could get worse; they weren't getting any worse, they were just getting smaller. It was the same stuff."

Lionel Speller was sent to Suwa: "That's where I was up until the last six months, when they disbanded and some went to Sendai, some went to Niigata, and I was shipped off. Suwa, we were supposed to be — at Suwa was a mixture of everything and we were supposed to be the bad guys. Like when I say, we'd either been caught at something or you'd struck the Japanese back or something. I don't know, I was like most of them, I took a chance and struck back once, but it wasn't worth it. You were black and blue for months afterwards if you ever."

Leonard Birchall took Speller and the other Canadians there. Birchall: "They put us in these boxcars. We went for 48 hours up into the mountains. This was an open face mine; we were up on one hill and we had to come down the side of the mountain, across the valley and up the other side to this open face mine, where they dug out — I don't know what kind or ore it was, but there was a big endless chain which came from about two or three mountain ranges or hills back. We came across the hills. Great big tubs on this endless chain. The tubs would come around and the guys would have to fill this. They would blast out and dig out the ore, put it on the little carts, bring it out to the loading platform, put them on the tubs and the tubs would go back to wherever the smelter was . . . We got to this camp after about 48 hours, cold, raining, miserable up in the mountains. The camp wasn't anywhere near finished. The buildings weren't finished. There was no cooking facilities. The iron bells were lying down on the ground. There was no water, there was *nothing*."[11]

Marsh was with the Sendai lot: "Under the Command of Captain Reid around two hundred Canadians entrained for our journey to Camp Sendai . . . We left Camp D3 one afternoon in April 1945.[12] We were under Captain Reid and a Lieutenant Finn, an American Naval Officer, who had accompanied us from Hong Kong. Traveling all night we arrived the following morning at a way station near the coal-mining town of Sendai in northern Honshu Island. By Japanese standards we were well equipped when we left D3, each man had a uniform, overcoat, shirt, underwear and new boots. Most of this was from our own British Army stores. The boots were from a shipment of Red Cross supplies. In comparison to what had happened to us in the last three years we now considered ourselves well off. Most of us now felt that the war could not last much longer and that we had a fair chance of survival. We had also been issued a little extra food from Red Cross stories on our departure. This bucked us up a lot."

Marsh continued: "Our first inkling of the conditions at Sendai was when we saw a group of human scarecrows standing near the gate. They were half naked, emaciated to the point that it was difficult to imagine how life could possibly remain in such a pathetic form. Their faces were pale, gaunt and haggard with hollow unseeing eyes, which stared at nothing. Their almost lifeless bodies were crippled and covered with scabs and sores. They were supposed to be brushing grass mats, but each movement was one of utter exhaustion as if in slow motion."[13]

Soon after, Bill Oxley, although at Sendai #2B, witnessed the arrival of the Canadians of Sendai #1B at his coal mine: "One day we came up to find we had been joined by 200 Canadians, an American doctor, and two American civilians. They went through the same routine as us. There were two French-Canadian brothers with whom I made friends, and my companion who slept next to me on the platform; he came out with us. He was Royal Corps of Signals, and his name was Bob Coghill. I liked Bob very much, and also Les Gibson, who was working in the Naval Dockyard in Shau Kei Wan. All three of us got on very well. We met another Hong Kong Volunteer, an Englishman, whose name was Vic Cropley. He had a bent spine, caused by an accident driving his motorcycle. He spoke Japanese, which was to cause him a lot of trouble."

Saturday, 17 March. Poulter: "St. Patrick's Day, March 17th and about 1.50 am the general Alarm sounded and then the local alarm and we could hear the sound of planes overhead. Without any orders from the Japs every man got up and packed his kit ready to go. All this took place in the dark, but as we use most of our clothes as a pillow there was very little confusion. Outside we could hear the barking of the AA guns and just near us was the gun on the Naval HQ banging away as well, and across the road we could hear the chatter of small arms fire. Being shut in as we were, it possibly sounds worse than it is. Over all this noise we can hear a sound as though a big pile of empty drums falling. I suppose this must be the incendiary. We lay on our bed spaces chatting and all this time we were in the dark. Round about 4 am we noticed a red glow through the cracks in the shutters, this can only mean that the fires are quite near us. Over the PA system came the order, 'Out side everybody and take all you can carry'. We trooped out and as we went I noticed that the Navy HQ is well alight, some cad has dropped an oil bomb on it! Later I learned that they had scored a direct hit on the gun. We showed the Japs what control really meant. We marched to our Air raid Shelter, formed up in sections and then sat down quietly waiting. I noticed that we were completely ringed with fire, but fortunately for us the wind is in our favour."

Wednesday, 21 March. 109 patients, four doctors, and five nursing orderlies moved from Bowen Road Hospital to huts at Shamshuipo, leaving four doctors and 56 staff with twelve so called 'strong' patients.

Friday, 23 March. The remaining patients and staff moved from BRH to Shamshuipo. At this point, BRH was finally closed.[14]

Friday, 30 March. Weedon at Kobe House: "Called in suddenly from digging on field in afternoon — all officers to parade in Takanaka's office, where told we should be leaving tomorrow morning for another camp." (p. 158)

On hearing this news, Poulter commented: "The officers have been told that they are leaving us and I don't like it. They have to a certain extent acted as a buffer between the Japs and us. I expect that they will miss the things that we used to get for them, on the other hand they might be better off, if such a thing is possible. The officers left for parts unknown on March 30th. RSM Challis took over as our camp commandant and 'Pug' Baron took over the Takahama section from him. Rumour says that the war is nearly over, well the sooner the better and that's not soon enough for me!"

Saturday, 31 March. Weedon continued: "Paraded on road at 5.30, and had to lay out kits, but no search — much to our surprise and greatly to my relief . . . Assembled at station with officers from several other camps in Osaka area, including Keith Goddard from Showa Denki. All had tales to tell of air raids, and Osaka area even worse than Kobe. Altogether forty officers in party — including an English padre who, in 1935, christened Andrew Man's daughter . . . Heavy kit dropped at station and set off to march to new camp . . . After about 1.5 miles reached new camp, a collection of long low camps like Argyle St., beside a stream in a little valley between steep wooded hills — a very attractive site. Camp already occupied by about 400 men, mostly RAF, 3rd Hussars, and RASC — all from Malaya or Java — who arrived two or three days ago from Wakayama, other side of Osaka . . . This camp apparently called Ikuno . . . Houghton officially appointed i/c, but majority of Nips seem to regard Lieutenant Frow (3rd Hussars), who was i/c at Wakayama, as i/c here." (p. 158)

James Ford at Tokyo #19D: "In March 45, two Americans joined us: Capt. Sedgie V. Hinson, U.S. Artillery, and Lieut. C.M. Bransfield, U.S.N. (A). There was no Allied doctor at this camp. A Jap civilian doctor made two routine calls a week and visited us in the case of emergencies such as injuries sustained at work. A British orderly held a sick parade every evening to attend to minor complaints. The housing was comparatively good. The officers maintained a high standard of cleanliness, Hard and I, with the help of Hinson and Bransfield after they arrived, doing most of the routine fatigues ourselves. Until the latter days of this camp, the officers did not have to go out on working parties. We had only about 30 books, most of which were entirely unsuitable for our men. I tried often with little success to obtain books from H.Q. and to buy books with officers' money. At this camp, we received 24 parcels and some comforts, details of which will be found in my diary. The chief factor contributing to the unrivalled health in 19 D was the extra food stolen from ships on which the prisoners were working.
Camp 19D Jap officials:
Camp Commandant: Lieut. J. Hayashi till Dec. 44.
Lieut. R. Kanetsuna"

April 1945

Hamilton at Osaka #1: "In April 1945, officers were taken to Oeyama camp and were compelled to work on a farm."[15] That same month, Hill was transferred from Hiroshima #1B to Tokyo #12B.[16]

Wednesday, 4 April. In Hong Kong, the French Hospital was bombed.

Saturday, 7 April. Redwood reported that Jackie Anderson married Keith Mackie in Stanley Camp.

Tuesday, 10 April. The Central British School (CBS) opened as the replacement hospital for Bowen Road with 119 patients, 6 officer staff, and 34 OR staff.

Sunday, 15 April. Tokyo #14B was destroyed by bombing and moved.

Friday, 27 April. Bowie at CBS: "One Volunteer died at 11.15 am on 27 April and having no acceptable mortuary we conducted the funeral at once to a site near Argyle Street, a short distance from the hospital."

May 1945

Wednesday, 9 May. Kiangwan Camp near Shanghai was closed down. With the exception of some twenty-five men (who were sent to Municipal Police Hospital in Shanghai, their number including Heather of the Middlesex)[17] too sick or injured to make the trip, the entire POW population was sent on their way to Japan. They stayed at a makeshift camp at Fengtai near Beijing, arriving on 14 May at noon, for about a month, then went on to Pusan, Korea for a few days. Almost 1,000 strong (though with only 30 or so from Hong Kong) they arrived in Japan in late June 1945, and were sent to the Hakodate camps on the northern island of Hokkaido.

Thursday, 10 May. The Narumi POWs were sent to Toyama (Nagoya #8B). Alec Howard at Narumi: "300 men left camp at 7 am arrive Toyama 8.30 pm." Thus, they arrived at Tatayama Heavy Industry Co. This would be a unique camp, holding only — with the exception of Riley, the senior officer — Hong Kong POWs.

Friday, 11 May. The Osaka #5D POWs were moved to camps under Fukuoka and Hiroshima's jurisdiction.[18]

Monday, 14 May. Some men, including Earnest Rowland, transferred from Omori to Sendai #5B.

Friday, 18 May. The Sakurajima POWs were transferred to Akenobe. Robert Bede Moore was included in this transfer: "Before the Japanese surrender we were shifted to 'Akenobe' and put to work in a copper mine."

Friday, 18 May. Bertram on the Yokohama bombing: "Now we drove to work from our little green oasis at Omori beside the silent, rusting tracks of the Yokohama electric railway, through a desert of ash and rubble in which lathes and all the machinery of small-shop industry stood up amid the wreck of what had been called a 'residential area'. Tokyo, the Tokyo we had known so well, was crumbling from day to day beneath our eyes." Bertram had considerable respect for the firemen: ". . . We always gave the Tokyo firemen an ironical cheer whenever their veteran engines — often built into old automobile chassis — chugged past us down the road, and we seldom failed to get grins and a shouted *'Buggeru!'* in response." (p. 196)

Sunday, 20 May. Fisher at Shamshuipo: "Most of our working parties are now engaged in digging tunnels into the hillsides, probably as air raid shelters. They are never properly shored up with broken wood, and we are very unhappy about the whole setup." (p. 170)

Sunday, 20 May. Ross Lynneberg: "On the 20th of May we were sent inland to a punishment camp in the lake area near Kyoto — the village name was Notogawa. Here we worked on reclaiming land from the lake making an area for paddy fields, and here we came under the control of army guards who gave us a pretty rough time. On the job site were leeches and on one occasion there was a very colourful water snake. Our food ration was cut and as there was nothing to loot we all started to lose weight, about 20 lbs in the first month. This was not enough for the Japs who started feeding us green wheat with more success, so successful in fact that if the war had lasted another month there would have been very few left alive. Sources of news were now practically nil the civilians being very simple and obedient to the military authority — unlike in Osaka where we were able to buy English printed papers with rice and sugar and steal Japanese printed papers which we had translated by the Chinese in the camp. In this camp we were subjected to more camp searches than at Osaka apparently looking for articles now not available in the stores. There was a hand cart at this camp which a work party I joined would drag to some of the nearby towns to gather up provisions. At this time there would be air raids by Grumman fighters, and we would see evidence of the strafing raids in the towns by bullet holes about three or four feet high on the buildings lining the side of the streets. It was while on one of the working parties that we came across a crashed fighter plane and the guard told us it was a USA fighter but when inspecting the cockpit we noticed that the instruments were identified by Jap signs so it was possibly the plane reported later as attacking the lame duck. On some of these work parties we would pass small buildings — one which had earlier been a sewing factory now had the sewing machines lying on the road side uncovered from the elements, no doubt with some more valuable war loot being concealed inside. It seemed towards the end of the war that this practice was fairly common."

Friday, 25 May. Changes were occurring in Hong Kong too. Redwood at Stanley noted: "Rosary Hill inmates, majority, have gone to Macau."

Edie Badger was at Rosary Hill: "It was in April of 1945 that Mr. Zindel and Mr. Suter of the Red Cross came to the camp with a Mr. Watanabe to tell the residents of the Camp that due to the American Blockade food in Hong Kong was getting very scarce and the Japanese will reduce our rations. We would be getting two meals of congee instead of the rice and beans we were getting each day. Then in early May we were told that the Macau Governor has agreed to allow passage to any Portuguese and Europeans interned in Rosary Hill with permission from the Japanese Commandant of all POW camps to proceed to Macau for humanitarian purposes. Col. Tokunaga gave his permission for anyone who wanted to leave. The first six junks loading between 30 to 40 per persons per junk left in mid-May. The next six junks left in early June. My mother did not want to leave, but when the congee became rice water with bran thickened with starch, she decided we had to go or we would all die. When we left, there was hardly anyone remaining in the camp. There were only three Junks in our convoy. We sailed out of Hong Kong harbor in early July of 1945 at about 11 a.m. heading towards Castle Peak."[19]

Badger continued: "We arrived in Macau three days later. It was in the late afternoon when we tied up to the dock and a Mr. Rodrigues from the Macau Red Cross met us and loaded us on a lorry and took us to a monastery high up on a hill. Only one way up about 200 very narrow steps and the same way down. We settled in a corner of a huge room. There were about thirty of us and we all settled in this room taking various nooks and corners to make ourselves comfortable. There were mattresses stacked in a corner. Each family was given enough for their use. We were getting settled in when someone said that food was coming up. All the kids ran to the front balcony and looked down the steps and we could see several Chinese coolies carrying two huge buckets of something steaming on a bamboo pole. We could hardly wait to see what it was. We did have some rice and veggies on the Junk, the first solid food for weeks, but that was only a little. Then all the children were called to the kitchen and each given a bowl of fried rice with everything under the sun in it. Char siu, shrimp, chicken, peas, carrots, onions, rice and spinach, other things I cannot remember. I sat down on the back steps by the outside kitchen in the back of the building with [my brothers] and we gobbled the food down. We were told to eat slowly, but no one listened. We sat there filled and exhausted, suddenly I started to get up and run to the outdoor latrine I was upchucking everything I ate a few minutes ago, Johnny came rushing in and George not making it to the latrines just did it out in the yard. We were so sick. After a while we were hungry and we ate again and brought it all up again. We did it three times. But you have to realize we had not seen food like this for four years."

Tuesday, 29 May. Bush, in hospital at Yokohama, reported: "On the morning of May 29th I was shaving. The air raid warnings had already sounded and I looked out of the window. A formation of some 25 bombers was approaching, then another formation came in sight and yet another. Suddenly great eruptions of black smoke soared skywards.

Within five minutes one could not see the sky for smoke and above it all was the roar of those great bombers and the bark of the anti-Aircraft guns. Then came a noise like hailstones on a corrugated and iron roof, the wind started to roar, and soon the houses were burning all around us. . . . It was like a dense, black London fog and the wind was howling and flames licked out from the burning houses and tress like the tongues of giant serpents. People bumped into us from out of the blackness which enshrouded everything, and that ghastly hail of incendiary bombs showered all around us, as wave after wave of B29s passed over."[20] (p. 220)

Thursday, 29 May. Tokyo #17D was destroyed by bombing, and moved temporarily to #18D.

Saturday, 31 May. Some men, including Henry Taylor, Royal Scots, transferred from Omori to Sendai #10B.

June 1945

Friday, 1 June. Osaka #1B was destroyed by air raid, and the POWs were temporarily moved to Tsumori.

Friday, 1 June. Tokyo #19D was closed and the POWs were sent to Niigata #15B. Ford was at #19D: "This camp was burnt down during the fire-raid of May 29th, 45. With the exception of 11 men who were transferred to Omori, the complement was transferred to Camp 15D."[21]

Monday, 4 June. Tokyo#18D was closed and the POWs were sent to Niigata #5B.

Tuesday, 5 June. Osaka #2B (Kobe) was destroyed by an air raid. Poulter: "At about 5.45 am on June 5th the general alarm sounded. The Jap pay sergeant came and told us to hurry up and eat our food and get our kits packed. He said that Kobe was to get it this time and this would be the last meal in Kobe House. I didn't like the way he said that! We could hear the sound of planes overhead at 6.15 am and then the local alarm sounded. The AA guns opened up and we carried on with our packing. As we lay waiting we could hear the sound of incendiaries falling, the dull crump of oil bombs bursting and the barking of the AA guns. At about 8 am the bombing seemed to be getting closer. Suddenly everything went dead quiet for a few minutes and then we heard the whistling sound of a heavy bomb or bombs falling. I feel sure that everyone in the camp could sense that this one was for us and we just had to lay there and wait for it. There was a dull explosion and the shutters were blown open and big gobs of flaming oil were flung up. Three oil bombs had hit Kobe House. One has hit our building between the first and second floors and has set fire to the stairs. One flaming gob of oil just missed me. We quickly got the fire on the stairs under control and then the people on the top floor shouted down that the roof was on fire."

Wright, also at Kobe House: "With other prisoners I worked at the pumps, but the thin stream of water from the hose was of no avail. Kobe House was destroyed. In it was one man, Chief Petty Officer Ray, who had died the night before." (p. 114)

Poulter: "All that day we lay out in the open and every so often we could hear a roar and a crash as building fell down. At 7 pm we were given a meal and then told to be ready to make a march into the hills. A little later an officer and a few men arrived and the part that I didn't like was the fact that two of the soldiers carried automatic guns. I thought to my self that this is a one way trip with a bullet at the end of it. I don't think I was the only one with that idea! We set off on our march into the hills, carrying all our kit and the sick men. On the way up we passed burned-out Tramcars and Buses and some private cars and we could also see piles of burned bodies. As we got higher into the hills, we could look back and see Kobe still burning and it looked quite good from where we were."

Wright, at nightfall: "We must have walked five miles before we reached a plateau surrounded by hills, on which stood lines of huts, a small square at their centre. As we squatted in the square, we learned that the place was called Maru Yama,[22] and it had previously been occupied by Australian prisoners from Singapore." (p. 115)

Poulter: "Arrived at Kawasaki, this is where the hospital used to be. We were detailed to our various huts and told to go to sleep. There was no arguing about this, we made up our beds and tried to get some sleep as were just about all in. the place was infested with mosquitoes and fleas, and by the way they acted they must have been starving! The fleas drove us out from under the blankets and the mosquitoes drove us back, eventually we did get some sleep."

Wright, next day: "In the evening the Japs asked for a hundred volunteers to evacuate Commander Page's hospital, which had been severely hit during the bombing, many patients being killed." (p. 116)

The surviving patients, many badly burnt, were evacuated. But, away from the American bombing, things were no safer at Oeyama.

Beadnell: "On the 6th day of June 1945, H 6928 Pte. BELL, G. of the Winnipeg Grenadiers died at Oeyama Camp from undernutrition, melancholia and pulmonary tuberculosis. This soldier never worked except for a short period of camp work while I was in this camp. He suffered from under-nutrition and the prevailing conditions of inadequate food and crowded quarters in my opinion may likely have contributed to the state of tuberculosis from which he ultimately died. In 1944 he attempted suicide by cutting his throat with a razor blade and subsequently became more and more abnormal mentally. His melancholic psychosis was undoubtedly precipitated by difficulties inherent in Prisoner Of War life in Oeyama Camp. The psychosis in its turn probably contributed to the onset of tuberculosis as he refused to leave the sick quarters for fresh air and over a long period refused to eat other than small amounts."

Jim Hart was struggling with the American bombing at Amagasaki: "There was systematic bombing north and south of the camp, so Amagasaki was evacuated on the 9th and 10th June 45 via Osaka."

Tuesday, 12 June. Wiseman, at Shamshuipo, was feeling no safer: "During the morning about 50 B24s bombed and dropped incendiaries from West Point to Causeway Bay. It is rumoured that there were very heavy Chinese casualties." (p. 81)

Sunday, 17 June. The POWs from Amagasaki camp arrived at Nagoya #9B and Hiroshima #3B.[23] Jim Hart was at the Nagoya camp: "We knew there were other camps in the Toyama neighbourhood. Sometimes we found rat skins. Someone else was killing and eating the rats. Maybe they were on the night shift."

Monday, 18 June. Poulter: "On the 18th, one hundred and twenty four of us, all sick men were selected to go away from this camp. We are supposed to be moving up to the Lake District in Kyoto. I hope it will be a better place than this. When we were paraded for the final selection, Morita, the Jap CSM said to me, 'Wouldn't you like to stay with your brother?' and I replied that I would take my chances. Who knows it might turn out to be better, but on the other hand it might be worse."

Tuesday, 19 June. The entire ex-Shanghai group departed Fengtai at 6 am, travelling five days to Pusan, Korea. They boarded the *Darian Maru*[24] to Japan at 6 am on June 28, arriving at Susa, Japan at 4 pm the same day, and disembarking on the 29 June at 1 pm.

Spooner was one of the ex-*Lisbon Maru* POWs on this journey: "We were loaded into decrepit railway wagons, the occupants of each wagon were split into two groups, and each group penned in by barbed wire. So it was hey-ho for the open railroad, our ultimate destination, we were told, was Japan, by way of China. Then on to Korea and across the straits of Japan to our new prison camp. Little did we know that we would be digging fox holes along the China part of the journey for the Jap defensive positions, as they did not know at which point the U.S.A., with their initiative and predominance of the sea and air, would strike if they attacked the Chinese mainland at all. At certain times, we would disembark, defecate, and dig — in that order. At times we were employed in other tasks, such as unloading timber from railway wagons. Eventually, after much more digging etc., we arrived in Japan, and were rushed to the rail station in Tokyo. This coincided with the civilians finishing work. They chased us through the station, enraged at the severe bombing from the air by U.S. aircraft. Carpet bombing had made a mess of Tokyo, razing large areas to the ground. The Japanese troops guarded us, albeit with kicks, punches and slaps, no doubt to satisfy the civilians. Eventually, we got onto the rail station platform and waited, amid a hail of stones and bricks from the enraged crowd. The train arrived, and we were herded into the carriages. The blinds were pulled down, and the train moved, much to our relief. We arrived at our ultimate destination, a small coal-mining village named [Hakodate]. Needless to say there was no 'welcome in the valley'. On arrival, we were issued with mining tools and marched through the village to jeers from the villagers. We were set to work in the mine, only two of us, Welsh miners, having had previous experience of mining work. Reaching the coal face involved walking, or rather sliding, down a slippery tunnel about five hundred yards long, at the sides of which hung high powered electric cables from which a lot of the insulation was bared. At the coalface we met our foreman, or 'Honcho' in Japanese. He was too old for military service, and looked too bloody old for mining. He spoke no English, had no teeth, which did not help, and he did not like us one bit. I assumed that he would not be an ideal instructor. This was made evident whenever we planted explosives to blow the coalface. He steered clear of us on those occasions. Mind you, we also did not hang around to watch when it happened, in view of our inexperience. However, after a few months, we would have done credit to Huw Morgan of 'How Green Was My Valley'. We sustained no major casualties for all our inexperience of mining, but no thanks to our 'Honcho'. Of course there was a few minor casualties. For instance little Willy Mitchell dropped his jacket into the hole which served as our toilet. He attempted to slither down the sloping sides of the hole, and one of the chaps said, 'Leave it Willy, it will stink to high heaven even if you do reach it.' But Willy still tried to reach the jacket. 'Give it up Willy!' 'No,' said Willy, 'my sandwiches are in the bloody pocket, and I am f— hungry.' Needless to say, he did not get his jacket back, or his grub."

Tuesday, 19 June. Kobe was bombed and finally evacuated. A number of men were sent to Nomachi. Poulter: "On the 19th we moved. We had a lousy meal at 4.30 pm and then we were marched to Kobe Station under an armed escort. We moved off from Kobe at 7 pm and our first stop was Osaka, where we changed trains. Here we were joined by one hundred and fifty yanks from the Osaka camp. We were all herded into three coaches and it was murder, there was barely enough room to move and, only a few could sit down. On this journey we had nothing to eat or drink, not a very nice trip. I got talking to one of the Jap sentries on the train and during the conversation I said to him that we would not be long at this place as the Americans will be here soon. He didn't get annoyed, but he said, 'Americanos come, all prisoners will be shot!' Now that's what I call real matey, so it looks as though even if our side wins we lose. We arrived at a place called Nomachi at 10 am on June 20th, a total of fifteen hours. I was dog-tired."

Thursday, 21 June. Wright and those at Maru Yama were marched on again: "We had arrived at a U-Shaped modern building, which had once been a school, and this was to be our new home . . . On being roused in the morning we were told that there were to be no working parties, and this gave us the opportunity to take stock of our surroundings. The school was in the Wakinohama district[25] at the foot of a range of hills, and below the viaduct, which served as a link in the Kobe-Osaka railway. Adjacent to the school was a large burnt-out building, once the Dunlop Rubber Company of Japan." (p. 126)

Friday, 22 June. The European prisoners in Stanley Jail, including Charles Boxer, Commander Young, Lt. Dixon, Commander Craven, Haddock, Routledge, Hardy and civilians such as W. J. Anderson (fourteen in total), were taken by train to Guangzhou and incarcerated in the city's Tungshan jail.

Friday, 29 June. Baird at Shamshuipo: "They took Harry [Hook] to the hospital over near our old prison camp at Argyle. I don't think he will live very long. He has put up an awful fight, but his heart has all gone to pieces and he weighs about 90 pounds. I hope they will be able to make things easier for him over there. The hospital here is like a barn with a roof that leaks like a screen door. After every rain the place is flooded. After reading this over, it seems pretty blue. I guess it is seeing Harry off that does it." (p. 254)

July 1945

Friday, 13 July. Cambon at Niigata: "Some of the men working at the Marutsu Docks were unloading glycol. It had a sweet taste and they mistook it for something good to drink. They came into the camp intoxicated or so we thought. However, in the middle of the night they became violently ill and passed into a stupour, breathing with difficulty. It was only then that anyone realised the seriousness of it all. Ten of the most serious cases were carried into the hospital and we all worked desperately to revive them, passing stomach tubes and doing whatever else possible with our limited supplies. Despite our efforts, four died, four young lads all in the prime of their youth, Bobby McLeod, a jolly lad who was very popular in the camp. Mac Hawes, the group leader, Jimmy Gard and Roy Kirk who had both recovered from severe amoebic dysentery." (p. 91)

Saturday, 14 July. The US Navy bombarded Kamaishi. The USS *Indiana*, one of three battleships in the bombardment (the others being USS *Massachusetts* and USS *South Dakota*)[26] filed a report from which these words are taken: "Task Unit 34.8.1 detached from Task Force 38 at 0600 and proceeded directly to Kamaishi. No training was conducted en route. Mission: Bombard 'certain vital areas of the Japanese mainland in order to destroy vital industries, demoralize transportation, and lower the will to resist of the Japanese people'. Own forces: Task Unit 34.8.1 approached Kamaishi in a circular air defense disposition, 4 V-Bomb. The final approach and bombardment was made in a column of battleships and cruisers with destroyer screen ahead, astern and on the disengaged sides. 0558 U.S.S. INDIANA left station in Task Group 38.1 to form on U.S.S. SOUTH DAKOTA as part of Task Unit 34.8.1. 0603 Battleship Division Eight formed column. 0705 Formed cruising disposition 4 S-Bomb, U.S.S. QUINCY and U.S.S. CHICAGO joined Task Unit 34.8.1. 0910 Sighted land bearing 235*(T). 1040 General Quarters. 1053 Deployed in bombardment disposition. 1100 Signal on Flagship 'Never Forget Pearl Harbor'. 1210 Opened fire with main battery. 1418 Ceased fire main battery. 1424 Formed cruising disposition 4 S-Bomb. 1436 Secured from General Quarters. 2152 Ships of Task Unit 34.8.1 ordered to report to previously assigned Task Groups. B.1 Weather: Wind 13 knots, from 084* (T)."

Hits in Target Area
1. 2 in Coke Ovens, Area 9451 U
2. 4 in Open Hearths, Area 9451 P&U
3. 1 in Foundry, Area 9315 T
4. 1 in Soaking Pit, Area 9351 T
5. 1 in Gas Holder, Area 7450, causing a violent explosion.
6. 1 in Rolling Mill South, Area 9351 Y
In addition to the above, 26 salvos were seen to land in the target area. But heavy smoke did not allow good spotting."

Five Dutch and American POWs were killed by this bombardment, but the Hong Kong POWs were unharmed.

Charles Trick was at Ohashi: "The American fleet came and they levelled hundreds of smokestacks at the iron smelter at Komitchi from just offshore. I forget how many thousand Japs they killed. They came down to our camp and loaded up a bunch of us to bury these Japs. They were already buried actually because they were in holes in the ground. They'd dig a hole for an air raid shelter and put some bamboo trees across and a bit of mud. They were buried already; their heads and legs and arms were sticking out. You could see the American navy laying right off the shore."

Thursday, 19 July. Les Fisher at Shamshuipo: "For the past three days our working party have been on a new job, dismantling the 'bamboo' pier which was used to take men across the harbour for Bowen Road Hospital when they were very sick. I suppose they think there might be a landing here. We had a wonderful time, dropping beams into the sea by accident and having to swim to get them back. I managed to get some small shell fish, which cooked up very well." (p. 218)

He continued on the same day: "Two deaths have been reported from the Central British School Hospital, Major Hook who had got over the cerebrospinal fever, and a Volunteer called Silva who had been in hospital almost since its inception. What a way to end your life!"[27]

Thursday, 19 July. At Innoshima, a new camp commandant, Mori, replaced the outgoing Nomoto. In his inaugural speech, Coxhead quoted the new commander as saying: "You may be dissatisfied with your food rations. But throughout Japan the food situation is difficult at present. You are receiving almost as much food as the Japanese soldiers".

Saturday, 21 July. Warrant Engineer Taylor at Niishin Camp: "21st — Cig issue, 5 per man. — Sunday 22nd."[28]

Wednesday, 25 July. In an air raid on Mitsui, one Hong Kong POW, Warrant Engineer Taylor, from Tokyo #2B, was killed.[29]

Poulter at Nomachi: "Pte. Andrews of the Middlesex Regiment died on the night of 30/31st of July. He appears to have died quietly in his sleep and his was the third death since we came here.[30] After his body was cremated, I took his ashes and kept them."

August 1945

Wednesday, 1 August. Redwood at Stanley: "Mrs Byrne, whose husband died while grinding rice last year, had news that her only son was dead."[31]

Wednesday, 1 August. Alec Howard: "Toyama burnt out by incendiary raid (Wed — our holiday)". For those, like Howard, at Nagoya #8B, their safety was provided by the rice fields that separated their camp and factory from the town, which according to American intelligence at the time was 75% burnt out.

Poulter watched the same raid from Nomachi: "On the night of 1/2nd August, we had another raid. It was quite close this time. They were bombing the town of Toyama, which is about five miles from us. Nearly all the camp was watching the raid; in fact we had a grandstand view. As the raid started we could see the planes, they looked all silvery and it looked like lots of little stars were falling from them. Later as the incendiaries took effect, the planes changed from silvery to rose red; it was a lovely sight from where we were. None of our sentry was visible; in fact I think the camp was deserted, except for the prisoners. After the raid was over and we were all supposed to be in bed, the Jap sentries turned up and walked round the camp."

But, by this point in the war, events had taken an utterly unexpected turn. On the tiny island of Tinian, in the Northern Marianas group north of Guam, a unique aerial task force had been assembled. Their mission was to take new, experimental, weapons and detonate them over Japanese cities. Until the test of the plutonium device 'Gadget' in New Mexico on 15 July, the effectiveness of these new weapons had been theoretical. Now they were proven. The components of the new bombs were rushed to Tinian. Early in the morning of Monday, 6 August, B29 Enola Gay took off carrying an untested uranium-based bomb, bound for Hiroshima.

Monday, 6 August. Collyer in Stanley felt something was in the air: "It appears as though we may be out soon. Everyone is very optimistic. I stand to lose a bottle of whisky & a pound if we are not out in September, or rather if we are not free."

Monday, 6 August. Coxhead at Innoshima, just 45 miles from Hiroshima, was aware of nothing, and was happy with minor variations of his day-to-day slog: "V. Gd. indeed. Soapy Hudson on. The Ape[32] unexpectedly away! A quiet day (5 men)."

At 8.15 a.m. the first uranium bomb ever detonated erupted in stellar fury over Hiroshima. Tens of thousands of innocent people died or suffered horrific burns. But the end of the war had been announced.

Thursday, 9 August. A second bomb, plutonium-based like Gadget, was detonated over Nagasaki.

Thursday, 9 August. The three American battleships returned to the bombardment of Kamaishi, this time with tragic results. Twenty-seven American, Dutch, and British POWs were killed, including two men from the RAMC in Hong Kong (who had been on the first draft to Japan): Staff Sergeant William Charles Tyner, and Private James Westby Downs. At least two other Hong Kong men from the first draft, Gerald Griffin, RA, and Earnest Rowland, Middlesex, were badly burnt, but survived.

Friday, 10 August. Gittins at Stanley: "The authorities issued an order: every man with a technical qualification was to assemble at 2 p.m. with his family outside his block ready for immediate transfer. In a typically Japanese manner, there the order ended. An atmosphere of doubt and excitement pervaded the camp. Engineers and technicians pulled their possessions from under their beds and threw them into whatever containers they had entered the camp with . . . The rest of the camp speculated wildly. Some argued that the party was destined for Japan. Others said they were needed for the city services because the Japanese themselves were going to leave. One theory claimed they were going to be used as hostages. Whatever the intention, we never found out. The transferees, over 170 in all, were packed into a junk and disappeared into the distance. Thrown into a makeshift camp in Kowloon, where conditions were fare worse than those they had left behind in Stanley, all they could do was wait. When the end came, they were still waiting."

Meanwhile, in Japan, the first overtures of surrender were being made. It was to be unconditional, except — the Japanese proposed — that the

Emperor would be retained as head of state. On the 12th, the United States gave agreement that the Emperor could remain, though only in a ceremonial capacity. On the 14th, the Emperor recorded a surrender message to the Japanese people, that could be taken from the palace (to prevent it being seized by elements of the forces opposed to surrender), and broadcast over the radio the following day.

Surrender

Unfortunately, for a number of men who had struggled to keep their spirits and health until this day, the Japanese surrender simply came too late.

Wednesday, 15 August.   Poulter: "On the morning of the 15th at 3 am Pte Tom Keeler died. He had got steadily worse since coming up here. I think he would have made it if he had had proper medical treatment."

But as the Japanese heard the broadcast, the message started to spill over into the camps.

Bertram: "And a few seconds later that magic phrase — the one scrap of Japanese that every prisoner knew — was being whispered through the yard in tones that ranged from agony to jubilation. 'Senso o wari! The war is over.' We didn't wait for details. There was wine (of a sort) in the warehouse, and even if it did belong to the Japanese navy there wasn't any Japanese navy left to worry about. Petty Officer [Geoff Josey], the Rabelaisian Shibaura toban who could smell alcohol at any distance up to half a mile, led the way. 'Come on, men, fill up your cans. It isn't straight Jamaica, but it's the best this benighted county can do!' By the time we piled into the lorries for the return trip to Omori, most of the working party, including the sentry and the fu's, were well passed caring what the consequences of the Emperors' broadcast might be for Allied prisoners in Japan." (p. 208)

Jim Hart at Toyama: "Timmy the navy lad [Stoker Timothy Kearney] saw them all the Japs reading the newspaper. He dropped his vegetables, and when he picked them up he picked up a copy of the paper too. 'I think something happened,' he said. 'Everyone's reading the newspaper. Some are laughing, some are crying.' I took it away and sat down. I knew enough characters to work it out; the newspaper said the war was over."

As rumours began, according to Parker in Shamshuipo: "Colonel White[33] asked for an interview, so with tongue in cheek he told the Commandant that he had heard the news. He insisted that the guards be put on the outside of the wire, where they had always belonged, and asked him to bring in more rations. I can only think that when Colonel White pulled this one he probably ducked automatically and put up his hands to protect his face because in former times they had always slugged him when he had made more reasonable requests. When he didn't receive the expected treatment he knew that the news was true, and immediately informed the camp of what he had said."

And on the same day, Bowie in Hong Kong reported: "On 15th August one British patient died, thus making the fifth death that had occurred at the British Central School." The other four had been: 27 April – HKVDC, 24 May – Canadian soldier, 7 July Canadian officer, 8 July – HKVDC. But Bowie's work would be increased from an unexpected source, as Baird noted that same Wednesday: "Some men have become actually ill and taken to hospital from excitement." (p. 258)

News of the Japanese surrender travelled more slowly in some camps, and men tried to find evidence to support what they heard.

Thursday, 16 August. Weedon: "The man who spent four months in Nip gaol (and lucky to survive) for stealing Red Cross Parcels, and who still sleeps in Nip guardroom and cleans up guardroom each morning, has redeemed somewhat his undesirable reputation by regularly stealing the guards' paper, sometimes right under their noses. Paper subsequently translated by Houghton." (p. 203)[34]

But in Hong Kong there was by this time no doubt.

Friday, 17 August. O'Toole: "Officers take over but Japanese still responsible for us but we now run the camp. Our 'worthy' liaison officer Major Boon arrested and about time. Major Ryan (I.G.) R.A did the job, later they arrested Philpotts, Bevan,[35] Hitchens and Strangler Evans, as stooges — a fine riddance."

Friday, 17 August. Bowie: "Later that night, 17 August, Major Harrison and I walked out of the hospital and went to a nearby Internment Camp [Ma Tau Wai] where we saw Dr and Mrs Selwyn-Clarke and Dr and Mrs Canaval who had worked with us during hostilities. I got back to the hospital at 1.30 am to find the place deserted by the Japanese and our men collecting souvenirs."

Saturday, 18 August. Bowie continued: "Major Ashton Rose brought in one patient from Sham Shui Po and said he had about 60 still to come."

Saturday, 18 August. Fisher at Shamshuipo: "Yesterday afternoon we started a round-up of the camp stooges. They were mostly in the camp office with Boon. Bevan, Hitchens and Philpotts were arrested. They say that Philpotts broke down; he was the one who gave away the tunnelling effort by the REs in 1942." (p. 226)

Saturday, 18 August. Poulter at Nomachi: "On the 18th August we were paraded and told officially that the war was over. There was no excitement, no clapping or cheering. All we have to do now is wait patiently to go home, the sooner the better. We now have nothing to do but sit around, talk and sleep. We are supposed to be going to Yokohama on the 23rd. I hope we do move soon, even though the war is over, I still feel that I am a prisoner and will do so until we get moving."

At Ohashi, the situation was similar. George MacDonell recounts that having told their camp commander that the war was over, they met with denial. "So we took him into the barracks and showed him the radio, now tuned into the American armed forces radio station set up in Tokyo. The camp commander was dumbfounded. He suddenly realised that we had known what was going on for weeks and he had not."[36]

Sunday, 19 August. Bowie: "On 19 August I went early to Sham Shui Po where I saw the senior officer who remained, Lieutenant Colonel F. Field and others. Major John Crawford, the senior Canadian medical officer, was in charge of the officers' camp and Captain Strahan moved to give professional help in the Indian camp . . . Ashton Rose would go to the Indian camp as Senior Medical Officer, Swyer would be S.M.O. Sham Shui Po."

Sunday, 19 August. The "Requirements of the Supreme Commander for the Allied Powers" presented to the Japanese in Manila, required the Japanese surrender delegation to be prepared to furnish all available information pertaining to "prisoner of war and civilian internment camps and places of detention, wherever located, within Japan and Japanese controlled areas". The Japanese asked to be notified as soon as possible as to where and when the Allied Nations would have the necessary ships for the prisoners' repatriation, and indicated that the following ports had been selected as embarkation points: Hakodate, Niigata, Omori, Fushiki, Tsuruga, Sendai, Yokohama, Nagoya, Kobe, Shimonoseki, Nagasaki, and Hakata.

Monday, 20 August. Unknown to the POWs, a part of the fleet that was being assembled for the invasion of Japan was now being swiftly repurposed for liberating POWs. The carrier HMS *Speaker*, for example, was instructed to report how many additional officers and men could be accommodated, and — though they did not know why at the time — this was shortly followed by an order to transfer the remaining airworthy aircraft to HMS *Ruler* to make more space available on the hangar decks.

Tuesday, 21 August. About a hundred close relatives, from Shamshuipo, arrived at Stanley. Simon White, Bob Cherry, and Henry Eardley were amongst the visitors.

Tuesday, 21 August. Baird: "Yesterday was a wonderful day for the Hong Kong Volunteers officers and men. Their wives and families were allowed to come and see them. It was both wonderful and pathetic, and the stories of atrocities and terrible treatment are really awful." (p. 262)

Tuesday, 21 August. Wiseman: "Having heard that Charles Boxer and the other 'convicts' had arrived at Central British School (CBS), still functioning as the BMH, I made my way there and found them. They were in surprisingly good shape and in tremendous form. It was a delight to see them and know that none were missing. While at the CBS a stream of visitors flowed through the ward, the most colourful being the Indian soldiers and Chinese cooks who had been in the Canton Jail with them. They included a gangster who was armed to the teeth and only too willing to get cash or anything else that Charles might fancy. I realised that we had led a very sheltered life as ordinary POWs." (p. 43)

Tuesday, 21 August. Fisher at Shamshuipo was catching up with news from Stanley: "Lady Grayburn has adopted little Michael Hyde whose father was executed. He used to go yachting with Andy and I, and was always full of fun. Mrs Hyde died shortly after her husband." (p. 229)

Tuesday, 21 August. Alec Howard at Toyama: "The SBO, Flt Lt Riley announces at 5.00 pm that war is over. A Nipponese officer arrived and intimated that the war was over. Guards were withdrawn to outside camp. Hara San and the Disciplinary Corps are now hopelessly drunk and competing for favours . . . Rations were increased by 50% and now get three rice meals a day. The only events now are roll call (instead of Tenco) held by Riley and meals. Nip Officer gives speech; says Emperor decide to make peace not only for Nip nation but for benefit of whole of mankind. Wished to thank us for co-operation during our stay. Was sorry that at present stage could not provide the kind of meals they would have liked to have presented. Hoped we would be soon safely home. The food was put up by Kaisha."

Wednesday, 22 August. A number of Shamshuipo POWs had the opportunity to visit Stanley via the sea route. O'Toole: "Trip to Stanley by launch 'Clara' across the harbour two trucks in very poor condition to Stanley. Alan just the same not changed in the least. Peggy Harrison also same. All look very fit especially the children & there is plenty of them. Couldn't see Joan Whiteby. Mrs Gill lost her little boy in the fresh water plunge on beach. A day is rather short to see and talk to everyone. Betty's last letter year old then very well. Rosie Spry looks older but is well. Got home at 11.30. Long day but enjoyable. Had a good swim at Tweed Bay."

Wednesday, 22 August. Weedon: "Warned at lunch time, with five other officers, including Chris, for immediate return to Kobe. Troops apparently a bit out of hand, and Nips want us to restore order . . . Our troops living in school buildings near chimneys we used to see from Kobe House. Had had miraculous escape when Kobe House received direct hits with incendiaries." (p. 209)

On the same day, back in Hong Kong, feelings at Stanley were running high. Collyer: "One of the R.C. Fathers from town stated that it is estimated that there have been about 50,000 official executions in town. On top of that you have the unofficial, those that have been bumped off 'for fun', etc. in the streets and various accidents. I should say another 100,000. Some of the executions were carried out in the following various forms: shot, beheaded; tied up by the feet & savaged by trained Alsatian dogs; burning alive; crucifixion; stoning; beaten to death; starved. These are the forms known to us; they probably have more, the tortures we do not know much about, but now the war is over, the fellows who have been in their hands will probably speak. One form of execution I did not mention was meted out to an American Airman who was brought down on 16th Jan. He, after torturing, was tied by the feet to a lorry & dragged through the streets until he was dead. I am certain people will not believe it when the tale is told. People have been beaten up in the Camp for trivial offences & then admitted to our own hospital with a broken back or ribs, or with the skin completely off their backs & legs. They should put those responsible on trial & let us be the judges. Or, better still, put every Jap back into Japan & remove all other nationalities from there & then bomb the whole place intensively with the new atomic bomb for a month. Wipe them out is the only answer."[37]

Wednesday, 22 August. Coxhead: A letter from another camp brings "detail of the terrible bomb-drafting of Hiroshima, in particular an account of a new bomb — the atomic bomb — which kills every living thing, plant and animal, within a radius of 5 miles."

Bill Oxley at Sendai was also hoping for news: "The committee was now in session, debating what we could and could not do. We had not got very far, when there was a lot of shouting. My heart missed a beat, I thought the Japs had come back, but it wasn't them. The men shouted, 'Planes, a lot of them.' We all ran out of our committee room, and there in the distance, about a mile away, coming towards us what looked like bombers — but whose? Yanks or Japs? Those with good eyesight could see the stars on the planes. They were Yanks. There was shouting and waving of hands — it seemed they would not see us. The Doc said, 'there are white sacks in the cook house.' Men ran in and grabbed armfuls of sacks which were waved. Surely they must see us! But at about a thousand feet away, they began to turn away. Our hearts sank. Suddenly a lone plane behind the others spotted us. He must have given a signal, because they all turned and came low over us. Nearly all of us were in tears — at last, oh, God, at last! My heart beat so fast I knew I had to calm down."

Nat Rakusen noted: "Well, I cannot describe the scene. Everyone cheered — shook hands — embraced — some cried. I must say that in my life I have had some thrilling moments, but none could compare with that. I went cold all over, then a cold sweat broke out, and I could hardly talk."

Marsh saw the same planes at Sendai: "The British and the Dutch had each made flags of the respective countries and flew them when our planes appeared. Some of us felt that we too should have a flag and I spoke to Captain Reid about this. He reminded us that American planes were dropping our supplies and that our own Lieut. Finn was an American Naval Officer. 'I'm sure he would like to see an American flag.' It was a great idea and with the Captain's blessing a few others and I formed a flag committee and got busy . . . It was suggested that we form a color party so that the flag could be presented with full military honors to Lieut. Finn. At this time we had recovered our old uniforms and the American planes had dropped other supplies. We were therefore able to turn out a fairly smart guard dressed in khaki shirts, shorts, socks and boots, and even our old Grenadier wedge caps with badges. I was the Sergeant in charge of the color party. When all were ready it was decided to draw Lieut. Finn over by subterfuge. Sgt.-Major 'POP' Corrigan of the

Rifles was detailed to go over to Finn's quarters and tell him there was trouble among the men and to come immediately. Soon Lieut. Finn could be seen hurrying across the compound prepared to deal with the same trouble he had been dealing with for many years. Most of the other Canadians were gathered around our small group and as Lieut. Finn approached I called the color party to attention. The flag was unfurled and our impromptu bugler, a bandsman who had recovered a cornet somewhere, blew the general salute. We all turned to the flag and saluted. Every man within the camp stood to attention with hand raised. Lieutenant Finn looked perplexed as if he were still ready to deal with some dispute. When he saw the flag and the color party he stopped, stared, and slowly raised his hand giving a salute with tears welling up in his eyes. I presented it to him and asked that he accept it on behalf of all the Canadian prisoners. The flag was a tribute to the United States of America, its armed services that had liberated us and to Lieutenant Finn who, at all times under the most adverse circumstances, had conducted himself towards the prisoners and towards the enemy as an American Officer and a man. As I presented the flag to him I could see his lips quivering with emotion. He accepted it and said, 'It's just what I wanted.' Clutching the flag close to his chest he hurried quickly away to his quarters and the boys gave him a great cheer as he went."

Thursday, 23 August. Cambon at Niigata noted, in his last diary entry: "I have literally grown up in a prison camp. Most of all my experience has been on the more unpleasant side of life . . . starvation, sickness, cruelty, robbery, torture, depravity . . . all overshadowed by death." (p. 97)

Saturday, 25 August. Alec Howard at Toyama Camp: "News from Warumi Camp tells that the Nip Staff are frightened to appear. The Bengo bullock was bought for 8000 yen immediately on news of war over and eaten . . . POW painted on roofs of huts for expected supply drop."

In Ohashi, George MacDonnel and comrades also needed food. "We sent out into the countryside teams of 10 men, under an NCO, to carefully and quietly barter with the peasants for food: pork, eggs, vegetables, soya sauce, beans — anything we could buy. In exchange for fresh food, we traded army boots, tinned army rations, soap, and other military supplies that we took from the camp's military stores." (p. 138)

Sunday, 26 August. At Oeyama, while waiting for relief, a system of 'outings' was arranged. J. I. Bevan: "Today was my turn for an 'outing' (200 a day) one hundred in the morning one hundred p.m. Travel by barge (the coal barge that so often we unloaded). A trip of approx. 1/2 hour. Very little money, two shops, and not very much there to buy. Received a cup of Japanese tea from one of the inhabitants."

Tuesday, 28 August. A B29 dropped food at Oeyama, together with notes containing news. Bevan again: "Atlee is prime minister with an overwhelming majority . . . The Allied forces will soon release you . . . The surrender was unconditional . . . Ford is turning out 1946 models . . . There's a new speed boat record . . . England we are told is now nationalised."

Wednesday, 29 August. The USS *San Juan* entered Tokyo Bay and landed parties which liberated prisoners at camps at Omori, Ofuna, and Shinagawa hospital.

Wednesday, 29 August. Bertram was at Omori, and on receiving a message dropped from a Grumman Hellcat saying that boats were being sent to pick them up, recalled the excitement of the moment: "Pandemonium. 'Get out the flags!' bawled a score of voices. And out they came, the hidden flags we had painted on army sheets during the night watches. The Stars and Stripes, the Union Jack, the red-white-and-blue of the Netherlands. Men had plunged into the bay and were swimming out to meet the landing craft. Low-flying planes were guiding them in now, through the maze of piles and overhead wires that lined the shores of Omori. A surge of half-naked prisoners burst out from the walls of the camp, down to the narrow sandspit with its little jetty. The flags were lined up by the landing stage. In front of them we danced about like savages. So suddenly, with so short a warming, had come the Day — and the Hour." (p. 216)

The POWs were transferred to the hospital ships *Benevolence* and *Rescue*. Lewis Bush at Omori: "Late that evening I was one of the last to board a landing craft which headed out into the bay to berth alongside USS *Benevolence*, a beautiful white hospital ship. Its name was more than upheld for never was such kindness, gentleness and understanding displayed as by the officers, nurses, doctors and men of that magnificent American vessel." (p. 225) The liberation of the POWs in Japan, a predominantly American operation — and one of unmatchable confidence, efficiency and compassion — was gathering speed.

From the hospital ships, the Omori men were transferred to HMS *Speaker*, with some 2,000 POWs in total.

Wednesday, 29 August. Alec Howard at Toyama Camp. "10.00 am Planes heard: great excitement. Circle over then come lower and after a couple of test runs one plane drops first parachute flying very low. Returns for second run and drops a third and on the next run the 4th package drops and then the plane sideslips and crashes 50 yds from us. Rush out to find plane has demolished a house and lies upside down. 2 men are brought out — one injured. The pilot is dead: a regrettable accident. Cases contain emergency rations, cigarettes, bag of bread and magazines. Had a slice of bread — delicious, just like cake!"

Thursday, 30 August. Howard continued: "Had just appeared for funeral service of pilot when planes appeared; dropped more supplies and note asking for information about airmen and indicating how to convey the information to them. Three men arranged on parade ground: one lying flat (dead Pilot), one sitting up (wounded air gunner) and one standing (uninjured). Sqd Leader indicated that he had got the signal and later when service was held they returned in formation and flew over." Mears of the Royal Navy died that day having been taken ill after drinking some synthetic alcohol found in the crashed plane.

Thursday, 30 August. Poulter at Nomachi: "About 9.30 am on August 30th, eight pursuit planes came over and dropped some parcels to the other camp, they then dropped a note to us saying that they would be back at 4 pm with more supplies. They came back at 4 pm and dropped one carton of cigarettes and one box of Navy Rations. Each man received half a tin of Pemmican, one small square of chocolate, one cigarette and ten malted milk tablets. Even the Yanks didn't consider this a very good show and we gave them a good ribbing over it. Never mind Yanks, there is always tomorrow and maybe it will be your turn."

Thursday, 30 August. Harcourt's relief fleet arrived in Hong Kong. It consisted of:
HMS *Anson* (Battleship)
HMS *Euryalus* (Cruiser)
HMS *Indomitable* (Aircraft Carrier)
HMS *Kempenfelt* (Destroyer)
HMS *Maidstone* (Submarine depot ship with eight submarines)
Hospital ship *Oxfordshire*
HMCS *Prince Robert*
HMS *Pyrias* (Destroyer)
HMS *Quadrant* (Destroyer)
HMS *Swiftsure* (Cruiser)

HMS *Toscin* (Destroyer)
HMS *Ursa* (Destroyer)
HMS *Venerable* (Aircraft Carrier)
HMS *Whirlwind* (Destroyer)

Redwood was in Stanley when the fleet landed: "In came two cars, the first of which Admiral Harcourt in full rig and Mr Gimson (who is now Governor). Then came some Marines on small amphibians, all looking so huge and healthy, their white starch uniforms gleaming, and their faces so pink that it looked as if they were wearing make-up."

Thursday, 30 August. Fisher at Shamshuipo: "Andy had been released from a Canton prison, where he had spent three months. He had been sentenced to death with 33 others, but with three more he had been pardoned and sent to prison in Canton instead." (p. 239)

Friday, 31 August. O'Toole: "First issue of *Hong Kong Telegraph* under our rule. Admiral Harcourt arrives with his Battle Fleet & comes to camp gets good reception, looks as if we shall be in here for week or two yet owing to danger of sea sickness in weak state. No effort been made yet to let us send messages home blast them. 8 subs in also no troops as yet. Hope to go to C.B.S. tomorrow to see Joan Whiteley."

Friday, 31 August. One hundred and one patients were transferred to the hospital ship, *Oxfordshire*. Later she took a further 90 patients, and steamed off for the UK, being replaced by the New Zealand hospital ship, *Maunganui*.[38]

Meanwhile, those who could wasted no time visiting Harcourt's vessels.

Thursday, 31 August. Bromley of the HKDDC visited a Canadian vessel: "I went on board an Armed Cruiser, the 'Prince Rupert', she was a Canadian vessel really. We were made very welcome indeed. Tons of food and drink."

Major Maurice Parker of the Royal Rifles of Canada visited a British one: "Two of us went aboard the Submarine Mother Ship the MAIDSTONE. A couple of ABs took us in tow and we ended up drinking their ration of beer. Things were tough aboard the British ships and we afterwards wished the sailors had not been so kind because we could have very easily done without it."[39]

September 1945

Saturday, 1 September. Bush on HMS *Speaker* off Yokohama: "Those were hectic and bewildering days. The whole pattern of naval and military life had changed since we had been taken prisoners and even the new wartime language was at times quite incomprehensible." (p. 227)

News of the surrender was still only starting to filter through to the more remote camps. Jack Etiemble was one of those sent to tell the Notogawa POWs that the war was over: "Some of us went to a camp at Lake Biwa. Shortly after the war ended, and the Americans had dropped us some clothing. R.S.M Mathieson called on five of us who had already been to Sen Riiyama up in the hills, where the Japanese HQ staff went shortly before the war ended, and brought back Colonel Murata, the Camp Commandant, as the Americans would want to question him. On return we were told to go and find the camp at Lake Biwa somewhere in the Kyoto region as he had a feeling that they had never been told the war had ended. On arrival in Kyoto we went to the Police HQ and asked for a guide, at first they refused but after some gentle persuasion they agreed. We eventually found the camp. The P.O.Ws were not at work but were standing around in the compound. We were recognised by some, who then asked what we were doing walking around in U.S. clothing, you can imagine the feeling, as they had not been told that the war had ended."

Ross Lynneberg was amongst those waiting POWs: "One afternoon on our return to camp from a working party there was a strange Jap officer asking if anyone knew anything about radiation poisoning — we had never heard of it. Shortly after this while at work a guard came cycling on to the job site shouting something to our guard who immediately dropped his rifle and took off on the push bike never to be seen again. One night while wondering what was happening an Aussie came over the back fence somewhat intoxicated with two silver plated revolvers housed in holsters hanging from his hips. He kept telling us that the war was over and to break out, but fearing that this was a trap for us to break out of the camp thereby giving the guards the right to shoot us down we stayed put and helped the Aussie back over the fence."

On the same day at 10.00 a.m., George MacDonnel at Ohashi was anxiously watching an American fighter searching for remote POW camps. Finally the aircraft zoomed over the camp, and dropped a metal box with a streamer attached. Inside was a handwritten note that said: " 'Lieutenant Claude E. Newton, from the *John Hancock*, 50 miles offshore.

Have radioed location. Put out markers.' In the tin box were several fluorescent-covered strips of cloth and instructions that said: 'If you need food, arrange the strips to read F; if you need medicine, arrange the strips to read M; if you need a combat paratroop drop, arrange the strips to read P'." (p. 139)

Saturday, 1 September. O'Toole at Shamshuipo: "Went to C.B.S. saw Joan & Taylor etc. Later in day they were all put on Hospital ship *Oxfordshire*. Went aboard sub talked to crew. They gave us milk in tea and 50 woodbines. *Maidstone* mother ship to subs. Very welcome aboard."

Sunday, 2 September. O'Toole: "Take worst cases from here on Hosp ship. Bill Bashford, Clancy, Roberts, Collinson, all RAOC. Fancy Bill Bashford got his wish in the end. Gordon Horrop also went had a drink of Saki with him before. Gave my white rabbit to Soares boys. We may go any day now. Pictures (Bitter Sweet) in the evening in camp. Nice to smoke a Players cig."

Sunday, 2 September. Bromley noted that some HKDDC men were also taken on board the *Oxfordshire*: "Several of our chaps have been sent off to a Hospital Ship."

Monday, 3 September. Weedon: "Held ceremony of raising Allied flags again, having had news of signing of surrender yesterday. Managed to unearth French flag, to add to those we already have — Union Jack, Stars and Stripes, Australian, Chinese, Greek. Quite a number of civilians to witness parade, and RSM Challis took photos. Quite impressive little ceremony. Later in day Campbell and Houghton arrived unexpectedly. Rather a shame, as we've already done all the heavy work, and Chris deserves the credit of handing over the camp to the Allies when they come. Houghton, luckily, very pleasant about it, and leaving all administration in Chris' hands."[40] (p. 217)

Tuesday, 4 September. The *Empress of Australia* arrived in Hong Kong.

Tuesday, 4 September. Poulter at Nomachi: "At about 2 am on the 4th an American Air Corp. Officer arrived in the camp. He told us that it was an Atomic Bomb that had finished the war. I don't care what they called it or what it was, it's finished and that's all I'm concerned about at present. He says that we are flying from Nomachi to Tokyo and that all prisoners will get top priority. That's OK by me — let's go! . . . Three Yanks from the other camp broke out and caused a spot of bother. Our camp, No. 10 Nagoya Area is in fairly good order even if it is in not very good hands."

Marsh, at roughly the same time, left Sendai by train for Tokyo: "How quickly we packed. The prisoners were loaded down with duffle bags filled with cigarettes, chocolate bars and spare clothing. The Jap Commandant, without his sword, and his crew came to see us off and stood at salute as the train pulled out. Some, still keeping up a pretence of responsibility, came with us and were the best behaved although a little nervous. They were unsure how the Americans would receive them at the other end of the line. Although we were packed in coal cars all that mattered was that we were on our way home. We laughed and sang and each section waved its flag from the side of the train. We still had Old Glory and Gooch was there to wave it. Our route was a hundred and twenty miles long and we threw gum and chocolate to everyone we saw. As we neared Tokyo we witnessed the incredible devastation the American bombing had caused in the towns we passed until finally we reached Tokyo and disembarked to change trains. As we detrained on an open platform another train came to a stop opposite us. It was full of Japanese troops returning to their homes. We stood staring at each other and all became very quiet. This had been our enemy. Long tense moments passed. Then someone laughed and threw over a package of American cigarettes and a dozen Japanese went to pick it up. This broke the tension and more cigarettes were thrown over and the Japanese began throwing back oranges. This was my last contact with the Japanese. Shortly afterwards we arrived at Yokohama and were met by a regiment of American Cavalry with their band. We were overjoyed to finally see our liberators. I jumped out of the train carriage before the train had even stopped and flung myself upon a stout, red faced, American Major. I thumped him on the back, shook his hand and all but kissed him. Others joined in and began pounding him on the back from all sides. The Major struggled to keep his parade dignity for this was a formal reception and the American troops were not allowed to break ranks."

Cicero Rozario was on the same trip: "We went to Tokyo by train. The city, except for a few chimney stacks, had been flattened by B29s. The doctor examined each one of us and we were issued with GI uniforms and then sent on to Manila on an American Destroyer for rest and recreation."

Wednesday, 5 September. Alec Howard at Toyama: "Only sick to go by plane now. We move off for train at 2 pm — 13 hrs journey they say.

All the village [sic] turns up to see us leave at the train station the works bosses are lined up, salute and later wave hands. How two-faced these people can be. 2.30 leave on short journey to Toyama steam train station. All buildings here completely destroyed and ticket office functions on platform. 1/2 hr wait and train arrives with No. 9 & 11 camps on board. Special train. We now number about 800. We all get a seat but dilapidated and uncomfortable coaches. Pass numerous stations completely burned out."

Wednesday, 5 September. Weedon: "Just starting supper, when news brought that party of Americans arriving Kobe 8 p.m. to collect us and evacuate us. Hamilton and I sent by Houghton to establish contact with them." (p. 219)

Wednesday, 5 September. The Niigata POWs were sent to Tokyo. Cambon: "A fleet of lorries took us to the railway station . . . In Tokyo station we were greeted by nurses and female soldiers. This last was a surprise as there had been none when we left Canada. The Americans were so kind and anticipated everything."[41]

At about the same date, Leonard Birchall led the Suwa POWs out of their camp: "After we'd had about two weeks of [being supplied from the air], of building up our strength and what not, we then commandeered a whole flock of trucks, and we found out the railway schedule. So we got the trucks and we went down, late one night, to the railway station. The train came through for Tokyo. Well, when the train stopped we just commandeered the coaches that we needed, put everybody on board, and down we went to Tokyo. We got in the next day. We got in there and got out at the rail station and there was nobody around. So we commandeered some more trucks, because a lot of the guys, as I say, had no feet, no hands, and were blind. We got the sick and the wounded on to the trucks and there was an electric railway line that runs from Tokyo to Yokohama. So we knew where this was and so we moseyed over to that, and again commandeered whatever railway coaches we needed to cart them in. Down we went to Yokohama, and we got out of the train and went out in front of the railroad station, and I've got a picture of the railroad at this time, I went out and got the actual pictures of that railway station, on this last trip. We got out, and we had made flags out of old pieces of sheet and crayons. So we got out and we sat out in front of the railway stations with our flags. Eventually an American guy came along in a jeep, took one look and asked us what the hell the story was. We told him. In no time flat, busses and trucks, and then they took us off down to the godowns and processed us through."

Thursday, 6 September. Poulter: "We left Nomachi at 6.30 am on September 6th, by train. We took all the camp staff with us and they do not look at all happy, maybe they realise what they have got coming to them, I bloody hope so! We are still travelling at 6 am the next morning . . . Arrived at a place called Arai Machi at 1 pm and a crowd of Yanks met us off the train. They took us in tow and placed us in lorries, this was in order to move us a distance of four hundred yards. We then boarded some landing craft and then away. These boats took us to the US Hospital ship 'Rescue'. Here we were told to dump all of our Japanese kit over the side except for our underpants. They then took us to the showers and afterwards dusted us with powder, no not talcum powder but DDT. They then issued us with US Naval kit, sweets, cigarettes, writing pad and pencil and a Red Cross Bag containing washing materials. We were then medically examined, a few particulars taken and then we were given a ticket with a special marking on it. Those of us that were marked fit for further travel were taken to the USS *Gosselin*. Nobody could fiddle his way, because of the cards that we had been given. Those that were not marked fit for further travel were kept onboard the 'Rescue'."[42]

Thursday, 6 September. Individual POWs were still being handed over to Allied forces in Japan. On this day, Arthur Herbert Betts, 2883762, Middlesex, was given over to "Man" at Sannomiya station.[43]

Friday, 7 September. Weedon: "Arrived Yokohama 10 a.m. . . . Eventually names called out in batches of twenty (mine luckily with Chris) and put on lorries, in which drove out to Atsugi airfield — fifteen miles outside Yokohama, and the centre of things at present as MacArthur only recently arrived there. We're terribly lucky to be seeing all these key places. It's astounding the amount of stuff the Americans have already got in — 1st Cavalry Division much in evidence, but many other troops as well, and a vast amount of equipment . . . Took off at 5.15 pm." (p. 222)

Saturday, 8 September. O'Toole: "Looks as if we are going tomorrow at 8 o'clock. Ye Gods Manila first stop. The American crew of a ship that were here during the war were flown out today by Yank air force."

Saturday, 8 September. The Niigata POWs embarked on USS *Ozark*, with a total of 950 returning POWs. She returned to America via Guam and Pearl Harbor.

Saturday, 8 September. Poulter, who had been transferred from *Rescue* to *Gosselin*, was trans-shipped to HMAS *Warramunga* which took him to

Tokyo Bay: "Later taken aboard USS *Monitor*, we are supposed to be going to Manila on this ship."

Sunday, 9 September. J. I. Bevan at Oeyama: "Board train 9 a.m. Sept. 9. On short time rations now. Goodbye Oeyama, hello Frisco, here we come." He described the excitement, the many stops, and the long journey: "One thing that's very unpleasant — travelling through tunnels — and there are very many of them — the sulphur fumes — really stifling, and the seat so very hard to sit on for any length of time — wooden and straight back." He listed the stations they passed through or stopped at: Ayabe, Nigo, Kyoto Yamas (where he received a memento, a small Buddha), Marbard, Ogaki, Ofuna, and finally Yokohama at 5.58 a.m. to be welcomed by an American band. There he boarded the US Navy hospital ship *Tryon*.[44] On board, he kept up with the latest films: *The Constant Nymph* and *Between Two Women*.

Sunday, 9 September. R. B. Moore, R. N. Y. Police: "Left Akenobe P.O.W. Camp on 9th Sept at 7.30 a.m. travelled by motor lorry to Watahama Railway Station (a little rain). Arrived at 9.20 a.m. — left at 12.30 for Yokohama where we arrived at, at 12 noon on 10th our rail journey was fairly comfortable and saw plenty of war ruins factories etc. burnt to a heap of rusted iron. On arrival at Yokohama was given a great welcome by American Air Corp the band was on Railway Station where we marched from the trucks which conveyed us to the wharfs[45] which were ready for us. First a good hot meal then a bath, next came new clothes and boots then a cable home, when this was through we filed a medical report, were allotted our compartment on the boat, and last but not least came red cross comforts soap, cigarettes, sweets, shaving cream, pencils, paper etc."

Sunday, 9 September. In Hong Kong the *Empress of Australia* took on board all who were being evacuated from Stanley. Bromley: "Left Hong Kong Naval Yard for Kowloon Godowns and boarded the Empress of Australia at 11 a.m. She was loading POWs and Internees from Stanley Camp all day. We are down on E13 deck right down in the heat, darkness and bloody bilges it's terribly hot down here. We are all strung up in hammocks."

Parker was just one deck above: "We left Hong Kong and as we got out into the China Sea, the EMPRESS began to roll. I had had a meal down in our mess room in "D" deck, four decks below and right on top of the boilers, or so it seemed, where the temperature was, I'm sure, one hundred and thirty five degrees Farenheit. Under these conditions food doesn't taste good. I was dripping with sweat and sat in a puddle of perspiration; the EMPRESS was rolling."

Monday, 10 September. Bromley: "Left Kowloon for Junk Bay to anchor and pick up more people from Stanley." The next day, at 8 a.m., they would depart for Manila.

Wiseman: "In September 1945 most HK POW were shipped Home via Suez on the C.P. liner *Empress of Australia* but a minority, including myself, went on from Manila in the US Attack Transport *Admiral F. Sharpe* bound for San Francisco." (p. 46) The British POWs on board were set off at British Columbia.[46]

Monday, 10 September. Poulter: "On September 10th moved to USS *Oconto*, this one is definitely taking us to Manila."

Monday, 10 September. As the repatriation effort gathered speed, POWs from the Tokyo area and beyond were concentrated in Yokohama. At Atsugi airfield there, in groups of twenty, they were allocated to Consolidated B24 Liberators — converted for passenger use by the addition of twenty plywood seats in the bomb bays — to fly them down to APO903 Okinawa. From APO903 they were ferried to Nielsen Field, Philippines. But on 10 September, something went horribly wrong.

As the fleet of Liberators headed south, B-24J #44-40666, *Les Miserables* with its cargo of POWs, was lost at 11.50 in the morning of 10 September 1945, 50 miles southwest of Taiwan.

With pilot Robert Armacost at the controls, the plane met with difficulties. Armacost recalled:

> It was dangerous, to have them with no experience. Before we went on these missions we briefed these ex-POWs on what to do in case of an emergency, and they'd be there pulling on a prop, looking around. They were not in good shape anyway. Some had been prisoners for five years.
>
> Anyway, I had made one trip down there and back and was making my second one. We took off early in the morning, climbed to 10,000 feet, everything was going along fine. I'd set the autopilot. I told my co-pilot, 'You watch it for a while, I'm going to rest my eyes.'
>
> Just as I leaned back he said, 'Watch number one.' Oil pressure was going down, and oil temperature was going up.
>
> He said, 'Should I feather?'
>
> I said, 'Just come back to half power. See how it is.'
>
> We did, and it cooled down. Oil pressure came back.

He said, 'Shall I put it back up?'

'No, just leave it where it is, we're going along fine.'

And about that time the prop ran away and it would not feather. It was like having a bit of plywood the size of that propeller hanging out on the end of that wing. We'd lost that engine at 10,000 feet, and circled back towards Formosa — we were in the Formosa Straits — and didn't know where we were going to land, but wanted to get back somewhere approaching civilisation.

Anyway, we got 10,000 feet, 2,000 feet, and were still losing it. We came across a ship. I decided — we were right on the edge of a typhoon — the ocean was swelling up twenty feet high, there was no way to ditch the airplane. So I decided everyone had to bail out. We had parachutes for everybody.

Anyway, between the tail gunner and the bomb-bay was a little hatch, we called a camera hatch, probably 3 feet by 2.5 feet, and I told my engineer, I said: now take these prisoners of war back where they can't be hit by anything, tell them to bail out of that camera hatch. And he did. Three of them popped their chest type parachute inside the airplane. He bundled them up altogether threw them out and they all worked, but some of them never did open their parachute going down.

Some of them would hang on the side of the airplane. Banging up against . . . wouldn't let go . . . he had to pry their hands off. Some of them worked, some of them didn't. It must have been a horrible experience for him.

2,000 feet, still losing altitude. My navigator came up, 'Boss, are you going to go out?'

I said, 'Yes, I am.' He said, 'You always said you'd never bail out.'

'Well, I guess I'll have to.'

When they were all gone except my co-pilot and I, I told my co-pilot to make a trip back and make sure they're all gone, and come back and tell me.

He came back up and said, 'Yes, they're all gone.'

I said, 'Good. Put on that raft on your chute and get on out of here.'

He strapped his raft on, then took it off and threw it down.

'That'd be kind of chicken, wouldn't it, sir? Bail everybody else out with just a Mae West, and we're going bailing out with a raft?'

'Well,' I said, 'OK, leave it there and get on out.'

And he did. I followed him right on out. I bailed out too.

We got picked up by that ship, which happened to be a British destroyer. I was probably in the water 45 minutes. I had no idea I wouldn't be picked up, but there were times, with the ocean swell that I could never see the ship. I knew they were around somewhere. Anyway by the time they picked me up, got me on board, all my crew members were already there.[47]

The Liberator was quite capable of holding altitude with three engines, but could not cope with the drag of a windmilling propeller that would not feather.

The British destroyer HMS *Ursa*, which had arrived with Harcourt's fleet, was the ship that had been seen. They picked up the crew and thirteen surviving POWs, the ones — as Armacost recalled — who had the good fortune to correctly deploy their parachutes. Three of the seven men lost were ex-Hong Kong POWs:

Clapperton, James	Private	Royal Scots
Clarke, John	Gunner	7 Bty, 5AA Regt.
Gollege, Gerald	Staff Sergeant	1 HK Regt HKSRA[48]

Amongst those from Hong Kong who survived were:

Hanley, Thomas James	Gunner	RA
Pope, William	Private	Middlesex
Evans, Taffy	Private	Middlesex
McDonagh, William	Private	Royal Scots

First Lieutenant Terence D. Adams, Pilot, 866th Bomb Sq (H) was circling above, watching as HMS *Ursa* searched for the survivors, and an Air Sea Rescue unit ('playmate') was called to the scene.

"We picked up the S.O.S. from aircraft 44-40666 and headed for their position. We saw what we believed to be the smoke from their plane when it crashed. I circled and made contact with a British warship, call sign Oscar. I dropped smoke bombs near survivors. A boat from the warship was seen picking up survivors. Before I left, because my gas was running low, I made contact with a Navy Privateer, call sign Cannonball and it was circling when I proceeded on course."[49]

News of the disaster quickly spread to the other POWs. Cicero Rozario noted: "The previous lot that were sent to Toyama Docks went by bomber plane, but the bomb bays opened and ten or more prisoners fell through it and into the sea. Our good friend, Doxford, who taught us karate and self-defence, was one of those who fell through."

But Doxford had in fact been lost in a second aircraft, *Ginny*, which had disappeared on the same day, but whose loss was not reported for seventy-six hours thanks to the aircraft being confused with one that had landed safely. Neither the aircraft nor those on board were ever found. Those ex-Hong Kong POWs lost on *Ginny* were:

Houghton, Alfred C.	Captain	RE
Gilham, Sidney Fred	Sergeant	Middlesex Regt.
Harrington, Desmond	Signalman	HK Sig Coy
James, William Richard	Sergeant	8th Coast Regt RA
King, Thomas Patrick	Private	Middlesex Regt.
Pargeter, Ernest Arthur	Private	Middlesex Regt.
Price, Charles Henry	Lance Corp.	HK Sig Coy
Bates, Sydney Francis	Gunner	8th Coast Regt RA
Burke, John	Lance Corp.	Middlesex Regt.
Doxford, William	Corporal	HKVDC

Ginny was from the 98th Bomb Squadron of 11 group, serial #44-40491.[50]

Wednesday, 12 September. James McHarg Miller of the Royal Scots[51] had arrived at Yokohama dock by train from Notagawa: "The American officer then told us what was going to happen. We would strip off all our clothes and leave them to be burnt on the dockside. The next move, we were to be deloused before entering the medical centre where we would get a complete medical and dental checkout. We would then be graded as to how we would travel, whether it would be by hospital ship, troopship or by air. At the end of the inspection, and on the way out, we would be issued with a complete American uniform and accessories and billeted in one of the warehouses which had been transformed into a hospital, there to await on our grading for travel. This procedure was duly carried out and we settled down for the wait. Everything was done to make us comfortable, everybody was so concerned about our health and that we should get the best attention possible. A few days passed before I got my grading, I was transferred to a hospital ship, which was tied up at the quay, they said I had amoebic dysentery. I stayed on the hospital ship for two days without any treatment but during that two days, the doctor discovered that I was wrongly diagnosed and that I would be transferred to a troopship which was enroute to Manila in the Philippines. This ship was carrying a large batch of our regiment and I was glad, I was among some of my old mates whom I had not seen since we were split up, years ago. This ship was named the 'U.S.S. Goodhue' and I must say, the Captain went out of his way to make the cruise to Manila a pleasant experience. I will always remember our first meal, aboard ship, the ships doctors had warned us to take it easy, on the amount of food we consumed, as our stomachs were in no condition to accept large amounts, but, like most people in our position, we gorged ourselves." The ship departed that day.

Wednesday, 12 September. Poulter on the USS *Oconto*: "At 11 am on the 12th we weighed anchor."

Wednesday, 12 September. Australian Robert Bede Moore was on the same ship: "Our next step was on board the Trooper *A.P.A. OCONTO* after a good supper and a long wanted sleep we shoved off the next day for Manila. Two days at sea brought us further comforts a pair of socks, underpants, singlet, soap shaving cream and a box of candy. Nothing of interest on journey, very good seas."

Wednesday, 12 September. Coxhead and the other Innoshima POWs took a train from Innoshima to Yokohama.

Thursday, 13 September. The Innoshima POWs at Yokohama were taken by ferry to HMS *Ruler*.

Thursday, 13 September. Bromley on *Empress of Australia*: "Arrived Manila Bay. We landed at 24.00 and proceeded to get into lorries. When our convoy was ready we were taken to a US Replacement Camp (C). On arrival we all had to be fumigated before touching anything or going into any tents or buildings. The Yanks were very good to us. We all had a hot bath, new clothes and a good hot meal, nice clean beds."

Parker had been sick on the voyage: "When we docked at Manila the American Medical Corps came aboard and took such men as were on the sick list to Field Hospitals by ambulance. My name was on the list and so my body had to be moved thence. I remember four big Yankees standing over me. Any one of them could have put me in his pocket. They wanted to know if I was hurt. I told them 'No'. They were tough boys, these chaps, but there was a glisten of a tear in their eyes as they transferred me, gently, to the litter. What had got them undoubtedly was the thought 'how could any human beings, no matter what color, let a fellow get so thin and so weak and so small . . . and why?' It felt good to be in their hands . . . it was good."

Parker and the other sick men were taken to No. 313 Field Hospital. There they found this reception:

> Greetings.
>
> After the hardships of separation you are here among friends whose primary concern is to get you back to health and strength for your return to home and loved ones. We deeply appreciate the bitterness of

your trials as you languished in enemy camps as prisoners of war. There were times, no doubt, when Hope and Faith were the only ties that kept your stout hearts from breaking. Now the scene has shifted and the darkness of the past has given way to glorious dawn.

The duty personnel of the 313 General Hospital considers it their greatest privilege to serve and nurse you back to the health you enjoyed before your sacrifices. Be quite sure that what-ever is required to secure that objective will be done by cheerful American hearts and hands. Nothing is too good for you who have suffered so nobly in a cause so grand. All that is within the power of Medical Science is at your disposal. However, we feel you need more than this. For years you have been without the comforts of life, a friendly atmosphere, kindness, and human affection. We are happy to be among the first to offer these to you. As you leave this Hospital cured in mind and body, it is our wish that God may grant you long life, happiness and every blessing that you so richly deserve.

Signed; Aubrey R. Carter Lt-Col. M.C Commanding

Friday, 14 September. Henry Taylor, 3050109, Royal Scots was handed over to Major Price of the US Army at Shiogama port.[52]

Friday, 14 September. Bromley at the US Replacement Camp: "This is a large Camp, about 30 miles from Manila. I met Harry Gorman today he had just flown in from a POW Camp in Japan, he didn't look too bad. He was one of the survivors from the *Lisbon Maru* disaster."[53]

Saturday, 15 September. HMS *Ruler* departed for Sydney via Manus in the Admiralty Islands (which was reached on the 21st).

On the same day, the Canadians from Ohashi finally reached the American fleet in Kamaishi harbour. There, a hospital ship, the *Mercy*, awaited. George MacDonell: "In minutes we were ferried to the *Mercy*, where we were welcomed by the captain, who shook each of us by the hand as we came aboard. In moments we were stripped and our brand-new uniforms — including socks, shoes, and underwear — were thrown over the side into the harbour. Next, we filed naked into the ship, where a gang of sailors in bathing suits sprayed us with DDT and scrubbed us with navy soap in hot showers, until we glowed." (p. 147)

Sunday, 16 September. The formal surrender of occupying Japanese forces in Hong Kong took place at Government House.

Monday, 17 September. *Joseph T. Dickman* arrived at Manila.

On the same day, in Tokyo Bay, the Ohashi POWs who were not hospitalized on the *Mercy* were transferred to APA *Hyde* which soon set sail for Guam.[54]

Tuesday, 18 September. R. B. Moore: "Arrived Manila 8 a.m. 18th Sept. laid at sea till 19th came to camp very good R. Cross issues 2 pkts cigs 4 cigar 1 tob 3 cans beer 1 chocolate daily."

Tuesday, 18 September. The *Empress of Australia*, having arrived in Manila on the 13th, re-embarked her passengers and departed for Liverpool.

Wednesday, 19 September. J. I. Bevan and the other men on hospital ship, *Tryon*, disembarked at Manila.

Wednesday, 19 September. Poulter at Manila: "Disembarked at 7.30 am on the 19th. From here we were ushered along to some lorries and then loaded. Then taken to a camp about fifteen to twenty miles outside Manila. Billeted with No. 292 Replacement Coy."

Saturday, 22 September. The Omine POWs left camp for Nagasaki, from where they would be taken to Okinawa on HMS *Speaker*.

Monday, 24 September. Bromley at the US Replacement Camp: "We left our Camp at 0800 in the USA Convoy of lorries for Manila Quay ready to board the US Troop-ship Admiral Hughes, expecting to leave today. We left at 5 p.m. for San Francisco. The Captain made an announcement that he was very pleased to have us liberated POWs on board his ship and we were going to a Western port where we would be nearer our loved ones. Hoping we would have a pleasant and safe passage. He seems quite a nice Officer."

Monday, 24 September. Parker: "At long last the day came when we were detailed to board our ship which would bring us home. Our ship was the A.P. 13, now the JOSEPH T DICKMAN. Forty-four of us Canadians, some British and about 2,800 Americans from Bataan, went aboard her. We travelled down the accepted lanes of shipping southward through the Islands, then swung up in the direction of Pearl Harbour. At Honolulu we ran across Nursing Sister Waters, one of our repatriated nurses who had served with us during the Hong Kong attack. She had volunteered to come out and bring us home on the Hospital Ship

SAZACIA. We stayed in Honolulu about a day. Admiral Halsey's fleet was in port just ahead of us. We watched his fleet of thirteen Capital ships sail past Diamond Head on their way to San Francisco for Navy Day. Believe you me this was some sight and we watched until the last ship had disappeared over the horizon. We had a pretty fast ship ourselves and arrived at San Francisco just about the same time as the fleet."

Tuesday, 25 September. Poulter at Manila: "On the 25th paraded, only those that had been marked for further travel. This time we had a much quieter trip to the harbour. Boarded a tug and away we went. We stopped alongside the Aircraft Carrier HMS *Implacable*, what a ship! We pulled up the anchor at 5.30 pm, on the way to Vancouver."

Thursday, 27 September. J. I. Bevan and others boarded USS *General R. L. Howze* (AP-134).

Thursday, 27 September. HMS *Ruler* arrived at Sydney harbour.

October 1945

Wednesday, 3 October. R. B. Moore at Manila was one of the Australian POWs who *Formidable* would take straight to Sydney: "Passed med insp on 23-Sept. Left 3 Oct to go on board aircraft carrier Formidable. Too rough, back to Camp."

Friday, 5 October. Rakusen: "We learned on arrival that all the British were being repatriated to England, and that no one could go back to Hong Kong, as it was being entirely evacuated of Europeans, and only the military and navy were going to be there for months, except for a number of government staff who were being flown out from home. They said that everything there was in a chaotic state, business was impossible for many months, and the authorities were not permitting anyone to return at present. I had intended returning there to find out my position with the firm; whether they intended to recommence business and also if they required me there right away. Besides, I didn't relish the idea of going all the way home in the inevitable conditions which necessarily prevail on a crowded troop ship, also to arrive in England in mid-winter as I had in mind my last experience in 1930/1 when I was so ill. Besides myself there were many similar cases and nearly 100 of Hong Kong born Eurasians and Portuguese (H.K.V.D.C.) and it would have been senseless to send them to England where they had no friends, relatives or connections, whereas all their people were in Hong Kong. We explained this to the authorities who finally agreed that we could stay in the camp until a boat could be provided to take us back to Hong Kong. We sailed on the aircraft carrier 'Collossus' on October 5th — again we were treated very well, but not as good as on the U.S. transport — and landed in Hong Kong on the 8th."

Around 100 HKVDC left the camp in lorries at 9 a.m. They arrived at the quayside in Manila at about 10.45 a.m. and were on board HMS *Colossus* by 11.45 a.m., going out in a landing craft. The aircraft carrier sailed at 12.30 p.m. The men and a few officers were on camp beds in the hangars, the rest (mainly senior officers from other units, heading for India) being in cabins. The ship arrived in Hong Kong at 1.45 p.m., Sunday, 7 October 1945.

Friday, 5 October.   HMS *Formidable* finally left Manila, bound for Sydney.

Friday, 5 October.   Poulter on board HMS *Implacable*: "Arrived at Pearl Harbour on the 5th at about noon."[55]

Sunday, 7 October.   *Takliwa* set sail from Hong Kong carrying 802 RAPWI Indian troops from Hong Kong:

Unit	Officers	VCOs	IORs
2/14 Punjabis	6	12	497
HKSRA	1	1	107
HK Mule Corps	2	3	148
5/7 Rajputs	–	1	18
IMS	–	2	2

Tuesday, 9 October.   Bromley on *Admiral Hughes*: "Arrived at Victoria B.C. at 1200 Esquimault Naval Yard[56] we received a marvellous welcome here, ships' sirens and everything that could make a noise also guns from the Forts. We all went to Fort Macauley, I mean us British POWs, the Canadians our Chums from Hong Kong went on by C.N. Railway to Winnipeg and Quebec."

Tuesday, 9 October.   HMS *Glory*, loaded with POWs (primarily ex-Omine), left Manila.

Saturday, 13 October.   Bromley at Victoria: "Left Victoria for Vancouver on a River Steamer 'Princess Elizabeth', arrived Vancouver and boarded our train and left for the East Coast."

Saturday, 13 October. R. B. Moore arriving at Sydney's Circular Quay on HMS *Formidable*: "Arrived Sydney 13 Oct weekend leave med insp X Ray O.K. indef — leave 16 Oct for Ilford."[57]

Sunday, 14 October. For those on the *Takliwa*, until 13 October the weather was fine, and the men — despite 25 cot cases — were well. However, on 14 October the weather worsened quickly. At about 02.50 on the 15th, a jolt was felt throughout the ship, and the captain instructed all passengers onto the main deck. Paddock:[58] "At about 0345 hours I was informed that fire had broken out in the Stoke Hold, and troops were ordered to their Emergency Stations . . . At about 0430 hours the ship's crew got a line to the shore, and soon after, the Nursing Officers, Nurses, Hospital Cases and staff, and certain RAPWI personnel went ashore by the ship's boats." By 10.00 all men had left the ship and the fire was spreading rapidly.[59]

Tuesday, 16 October. *Dickman* and *General R. L. Howze* reached San Francisco. Those on board took a boat to Oakland, then a train from Oakland to Montreal to board the *Queen Elizabeth* at Halifax.

Thursday, 18 October. *The Dominion Monarch*, carrying many men who had arrived on HMS *Ruler* and other ships, departed Sydney harbour. She would dock at Southampton on 15 November.

Thursday, 18 October. Bromley was on a train across Canada: "We arrived at Debert where again the welcome was grand."

Wednesday, 24 October. Bromley at Debert continued: "Arrived on board at Halifax the Ile De France 8 p.m."

Thursday, 25 October. Poulter: "We left DeBert at 10 am on the 25th October. Arrived at Halifax, Nova Scotia at about noon. We boarded the *Ile de France* and sailed for England at 6 pm."

Saturday, 27 October. The British aircraft carrier HMS *Glory* arrived in Canada.[60]

Sunday, 28 October. The *Empress of Australia* landed in Liverpool.

Wednesday, 31 October. Bromley on the *Ile De France*: "Breakfast 7 a.m. Paid all Tips as per peace time to the French Stewards. Ashore at

1030. We caught Special Buses that took us to the Great Western Hotel, which was being used as a RN Reception Station for us."

Wednesday, 31 October. Others boarded the *Queen Elizabeth* at Halifax. They would arrive in the UK on 5 November.

Finally, British, Indians, Hong Kong, and Canadian alike were home.

Bill Oxley: "When Irene and I were married and she saw my back, she gave me a look of sadness and said, 'Never tell me what punishment you all took.' I told her I wouldn't tell her even if she asked. She said, 'Why?' I said, 'People would not believe me, what all of us went through. The body of a man or woman is very strong under those conditions.' "

Oxley continued: "I was making my way to Irene when I saw her coming out of the local shop, having bought something. We walked to her house together. Suddenly I said to her, 'Would you do me a kindness?' She replied, 'Of course.' I said, 'Will you explain to your Mum that I still have a little tension. Please ask her not to ask me about the war; it will all come out when I am ready to tell it.' "

But let the last words for 1945 be spoken by Maurice Parker of the Royal Rifles of Canada, at Gordon Head, DC: "Well do I remember the long distance call I put in to Beryl, my wife. She answered the phone. I tried to speak but my voice would not come. I could not say a word . . . I just gulped. Beryl took over and brought me over the hump. She's like that. She was so excited to hear me, when I did speak, that I guess neither of us knew what we were saying to each other . . . and you can be sure, if I did, I wouldn't tell you."

ROLL OF HONOUR FOR 1945

Sham Shui Po

Name	Rank	Number	Unit		Date
Leung Tak Shun	Sapper	628	HKVDC		U 1.45
Williams, Hugh Hoskyn	Master		MN SS Henry Keswick HK		K 1.1.45
MacCulloch, David M.	Corporal	7588090	RAOC		K 9.1.45
Cullup, Leonard	Gunner	998464	HKSRA		K 10.1.45
Williams, Herbert Joseph	SSM	S/13005	RASC		K 16.1.45
Lumby, Walter Ernest	Private		HKDDC	BRH	K 17.1.45 Ci
Stainfield, Harry	Ch Eng Off		MN SS Shun Chih HK		K 9.2.45
Goldman, Harry	Chief Eng.		MN US Merchant Service		UX 18.2.45[61]
Cullen, Fred	Private	64	HKVDC	BRH	K 2.3.45
Spark, William	Purser		MN SS Fausang HK		K 14.3.45
Tansley, William Arthur	Bombardier (ART)	3793	HKVDC		K 2.4.45[62]

Owens, James	Ch. Off		MN		K 17.4.45
Lesieur, Beryl	Rifleman	E/30312	RRoC		K 29.5.45[63]
Hook, Henry William	Major		WG MiD	BRH	K 7.7.45[64]
Silva, Ambrosio Caeser	Private	3615	HKVDC	BRH	K 8.7.45[65]
Frain, Albert Victor	2nd Eng Off		MN SS St. Vincent de Paul		K 23.7.45
Sutton, Arnold Arthur	Sergeant		HKDDC	BMH	K 15.8.45 Ci

Fukuoka #1 Branch Camp (Kumamoto)

Easter, Stanley William	Sapper	2124419	RE	(XD3)	K 21.7.45 Y[66]

Fukuoka #5 Branch Camp (Omine Coal Mine, Kawasaki-machi)

Blank, Elmer Walter	Rifleman	E/30291	RRoC	(XD3)	K 28.1.45 Y TB[67]
Chaboyer, David	Private	H/41688	WG	(XD3)	K 13.3.45 Y Pa
Bent, Howard N.	Rifleman	F/40828	RRoC	(XD3)	K 7.9.45 Y Al
Cyr, Clement	Rifleman	E/30414	RRoC	(XD3)	K 7.6.45 Y Al[68]
Devaney, Peter Gavin	Sapper	1880606	RE	(XD3)	K 7.9.45 Y Al
Moore, Fred	Sapper	1874085	RE	(XD5)	K 7.9.45 Y Al[69]
Morris, James Stuart	Sapper	1874306	RE	(XD3)	K 7.9.45 Y Al
Pemberton, George	Lance Corp.	1871779	RE	(XD3)	K 8.9.45 Y Al

Nagoya #2 Branch Camp (Narumi)

Rogers, James	W.O.	105	HKRNVR	(XD5)	K 15.1.45 Y Cbi/Pa[70]
Matheson, Harold M.	Rifleman	E/29927	RRoC	(XD5)	K 26.1.45 Y Cbi
Angus, George Ian	Private		HKVDC	(XD5)	K 29.1.45 Y Cbi
Burgin, Ernest	A.S.	D/SSX20669	RN	(XD5)	K 14.2.45 Y Pu[71]
Gittins, William Minto	Sergeant	3161	HKVDC	(XD5)	K 5.3.45 Y Pa

Nagoya #8 Branch Camp (Toyama Tateyama)[72]

Mears, Albert Edgar	Leading Seaman	D/JX141563	RN	(XD5)	K 31.8.45 Y Al[73]

Nagoya #10 Dispatched Camp (Fushiki-Kairiku, Takaoka)

Andrews, James Henry	Private	6204080	MX	(XD2)	U 31.7.45 Es[74]
Keeler, Alfred	Private	6195957	MX	(XD2)	K 15.8.45 Acton Es

Osaka #1 Branch Camp (Minato-ku, Osaka)

Bell, Thomas Baxter	Private	3054412	RS	(XD2)	K 6.1.45 Y Gu
Banham, Thomas William	BSM	545435	RA	(XD2)	K 11.8.45 Y Bi

Osaka #2 Branch Camp (Kobe)

Ellender, William Hubert	QMS	1863600	RE	(XD2)	K 6.6.45 Y

Osaka #3 Branch Camp (Oeyama)

Clarke, Stanley Reginald	Bombardier	838446	RA	(XD4)	K 10.2.45 Y[75]
Rees, Ralph Charles	Private	H/6297	WG	(XD4)	K 14.3.45 Y Pa
Hooker, 'Rosey' James W.	A.S.	P/SX21736	RN	(XD5)	K 23.4.45 Y[76]
Bell, Gordon	Private	H/6298	WG	(XD4)	K 6.6.45 Y Cs
Bazinet, Henry J.P.	Private	H/6878	WG	(XD4)	K 12.6.45 Y Sa
Phillips, John	Gunner	1414646	RA	(XD4)	K 24.6.45 Y Cbi

Osaka #4 Dispatched Camp (Sakurajima)

Brewin, Alan	Private	HKDDC RN / DYP	(XD3)	K 8.1.45 Y Pu diw
Tynemouth, Robert	Sergeant	HKDDC	(XD3)	K 4.2.45 Y Pa
Ogle, George Henry	Private	HKDDC	(XD3)	K 5.2.45 Y Cbi
May, Francis Cecil	Private	HKDDC	(XD3)	K 16.4.45 Y Es
Knight, William Charles	Private Draftsman	HKDDC	(XD3)	K 12.5.45 Y[77]

Osaka #6 Dispatched Camp (Amagasaki)

Brenchley, Harold B.	Corporal	524960	RAF	(XD3)	K 5.1.45 Y Pa/Es dkoh
Pollitt, Robert Henry	L Stoker	P/KX83981	RN	(XD3)	K 21.5.45 Y TB diw
Cook, Jack Roland M.	Driver	T/61815	RASC	(XD3)	K 5.6.45 Y Pu dkoh

Sendai #2 Branch Camp (Yoshima Coal Mine)

Thelin, Henry Antonia	Private	29	HKDDC RN/DYP	(XD6)	K 3.1.45 Y Bi/Es dsgh
Organ, William Henry	Private		HKDDC	(XD6)	K 4.1.45 Y[78]
Blueman, Henry Kendall	Lance Corp.	H/6379	WG	(XD6)	K 19.1.45 Y Bi[79]
Franco, Eluardo Miguel	Private	2447	HKVDC	(XD6)	K 29.1.45 Y Pa
Law, Arthur Sidney	Staff Sergeant	S/54306	RASC	(XD6)	K 6.4.45 Y Bi/Es/Ul dsgh

Sendai #5 Branch Camp (Kamaishi)

Tyner, William Charles	S/Sergeant	6630623	RAMC		(XD1)	K 10.8.45 Y Ff[80]
Downs, James Westby	Private	7263665	RAMC	20.8.45	(XD1)	K 10.8.45 Y Ff[81]

Tokyo #1 Branch Camp (Oshima-cho, Kawasaki)

Fenn, Albert V.	Private	6208367	MX	2.2.45	(XD1)	U 6.2.45 An[82]

Tokyo #2 Branch Camp (Ogi-cho, Kawasaki)

Taylor, Arthur William F.	Warrant Eng		RN	(XD1)	K 25.7.45 Y Ff[83]

Tokyo #5 Branch Camp (Niigata-Rinko)

Gard, James Phillip	Private	H/6776	WG	(XD4)	K 14.7.45 Y Gl[84]
Kirk, Roy Lomax	Lance Corp.	H/6178	WG	(XD4)	K 14.7.45 Y Gl
Hawes, Malcolm John	Private	H/6204	WG	(XD4)	K 15.7.45 Y Gl
McLeod, Robert	Private	H/6466	WG	(XD4)	K 15.7.45 Y Gl
Moore, Bertrand Cyril	Private	H/6621	WG	(XD4)	K 15.7.45 Y Bi/Pa

Tokyo #6 Branch Camp (Suwa)

Russell, Robert Leslie	Sergeant	E/22946	RRoC	(XD3)	K 15.6.45 Y TB dsgh

Tokyo #10 Branch Camp (Sumidagawa)[85]

Neufeld, Benjamin	Private	H/6156	WG	(XD3)	K 19.7.45 Y Je
Dunnell, Kenneth Stanley	Private	3053771	RS	(XD1)	K 29.8.45 Y[86]

Tokyo #14 Branch Camp (Toshiba, Tsurumi)

Forth, Albert	Sapper	2057662	RE	(XD1)	K 11.1.45 Y Cbi[87]
Morgan, Herbert Francis	Sergeant	T/45960	RASC	(XD1)	K 19.2.45 Y Es dsgh

Tokyo #17 Branch Camp (Nisshin Oil)

Megson, Frank Cyril	QMS	1866583	RE	(XD1)	K 16.2.45 Y Ul dsgh[88]

Air Crash

Gollege, Gerald	Staff Sergeant	1415975	HKSRA	8.9.45	(XD2)	U 10.9.45 PC
Bates, Sydney Francis	Gunner	1712468	RA		(XD1)	U 10.9.45 PC
Burke, John	Lance Corp.	6203596	MX		(XD1)	U 10.9.45 PC
Clarke, John	Gunner	4914894	RA		(XD2)	U 10.9.45 PC
Clapperton, James	Private	3055328	RS		(XD2)	U 10.9.45 PC
Doxford, William	Corporal	3736	HKVDC		(XD5)	U 10.9.45 PC
Gilham, Sidney Frederick	Sergeant	6200749	MX		(XD2)	U 10.9.45 PC
Harrington, Desmond M.	Signalman	2323399	RCS		(XD2)	U 10.9.45 PC
Houghton, Alfred C.	Captain	49536	RE		(XD2)	K 10.9.45 PC[89]
James, William Richard	Sergeant	847074	RA		(XD2)	U 10.9.45 PC
King, Thomas Patrick M.	Private	6213522	MX		(XD2)	U 10.9.45 PC
Pargeter, Ernest Arthur	Private	6203984	MX		(XD2)	U 10.9.45 PC
Price, Charles Henry	Lance Corp.	2324244	RCS		(XD2)	U 10.9.45 PC

Hospital Ships

Forsey, William Edward	Private		HKDDC		U 3.9.45[90]
Hart, William Henry E.	Gunner	6202039	RA	(XD2)	K 24.9.45 Y[91]
Benjamin, Vivian	Private	4989	HKVDC		U 21.9.45[92]
Airries, Frank W.	Private	L/2865	WG	(XD3)	K 15.9.45 Y[93]

Ma Tau Chung

Munshi Singh	Sepoy	12263	RP		U 2.1.45
Mehnga Ram	Sepoy	16111	PJ		U 5.1.45
Indar Pal Singh	Lance Naik	15095	RP		U 6.1.45
Tawaqal Khan	Gunner	5080	HKSRA		U 13.1.45
Akbar Ali	PC		HKDDC	RN / DYP	U 14.1.45
Nur Muhammad	PC		HKDDC	RN / DYP	U 14.1.45
Shafi Muhammad	PC		HKDDC	RN / DYP	U 14.1.45
Mohar Singh	Lance Naik	13245	RP		U 19.1.45
Mubarak Ali	Gunner	5240	HKSRA		K 21.1.45
Munshi Khan	Jem	3169	HKSRA		U 21.1.45[94]
Charan Singh	Gunner	4866	HKSRA		U 6.2.45
Nawab Khan	Gunner	4936	HKSRA		U 22.2.45
Niaz Ali	Sepoy	9169	RP		U 15.2.45
Sukh Ram Singh	Sepoy	13854	RP MiD		K 28.2.45
Ghulam Muhammad	Gunner	3024	HKSRA		U 22.3.45
Bala Singh	Sepoy	7232	RP		K 26.3.45
Khushi Muhammad	Gunner	8164	HKSRA		U 3.4.45
Muhammad Yaqub	Gunner	5387	HKSRA		U 3.4.45

Name	Rank	Number	Unit	Status
Harbhajan Singh	Religious Teacher R.T./1	36	HKSRA	U 4.4.45
Sheo Raj Singh	Sepoy	14445	RP	K 6.4.45
Karam Singh	Gunner	7802	HKSRA	U 13.4.45
Asa Singh	Gunner	4700	HKSRA	U 20.4.45
Ram Karan Singh	Lance Naik	12666	RP	U 23.4.45
Hari Singh	Gunner	4776	HKSRA	U 24.4.45
Gurbachan Singh	Gunner	4781	HKSRA	K 27.4.45
Karnail Singh	Gunner	4740	HKSRA	U 27.4.45
Sohan Singh	Gunner	4831	HKSRA	U 27.4.45
Kamal Singh	Lance Naik	13629	PJ	U 28.4.45
Maskin Shah	Naik	8692	PJ	K 13.5.45
Muhammad Khan	Gunner	5339	HKSRA	U 16.5.45
Sultan Muhammad	Sepoy	12575	PJ	U 18.5.45
Murli Singh	Sepoy	7237	RP	U 28.5.45

Ma Tau Wai

Name	Rank	Number	Unit	Status
Sai Khan	Sepoy	18821	PJ	K 5.6.45
Abdul Satar	Lance Naik	174019	HKMC	U 6.6.45
Khair Gul	Sepoy	11859	PJ	U 14.6.45
Muhammad Yaqub	Gunner	5208	HKSRA	U 15.6.45
Sher Khan	Gunner	5276	HKSRA	U 15.6.45
Ghulam Bari	Gunner	5201	HKSRA	U 15.6.45
Muhammad Shafi	Sepoy	16453	RP	U 17.6.45
Nur Muhammad	Gunner	5167	HKSRA	U 1.7.45
Wali Dad	Gunner	3178	HKSRA	U 3.7.45
Ziyarat Khan	Sepoy	19586	PJ	K 10.7.45
Bagh Ali	Jemadar	–	RP	U 29.7.45
Mir Qasim	Sepoy	12062	PJ	K 31.7.45
Sardar Ali	Gunner	5349	HKSRA	U 5.8.45
Sahib Din	Sepoy	19893	PJ	K 13.8.45
Niranjan Singh	Tailor	181195	HKMC	K 15.8.45
Fazl Din	Gunner	7957	HKSRA	K 18.8.45
Nain Singh	Lance Naik	9088	PJ	K 22.8.45
Sardar Khan	Lance Naik	9811	RP	U 30.8.45
Karam Khan	Sepoy	10589	RP	U 1.9.45
Sardar Khan	Havildar	11187	PJ	U 7.9.45[95]
Karam Singh	Cook	L/141	HKSRA	U 3.10.45
Muhammad Shafi	Sepoy	179376	HKMC	U 24.10.45
Firoz Khan	Sepoy	16160	RP	U 15.11.45
Mehman Singh	Gunner	3904	HKSRA	U 15.11.45
Muhammad Husain	Sepoy	175729	HKMC	U 15.11.45
Munawar Khan	Sepoy	178772	HKMC	U 15.11.45
Mir Sanad Sar	Sepoy	7484	PJ	U 18.12.45

Stanley

Name	Rank	Number	Unit	Status
Jeffery, Olive Susanna	CV		34, Hospital sister	UCWD 4.1.45
Page, Harry William	CV		70	UCWD 12.1.45

Balfour, Stephen Francis	CV	39, Husband of Anne G. Balfour	UCWD 16.1.45
Bishop, Sidney Frank	CV	51	UCWD 16.1.45
Davies, Margaret Louisa	CV	37, Mrs.	UCWD 16.1.45
Dennis, Albert James	CV	56, at Stanley, husband of E. Mary	UCWD 16.1.45
Eager, Oscar	CV	57	UCWD 16.1.45
Guerin, Aileen Elizabeth	CV	37, wife of J. Guerin. ARP	UCWD 16.1.45
Holland, Adam Morrison	CV	43, Inspector of Works, Hong Kong	UCWD 16.1.45
Hyde-Lay, Alexander	CV	51, ARP	UCWD 16.1.45[96]
Hyde-Lay, Elizabeth F.	CV	42	UCWD 16.1.45
Johnson, Isabella	CV	54, Wife of Maj. Maurice Alfred	UCWD 16.1.45
Searle, Edward Valentine	CV	53	UCWD 16.1.45
Searle, Mabel	CV	40	UCWD 16.1.45
Stopani-Thomson, George	Lieutenant	HKRNVR	K 16.1.45
Willoughby, George	CV	36, Chemist, 224 Nathan Road, KL	UCWD 16.1.45
Livesey, Charles F.	CV	59	UCWD 19.1.45
Martin, Kathleen Louisa	CV	59, wife of the Revd. E. W. L.	UCWD 19.1.45
Balean, Hermann	CV	59, husband of Isabel Balean	UCWD 30.1.45
Owen-Hughes, John	CV	74, ARP, husband of Susan E.	UCWD 4.2.45
Batty-Smith, Sydney H.	CV	54, A.D.C. to H.E. the Gov.	UCWD 12.2.45
Ryan, Lionel Ernest N.	CV	56	UCWD 27.2.45
Gibson, James Smith	CV	72, husband of Alice Maud	UCWD 6.3.45
Barber, Norman Charles	CV	45, Merchant, 10 Carnarvon Rd., KL	UCWD 3.5.45[97]
Osborne, John Joseph	CV	58, husband of M. B.	UCWD 5.7.45
Morris, Alfred	CV	71, of Villa Miramare, Pokfulam	UCWD 8.7.45
Pederson, Olaf	CV		UCWD 15.8.45
Hassard, Muriel	CV	59, Matron of Diocesan Boys School	UCWD 26.8.45
Overy, Hubert	CV	60	UCWD 26.8.45[98]
Tanner, Richard Lancelot	CV	40, husband of Doris Tanner	UCWD 30.9.45

British Army Aid Group

Wun Fah		BAAG	U 21.2.45

Release

The first time I saw my father to remember him was getting off a train at Colchester station with my Mother. She had gone to meet him in London the day before. I was nine years old. He picked me up and held me up in the air, looked at me, hugged me tightly and cried. I was impressed and proud of this man and it was only later as I got older that I began to learn what had happened to him. Over the following months he borrowed an old typewriter and transferred from old pieces of paper and exercise books all the events that had befallen him and his comrades.

— Robin William Poulter, schoolboy[1]

I was a child when I went up to London with my grandfather to meet my aunt Bee Bicheno when she came home from Stanley Camp. My grandfather groaned when he saw her coming off the boat train. She was skin and bone and this was after a long sea voyage back to England. My grandfather, a very stiff upper-lip retired Army officer, was not a person to show emotion and I was amazed to see how upset he was. Of course I had never met my aunt before so had no idea what she was like.

— Jill McNichol, schoolgirl

And so the camps were finally emptied, or turned to other purposes.

During 1945, some 178 more of Hong Kong's POWs and internees had perished. This would bring the totals, from 1 January 1942 to the end of the war and the journey home, to some 2,340. More, of course, would continue to die of the war's effects in 1945, 1946, and every year that followed.

Those 2,340 added to the 1,550 who had perished in the initial Japanese invasion of Hong Kong. The Garrison — never more than 15,000 strong, however one chooses to count — had suffered badly; almost 4,000 had been lost.

The disruption to ordinary human life had been incalculable. So many families had been evacuated to Australia, and a large percentage would never be whole again. Those men who survived never truly threw off the effects of battle and incarceration, and those effects reverberated through the next generation. Yet, the sufferings of the Chinese population of Hong Kong were still immeasurably greater.

For the prisoners of war, release brought enormous challenges. For young men, with no real career before the war, the loss of their one great aim in life — survival — could be traumatic. For others, it was the attempt to return to 'normality' that created painful obstacles.

But most tried, and they are not forgotten. At the time of writing, in 2008, the Little Hong Kong Ordnance store which featured in the first chapter as the last part of Hong Kong to surrender, is now preserved as a very tasteful Wine Cellar and Club, patronized by the elite of Hong Kong's movers and shakers.[2] At events there, even today, the first toast is always to: 'The Boys'.

Interestingly, "Give my regards to all the boys, Major", was also the last thing that Major Young heard from the driver as a taxi he had taken in Toronto in 1946 sped away. He realized, belatedly, that the driver was Rifleman Riley who had spent the early war years in Stanley camp as a 'civilian', before being repatriated to Canada in 1943.[3]

But I will give the last words to Bill Lowe, who introduced this work. He (as others did, and, at time of writing, still do) made the pilgrimage back to Japan, after the war, to confront his memories head-on:

> And I did go back to the Hachi Dock — Mianoshta — as I always said I would. I did have grey flannels & a sports coat, but instead of a walking stick I had an umbrella & I met Arthur Achey (my gangboss) & his offsider the one eyed Gondoo Coolie & I gave 'em cigarettes & chocolates — & they cried damn it & I did.[4]

Appendices

APPENDIX 1: AMERICAN POWS

Aside from the American civilians in Stanley, the military POWs included a number of Americans who fought with the Canadians as members of C Force, a few members of the HKVDC/HKRNVR, and a number of Merchant Marine men in Hong Kong at its fall. Later, a handful of other Americans were captured in Hong Kong and became POWs after bailing out from USAAF and USN aircraft once the bombing began, or passed through Hong Kong as POWs on 'hell ships'. Their fate is outside the scope of this work. A number of Americans who passed away on the *Hokusen Maru* were either buried near the harbour, or possibly at sea, and the fate of their remains is currently unknown.

APPENDIX 2: DUTCH POWS

The crew of the Dutch submarine *O-20*, minus their captain and six men who went down with the boat, ended up as POWs in Hong Kong. Two, as noted in the text, escaped with Proulx from North Point. Although the fate of these POWs is outside the scope of this work, the remainder stayed in the Hong Kong camps until liberation.[1]

APPENDIX 3: DRAFTS TO JAPAN

(Camp transfers following each draft are indicated by indentations, though these will not be complete as a number of men were moved individually or in very small groups.)

Maru Shi

Boarded:	3 September 1942
Departed:	4 September 1942
In command:	Captain Caesar Otway, Royal Engineers
Arrived:	15 September 1942, Yokohama
On Board:	618 British Regulars[2]

Camps: Tokyo #3B (Yokohama Stadium) (closed 1 May 1944)
- Tokyo #19D (Yokohama Senpaku, Stevedore Camp) (Burnt down during the fire-raid of 29 May 1945.)
- Tokyo #15B (Niigata-Tekko) (1 June 1945)
- Tokyo Main Camp (Omori HQ) (1 June 1945) 11 men
- Tokyo #13D (Asano Dock)
- Sendai #5B (Kamaishi)
- Tokyo #17B (Nisshin Oil)
- Tokyo #18D (Yokohama Taika Renga, Firebrick Factory)
- Tokyo #15B (Niigata-Tekko) (4 June 1945)
- Tokyo #14B (Toshiba, Tsurumi)[3]

Tokyo Main Camp (Shinagawa) (closed 20 July 1943)
- Hiroshima #1B (only Lieutenant Hill)
- Tokyo #12B (Hiraoka, Mitsushima)

Tokyo Main Camp (Omori HQ Camp)
- Tokyo #10B (Sumidagawa)
- Sendai #10B (Wakagawa) (May 1945)
- Sendai #5B (Kamaishi)

Tokyo #1B (Oshima-cho, Kawasaki)
- Tokyo #23D (Ajinomoto)

Tokyo #2B (Ogi-cho, Kawasaki)

Lisbon Maru

Boarded: 25 September 1942
Departed: 27 September 1942
In command: Lieutenant-Colonel Moncrief Stewart, Middlesex
First Hold: Polluck (Royal Navy)
Second Hold: Cuthbertson (Royal Scots)
Third Hold: Pitt (Royal Artillery)
Arrived: Sunk, 2 October 1942, off Zhoushan. Over 800 died, and three escaped. Surviving POWs were taken to Shanghai where some would remain. The others would be shipped to Moji on the *Washington Maru* (also called *Shinsei Maru*), arriving 10 October.
On Board: 1,834 British Regulars[4]
Camps: Woosung (China)
Kiangwan (China)
Darian Maru[5]
Drafts: *Washington Maru*

Washington Maru

Boarded: Shanghai, 8 October 1942
Departed: 8 October 1942
In command: Lieutenant-Colonel Moncrief Stewart, Middlesex
Arrived: Moji, 10 October 1942

On Board: 980 British Regulars
Camps: Osaka #1B (Minato-ku, Osaka)
              – Osaka #9B (Notogawa) (see Miller/Lynneberg)
              – Osaka #3B (Oeyama) (according to Hamilton)
              – Hiroshima #1B (six officers)
              – Fukuoka #9B (Miyata)
              Osaka #2B (Kobe)
              – Nagoya #10B (Fushiki-Kairiku, Takaoka) (open 18 June 1945)
              – Osaka #4B (Ikuno) (Weedon, Houghton and some officers)
              – Osaka #5D (Kawasaki-Juko, Kobe)[6]
              Ichioka Ward (Staff)
              – Osaka #12B (Hirohata) (Hastings only)
              – Nagoya #1D (Kamioka) (Jackson only)

Tatsuta Maru[7]

Boarded: 19 January 1943
Departed: 19 January 1943
In command: Surgeon Commander Page, RN
Arrived: Nagasaki, 22 January 1943
On Board: 1,176: 664 Canadians, 82 HKVDC, 430 British Regulars
Camps: Fukuoka #5B (Omine Coal Mine, Kawasaki-machi) – Canadians
              Tokyo #3D (Tsurumi Shipyard) (Kawasaki 3D) – Canadians
              – Tokyo Main Camp (Omori HQ Camp)
              – Tokyo #10B (Sumidagawa) (March 1945)
              – Sendai #4B (Ohashi Mine)
              – Sendai #1B (Yumoto)
              – Tokyo #6B (Suwa)
              Osaka #4D (Sakurajima) – British Regulars
              – Osaka #6B (Akenobe)
              Osaka #6D (Amagasaki) – British Regulars
              – Hiroshima #3B (Tamano)
              – Nagoya #9B (Toyama)
              Hiroshima #5B (Innoshima) – HKVDC

Special Draft

Boarded: 4 August 1943
Departed: 4 August 1943
In command: General Christopher Maltby
Arrived: Maltby's party of 21 arrived at Shirakawa Camp, Taiwan, on 9 August, but Sir Mark Young and his batman Waller arrived there on 12 September. Flown to Japan in October 1944, then to Manchuria.
On Board: 21 Senior Officers

Camps: Karenko Camp, Taiwan
Tamazato (2 April 1943)
Karenko Camp – 89 men (5 June 1943)
   Shirakawa
      Draft: *Oryoku Maru* via Moji 350 men (10 October 1944)
         Cheng-Tai-tun
         Shenyang Main Camp (20 May 1945)
   Taihoku Camp #5 – 28 senior men (24 June 1943)
      Heito Camp – Governors and senior officers (5 October 1944)
         Cheng-Tai-tun (via Japan)
            Hsi-an Camp – 32 (senior offices and batmen) 1 December

SS *Morning Star* (*Manryu Maru*)[8]

Boarded:	15 August 1943
Departed:	15 August 1943
In command:	Sub Lieutenant Lewis Bush, HKRNVR
Arrived:	Osaka, 1 September 1943
On Board:	470: 370 Canadians, and 100 British Regulars
Camps:	Tokyo #5B (Niigata-Rinko) 270 Canadians
	Osaka #3B (Oeyama) 100 Canadians, 100 British Regulars
	– Nagoya #2B (Narumi) (some)
	– Nagoya #8D (Toyama) (some)
	– Sendai #10B (two Canadians)[9]

Soong Cheong

Boarded:	15 December 1943
Departed:	15 December 1943
In command:	Lieutenant Miles Abbott, Middlesex
Arrived:	Kaohsiung, Taiwan, 19 December 1943
On Board:	496: 98 Canadians, 204 HKVDC, 194 British Regulars
Camps:	None
Drafts:	*Toyama Maru*

Toyama Maru[10]

Boarded:	Kaohsiung, Taiwan, 20 December 1943
Departed:	20 December 1943
In command:	Lieutenant Miles Abbott, Middlesex
Arrived:	Moji, 5 January 1944
On Board:	496: 98 Canadians, 204 HKVDC, 194 British Regulars
Camps:	Nagoya #2B (Narumi) – 50 Canadians, British Regulars, HKVDC
	– Nagoya #8D (Toyama) (April 1945)
	– Nagoya #9B (Toyama Nippon Express) (18 June 1945)

Osaka #3B (Oeyama) – 48 Canadians, British Regulars
Omori (Bertram, Abbott, Rae Watson, Ken Seyer)

Naura Maru

Boarded:	29 April 1944
Departed:	29 April 1944
In command:	Captain James Robinson, RAMC
Arrived:	Moji, 11 May 1944
On Board:	220: 47 Canadians, 115 HKVDC, 58 British Regulars
Camps:	Sendai #2B (Yoshima Coal Mine)

Darian Maru[11]

(Taking the ex-*Lisbon Maru* chaps from Pusan to Japan)

Boarded:	28 June 1945
Departed:	28 June 1945
In command:	Unknown
Arrived:	28 June 1945, disembarked 29 June 1945
On Board:	996: of which 30 British Regulars ex-*Lisbon Maru*
Camps:	Hakodate #2B (Akahira)
	Hakodate #4B (Nishi-Ashibetsu)

APPENDIX 4: PRISONER-OF-WAR CAMPS AND HOSPITALS

Note that there were of course many more camps in China, Korea, Taiwan, Southeast Asia and Japan than those listed here. The purpose of this section is simply to document those camps that held prisoners-of-war originally captured in Hong Kong.

Hong Kong Camps

Sham Shui Po

Shamshuipo Camp was originally established as a barracks for the regular British army. It consisted of two mirror-image barracks known as Nanking and Hankow. Later, these were added to by the addition of a well-built two-building married quarters known as Jubilee Buildings. The facilities were still in use as barracks when the Japanese attacked in early December 1941, and by the end of the month, following Hong Kong's surrender, it was already the biggest of the POW Camps. It would retain this position until the Liberation. The camp remained in existence until around 1990, when the site was redeveloped for housing. A few memorials exist today in a little park at the southern end of the old site.

North Point

North Point Camp was originally established as a refugee camp for those fleeing the invading Japanese in China. Its position on the Island, in an area captured soon after the Japanese invasion, resulted in it being used as a POW camp almost immediately after the fighting started. After the reorganizations towards the end of January 1942, the camp primarily held the Canadians of C Force, and the Royal Navy. The latter were moved out to Shamshuipo in April 1942, and the former in September 1942 following the departure of almost 2,000 POWs to the ill-fated *Lisbon Maru*. At that point, the camp was closed. Parts of the site are now the Tin Chiu Street and King's Road Playgrounds, though there are no memorials and nothing of the camp itself survives.

Argyle Street

Argyle Street Camp, like North Point, was originally established as a refugee camp. It was already occupied by POWs — many of them Indian — before Hong Kong surrendered, but was emptied during the January 1942 reorganization. In April 1942, the majority of Hong Kong's commissioned officers moved into the camp, together with 100 men who acted as batmen and cooks. This group stayed until May 1944, when they were transferred back to a wired-off part of Shamshuipo Camp. In June 1944, the remaining Indian POWs moved from Ma Tau Chung into Argyle Street, where they remained until Liberation. After the war, Argyle Street camp was initially used to hold displaced persons returning to Hong Kong from abroad. Today, nothing is left of the camp.

Ma Tau Chung

Ma Tau Chung was the third of Hong Kong's camps to be originally established as a refugee camp. It was closed in 1944 when the remaining Indian POWs moved back to Argyle Street Camp. It would then reopen as Ma Tau Wai internment camp.

Ma Tau Wai

Ma Tau Wai (Ma Tau-wei) Civilian Internment Camp was established in the facilities of Ma Tau Chung Camp, when the latter was closed in June 1944. This camp held third-nationals such as South Americans, Chinese of foreign decent, Thais, and others. There were also a number of British internees here, such as Sir Selwyn Selwyn-Clarke and his family, following his release from interrogation. After the war, like Argyle Street, this camp held returning displaced people. Today, the widened Ma Tau Chung Road covers part of the site, with housing estates accounting for the remainder. Nothing remains of the camp itself.

Stanley Civilian Internment Camp

Stanley Civilian Internment Camp was established in late January 1942 in the grounds of St Stephen's College and Stanley Jail. Although the jail itself was not part of the camp, the prison warders' accommodation and facilities housed a number of internees and POWs from time to time. A number of repatriations (the Americans in June 1942, the Canadians in September 1943, and a number of smaller groups departing for Shanghai) reduced the numbers resident at

Liberation. In January 1944, Stanley became a Military Internment Camp. Today, with the exception of a few of the 'Indian Quarters' blocks (demolished for new buildings), the site is largely unchanged from those days.

Rosary Hill

Rosary Hill was established on 26 August 1943 in the facilities of St Albert's Convent on Stubbs Road. The site is now 41 Stubbs Road, the rear part of which is Rosary Hill School.

Sun Wah Hotel

Sun Wah Hotel, although never officially being an internment camp, housed expatriate bankers forced to work for the Japanese. It finally closed in June 1943, with the last bankers moving to Stanley Internment Camp.[12]

Hong Kong Hospitals

The key hospital for the POWs was the Bowen Road Military Hospital.[13] This was kept operational throughout the war, relocating at the very end to the Central British School (now KGV). Until August 1942, St Teresa's Hospital on Prince Edward Road provided services to the POWs in Kowloon. Each camp also had a 'hospital', but with one exception these were simple affairs with little or no equipment. The exception was Stanley, where the Tweed Bay hospital performed an outstanding service. Stanley was unique in that such a large percentage of the inmates were doctors and nurses.

China Camps

Woosung, Shanghai

Woosung Camp was originally established as an army barracks, consisting of seven long huts, some smaller buildings and a large parade ground. The first POWs to arrive, in mid-January 1942, were some 1,200 American civilians and soldiers captured on Wake Island. At the beginning of February, they were joined by 200 US Marines from Nanking. In early October 1942, some thirty POWs from the *Lisbon Maru*, too sick to travel further, and several RAMC orderlies escorting them, were left at Woosung while their colleagues went to Japan. They were joined by a handful of other ex-*Lisbon Maru* POWs who were discovered on islands off Shanghai in the ensuing few weeks. Some American POWs were later moved to Japan, and in December 1942, the remaining men — including the Hong Kong POWs — were moved to Kiangwan.

Kiangwan, Shanghai

In December 1942, the Woosung POWs were moved to Kiangwan. In August 1943, some of the American POWs were sent to Japan. In the spring of 1945, most remaining POWs, including the ex-*Lisbon Maru* Hong Kong men, were sent to Hokkaido to work in the coal mines of the Hakodate POW Camps.

Guangzhou (Canton)

On Friday, 22 June 1945, a number of European prisoners in Stanley Jail, including Charles Boxer, Commander Young, Lt. Dixon, and civilians such as W. J. Anderson, were taken by train to Guangzhou and incarcerated in the city's Tungshan (Tongshan) jail. They would stay there until late August 1945, when they would take a train back to Kowloon.

Shenyang (Mukden, Manchuria)

Shenyang Camp was originally established at North Camp, POW Camp Hoten No. 1 (then a group of Chinese Army barrack huts built partly underground) with the arrival of 1,202 American POWs from Manila in November 1942. In July 1943 the camp was moved some four miles, to two-storey above-ground brick buildings close to the Manchu Kosaku Kikai Kabushiki Kaisha (Manchu Work and Machine Tool Corporation Ltd.) factory, a former Ford factory where some of the camp inmates worked. A number of work-party sub-camps were established in 1944. Hoten Sub-camp No. 1 with POWs working at the Manshu Hikaku leather company, Sub-camp No. 2 with POWs working at the Manshu Hanpu cloth company, and Sub-camp No. 3 with POWs working at the Nakayama Seikosho steel company and Toyo Mukuzai lumber company. On 7 December 1944, US bombers attacked the city killing nineteen POWs and injuring more than thirty. The Hong Kong POWs, including Maltby and Collinson, were imprisoned here, having been shipped via Japan and Korea. Sir Mark Young arrived via Taiwan. They were liberated by the Russians.[14]

Taiwan Camps

Maltby, with his senior officers and batmen, together with Governor Sir Mark Young and his batmen, were in a variety of camps in Taiwan before moving to Shenyang, China. These camps were:

- Heito Camp
- Karenko Camp
- Shirakawa
- Taihoku Camp #5
- Tamazato

Southeast Asian Camps

The only camp known to have housed ex-Hong Kong POWs in Southeast Asia was in Saigon, where six RAF officers were held temporarily from February 1942. This was presumably Saigon Central Prison.

Japanese Camps

Note on camp names

There were two main classes of POW camps in Japan: branch and dispatched camps. The dispatched camp was one that provided workers to a particular

APPENDICES 253

company. In all camps the Japanese army provided staffing, and in branch camps the Japanese Army supplied all the housing, food, and clothing for the POWs. However, in a dispatched camp these items were provided by the companies being served by the POWs.

The following camps held Hong Kong POWs, and are listed by their vernacular[15] and official last names:

Ajinomoto:	Tokyo #23 Dispatched Camp
Akenobe:	Osaka #6 Branch Camp
Amagasaki:	Osaka #6 Dispatched Camp
Asano Dock:	Tokyo #13 Dispatched Camp (Nippon Steel Tube Asano Ship-building)
Firebrick Factory:	Tokyo #18 Dispatched Camp (Yokohama Proof-brick)
Hakodate:	Hakodate #2 Branch Camp (Akabira)
Hakodate:	Hakodate #4 Branch Camp (Nishi Ashibetsu)
Hiraoka Mitsushima:	Tokyo #12 Branch Camp (Hiraoka Mitsushima)
Hirohata:	Osaka #12 Branch Camp
Ikuno:	Osaka #4 Branch Camp (Ikuno)
Innoshima:	Hiroshima #5 Branch Camp
Kamaishi:	Sendai #5 Branch Camp
Kamioka:	Nagoya #1 Dispatched Camp (Kamioka Branch Camp)
Kawasaki:	Tokyo #1 Branch Camp (Oshima-cho, Kawasaki)
Kawasaki:	Tokyo #2 Branch Camp (Ogi-cho, Kawasaki)
Kawasaki:	Osaka #5 Dispatched Camp (Kobe Kawasaki)
Kawasaki 3D:	Tokyo #3 Dispatched Camp (Tsurumi Shipyard)
Kobe House:	Osaka #2 Branch Camp (Kobe)
Kosaka:	Sendai #8 Branch Camp (Kosaka)
Kumamoto:	Fukuoka #1 Branch Camp (Kumamoto Branch Camp)
Miyata:	Fukuoka #9 Branch Camp (Miyata)
Mitsubishi-Yokohama:	Tokyo #1 Dispatched Camp
Narumi:	Nagoya #2 Dispatched Camp
Niigata:	Tokyo #5 Branch Camp (Niigata-Rinko)
Niigata:	Tokyo #15 Branch Camp (Niigata Tekko)
Nisshin Oil:	Tokyo #17 Branch Camp
Nomachi:	Nagoya #10 Dispatched Camp Fushiki Sea and Land Transportation
Notogawa:	Osaka #9 Branch Camp
Oeyama:	Osaka #3 Branch Camp
Ohashi:	Sendai #4 Branch Camp
Omine:	Fukuoka #5 Branch Camp (Kawasaki-machi)
Omori:	Tokyo Main Camp (July 43 onwards)
Osaka:	Osaka #1 Branch Camp (Minato-ku, Osaka)
Sakurajima:	Osaka #4 Dispatched Camp
Sendai 2:	Sendai #2 Branch Camp (Yoshima Coal Mine)
Shinagawa:	Tokyo Main Camp (until July 43, then hospital)
Sumidagawa:	Tokyo #10 Branch Camp

Suwa:	Tokyo #6 Branch Camp
Tamano:	Hiroshima #3 Branch Camp
Toyama:	Nagoya #8 Dispatched Camp (Toyama Tateyama Heavy Industry)
Toyama:	Nagoya #9 Branch Camp (Toyama Nippon Express)
Tsurumi:	Tokyo #14 Branch Camp Toshiba Electric (see also Kawasaki 3D above)
Wakagawa:	Sendai #10 Branch Camp
Yokohama Stadium:	Tokyo #3 Branch Camp
Yokohama Stevedore:	Tokyo #19 Dispatched Camp (Yokohama Ship Loading)
Yumoto:	Sendai #1 Branch Camp (Yumoto)
Zentsuji:	Hiroshima #1 Branch Camp (Zentsuji)

Note: As some of these camps just had (literally) one or two Hong Kong POWs, there may still be some missing from this list. This is especially true for medical officers, who were highly valued and were often distributed individually to camps in need.

Vernacular camp and work-party names also often included references to the type of work involved. The following are the most common to be seen in diaries and letters:

Denka or Denki:	Electric
Kogyo:	Industries or Mining
Kogyosho:	Industries
Kokan, Seitetsu, or Tekkojo:	Steel Mill/Iron Works
Koun:	Shipping
Kozan or Tanko:	Mining
Seifun:	Flour Mill
Tsuun or Unso:	Transport
Zosen:	Shipbuilding[16]

Note on Hospitals

Only two dedicated POW Hospitals existed in Japan during the war. One was Shinagawa Hospital attached to Tokyo POW Camp (and which itself had originally been Tokyo Main Camp), and the other was Kobe Hospital (originally, Ichioka Ward) attached to Osaka POW Camp. However, POWs were sometimes admitted to the Japanese Army Hospitals or the hospitals attached to the companies that employed the POWs.

Hiroshima Military Hospital:	Hiroshima
Ichioka Ward:	Osaka
Kokura Military Hospital:	Fukuoka (Kokura City, today Kitakyushu City)
Kobe Hospital:	Osaka (Kobe City)
Osaka Military Hospital:	Osaka
Sagamihara Military Hospital:	Tokyo (Sagamihara City, Kanagawa Prefecture)
Shinagawa Hospital:	Tokyo
Tokyo #2 Military Hospital:	Tokyo[17]

Fukuoka

The Fukuoka POW Camp administration was established on 1 January 1943, initially controlling the branch camps in the Kyushu area, and part of the Chugoku and Shikoku areas. Later, the branch camps in the Chugoku and Shikoku areas were separated from Fukuoka when the Zentsuji and Hiroshima POW Camp administrations were established. The first commander was Colonel Ijyu Sugasawa, who was succeeded by Colonel Manjiro Fukumoto. Three camps under Fukuoka's administration housed Hong Kong POWs.

Fukuoka #1B (Kumamoto Branch Camp and Fukuoka Branch Camp)

Established as Kumamoto Branch Camp of Yawata Temporary POW Camp at Aza-Saburotsuka, Kengun-cho, Kumamoto City, Kumamoto Prefecture on 26 November 1942, it was reorganized as Kumamoto Branch Camp of Fukuoka POW Camp on 1 January 1943. It was then renamed Fukuoka Number 1 Branch Camp on 1 March 1943. The POWs here worked for Seibu District Army, building Kengun Airfield at Kumamoto City. The camp moved to Tatara-cho, Kasuya-gun (now Tatara, Higashi-ku, Fukuoka City), Fukuoka Prefecture on 20 September 1943, and moved again to Oaza-Mushiroda, Fukuoka City on 17 April 1944. Finally, it moved to Hakozaki-cho, Higashi-ku, Fukuoka City on 20 January 1945. In all, 147 POWs died in this camp, one of whom was Stanley Easter, RE, who appears to have been the only Hong Kong POW imprisoned here.

Fukuoka #5B (Kawasaki Omine)

Fukuoka Number 5 Branch Camp was established as Omine Branch Camp of Fukuoka POW Camp at Omine Coal Mine in Kawasaki-cho, Kawasaki-gun, Fukuoka Prefecture on 22 January 1943. It was renamed Fukuoka Number 5 Branch Camp on 1 March 1943, then Fukuoka Number 8 Dispatched Camp on 1 December 1943, and finally Fukuoka Number 5 Branch Camp in August 1945. The Hong Kong POWs, including Sydney Skelton, arrived on 24 January 1943. The POWs worked for Furukawa Mining Company. In all, 21 POWs died in this camp, including 16 Hong Kong POWs: 4 British Royal Engineers, and 12 Canadians, all from the third draft from Hong Kong.

Fukuoka #9B (Miyata)

Fukuoka Number 9 Branch Camp was originally established as Fukuoka Number 20 Branch Camp at Onoura Coal Mine in Miyata-cho, Kurate-gun, Fukuoka Prefecture on 4 December 1943. It was renamed Fukuoka Number 12 Dispatched Camp on 10 April 1944, and again renamed Fukuoka Number 9 Branch Camp in August 1945. The Hong Kong POWs were officers arriving from Zentsuji in July 1945. The POWs worked at Kaijima-onoura Coal Mining Company. No Hong Kong POWs died in this camp.

Hakodate

The Hakodate POW Camp administration was established on 26 December 1942, to administer the branch camps on Hokkaido Island and part of the northeastern corner of Honshu Island. However, following the establishment of the Sendai

POW Camp administration in April 1945, Hakodate's area of control became restricted to Hokkaido. The first camp commander was Colonel Toshio Hatakeyama, the second was Lieutenant Colonel Shigeo Emoto, and the third was Colonel Atsuo Hosoi. Only two camps in this administration housed Hong Kong POWs.

Hakodate #2B (Akabira)

Hakodate Number 2 Branch Camp was established at Akabira-cho, Sorachi-gun (now Akabira City), Hokkaido on 7 June 1945. The POWs worked for the Sumitomo Mining Company. Twenty-eight of the British POWs were ex-Shanghai *Lisbon Maru* POWs who arrived on 29 June 1945, including Bill Spooner and Cyril Mace.[18] No POW deaths were recorded in this camp.

Hakodate #4B (Nishi Ashibetsu)

Hakodate Number 4 Branch Camp was established at Aza-Nishiashibetsu, Ashibetsu-cho Sorachi-gun (now Ashibetsu City), Hokkaido on 29 June 1945. Two of the British POWs here were Fairbairn and Haywood from Shanghai (and the *Lisbon Maru*) who arrived on 29 June 1945. No POW deaths were recorded in this camp.

Hiroshima

The Hiroshima POW Camp administration was established in April 1945 and controlled the branch camps in the Chugoku and Shikoku areas. The branch camps that had previously been included in the jurisdictions of Fukuoka and Zentsuji were transferred to Hiroshima's administration. The Camp Commander was Colonel Gyokuei Kondo. Three camps under Hiroshima's administration housed Hong Kong POWs.

Hiroshima #1B (Zentsuji)

Hiroshima Number 1 Branch Camp was originally established as Zentsuji Main Camp at Oaza-Sakino, Zentsuji-cho, Kagawa Prefecture on 14 January 1942. It was transferred to Hiroshima's jurisdiction as Hiroshima Number 1 Branch Camp on 13 April 1945. The POWs worked at Nippon Express Company. Ten POWs died in this camp, none of them from Hong Kong. The officers from Hong Kong interned in this camp for a period (all from the *Lisbon Maru*) were: Lieutenant Henry Bevis (RN), Lieutenant C. D. W. Brown (Royal Signals), Lieutenant C. E. Bucke (Royal Signals), Chief Skipper J. H. Cowling (Merchant Service), Lieutenant Graham Hill (Middlesex), Lieutenant Hargreaves Howell (RASC), and Lieutenant Claude Woodcock (RE). In around April 1945, Hill was transferred to Tokyo #12B Mitsushima, with some other officers from Hiroshima #1B, but none of the others from Hong Kong. The other Hong Kong officers were transferred, around July 1945, to Miyata Fukuoka #9.

Hiroshima #3B (Tamano)

Hiroshima Number 3 Branch Camp was established at 448 Hibi, Tamano City, Okayama Prefecture on 1 June 1945. The Hong Kong POWs arrived the following day, including Reginald Danny Gunstone. The POWs worked for the Mitsui Mining Company at the Hibi refinery. No POWs died in this camp.

Hiroshima #5B (Innoshima)

Hiroshima Number 5 Branch Camp was originally established as Innoshima Branch Camp of Yawata Temporary POW Camp at Innoshima-cho, Mitsuki-gun (now Innoshima City), Hiroshima Prefecture on 27 December 1942. It was reorganized as Innoshima Branch Camp of Fukuoka's administration on 1 January 1943 and renamed Fukuoka Number 12 Branch Camp on 1 March 1943. Transferred to Zentsuji's jurisdiction as Number 2 Branch Camp on 14 July 1943, it was renamed Zentsuji Number 2 Dispatched Camp on 1 December 1943. Next, it was transferred to Hiroshima's jurisdiction as Number 2 Dispatched Camp on 13 April 1945, and was finally renamed Hiroshima Number 5 Branch Camp in August 1945. The Hong Kong POWs arrived on 24 January 1943, including Bill Lowe and Geoffrey Coxhead of the HKVDC. The POWs worked for Hitachi Dockyard Company. Twelve POWs died in this camp, four of them HKVDC from the third draft from Hong Kong.

Nagoya

The Nagoya POW Camp administration was established in accordance with the establishment of Tokai Army District in April 1945 and controlled the branch camps in the Tokai and Hokuriku areas (which had been under the jurisdiction of Osaka and Tokyo). The camp commander was Lieutenant Colonel Michiji Otake. Five camps under Nagoya's administration housed Hong Kong POWs.

Nagoya #8B (Toyama Tateyama Heavy Industry)

Nagoya Number 8 Branch Camp was established at 1-Banchi, Shimookui-cho, Toyama City, Toyama Prefecture on 10 May 1945. The POWs worked for Tateyama Heavy Industry Company. The Hong Kong POWs arrived from Narumi on 10 May 1945. One POW died in this camp, Albert Mears, RN, from Hong Kong.

Nagoya #9B (Toyama Nippon Express)

Nagoya Number 9 Branch Camp was established at Ohirota, Higashiiwase-cho, Toyama City, Toyama Prefecture on 28 May 1945. The Hong Kong POWs arrived on 18 June 1945, the RAF men having previously been at Narumi. The POWs worked for Nippon Express Company. No Hong Kong POWs died in this camp. The known Hong Kong POWs included: Frederick George Cocks (RASC), John Joseph Emmons (RASC), Walter Harold Field (HKRNVR), Archibald Greenwood (RASC), James Hart (RASC), John R. Harvey (RAMC), Robert Edward Haycock (RAF), David Campbell Highlands (RAF), Norman H. Hildersley (RAOC), John Arthur Maynard (RAF), Albert E. McDonough (RASC), James Steele Moore (RAF), George Hetherington Stewart (RAF), and Henry William Way (RAOC).

Nagoya #1D (Kamioka)

Nagoya Number 1 Dispatched Camp was established as Kamioka Branch Camp of Osaka POW Camp at Wasaho, Aso-mura, Yoshiki-gun (now Kamioka-cho,

Hida City), Gifu Prefecture on 8 December 1942. It was renamed Osaka Number 7 Branch Camp on 18 February 1943, and was transferred to Nagoya's jurisdiction as Nagoya Number 1 Branch Camp on 6 April 1945. The POWs worked for Mitsui Mining Company. Surgeon Commander Jackson was the only Hong Kong POW interned here.

Nagoya #2D (Narumi)

Nagoya Number 2 Dispatched Camp was originally established as Osaka Number 11 Branch Camp at Arimatsuura, Narumi-cho, Aichi-gun (now Midori-ku, Nagoya City), Aichi Prefecture on 28 December 1943. The Hong Kong POWs arrived on 7 January 1944, including Alec Howard, HKVDC. The camp was transferred to Nagoya's jurisdiction as Nagoya Number 2 Branch Camp on 6 April 1945. The POWs worked for Nippon Rolling Stock Company. There were 22 POWs who died in this camp; 18 of these were Hong Kong POWs: 16 British (HKVDC, Royal Scots, Middlesex, RN), and 2 Canadian (RRoC), all from the fifth draft. The surviving Hong Kong POWs were transferred to Nagoya #8B on 10 May 1945.

Nagoya #10D (Fushiki Sea and Land Transportation)

Nagoya Number 10 Dispatched Camp was established at Tatenoue, No-machi, Takaoka City, Toyama Prefecture on 18 June 1945. The POWs worked for Fushiki Sea and Land Transportation Company. Thirty-one Hong Kong POWs were held here altogether, arriving on 18 June, including Dennis Morley, Bill Poulter, and Sam Atkins. The senior Hong Kong officer was Lieutenant Evans (RE).[19] Five POWs died in this camp, of whom two were from Hong Kong, having arrived via the *Lisbon Maru*.

Osaka

The Osaka POW Camp administration was established on 23 September 1942, and initially controlled the branch camps in the Kinki and Tokai areas. Later, the branch camps in the Tokai area were separated when Tokai Army District was established in April 1945. Towards the end of the war, in order to avoid the worsening air raids and in preparation for the expected battles in the Japanese mainland, many camps in the Kobe and Osaka areas were evacuated inland and towards the Inland Sea. The camp commander was Colonel Sotaro Murata. Ten camps under Osaka's administration housed Hong Kong POWs.

Osaka #1B (Main Camp and Osaka)

Osaka Number 1 Branch Camp was established at 3-chome, Gojo-dori, Minato-ku, Osaka City on 23 September 1942. The camp was burnt down in the air raid on 1 June 1945, and the camp office was moved to an elementary school building at Aza-shimoshinden, Shinden-mura, Mishima-gun (now Senriyama, Suita City), Osaka Prefecture on 10 July 1945. At that time, the POWs were moved to Nishinomachi, Kitafukuzaki, Minato-ku, Osaka City and Osaka Number 1 Branch Camp was established there. The POWs worked for Nippon Express Company, at Osaka Harbour, ironworks, and railway stations in Osaka City. The Hong Kong POWs, including Geoffrey Hamilton of the Royal Scots, arrived from

Shanghai on 12 October 1942. In all, 154 POWs died in this camp; 97 of these were Hong Kong POWs, all from the *Lisbon Maru*.

Osaka #2B (Kobe)

Osaka Number 2 Branch Camp was originally established as Kobe Branch Camp of Osaka POW Camp at Ito-cho 28, Kobe-ku (now Chuo-ku), Kobe City on 23 September 1942. The Butterfield and Swire warehouses were used as the POW compound. Renamed Osaka Number 1 Branch Camp on 18 February 1943, it was burnt down in the air raid of 5 June 1945, and moved to the old site of the Kobe Kawasaki Branch Camp at Maruyama-cho, Kobe City, then to the old site of the Wakinohama Branch Camp at 3-chome, Wakinohama-cho, Kobe City on 21 June. It was again renamed Osaka Number 2 Branch Camp in August 1945. The POWs worked for Nippon Express Company, Kobe Ship Transport Company, Toyo Steel Company, Showa Denkyoku Company, and Yoshiwara Vegetable Oil Company in the suburbs of Kobe City. The Hong Kong POWs, including Martin Weedon of the Middlesex, arrived from Shanghai on 12 October 1942. There were 134 POWs who died in this camp, 117 of these were Hong Kong POWs, all from the *Lisbon Maru*.

Osaka #3B (Oeyama)

Osaka Number 3 Branch Camp was originally established as Osaka Number 12 Branch Camp at Sutsu, Yoshizu-mura, Yosa-gun (now Miyazu City), Kyoto Prefecture on 20 September 1943. It was renamed Osaka Number 3 Branch Camp in August, 1945. The POWs worked for Nippon Yakin Kogyo Company, and Oeyama nickel mine in Kaya-cho. The first Hong Kong POWs arrived on 1 September 1943, with a second group — including Frank Evans — joining on 7 January 1944. In all, 62 POWs died in this camp, 52 of whom (21 Canadians and 31 British) were from Hong Kong, the vast majority being from the initial group to arrive at this camp.

Osaka #4B (Ikuno)

Osaka Number 4 Branch Camp was originally established as Osaka Number 19 Branch Camp at Kuchikanaya, Ikuno-cho, Asago-gun (now Asago City), Hyogo Prefecture on 28 March 1945. It was renamed Osaka Number 4 Branch Camp in August, 1945. The POWs worked for the Mitsubishi Mining Company, at the Ikuno Copper Mine. No POWs died in this camp. The camp held Major Houghton, Captain Martin Weedon, and other officers from the *Lisbon Maru*, who arrived on 31 March 1945.

Osaka #6B (Akenobe)

Osaka Number 6 Branch Camp was originally established as Osaka Number 21 Branch Camp at Wada, Minamitani-mura, Yabu-gun (now Yabu City), Hyogo Prefecture on 18 May 1945, it was renamed Osaka Number 6 Branch Camp in August, 1945. The POWs worked for Mitsubishi Mining Company, at the Akenobe Copper Mine. The Hong Kong POWs, including Robert Bede Moore, arrived on 18 May 1945 from Sakurajima. No Hong Kong POWs died in this camp.

Osaka #9B (Notogawa)

Osaka Number 9 Branch Camp was originally established as Osaka Number 24 Branch Camp at Iba, Notogawa-cho, Kanzaki-gun, Shiga Prefecture on 18 May 1945. It was renamed Osaka Number 9 Branch Camp in August, 1945. The POWs worked for Shiga Prefectural Office and were engaged in land reclamation work at Lake Biwa, and growing rice. The Hong Kong POWs, including New Zealander Ross Lynneberg, arrived on 20 May 1945 from Osaka #1B. No POW deaths were reported at this camp.

Osaka #12B (Hirohata)

Osaka Number 12 Branch Camp was originally established as Hirohata Detached Camp of Kobe Branch Camp at Sai, Hirohata-cho, Shikama-gun (now Himeji City), Hyogo Prefecture in October 1942. It was reorganized as Hirohata Dispatched Camp of the Osaka camp administration on 10 December 1942. Renamed Osaka Number 1 Dispatched Camp on 18 February 1943, it moved to Kosaka, Hirohata-cho in September 1943, and was again renamed Osaka Number 12 Branch Camp in August 1945. The POWs worked for Nippon Steel Company. The only Hong Kong POW was medic Wallace Hastings, who had been aboard the *Lisbon Maru* and had served at Ichioka Ward.

Osaka #4D (Sakurajima)

Osaka Number 4 Dispatched Camp was originally established as Sakurajima Branch Camp of Osaka POW Camp administration at 3-chome, Takami-cho, Konohana-ku, Osaka City on 20 January 1943. Renamed Osaka Number 8 Branch Camp on 18 February 1943, it was again renamed Osaka Number 4 Dispatched Camp on 1 October 1943, and closed on 18 May 1945. At that point, the POWs were transferred to Akenobe. The Hong Kong POWs arrived at Sakurajima on 24 January 1943, including Robert Bede Moore. The POWs worked for the Hitachi Dockyard Company. Thirty-eight POWs died in this camp, thirty-three of them from Hong Kong.

Osaka #5D (Kobe Kawasaki)

Osaka Number 5 Dispatched camp was originally established as Kobe Kawasaki Branch Camp of Osaka POW Camp at 2-chome, Maruyama-cho, Nagata-ku, Kobe City on 8 December 1942. Renamed Osaka Number 5 Branch Camp on 18 February 1943, it was again renamed Osaka Number 5 Dispatched Camp on 25 October 1943. It closed on 21 May 1945, and the POWs were moved to camps under Fukuoka and Hiroshima's jurisdiction.[20] The POWs worked for Kawasaki Heavy Industry Company. Fifty-five POWs died in this camp, including one Hong Kong POW, William Andrews, from HMS *Tamar*.

Osaka #6D (Amagasaki)

Osaka Number 6 Dispatched Camp was originally established as Amagasaki Branch Camp of Osaka POW Camp at Nishitakasu-cho 31, Amagasaki City, Hyogo Prefecture on 20 January 1943. Renamed Osaka Number 9 Branch Camp on 18 February 1943, it was again renamed Osaka Number 6 Dispatched Camp on 20

October 1943. The Hong Kong POWs, including James Hart, RAOC, arrived on 25 January 1943. It closed on 16 June 1945, and the POWs were moved to Hiroshima #3B and Nagoya #9B. The POWs worked for Otani Heavy Industry Company. Twenty-eight POWs died in this camp, including twelve from Hong Kong.

Ichioka POW Hospital Ward

Established using the field athletics stadium stand at Yawatayamatsuno-cho, Minato-ku, Osaka City on 18 October 1942, it housed seriously ill POWs from all the Osaka POW Branch Camps. It closed on 10 June 1944, and the POWs were moved to Kobe POW Hospital.

Kobe POW Hospital

Established using the building of Kobe Central Theological School at Kumochi-cho, Fukiai-ku (now Chuo-ku), Kobe City on 10 June 1944, it housed seriously ill POWs from all the Osaka POW Branch Camps. It was burnt down in the air raid on 5 June 1945, and the POWs were moved to the old site of the Kobe Kawasaki Branch Camp until the end of the war.

Sendai

The Sendai POW Camp administration was established on 14 April 1945 in accordance with the establishment of the Tohoku Army District, and controlled the branch camps in the Tohoku area of northeast Honshu. Some branch camps that had previously been controlled by the Tokyo POW Camp administration or the Hakodate POW Camp administration, were transferred to Sendai. The camp commander was Lieutenant Colonel Riichi Kitahara. Six camps in this administration housed Hong Kong POWs.

Sendai #1B (Yumoto)

Sendai Number 1 Branch Camp was originally established as Tokyo Number 6 Branch Camp at Mizunoya, Yumoto-cho, Iwaki-gun (now Joban Mizunoya-cho, Iwaki City), Fukushima Prefecture on 15 April 1943. It was renamed Tokyo Number 4 Dispatched Camp on 1 August 1943, and transferred to Sendai's jurisdiction as Number 1 Branch Camp on 14 April 1945. The POWs worked for the Joban Coal Mining Company. The Hong Kong POWs arrived after Tokyo #3D was closed in spring, 1945. They included Tom Marsh, Winnipeg Grenadiers. No Hong Kong POWs died in this camp.

Sendai #2B (Yoshima)

Sendai Number 2 Branch Camp was originally established as Tokyo Number 14 Dispatched Camp at Kami-yoshima, Yoshima-mura, Iwaki-gun (now Yoshima-cho, Iwaki City), Fukushima Prefecture on 30 March 1944. It was transferred to Sendai's jurisdiction as Number 2 Branch Camp on 14 April 1945. The POWs worked for the Furukawa Mining Company. The Hong Kong POWs arrived on 13 May 1944, including Cicero Rozario, HKVDC. Eight POWs died in this camp, six of them — three British, two Portuguese, and one Canadian — from Hong Kong.

Sendai #4B (Ohashi)

Sendai Number 4 Branch Camp was originally established as Hakodate Number 2 Branch Camp at Kamaishi City, Iwate Prefecture on 30 November 1942. It moved to Ohashi, Kasshi-mura, Kamihei-gun (now Kasshi-cho, Kamaishi City), Iwate Prefecture on 1 April 1943, and was transferred to Tokyo's jurisdiction as Number 6 Branch Camp on 20 April 1944. It was transferred for a second time, to Sendai's jurisdiction, as Number 4 Branch Camp on 14 April 1945. The POWs worked for the Nippon Steel Company. The Hong Kong POWs, including Jim Trick, Winnipeg Grenadiers, and George MacDonell, Royal Rifles of Canada, arrived when Tokyo #3D was closed in spring, 1945. No Hong Kong POWs died in this camp.

Sendai #5B (Kamaishi)

Sendai Number 5 Branch Camp was originally established as Hakodate Number 3 Branch Camp at Dai 4 Jiwari 68-1, Oaza Kamaishi, Kamaishi City, Iwate Prefecture on 10 November 1943. It was transferred to Tokyo's jurisdiction as Number 7 Branch Camp on 20 April 1944, and transferred again to Sendai's jurisdiction as Number 5 Branch Camp on 14 April 1945. An American fleet bombarded the camp in August 1945, and destroyed it. The camp was moved to Yanoura, Kamaishi City immediately after the war. The Hong Kong POWs arrived from Omori on 14 May 1945, including William Tyner and Earnest Rowland.[21] The POWs worked for the Nippon Steel Company. Fifty POWs died in this camp, thirty-two of whom — including two from Hong Kong — were killed by the US fleet's fire.

Sendai #8B (Kosaka)

Sendai Number 8 Branch Camp was originally established as Tokyo Number 10 Branch Camp at Kosaka-cho, Kazuno-gun, Akita Prefecture on 1 December 1944. It was transferred to Sendai's jurisdiction as Number 8 Branch Camp. The POWs worked for the Fujita-gumi Construction Company. No Hong Kong POWs died in this camp. The only Hong Kong POW known to be present was Lieutenant-Colonel Cedric Shackleton.

Sendai #10B (Wakagawa)

Sendai Number 10 Branch Camp was established at Wakasennin, Oaza-Yamaguchi, Iwasaki-mura, Waka-gun (now Waka-cho, Kitakami City), Iwate Prefecture on 20 May 1945, with 300 POWs from the Tokyo and Yokohama areas. The POWs worked for Tohoku Electrical Ironworks. From Hong Kong, the camp held Lieutenant-Colonel Harry Rudolf and a number of men from the first draft, who arrived in May, 1945, and Canadians George Chanell and Arthur Hunter from the fourth draft. No POWs died in this camp.

Tokyo

Tokyo POW Camp administration was established on 25 September 1942. Initially it controlled the branch camps in the Tohoku, Kanto, Koshinetsu and Hokuriku areas. However, following the establishment of the Sendai and Nagoya administrations on 14 April 1945, the branch camps in the Tohoku and Hokuriku areas were separated. Towards the end of the war, in order to escape worsening air raids (or as a result of being burnt out), and in preparation for the expected invasion of the Japan proper, the camps in the Tokyo and Yokohama areas were evacuated and the POWs were moved away from the coast. The first camp commander was Colonel Kunji Suzuki, and the second was Colonel Kaname Sakaba. Seventeen camps under Tokyo's administration housed Hong Kong POWs.

Tokyo Main Camp

Shinagawa POW Camp was established at 3-chome Higashi-Shinagawa, Shinagawa-ku, Tokyo using the office building of Keihin Canal Construction Company on 12 September 1942, it was renamed Tokyo POW Main Camp on 25 September 1942. Tokyo Main Camp was moved to Arai-cho, Omori-ku (now Heiwajima, Ota-ku), Tokyo on 2 July 1943 (after which the original site became Shinagawa Hospital). The Hong Kong POWs arrived initially on 15 September 1942, but were joined by four others from Hong Kong in January 1944 (including James Bertram, HKVDC), and eleven more from Tokyo #19D on 1 June 1945 (others may have passed through in 1945, as Omori appears to have been used for men in transit). The POWs worked for the Nippon Express Company. Forty-one POWs died in this camp, fourteen of them being British POWs from the first draft from Hong Kong.

Shinagawa POW Hospital

This hospital was established at 3-chome, Higashi-Shinagawa, Tokyo using the original site of Tokyo Main Camp (Shinagawa) on 1 August 1943. It held seriously ill POWs sent from all the camps under Tokyo's jurisdiction.

Tokyo #1B (Kawasaki)

Tokyo Number 1 Branch Camp was originally established as Kawasaki Temporary POW Camp at 4-chome Oshima-cho, Kawasaki City on 24 August 1942. It was renamed Tokyo Number 1 Branch Camp on 25 September 1942. The POWs worked for the Nippon Express Company and others. One hundred Hong Kong POWs arrived on 15 September 1942, including Alfred Condon. Sixteen POWs died in this camp, five of whom were British from Hong Kong, all from the first draft.

Tokyo #2B (Kawasaki Ogimachi)

Tokyo Number 2 Branch Camp was originally established as the Wharf Branch of Tokyo Number 1 Branch Camp at Ogimachi, Kawasaki-ku, Kawasaki City on 12 November 1942. It was renamed Tokyo Number 2 Branch Camp on 1 August 1943. The POWs worked for Mitsui Wharf Storage Company, Kawasaki Ship Loading and others. It is not clear whether the Hong Kong POWs here actually transferred from Tokyo #1B or were simply on a working party to #2B. Forty-seven POWs died in this camp, twenty-two of whom were killed in an American air raid on 25 July 1945. One Hong Kong POW died in the bombing: Arthur Taylor, Royal Navy, who had been on the first draft.

Tokyo #3B (Yokohama)

Tokyo Number 3 Branch Camp was originally established on 12 September 1942 as Yokohama POW Camp, in the Yokohama Baseball Stadium in Yokohama Park, Naka-Ku, Yokohama City. The Hong Kong POWs, including James Ford, arrived on 15 September 1942. The camp was renamed Tokyo Number 2 Branch Camp on 25 September 1942, and again renamed Tokyo Number 3 Branch Camp on 1 August 1943. It closed on 1 May 1944, and the POWs were transferred to Nisshin Oil Branch Camp, Yokohama Fireproof Brick Dispatched Camp, and Yokohama Ship Loading Dispatched Camp. The POWs worked for Yokohama Ship Loading Company and others. Seven POWs died in this camp, five being British from the first draft from Hong Kong.

Tokyo #5B (Niigata Sea and Land Transportation)

Tokyo Number 5 Branch Camp was established at Nutari, Niigata City, Niigata Prefecture on 20 August 1943, it moved to Kawato Shinden, Ogata-mura, Nakakanbara-gun (now Kogane-machi, Niigata City) on 4 December 1943. The Hong Kong POWs, including Ken Cambon and Tom Forsyth, arrived on 1 September 1943. During the period from late December to April 1944, the POWs were temporarily moved to the factory of Niigata Sea and Land Transportation Company and Niigata Ironworks Company. The POWs worked for Niigata Sea and Land Transportation Company and others. In all, 99 POWs died in this camp, including 73 Canadians from Hong Kong.

Tokyo #6B (Suwa)

Tokyo Number 6 Branch Camp was established at Kitayama-mura, Suwa-gun (now Kitayama, Chino City), Nagano Prefecture on 4 June 1945. The Hong Kong POWs arrived on 15 March 1945, from Tokyo #3D. They included Lionel Speller. The POWs worked for Nippon Steel Tube and Mining Company. Four POWs died in this camp, one of whom was a Canadian — Robert Russell — from Hong Kong.

Tokyo #10B (Sumidagawa)

Tokyo Number 10 Branch Camp was originally established as Tokyo Number 20 Dispatched Camp at Minami-senju, Arakawa-ku, Tokyo on 1 July 1944. It was renamed Tokyo No. 10 Branch Camp in August, 1945. The first Hong Kong POWs arrived from Omori when this camp was established, with Canadians — including William Allister — joining from Tokyo #3D in spring, 1945. The POWs worked for the Nippon Express Company. Two POWs died in this camp: one Canadian, and one British. Both were from Hong Kong.

Tokyo #12B (Hiraoka Mitsushima)

Tokyo Number 12 Branch Camp was originally established as Tokyo Number 3 Branch Camp at Mitsushima, Hiraoka-mura, Shimoina-gun, Nagano Prefecture, on 18 November 1942. It was renamed Tokyo Number 2 Dispatched Camp on 1 August 1943, and again renamed Tokyo Number 12 Branch Camp in August,

1945. The POWs worked at Kumagai-gumi Construction Company and were engaged in the construction of Hiraoka hydro-electric power station and dam. Lieutenant Graham Hill was the only known POW from Hong Kong in this camp.

Tokyo #14B (Toshiba Electric Tsurumi)

Tokyo Number 14 Branch Camp was originally established as Tokyo Number 3 Dispatched Camp at Suehiro-cho, Tsurumi-ku, Yokohama City on 25 December 1943. It moved to 2-4 Suehiro-cho, Tsurumi-ku on 15 April 1945. It was destroyed in an air raid on 15 April 1945, which killed thirty-one POWs, and moved to the site of Toshiba Electric Company. It was renamed Tokyo Number 14 Branch Camp in August, 1945. The Hong Kong POWs presumably arrived after the Stadium camp was closed. The POWs worked for Toshiba Electric Company. Forty-four POWs died in this camp in total. Two of the dead (Albert Forth and Herbert Morgan) were Hong Kong POWs from the first draft.

Tokyo #15B (Niigata Ironworks)

Tokyo Number 15 Branch Camp was originally established as Tokyo Number 15 Dispatched Camp at Akiba-dori, Yamanoshita, Niigata City, Niigata Prefecture on 1 April 1944. It was renamed Tokyo Number 15 Branch Camp in August, 1945. The Hong Kong POWs arrived on 1 June 1945 from Tokyo #19D and on 4 June 1945 from Tokyo #18D, and the Canadians were present from late December 1943 to April 1944 (from nearby Tokyo #5B; this group included Tom Forsyth). The POWs worked for the Niigata Ironworks Company. Six POWs died in this camp, two of whom were Canadians from Hong Kong.

Tokyo #17B (Nisshin Oil)

Tokyo Number 17 Branch Camp was originally established as Tokyo Number 17 Dispatched Camp at Chiwaka-cho, Kanagawa-ku, Yokohama City on 1 May 1944. It was destroyed in the air raid on 29 May 1945, and the POWs were temporarily moved to Tokyo #18D. It was renamed Tokyo #17 Branch Camp in August, 1945. The Hong Kong POWs arrived on 1 May 1944 from Tokyo #3B, and on 20 December 1944 from Tokyo #1B (including Arthur Taylor). The POWs worked for Nisshin Oil Company. One POW died in this camp, from the first draft from Hong Kong.

Tokyo #1D (Mitsubishi Yokohama Ship-building)

Tokyo Number 1 Dispatched camp was originally established as a Branch of Yokohama Branch Camp of Tokyo POW Camp at 1-1 Hashimoto-cho, Kanagawa-ku, Yokohama City on 18 November 1942. It was renamed Tokyo Number 1 Dispatched Camp on 1 August 1943. The POWs worked at the Mitsubishi Heavy Industry Yokohama Ship-building Company. The camp was closed on 13 May 1945 and the POWs were moved to Omori and Mitsushima. Only one Hong Kong POW, Dr A.C. Price, is known to have been at this camp.

Tokyo #3D (Nippon Steel Tube Tsurumi Ship-building)

Tokyo Number 3 Dispatched camp was originally established as Tokyo Number 5 Branch Camp at 1-124 Suehiro-cho, Tsurimi-ku, Yokohama City on 21 January 1943. The Hong Kong POWs arrived on 23 January 1943, including Tom Marsh and Leo Berard. The camp was renamed Tokyo Number 3 Dispatched Camp on 1 August 1943. The POWs worked for Nippon Steel Tube Tsurumi Ship-building Company. Twenty-three POWs died in this camp, all Canadians from the third draft from Hong Kong. The camp closed in the spring of 1945, and the POWs were moved to Tokyo #10B, Sendai #4B, Sendai #1B, and Tokyo #6B.

Tokyo #13D (Nippon Steel Tube Asano Ship-building)

Tokyo Number 13 Dispatched Camp was established at 29 Mitsuzawashimo-cho, Kanagawa-ku, Yokohama City on 20 March 1944. The Hong Kong POWs arrived from Tokyo #3B on 1 May 1944. The POWs worked for Nippon Steel Tube Asano Ship-building Company. No POW deaths were recorded in this camp. It was closed on 13 May 1945, and the POWs were transferred to Sendai #5B.

Tokyo #18D (Yokohama Firebrick)

Tokyo Number 18 Dispatched Camp was established at Baba-cho, Nishinegishi, Isogo-ku, Yokohama City on 1 May 1944. The Hong Kong POWs arrived from Tokyo #3B on 1 May 1944. The POWs worked for Yokohama Fire-proof Brick Company. No POW deaths were recorded in this camp. It was closed on 4 June 1945, and the POWs were moved to Tokyo #15B.

Tokyo #19D (Yokohama Stevedore)

Tokyo Number 19 Dispatched Camp was established at 32 Yamashita-cho, Naka-ku, Yokohama City on 1 May 1944. The Hong Kong POWs arrived from Tokyo #3B on 1 May 1944, including James Ford. The POWs worked for Yokohama Ship Loading Company. No POW deaths were recorded in this camp, which was destroyed in the air raid on 29 May 1945 and was closed on 1 June. The POWs were then moved to Tokyo #15B (the majority) and Tokyo Main Camp (Omori, eleven men).

Tokyo #23D (Ajinomoto)

Tokyo Number 23 Dispatched Camp was established at Kawasaki City, Kanagawa Prefecture on 20 September 1944. The Hong Kong POWs were all from the first draft, working at the Dainippon Chemistry Company. No Hong Kong POWs died at this camp. The camp was closed on 30 June 1945, and the POWs were moved back to Tokyo #1B (Kawasaki).

APPENDIX 5: LIBERATION VESSELS AND ROUTES

In general, Far Eastern POWs were concentrated in Manila before being shipped home. The main route for the British POWs led (via Honolulu or Guam) to the west coast of North America, followed by a train ride to the east coast and a ship home. This list of vessels will not be comprehensive, as some individuals left

APPENDICES   267

their camps independently and joined other groups in the evacuation. Also, some ships in this list made more than one repatriation voyage. The Indian POWs were, it appears, exclusively shipped home on the *Takliwa*.

Vessel	Departure	Arrival	
Empress of Australia	Hong Kong 9.9.1945	Manila	13.9.1945
Oxfordshire	Hong Kong 2.9.1945	Manila	5.9.1945
HMCS *Prince Robert*	Hong Kong 20.9.1945	Manila	?
Takliwa	Hong Kong 7.10.1945	Madras	15.10.1945[22]
Maunganui	Hong Kong	New Zealand	?[23]
(Air Transport)	Yokohama	Okinawa	various[24]
(Air Transport)	Okinawa	Manila	various
USS *Benevolence*	Yokohama 27.11.1945	San Francisco	12.12.1945[25]
USS *Goodhue*	Sagami Bay 12.9.1945	Manila	18.9.1945
USS *Hyde*	Yokohama (after 8.9)	Guam	23.9.1945
USS *Oconto*	Yokohama 12.9.1945	Manila	?
USS *Ozark*	Tokyo 8.9.1945	San Francisco	2.10.1945
USS *Rescue*	Tokyo 19.9.1945	San Francisco	8.10.1945 ?
HMS *Ruler*	Tokyo 13.9.1945	Sydney	?
HMS *Speaker*	Tokyo 3.9.1945	Manila	9.9.1945
USS *Tryon*	Yokohama (after 1.9)	Manila	18.9.1945
Admiral Hughes	Manila 24.9.1945	Victoria	9.10.1945
USS *Catron*	Manila (after 29.9)	San Francisco	19.10.1945
HMS *Colossus*	Manila 5.10.1945	Hong Kong	7.10.1945
HMCS *Crescent*	Manila ?	Esquimalt	21.10.1945[26]
Empress of Australia	Manila 18.9.1945	Liverpool	28.10.1945
HMS *Formidable*	Manila 5.10.1945	Sydney	13.10.1945
General R. L. Howze	Manila 27.9.1945	San Francisco	15.10.1945
HMS *Glory*	Manila 9.10.1945	Esquimalt	27.10.1945
USS *Goodhue*	Manila 11.10.1945	Esquimalt	?
USS *Gosper*	Manila (after 15.9)	Victoria	12.10.1945
HMS *Implacable*	Manila 25.9.1945	Esquimalt	11.10.1945
Joseph T. Dickman	Manila (after 17.9)	San Francisco	16.10.1945
Oxfordshire	Manila (after 5.9)	Sydney	24.9.1945
HMCS *Prince Robert*	Manila 29.9.1945	Esquimalt	20.10.1945
Dominion Monarch	Sydney 18.10.1945	Southampton	15.11.1945
Ile de France	Halifax 26.10.1945	Southampton	31.10.1945
Queen Elizabeth	Halifax 31.10.1945	Southampton	5.11.1945

APPENDIX 6: DISEASE

Aside from the *Lisbon Maru*, the vast majority of deaths in the POW and Internee camps were caused by disease. Some were caused by the poor hygiene (the various dysenteries and diahoreas, tuberculosis, and diphtheria being obvious examples), some were caused by general weakness and debility (pneumonia), some through previous infection (malaria), and the remainder primarily through vitamin starvation (wet and dry beri-beri, and pellagra).

Diphtheria had been a big killer in Europe before the serum became available, and was thus easily recognized when the epidemic began. Pneumonia, TB, and Malaria were also familiar. However, beri-beri and pellagra were not well known to many Western doctors.

Pellagra manifested itself as a skin disease, but without treatment could lead to depression, dementia, and death. As a skin disease, it was popularly known to the POWs as "Strawberry balls", or "Hong Kong balls", for the painful sores it left on the scrotum.

On dry beri-beri, Allister noted: "On the way to the benjo, the outdoor latrines, during the night, it was a common sight to see hunched prisoners wrapped in blankets, with their burning beri-beri feet submerged in fire buckets. These fire buckets, which lined the centre aisle, turned to ice during the night; the sufferer would break the ice to shove his feet into the water for relief while he shivered under his blankets. A more desolate portrait of misery would be hard to find."

Fisher added: "Some 'electric feet' sufferers — as they were called — used to sleep with their feet on a piece of cold stone, or sleep outside in the cold weather with their feet exposed. On one occasion I went into the washhouse in the middle of the night, and found a group sitting perched like fowls with their feet in the ice-cold water. Night after night, week after week and month after month this went on until we got nicotinic acid, and my heart bled in sympathy for these poor creatures. One fellow put his feet into almost boiling water without realising it and the subsequent burns left an almost permanent injury."

Fisher describes wet beri-beri thus: "Limbs became swollen to huge proportions and then the body. This was the dangerous stage because when a man laid down the water crept up and often proved fatal by a death similar to drowning. I shall never forget Muskett in B4 who one night woke us all by dreadful gargling noises. We got him upright and by a miracle he lived to tell the tale, but only after dreadful suffering."

Almost every man had dysentery sooner or later. It was the most debilitating of diseases, and could reduce a previously fit man to child-like weakness in days. Fisher: "For three or four days I could eat no food but just lay there tormented nearly to distraction by visions of ham and eggs. The food at the time was rice and Chinese vegetable with no salt or oil because we had none, and a piece of bread. I gave the whole of mine away and was content to lie there in a world of my own. On the fourth day my hands and feet began to go numb and useless and then my forehead became the same. I found it difficult to move my lips and speak. Fortunately, at this stage, I woke up to the real seriousness of the situation. Hickman, a few beds away, who had piles and dysentery went delirious and died. A Canadian became obstinate and insisted on sitting up when told to lie down. As the sun began to set at about 7.00 pm, I watched him begin to breathe harder and harder and them more slowly until with a faint gasp he lay still forever. This shook me, and I fell off the bed and padded outside to see if I was alive myself or not."

On Monday, 9 November 1942, Bill Lowe of the Volunteers summarized the health situation as follows: "A few notes on the various complaints in & around camp. Main one is Electric or Happy Feet. Terrific pains in toes & extremities do not allow owner to sleep. Only temporary relief is holding 'em under cold water. Young & old affected (Suter 21, other people over 60) no outward signs whatever. Pellagra of mouth, nose & throat. Also blotches all over body, seems to be symmetric in so much as if on shin of rt leg appears in similar spot on left leg. Sun seems to irritate it yeast helped. Strawberry balls are damn painful, cured more with Lions Tooth Pdr. Also swollen penis — so bad in some cases that foreskin has to be cut — 2 deaths of this latter. General malnutrition has killed many & two middies who died yesterday weighed only 40 & 50 lbs respectively! Also many more have partially lost sight — temporarily we hope. Ed Murphy is like this & has much difficulty in recognising people at a couple of yards. Ringworm, tinia, scabies are also rife & no segregation for such people using Theoflav, Mal Green & Men chrome to cure. Small cuts go septic in a day — 8 men so far have died from sheer exhaustion due to Electric feet! Dermatitis also going strong. Fortunately, dip & typhoid are now on the wane, but dysentery & diarrhoea are still going strong & men are dying like flies. They get to the bog & then fall exhausted in the shit & are found later by the orderlies — if they're lucky if not they just peg out. Another type of malnut is a kind of swollen gland on the neck, neck just swells out to shoulders & eyes protrude, face swells. Two deaths so far & don't know what it is."

He continued later, on electric feet: "These damned E.F. defy all attempts to clear 'em they are no respectus of age, colouring or race. Bill Joel (50 odd), has 'em, Hands 65 hasn't, Hatch (25), Cainc (20) has 'em, Miller (30), Day (28) haven't, Paterson (fair) hasn't. Cornec (fair) has 'em, Toikin (dark) has; Partridge (dark) hasn't, Bill Gegg big athlete & 100 yd champ has 'em, Crawford who in Civil life never walked an inch hasn't. Portuguese have 'em, Chaps who were born here have 'em. Fat fellows & thin fellows have. Marriott, Seb Newton, Busty Bowers, who rush about haven't, Labrousse who walks slowly & doesn't wash hasn't. Spores who was champion strong man has 'em, Miller & Lionel who never did any work haven't."

APPENDIX 7: INDIAN ESCAPES

BAAG accepted a total of 367 Indian escapees and refugees, far too many to list individually in this work. Few, if any, were from Ma Tau Chung or other formal POW camps. Most of the servicemen escaped from working parties and guard units at other locations (for example, I.R. Nos. 308, 347 and 348 below escaped from Canton). A list of all names can be found in the Ride Papers, Series 9, No. 16, pp. 5–29. The first page is reproduced here as a sample:

Name	I.R. No.	Pre-war Occupation
Advani, H.L.	26	Merchant
Assumal, T.	55	Merchant
Allah Din	65	Merchant
Abdul Latif	69	Tailor
Aziz Ahmed	92	Merchant
Amin, M.	95	Merchant
Amin, M. Mrs	96	Wife of I.R. No. 95
Ajun Khan	146	Driver
Abdom Yarkoob	160	Accountant
Abdom Yarkoob Mrs	161	Wife of I.R. No. 160
Amin Yarkoob Master	162	Son of I.R. No. 160
Abdul Hamid PC B673	165	Constable HK Police
Amir Din B33	168	Constable HK Police
Atma Singh	188	Gnr.4830 HKSRA 36 Coast Bty.
Abdul Rashid	190	Gnr.3680 HKSRA 4th Med Bty.
Abdullah Ali	194	Ex-HK Police Reservist
Abdul Haq B121	215	Constable HK Police
Amir Hussain B722	220	Constable HK Police
Adalat Khan B90	223	Constable HK Police
Allah Ditta S.20	231	Watchman Guards Office
Angreza Singh	238	Gnr.4711 HKSRA 26th Coast Bty.
Abdul Rashid Abbas	253	Clerk HK Royal Naval Yard
Abdul Rashad Abbas Mrs	254	Wife of I.R. No.253
Allah Dad	256	L/Nk.5273 HKSRA 17 AA Bty.
Abdullah Sher Moh'd	261	Clerk C. Rahim & Co.
Abdul Manak Ramjahn	270	Stenographer
Alim Din B114	273	Constable HK Police
Ali Ahmed	282	Constable No.263 HKRNY Police
Akber Ali	284	Nk.172755 HK Mule Corps
Akber Shah	285	Sepoy 8911 2/14th Punjab Regt.
Ahmed Khan	286	Gnr.3355 HKSRA 1st Mtn. Bty.
Abdullah Khan	288	Gnr.5190 HKSRA 1st Mtn. Bty.
Ahmed Khan	295	L/Nk.3383 HKSRA 1st Mtn. Bty.
Allah Wasaya	308	Nk.11679 5/7th Rajput Regt.
Ahmed Din B523	315	Constable HK Police
Ahmed Din Mrs	319	Wife of I.R. No.315
Amanat Ali	321	Havildar 7564 5/7 Raj. Regt.
Azim Khan	323	L/Naik 10192 5/7 Raj. Regt.
Alam Khan	324	L/Naik 13924 5/7 Raj. Regt.
Allayar Khan	335	PC B299 Hong Kong Police
Abdul Namid	346	Eye Specialist HK
Ahmed Hassan	347	Jemadar HK Mule Corps
Allayar Khan	348	Havildar No.2675 HKSRA 36 Bty.
Amir Khan	352	Sepoy No.9091 2/14 Punjab Regt.
Asha Khan	362	Sepoy No.19894 2/14 Punjab Regt.
Abdul Hassan	364	Sepoy No.13571 2/14 Punjab Regt.

APPENDIX 8: INDIAN POW ETHNIC GROUPS AND NUMBERS

After the reorganization of the Indian Army in 1922, each battalion was constituted with one company each of different castes (partly as a result of the experience of the Mutiny of 1857, when entire battalions were of one ethnic group, and so mutinied in entirety.) The Dogras (Hindus of pastoral stock, hailing from the Himalayan foothills of Jammu in the north) were one such group. They rose to prominence as a martial race in the Army of the Punjab under Maharaja Ranjit Singh, and sacked Kabul in the 1820s in campaigns under his famous commander, General Zorawar Singh. As a result of service with the Punjabis, Punjab Regiments had one company of Dogras, and one of P.M.s, mixed with one or two companies of Rajputs and/or Brahmins. The P.M.s were Punjabi Musalmans, of the agricultural castes of the Punjab, also known as Jats, and Rajputs (there were Muslim Rajputs in Pre-partition India, and all lived, ate, fought, and died side by side with Hindus under the banner of the Regiment).

BAAG believed that 3,831 Indian POWs were captured in Hong Kong, and the Japanese stated 3,829. These numbers are far too close to be coincidental, and the minor variation might even be explicable simply through deaths between Hong Kong's surrender and the initial Japanese census.

By the end of 1942, BAAG had been informed by Indian escapees that a total of 2,712 Indian POWs had been moved out of Ma Tau Chung. One thousand and three hundred went to Canton in July, 300 went to Hainan at the same time, and the remainder — in smaller groups — went to a large number of different sites in HK as described in the text. BAAG was also informed that 54 men had died up to September 1942, so calculated that 1,065 (3,831 – 2,712 – 54) were still at Ma Tau Chung. However, 500 men (not included in the 2,712) had been taken from Ma Tau Chung to Gun Club Hill in September, which left 665 in Ma Tau Chung. This fits quite well the September 1943 estimate of 600 left in Ma Tau Chung, and perhaps general attrition accounts for the estimate of 500 who moved to Argyle Street in 1944 when Ma Tau Chung reverted to civilian use.

APPENDIX 9: WAR CRIMES AND COLLABORATION TRIALS

Following the *Lisbon Maru* disaster, the interpreter on board (Niimori) and the master of the vessel (Kyoda Shigeru) were tried and found guilty. They were sentenced to fifteen and seven years respectively.[27] A number of the more infamous guards of the Hong Kong camps (such as the "Kamloops Kid") were also brought to the courts. Those convicted were held or executed at Stanley Jail.

A large number of guards from the camps in Japan were also tried (the greatest numbers coming from Narumi, Nagoya #2B, with 22 war criminals, Niigata Sea and Land Transport Branch Camp, Tokyo #5B, with 18 war criminals, and Niigata Ironworks Branch Camp, Tokyo #15B, with 17 war criminals). Sentences varied from terms of imprisonment to capital punishment.

After the war, a number of POWs were charged with Collaboration and tried. These included Cecil Boon, John Harvey, and Marcus Tugby.

Frank Evans: "In the courts martial after the war, it was held that conditions of captivity were so extreme in that horrible atmosphere that conduct could not be judged by normal standards. The accused persons were considered to have suffered enough, and in fact they had suffered nearly a year of suspense and ostracism before their trials, resulting in the total loss of the joy of homecoming."

Boon's Court Martial

The court martial of Major Cecil Boon was the most awaited. The case against Boon opened at Curzon Street, Mayfair, London, on 27 August 1946.[28] Colonel J. A. C. Birch was presiding, while Colonel R. C. Halse was prosecuting, with the defence counsels being G. O. Slade and Neville Faulks.

Eleven charges were brought against Boon:

1. Having been made a prisoner of war, he voluntarily aided the enemy that in Hong Kong, on or about 21 August 1943, he communicated to the enemy information obtained by him of a discussion relating to a proposed escape of members of H.M. Forces who were then prisoners-of-war.

2.. In Hong Kong, on or about 1 September 1943, he voluntarily aided the enemy by conducting a search for, and delivering to the enemy, wireless components hidden in the precincts of Shamshuipo prisoner-of-war camp by members of British and allied forces who were prisoners of war.

3. On or about 12 September 1943, he communicated to the enemy information obtained by him relating to conduct of Hubert George Carkeet,[29] a member of the forces then a prisoner.

4. On or about 20 October 1943, he communicated to the enemy information relating to a document found in possession of Maurice Richard Jones, a member of the forces and a prisoner.

5. On or about 14 December 1943, he communicated to the enemy information relating to documents in the possession of William Joseph Buckley.

6. On or about 18 October 1944, he wrote a letter addressed to the commander of the American Air Force detachment which attacked Hong Kong on 16 October 1944, and handed the letter to the enemy, well knowing that it was intended to be used by the enemy for propaganda purposes.[30]

7. In May 1945, he communicated to the enemy information relating to the conduct of Petty Officer H.A.W. Waardenburg, Royal Netherlands Navy, a prisoner of war.

8. Between 21 August 1943 and 17 August 1945, he interrogated, on behalf of the enemy, persons who were prisoners of war, as to the details and nature of their occupation and duties in the forces.

9. Between 21 August 1943 and 17 August 1945, he was interrogating and procuring for the purposes of the enemy information regarding the organization and equipment of the Royal Signals and British artillery.

10. Between 21 August 1943 and 17 August 1945, he conducted, for the purposes of the enemy, a system of spying on quarters, parcels, and personal affairs of members of British and allied forces and others then prisoners.

11. Between 21 August 1943 and 17 August 1945, procuring the writing for the purposes of the enemy of an account of the defences of Hong Kong, and of reports to the enemy of the conduct of members of the British and allied forces then prisoners in their hands, and of preventing the prisoners from communicating with persons outside Shamshuipo prisoner-of-war camp, and by delivering to the enemy a parcel of medicine intended to be used for the succour of the sick among the prisoners, and by giving assistance and information to the enemy on the use of medically unfit prisoners on working parties and in the use of the prisoners on work of the enemy connected with operations of war.

Major Boon, 49, who had been commissioned into the RASC in 1918 and was Deputy Assistant Quartermaster General, China Command when the Second World War started, pleaded "not guilty" to all the charges.

The prosecution brought 44 witnesses, including: Simon White, Leonard Crosby, George Ryan, Albert Tovee, Staff Sergeant Hitchings, David Samuel Bevan, George Huxham, Ronald Cushley, Henry Evans, Reverend H. Davies, Arthur Grieve, William Angus, Maurice Jones, Harold Cole, William Buckley, Myles Abbott, Hendrikus Waardenburg (NL Navy), Lance Sergeant Jeffery, Henry Field, Captain Valentine, William Robertson, Raymond Lancaster, and James Gray. There were no witnesses for the defence. This latter point was a cause of protests. Mr Slade, on hearing that prosecution witness William Robertson had arrived from Hong Kong by air the previous day, complained: "I am going to renew my submission of the unfairness of holding this trial in England. The Court was told no witness was coming here from Hong Kong. When I want a witness from Hong Kong, I am told I have to pay the expense. When the prosecution want one he can come all the way by air."

By the twelfth day of the case, 26 of the prosecution's witnesses had been called. They had described Boon's alleged activities, including putting eggs and Red Cross parcels aside for the Japanese camp commandant, organizing searches for hidden revolvers and other items, looking for those trying to escape, preventing parcels being sent in to the men, and reporting letters written by the men. Entries from Boon's diary (written in Russian from 12 September 1942 to 28 November 1944, and found in his offices by Major George Ryan, RA, after the Japanese surrender): "July 16 — All day, long searches on the roof, binoculars in the room of the Canadian officers. January 7, 1943 — Philpot came to see me, and said he had heard men talking about the draft to Japan, and heard them say that if they were drafted they would try to escape. I ordered him to find out the names of the men."

One witness, Lieutenant Edward Field, related how he had sent a letter to Boon protesting that the work of constructing an airfield was against an agreement signed by Japan at The Hague, whereby prisoners should not be called on to perform work directly connected with the progress of the war. He was beaten up by the adjutant at the Japanese office. However, "the witness agreed with Mr Faulks (for the defence) that Boon, had be attempted to intervene, would himself have been beaten up."

The case for the prosecution concluded on 10 September.

The case for the defence rested on three points:
1. What acts constituted "aid the enemy".
2. The meaning of the word "voluntarily".
3. The intent which the criminal law required should be proved to constitute the offence.

The defence was attempting to establish that Boon had merely been passing on the instructions of the Japanese, and carrying out their instructions, and had never initiated any pro-Japanese action of his own accord.

On 12 September, Boon was found not guilty on six charges (1, 3, 7, 8, 9, and 11) as no prima facie case had been established.

For the remaining five charges, the dispositions and statements of witnesses tended to support the defence's point that Boon's 'errors' were of omission rather than commission. A disposition from Major Grieve, for example, noted: "On many occasions I asked Major Boon to have the parade cancelled owing to extreme cold or rain, but this he refused to do, and told me to ask the [Camp Commandant] myself. This I did and I was never refused." And from Captain Crew: "Official [pilfering of foodstuffs] by the Japanese officials, including Col. TAKANUGA — 'the fat pig' as popularly known, continued throughout. Such action was invariably supported and condoned by Major Boon."

Although some attempts were made to imply that Boon had initiated searches and so forth of his own accord, the prosecution's case seemed to be running out of steam. For the prosecution, Colonel Halse summed up: "All this I suggest indicated that [Boon's] intentions were to aid the enemy, that he had a hostile intent, and that he intended throughout the period he was in a prisoner of war camp to aid the enemy . . . He is a Regular soldier. He has been brought up in the service of arms, and he quakes because someone lifts a bamboo stick, and fears for his life because he hears someone in the Kempeitai yell. You may think he is a coward, but you are not trying him for cowardice."

But the court sided with the defence. Mr Boon was found not guilty on all charges.

Two further trials were carried out in Canada (Canadian Army Routine Orders, Nos. 6746-6752, 12 September 1946).

Tugby, Marcus Charles, a warrant officer in the Canadian Army was tried from 18 March to 6 April 1946 on nineteen charges. He was found guilty of eight charges (all relating to hitting or assaulting fellow prisoners) and exonerated of the other charges. He was sentenced to be "severely reprimanded".

7260898, Corporal, acting sergeant, John Hugh Harvey, Royal Army Medical Corps, was indicted under twenty-nine charges, including the manslaughter of Friesen, at a court martial in Winnipeg on 2 March 1946. He was acquitted on the charge of manslaughter, and nineteen other charges, but convicted on the remaining nine. However, on 26 August 1946, the *Times* reported that Harvey had received a letter from the War Office stating that the nine convictions had been quashed and that "he is relieved of all consequences of the convictions".

On 10 March 2001, rumours of Major Charles Boxer having been a collaborator surfaced, and were unfortunately given prominence in the *Guardian* newspaper. The original spark for this rumour may have been inspired by a visit by a member of the Japanese royal family to Argyle Street in May 1942. Colonel Price, a Canadian from a wealthy family, had met and entertained one of the visiting Japanese princes before the war, and the latter asked Price if he needed any special treatment. Quite rightly, Price turned him down, but pointed out that his colleague Boxer needed medical attention, or would lose the use of an arm that had been injured in the fighting. Brian Baxter, HKDDC, confirmed: "Until the intervention of Colonel Price, he had received no satisfactory treatment." Equally, Boxer's 1940 separation from his very English wife, Ursula Tulloch, and then taking up with the flamboyant American Emily Hahn, had earned him enemies in the more conservative parts of British Hong Kong society. Lastly, the fact that he was a fluent Japanese speaker, and an intellectual heavyweight, did not endear him to the military establishment.

After this newspaper article was published, the late Roger Rothwell, Middlesex, noted of Boxer: "In prison he was a model of courage and endurance and was an example to us all and any suggestion that he could have been involved in any act of treachery which could have betrayed us to our hated captors is as ludicrous as it is libellous."[31]

APPENDIX 10: OTHER BAAG DEATHS

BAAG deaths not included in CWGC records include:
Chan King
Chan Kai
Chan Kwok Kwong
Chan Kwong Man
Chan Wing Chiu
Chan Yeung
Cheng Yuet
Cheung Yung Sam
Feroz, M.
Fung Him
Ip Kam Wing
Lam Chow Kwang
Lam Ho Kwan

Lam Kwok Yiu
Lam Seng
Lau Fook
Lau Teng Ke
Leung Hung
Li Tam On
Loie Fook Wing (David)
Lok Cheng Liang
Ma Tai
Ng Tak Chueng
Ng Tak Wing
Ngai Yiu Ming
Shui Man Lee
Tai Kar Yin
Tsan J.
Tso Lee
Wong For Yau
Wong Kwong Sheung
Wong Man
Wu Hung
Wun Mah Shin

APPENDIX 11: REMAINS OF POWS IN BUDDHIST SHRINES

Juganji Temple
3–12 Yamatecho, Hirakoa, Osaka

Dear Sir,

September 1, 1966
Osaka, Japan

I, the undersigned and a chief Buddhist priest of Juganji Temple in Osaka, Japan, take the liberty of addressing you that I had been safely keeping the ashes of 1,086 POW's of the last World War from July 1942 toll October 20, 1945 in the main building of my temple to enshrine them, and had been praying for the repose of their souls every day and night.

They were from eight different countries: England, USA, Canada, Netherlands, Australia, India, Italy and Norway, who came to Japan as POW and died unfortunately of sickness. On October 20, 1945 they were officially delivered to the then Occupation Forces in Japan and sent back to their homes. Since then I have been always praying for the repose of their souls every day.

It is the Buddhist's custom that we hold a memorial service at my temple every year for the repose of these souls. And I have been holding an annual memorial service at my temple every year for 1,086 sacred servicemen. And through all these daily and annual services I have been praying not only for the repose of these souls but also for the true world peace.

The year 1966 is the twentieth anniversary of the end of the last war. And the people of the world seem to have been enjoying the peaceful life everyday. But do you believe that they are really enjoying the world peace now? I dare say they are not, and I also say that if the war would happen again in future, many people would suffer very much from the war and will also have the same or more sad and miserable experiences you had in the past. It will surely be a great tragedy for all the people of the world and I believe that it is our own responsibility that every one of us must think it over very seriously to stop the war, and to try our best for the establishment of world peace in future.

The first memorial grand service praying for the repose of the 1,038 souls and for world peace was solemnly held at my temple in Osaka on October 20, 1955 in memory of the official delivery date of the ashes. Since then the temple was moved to the present site from Osaka and we have built a new Pagoda of World Peace as an enclosed picture. And all the pictures of the late servicemen we received from their bereaved families in eight countries were seriously and solemnly enshrined in this new pagoda.

It is my earnest desire that when we hold a grand memorial service at my temple exactly at 2 o'clock in the afternoon October 20 every year praying for the repose of their souls and for world peace, you will also be kind to join the prayer together with us regardless you are a Buddhist or not.

The annual grand service this year in memory of the twentieth anniversary of the end of the last war will be held at my temple supported by many Buddhist peace organisations in Japan who sincerely and earnestly hope to establish world peace. The grand service on that day will be attended by many leading people in Osaka and they will pray for the repose of the souls of these brave patriots who died for their countries, and at the same time we also pray for world peace expecting there will be no more war in any future.

Though we are several thousand miles away from each other and we have different color and creed, let us join to pray for the repose of these souls and the world peace at 2 p.m. October 20, 1966 when the grand memorial service will be held at the temple in Japan.

Jesus Christ said, "Love your neighbours", and we are the neighbours of the world, and let us love each other and let us try our best to establish world peace forever.

To attain this very serious objective to establish world peace, I am asking your kind cooperation to pray for this very solemn purpose. This is the very reason why I am writing this letter to you.

Please remember that at 2 o'clock in the afternoon October 20 every year, a very solemn grand memorial service praying for the repose of these souls and for world peace is held at Juganji Temple in Osaka, Japan, and I seriously hope from the very bottom of my heart that you will volunteer to join the prayer at that time wherever you may be to attain this very sacred desire of all people in the world.

Hoping that you will always be happy and healthy,

Sincerely yours

(signed) Shinkai Yamaguchi

Shinkai Yamaguchi
Chief Priest
Juganji Temple
12-3 Yamatecho
Hiraoka, Osaka
Japan[32]

APPENDIX 12: ROLL OF HONOUR FOR THE ST JOHN'S AMBULANCE

The St John's Ambulance roll of honour for the war years does not give dates of deaths. The majority were most probably killed in the massacres in and around Wong Nai Chung and Stanley during the fighting, and the others presumably in the occupation years. The only exception known is Lieutenant Potter, shot while aiding the break out from the *Lisbon Maru*. The full list is reproduced here:

Name	Rank	Category	Status
Chan Chung		Military	Killed
Chan Hing Lun		Civilian	Killed
Chan Kin Ting	Corporal	Civilian K.C.O.B.Div.	Killed
Chan Kwan Ping	Corporal	Military Eastern Div	Killed
Chan Lai Chuen		Military	Killed
Chan Ping Shan		Civilian	Killed
Chan Ping Kwong	D/S	Military C.A.A.	Killed
Chan Yiu	Private	Civilian	Killed
Cheng Kwai Chun	Amb Sister	Civilian K.C.N.	Killed

Name	Rank	Unit	Status
Cheung Chung Hong		Civilian	Killed
Chu Hung Wah		Civilian	Killed
Fan Shiu Nam	D/S	Civilian Mongkok Div.	Killed
Fok Fat	Private	Civilian	Killed
Fong Sau Kuen	Lance Corp.	Civilian Mongkok Div.	Killed
Ha Ling		Civilian	Killed
Ho Hin Cheong		Civilian	Killed
Ip Cheong	Lance Corp.	Civilian Motor Transport Div.	Killed
Katima El Arculli		Civilian V.N.	Killed
Kwok Big Chuen		Military S.C.A.A.	Killed
Lai Yuk Ching		Civilian Kowloon N.	Killed
Lau Chun Pong	Sergeant	Civilian	Killed
Lau Man Lim	Private	Civilian	Killed
Leung Hung Kwan		Civilian	Killed
Leung Kwai Fong		Military	Killed
Leung Kwok Wah		Military	Killed
Leung Yat Tung	Corporal	Civilian	Killed
Li Cheuk Wai		Military	Killed
Liu Shing		Military	Killed
Lo Kwan Dic		Civilian	Killed
Lo Kwan Yam	Lance Corp.	Civilian	Killed
Lo Wai Fan		Civilian	Killed
Mo Yee Ching		Civilian L.C.N.	Killed
Ng Wing Chiu		Military	Killed
Pat Yuen		Military	Killed
Potter, Alan Stanley	Corps Officer	Military	U 1.10.42[33]
Shiu Wai		Civilian	Killed
Sin Chi Ling	Private	Military	Killed
Sin Wing		Civilian	Killed
Sin Yuen Ping	Lance Corp.	Military Mongkok Div.	Killed
Tong Chan Ying	Sergeant	Civilian	Killed
Tong Chiu Hon		Civilian	Killed
Tong Hung Lay	Private	Civilian	Killed
Tso Leung	Private	Civilian	Killed
Wan Hau Kwong	Private	Civilian K.C.R.	Killed
Wan Pui Chee		Civilian	Killed
Wong Hon Sing	Private	Civilian Kowloon Godown	Killed
Wong Kam Moon		Civilian	Killed
Wong Kin		Civilian	Killed
Wong Wai	Private	Military Kong Wah Div.	Killed
Yau King Shun	Private	Military	Killed
Yau U Kam	Lance Corp.	Military H.K.Y.M.C.A.	Killed
Yeung Man On		Military	Killed
Yeung Yuet Wah	Sergeant	Civilian Wanchai A Div.	Killed
Yue Yee Chick	Private	Military	Killed

APPENDIX 13: ROLL OF HONOUR FROM 1946 ONWARDS

The survivors of the garrison did not, in general, have an easy time after the war. The majority appear to have suffered mentally, physically, or both from their experiences. Although no formal study has been done, it appears that post-war there were four peaks of deaths. The first was in the period after the liberation until perhaps 1947. Here, men who never really recovered from their experiences passed away.

"In September 1945 the Commander-in-Chief of the British Pacific Fleet requested the New Zealand Government to assist with the provision of hospital facilities for sick prisoners of war and civilian internees from Hong Kong and China and other territories which had been occupied by the Japanese. The Government agreed to receive 400 hospital cases and 500 convalescents. It was arranged that the Health Department through the hospital boards should provide treatment for the hospital cases and that the Army Medical Service should provide accommodation for the convalescents. For the hospital cases Auckland Hospital provided 200 beds, Waikato Hospital 50 beds, Palmerston North Hospital 50 beds, and Hutt Hospital 100 beds. For the convalescent cases the convalescent depots at Raventhorpe and Burnham provided 200 beds each, and the camp hospitals at Papakura[34] and Trentham 150 and 75 respectively.

Records of medical examination and treatment for all service personnel, whether attached to British or Allied forces, were the responsibility of the Army Department, and those for all civilians that of the Social Security Department.

Early in October the Hospital Ship *Tjitjalengka* brought over 300 ex-prisoners of war and internees to Auckland, and the Hospital Ship *Maunganui* brought 362 to Wellington and the South Island. These persons were admitted to hospitals and convalescent depots as arranged, in all cases the actual admissions being proportionately less than originally provided for owing to the lesser number of patients concerned. Of the army medical units, Raventhorpe Convalescent Depot admitted 162 patients, Papakura Camp Hospital 87, Trentham Camp Hospital 25, and Burnham Convalescent Depot 172. These patients remained in New Zealand from six weeks to four months before moving on to their home countries.

Most of them on arrival in New Zealand, however, were debilitated and suffering from avitaminosis, chiefly of the beri-beri type. In general, the severity of this condition varied inversely with the ability of the prisoners to secure fresh food at their various prison camps. Other symptoms associated with avitaminosis were oedema, neuritis, dyspepsia, gall-bladder disease, anaemia and impaired vision. Appropriate diet to supply vitamin deficiencies and enable the prisoners to regain the capacity to eat a fair meal without discomfort were important features of their convalescence.

Their mental condition was in some ways the greatest rehabilitation problem of these ex-prisoners. They were in a hyper-emotional state and at first restless and aimless in their demeanour. With freedom from irksome regulations they gradually reverted to normal and their behaviour was exemplary.

When they left New Zealand's shores most had recovered from beri-beri, and all were heavier, stronger, more physically fit and healthier in mental outlook and very thankful for the care and attention they had received."[35]

Those who died while recuperating in New Zealand and are interred at Auckland (Waikumete) Cemetery (all ex-*Lisbon Maru*):
- Everard, Henry Joseph, Able Seaman, C/JX188399, RN, HMS *Pembroke II*, 17 April 1946. Of Newfoundland.
- Allan, Thomas, Serjeant, 3054398, Royal Scots, 2nd Bn. Died 14 March 1946.
- Minchinton, Leonard Stanley Douglas, Gunner, 850333, Royal Artillery, 30 Heavy Bty. Died Age: 26, 26 January 1946, Son of Charles George and Florence Jessie Minchinton, of Eltham, London, England.

Those who died immediately after the war, but after leaving the forces (such as Lieutenant Harry James Taylor, 7HAA, who died in 1946 "as a result of illness from POW camp" are of course not included in CWGC records. Another example is John Mosionier of the Winnipeg Grenadiers, who died in 1946 in Canada of tuberculosis and is buried in Rose Du Lac Cemetery.

There were also suicides, such as that of nurse Ivy Lily Morgan in August 1947.[36]

Others died in their forties, perhaps (as their families often believe) directly from the effects of their incarceration. Gunner Robert David Curran, for example, joined up from Dingle, Liverpool. He survived the battle of Hong Kong, the *Lisbon Maru*, and POW camps in Japan, but wasn't comfortable with civilian life post war. He rejoined the army, becoming RSM of his Regiment. He died young, aged only 46, as a result — his family says — of his treatment as a POW. William Robert Josiah Wilkinson of 3 Company of the HKVDC was another example; he also never really recovered from the war experience, and died at the age of 44.

Other died of accidents and other causes. Vivian Ferrier of the HKRNVR was killed on 18 October 1951 when he crashed his Lincoln into the wall bordering the junction of Garden Road and the slip road from Upper Albert Road opposite the Helena May Institute. Bill Evans of the same unit, who successfully escaped and evaded from the *Lisbon Maru*, was killed by bandits in Saigon during a brief visit to Indo-China in 1952.

A further peak appeared as these men were in their fifties and sixties. Gunner Stanley Gillmore, wounded on 22 December 1941, died of stomach cancer in Auckland in November 1969, aged 52. His doctors noted that the cancer "may have been caused by shrapnel which they found embedded in the stomach wall". Evan Stewart of the HKVDC had not been properly treated as a POW, and was immediately evacuated to the UK on the hospital ship *Oxfordshire*. After a period in Stoke Manderville Orthopaedic Hospital, he was able to return to Hong Kong in 1947 despite a 'dropped-foot' resulting from an inadequately treated shrapnel wound in his spine. He died in 1958, still headmaster of St Paul's College, aged only 66. Four months after his sixty-fourth birthday, Bill Poulter of the Middlesex Regiment died of a massive heart attack on 31 July 1973. Sergeant Breese, Royal Marines ('he never really recovered'), died in 1976.

At the time of publication, we have already been in the fourth phase for some years. Here, men are passing away in their eighties and nineties. Even while I have been preparing the final draft of this work, we have lost Arthur Gomes, Wallace Hastings, Ken Cambon, Robert Billingham, William Allister and others. One day, only one will be left. The one thing he believed would be a talking point for his whole life — the defence of Hong Kong with some 14,000 colleagues and many others present — will suddenly, shockingly, become a monologue. In silence he will sit alone, contemplating for the last time the fate of all his fallen comrades.

APPENDIX 14: ROLL OF HONOUR: OTHER WARS

Korea

There are many stories of ex-Hong Kong POWs losing their lives in Korea. However, no verifiable examples have as yet come to light. The three Royal Scots fatalities in Korea were all as a result of accidents: Captain Bill Bramall died in a tent fire on 4 March 1953 and Privates James Logan and Ian Stewart drowned in the Imjin on 27 July 1953. The ceasefire was signed 48 hours before the First Battalion arrived on the front line, so there were no battle casualties — and none of the three had served with the Second Royal Scots in Hong Kong.[37]

The Middlesex were heavily engaged in Korea, losing six officers, eleven NCOs, and 25 privates. However, no names or serial numbers of the HK POWs match those lost (although some of the men killed in Korea have serials of WWII vintage).

However, other sources claim that Private Joseph Gallagher, 3054444, Royal Scots — an escaper — died in Korea in 1951,[38] and that another escaper, C.P.O. Telegraphist Gilbert Thums (ex-*Cicala*), was killed in Korea in 1953 by American 'friendly' fire. Thums did not die in Korea; the fate of Gallagher is unknown.

Walter John Butler Keates, a schoolboy interned at Stanley, is recorded on the Roll of Honour at KGV as having lost his life in Korea.

Malaya

Lancelot Searle, the policeman and ex-Stanley internee described as "one of the bravest men I have known" by George Wright-Nooth, was killed on 20 April 1954 with the rank of assistant commissioner, in an ambush in Malaya — a 'friendly fire' encounter in an operation against the Communist Terrorists (CTs), as they were then called. As related above, at least one other Stanley internee also lost her life there.

Suez

Captain David Pinkerton, Royal Scots, who had been seriously wounded in the 1941 fighting in Hong Kong, was killed by either a stray bullet or a sniper in the Suez Campaign of 1956.[39]

Vietnam

A number of Americans served with the Canadian forces in Hong Kong. At least one, John L. McCoy, went on to fight and die in Vietnam. He was a young American jockey who had volunteered for the US Army in 1941. Rejected, he instead went to Canada and enlisted there. He joined the Winnipeg Grenadiers as H/67020 at the age of sixteen and fought in Hong Kong. In 1945, at the age of twenty, he was released from Oeyama POW Camp. He testified at the war crimes trials of the American-born Japanese Oeyama POW camp director in Los Angeles. He then joined the US Army, and during the Korean War served with the 23rd Raiders, conducting reconnaissance patrols and ambushes on strategic hills in no-man's land. In 1953, he was wounded. After serving at Fort Dix, New Jersey as an Escape and Evasion instructor, he volunteered for Vietnam and was sent in June 1964 as a Ranger Advisor. On 26 September 1964, McCoy was engaged in a firefight in a rice paddy when he yelled to a colleague to keep his head down. Seconds later, he was killed by a shot to the head. He was 39.[40]

APPENDIX 15: KANE BUSH

Kane Bush, wife of Lewis Bush of the second MTB Flotilla, was Japanese. At the time of Hong Kong's surrender, she was at Marina House on Queen's Road, but was swiftly taken by the Japanese military to the Exchange Building where she was used as an interpreter. On 2 January, she was arrested by the Kempetai and taken to Eastern Kempetai Headquarters at St George's Building on Chater Road. There she was interrogated for several days, with the Kempetai trying to force her to confess that she was working with Ryutaro Takeuchi (also known as Ryutaro Nosu), a Japanese deserter. Takeuchi had defected from the Chinese border in October 1941, and had volunteered to serve the British. However, the British suspected that he was a 'plant' from Japanese intelligence and thus confined him at Central Police Station.[41]

Next, questions centred around the role of her husband, who the Japanese accused of being involved in British Intelligence.[42] From then on, she was forced to do menial work and was normally woken at three each morning for further interrogations. She was told that her husband had been executed, and was forced to watch the tortures of Chinese civilians "who were subjected to brutal beatings, water poured down their noses, their finger nails set on fire, made to walk on burning charcoal etc. In a dungeon six feet square, thirty or so wretched Chinese were huddled together and starved and tortured and when the dungeon could contain no more they were taken out and beheaded after having been forced to dig their own graves."

In June 1942, Kane Bush was deported to Japan, "being forced to travel in the hold of the steamer like a piece of baggage and not allowed on deck. All my clothes had been confiscated by the kempei and I arrived in Kobe almost naked."

There, she was put under house arrest at her parents' home. When her story became known, she: "[i]mmediately received dozens of letters from various people urging me to commit suicide, telling me that I was a disgrace to the land of my birth and hurling all manner of insults upon me. On one occasion I was picked up in the street by kempei who took me by train to Sakai where I was confronted by a high ranking kempei officer who stared at me without speaking for twenty minutes and then said: 'I only wanted to see the woman who would rather be an enemy than a loyal Japanese'."

Having seen what the Kempetai could do, she concluded: "It is my considered opinion that every member of the kempei should be treated as a war criminal. From the highest to the lowest they are a brutal and inhuman clique who openly boasted of their brutalities towards Chinese, British, and others."

After the war, Lewis and Kaneko Bush returned to Japan.[43]

Notes

Introduction

1 These are the first words of "Willy" Lowe's wartime diary. Lowe was in the Armoured Car Platoon of the HKVDC, and was a POW at Shamshuipo and Innoshima. Eli was his wife Elah Mary Lowe (who herself served with the HKVDC VADs, and spent the war years as a civilian internee at Stanley in Room A1/15). All such quotes from Lowe are taken from a diary in the possession of his family.

Capture

1 All quotes from Hewitt are taken from his book, *Bridge with Three Men*.
2 For a blow-by-blow account of the fighting, and an analysis of these deaths, see Tony Banham, *Not the Slightest Chance*.
3 A number inflated by numerous Indian soldiers who escaped from various duties in Hong Kong and around China. See Appendix 7.
4 See G. S. P Heywood, *Rambles in Hong Kong*, p. 101.
5 There were many escapes and evasions from Hong Kong, beginning on 8 December and ending with the last escapes in 1944. Many of these men went on to fight in clandestine units in China, and also more conventional units elsewhere. However, their activities outside POW camps are also outside the scope of this work.
6 All quotes from Ross are from the memoirs kindly supplied by his son. Ross escaped from Hong Kong on 25 December 1941.
7 Fragmented bones and a helmet were found by workers digging just north of Argyle Street, Kowloon, in April 2004. Despite the fact that I believed them most likely the remains of Gray, conscientious and skilful work by the Canadian Department of National Defence finally proved, in November 2007, that they were not.
8 However, it seems plausible that some of the Indian prisoners initially housed at Argyle Street would have been captured here.
9 All quotes from Marsh come from his memoirs.
10 This quote comes from Bevan Field's long and detailed diary, held by his grandson.

11 From "Report of the Director of Public Works for the year 1939": "Camp for Chinese Interned Soldiers: The site is at Argyle Street, Kowloon, and the work consisted of the erection of a hutment camp of timber construction with concrete floors, except the kitchen which has brick walls and a roof covered with asbestos sheets, together with water and fire services, drainage, channels, recreation ground and approach road. The camp is surrounded by a wire mesh fence with barbed wire entanglements and seven sentry watch towers are provided. There are eleven sleeping huts with accommodation in each one for seventy two persons; one dining hut; one kitchen with store and office; one sanitary hut containing latrines, ablution and wash house; one hospital hut with an office for the medical officer, three wards for eight, four and two persons respectively, dispensary, store and latrines; two huts for the outer and inner police guards with an office, quarters, mess room, kitchen, store and lavatories; a gate keeper's hut; lock up; incinerator and refuse bunker. The contract was let to Messrs. Tung Shan and Company on 17th October and the work was satisfactorily completed on 15th December."
12 All quotes from Trick are from his diary, held by his son, and from a transcript of an earlier interview.
13 From the Government Gazette: "Public Works Department. No. S288. It is hereby notified that sealed tenders in triplicate, which should be clearly marked 'Tender for a Refugee Camp, North Point' will be received at the Colonial Secretary's Office until noon of Tuesday, the 6th day of September, 1938, for erecting temporary wooden huts for sleeping, dining, kitchens, latrines & quarters, etc., surface water channels, drains, and fences, etc. As security for the proper performance of the works under this contract, the successful tenderer will be required to deposit, in cash, a sum of $2,000 with the Accountant-General. No work will be permitted on Sundays. For form of tender, specification, and further particulars apply at this Office. The Government does not bind itself to accept the lowest or any tender. R. M. Henderson, *Director of Public Works*, 16th August 1938."
14 Riley appears in the Stanley list as James Riley Ryan. See Grant Garneau, *The Royal Rifles of Canada in Hong Kong*, p. 181.
15 Presumably either Richard Alfred Wynne, or Charles T. Wallington.
16 All quotes from Hart are from personal correspondence or interviews with the author. The Japanese attacks he witnessed were across St Stephen's College playing fields.
17 This work uses current spellings for the text (thus it would have been "Wong Nai Chung Gap" in this example), but retains earlier spellings in quotes.
18 All quotes from O'Toole are from his diary, kindly transcribed by Mike Peaker.
19 In the next morning, the survivors were forced to cremate all the bodies, including those from the heavy fighting in the area. Witnesses speak of perhaps 150 bodies altogether. A memorial was built in the old cemetery. Stericker, writing about the massacre, noted: "It must be noted that when we arrived in [Stanley Camp] we found the remains of the victims amongst

20 Williams' quotes are taken from her war crimes trials dispositions. Miss Williams had helped a nurse escape at five o'clock on the morning of the 26th by dressing her in a Chinese gown. She had got through to Bowen Road Hospital with the story, and they had informed Selwyn-Clarke.
21 All quotes from Forsyth are taken from his diary.
22 Young's account is taken from materials loaned by Lt.-Col. E. E. Denison, E. D. to Grant Garneau, and kindly supplied by the latter. A longer account appears in his book, *The Royal Rifles of Canada in Hong Kong*.
23 On 28 December, according to Young.
24 Davidson's quotes are from an account of his experiences held by his daughter.
25 Although Murray House has today been reassembled at Stanley, in 1941 it — and the rest of the barracks — was in Central.
26 All quotes from Bush are taken from his book *The Road to Inamura*.
27 For his wife's unique experiences, turn to Appendix 15.
28 This was Major Dewar, an Australian attached to the RASC. An RAOC Ammunition Examiner (AE) present on the occasion, in 2007 told me: "66 years on, and at the age of 92 I still remember Major Dewar with respect and admiration. He was a soldiers' officer, friendly, decisive, and courageous. Someone you could trust and believe in, and that was something of a rarity in Hong Kong in 1941."
29 New to Hong Kong, Briggs had left Pasadena, California, on 14 August 1941, to return to the Far East for his employer, Standard Vacuum Oil Company. All quotes from Briggs are from his memoirs, *Taken in Hong Kong*, though the version used here was the original manuscript kindly supplied by his daughter.
30 All quotes from Proulx are from his book, *Underground from Hong Kong*.
31 Email communication with author.
32 From an annotated version of Barbara Anslow's (née Redwood) diary, which she kindly gave to the author. The original version is at the Imperial War Museum.
33 All quotes from Hill are taken from his diary.
34 All quotes from Evans are taken from his book, *Rollcall at Oeyama*.
35 All quotes from Whitehead are from his book, *Escape to Fight On* (co-authored by George B. Bennett).
36 All quotes from Fisher are from his book, *I Will Remember*.
37 From a report by Baugh held by the family of Major Munro, with whom Baugh would later escape. Baugh was killed before the war's end, flying the hump.
38 This work included a list of St John's Ambulance orderlies who lost their lives in the period from December 1941 to August 1945, and those names are repeated in Appendix 12.
39 The original date in CWGC records is 22 December 1944. It must be assumed that this date is in error, and that Corporal Ryan should be added to the list of those lost during the RAOC/RASC massacres in Hong Kong on 22/23 December 1941.

40 As for Ryan in the above note, the CWGC date in Stacey's case being 22-23 December 1944.

41 Two Petty Officer Youngs died this day, hence the unfortunate omission of one. From a damaged letter from Henry Collingwood Selby (*Redstart*'s commander) to Young's wife: "Prior to the fall of Hong Kong, I was . . . HMS *Redstart*. I have recently been . . . from the POW camp there and, at last, have obtained your address. I am writing to convey my deepest sympathy at the loss of your husband. SPO Young was a man I much admired and appreciated in having in my ship. His sensible kindliness and good humour did much, I feel, to make the *Redstart* the happy little ship that she was. When we landed to assist the soldiers, SPO Young came with my party. On the morning of Sunday 21st December 41, we were attacking a bungalow which was in the possession of the enemy. After a little, I got knocked out by a couple of bullets and a bit later pulled myself together and began to crawl away. As I did so, I became aware that SPO Young was lying alongside me seriously wounded. He was in a drowsy state from loss of blood but managed to recognise me and then, with the most marvelous unselfishness, he said, "I've got some rum and water in my bottle sir, wouldn't you like to take a swig?" I simply cannot express my admiration at the wonderful Christian spirit he exhibited when he was so far gone himself. . . . arrived at the dressing station . . . a party was sent out but arrived just . . . passed away. I was told that he wouldn't have suffered much as the loss of blood would have made him drowsy. He rests in a very beautiful spot high on a hillside with a view of the blue waters and picturesque junk harbour of Aberdeen."

1942

1 It has not proved possible to accurately enumerate these evaders, as no complete lists of Chinese members of local forces appear to exist. However, BAAG records show a very large number passing through their hands in China in the early months after the Group was formed.

2 Although the Stanley Camp was for civilians, a number of older members of the HKVDC were interned there. The Hong Kong Police Force was also resident, minus a few of their number who were in Shamshuipo, having been captured during the short period that the police officially acted as a militia force against the invaders. Other civilian internment centres would later be opened at Rosary Hill and Ma Tau-wai.

3 From document 10591, NARA: Article 1: The term 'intern,' as used in these Regulations, shall mean the detaining of enemy nationals or neutrals at a specified place with the purpose of restricting their activities and of extending protection to them; the term 'army internee' shall mean any enemy national or neutral interned; and the term 'internment camp' shall mean any such place in which an army internee is interned.

4 All quotes from Goodwin are from his book *Hongkong Escape*.

5   All quotes from Wright-Nooth are taken from his book *Prisoner of the Turnip Heads*.
6   Letter to author.
7   These included the Bacteriological Institute, Kowloon Hotel, Stag Hotel, Hong Kong Hotel, the University of Hong Kong, La Salle Relief Hospital, Luk Hoi Tong Boarding House, Maryknoll First Aid Post, Mee Chow Hotel, the Exchange Building (British staff of the Hong Kong Telephone Company), the Peak, the Mental Hospital, Matilda Relief Hospital, New Asia Hotel, Nam King Hotel, Nam Ping Hotel, the Chinese YMCA, Kowloon Hotel, the Prison Hospital, St Paul's Hospital, Sun Wah Hotel, Tung Fong Hotel, Tai Koon Hotel, University Relief Hospital, and the War Memorial Hospital.
8   John Stericker worked for British American Tobacco. Quotes here are taken from his book, *A Tear for the Dragon*.
9   Uniquely, at time of writing it is almost perfectly preserved. While many buildings have been added to the area, and the cemetery was extended during and after the war, only four of the original buildings have been demolished.
10 Correspondence with author.
11 All quotes from Baird are from his book, *Letters to Harvelyn*.
12 Although the first to take this route very probably were relatively recent refugees to Hong Kong, before long many resident families would follow.
13 Lee had originally served in 3 Coy, HKVDC.
14 Although others had simply walked out of camps before any formal security was established, this was probably the first real escape. All successful British escapes from Hong Kong would be made between this date and April, although one New Zealander would escape in 1944, and numerous Indian personnel would escape once they were removed from Hong Kong. It should be noted that almost all the British escapes were led by, or comprised entirely of, men with considerable experience of the region. The Canadians of C Force had no such experience to fall back on, though on one occasion would try to escape anyway. However, the only successful Canadian escape was by Proulx of the HKRNVR, who had lived in Hong Kong for a considerable time.
15 Ride's was arguably the most significant single escape, as later he would form the British Army Aid Group in China and would facilitate many other escapes and evasions, as well as aiding those in the Camps, assisting shot-down aircrew, and providing vast quantities of high-quality intelligence to the Allies.
16 Jones, always a noticeable man, caused great comment by arriving in a woman's fur coat which he had found in the house in Fanling where he and the others were initially held.
17 From document No. 1547-A, Exhibit No. 1960, NARA: "Japanese rules for hospitals: 1. The medical treatment of prisoners of war who are patients (henceforth called patients) shall as a general rule be rendered at an infirmary established at the prisoner of war camp (henceforth called the camp). Those prisoners of war patients requiring special treatment or suffering from contagious diseases may be admitted to an army hospital by an arrangement made between the commandant of the camp and the director of the nearest

army hospital. 8. Documents for evidence such as clinical diaries and death certificates shall be prepared in the same manner as that prescribed for the Army and they shall be kept in safe custody." The scale of the damage in the position — still extant — in which Thompson was wounded makes it very surprising that any of these men survived.

18 Food was naturally a dominating topic for all POWs. Diaries attest to continuous discussions on recipes, meals once had, and meals to be. Some diaries consist of nothing but lists of foods received in camp, while the more sophisticated diaries (Coxhead's, for example) often include running commentaries on all that was comestible. Although this was such an important topic at the time, I have limited the coverage in this work so as to reserve space for other subjects.

19 All Priestwood quotes are from her book, *Through Japanese Barbed Wire*. As this was published in 1944, following a successful escape, the author did not believe it appropriate to reveal names and details of those still in Japanese hands. This quote is from page 42.

20 Fisher noted that he was initially in hut E1. In April, he would move to C5, and then B4. It seems that such moves were common as POWs came into and out of Shamshuipo.

21 The bungalow, still inhabited at time of writing, had been fought over to the death twice on 25 December. Initially a mixed force of Middlesex and 1st Battery HKVDC had held the building until the Japanese brought up flame-throwers. Later, D Company of the Royal Rifles of Canada had recaptured it during a counter attack, before being pushed out in turn. In January 1945, it would be the scene of yet more deaths.

22 Brown uses the pseudonym 'Bayne' for their leader (though possibly by accident, as Brown was a notoriously poor observer). See *Hong Kong Aftermath*, p. 129.

23 All quotes from Gittins are from her book, *Stanley: Behind Barbed Wire*.

24 Their role, according to Frank King's comprehensive *The History of The Hongkong and Shanghai Banking Corporation*, Volume III, p. 573, was "to assist in the liquidation of the Bank".

25 Banfill had been captured at the Salesian Mission, a medical post at which most of those captured were marched out to a catchwater above the building, and shot.

26 Bertram was a New Zealand reporter who had joined 1 Bty HKVDC at the last minute and had taken part in the defence of Stanley. All quotes are taken from his book, *Shadow of a War*, which had the advantage of being written soon after liberation. (The book was also published under the title, *Beneath the Shadow*.)

27 While the focus of this work is purely the Hong Kong garrison, it should be noted that this crew were from submarine *O-20* which had left Singapore on 16 December 1941, and was sunk by Japanese destroyers off Kota Baru on 19 December. The crew, minus their captain and six others who went down with the boat, were picked up on the 20th. The wreck was discovered

in 2002 approximately 35 miles northeast of Kota Baru at a depth of 44 metres.
28 Ride Papers, Series 13, No. 11, p. 8.
29 This was in response to a query, via Argentina, from the British government. Document No. 847 F, Exhibit No. 1956, NARA.
30 Baugh's quotes come from his official report.
31 National Archives WO 0103/3619. These numbers exclude Internees at Stanley.
32 However, the Japanese claimed they had been executed, and produced three headless corpses in uniform.
33 See Fairclough, *Brick Hill and Beyond*. This quote is from page 42.
34 Although no exact date is given, it appears this visit, chosen as being representative, was between 1 February and 22 February.
35 This comes from a 1999 letter to Alan Gray, to whom I owe these details. While their fellow POWs believed the move was made as punishment for the escapes, the RAF men believed the Japanese wanted to interrogate them about RAF techniques in the battle for Singapore. Fortunately for them, Singapore fell shortly after they arrived and they were soon shipped back to Hong Kong.
36 Some attempts at sabotage were made. Alexander Gordon, Royal Scots: "Working party at oil dump Aberdeen, Hong Kong. Piercing oil drums putting sand in oil. Only small damage possible." WO344/378/2.
37 Taken from Vos Dos Macaenses de Vancouber, Vol. 3, No. 4, November 2001.
38 At Saikung he met Hank Marsman, a Dutch/American businessman who had stayed out of camp by claiming Filipino nationality, and was also on his way to China.
39 Bentley would later run the Hong Kong Government Relief Office from a houseboat at Kukong.
40 Governor Young and his batman Waller arrived at Karenko Camp, Taiwan, on 15 September 1942. In all, 117 senior officers and governors were sent to Tamazato on the east coast on 2 April 1943 to 5 June 1943 — 28 of the top officers and governors were separated from the rest. The remaining 89 returned to Karenko Camp on that date, though this camp closed later that month and they transferred to Shirakawa on the west side of Taiwan. On 23 June, the twenty-eight started on their journey to Taihoku, arriving the following day and going into Taihoku Camp #5 at Mucha. They remained there until 5 October 1944 when Generals Percival and Wainwright and some of the governors and others were moved by train to Heito Camp in the south of the island and then flown to Japan the next day, and from there to the camp at Cheng-Tai-tun. On 10 October, about 350 senior officers and enlisted men left Shirakawa for Keelung and were transported on the hellship *Oryoku Maru* to Moji and from there on to Cheng Tai-tun. On 1 December, 16 of the senior officers and governors and their batmen (32 in total) were moved to Hsi-an Camp about 100 miles north of Shenyang. Here they stayed until liberated by the Americans and the Russians. The rest spent the long winter

at Cheng Tai-tun and suffered greatly from the lack of food and the cold. The men refused to do any work so on 20 May 1945. They were moved to the main camp at Shenyang where they finished out the war. I am indebted to Michael Hurst, MBE, for his help in this area of research.
41 I have only included mentions of death in this work if they add something to our knowledge of the circumstances. Many diaries record the passing of individuals, but without adding any more information than appears in the rolls at the end of each year.
42 All such quotes are taken from Gray's war crime affidavit.
43 Quotes from Oxley are taken from his diary.
44 The two Royal Scots repaid the guerrillas who helped them by giving them extensive training in the use of the British arms (specifically 2-inch mortars, the Vickers gun and anti-tank rifles) that had been found after the fall of Hong Kong. Their escape is further documented in WO 106/3560. Grimsdale was Military Attache; he sent this report to GHQ India on 2 June 1942.
45 Cambon attributes his survival to 'M & B sulfa tablets' given to him by Gunn. All quotes from Cambon are taken from his book, *Guest of Hirohito*.
46 From "Report of the Director of Public Works for the year 1939": "Hospital Huts for Refugee Camps at King's Park, Ma Tau Chung and North Point: The erection of a hut of timber construction with a concrete floor at each of the three camps, containing three wards for twelve children, four females, and two males respectively, a consulting room for the medical officer, dispensary, store, lavatories and drainage, was commenced on 30th September and completed on 15th December. The contract was let to Messrs Sang Lee & Company" (these camps had been listed as completed in the 1938 report, but in fact minor work was still being done in 1939).
47 Poulter's diary records: "One roll call we had was over two men of the Royal Engineers that escaped. A few days later the Japs said they had caught them and shot them, maybe it's true, as we never saw them again." This was a remarkably persistent rumour, with others claiming that the bodies were seen. The two sappers were Ferguson and Howarth.
48 She had died through worry and anxiety about her son, two days earlier on 27 February.
49 Called 'Anthony Bathurst' in Priestwood's account, as he was — at time of publication in 1944 — still with the British forces in China. (Anthony Bathurst was the name of a fictional detective in a series of books that spanned the war.)
50 Such stories, though inexact, were not uncommon.
51 Ride Papers, Series 9, No. 24, pp. 12–17.
52 He was given shelter at the house of a colleague's wife until February 1943. Making his way to BAAG in China, Salter arrived back in the UK on 12 August, and reported for duty with No. 1 Infantry Depot, Redford Barracks, Edinburgh on 11 September, after a short period of leave. WO 208/3035.
53 Chia Kee Sian was released 16 May. Ride Papers, Series 11, No. 10, p. 29.

54 They returned to Stanley on 20 June 1944. For unknown reasons, Wright-Nooth's account of this escape refers to Bidmead as 'Smythe'.
55 All quotes from Bosanquet are from his book *Escape through China*. Clague would go on to an extremely important role in BAAG, culminating in being flown into Thailand at the end of the war in Operation Swansong to ensure the safe release of some 30,000 surviving Allied POWs there.
56 All quotes from Laite are taken from his diary.
57 The only Indian officer to be interned there was Kamta Prasad of the Punjabis. Ansari of the Rajputs also held the King's Commission, but stayed with his men in Ma Tau Chung. The other ethnically Indian officers were VCOs (Viceroy Commissioned Officers).
58 Charles Barman was in charge of all Other Ranks in Argyle Street.
59 For more on the possible consequences of this visit, see Appendix 9.
60 His father, Sapper Andrew Spoov of the HKVDC was a POW. The Stanley Internees on board also included Evelyn Boyd, William Hunt (American), and Irene Spice Raymond.
61 The entry continued with the strange text, 'Our troops at Saarbrucken, fighting in Malaya'.
62 Document No. 1547-A, Exhibit No. 1960, NARA. An expanded version of this text is also in the files, dated a month later. It can be assumed that all POW Camp commanders were familiar with this instruction.
63 All quotes are from Wiseman's book, *Recollections of a British Prisoner of War*. He was there for eighteen days before being moved to Argyle Street, his original destination. The imprisonment had resulted from a letter to a fellow POW being found smuggled in his wooden leg. In Argyle Street he was in the hut commanded by Major Curran, with the 5AA and small units such as the RAF, RAPC, CMP, RASC, RAOC.
64 When returning from Bowen Road to the POW Camps, it was not unusual to be asked to take drugs back for the 'hospitals' at the latter. For example, Maurice Parker records: "The day we were going out, a Doctor gave us small packages of pills, tablets and drugs that we were to conceal on our person and hand over to another medical Officer in whatsoever camp we were sent. We were searched both on leaving the Hospital and upon arriving at our new place. The man who was taking the most chance was the one who had given us the drugs at the Hospital but we got away with it."
65 The wife of Hargreaves Howell, who would later lead the escape from the *Lisbon Maru*. There is still a school of dance in her name in Hong Kong today.
66 Bickley of the RAMC had lost his sight when guiding a lorry load of wounded from Tai Tam to Bowen Road Hospital. Japanese machine guns opened up on the vehicle, showering him with broken glass from the windscreen.
67 This is possible. At around this time, director Tanaka Shigeo was making *The Battle of Hong Kong*, produced by the Dai Nippon Film Company, which was first shown in cinemas on the first anniversary of the battle.
68 A full-length report on the American experience in Stanley, by the US Consul Samuel Sokobin (written on board the *Gripsholm*) is at CO 980/120 26243.

George E. Baxter, former manager of the Hong Kong Bureau United Press Associations, also wrote a report. See bibliography.

69 Thus Heyworth, in effect, engineered his escape from Hong Kong. Those transferred included: Norris Asquith, Leonard Bidmead, Aubrey Burgoyne, the Cammiades, Andrew & Winifred Christie, Richard Down, Reginald Duncan, Arthur Ffoulkes, Norman Fox, Ronald Fuller, Ray Gabbat, Alfred Glover, Harold Goddard, William Gomershall, George Hankinson, Alexander Harvey, Sydney Hayes, Edmund Hewitt, Roger Heyworth, Arthur Hill, Henry Hobden, Lilian Hope, Winifred Howkins, Percival Jennings, Stanley Johnson, Joseph Leslie, Arthur Lindsay, Percy Maley, Cyril Marshall, Eugenia Martin, Cecil Mason, Charles Mitchell, Denis Palfreeman, Edith Palmer, the Pearsons (Godfrey, Suzanne, and Wilfred), Henry Proud, Stanley & Alfred Rogers, George Shepherd, Robert Southerton, Thomas Spedding, and William Ward.

70 The three who would survive were all later shipped to Japan, two of them in the first draft of 'undesirables'.

71 All Plumber's statements are from the report of No. 1 Canadian War Crime Investigation Unit.

72 Two Connollys were in the HKVDC, and may have been brothers of Paul (who was in the HKDDC). It is not clear which is referred to here.

73 This was Corporal Hurn. On the subject of food, Jim Hart also reported: "Quite a few officers had dogs. The Royal Artillery were selling soup for cigarettes for months afterwards. All of a sudden, there were no dogs!" (Conversation with author.)

74 Reported by James Gray, RAMC, in his war crimes affidavit. This was presumably Corporal Leonard Hunt, RAF, though many diphtheria deaths had already occurred in St Teresa's.

75 All quotes from Bowie are taken from his account, "Captive Surgeon in Hong Kong".

76 From a report that Stott wrote to Lindsay Ride at Guilin, 6 October 1942, now in the Ride Papers at the University of Hong Kong Library Special Collections.

77 Tse Dickuan's report, mentioning this incident, is quoted in full in *The Sinking of The Lisbon Maru: Britain's Forgotten Wartime Tragedy*, Appendix 2.

78 Parker commanded D Company, Royal Rifles of Canada. All quotes are from his diary. Ferguson and Howarth's escape seems to have gone almost unnoticed, though later the Japanese would claim that they had been shot and show Boon two unknown but presumably uniformed bodies to identify.

79 From the report of No. 1 Canadian War Crime Investigation Unit.

80 The Canadians also interviewed Corporal Harris 6201831 of the Middlesex who had been in PB19 at Repulse Bay during the fighting, and confirmed that Berzenski had shared the same pillbox.

81 Aside from these two parties, two other men who were executed after an escape attempt are buried in Hong Kong. These are Thomas Henry Fletcher and Henry Edward Weeks of MV *Tantalus*. *Tantalus* had been towed from Hong Kong to Manila in December 1941, and was bombed off Bataan during the Japanese attack on the Philippines. All the crew were taken prisoner when

Manila fell, with these two men being executed on 15 February 1942 after a failed escape. After the war, they were re-interred in Hong Kong.

82 Lowe actually believed they were going on the *Lisbon Maru*. This is probably explained by the fact that both drafts boarded in September, and the *Lisbon Maru* had been docked in Hong Kong for some time.

83 All numbers listed here are the actual counts of the names of the men shown as being on each vessel in the Shamshuipo camp list, with some later corrections. Transliterations vary for many of the names of the ships. Most men did not know the name of this vessel. To quote James Ford, MC: "A comrade of mine told me that it was the *Fukuku Maru* — but I think that was a POW jest." (Letter to author.)

84 Example POW Index Cards from this draft read: WO 344/393/1 Albert Ernest Moralee, Middlesex, 10 Derby Terrace, South Shields:

Sham Shui Po	25.12.41 — 3.9.42	
Tokyo No. 3	15.9.42 — 20.3.44	Sqdrn Ldr. Burchell
Tokyo D13	20.3.44 — 12.5.45	Captain Marsden
Kamaishi	14.5.45 — 9.9.45	Captain Grady (US)

And: Gunner Job I Bevan: Shamshuipo — departed 4/9/42 — Shi Maru?
Tokyo No2, 15/9/42 to 13/1/43 — Oi/c Sqn Ldr Birchall RCAF
Tokyo mil Hospital, 13/1/43 to 8/8/43
Shinagawa POW Hospital, 8/8/43 to 12/10/43
Tokyo No 2, 12/10/43 to 20/03/44 — Oi/c Sqn Ldr Birchall RCAF
Tokyo 13 detachment — 20/03/44 to 12/5/45 — Oi/c Capt Marsden RCS
Kamaishi POW camp — 12/5/45 to 9/8/45 (release) — Oi/c Capt Grady H.S.A.S Corps??

85 Letter to author. Ford's brother, Douglas, would later be executed by the Japanese.

86 Blomfield's diary is in the Imperial War Museum. See pp. 56–57: "composition of the camp: including a description of the arrival of prisoners from Hong Kong on 15 September 1942."

87 When the POWs left to go to Omori, Shinagawa became an important POW hospital.

88 Price may have been the oldest POW to be taken to Japan. Born in 1889, he was educated in Eltham College and was a graduate of Edinburgh medical school and a qualified surgeon. He served in the Great War, and by April 1941 was based in Amoy, China, from where he wrote: "about two months ago I heard that it was possible to get RAMC commissions out in the Far East. They made me go down to Hong Kong to be medically examined, but I am fit enough and now it is all fixed. I have to report at Hong Kong when my affairs are in order." Interestingly, and perhaps because he received his commission where and when he did, he is not mentioned in Drew's *Medical Officers in the British Army 1660–1960*. Thanks to Ceri Harris.

89 Leonard J. Birchall was dubbed the 'Saviour of Ceylon' after the war by Sir Winston Churchill. Early on 4 April 1942, Birchall and his eight-man crew boarded their Catalina flying boat and began a day-long patrol southeast of

Ceylon. Towards the end of the mission they sighted a large Japanese naval force heading towards Ceylon, intending to surprise the Royal Navy there. As they came under fighter attack, Birchall and his crew sent signals to alert Allied units on Ceylon, allowing them time to prepare their defence. After ditching, they were picked up by a Japanese destroyer and taken prisoner.

90 All quotes from Birchall are from an interview with Dr Charles Roland recorded on 22 February 1986.
91 From a post-war letter provided by Roger Mansell.
92 Birchall's diary, which was turned over to the US authorities in Yokohama, contains details of Red Cross issues, complete with notes of Jap pilfering. "So far as I remember, we received: Christmas 42 1 British parcel per man; Spring 43 British food (corned beef, cereal, dried fruit, cocoa, sugar, salt in bulk); Christmas 43 1 American parcel per man; Spring 44 1 American parcel per man. All I can remember is that, in all the time I was in Japan, I received 78 [7–8?] letters or postcards, and sent 7 letters or postcards and 1 [one] 200 word radio message."
93 Ride Papers, Series 10, No. 33, p. 18. Many students, several hundred in total, escaped from the University of Hong Kong, but one small group was captured and executed trying to escape via Tai Po. See Chan Lau Kit-ching and Peter Cunich (ed.), *An Impossible Dream: Hong Kong University from Foundation to Re-establishment, 1910–1950*, pp. 111–112.
94 See *The Maryknoll Mission, Hong Kong 1941–46*.
95 Morley wrote: "Thank you very much for the info on Paul Connolly. My mind is now at rest. Did I tell you that we did make an attempt in the early days but were observed by a sentry and had to get back quick? I knew he would try again but would not put me at risk. He was the best friend I have ever had. Thank you once again." (Letter to author.)
96 Some would be removed from the draft before they were ferried out to the ship, and a lucky few more were actually removed from the ship before she sailed.
97 All quotes from Poulter are from his diary.
98 This draft is fully documented elsewhere. See Tony Banham, *The Sinking of the Lisbon Maru*.
99 From an account provided to the author.
100 All quotes from Wright are from his book, *I Was a Hell Camp Prisoner*.
101 This quote from Hamilton is taken from his unpublished memoir, "Prisoner of War in Hong Kong and Japan".
102 Speller had also noticed the mixed opinions on Ashton-Rose: "I can only speak well of him. Whether he was only a Lieutenant or what he was, that part of it I could care less. As a medical doctor, to me, he knew what he what he was talking about, to me he did everything to restore my eyesight, and did that. I can't remember a day went by 'Well young feller how are you today?' I can only speak too well of Ashton Rose. I've heard all kinds of stories about him after. But for me he was a gentlemen and he was a good doctor, and he certainly looked after me, so I can only speak as I find." All quotes

from Speller are from an interview with Dr Charles Roland recorded on 27 May 1990.
103 In Dora's tiny cottage at time of writing, part of a small cupboard is 'Wilf's Corner' containing the few possessions that he had salvaged from his Service days. Amongst them is the photograph of a pretty sixteen-year-old Dora that he had managed to keep hidden from the Japanese throughout those years, and next to it a sprig of heather that they had picked on the last day before he had been sent overseas. Thanks to Andrew Suddaby for this quote.
104 Letter to author.
105 Actually five Canadians and one British, though on the same day in Japan a further six ex-*Lisbon Maru* men died.
106 Budden would never be reunited with his family. He died as a POW a year later.
107 I am indebted to Kathleen Porter, sister of John Cassidy RN (who died in Japan the following year) for this message. The exact date of the broadcast is not clear from the headings, and could be either 11 October or 15 October; 15 October seems more likely. Many further broadcasts were made by POWs as the war went on, with the next being on 29 October. In some cases, such as Kenneth Baird's message of 17 December 1943 from Hong Kong, the broadcast was read by a Japanese announcer.
108 As Norah Stutchbury, she would be murdered by guerrillas in Malaya when her transport was ambushed in the summer of 1950. Redwood's diaries also mention Stanley internee Joyce Moxon, who became a headmistress postwar, and lost her life in one of the infamous De Haviland Comet crashes.
109 Ichioka Ward was established under the stand of Osaka municipal field athletic ground at Yawataya-Matsuno-cho, Minato-ku, Osaka City in October 1942, and closed in July 1944. When it was closed, Kobe POW Hospital was established at Kumochi-cho 1-chome, Fukiai-ku, Kobe City and the POW patients were transferred there. There was only one other dedicated POW Hospital in Japan during WW2: Shinagawa Hospital, which was established in 1943. However, POWs sometimes entered the Japanese Army Hospitals or the Hospitals attached to the companies that employed POWs. The army hospitals used by POWs were: Hiroshima Military Hospital, Kokura Military Hospital, Osaka Military Hospital, Sagamihara Military Hospital (at Sagamihara City, Kanagawa Prefecture, Tokyo) and Tokyo #2 Military Hospital.
110 Correspondence with author.
111 Stericker noted: "Where there is youth there is generally a certain amount of happiness, and the young men and maidens were not slow to make the most of things. After a time there was a good deal of pairing-off. This latter could be divided into two groups; the permanent and the convenient."
112 Note that the very large number of Indian escapes precludes the inclusion of all but a representative few. See Appendix 7.
113 All from AWM PR/82/068 — Series 10, No. 31, p. 33.
114 Red Cross parcels were enormously important to the POWs, and their

distribution disrupted all other focuses for days. Diaries discuss in great detail the contents, how they were swapped and exchanged, and how they were eked out over weeks in order to bring taste to otherwise excruciatingly dull diets. I have resisted the temptation in this work, to report on each and every distribution; but those involved in their manufacture, packaging, and delivery should be in no doubt as to the high esteem in which they were held by the recipients.

115 Oxley continued: "... I was determined I was not going like that. I knew of a civilian in the camp who had a rough-haired lavatory brush ... he let me have it. I went to a makeshift shower where there was nobody around, took my shorts off, stood under the shower, and scrubbed my back until all the big sores were gone. The blood ran down my legs; how could I stop it?"
116 The only other person to die that day there was Mann, Rifleman Maxwell Alastair.
117 These included the Begleys (Australian), Victor Billon, the Binks, Sir and Lady Blackburn, Margaret Davies, John and Robert Davis, Linda Day, Arthur and Charles Evans, Joseph Faly, Dorothy Focken, the Gilchrists, the Greenalands, Harry Greenwood, Sidney Herrett, Richard Knox, Mrs Manners, the Metcalfes, Thomas and Donald Mulholland, the Murdochs, Walter Noble, Laurence Olsen, William O'Neill, Melville Pearce, Henry Reed, Percy Rosser, Alexander and Nina Smith, Andrew Swanson, Douglas and Edith Weir, Reginald Westcombe, Edward Williams, the Woulfes, Ethel Wyllie, and Smith Yates.
118 Delaney, Polson, Gillies, Wojnarsky, and Remer were hospitalized at the QMH on 28 December.
119 Causes of death are taken from a number of sources including HK PRO HKRS 112-1-1 (the 'Provisional List' which contains the remaining wartime hospital records) and the Ride Papers for Hong Kong, NARA for Japan camp records and Shinagawa, Kobe, Tokyo and other hospitals (cross-checked with the Japan POW Network), previous research for *The Sinking of the Lisbon Maru* (and associated CWGC records), personal diaries and unit records in private and public hands.
120 QMH records include a Private Foster, J. HKVDC who was hospitalized on 26 December at QMH and died either on 27 December 1941 or 4 January 1942. As no one of that name is officially recognized as dying, this may be a duplicate of Polson, J.
121 Wounded at Wong Nai Chong Gap police station on 19 December and taken to QMH. Leg amputated.
122 Died of grenade wounds sustained near PB 29, morning of 22 December.
123 Grenade shrapnel wounds sustained on 20 December.
124 Wanchai. Originally buried RNH.
125 Multiple wounds, toxaemia. Had been wounded at Wong Nai Chung Gap.
126 Compound fracture of leg, multiple GSW.
127 Shot in both knees at North Point Power Station.
128 A number of such partial records for Chinese personnel imply that they actually died out of the camp, possibly after evading capture.

129 Intestinal obstruction.
130 An 'Unknown' for a regular at this date is unusual.
131 Had been wounded on 25 December.
132 Initially hospitalized on 22 December, at QMH, then transferred to SAH.
133 From toxic poisoning caused by eating soil.
134 Multiple injuries. Killed by a landslide at Kai Tak.
135 Wiseman: "He had been a lab technician in the hospital dispensary where he had been making 'hooch' and had drunk so much that it killed him. The Nips regarded him as a hero, driven to suicide by the shame of the Surrender, and gave him a slap-up funeral to which all the doctors, nurses and up-patients had to go."
136 CWGC internal documents give an alternate date of 3 April.
137 Compound fracture of the skull, septic GSW.
138 Initially taken to QMH, 25 December, with GSW.
139 His brothers Leslie and Robert also died during the war. Leslie was in the King's Own Royal Regiment and died on 14 July 1943. He is buried in Poland. Robert was in the Royal Corps of Signals and died on 15 September 1943. He is buried at Kanchanaburi, Thailand. Basnett had been wounded on 9 December.
140 In 1946, Sergeant Kawamoto was executed, having been found guilty of killing Lloyd through water torture. The annotated list of POWs which was smuggled out of Shamshuipo (the 'smuggled list') states 'cardiac failure', which was either a euphemism or, quite likely, the clinical cause of death.
141 Malaria, anaemia, dysentery, colitis, beri-beri.
142 See comment for Walker above.
143 Stephens had been taken to WMH on 21 December with GSW to spine.
144 Not in the personnel list in the HKDDC war diary.
145 Cellulitis at scrotum.
146 Pemphigus.
147 STH records quote a Private A. Miller, Royal Scots dying there of acute appendicitis the following day, but he neither appears in the smuggled list nor CWGC records.
148 CWGC internal documents give 6 July as an alternative date.
149 Other documents claim June 1943 as date of death.
150 CWGC internal documents give an alternate date of 2 March 1942.
151 Broncho-pneumonia, paralysis of diaphragm following diphtheria.
152 Yoong Yew Moy George's death was confirmed by the late Arthur Gomes of the HKVDC: "I have a G. Yoong No 5183 Sgt. Corps Signals, HKVDC whom I presume is the name you seek. He died in Shamshuipo POW Camp 8/9/42" (letter to author). He was awarded a posthumous Engineering degree by the University of Hong Kong in 1942. See Clifford Matthews and Oswald Cheung (ed.), *Dispersal and Renewal: Hong Kong University during the War Years*, p. 301. He does not appear in CWGC records.
153 The execution was also mentioned in the *South China Morning Post* of Tuesday, 18 September 1945.

154 Paralysis of diaphragm, broncho-pneumonia.
155 First buried at BRH No. 1 HP Cemetery.
156 Auricular Fibrillation. Not in CWGC but reported dead in the smuggled list under 'Merchant Seaman'.
157 Capes was also in the HKDDC. Malnutrition, at 16.15. The HKDDC war diary confirms the 18th, though other records state the 16th. The smuggled list states the 18th.
158 The smuggled list states 4 October 1942.
159 The smuggled list states 22 December 1942.
160 CWGC internal documents give an alternative date of 21 November 1942.
161 In some documents as 'Lavoix'.
162 CWGC internal documents give a date of 2 April 1942.
163 Died of wounds from the 16 December bombing of Lyemun (according to the late Ray Smith, RRoC: correspondence with author).
164 Hospitalized at QMH on 28 December 1941. GSW. "His wounds never healed." See Grant Garneau, *The Royal Rifles of Canada in Hong Kong*, p. 294.
165 Depressed fracture of skull. "Had a bad head wound and was in hospital ten months". See Grant Garneau, *The Royal Rifles of Canada in Hong Kong*, p. 298.
166 Atrophy of yellow of liver.
167 Post-diphtheria paralysis and myocardial degeneration.
168 Mal. BT. Ankyol.
169 Hospitalized on 24 December 1941.
170 Inanition.
171 Wounded in the 16 December bombing of Lyemun.
172 Initially at RNH. Shell wound perineum and rectum. GSW and anaemia.
173 Amputation at hip joint at RNH. Died of thrombus.
174 Initially hospitalized at QMH on 28 December 1941, GSW to leg and rectum.
175 First buried at BRH No. 1 HP Cemetery.
176 Endocard.
177 C. Beri and cystitis.
178 Diphtheria and intoxaemia.
179 First buried at BRH No. 2 HP Cemetery.
180 The CWGC lists some deaths as 1 October or 1–2 October. As research has shown that the first two men to die (while still aboard the boat) were CERA Herbert Thomas Bevis of HMS *Tamar* and Shipwright First Class Cyril Alfred Lifton of HMS *Tern*, and they died after midnight on the 1st, these dates have all been corrected to the 2nd.
181 Some might question why these men are not listed as 'Ff' — 'Friendly fire'. This is due to the fact that the fire in question was directed at a purely legitimate target (i.e. a Japanese freighter), and the deaths of these men could perhaps be described therefore as 'collateral damage'. However, the latter term lacks the necessary respect to be used in this context.
182 The smuggled list shows him to have died on the *Lisbon Maru*.
183 The smuggled list says *Lisbon Maru*, but this is not noted by the CWGC. This is true of many RN records for 2 October 1942.

184 The smuggled list states he was lost on the *Lisbon Maru*. His POW Card says: "42.Sep.27 dept from HK to Japan by Lisbon Maru and assumed that on 1/Oct at East China sea N30.17 E123.13 got shipwrecked and drowned." We can assume the CWGC date is a mistyping of 1–2 October 1942.
185 The smuggled list states that he died on the *Lisbon Maru*.
186 His brother Frank, of 36 Bty. 8 Coast Regt, predeceased him on 26 October 1940. However, CWGC internal documents contain a strange note giving date of death as '1943', and place of burial as BRH.
187 Confusingly, the CWGC record Burrows under HMS *Sultan*, and the smuggled list repeats the number of Bow. CWGC gives the serial as C/KX 83472.
188 The smuggled list puts him, and all other police who were on the *Lisbon Maru*, in the Dockyard Police.
189 An eyewitness, Jack Etiemble, describes Childs being kicked in the head and thrown overboard, having previously gained the deck of a Japanese patrol craft.
190 The smuggled list states that he died on the *Lisbon Maru*. His POW Index card says: "42.Sep.27 dept from HK to Japan by *Lisbon Maru* and assumed that on 1/Oct at East China sea N30.17 E123.13 got shipwrecked and drowned." We can assume that the CWGC date is a mistyping of 1–2 October 1942.
191 Foster's POW Index Card states: "27 September 1942 Unknown." Most probably he was muddled by the CWGC with J. Foster RA, 872412, who died in Japan on 11 October 1942.
192 The smuggled list claims he survived the *Lisbon Maru*, but this seems to be incorrect.
193 The Signals war diary claims he died on 11 November 1942.
194 Incorrectly described as 'Major' Greenwood in BAAG reports at the time.
195 Shot. See Tim Carew, *Hostages to Fortune*, p. 132.
196 Not recorded as dying on the *Lisbon Maru* in the smuggled list, though this seems to be incorrect.
197 The smuggled list gives Jones, Thomas Davy the serial 6204938, listing him as surviving the *Lisbon Maru*. Possibly there were two men, and Jones, Thomas David 6213447 was simply inadvertently left off this list.
198 The smuggled list claims that McKay [sic] was on the 5th draft and survived. Presumably that was in error.
199 This name does not appear at all in the smuggled list.
200 The smuggled list claims he was lost on the *Lisbon Maru*. Investigation of his POW Index Card indicates that on Showa 17 September 12 he died of chronic enteritis between 06.00 and 07.00. However, this is clearly in error as it continues: "Showa 17 September 27 transported to inland by *Lisbon Maru*. On the way, October 1, shipwrecked in East China Sea and assumed to drown. Shipwreck position: N30.17 E123.13."
201 Platoon Sergeant Major was a short-lived rank, better known as WO III.
202 The smuggled list implies that Robertson survived the *Lisbon Maru*. This is presumably incorrect.

203 CWGC internal documents include a strange note that Samuels was originally buried at Barton's Bungalow (Bungalow C) Stanley.
204 The smuggled list implies that Seager survived the *Lisbon Maru*. This is presumably incorrect.
205 Commemorated by the UCWD as Clerk, of 69 Elia Tervon Stra., Athens, Greece.
206 The smuggled list claims he was lost on the *Lisbon Maru*. The CWGC probably had the date muddled with Webster, George Alfred 6201926.
207 See *Hostages to Fortune*, p. 116, which maintains that Wigzell died of diphtheria onboard the *Lisbon Maru* before the sinking. Interestingly, the CWGC internal documents claim he was buried at Argyle Street in September 1942.
208 The brother of Robert William Richards, also lost on the ship.
209 "Died and was buried at sea", PRO ADM 1-24284, p. 241.
210 The smuggled list claims he died on the *Lisbon Maru*.
211 Died on the *Shensei Maru*. The smuggled list claims he died on the *Lisbon Maru*, but adds 'Sea burial'.
212 Poulter's diary states: "Our Signal Officer Lt Young died today. He was given a proper burial at sea." The date is uncertain, but the context indicates he was on the *Shensei Maru*. Wright concurs: "More men died on the journey to Japan, among them Lieutenant K.E. 'Chippie' Young, Signal Officer of the Middlesex Regiment. The passing of this fine officer filled us with sorrow. He was buried at sea, and there was not a man of the Middlesex group, well or ill, who was not present to see his body committed to the water." From the context, 8 October is probably the most likely date.
213 The smuggled list claims that he died on the *Lisbon Maru*, and states 'Sea burial'. Uniquely in this list, Stewart is commemorated on the New Zealand Naval Memorial in Auckland. Stewart's burial at sea was witnessed by Lynneberg.
214 The smuggled list implies he survived the *Lisbon Maru*. Osaka #1 Branch Camp (Minato-ku, Osaka). Makel's POW Index Card states: "42.10.11 Transferred to Osaka prison camp. No acceptation of death on the ship (related to *Lisbon Maru*) / died on the ship and Osaka did not receive him." The most likely explanation seems that he was lost on the *Shensei Maru* on or around the 10th.
215 His POW Index card states: "42.10.11 Transferred to Osaka Prison Camp. *Lisbon Maru*. On the way to Japan, died on a ship. No death certificate. Unknown the time got sick." Despite the CWGC date, it seems most probable that he died and was buried at sea from the *Shensei Maru*.
216 His POW Index Card says: "42.10.11 Transferred to Osaka prison camp. Died on the ship. No acceptation. Not processed in Japan. (Related to *Lisbon Maru*). Date of sickness: Unknown. No death certificate." It seems most likely he died on the *Shensei Maru*.
217 The smuggled list has provided the correct dates here in most cases.
218 The smuggled list claims he died on board, but adds "Dysentery" and the

correct date. PRO ADM 1-24284, p. 243, states: "Following are known to have reached safety and been recaptured, Skipper Bailey RNR . . ." His POW Index Card states: "42.2.Oct got sick. Since 9 Oct, admitted to Woosung prison camp. On 7 Oct [sic], died of bacillary dysentery (sat) a.m. 5.30. Place of death: Jiangsu, Shanghai. Burial: Buried at Shanghai prison camp."
219 The smuggled list has a S/Sgt with this name under 'Miscellaneous' and dying on the *Lisbon Maru*. Campbell's POW card states: "4 Oct got sick. Since 42.Oct 9 admitted to Jiangsu. 23 Oct died of dysentery 14.00 (sat). Place of death: Jiangsu, Shanghai prison camp. Buried at cemetery in prison camp."
220 For POWs who died in Japan, the draft they arrived on is listed. For this, I have created a code which is simply XD (transferred draft) followed by a number from 1 to 6 indicating which draft it was. XD2, as in this case, is the *Lisbon Maru*. These are from the smuggled list, and experience shows that they are around 98 percent accurate.
221 Tim Carew claims 6 November rather than October; see *Hostages to Fortune*, p. 158.
222 The smuggled list claims he died on the *Lisbon Maru*.
223 Other documents claim November 1942 as time of death.
224 The Signals war diary says he died at Moji.
225 Osaka #1 Branch Camp (Minato-ku, Osaka). Died at Osaka Military Hospital.
226 Brother of Harry Badger of Command HQ.
227 Harry's father, Edwin Jones, was CSM of the Middlesex in WWI, posted missing 2.5.15.
228 His POW Index Card says: "42.10.4 Became sick. 42.10.11 Transferred to Osaka prison camp. 42.10.17 Died of anaerobic cellulites and sepsis. Place of death: Osaka Kobe Office. Ash: Jyugan-ji. 45.11.9 Handed over to QM Corps 1st Lt. Guymen, Clarence B."
229 The Signals war diary says he died at Moji. Osaka #2 Branch Camp (Kobe) acute pneumonia. However, his POW Index Card says: "42.10.11 Transferred to Osaka Prison camp. 42.10.19 Got sick. 42.10.21 Died of acute pneumonia at Osaka prison #1 office. Handed over to QM Corps 1st Lt. Guymen, Clarence B at Jyugan-ji." See Appendix 11.
230 Thorpe's brother Ronald Clive of the Northamptonshire Regiment died on 26 August 1942.
231 Blood poisoning.
232 Other documents give an alternative date of death of 30 November.
233 However, his index card reads: "Sep 15 1942 transferred to Tokyo #1 prison camp. Feb 5 1943 became sick. Feb 20 1943 at 15.40 died of malaria. Place of death: Oshima-machi, Kawasaki City, Tokyo #1. 1945 Sep 10 Handed over to Lieutenant Bryan, James (American army #8) at Tokyo main prison camp. Cremated."
234 "During the air raid on Oct 25th and 26th/42 when ordered to fire anti aircraft guns [the HKSRA] refused. Two Indian officers [sic] were shot and the remainder were returned to prison camp." WO 208/3035.
235 Beaten to death with rifle butts. See Russell Clark, *An End to Tears*, p. 53.

236 Died in Stanley Camp. Probably the 'Shepherd' noted by Stott to have died of dysentery in Tweed Bay Hospital.
237 According to the *South China Morning Post* of Monday, 24 September 1945, Jackson was killed by a shark on the 23rd. Wright-Nooth claims that Goldie was killed by the fish, but other documents show Goldie repatriated after the war's end and then rejoining the police. Jackson is shown as being in Hong Kong immediately after the Japanese surrender, but does not appear later. It seems therefore that the CWGC date is incorrect. Thanks to force historian Mike Watson for confirming these details.
238 The Civilian Roll also lists: "MacNAUGHT, Civilian, MISS, Civilian War Dead. 8th July 1942." In the absence of any other evidence, I suspect this is a duplication of the McNaught entry.
239 At Stanley. Listed as 'Hotel proprietor', while the other two Ellis' are 'Café owners'.
240 BAAG members already listed in the unit roles above will be repeated in the BAAG lists between parentheses for completeness.

1943

1 Parker, a cellist, also noted, after a donation from the Vatican for POWs had been partly spent by the Japanese on band instruments: "with the band instruments it was possible to put on some pretty good shows and it can be said that the shows were as good as you could want to see anywhere. Altogether there were about eight shows put on that would have been a success in any large city both from a point of view of talent and scenery. Everything was made from bits and pieces picked up here and there. The colours in the stage settings were beautiful to look upon, the plot of the plays and the musical scores were composed by talented people who worked long and hard but were glad to have something to occupy their minds."
2 Major Cecil (commonly known as 'Queenie' or 'Cissy') Boon would be tried on charges of collaboration after the war, and acquitted. See Appendix 9.
3 Hideo Wada had of course been in charge of the POWs on the *Lisbon Maru*, and was widely held responsible for the deaths of so many. Interestingly, he was not generally disliked in this new role.
4 A number of such benefactors were recognized by official letters of thanks from the camps soon after liberation.
5 Men were graded by health, with 'A' being best.
6 In most respects, the experiences of the British and Canadian members of the garrison were remarkably similar. However, I have yet to discover why only one Canadian officer accompanied Canadian men to Japan, whereas some seventy-five British officers (excluding the thirteen sent to Taiwan as a 'punishment') travelled with theirs. These numbers are so skewed as to imply that this was a policy, but whether set by Japanese or others is as yet unknown.

7   All quotes from Skelton come from Rifleman Sydney Skelton's Diary, as kindly supplied by his son.
8   Some of the best coverage of the HKVDC at Innoshima comes from an RAF pilot there. See Terence Kelly, *Living with Japanese*.
9   Quotes from Bob Moore are taken from documents in the possession of his daughter.
10 Gunstone's index card is a good example of an Amagasaki POW, though unlike Hart he would be transferred to Hiroshima #3B: "Showa 18 Jan/22 Transferred to Osaka prisoner camp, Showa 20 Jun/2 Transferred to Hiroshima camp (2nd branch), Showa 20 Sep/2 At Hibi, Tamano-shi, Okayama pref, pass to RA Condr. Davies Thomas John." (It is not clear why it states #2B, as Tamano was in fact #3B.)
11 All quotes from Berard are from his book, *17 Days until Christmas*.
12 All quotes from Speller are from an interview with Dr Charles Roland recorded on 27 May 1990.
13 Poulter adds: "We had to carry them from the barge, across the quayside, into the Godown and up a series of steep planks. This job is much too heavy for us as well as being very tricky work, going up a steep plank with a two hundred-pound load on your back. We went on strike! They went mad and some of us got beaten up but we stuck it out and refused to carry the stuff up the planks. We won! In the afternoon I fell into the harbour. It was bleedin' cold! Our chaps threw me a line and pulled me out and then carried me to one of the Jap rest huts. They stripped me off and, lit a fire and let me dry my clothes off. Drummy had pinched some rice and I cooked it and we had a good feed. My clothes were not quite dry by the time we had to leave for camp, so I had to march back in them. When we got back to camp we were again searched for cut blankets."
14 All quotes from Weedon are from his book, *Guest of an Emperor*. He often notes how the men, working at the docks, would bring extra food back for the officers who lacked their opportunities for foraging. This is also emphasized in Poulter's diary and Wright's account.
15 Ride Papers, Series 11, No. 6, pp. 36–41.
16 Note that the poor quality of the original copy does not permit certainty in the spelling of some names therein.
17 A handwritten addition notes '? — Punjabs'.
18 Wright would write, date uncertain: "The sick men back from Kowsaki [*sic*], the resort to which they had been transferred, were much fitter, but news of Private Bowles was not so good, for he seemed likely to lose some of his toes through beri-beri." Osaka #5D is now Maruyama Hospital.
19 For anyone interested in 1941 cocktail recipes, here are two examples verbatim: "THE FRENCH CANADIAN. (Major F. T. Atkinson, Royal Rifles of Canada). + Maple Syrup, + Lemon Juice, + Scotch Whisky. Ice and shake. Tim Atkinson gave me this one. Need I say more? THE GLENCORSE. (Capt. C. R. Jones, The Royal Scots.) + Scotch Whisky, + French Vermouth, + Lime Juice. Ice and shake. This one comes from an Englishman with a Welsh name who lives in Edinburgh and wishes to remain anonymous."

20 This arrest concerned money being smuggled by Dr Talbot at the request of Grayburn and Hyde. Neither Grayburn nor Hyde survived. It is hoped that a future volume will cover this episode in appropriate detail.
21 BAAG. Dated 2 April 1943.
22 Ride Papers, Series 10, No. 35, p. 14.
23 Ansari was a highly respected Indian officer of the 5/7th Rajputs. Although very much pro-Indian independence, he was equally anti-Japanese and actively resisted their attempts to popularize the Indian National Army in Ma Tau Chung POW Camp. Soon after sixty was arrested, he too was tortured and executed, later being awarded the George Cross.
24 On George's death, his brother Jimmy promptly joined the BAAG well knowing what his fate might be. He lost his life in similar circumstances to George in 1944. The detailed story of George's betrayal and arrest are in the Ride Papers: AWM Series 11, No. 32, p. 130. Note that Edwin Ride's book, *British Army Aid Group: Hong Kong Resistance 1942–1945*, confuses the two brothers; see *British Army Aid Group*, p. 160.
25 Ride Papers, Series 10, No. 35, p. 15. It was believed that 'Inky custodian' was Ansari's reference to himself as the hockey goalkeeper for the Rajputs, whereas Clague (an R.A. officer at Lyemun, who had sent him two previous messages) played on the right wing. 'Overhauled' was recognized as a reference to health recovering after interrogations, and "always ready to rush out" as a willingness to attempt to escape.
26 From his autobiography, *Footprints: The Memoirs of Sir Selwyn Selwyn-Clarke*.
27 The arrival of letters from home was of course a major event. Men evolved all sorts of ways to eke them out (reading a sentence per day, for example). Most arrived between a year and eighteen months after they were sent. Diaries make many mentions of them, though I have limited the repetition in this work.
28 The book *USS Arizona's Last Band* lists a Musician 2nd Class by the name of James Harvey Sanderson as being amongst those killed during the attack on Pearl.
29 Ride Papers, Series 10, No. 38, p. 9. Quotes WIS 38 (11 July 1943) as saying: "All bankers, with the following exceptions, were interned in STANLEY with their families on 2 July. They were given 1 week's notice to get ready and took all their belongings with them. The following were still working in the YOKOHAMA SPECIE BANK: OLIVE — Inward Bills Department, MACLATCHIE, DAVIS — Sub-Accountants, PERRY — Cashier, MAC — Bookkeeper. Their families are still with them residing in Chinese hotels. All above are HONGKONG & SHANGHAI BANK. HAWKINS (Mercantile Bank Manager) and 1 Chartered Bank man (name NOT known) are also still at 'liberty'."
30 Ride Papers, Series 10, No. 37, p. 24.
31 Meaning HKVDC.
32 Some forty-eight people would be arrested concerning this matter. It is hoped that a future volume will cover this incident in appropriate detail. Meanwhile, the fullest coverage can be found in Anderson PRO WO 325/42.

33 Actually Zindell. Rudolf Zindell was a Swiss businessman based in Hong Kong, appointed by the Red Cross as their representative. He visited the camp this day.
34 It is hoped that a later volume will cover this incident with appropriate detail. Meanwhile, probably the most complete coverage is Boxer PRO WO 311/561.
35 In fact Bertram himself would arrive, with three others from the fifth draft, at Omori in January 1944.
36 Bertram noted another example while on a ten-day sentence for dropping a pack while on parade at Omori: "Some months before, Alf Mansfield, a genial and incorrigible thief in the Middlesex had done a stretch in the guardhouse for stealing red cross parcels. By a triumph of legerdemain he had succeeded in stealing sixteen more parcels *while within the cell*" (my emphasis). This was presumably Joseph Mansfield.
37 Goodwin continued: "Before he left the Brigadier bequeathed me a tin of 'Bemax', a heart of wheat meal, and that formed a valuable item of food during my subsequent escape."
38 Rose was an original 'old contemptible' who had won his MC in France. Of the Wiltshire Regiment, he was assigned to command The Volunteers in 1938. Following Lawson's death in the Hong Kong fighting, he took over West Brigade and Mitchell replaced him commanding the HKVDC.
39 Winkworth's interview card, WO 344/409/2: 13 Burlington Gardens, Acton, London, states he was in Hong Kong from 25 December to 4 August 1943, in Formosa from 9 August 1943 to 9 October 1944, and Manchuria from November 1944 to August 1945. In the latter two camps, the camp commander is correctly listed as Air Vice Marshal Maltby, General Maltby's brother.
40 See Bush, *The Road to Inamura*, p. 173. In fact the printed date is the 25th, but it seems certain this is an error. See also his diary at NARA RG407 Box 128.
41 Cambon notes with regret that he died an alcoholic in Vancouver after the war. See *Guest of Hirohito*, p. 80.
42 Almost certainly Harold Barlow Shepherd, Winnipeg Grenadiers, who Bush notes was very keen on seizing the ship and making for China.
43 Bush makes it clear that 'Cardiff Joe', a Japanese man by the name of Matsuda who had been the Cardiff manager for Yamashita Steamship Company until late 1940, was of great help to the POWs.
44 He continues: "His brother, an unarmed stretcher bearer, was killed by Japs while tending wounded men during the battle of Hong Kong."
45 Though Bush himself was sent to Omori.
46 All quotes from Bevan come from his diary.
47 Shinagawa.
48 Ride Papers, Series 10, No. 39, p. 23. It also states: "HK News of 9 Sep 43 quotes Mr ZINDEL, HK representative of the International Red cross as saying that the first batch would move in on the following week. A total of 800 persons is [sic] expected to live at this centre. A Mr. SUTER is mentioned as

Superintendent of the Home." Later (Series 10, No. 39, p. 35) reports on 10 October 1943: "An advertisement issued by the ROSARY HILL RED CROSS HOME, 43 STUBBS RD., announces visiting hours as twice weekly — Sundays and Wednesdays, 1400–1700 hrs." Series 10, No. 14 (p. 5) includes names of all Red Cross in Hong Kong, and the 'Administrative Council' of Rosary Hill.

49 This, and the 'daily menu', come from Peter White's memoirs of Rosary Hill, which he kindly supplied to the author.
50 Others called this plane 'Hank' (presumably Hank the Yank).
51 Ride Papers, Series 10, No. 39, p. 17.
52 Prata is buried in a grave in the Catholic Cemetery in Happy Valley. However, even today his family cannot be certain that the bones therein are truly his.
53 It is hoped that a later volume will cover this incident with appropriate detail. Meanwhile, a good narrative version exists in Goodwin's book, *Passport to Eternity*.
54 The *Teia Maru* was built as *Aramis* — the second craft of that name — for Messageries Maritimes' Marseilles-Far East service in 1932. It was seized by the Japanese at Saigon in April 1942 and renamed. She was sunk by submarine USS *Rasher* off the Philippines on 18 August 1944.
55 All quotes from this work under Taylor are from his diary, now held privately by his family. Thursday, 21 October 1943 is the first entry.
56 Rumours persist that this was the result of executions following an escape attempt, but nothing exists in known files to corroborate this.
57 Though when the ship sailed, O'Toole noted: "Selection leaves. Smith & Wright taken off, also Jefferys who had malaria. All given wind-breaker and two blankets all quite orderly. Marched off after breakfast. Taken by tug from Bamboo Pier to boat so they didn't have to walk through."
58 To Chiu. Her brother was To Kom Wing (see Ride Papers, Series 11, No. 22, p. 2). The report itself comes from Ride's papers, Series 11, No. 21, p. 142.
59 A sample POW Index card for this voyage (from WO344/378/2): Alexander Gordon, Royal Scots, 36 Glasgow Road, Perth Scotland.
Sham Shui Po 25.12.41 — 18.12.43 Major Boon Captain Ford, later Capt. Campbell
Narumi 7.1.44 — 20.6.45 Lt. Riley RAF
No. 8 Toyama 21.6.45 — 5.9.45 Lt. Riley RAF RSM Ashman RAEC
The reference to Humphreys suggests that his recorded date of death in 1942 is incorrect.
60 Presumably at Kaohsiung (previously known as Takao).
61 These three men would be posthumously awarded the George Cross, as were Ansari and Fraser.
62 The smuggled list claims 10 January 1942.
63 Hydrocephalus avitaminosis.
64 Endocard.
65 Killed by accident on Shamshuipo's electric fence.
66 The Stanley grave register notes: "Served as Rosario, Peter Norman . . . Also served in British Army Aid Group." The type of grave ('Special Memorial C')

is one of 24 that refer to people buried in the cemetery, but whose exact grave location is not known. The 1955 Sai Wan Memorial book also listed him as U 29 October 1943.
67 The smuggled list notes "tortured".
68 Burns was also in the HKVDC.
69 The smuggled list claims 16 November 1942.
70 Nephritis.
71 Not recorded in the HKDDC war diary. It would appear that the CWGC recorded the majority of Royal Naval Dockyard Police fatalities as HKDDC, whether or not they were actually in that unit.
72 Not recorded in the HKDDC war diary.
73 I assume this is the "Fred Charles Granville" referred to as a Boom Engineer in the smuggled list.
74 Gardiner's POW Card states: "42.10.11 Transferred to Osaka prison camp. 43.4.9 at 21.50 died of beri-beri. 43.2.19 got sick. Place of death: Osaka prison, Kobe office. Place of ash: Osaka minami tani-cho, Jyugan-ji. Handed over to QM Corps 1st Lt. Guymen, Clarence B, at Jyugan-ji."
75 Osaka #2 Branch Camp (Kobe). Sturges' POW Card states: "42.10.11 Transferred to Osaka prison. 43.1.25 got sick. 43.7.2 died of acute colitis. Place of death: Osaka Kobe office. Place of ash: Jyugan-ji, Minami-ku, Osaka City. Handed over to QM Corps 1st Lt. Guymen, Clarence B, at Jyugan-ji (Osaka American occupation force, 1st Division)."
76 Other documents state he died on 5 November or 26 November.
77 The Signals war diary states that he died at Moji.
78 Fracture of left ribs, internal haemorrhage of the lungs. A 'factory accident' according to Bevan's diary.
79 Fracture of the skull and legs.
80 Fracture of pelvis and left fibula and tibia.
81 Contusion of brain.
82 Cerebral haemorrhage.
83 Handwritten in CWGC internal documents is a date that looks like 27 June 1943, followed by the words: "cardiac beri-beri". However, the *Royal Rifles of Canada in Hong Kong* (p. 330) reports that one Canadian died on board the draft. From the context, it looks like the date of death should be 21 January 1943, and this may well be Lawrence. Further research is required.
84 At the age of eighteen, thus he was sixteen at the time of the battle.
85 From the *London Gazette* of 18 March 1946: "Awarded the George Cross for most conspicuous gallantry in carrying out hazardous work in a very brave manner." All the military GC winners had the same text. Only Fraser's civilian award had more detail: John Alexander Fraser was interned by the Japanese in the Civilian Internment Camp at Stanley. Fully aware of the risks that he ran he engaged continuously in most dangerous activities. He organized escape plans and a clandestine wireless service and succeeded not only in obtaining news from outside but also in getting important information out of the camp. Subjected by the Japanese to prolonged and most severe torture he steadfastly

refused to give any information, and was finally executed. His fortitude was such that it was commented upon by the prison guards, and was a very real source of inspiration to others. His magnificent conduct undoubtedly saved the lives of those others whom the Japanese sought to implicate."
86 Also recorded as "unknown" on the Sai Wan Memorial.
87 CWGC lists him as a civilian. He died of an internal haemorrhage and is buried in Stanley.
88 A note says, "Of Hong Kong Dockyard."
89 The CWGC lists Private Ivan Patterson, 7536265, RADC, K 10.2.43 as being "BAAG", and this is echoed in Edwin Ride's *British Army Aid Group: Hong Kong Resistance 1942–1945*. However, as yet there seems to be no evidence that Patterson was involved in BAAG, and in fact he was a POW in Taiwan who was re-interred in Saiwan after the war (though it should be noted that Taiwan was within BAAG's jurisdiction for some time).

1944

1 It is not always clear when individual medical officers were sent to their camps, thus these may not feature in such lists. However, their POW Index cards should record this information.
2 Although not all of the BAAG victims had, strictly speaking, been POWs or Internees, all had been prisoners before execution.
3 However, at Moji, Bertram, Abbott, Rae Watson (HKVDC) and Ken Seyer (HKVDC) — all with pre-war media experience — were separated from the draft and taken, via Moji Camp, to Tokyo, to be 'encouraged' to join the Bunka centre that provided pro-Japanese propaganda in English. When this failed, they were posted to Omori HQ Camp. All quotes from Howard at Narumi are from his diary.
4 This view was endorsed by Stenning, the senior medical officer there at the time: "Generally this was a very bad camp with much sickness, bad water supply, and most severe weather and working conditions . . . Hard work working in the wet and cold and snow and the incessant driving of the work bosses to make men work harder and harder and harder, made this the worst camp in the Osaka area for the percentage of deaths and sickness."
5 From *It Was Like This* . . . In her diary, Barbara Redwood had also noted that an internee by the name of Betty McGowan was in Stanley, who appeared on stage in London after the war as Chin Yu. She also mentioned the 'Misses Woods' who had a stage/film career before the war.
6 Her book, *Twilight in Hong Kong*, gives a good description of Rosary Hill.
7 Mortimer had been caught trying to find Red Cross parcels in a storeroom. He was with an American POW by the name of Yetman, who was also killed.
8 Cambon says he died two months later. See *Guest of Hirohito*, p. 77: "Mortimer showed incredible courage and tenacity, knowing he had almost no chance of survival. He never complained, joked about his black feet and

actually comforted those beside him. He fought the inevitable for almost two months and died in his sleep. I cannot forget this change of character into a person of such strength, a model for us all."
9   From Stenning's (senior medical officer at Oeyama, 15 October to 23 June 1944) war crimes affidavit.
10 See Appendix 9.
11 The child, presumably still born, does not appear in the Stanley lists or CWGC records, but there is a grave in Stanley Cemetery.
12 Presumably Private Albert V. Fenn, 6208367, from the first draft.
13 Mynatt is not in Hong Kong records. The majority of deaths and diseases reported by Taylor appear to be in Merchant Navy men — such as David Wilson — at the same camp, few of whom came from Hong Kong.
14 Presumably Sapper Dennis Edge.
15 Also from the *Lisbon Maru* and the Hong Kong garrison.
16 I once asked Dennis Morley of the Royal Scots what he thought of Jackson. He answered in just three words: "He was God." Weedon noted, 8 July 1945: "Talk in next-door hut after supper by new Dr. (Hockman) giving us resume of news he knew . . . Is convinced that Nips are trying to kill off Dr. Jackson (who did such heroic work in early days) because he knows too much. Was sent to punishment camp on framed up charges about February this year."
17 For this 'crime', Coxhead was assigned to the 'bottles' (particularly hard physical work), though his diary makes no complaint. Most POWs believed that survival was primarily a matter of one's mental state and thus ability to withstand such blows, and Coxhead's survival is very probably an example.
18 All Hong Kong's senior officers and, in practice, the majority of those ranked Major and above, had served in the first war.
19 Fisher's writings are full of such references to Boon, a man who he clearly detested. I have not included most as they are repetitive in nature.
20 As an example POW MI9 interview for this draft: Samuel Hewitt, RASC, 52 Philips Park Road, Lancs.

Sham Shui Po:	28 Dec 41 — 19 Dec 42.	Maj Gen Maltby	
BRH:	19 Dec 42 — June 43		
Sham Shui Po:	June 43 — April 44	Major Boone [sic]	QMS Keast
Sendai:	May 44 — Dec 44	Captain Robinson	QMS Casey
Tokyo Hospital:	Dec 44 — July 45	Commander Cleaves	
Sendai:	July 45 — 18 Aug	Captain Smyth	QMS Casey

21 Misidentification of ships was common, although it is still not completely clear which ship this really was. The *Naura Maru* does not appear in other known records.
22 All quotes from Rakusen come from his letters, kindly supplied by his son Ron.
23 See entry for 26 July.
24 On the subject of Stanley's younger internees, Stericker noted: "They were undisciplined children and quite without class-consciousness. Their friends were of all colours, and their vocabularies were unprintable. However, they

were happy children. What they had never known they never missed. They knew nothing of Christmas or birthdays, nor of special food or treats. To toys they were also strangers."

25 Dodwell's grave, as one enters Stanley Cemetery, is immediately behind the cross of remembrance, and thus the first that one sees on arrival.

26 Letters from home were of course extremely good for morale, and diaries make it clear that they were as welcome as Red Cross parcels. Readers of Coxhead's diary may notice use of the word 'jeep'. This is not an anachronism. As Kelly explains: "We had others employed by the dockyard who were dressed in a quasi military uniform whom we called jeeps for whom the official title was, I understand, gunzoku."

27 Often spelled 'Ma Tau-wei'.

28 News of the military situation in the wider world was another dominant theme in diaries. This manifested itself particularly in comments on visible activities (such as Allied bombing of areas adjacent to camps), and — especially post-6 June 1944 — on advances reported as the Allies recaptured territory. While the documentation of these facts tells us nothing new, their perceived importance is clearly indicative of the implications as to the coming of the end of the war, and subsequent liberation.

29 Hatt died in the UK in June 1946.

30 Shrigley's repeated arrest and death are something of a mystery. However, according to Geoff Knee, a relative: "One Sunday morning in about 1947, as my parents and I were walking home from church, a man approached my father, saying, 'You are Mr Knee, aren't you?' He went on to explain that he was a Barnsley man and had been in a POW in Hong Kong with Ralph Shrigley. He and Ralph had shared many conversations about Barnsley and our family. He said he had a message for my Dad from Ralph. After the first interrogation, Ralph had told him that the Japanese had found his (Ralph's) groundsheet with his name on it, in a tunnel that had been started for an escape. Ralph had given the groundsheet to the escapees for dragging earth out of the tunnel. The Japanese wanted to know the names of the escapees, but he would not tell them. They had beaten him up badly and he told his friend that if he (the friend) got back to England he should try to tell my father about it. After a second interrogation, Ralph did not return to the camp." When hostilities commenced, Shrigley had hidden the HKVDC's Regimental Colours. As he did not tell anyone where they were, they were only discovered by accident when the foundations of the American Consulate in Garden Road were laid in the 1970s.

31 Such notes, usually tucked into Red Cross parcels, were not uncommon and were the source of much entertainment. Packers sometimes also deliberately used newspapers with interesting articles as wrapping; for example, this is how the Stanley internees learned of Bill Evans' escape and evasion from the *Lisbon Maru* and his repatriation to Canada to rejoin his wife.

32 Goodwin was concerned about the strength of his right leg, which had been severely injured in the fighting.

33 Baird was right in that there were extra parades, missed meals, slapping and extra discipline, and the purchase of cigarettes was stopped. However, Baird went on to say that it: "takes lots of guts to do what that chap did", and "I hope he is safe." Goodwin himself noted: "The two officers who slept either side of me, Lt. (E.) Chown, RNVR, and Lt. Trapman, 12 CRRA, were arrested for interrogation, as also were my closest friends, Lt. Glover, HKRNVR, and Lt. Thomson, RNR . . . However, no one suffered any very severe beatings, and reprisals against the camp were very much lighter than they might have been." Parker reported that these reprisals were so comparatively light that "it should have been easy for us to realize that the end of the war was much closer than we had believed."
34 Saipan fell on the 9th, and next-door Tinian was invaded on 2 July. This loss so close to the Japanese heartland would lead to the resignation of Tojo's cabinet. Slightly over a year later, from Tinian, the two atomic bombs would be flown to Japan, bringing the war and the POWs' incarceration to an end.
35 Both these remains would be lost. Coils and Barry were presumably captured in Singapore.
36 Ride Papers, Series 10, Number 20, p. 19.
37 Presumably a reference to Sapper Hale, whose parents hailed from Vancouver.
38 Charles Frederick Hyde, of Hong Kong Bank. Michael Hyde would die in a freak accident on a firing range during National Service in 1956.
39 Ride Papers, Series 10, No. 17, p. 8.
40 Beadnell had been captured in Java, having been sent there from Singapore. He arrived at Oeyama on 26 June 1944 — taking over from Stenning — and was senior officer there until 9 September 1945 when all Oeyama POWs were put on the train to Yokohama. All quotes from Beadnell are from his war crimes affidavit held in the Canadian archives.
41 In August 1944, approximately 200 American POWS arrived at Oeyama. However, initially these men were relatively fit, and thus the men discussed in this letter are the Hong Kong POWs (though Beadnell notes that the Americans' health, too, deteriorated rapidly after their arrival, and the senior American officer produced an addendum to this letter, listing the 32 sickest American POWs).
42 In early 2007 I received an email from the grandson of Lance Corporal John Laird, Royal Scots: "After rescue [from the *Lisbon Maru*] he was transported to Kobe. Not sure on the camp exactly, I do know his work detail was in the docks in Kobe. Would there be record or diaries of this time there? I know he rescued the Harbor Master's daughter from drowning when she fell into the dock; he jumped in and saved her. I think he got slightly better treatment from his work masters as a result of this bravery."
43 Ride Papers, Series 10, No. 19, p. 43.
44 The exact medical circumstances of the deaths of Corporal Townsend H/6135, Corporal Grainger H/6578, Lance Corporal Rees 6297, Private Delorme H/6758, Pte. Paul H/40700 and Private H. Bazinet, all of the Winnipeg Grenadiers, are also given in Beadnell's war crimes affidavit. See also 6 June 1945.

45 Edward James Tandy was the brother of Jessica Tandy, the celebrated actress. Jessica became well known shortly after the war for her role on Broadway in *A Streetcar Named Desire*. Her Hollywood career was even more impressive, encompassing such classics as Alfred Hitchcock's *The Birds*, and culminating in an Oscar for best actress in 1994 for *Driving Miss Daisy*.
46 See Appendix 11.
47 Presumably Stoker P. O. James South, from the first draft.
48 Presumably Leading Stoker Thomas Ostend Yates, from the first draft.
49 The spelling of the three American officers is uncertain, and none of the three appear to match the liberation rosters of the camps, indicating perhaps that they had been transferred elsewhere by then.
50 From Consuelo Delgado y Perez' granddaughter, Joyce.
51 Myelitis.
52 King also served in the HKDDC. CWGC records state the date of death as 15 February 1944.
53 Davis' details appear in the smuggled list but not on CWGC.
54 Stevenson's shipmates were captured at sea on SS *Ben Nevis* on 23 December 1941 and interned at Osaka #13B (Tsumori) where three of them perished.
55 The smuggled list says 13 April 1944.
56 The smuggled list says 2 May 1943.
57 Killed in a fall from a second floor window in Yaumatei while under interrogation. It is not known whether he jumped or was thrown. See Goodwin's second book, *Passport to Eternity*. The smuggled list says 'beri-beri', 2 July 1944.
58 As another man of this name exists in CWGC records for 1940, when the *Glenmoor* was actually sunk, the addition of the vessel's name in Stanley Cemetery's printed register is probably incorrect.
59 Aged fifty-five and believed to have retired. Buried in Stanley.
60 Cancer of the oesophagus.
61 Mining accident. See Grant Garneau, *The Royal Rifles of Canada in Hong Kong*, p. 377. Pelvic fracture.
62 Mining accident. See Ken Cambon, *Guest of Hirohito*, p. 122 and Garneau, *The Royal Rifles of Canada in Hong Kong*, p. 377. Cranial fracture and brain haemorrhage.
63 Fleming had been with the Blue Funnel Line. He died of suspected stomach ulceration after eating food found in a barrel at Innoshima. See Terence Kelly, *Living with Japanese*, p. 156.
64 At Narumi, as a result of beating by Niimori, having been unable to produce a sweater for inspection. See Grant Garneau, *The Royal Rifles of Canada in Hong Kong*, p. 139.
65 Contusion in the middle of forehead, epithelial exfoliation, pneumonia.
66 Served as Baladin, G.
67 Ling's POW Index Card, as an example, states: "43.9.1 Transferred to Osaka 12 Office. 43.12.14 got sick. 44.1.21 at 18.15 died of beri-beri. Place of death: Osaka #12 office. Place of Ash: Jyugan-ji. Handed over to Lt. Guymen."

68 Beri-beri and acute colitis.
69 After the war, Harvey of the RAMC was charged with Friesen's murder, but was acquitted. See Appendix 9.
70 And rheumatism in the lambrosacral region.
71 Atrophic libereirrhose [sic].
72 George Alfred Webster's POW card, as an example:
    43.1.22 Transferred to Osaka prison camp
    44.3.19 got sick
    44.3.21 died of chronic enteritis
    Place of death: Osaka City, Osaka #4 office. Place of ash: Jyugan-ji
    45.11.9 Handed over to QM. Corps 1st Lt. Guymen, Clarence B. at Jyugan-ji
73 The *South China Morning Post* for Tuesday, 18 September 1945, gives the following alternative dates of death: Bearman 28 April 1944, Blair 28 March 1944, Cole 5 February 1945, Deakin 20 January 1944, Stoneham 15 December 1945. The provenance of these dates in not known, though the last is clearly in error.
74 Right wet pleurisy.
75 Mann's father, also Alexander, was lost in Hong Kong on 22 December 1941 as a CQMS of the RASC and has no known grave.
76 Acute pneumonia.
77 Reed, Stephen Arnold is also attributed to this serial number. Japanese records state 3586. Dislocation and fracture of the 11th thoracic vertebrae.
78 A letter from Alfredo Prata, HKVDC, notes that: " 'Fuzzy Fernandes' was killed in a mine collapse during an earthquake." Thanks to Prata's daughter Francesca Sankey.
79 Condon's POW index card confirms that he was transferred to the main building of the Tokyo POW Camp on 15 September 1942. He died of heart failure at 22.30 (the card adds 'Methanol Intoxication'). His remains were handed to a Lt. Bryan, James of the Salary Section of the Eighth American army on 10 September 1945. A letter from Kawasaki City Council states that his remains were sent to Hong Kong in error at the end of the war. As he is commemorated on the Sai Wan Memorial, despite dying in Japan; it is possible (though certainly not proven) that his remains were lost in the B24 Liberator crashes of 10 September 1945.
80 Father of Bliss Cole. He died in Kawasaki #3D.
81 Fracture of 2nd and 3rd cervical vertebrae. Lacerations.
82 Killed by a building collapse at Niigata Camp #5B. See Charles G. Roland, *Long Night's Journey into Day*, p. 234, although the cause is also recorded as chronic enteritis. Date of death suggests the former cause is correct.
83 Acute pharyngitis, catarrh pneumonia.
84 Catarrh pneumonia, acute pharyngitis.
85 The smuggled list is approximately 98% accurate in the listing of drafts. This is an example where it is probably incorrect.
85 Scars of pleurisy, malaria.
86 Beaten and left in the snow for more than twenty-four hours after allegedly stealing a Japanese workman's lunch, Mortimer died two months later.

87 Address given as: Repulse Bay Hotel.
88 A note says: "Also known as William PATTINSON."
89 One-armed Sutton.
90 Room 2A, Church Guest House.

1945

1 MacCulloch AE (Ammunition Examiner) had led the party that had reopened the Little Hong Kong magazines during the fighting.
2 Ian Quinn, the expert on the topic, notes: "These were two Avengers, witnessed by Stanley Camp 'guests' as well as other crews.' Chutes were seen, one wrapped around the tail of one Avenger, but one or two may have survived. There was a report of someone picked up in the hills that day, but that was the day Major Houck of the 118th flying a P-51 was shot down (he was the one later executed) so not sure if that was him but very likely it was Lt Hunt, pilot of one of the Avengers who later died in a POW camp in Japan from 'untended burns' . . . Two gunners were picked up that day from Helldivers (survived as POWs in Japan) and one Hellcat pilot was seen in a raft near Repulse Bay but consensus is that he was executed that day . . . several luckier pilots made it to Kunming after being picked up by junks and taken to Macau." Those last men referred to, were escorted to British lines in China by Nelson Mar, BEM, a friend of the author today.
3 Watanabe was a Japanese interpreter who took great risks to give humanitarian aid to POWs and Internees when possible. His story is documented in the book, *Small Man of Nanataki*, by Liam Nolan.
4 Redwood: Including "Mr Holland (whose wife had been killed during the war)" (see *Not the Slightest Chance*, note 103). On 26 January Redwood noted that the bungalow "isn't nearly as wrecked as I had imagined". Wally Scragg, a policeman interned in Stanley, noted that the bomb fell on the concrete roof of the garage, hence the fact that blast caused the fatalities and the bungalow itself was relatively undamaged. While it has often been said that the USN were aiming their bombs at a lighter just offshore, Scragg also noted that the Japanese had a mobile gun on the road nearby, and this may also have been the target (conversation with author).
5 All quotes from Collyer (Head Attendant at the Mental Hospital before the war) are from his diary.
6 Wiseman noted: "SSM Williams RASC died of heart failure, being very weak from malaria. In our Camp C.A. Stansfield (Major RIASC) and R.S. Richards (Lt QM RASC) were slightly wounded by AA fragments."
7 Née Mason.
8 This compliment is amplified by the context of Collyer's many negative remarks about women in Stanley who "should not be here". There was widespread resentment amongst internees, about women who had found ways to avoid the 1940 evacuation. Stericker noted: "Now that we were

interned it was obviously a perfect nuisance that a situation which was desperate and difficult as it was, would have been enormously complicated by the large numbers of women and children, as well as babies, many of whom belonged to government employees." Others, however, complained of the presence of missionaries. It seems that each group had different definitions of who should or should not have been in Hong Kong.

9 Fenn was another of those who died in Japan whose remains were subsequently lost. He had died on the 6th.
10 In fact Maurice had died in March, but news was slow to arrive. Further confusion is added by the fact that Weill's date of death is officially recorded as 27 April 1944.
11 Speller had the following to say about Birchall: "As far as I'm concerned, Birchall was the best officer ever seen for standing up. Now, in other places he might not have done the men any good, but the Japs sure respected him. It was surprising. The Camp Commandant there would, as mean as he was — 'little Fat Pig,' we called him -- he respected Birchall. 'Birchall comma here.' And Birchall would say, 'What the hell do you want now? Is it important? You come here.' Just that way. Oh no, he was a fine man, old Len Birchall. I get a kick out of him."
12 There is some uncertainty over the date of these moves. Trick notes that he moved on 31 March, Marsh says 'April', Birchall says 'May', and Speller — at different times — states that he was at Suwa for five or six months (which would imply March). Other sources state that Kawasaki 3D was closed on 13 May rather than March. All agree that this move happened after a heavy air raid, but as the three biggest raids were Tokyo on 10 March, Kawasaki City on 15 April, and Yokohama City on 29 May, it is still unclear.
13 Later Marsh noted: "The British were the survivors of Singapore and had been sent to help build that infamous railroad along the peninsula through Indo China. They were riddled with malaria and other tropical diseases as well as severe malnutrition. The Japanese hated the British for their defiant stubbornness and unwillingness to cooperate. The Japanese had reduced them to dumb driven beasts, sick both in mind and body. Later when we spoke to them they told us it was only a matter of time until we would all die. They had seen thousands of their comrades die. They had heard no news from anywhere for years, no letters, no Red Cross parcels, nothing. We told them that Germany had surrendered and that Japan too would soon fall. They refused to believe us. They hated the Jap and lived to thwart him. Perhaps it was only hate that kept them alive."
14 The building remains though. Both of the author's children attended kindergarten there, the younger 'graduating' in 2007.
15 This quote comes from his War Crimes depositions, Record Group 331, Box 496, NARA.
16 Presumably the six other ex-*Lisbon Maru* officers left Hiroshima #1B for Fukuoka #9B (Miyata) at the same time, though some sources state that this move was in July.

17 Heather's POW Index Card states: "42.Nov.9 transferred to Shanghai prison camp. By the order from stationary troop at Shanghai prison camp, hospitalised to entrust to Shanghai army internment on May 8 45 because of seriousness sickness. Next day: Released by 13th army's 66th order." Heather was one of twelve men released from St Luke's Hospital in Shanghai and transferred to 'Peking Military Internment Camp'. From there he was liberated by the Americans and flown home, becoming the first London FEPOW to be reunited with his family.

18 Unfortunately, it has not yet been possible to determine precisely which camps these were.

19 Email communication.

20 Bush noted, however, that the B29s were not invulnerable, having seen at least a dozen hit on a previous night.

21 The reference to #15D is not a mistake. Although this work consistently uses the final camp designations in the text, all quotes have been left with the designations used at the time. #15D would not be renamed #15B until August.

22 This was the old site of Kobe Kawasaki Branch Camp (Osaka #5D), which had been closed on 21 May 1945.

23 Hiroshima #3B (Tamano), opened on 1 June. However, there is some doubt about the date of the POW's arrival, as Gunstone's POW card indicated 2 June.

24 The vast majority of the 996 men on board were American. All quotes from Spooner are from his diary.

25 This was the original site of the Kobe Wakinohama Branch Camp (Osaka #18B) which was closed on 20 May 1945.

26 The USS *Massachusetts* is today preserved at Battleship Cove, Mount Hope Bay, Massachusetts.

27 Hook died on 7 July. Baird added: "He was a damn good officer and soldier, the best on the force that came out here and to think that now it is nearly over, to have to pass on."

28 Taylor's diary ceases at this point. This diary, being written in its entirety in Japanese camps by someone who lost his life in one, is probably unique. His granddaughter notes: "My Gran received his diary and some belongings after the war from a Scotsman who just turned up after door some time after the end of the war. No-one knows his name but the information we have is that he had made a pact with my grandad that whoever survived would ensure their belongings were returned to their family."

29 A Sergeant Bentley of 7HAA Regt. RA was killed in the same manner. That being a Hong Kong Regiment, one would assume he was also a Hong Kong POW. In fact, his index card shows that he was captured on 10 May 1942 on the SS *Nankin* in the Indian Ocean by a German raider, and was handed over to the Japanese on 25 August 1942. Most probably the regimental information is incorrect.

30 Poulter and 123 of his comrades had been transferred to Nomachi. Andrews was Private James H. Andrews, Middlesex Regiment.

31 Presumably Brian Byrne, buried in Burma, 18 January 1945, son of George Thomas Byrne and Ethel Byrne, of Fairhaven, Lytham-St.-Annes, Lancashire. Gittins confirms that their only son, a Cambridge graduate, was killed in Burma.
32 The Japanese foreman of Coxhead's working party.
33 Lt.-Col. Simon White was in command of the 2nd Battalion the Royal Scots, and was at this time the Senior Officer in Shamshuipo.
34 The following day, Weedon names this man 'Benson', though Bertram had claimed it was Mansfield. As Benson was CQMS of the Royal Scots, perhaps Mansfield is more likely.
35 This was not the J. I. Bevan quoted elsewhere in this text.
36 Quotes from George MacDonell come from his excellent work, *One Soldier's Story*. This is from page 137.
37 Later, when Harcourt's fleet arrived, Stericker was to note: "Then, and only then, did the Chinese turn on the hated aggressors. Some were torn limb from limb. Others were thrown from the tops of tramcars. The executioner from the gaol, recognised on a ferry, had a rope slung round his neck and was towed across the harbour, ending up a very drowned man."
38 Sadly, the transfers went both ways. *Swiftsure* alone left at least three of her young crew in the cemeteries of Hong Kong — victims of accident or disease in those early days of September.
39 Parker continued: "Later, some Flying Officers from the Aircraft Carrier VENERABLE invited Charlie and me to dinner. We passed a very pleasant evening. When we left to go home it was raining cats and dogs. The fliers commandeered a car that wasn't running too well to take us safely home. One of them had to sit on the bonnet and hold a wire in place but we got home, wet inside and out. They came into camp with us and after polishing off a $100 bottle of Gin we went to bed and they went back to their ship."
40 Seven days later, Houghton was dead. His POW Index Card simply says: "Showa 17, Oct 11th; transferred to Osaka P.C. Showa 20, Sept 9th; handed over to Pit at Ikuno station." At the time of writing it is not clear how he ended up in a grave in the UK, with a headstone dated September 10th, as he was lost on *Ginny* (see below).
41 Cambon goes on to describe his deep gratitude to the Americans, and then notes: "Not that I agree too often with their foreign policy!"
42 *Gosselin* stayed moored in Yokohama, acting as a barracks for shore-based personnel, until 15 December.
43 This was the main station of Kobe. Possibly this was Captain Man of the Middlesex, though most such transfers seem to have been to American officers.
44 *Tryon* had brought Occupation troops to Japan, having picked them up at Leyte, Philippines, on the way.
45 The original is hard to read, but "wharfs" seems most likely.
46 It is not clear which ship Wiseman refers to, as neither an AP nor APA of this name appears to have existed. However, the *Goodhue's* captain was called Sharp.

47 From an interview conducted in 2004, and kindly supplied by Mr Armacost. In his reply to my formal request to quote him, Bob rather nicely noted: "Any little kid who can track down total strangers half-way around the world is most certainly entitled to use whatever material in whatever way he pleases". Of course, the "tracking down" was done with the help of a number of kind people, and the indispensable Internet.

48 Gollege's CWGC record states 8 September 1945, but his name was on this aircraft's manifest.

49 From MACR # 14936. The aircraft was also carrying twelve other British POWs who were not from Hong Kong (five of whom survived and were picked up at sea), one Dutchman who survived, and four Americans, two of whom survived (though there is some doubt about the identity of Taylor). MACR # 14972 B-24M #44-42052, describes another aircraft, "Liquidator", also lost on 10 September 1945, flying from APO 903 (Okinawa). Five on board were Australians. They were not members of the Hong Kong garrison, but were reinterred in Hong Kong after the war as they had initially been buried in Taiwan. A further fifteen passengers, all but two (who were Dutch) being American, were also lost in this crash, as were the crew. The bodies were retrieved from Kanzan Mountain, north of Tai To, in an epic recovery.

50 See RG407 Box 185.

51 Miller was a survivor of the *Lisbon Maru*. This account was provided by his daughter.

52 Shiogama is on the coast between the city of Sendai and the town of Matsushima.

53 When transferred to this camp, Parker reported: "When one of these Doctors was checking up a HKVDC soldier, then only a mere private, he asked the man all about the troubles he was having and was getting the most intelligent replies imaginable. It amused me to see the Doctor sort of prick up his ears and I heard him say to this man, 'Who are you?' The reply was I am so and so, formerly Professor of Surgery at the University of Hong Kong and a Fellow of the Royal College of Surgeons etc. I mention this because in the HONG KONG VOLUNTEER DEFENSE CORP there were many just such men . . . privates, but serving their country."

54 From Guam they would return home on the *Catron* to San Francisco. MacDonell recounts how one of his men, on landing, demanded silence from the huge crowd that met the ship, and said: "If you Yanks have any more trouble with the Japanese, you know where to find us!" After a short stunned silence, the whole port howled with glee at the sheer audacity of the remark.

55 Aboard these ships, and in the temporary camps, a number of publications took the place of regular newspapers. These included "Aquidaily", "Pair O' Dice", "Renville Informer" and others.

56 Esquimalt is a municipality at the southern point of Vancouver Island, British Columbia, and is the base of Canada's Pacific Naval Fleet.

57 Ilford was his hometown — a small farming community 214 kilometres west of Sydney.

58 Major Paddock of the Gloucestershire Regiment was OC Troops, HT *Takliwa*. From the papers of Major Kamta Prasad, 2/14th Punjabis, kindly provided by his son, who notes: "This is all I have on HK from my father's records. Everything was lost on the *Takliwa*, and then the Regiment was transferred to Pakistan after Partition."
59 Although all concerned claim that there was no loss of life, four Indian ex-POWs were reported lost this day. Major Hancock of the Hong Kong Mule Corps, who was on board, was kind enough to send me a cutting from the *Madras Weekly* of 20 October 1945: "Eight hundred prisoners of war from Hong Kong who were rescued from the ill-fated S.S. *Takliwa* which caught fire and was abandoned off the coast of the Nicobar Islands last Monday while on its way to India, arrived in Madras Harbour this evening . . ."
60 Rifleman Arnold Joseph Carrier (suffering from diphtheria and wet beri-beri) was on this carrier and will suffice as a medical example. On arrival in Canada, he was placed in a military hospital in Vancouver until the end of November. From there, he was put on a hospital train and taken to a military hospital in Quebec City. He left that hospital on 30 March 1946 and was taken to Lancaster Hospital in Saint John, N.B. In April 1946, he was transferred to Sussex Hospital, but a year later in April 1947 he was transferred back to Lancaster Hospital. In April 1948, he was shipped to a convalescent centre in London, Ontario, from where he was finally discharged in November 1949.
61 This is not in CWGC records. It appears that he was American.
62 Also known as Mok Fook Hing. Tortured to death by the Kempetai. His wife was also tortured, and lost her sanity shortly after the war.
63 See Leo Paul Berard, *17 Days Until Christmas*, p. 163. It tells of Lesieur in Camp 12 Sendai being kicked by 'The Frog'. However, there is some uncertainty over the name, and Lesieur is buried in Hong Kong rather than Yokohama.
64 Admitted to BMH from Shamshuipo on 29 June 1945 with suspected Japanese B Type encephalitis.
65 Severe haemorrhage, BMH.
66 Easter's POW Card states: "43.1.23 Transferred to Fukuoka prison camp Omine Office #5. 43.3.1 Changed to Fukuoka #5 prison camp. 43.12.1 changed to #8 prison camp. 44.12.3 Transferred to #1. 45.7.2 at 12.30 died of acute enteritis and beri-beri. Place of death: Fukuoka City Hakozaki-cho Fukuoka #1 Office. Ashes at Fukuoka, Fuji Saki-cho cemetery. Around July / Showa 21 (1946), handed over to Lt. Tarjee (?) 108 regiment cemetery registry at the above cemetery."
67 And otitis media.
68 More likely 7 September 1945, as with the other cases of poisoning.
69 This is probably 'Moore, Donaghan Victor' listed at Argyle Street Camp and the smuggled list.
70 Died in Osaka.
71 Burgin was transferred to Narumi on 16 January 1944; he became ill on 4

April 1944 and died on 14 February 1945, 9.35 a.m. The remains were taken to Juganji Temple (see Appendix 11) and on 9 November 1945 were handed over to the QM Corps 1st Lt. Clarence B Guymen of the First Division of the US Army.

72   Only one death, British, is reported at #8B. Mears' POW Card confirms: "44.1.16 Transferred to Osaka prison camp 11 Office [Narumi]. 45.4.6 Transferred to Nagoya prison camp. 45.7.30 Died of cardiac failure 14.15 pm. Place of death: Toyama City, Shimo Okui Nagoya #8 Office. Handed over to British Air Force Lt. Riley at Toyama Prefecture Toyama City #8 Office."

73   As a result of synthetic alcohol poisoning after the surrender in Kobe. See James Bertram, *The Shadow of a War*, p. 177.

74   Sergeant Poulter carried the ashes of both Andrews and Keeler to the UK. While in Nomachi after the surrender, awaiting repatriation, he noted: "Twenty planes came over and restocked us with food. Later a correspondent from the 'Yank' came to the camp taking photographs and notes about the camp. Boy, does he hate the Nips, anybody would think that he had been a prisoner to hear him talk. He was very interested in the two white boxes that I have; they contain the ashes of Keeler and Andrews."

75   Emphema.

76   Motor Torpedo Boat and HMS *Tramp*.

77   Right wet pleurisy.

78   Shipped to Japan on the sixth POW draft, Organ and his friend Harold Hall were sent to Sendai camp. When Organ fell seriously ill, Mr Hall took him, unconscious, in a coal trolley to the nearest railway station and put him in a goods van with a label saying 'POW Hospital Tokyo'. Amazingly he arrived there, but died soon afterwards, on 4 January 1945, of beri-beri and dysentery. Shinagawa hospital records say that he was ex-#14D, and died of a "paralytic stroke", and that he entered hospital on 19 December 1944 (though the original mistakenly quotes the year as 1943).

79   Shinagawa hospital records give cause of death as beri-beri.

80   Both of burns, following the second US naval bombardment of the camp.

81   Camp records indicate that Downs also died on the 10th. This is born out by the fact that he does not appear on the list of those taken to hospital after liberation, so it can be assumed that the CWGC date is incorrect.

82   His POW Index Card reads: "Showa 17 September 15 Transferred to Tokyo #1 prison camp. Showa 20 February 5 got sick. Showa 20 February 6 (a.m.) died of angina pectoris. Place of death: Oshima-machi, Kawasaki City, Tokyo office #1. Showa 20 September 10 Handed over to Lieutenant Bryan, James (American army) at Tokyo main prison camp. Cremated." Probably he should be recorded as being at Tokyo #23D when he died.

83   In an air raid on Mitsui, Japan. Fragmental fracture of the skull, complete fracture of right humerus. His diary had indicated, in the previous few weeks, his fear of the ever-nearing American bombing raids.

84   From drinking glycol at Marutsu Docks. See Ken Cambon, *Guest of Hirohito*, p. 91. Glycol poisoning.

85 James Bertram notes that this camp was originally called "The Coconut job", when it was a railway job for Omori POWs. See *The Shadow of a War*, p. 161.
86 Induration of lungs. The Shinagawa Hospital records state that he entered on 28 August 1945 and died on 29 September 1945 of cirrhosis of the liver.
87 Forth's POW card states: "Showa 20 Jan 5 got sick. Showa 20 Jan 11 04.45 died of beri-beri. Place of death: Heian-mach, Turumi-ku, Yokohama City, Tokyo #1 Dispatch centre. Showa 20 Sep 10 Handed over to Lieutenant Bryan, James (#8 American army) at Tokyo main prison camp. Cremated."
88 Megson is listed under #18D in some reports. #18D is where #17D relocated to after the latter was destroyed in the fire raid of 29 May 1945.
89 A Major A.C. Houghton 49563 died on 10 September 1945 and is buried, or commemorated, in Surrey. See note 40 above.
90 His name appears in Bromley's diary as "Died after our release and on Hospital Ship to Australia, W Forsay Chargeman Foundry, F Jones, Chargeman Factory, P Tancy, F Bryce". The other three names appear neither in HKDDC nor CWGC records.
91 Hart's POW Card says simply: "42.10.11 Transferred to Osaka Prison camp. 45.9.8 Handed over to John Rock at Osaka Station."
92 According to internal documents at CWGC, he died at sea following release from POW camp. He was not in Japan according to the smuggled list so most probably he perished on the *Oxfordshire*.
93 Most probably on USS *Rescue*. Unfortunately, it has not yet been possible to locate the records of the hospital ships, so there is some doubt about these four men's fates.
94 Killed in an air raid. WMH or Matilda Hospitals, according to the internal records of the CWGC.
95 Died after being thrown against a wall by the Japanese. See Russell Clark, *An End to Tears*, p. 51.
96 Metals Control Office, St John's headquarters.
97 Husband of M.C. Barber.
98 Merchant, 16 MacDonnell Road.

Release

1 Sergeant Bill Poulter, Middlesex, finished that diary, and it has been quoted several times in this work.
2 In 2007, this institution received a well-deserved UNESCO Heritage award for preservation.
3 From Brigadier John H. Price, with thanks to Grant Garneau.
4 These are the final words of 'Willy' Lowe's wartime diary.

Appendices

1. Other Dutch personnel are interred at Sai Wan cemetery, but these men perished outside Hong Kong and were re-intered here after the war.
2. Note that the numbers listed for each ship and each group are taken from the 'smuggled list'. This can be estimated, as has been stated above, as 98% accurate on average.
3. Circumstantial evidence implies that the move to #14B came from the Stadium Camp, but this is not confirmed.
4. HKDDC, Police personnel, and ex-HKVDC officers now with other Regiments were also on board, but were treated as regulars.
5. Possibly the *Darien Maru*. No records of this vessel appear to have survived.
6. Initially as a hospital, but it seems that either some POWs stayed at #5D, or others arrived later.
7. The *Tatsuta Maru* would be sunk by the USS *Rasher* on 8 February 1943.
8. The *Manryu Maru* was the Norwegian *Bordvik*, captured by the Japanese at Surabaya in January, 1942. She would be sunk by USS *Sunfish* on 16 April 1945, off Kamaishi, Japan.
9. It is not certain whether these two were ex-Niigata or ex-Oeyama, but the latter appears more likely.
10. On 29 June 1944, the *Toyama Maru* was bound for Okinawa, carrying some 6,000 men of the Japanese 44th Independent Mixed Brigade when she was sunk by USS *Sturgeon*. There were fewer than 600 survivors.
11. Darian being the Chinese city today known as Dalian.
12. Many other hotels had housed civilian internees on their way to Stanley, but as these were only occupied for a matter of days, they are not listed individually here.
13. Other hospitals used during the fighting continued to operate for the first month or two of 1942. These included the Queen Mary Hospital, the Royal Naval Hospital, St Albert's Convent and the Indian General Hospital. When these were closed, the patients and staff were transferred either to the two main hospitals or to the camps themselves.
14. The 18 September 1931 attack on the northeastern city of Shenyang, which had been known as Mukden until 1911 and is situated northwest of China's border with Korea, led to the Japanese occupation of China's northeast. This was followed by the occupation of much of China in 1937.
15. Vernacular names appear to have varied amongst different groups of POWs, and sometimes duplicate each other. I have tried to steer the best course.
16. Thanks to Wes Injerd.
17. Thanks to Toru Fukubayashi of the POW Research Network Japan.
18. Where possible, for each camp one or two illustrative names of men in the text are provided.
19. Note that Nagoya #10D was virtually next door to Nagoya #6D (Fushiki Hokkai Electro-Chemical), and to some degree their records seem to be mixed.

20 Murata's report on the Osaka Camps, at NARA, does not specify which camps these were, and further research has not yet been fruitful.
21 Rowland's POW card reads: "Showa 17 Sep 15 Transferred to Tokyo #2 prison camp. Showa 20 May 14 Transferred to Sendai prison camp. Showa 20 August 26 Transferred to Morioka Army Hospital as result of burns. Showa 20 September 13 Discharged. Showa 20 September 13 Handed over to American Major Sign at Kamaishi port."
22 Ran aground and burnt out on the Nicobar Islands.
23 Via Keelung, Taiwan, and Manila. There were 111 patients embarked from Hong Kong, 108 from Taiwan, and finally 156 from Manila. Three hundred and sixty-two were brought back to New Zealand where, except for a number of Australians transferred to an American hospital ship bound for Sydney, they convalesced before being repatriated to their own countries (with British POWs travelling on the *Maunganui* again on 23 November).
24 In the early days of September, it seems that some 48 Canadians who had initially recuperated on the USS *Iowa* (including Leo Berard and Frank E. Christensen) flew from Okinawa to Iwo Jima, then via Guam, Johnston Island, and Honolulu, to Oakland CA.
25 *Benevolence* anchored off Yokosuka, Japan, on 29 August and started accepting liberated RAPWI. As a hospital ship, she was primarily concerned with treatment rather than transportation, and remained in Japanese waters until 27 November before carrying wounded back to San Francisco, arriving on 12 December.
26 *Crescent* was involved in an unusual incident less than four years later while supporting British Commonwealth diplomats during China's civil war. On 20 March 1949, at Nanjing (then just weeks away from being overrun by Mao's People's Liberation Army) 83 of *Crescent*'s crew locked themselves in their messdecks, refusing to obey orders until the captain had heard their grievances.
27 For coverage of Kyoda's trial, see *The Sinking of the Lisbon Maru*.
28 The majority of this information comes from coverage of the trial by the *Times*, and by the depositions of Major Arthur Grieve and Captain G. Crew at the PRO WO32/14550. My thanks to Jacky Kingsley and Keith Andrews for these details.
29 Carkeet had been accused of stealing food.
30 Said to have appeared in the 'Tokyo Times & Advertiser'.
31 Strictly speaking, this was not 'libellous' as the *Guardian* waited until the year after Boxer died before printing this article. Both quotes are from private letters to the author. Other officers who knew Boxer well expressed identical views, though employing less printable vocabulary. Towards the end of the war, as described in the text, Boxer and others were jailed by the Japanese in very poor conditions in Guangzhou.
32 This letter was kindly supplied by Kathleen Porter, sister of John McFerran Cassidy, RN, who was a *Lisbon Maru* survivor who died in Osaka #1B.
33 Potter is not on the St John's Ambulance memorial, but is listed at Sai Wan

as being an officer of that unit. Lt. Col. Ride described the situation vis-à-vis Potter in a letter to Col. Murray Brown of the Volunteers in 1962, quoted in full in *The Sinking of the Lisbon Maru*.

34 In New Zealand, Peter Gillmore, son of Stanley Gillmore, R.A., notes: "My grandparents saw an advertisement in a newspaper, which asked for home stays for British ex POWs while they recuperated. They replied that they were willing to have a young man stay with them and it was arranged that my father would travel from Auckland — I think he was at this time at the Papakura Army Camp — just south of Auckland to Te Ringa in Hawkes Bay. He had previously been in Auckland Hospital recovering from malaria and other diseases, as well as from some of the shrapnel still in his left leg." The astute reader will realize that these kindly New Zealanders had a daughter of marriageable age!

35 "Medical Services in New Zealand and The Pacific", XV: Ex-prisoners of War from Far East — Hospital and Convalescent Treatment in New Zealand.

36 See also Martin Booth's description of the suicide of 'Nagasaki Jim' in his autobiographical book, *Gweilo*, p. 132.

37 For these details, I am indebted to David Murphy of the Royal Scots Regimental Museum, Edinburgh.

38 Killed in Korea according to Oliver Lindsay's *The Lasting Honour* (p. 182), and John S. Whitehead and George B. Bennett, *Escape to Fight On*, p. 168.

39 The Royal Scots did not serve in Hong Kong after the war, but when they were en route to Korea, their troopship called in and Majors Ritchie and Pinkerton — with seven SNCOs who had served in the colony in 1941 — visited the area. This may well be when and where the well-known photo of a Royal Scots officer looking through binoculars at the Shing Mun Redoubt was taken.

40 He was survived by his wife who he had met in Korea, daughter Nina (ten years old at the time — who kindly provided these details), and two sons (aged eight and six). He was inducted into the US Army Ranger Hall of Fame in July 1999. McCoy's service record includes three Silver Stars for gallantry, two Bronze Stars for valor, two Purple Hearts and numerous campaign ribbons from the US, Canada and Vietnam.

41 He was not. He was sent to Guangzhou (Canton) by the Japanese soon after, and presumably executed there.

42 It seems likely that he was, though hard evidence has yet to surface.

43 I am indebted to the late Professor Jimmy Cummins for this information, the original of which can be found in WO 311/0563.

Bibliography and Sources

PUBLISHED (PRIMARY)

Allister, William. *Where Life and Death Hold Hands*. Stoddart, 1989.
Anderson, William S. (with Charles Truax). *Corporate Crisis. NCR and the Computer Revolution*. Dayton, OH: Landfall Press, 1991.
Andrea (Dorothy Jenner) and Trish Sheppard. *Darlings, I've Had a Ball*. Sydney: Ure Smith, 1975.
Baird, Kenneth G., Major. *Letters to Harvelyn*. Harper Collins, Toronto, 2002.
Baxter, George E. *Personal Experiences During the Siege of Hong Kong*. Printed for East Asian Residents' Association, Sydney. No date.
Berard, Leo Paul. *17 Days Until Christmas*. Canada: privately printed, 1997.
Bertram, James. *Beneath the Shadow*. New York: John Day, 1947.
———. *Capes of China Slide Away*. Auckland: Auckland University Press, 1993.
Bosanquet, David. *Escape Through China*. London: Robert Hale, 1983.
Bowie, Donald. Captive surgeon in Hong Kong: The story of the British Military Hospital, Hong Kong 1942–45. *Journal of the Hong Kong Branch Royal Asiatic Society*, Volume 15, 1975, pp. 150-290.*
Briggs, Alice. *From Peking to Perth*. Perth, WA: Artlook Books, 1984.
Briggs, Christopher, MBE. *Farewell Hong Kong (1941)*. Perth, Western Australia: Hesperian Press, 2001.
Briggs, Norman. *Taken in Hong Kong*. Publish America, 2006.**
Brown, Wenzel. *Hong Kong Aftermath*. New York: Smith and Durrell, 1943.
Bush, Lewis. *The Road to Inamura*. Japan: Charles E. Tuttle Co. Ltd., 1972.
Cambon, Ken. *Guest of Hirohito*. Vancouver: PW Press, 1990.
Dew, Gwen. *Prisoner of the Japs*. New York: Heinemann, 1943.
Evans, Frank. *Rollcall at Oeyama*. Llandysul, Dyfed: J. D. Lewis and Sons, Ltd., Gomer Press, 1985.
Fairclough, Gordon. *Brick Hill and Beyond*. Vancouver: Privately printed, 2004.
Field, Ellen. *Twilight in Hong Kong*. London: Frederick Muller Limited, 1960.
Fisher, Les. *I Will Remember*. Privately published, 1996.

---

*   Note that the version quoted here is the original manuscript, which I was fortunate enough to purchase through the Internet — together with several extra pages from Sims, RE — a few years ago.
**   Briggs' memoirs were compiled by his daughter Carol Waite. The quotes here are from the original diaries.

Gittins, Jean. *Stanley: Behind Barbed Wire.* Hong Kong: Hong Kong University Press, 1982.
Goodwin, R. B. *Hongkong Escape.* London: Arthur Barker, Ltd, 1953.
Gunning, Norman. *Passage to Hong Kong.* Bicester, Oxford Bound Biographies, 2005.
Harrop, Phyllis. *Hong Kong Incident.* London: Eyre and Spottiswoode, 1943.
Hewitt, Anthony. *Bridge with Three Men.* London: Jonathan Cape, 1986.
Leiper, G. A. *A Yen for My Thoughts.* Hong Kong: South China Morning Post, 1982.
Lockhart, Terry. *A Colonial Boy.* Devenport, Tasmania: Taswegia 1989.
MacDonell, George S. *One Soldier's Story.* Toronto: Dundurn Press, 2002.
Mathers, Jean. *Twisting the Tail of the Dragon.* Sussex: The Book Guild Ltd., 1994.
Priestwood, Gwen. *Through Japanese Barbed Wire.* London: George G. Harrap and Co., Ltd. 1944.
Proulx, Benny. *Underground from Hong Kong.* New York: Dutton, 1943.
Ream, Bill. *Too Hot for Comfort.* London: Epworth Press 1988.
Redwood, Mabel Winifred. *It Was Like This . . .* Essex: Anslow, 2001.
Selwyn-Clarke, Selwyn. *Footprints: The Memoirs of Sir Selwyn Selwyn-Clarke.* Hong Kong: Sino-American, 1975.
Stephenson, Ralph. *Colonial Sunset.* London: Pen Press Publishers, 2004.
Stericker, John. *A Tear for the Dragon.* London: Arthur Barker, 1958.
Verreault, Georges. *Diary of a Prisoner of War in Japan.* Quebec: Vero, 1996.
Weedon, Martin. *Guest of an Emperor.* London: Arthur Barker, 1948.
Whitehead, John S. and Bennett, George B. *Escape to Fight On.* London: Robert Hale, 1990.
Wiseman, E. P. *Recollections of a British Prisoner of War.* Ontario: Veterans Publications, 2001.
Wright, Robert. *I Was a Hell Camp Prisoner.* London: Brown, Watson Limited, 1963.
Wright-Nooth, George. *Prisoner of the Turnip Heads.* London: Pen and Sword, 1994.

A further three published primary sources were written in verse. While not quoted from in this work, they are still interesting to read — particularly in certain introductions to prose:

Franklin, Frederick. *Hong Kong.* Brisbane: Boolarong Press, 2004.
McNaughton, H. P. *Shadow Lights of Shamshuipo* (no publishing information).
Varcoe, Sid. *Oriental Odyssey* (no publishing information).

UNPUBLISHED (PRIMARY)

Alsey, Arthur. Royal Sots. Diary. Imperial War Museum.
Barman, Charles. HKSRA. Diary. Held by his family, and will be published by Hong Kong University Press.
Baugh, Norman. RAF. Statement given at AHQ 221 Group.
Bevan, Job. Royal Artillery. Diary. Held by his son David.
Billings, Adrian. RN. Diary. IWM PP/MCK/121.

Birchall, Leonard. RCAF. Transcript of interview with Charles Roland.
Bromley, Ernest. HKDDC. Diary. Held by his son Brian Bromley.
Collyer, Laurence. Civilian. Diary. Held by Don Collyer.
Coxhead, Geoffrey. HKVDC. Diary. Copies held at King George V School, Hong Kong, and the Museum of Coastal Defence, Hong Kong.
D'Almada, Chris. HKVDC. Diary. Held by Hong Kong University Library.*
Davidson, David. RASC. Diary. Held by his daughter Barbara Wrighting.
Deloughery, Francis. Canadian Chaplain Service. Diary. Held by the HKVCA.
Field, Bevan. HKVDC. Diary. Held by his grandson and the IWM.
Forsyth, Tom. Winnipeg Grenadiers. Diary. Held by his son Morley and with the HKVCA.
Hamilton, Geoffrey. Royal Scots. Memoir: "Prisoner of War in Hong Kong and Japan". Held by Imperial War Museum and his daughter Hilary.
Hill, Donald, RAF. Diary.**
Howard, Alec. HKVDC. Diary. Held by his nephew, Michael Longyear.
Jenner, Dorothy. Civilian. Diary. Mitchell Library: MLMSS 5184.
Kemsley, George. HKDDC. Diary. Held at Imperial War Museum and with his family.
Laite, Uriah. Canadian Chaplain Service. Diary. Held by his family and with the HKVCA.
Lamble, Robert. HKRNVR. Diary. Held by his family.
Lowe, Bill. HKVDC. Diary. Held by his daughter Jeni Zuber.
Lynneberg, Ross. RNZVNR. Memoirs. Held by the Lynneberg family.
Marsh, Tom. Winnipeg Grenadiers. Diary. Held by his son Vic, and with the HKVCA.
Miller, James. Royal Scots. Diary. Held by his daughter.
Moore, Robert. R. N. Y. Police. Letters and Documents. Held by his daughter Faye Powell.
Munro, John. RA. Diary. Held by Richard Goldsbrough.
Newnham, Lanceray. General Staff. Diary. Imperial War Museum.***
O'Toole, James, RAOC. Diary. Held by the FEPOW Community.
Oxley, Albert (Bill). Middlesex. Memoirs, "My Wind of Change". Held by his great nephew Steve Favell.
Parker, Maurice. Royal Rifles of Canada. Memoirs. Held by his son Ron Parker.
Poulter, Bill. Middlesex. Diary. Held by his son Robbie Poulter.
Rakusen, Manassah (Nat). HKVDC. Letters. Held by his son Ron Rakusen.
Redwood, Barbara. ARP. Diary. Copies with the family, the author and the IWM.
Ribeiro, Luigi. HKVDC. Memoirs. Held by Stuart Braga.
Ross, Ted. Ministry of Defence. Memoirs. Held by his son Warwick Ross.

---

* Permission is needed to view this diary.
** Although this short diary is available on the web, it also formed the backbone of a book by Andro Linklater titled *The Code of Love*.
*** His wife's diary is included.

Rozario, Cicero. HKVDC. Diary. Held by his daughter Anna Rozario.
Skelton, Sydney. Royal Rifles of Canada. Diary. Courtesy of Ken Skelton, Gravenhurst, Ontario PIP 1A5 Canada.
Speller, Lionel. RCCS. Transcript of interview with Charles Roland.
Spooner, Bill. Royal Scots. Diary. Held by his daughter Sue and the Burma Star Association.
Tandy, Edward James. HKVDC. Diary. Prisoner-of-war diary, 1942–1943. Box 11, Hume Cronyn and Jessica Tandy Papers, Manuscript Division, Library of Congress, Washington, D.C.
Taylor, Arthur. Royal Navy. Diary. Held by his granddaughter Susie Hunter.
Trick, Charles. Winnipeg Grenadiers. Diary. Held by his son Jim, and with the HKVCA.
White, Harry. Winnipeg Grenadiers. Diary. Imperial War Museum.
Williams, Amy. Nurse. War crimes trial deposition.
Woodward, William. Civilian. Diary. Imperial War Museum.

CORRESPONDENCE (PRIMARY)

Solomon Bard, HKVDC
Bunny Browne, Fortress Headquarters
Phil Doddridge, Royal Rifles of Canada
Jack Etiemble, Royal Artillery
Pat Fallon, HKVDC
James Ford, MC, Royal Scots
Ian Forsyth, 2/14 Punjabis
James Hart, RASC
Major Hancock, Hong Kong Mule Corps
Ross Lynneberg, RNZNVR
Dennis Morley, Royal Scots
Wally Scragg, Hong Kong Police
Edward Shayler, Winnipeg Grenadiers
Raymond Smith, Royal Rifles of Canada

PUBLISHED (SECONDARY)

This work relied in part on research completed while preparing two earlier books:

Banham, Tony. *Not the Slightest Chance: The Defence of Hong Kong, 1941*. Hong Kong: Hong Kong University Press, 2003.
Banham, Tony. *The Sinking of the Lisbon Maru: Britain's Forgotten Wartime Tragedy*. Hong Kong: Hong Kong University Press, 2006.

In the writing of *We Shall Suffer There*, I have been careful not to use any secondary sources, though as a form of peer review (mainly to ensure that I had not omitted any significant event) I consulted at the end a small number of those that I considered the more scholarly works on this subject. They were:

Birch, Alan and Martin Cole. *Captive Years.* Hong Kong: Heinemann Asia, 1982.
Boxer, Charles R. *An Uncommon Life.* Dauril Alden: Fundacao Oriente, 2001.
Endacott,G. *Hong Kong Eclipse.* Edited and with additional material by Alan Birch. Hong Kong: Oxford University Press, 1978.
Garneau, Grant. *The Royal Rifles of Canada in Hong Kong.* Sherbrooke, Quebec: Progressive Publications, 1970.
Lindsay, Oliver. *At the Going Down of the Sun.* London: Hamish Hamilton, 1981.
Roland, Charles G. *Long Night's Journey into Day.* Waterloo, Ontario: Wilfred Laurier University Press, 2001.
Snow, Phillip. *The Fall of Hong Kong.* New Haven and London: Yale University Press, 2003.

OTHER WORKS

Carew, Tim. *Hostages to Fortune.* London: Hamish Hamilton Ltd., 1971.
Chan, Lau Kit-ching and Peter Cunich (ed.). *An Impossible Dream: Hong Kong University from Foundation to Re-establishment, 1910–1950.* Hong Kong: Oxford University Press, 2002.
Clark, Russell S., *An End to Tears.* Sydney: Peter Huston, 1946.
Drew, Sir Robert. *Medical Officers in the British Army, 1660–1960.* London: The Wellcome Historical Medical Library, 1968.
Goodwin, Ralph. *Passport to Eternity.* London: Arthur Barker Ltd., 1956.
Kelly, Terence. *Living with Japanese.* Folkestone: Kellan Press, 1997.
Kent, Molly. *USS Arizona's Last Band.* Kansas City: Silent Song Publishing, 1996.
King, Frank H. H. *The History of The Hongkong and Shanghai Banking Corporation.* Cambridge: Cambridge University Press, 1988.
Lindsay, Oliver. *The Lasting Honour.* London: Hamish Hamilton Ltd., 1978.
Matthews, Clifford and Oswald Cheung (ed.). *Dispersal and Renewal: Hong Kong University during the War Years.* Hong Kong: Hong Kong University Press, 1998.
Nolan, Liam. *Small Man of Nanataki.* New York: E.P. Dutton & Co., 1966.
Ride, Edwin. *British Army Aid Group: Hong Kong Resistance 1942–1945.* Hong Kong: Oxford University Press, 1981.
Smith, Rev. James and Rev. William Downes, The Maryknoll Mission: Hong Kong 1941–46. *Journal of the Hong Kong Branch Royal Asiatic Society,* Volume 19, 1979, pp. 27–148.

OTHER SOURCES

"Chronological Chart of ex-Prisoner of War Camps in Japan Proper" (US National Archives GHQ/SCAP, RG331, Box No.1305).

"Roster of Deceased Allied POWs in Japan Proper" (Japan National Diet Library GHQ/SCAP LS 03399-03404).

"Reviews of the Yokohama Class B and Class C War Crimes Trials by the U.S. Eighth Army Judge Advocate 1946–49" (Japan National Diet Library).

NARA liberation rosters and other documents.

CWGC Internal Documents.

Hong Kong PRO HKRS 112-1-1, Provisional Lists of British and Foreign (other than Japanese) Casualties, Prisoners of War, and Internees in Hong Kong.

Canadian National Archives, RG 24, Box 2900 and Box 2902 (war crimes depositions).

National Archives:

WO344/361/1 to WO344/410/2 (ordered by surname) — MI9 Liberated POW Questionnaires

WO345/01 to WO345/58 (ordered by surname) — POW Index Cards

WO32/14550 Documents relating to the Prisoner of War Camps in the Far East, covering:
- POW Camp 'N', Lt. Col. F. D. Field
- Memoirs of a POW under the Japanese in Hong Kong and Japan, C. R. A. Holmes, 1st Middlesex Regiment
- Mrs. Kaneko Bush, wife of Lewis Bush RNVR, POW Hong Kong and Japan
- Report on the Shamshuipo POW Camp by the SMO
- Report on the general conditions concerning POWs of the Hong Kong Garrison by Major General Maltby
- Report on incarceration at Hong Kong as affecting RAF POWs, by Wing Commander H. G. Sullivan
- POW Burials
- Mark Young, report and correspondence
- Statement — Shamshuipo by Major Grieve RASC
- Statement — Shamshuipo by Capt. G. C. E. Grew RASC*
- Documents submitted by Lt. Col. S. E. H. E. White, Royal Scots, Commanding Camp 'N' Hong Kong

(This file also contains information on the Taiwanese and Manchurian Camps relevant to Hong Kong's senior officers' incarceration).

---

* These two statements refer to Major Boon's post-war trial, but his name has been carefully scratched out. This was done before the files reached the National Archives, but someone has inserted a slip of paper in these files with the Major's name on it.

Index

Notes:

1. Garrison personnel: Many of the works quoted here are personal diaries or letters, the writers of which assume familiarity with those named. Where a quoted name (for example, 'John') can be clearly resolved as a specific individual ('Adams, Private John H. [Winnipeg Grenadiers]'), that name has been indexed in full. Diarists are also typically cavalier with spelling. The spellings in their original texts have been left untouched (even when I suspect it was the transcription from the handwritten original that led to the error), but I have attempted to index with the correct form. Ranks and honours are, as far as possible, those at the start of internment.
2. Place names: Japanese mainland POW camps typically changed their names two or three times during the war, and they often had one or two vernacular names too. Whatever the name in the text, I have consistently indexed by using what I believe is the most accurate version of the Japanese name as at August 1945. Where place names have changed since 1945, I have indexed using the version that predominates in the text.
3. Lists: Rolls of honour and numbered lists have not been indexed, except for the camp name headers in the rolls of honour themselves. To keep the index to an acceptable size, appendices and notes have also not been indexed.

Abbott, Lieutenant Miles J. (Middlesex) 141–3
Aberdeen 8, 13–15, 34, 35, 134, 135, 140
Aberdeen Industrial School 65
Adams, Private John H. (Winnipeg Grenadiers) 52, 53, 55
Adams, First Lieutenant Terence D. (USAAF) 228
Adams, Private William R. (Winnipeg Grenadiers) 47
Admiralty Islands 231
Ahmed, Gunner Nasir (RA) 122
air crash 226–9, 239

air raid 68, 134, 135, 169, 170, 174, 175, 189, 190, 192, 195–201, 203, 204
Ajinomoto (Tokyo #23 Dispatched Camp) 176, 187
Akbar, Havildar Mohamed (HKSRA) 122
Akenobe (Osaka #6 Branch Camp) 198, 225
Ali, Lance Naik Bahadur (HK Mule Corps) 122
Ali, Havildar Major Iftikhar (Rajputs) 122
Ali, Gunner Sultan (RA) 122

Allister, Signalman William (RCCS) 1, 28, 37, 48, 63, 112, 187, 192
Altadena 15
Amagasaki (Osaka #6 Dispatched Camp) 109, 113, 114, 147, 154, 181, 187, 203, 238
American Block 28, 108
Amir, Sepoy Mohamed (Rajputs) 122
Andersen Meyer 172
Andersen, Jaqueline (Civilian) 197
Anderson, James L. (Civilian) 126
Anderson, William J. (Civilian) 126, 205
Andrews, Private James H. (Middlesex) 208
Ansari, Captain Mateen A. (Rajputs) 69, 123, 124
Arai Machi 224
Argyle Street 16, 27, 46, 177, 197
Argyle Street POW Camp 7, 8, 10, 18, 21, 22, 26, 29, 30, 41–43, 69, 74, 107–9, 121, 126, 136, 137, 139–41, 143, 144, 153, 165, 166, 170, 178, 187, 196, 205
Armacost, First Lieutenant Robert (USAAF) 226, 228
Air Raid Precautions (ARP) 16, 23, 134
Asama Maru 46–49, 112, 161
Asano Docks (Tokyo #13 Dispatched Camp) 158, 164, 192
Ashton Hill, Lance Corporal Robert (HKVDC) 173, 176
Ashton-Rose, Captain Leopold W. (IMS) 63, 212
Assesserow, Lance Bombardier Wadin F. (HKVDC) 165
Atana Factory 114
Atkinson, Captain Fred T. (Royal Rifles of Canada) 59
Atlee, Prime Minister Clement 217
atomic bomb 168, 214, 215, 221
Atsugi 224, 226
Australia 3, 202, 243

B24 190, 203, 226, 228
B29 168, 169, 190, 192, 200, 208, 217, 222
Badger, Edith (Civilian) 190, 199
Badger, Captain Harry S. (Middlesex) 45, 55, 135
Bailey, Charles (ARP) 72
Bailie, Major John A. (Winnipeg Grenadiers) 46
Baird, Major Kenneth (Winnipeg Grenadiers) 25, 26, 41, 66, 68, 110, 124, 159, 165, 168, 205, 211, 213
Bak, Dee Dee (Civilian) 6, 7
Bamboo Pier 60, 166, 207
Banfill, Captain Stanley (RCAMC) 29
Bardal, Captain Njall O. (Winnipeg Grenadiers) 110
Barman, BQMS Charles E. (HKSRA) 42
Barnett, Reverend Captain James A. (Canadian Chaplains Service) 127, 141, 169
Barnett, Lieutenant Ken (HKVDC) 18
Barron, CSM John W. (Royal Scots) 44, 195
Barrow, Mrs Katherine (Civilian) 10, 48
Barrow, Oriana (Civilian) 48
Barry, Major 170
Barton, Mrs Ester (Civilian) 46
Barton, Marie (Civilian) 178
Barton, Sergeant Thomas (CMSC) 64
Barwell, Dr Alan (Civilian) 26, 73
Bashford, Staff Sergeant Wilfred G. (RAOC) 111, 123, 221
Bataan 232
Bateman, Carol (Civilian) 46
Bates, Gunner Sydney F. (RA) 229
Bathurst, Anthony (*see* Thompson, W.P.)
Batty-Smith, Captain Sydney H. (ADC Governor) 188, 191
Baugh, Flying Officer Norman L. (RAF) 18, 19, 31, 32

INDEX

Beadnell, Major Herbert (RAMC) 173, 176, 202
Beijing 197
Belfast 66
Belgian Consul 44
Bell, Private Gordon (Winnipeg Grenadiers) 202
Bennett, Chester (BAAG) 126
Bennett, Wing Commander Hubert 'Alf' (RAF) 34
Bentley, Arthur (Civilian) 35
Berard, Leo P. (Winnipeg Grenadiers) 115, 116, 132, 158, 160
beri-beri 39, 56, 68, 73, 156, 158, 160, 162, 173, 175, 176
Bermondsey 72
Bertram, Gunner James (HKVDC) 30, 37, 67, 127, 128, 141, 142, 192, 198, 210, 217
Berzenski, Lance Corporal George (Winnipeg Grenadiers) 48, 52-55
Berzenski, Private Nick J. (Winnipeg Grenadiers) 53
Bethany 59
Betts, Private Arthur H. (Middlesex) 224
Bevan, Gunner Ivor J. (RA) 132, 216, 217, 225, 232, 233
Bicheno, Beatrice (Civilian) 243
Bickley, Private George R. (RAMC) 46
Bidmead, Superintendant Kenneth (HKPF) 40, 44
Bignal, Leading Writer Gordon H. (RN) 159
Birchall, Squadron Leader Leonard (RCAF) 57, 116, 193, 223
Bird, Captain Godfrey V. (RE) 166
Birkett, Lieutenant Ernald P. (RN) 65
Blackwood, Lieutenant Thomas A. (Winnipeg Grenadiers) 41, 124
Blair, Captain Ian (Punjabis) 34
Blazey, Gunner Dumont W. (RA) 141
Bliss, Eileen (Civilian) 138

Blofield, Staff Sergeant Herbert K. (RAOC) 111
Blomfield, Wireless Officer Charles J. (Merchant Service) 56
Bolt, Tom (Civilian) 188
Boocock, Sergeant Harold N. (RAOC) 111, 139
Boon, Major Cecil (RASC) 42, 108, 111, 126, 141, 160, 190, 211, 212
Bonney, Captain Robert (RAOC) 10
Bosanquet, Gunner David (RA) 40
Botelho, Captain Henrique A. (HKVDC) 166
Bowen Road Military Hospital 22, 35, 36, 39, 46, 50, 51, 54, 107, 123, 137, 143, 153, 156, 165, 174, 187, 191, 192, 195, 197, 207
Bowie, Lieutenant Colonel Donald C. (RAMC) 50, 51, 211, 212
Bowles, Private William N. (Middlesex) 120
Boxer, Major Charles R. (Lincs.) 50, 136, 138, 143, 205, 213
Braemar 6
Bransfield, Lieutenant C.M. (USN) 196
Branson, Private Victor (Middlesex) 49, 59
Briggs, Norman (Civilian) 15, 24, 28, 29, 46, 47, 51
British American Tobacco 62
British Army Aid Group (BAAG) 66, 69, 105, 117, 118, 122, 123-7, 129, 134, 135, 140, 151, 154, 170, 172, 175, 177, 185, 188, 241
British Columbia 226, 234
Bromley, Private Ernest E. (HKDDC) 219, 221, 225, 226, 230-5
Bross, Private Carl J. (Winnipeg Grenadiers) 157
Brown, Professor Wenzell (Civilian) 29
Bruce, Sheila (Civilian) 64
Buckley, Lance Sergeant William J. (RAOC) 124, 139

Budden, Private Henry E. (HKDDC) 65
Bull, Sergeant Edward A. (RAOC) 73
Bungalow C 28, 72, 174, 189, 190
Bunje, Doctor Frederick (Civilian) 125
Burke, Lance Corporal John (Middlesex) 229
Bury, Quebec 131
Bush, Captain Howard (RCASC) 130
Bush, Kaneko 13, 14
Bush, Sub Lieutenant Lewis (HKRNVR) 13, 130, 131, 135, 200, 217, 220
Bux, Havildar Karam (HKSRA) 122
Byrne, Ethel (Civilian) 208
Byrne, Professor George T. (Civilian) 166
Byrne, Lance Corporal William G. (Middlesex) 49, 59

Calcutta 30
Cambon, Rifleman Kenneth (Royal Rifles of Canada) 36, 37, 130, 131, 139, 157, 206, 216, 223
Camp Strength or Personnel Lists 122, 123, 129, 171–3
Canadian Pacific Railway 51
Canaval, Doctor Gustav (Civilian) 211
Canton 34, 36, 71, 108, 118, 121, 130, 140, 153, 205, 213, 219
Capsicum Pass 52
Carkeet, Captain Hubert G. (Merchant Service) 109
Carter, Lieutenant Colonel Aubrey R. (USAMC) 231
Cassidy, Joiner John (RNVR) 66
Castle Peak 52, 199
Causeway Bay 51, 203
Cautherley, George (Civilian) 55
Cecil Hotel 16
Central British School (CBS) 197, 207, 211, 213, 219, 221
Central Police Station 123
Challis, RSM Robert H. (Middlesex) 155, 165, 195, 221

Chambers, ERA James W. (RN) 63, 64
Chan, Sapper Peng Seng (RE) 58, 59
Chaplin, CSM Robert R. (Middlesex) 165
Chapman, Private James E. (Winnipeg Grenadiers) 54
Cherry, Private Robert M. (HKVDC) 213
Cheung Chau 39
Chiko Dock 131
China Fleet Club 15
China Light and Power 58
Chisholm, Frank (Civilian) 192
Choa, Rudy 126
Chown, Lieutenant John C. (RNVR) 168
Christensen, Lance Bombardier Neils O. (HKVDC) 74
Christie, Lieutenant (Nursing Sister) Kathleen G. (RCAMC) 136
Chung Am Kok (*see* Chung Hom Kok)
Chung Hom Kok 9, 11
Chungking 52
Clague, Lieutenant James Douglas (Royal Artillery) 33, 40, 71
Clapperton, Private James (Royal Scots) 228
Clara 214
Clarke, Gunner John (RA) 228
Cogbill, Signalman Robert J. (RCS) 194
Coils, AB Jimmy (RN) 170
Cole, Private Edward W. (Winnipeg Grenadiers) 47
Collard, Nurse Gladys (Civilian) 136
Collinson, Commander Alfred C. (RN) 42
Collinson, SQMS Arnold B. (RAOC) 221
Collyer, Laurence (Civilian) 190, 191, 209, 214
Colvin, Private Alexander (Winnipeg Grenadiers) 41
Combined Field Ambulance 25

Condon, Private Alfred (Royal Scots) 170
Connolly, Private Paul (HKDDC) 49, 50, 59
Conte Verde 47
Coomer, Private John (Middlesex) 125
Cooper, WO II James E. (RAOC) 73
Corneck, Private Ken (HKVDC) 74
Corps of Military Police 129, 132
Cosmo Docks 170
Coxhead, Gunner Geoffrey S. (HKVDC) 159, 166, 167, 173, 176, 207, 209, 215, 230
Craven, Commander Douglas H. (RN) 136, 138, 143, 205
Crawford, Sergeant George W. (HKVDC) 74
Crawford, Major John N. (RCAMC) 212
Cropley, Sapper Colin M. (HKVDC) 194
Crossley, Pilot Officer Eddie (RNZAF) 31, 32, 33
Cund, Sapper Henry G. (RE) 157

Dai Ichi Shinko 117
Daily Mail 62
Dalzeil, Sergeant James M. (HKVDC) 140
Damours, Signalman Roland N. (RCCS) 48
Dann, Private Milton R. (Winnipeg Grenadiers) 54
Darian Maru 203
Darmore, Doctor 177
Dauphin, Manitoba 132
Davidson, Corporal David (RASC) 11, 12
Davies, Lieutenant David F. (HKRNVR) 26
Davis, Private John J. (Winnipeg Grenadiers) 122
Deakin, Nurse Dorothy (HKVDC) 43
Debert 235

Deep Water Bay 8, 10
Deloughery, Rev. Captain Francis (Canadian Chaplains Service) 29
Des Voeux Road 16, 27
Diamond Head 233
Digby, Surgeon Professor Kenelm H. (Civilian) 43
Din, PC Alim (HKPF, BAAG) 134, 135
Din, PC Hussain (HKPF) 135
Dina House 16
diphtheria 22, 28, 47, 50, 56, 63, 64, 66, 67, 107, 108, 111
Director of Medical Services (*see* Selwyn Selwyn-Clarke)
Dixon, Private Aaron H. (Middlesex) 64
Dixon, Lieutenant Herbert C. (RNZNVR) 136, 143, 205
Dodwell, Gunner Michael C. (HKVDC) 165
Dominion Monarch 235
Douglas, Lieutenant J. (RNR) 30
Downs, Private James W. (RAMC) 209
Doxford, Corporal William (HKVDC) 228, 229
Drown, Elizabeth (Civilian) 46, 64, 156
Duddell Street 16
Dunkirk 127
Dunne, Lance Corporal Maurice T. (RAOC) 49, 59
Duro Paint Factory 8
Durrschmidt, Henry (Civilian) 29
dysentery 22, 36, 37, 39, 51, 54, 56, 59, 63, 64, 74, 107, 110, 111, 121, 139, 143, 158, 160, 206, 229
Dyson, Sergeant Robert W. (Middlesex) 165

Eager, Oscar (Civilian) 174
Eardley, Lieutenant Henry C. (HKRNVR) 175, 213

Earnshaw, Private Charles Eric (RAPC) 26
East Brigade 16
Easter, Sapper Stanley W. (RE) 176
Eastholm, Private Eric E. (Winnipeg Grenadiers) 66
Eddy, Catherine 167
Edge, Sapper Dennis (RE) 159
Edinburgh 141
Edmonston, David (Civilian) 121, 125, 172
Edmonston, Mary (Civilian) 172
Edmunds, Sergeant Joe (RAF) 130, 131
electric feet 72, 73, 113
Eley, Staff Sergeant Herbert E. (RAOC) 73, 139
Elliot, Private Harry G. (Middlesex) 74
Ellis, CSM Lyle L. (RCAPC) 158
Ellis, Private Percy J. (Winnipeg Grenadiers) 52, 53, 54, 55
Emo, CSM James T. (Canadian Provost Corps) 160
Empress of Australia 221, 225, 226, 230, 232, 235
Epstein, Israel (Civilian) 38
Esquimalt 234
Estes, Luba (Civilian) 24, 39
Etiemble, Gunner John (Royal Artillery) 220
Eucliffe Castle 9
Evans, Seaman Gunner Arthur J. (HKRNVR) 62
Evans, Owen (Civilian) 189
Evans, Private Thomas (Frank) (RAPC) 17, 26, 35, 37, 42–44, 50, 141–3, 155, 176
Evans, Private Thomas G. (Middlesex) 61, 228

Fabel, W.O. Fred A. (RAF) 114, 173
Faid, Professor William (Civilian) 169
Fairclough, Lieutenant Gordon (HKSRA) 33
Fairfax-Cholmondeley, Elsie (Civilian) 38
Fallace, W.O. James W. (HKRNVR) 62
Fan Ling 5, 26
Farmer, Lance Corporal Clarence L. (HKVDC) 137
Fay, ASP Brian (HKPF) 40
Fengtai 197, 203
Fenn, Private Albert V. (Middlesex) 158, 191
Fenwick, T.J. (Civilian) 66
Ferguson, Sapper Douglas (RE) 53
Ferguson family 178
Field, Lieutenant Bevan (HKVDC) 7
Field, Ellen (Civilian) 157
Field, Lieutenant Colonel Fred D. (RA) 136, 138, 166, 212
Field Ambulance 15
Finn, Lieutenant Charles R. (USN) 194, 215, 216
Fisher, Sergeant 'Les' Arthur (HKVDC) 18, 28, 36, 40, 42, 111, 126, 132, 134, 137, 140, 141, 155, 156, 158, 160, 165, 166, 170, 171, 188–92, 198, 207, 212, 213, 219
Food Control 23
Ford, Captain Douglas (Royal Scots) 56, 69, 122, 126, 139, 143
Ford, Lieutenant James A. (Royal Scots) 55–58, 164, 196, 201
Formosa (*see* Taiwan)
Forsyth, Second Lieutenant Ian N. (Punjabis) 64
Forsyth, Private Thomas (Winnipeg Grenadiers) 11, 16, 18, 22, 25, 28, 41, 46–48, 53, 54, 59, 63, 67, 107, 121, 122, 125, 130, 131, 139, 143, 154, 157, 160
Fox, Mrs B. 110
Fraser, John A. (BAAG) 126, 138
Fredericks, Lieutenant Colonel Ernest (RASC) 8
Freeman, Private Edward J. (Winnipeg Grenadiers) 67
French Hospital (*see* St Paul's)

INDEX

Friesen, Private John E. (Winnipeg Grenadiers) 157, 158
Frow, Lieutenant Kenneth G. (3rd Hussars) 196
Fryer, WOI James E. (Royal Artillery) 114
Fukuoka 198
Furey, Private Joseph (Winnipeg Grenadiers) 154
Fushiki 212

Gallagher, Private Joseph (Royal Scots) 36
gangrene 73, 176
Gard, Private James P. (Winnipeg Grenadiers) 206
Geneva Convention 31
Gibson, Lance Corporal Lachlan A. (HKVDC) 74
Gilham, Sergeant Sidney F. (Middlesex) 165, 229
Gill, Brian (Civilian) 165, 214
Gimson, Franklin (Colonial Secretary) 219
Gin Drinkers Line 4
Ginny 228, 229
Gittins, Jean (Civilian) 1, 29, 33, 169, 209
Gittins, Sergeant William (HKVDC) 33
Glasgow, Lieutenant Kenneth (Royal Scots) 34
Gloucester Hotel 23, 70
Glover, Lieutenant Henry C. (HKRNVR) 168
Goa 136
Goddard, Lieutenant Keith W. (AASC) 196
Golden, Captain David A. (Winnipeg Grenadiers) 59
Golden Hill 32
Gollege, Staff Sergeant Gerald (HKSRA) 228
Gooch, Private Arthur H. (Winnipeg Grenadiers) 222

Goodwin, Lieutenant Ralph (RNZNVR) 22, 36, 37, 42, 128, 167, 168
Gordon Head, DC 236
Gordon, Sister Kate (Colonial Nursing Service) 169
Gorman, Sergeant Thomas H. (Royal Naval Dockyard Police) 231
Gosano, Father Zinho (HKVDC) 161
Graff, Sapper Alex (RE) 124
Graham, Lieutenant Ewan C. (Middlesex) 120, 165
Grant, Signalman George C. (RCCS) 48, 192
Gray, Flight Lieutenant Hector B. (RAF) 69, 126, 139, 143
Gray, Major James (RAMC) 35, 45, 66, 68
Gray, Private John (Winnipeg Grenadiers) 4
Grayburn, Lady Muriel (Civilian) 172, 213
Grayburn, Sir Vandeleur (Civilian) 121
Griffin, Gunner Gerald (RA) 209
Grimsdale, Major General Gordon E. (Military Attache) 36
Gripsholm 40, 49, 136
Grooms, Corporal Eric L. (HKVDC) 160
Groves, Arthur (Civilian) 158
Groves, Sergeant Arthur G. (HKPF) 158
Groves, Mrs Doris (Civilian) 158
Groves, Joyce (Civilian) 158
Guam 208, 224, 232
Guangzhou (*see* Canton)
Gun Club Hill 69
Gunstone, Sergeant Reginald (RASC) 11, 12

Habu Docks 116
Haddock, Sub Lieutenant Joseph R. (HKRNVR) 126, 136, 205
Hahn, Emily (Civilian) 15
Hainan Island 34, 108, 153

Hakata 212
Hakodate 61, 197, 204, 212
Hale, RQMS Percy (Middlesex) 165
Halifax, Nova Scotia 235, 236
Hall, Frederick I. (BAAG) 138
Halsey, Admiral William F. (USN) 233
Hamilton, Second Lieutenant Geoffrey C. (Royal Scots) 62, 197, 223
Hamlen, CQMS Fred (RASC) 12
Hankow Barracks 30
Hanley, Gunner Thomas J. (RA) 228
Happy Valley 40, 191
Harcourt, Admiral Cecil H. (RN) 218, 219, 228
Hard, Pilot Officer (RAF) 164, 196
Harding, Gunner Norman (RA) 17, 18
Hardy, Sergeant Ralph J. (RAF) 69, 126, 205
Harrington, Signalman Desmond (RCS) 229
Harrington, LSBA William L. (RN) 49
Harrison, Rifleman Edmond C. (Royal Rifles of Canada) 131
Harrison, Major Gerald C. (RAMC) 211
Harrison, Margaret (Civilian) 73, 214
Harrop, Gunner Gordon (HKVDC) 221
Harrop, Phyllis (Civilian) 15
Hart, Driver James S. (RASC) 8, 9, 11, 17, 50, 114, 203, 210
Harvey, Corporal John H. (RAMC) 132, 157, 158
Hastings, LSBA Wallace G. (RN) 67, 68, 73, 159
Hatt, Sergeant Charles (HKVDC) 166
Hausamann, Private Ernest (HKVDC) 156
Hawes, Private Malcolm J. (Winnipeg Grenadiers) 206
Hay, Private John C. (Winnipeg Grenadiers) 54
Hayashi Lieutenant J. 58, 196

Haynes, Mr. Frank (RAOC) 124
Haywood, Second Lieutenant Roy (Royal Scots) 34
Hazami, Lieutenant 157
Heath, ASP Henry (HKPF) 44
Heath, Ian (Civilian) 64
Heather, Corporal Charles K. (Middlesex) 197
Heep Yuen School 192
Hellcat 217
Hewitt, Captain Anthony (Middlesex) 3, 18, 31–33
Hewitt, Corporal Robert B. (RAOC) 73, 139
Heywood, Private Graham (HKVDC) 4
Heyworth, Roger H. (Civilian) 49
Higashinada 117
Hildersley, W.O. II Norman H. (RAOC) 111
Hill, Squadron Leader Donald (RAF) 17, 19, 26, 27, 32, 34, 37
Hill, Lieutenant Graham S. (Middlesex) 55, 128, 197
Hillman, Staff Sergeant John (RAOC) 73
Hills, Lance Corporal William M. (Middlesex) 49, 53, 54, 59
Himeji 159
Hinson, Captain Sedgie V. (US Artillery) 196
Hiraoka (Tokyo #12 Branch Camp) 197
Hirohata (Osaka #12 Branch Camp) 159
Hiroshima 61, 198, 208, 209, 215
Hiscox, Corporal Sydney (Winnipeg Grenadiers) 6
HMAS *Warramunga* 224
HMCS *Prince Robert* 218, 219
HMRFA *Ebonol* 109
HMS *Anson* 218
HMS *Cicala* 67
HMS *Colossus* 234
HMS *Euryalus* 218

INDEX   341

HMS *Formidable* 233, 234, 235
HMS *Glory* 234, 235
HMS *Implacable* 233, 234
HMS *Indomitable* 218
HMS *Kempenfelt* 218
HMS *Maidstone* 218, 219, 221
HMS *Pyrias* 218
HMS *Quadrant* 218
HMS *Ruler* 213, 230, 231, 233, 235
HMS *Scout* 4
HMS *Speaker* 213, 217, 220, 232
HMS *Swiftsure* 218
HMS *Tern* 30
HMS *Thanet* 4
HMS *Thracian* 11, 12, 128
HMS *Toscin* 219
HMS *Ursa* 219, 228
HMS *Venerable* 219
HMS *Whirlwind* 219
Ho, Helen 125
Hobson, Sergeant Albert J. (Middlesex) 138, 165
Hodges, Private Daniel (Royal Scots) 36
Hogarth, Sergeant Cecil G. (RE) 124
Holdford, Sergeant Charles (Middlesex) 165
Holroyd P.O. Telegraphist Maxwell (RN) 30
Home, Lt. Colonel William J. (Royal Rifles of Canada) 46, 59
Hong Kong Dockyard Defence Corps 49, 59, 219, 221
Hong Kong Field Ambulance 25
Hong Kong Hotel 36
Hong Kong Mule Corps 122, 234
Hong Kong News 132
Hong Kong Observatory 4
Hong Kong Police Force 45
Hong Kong Royal Naval Volunteer Reserve 15, 25, 26, 62, 130, 168, 175
Hong Kong and Shanghai Banking Corporation 66, 121

Hong Kong and Singapore Royal Artillery 4, 33, 69, 118, 122, 135, 228, 234
Hong Kong Telegraph 219
Hong Kong University 11, 18, 29, 35
Hong Kong Volunteer Defence Corps 3, 16, 21, 26–28, 31, 32, 42, 58, 66, 74, 111, 113, 114, 123, 126, 130, 133, 134, 137, 153, 158, 162, 169, 172, 194, 197, 207, 211, 213, 229, 233, 234
Honolulu 232, 233
Hook, Major Henry W. (Winnipeg Grenadiers) 205, 207
Hooper, Colonel E. (BAAG) 140
Hordyke, Lieutenant (Royal Netherlands Navy) 30
Houghton, Captain Alfred C. (RE) 196, 211, 221, 223, 229
Howard, Staff Sergeant Alec H. (HKVDC) 155, 189, 197, 208, 213, 216, 218, 222
Howarth, Sapper Glen L. (RE) 53
Howell, 2nd Lieutenant Hargreaves M. (RASC) 62
Huggett, Private John (Middlesex) 64
Humphreys, Chief Engineer Joseph J. (Merchant Service) 141
Hurst, Lieutenant J.W. (RNR) 30
Hyde, Charles F. (BAAG) 126
Hyde, Florence (Civilian) 172
Hyde, Michael (Civilian) 172, 213
Hyde-Lay, Alexander (Civilian) 72
Hyde-Lay, Elizabeth (Civilian) 72

Ichioka Ward 67, 73, 159
Idema, Lieutenant (Royal Netherlands Navy) 30
Ikuno (Osaka #4 Branch Camp) 196
Ile de France 235
Indian Independence League 69, 123, 134
Indian Medical Services (IMS) 234
Indian POW Location Lists 70, 71, 119, 120

Ingram, Private Theodore R. (HKVDC) 74
Innoshima (Hiroshima #5 Branch Camp) 109, 113, 114, 116, 120, 156, 159, 166, 167, 173, 176, 178, 179, 207, 209, 230
Ito, Captain 131
Iverach, Corporal John A. (Winnipeg Grenadiers) 63

Jackson, Surgeon Lieutenant Charles A. (RNVR) 67, 73, 159, 175
Jacobs, Private Mike (RAMC) 32
James, Sergeant William R. (RA) 229
Japanese Indian Fifth Column (JIFC) 134
Jardine Matheson 18, 27
Jardine's Lookout 5
Java 156, 196
Jeffery, Corporal Reginald (RAOC) 111, 139
Jeffree, Sergeant George H. (Middlesex) 165
Jiangwan (see Kiangwan)
Jingle, Mr (Civilian) 178
Jockey Club Relief Hospital 10
Johnson, Isabella (Civilian) 174
Johnson, Superintendent Maurice A. (HKPF) 174
Johnston, Private David (Winnipeg Grenadiers) 125
Johnstone, W.O. William C. (HKRNVR) 62
Jones, Captain Cyril R. (Royal Scots) 26, 69
Jones, Private Harold B. (Winnipeg Grenadiers) 154
Josey, Leading Seaman Geoffrey L. (RN) 210
Joy, Father Patrick 125
Jubilee Buildings 17, 30, 31, 50, 67, 73, 111
Junk Bay 226

Kadoorie Avenue 39

Kadoorie, Michael (Civilian) 43, 44
Kai Tak 4, 34, 35, 42, 47, 54, 58, 59, 69, 134, 177
Kamaishi 231
Kamaishi (Sendai #5 Branch Camp) 192, 198, 206, 209, 238
Kamakura Maru 49
Kamigumi 116
Kamioka (Nagoya #1 Despatched Camp) 159
Kanetsuna, Lieutenant R. 196
Karoto Foundry 116
Kauffman, Captain Nelson N. (USMC) 57, 58
Kawasaki 113
Kawasaki (Tokyo #1 Branch Camp) 56, 102, 109, 138, 238
Kawasaki (Tokyo #2 Branch Camp) 208, 238
Kawasaki 3D (see Tsurumi Shipyard)
Kawasaki Kobe (Osaka #5 Dispatched Camp) 109, 120, 121, 147, 154, 198, 202
Kawasaki Station 138, 158, 170
Kearney, Stoker Timothy (RN) 210
Keeler, Private Alfred (Middlesex) 210
Keelung 131
Keenan, RSM Oscar C. (Winnipeg Grenadiers) 116
Kellett Island 52
Kempetai 40
Kennard, Eric J. (Civilian) 43
Kennedy Road 74
Khan, Jemadar Dadan (HKSRA) 118
Khan, Sepoy Didla 171
Khan, Gunner Hadayat (HKSRA) 135
Khan, Subedar Inmar (Rajputs) 71
Khan, Jemadar Lal (HKSRA) 134, 135
Khan, Subedar Maxim 69
Khan, Havildar Mehdi 117
Khan, Subedar Meher (Rajputs) 135
Khan, Lance Naik Raja (RA) 121, 122
Kiangwan POW Camp 72, 108, 109, 153, 187, 197
King, Gunner Frank G. (RA) 157

King, Professor Gordon (Civilian) 35
King, Second Lieutenant Ralph M. (Middlesex) 165
King, Private Thomas P. (Middlesex) 229
King's Road 6, 28
Kirk, Doctor Edward W. (Civilian) 43
Kirk, Lance Corporal Roy L. (Winnipeg Grenadiers) 206
Knight, Private Humphrey C. (HKVDC) 74
Kobe 114, 120, 201, 202, 212, 223
Kobe (Osaka #2 Branch Camp) 61, 62, 67, 68, 100, 109, 116, 117, 120, 125-7, 138, 146, 153, 154, 165, 168, 171, 174, 179, 187, 190, 195, 196, 201, 204, 205, 214, 237
Kobeco 117
Kock, Erwin (Civilian) 29
Kokura 61, 108
Korea 197, 203
Kota Bharu 30
Kotwall, Private George (HKVDC, BAAG) 123
Kowloon 4, 5, 7, 8, 10, 16, 17, 25, 28, 30, 31, 37, 39, 42, 46, 49, 59, 70, 112, 209, 225, 226
Kowloon Canton Railway (KCR) 134
Kowloon Cricket Club 40
Kowloon Docks 130
Kowloon Gaol 49, 53, 54
Kumamoto (Fukuoka #1 Branch Camp) 176, 187, 237
Kwangchowan 70
Kwanti Race Course 117
Kyoto 198, 203, 220, 225

La Salle Relief Hospital 26, 51
Labrousse, Corporal Ernest D. (HKVDC) 74
Lai Chi Kok 35, 134, 135
Laite, Rev. Captain Uriah (Canadian Chaplains Service) 41, 43, 53, 59, 64, 69, 72, 109, 110, 112, 124, 127, 133, 141, 161, 165, 169, 170, 174, 175
Lake Biwa 220
Lam, O.S. (Civilian) 177
Lamma Island 12
Lashio 30
Lau Fan Kiu 118
Lavarie, Private Cecil F. (Winnipeg Grenadiers) 117
Lee, Dorothy 125
Lee, Francis (Civilian) 29
Lee, Private Francis Yan Piu (HKVDC) 25, 26
Lee, Private Frank (HKVDC) 74
Lee, Lance Corporal John S. (HKVDC) 74
Leonard, Private David J. (HKVDC) 16
Leonard, Private Stanley L. (HKVDC) 161
Les Miserables 226
Lewis, Gunner Reginald (RA) 32
Lin Ma Hang Mine 118, 173
Lisbon Maru 22, 59-61, 62, 64, 66, 72, 81, 107-9, 112, 116, 127, 128, 141, 143, 153, 203, 231
Liverpool 232, 235
Lloyd, Sergeant Norman 'Lofty' (HKVDC) 40
Lo, Sergeant Hung Sui (HKVDC, BAAG) 66
Lomax, CQMS Robert (Middlesex) 165
Lourenco Marques 48
Lowe, Mrs Elah (HKVDC) 111, 112
Lowe, Private William (HKVDC) 1, 45, 48, 50, 55, 59, 64, 68, 74, 111, 113, 114, 116, 120, 153, 156, 159, 178, 244
Lucas, Private Harold F. (Winnipeg Grenadiers) 54
Luscombe, ASP Colin (HKPF) 44, 70
Lyemun 124
Lyle, Lance Sergeant Ian F. (RAPC) 141

Lynneberg, Telegraphist Ross (RNZNVR) 198, 220
Lyon, Jean (Civilian) 192

Ma Tau Chung POW Camp 21, 27, 69, 71, 72, 102, 107, 109, 119, 121, 123, 124, 126, 134, 135, 139, 149, 153, 166, 170, 175, 177, 183, 188, 239
Ma Tau Wai Civilian Interment Camp 166, 175, 177, 178, 187, 192, 211, 240
MacArthur, General Douglas (United States Army) 224
Macau 27, 39, 52, 124, 177, 199
MacCleod, Kenneth B. (Civilian) 50
MacCulloch, Corporal David M. (RAOC) 188
MacDonell, Sergeant George S. (Royal Rifles of Canada) 212, 216, 220, 231
MacGregor, Lieutenant Ian 121
Mackie, William (Civilian) 197
Macklin, Sergeant Robert (AEC) 74
MacNider, Gladys (Civilian) 170
malaria 54, 56, 125, 132, 165, 189
Malaya 196
Malekin, Lance Sergeant Edmond (RAOC) 73, 139
Maltby, Major General Christopher 13, 14, 30, 127, 129
Man, Andrew 196
Man, Captain Christopher M. (Middlesex) 165, 214, 221, 224
Manchester, Sergeant Robert (Winnipeg Grenadiers) 10
Manhattan 51
Manila 212, 222, 224–6, 229–34
Manners, Charles (Civilian) 176
Manning, Lieutenant Frank (HKRNVR) 14
Manryu Maru 130
Marina House 14
Marsden, Captain Eric (RCS) 166
Marsh, Private William (Middlesex) 127

Marsh, Sergeant Thomas (Winnipeg Grenadiers) 5, 7, 10, 41, 112, 115, 117, 169, 175, 194, 215, 221
Maru Shi 55
Maru Yama 202, 205
Marutsu Docks 132, 206
Maryknoll Missionaries 59, 110
Maryknoll School 7, 10, 26
Matheson, CSM Donald (Royal Scots) 220
Mathieu, Gunner Pierre B. (HKVDC) 133, 134
Matsuda 'Cardiff Joe' 131
Matte, Private Thomas (Winnipeg Grenadiers) 6
Matthews, Captain David 'Mathers' (Punjabis) 34
Maunganui 219
May Hall 58, 59
McAuley, Corporal William A. (Winnipeg Grenadiers) 41
McBride, Private Thomas A. (Winnipeg Grenadiers) 48
McDonagh, Private William (Royal Scots) 228
McInally, Private Joseph (Middlesex) 45, 64
McKillop, Lieutenant Orville (Winnipeg Grenadiers) 7, 8
McLeod, Private Robert (Winnipeg Grenadiers) 206
McMaster, Driver Thomas Y. (RE) 47
McNaughton, Staff Sergeant Henry P. (Winnipeg Grenadiers) 127
McNichol, Jill 243
Mears, Leading Seaman Albert E. (RN) 218
Meekings, Staff Sergeant Edward H. (RAOC) 111
Merthyr, Major, The Lord W. (RA) 43, 108
Meyer, CQMS Joseph (HKVDC) 12
Meyer, Father Bernard F. (Civilian) 165

INDEX 345

Middlesex Regiment, the 1st Battalion 3, 9, 16, 27, 30, 31, 35, 45, 49, 54, 55, 59, 60
Miller, Private James M. (Royal Scots) 229
Minamoto, Mr 58
Minatagowa 116
Ministry of Information 4
Mitchell, Sergeant Alfred C. (RAOC) 139
Mitchell, Mrs Amy (Civilian) 68
Mitchell, Lieutenant Eric (Winnipeg Grenadiers) 6
Mitchell, Robert (Civilian) 164
Mitchell, Rosemary (Civilian) 68, 164
Mitchell, Lieutenant William (Winnipeg Grenadiers) 6
Mitchell, PO William E. (RN) 135
Mitchell, Willy 204
Mitsubishi 128
Mitsubishi Shipyard 112
Mitsubishi Takehome 117
Mitsui 208
Mitsumosho 114, 116
Mogford, Corporal Edward M. (RAMC) 116, 156
Mohamed, Jemadar Dosht (Punjabis) 171
Moji 61, 155, 161
Monaghan, Private Thomas C. (HKVDC, BAAG) 126
Montreal 235
Mooney, Mr 178
Moore, PC Robert B. (Royal Naval Dockyard Police) 114, 123, 198, 225, 230, 232, 233, 235
Morgan, (Royal Rifles of Canada) 37
Mori 207
Morita, CSM 203
Morley, Private Dennis (Royal Scots) 59
Morley, Sub Lieutenant Denys W. (HKRNVR) (26)
Morosov, Staff Sergeant Vladimir (RE) 123

Morrison, J.A. (Civilian) 66
Morrison, Police Sergeant Vincent M. (HKPF) 178
Morrison, Police Officer William (HKPF) 40
Mortimer, Rifleman James L. (Rifleman) 157
Moulton, Corporal John (RAF) 42
Mount Austin Barracks 11
Mount Parker Road 6
MTB08 135
Muckden (*see* Shenyang)
Mullah, Reim (Civilian) 171
Munro, Major J. (RA) 31, 32
Murata, Colonel 220
Murphy, Corporal Edward O. (HKVDC) 74
Murray Barracks 13-15, 18
Murray Parade Ground 23, 24

Nagasaki 113, 155, 209, 212, 232
Nagoya 212
Naimat, Havildar Ali (HKSRA) 118
Nakayama, Medical Sergeant 157
Nankin Barrack 30
Nanking Hotel 23
Napaloff, Sapper Alexis I. (HKVDC) 124
Narumi (Nagoya #2 Branch Camp) 109, 154-6, 179, 187, 189, 197, 237
Nathan Road 4, 16, 17, 39
Naura Maru 160
Naval Dockyard 16
Nelms, Lance Corporal Phillip A. (Middlesex) 73
Ness, Parker Van (Civilian) 38
New Territories 121
New York 51, 167
Newnham, Colonel Lanceray A. (Middlesex) 69, 126, 139, 143
Newton, Lieutenant Claude E. (USN) 220
Nichol, 2nd Engineer Robert H. (Merchant Service) 109

Nichol, W.O. II William (RAOC)   30, 111, 123
Nichols, Sapper Alan (RE)   124
Nicolson, Doctor Murdo (Civilian)   125
Nielsen Field, Philippines   226
Niigata   212
Niigata Rinko (Tokyo #5 Branch Camp)   109, 131, 132, 139, 143, 148, 153, 154, 157, 160, 182, 187, 193, 201, 206, 216, 223, 224, 238
Niigata Tekko (Tokyo #15 Branch Camp)   143, 183, 187, 201
Niishin Oil (Tokyo #17 Branch Camp)   159, 164, 171, 177, 191, 200, 207, 239
Nippon Yusen Kaisha (NYK)   112
Nomachi (Nagoya #10 Dispatched Camp)   204, 205, 208, 212, 218, 221, 222, 224, 237
Nomoto   207
North Point   5, 8, 16, 18, 29
North Point POW Camp   6–8, 21, 27, 28, 30, 31, 36, 37, 41, 42, 47, 48, 50, 52, 54, 63, 69, 81, 108, 110, 121
North Point Power Station   5
Norris, Captain John A. (Winnipeg Grenadiers)   125
Notogawa (Osaka #9 Branch Camp)   198, 220, 229
Nunn, Sergeant Walter R. (RE)   123

Oakland   235
Oeyama (Osaka #3 Branch Camp)   109, 131, 132, 147, 153, 155, 157, 173, 176, 180, 187, 197, 202, 203, 216, 217, 225, 237
Ofuna (Tokyo Main Camp Detached Camp)   57, 217
Ogley, Olivia (Civilian)   55
Ohamigumi   117
Ohashi (Sendai #4 Branch Camp)   192, 193, 207, 212, 216, 220, 231, 232

Okinawa   226, 232
Omar, Jemadar Mohamed (Punjabis)   171
Omine (Fukuoka #5 Branch Camp)   109, 113, 117, 137, 145, 154, 176, 179, 187, 232, 234, 237
Omori (Tokyo Main Camp)   56, 57, 109, 127, 128, 135, 148, 153, 166, 177, 192, 198, 201, 210, 212, 217
Onagi   128
O'Neill, Honourary Captain Francis G. (Canadian Auxiliary Services)   174
O'Neill, Raymond (Civilian)   38
O'Neill, William (Civilian)   74
Onomichi   114
Onyette, W.O. Greenville C. (RCAF)   57
Osaka   131, 156, 159, 196, 203, 205
Osaka (Osaka #1 Branch Camp)   61, 62, 66–68, 99, 108, 109, 117, 127, 131, 145, 153, 179, 187, 197, 199, 201, 237
Osaka Iron Works   114
Otaki   58
O'Toole, Staff Sergeant James (RAOC)   10, 18, 21, 26, 30, 73, 74, 111, 123, 129, 134, 139, 160, 165, 188, 189, 211, 214, 219, 221, 224
Otway, Captain Caesar E. (RE)   57
Oxfordshire   218, 219, 221
Oxley, Private Albert 'Bill' (Middlesex)   35, 72, 135, 161, 162, 194, 215, 236

Paddock, Major (Gloucestershires)   235
Page, Surgeon Commander John A. (RN)   114, 171, 202
Palmer, Corporal Douglas (RAF)   19
Panco, Private Michael (Winnipeg Grenadiers)   132
Pargeter, Private Ernest A. (Middlesex)   229
Parker, Corporal Bernard (RAOC)   139

Parker, Writer Henry T. (RN)   135
Parker, Major Maurice A. (Royal Rifles of Canada)   52, 108, 136, 168, 211, 219, 225, 230, 232, 236
Parrott, Lance Bombardier Danny (RA)   32
Passmore, Lieutenant Phillip (RA)   33
Paterson, Major John (HKVDC)   18
Paul, Petty Officer Peter (RN)   128
Payne, Sergeant John O. (Winnipeg Grenadiers)   52-55
Peacehaven   66
Peak, The   15, 24, 28
Peak Mansions   11
Peak Tram Terminus   25
Pearce, Lieutenant Alec C. (RA)   44
Pearce, Second Lieutenant John C. (RA)   40
Pearl Harbour   125, 206, 224, 232, 234
Pears, Lt.-Commander Arthur (RN)   13
Pegg, Private Charles W. (Middlesex)   64
pellagra   56, 121, 167, 176
Peninsula Hotel   127
Perez, Consuelo Delgado Y (Civilian)   177
Perkins, Lieutenant (United States Army)   177
Petchey, Gunner Basil G. (RA)   45
Peters, Staff Sergeant Walter R. (RAOC)   111
Peveril-Guest family   178
Pickles, Private Maurice (RAOC)   139, 176
Piddington, Lance Corporal Reginald (Middlesex)   35
Plumber, Sergeant George E. (Middlesex)   49, 54
Plummer, Lieutenant Robert (RA)   18
pneumonia   139, 160, 176
Pokfulam   8, 110,
Pollock, Lieutenant Joshua T. (RN)   62
Pooley, Signalman Charles H. (RN)   66
Pope, Private William (Middlesex)   228
Portage, Canada   8
Potts, Peter (Civilian)   136
Poulter, Robin   243
Poulter, Sergeant William H. (Middlesex)   60-62, 67, 120, 125, 126, 138, 154, 165, 174, 190, 195, 201-4, 208, 210, 212, 218, 221, 224, 226, 230, 232-4, 243
Prata, Private Manuel G. (HKVDC)   126, 136
Prendergast, Lieutenant Alexander A. (Winnipeg Grenadiers)   59, 110
Price, Major (United States Army)   231
Price, Lieutenant Arthur C. (RAMC)   57
Price, Lance Corporal Charles H. (RCS)   229
Price, Major John H. (Royal Rifles of Canada)   126
Price, Sapper Leonard (RE)   141
Priestwood, Gwen (Civilian)   27, 38
Proulx, W.O. Benny (HKRNVR)   15, 25, 30, 31
Pugh, Lance Corporal Alfred (RAOC)   124, 160
Pugsley, Sergeant William (Winnipeg Grenadiers)   6, 10, 127
Punjabi Regiment, the 14th, 2nd Battalion   171, 172, 234
Pusan, Korea   197, 203

Queen Elizabeth   51, 235, 236
Queen Mary   51
Queen Mary Hospital   13, 27, 74, 191
Queen's Pier   28
Queen's Road   16, 23
Quick, Sergeant John H. (Middlesex)   165
Quilliam, Lieutenant Thomas H. (RN)   135
Quinsy   54

radio   66, 136, 137, 139
Rajput Regiment, the 7th, 5th Battalion   5, 71, 122, 124, 136, 234

Rakusen, Staff Sergeant Manassah N. (HKVDC)   163, 215, 233
Rance, Private Arthur W. (HKVDC)   48, 130
Randall, B.   125
Randall, Harold (Civilian)   40
Rashid, Naik Abdul (HKSRA)   118
Ray, Chief Petty Officer (RN)   201
Read, A/S.M. Arthur I. (RAOC)   111
Red Cross   5, 72, 107, 121, 132, 141, 167, 194, 199, 211, 224, 225, 232
Redwood, Barbara (ARP)   16, 23, 25, 27, 43, 46, 47, 50, 51, 55, 64, 67, 68, 72, 74, 136, 138, 156, 158, 164, 165, 169, 172, 174-6, 178, 188, 189, 192, 197, 199, 208, 219
Redwood, Mabel Jnr. (HKVDC)   46
Redwood, Mabel Sen. (ANS)   43
Redwood, Olive (Food Control)   23, 172
Rees, Hubert S. (BAAG)   126
Reeves, John (British Consul)   124
Reid, Captain John A. (RCAMC)   112, 116, 132, 194, 215
Reid, Rifleman Lloyd G. (Royal Rifles of Canada)   139
Replacement Camp   230-2
Repulse Bay   8-11
Repulse Bay Hotel   8, 9
Reuters   74
Richards, J. J. (Civilian)   177
Ride, Lieutenant Colonel Lindsay (HKVDC, BAAG)   25, 26
Ridge, The   8, 9, 11, 12
Riley, Rifleman James (Royal Rifles of Canada)   8, 244
Riley, Flying Officer Walter (RAF)   156, 197, 213
Rinko   132
Rio de Janeiro   51
Roberts, Private Edward A. (HKVDC)   66
Roberts, Lance Corporal William E. (RAOC)   221
Robinson, Captain James E. (RAMC)   162
Robinson, Corporal Roy (Winnipeg Grenadiers)   117
Roblee, Rifleman Lloyd L. (Royal Rifles)   160
Rodrigues, Mr   199
Rosary Hill   22
Rosary Hill Civilian Internment Camp   109, 132, 133, 156, 187, 190, 199
Rose, Dawn (Civilian)   165, 169, 170
Rose, Gerald (Civilian)   165, 169, 170
Rose, BSM Henley H. (HKVDC)   165, 169
Rose, Signalman Jack (RCCS)   48
Rose, Rachel (Civilian)   165, 169
Ross, Ted (Ministry of Information)   4
Rousoll, CSM Henry C. (HKDDC)   123
Routledge, Sergeant Ronald J. (RCCS)   69, 126, 205
Rowland, Private Ernest (Middlesex)   198, 209
Royal Air Force   17, 18, 21, 31, 32, 34, 114, 129, 130, 132, 164, 176, 196
Royal Army Dental Corps   51
Royal Army Medical Corps   32, 35, 37, 51, 57, 63, 116, 120, 132, 156, 162, 209
Royal Army Ordnance Corps   9, 21, 42, 49, 59, 111, 114, 130, 139, 221
Royal Army Service Corps   50, 108, 114, 196
Royal Artillery   16, 31-33, 43, 55, 60, 114, 118, 122, 132, 141, 157, 209, 228, 229
Royal Australian Navy   157
Royal Canadian Air Force   57
Royal Canadian Army Medical Corps   112
Royal Canadian Army Service Corps   130
Royal Canadian Corps of Signals   187
Royal Corps of Signals   60, 114, 194, 229

Royal Engineers 14, 34, 50, 51, 57, 60, 129, 132, 141, 157, 212, 229
Royal Marines 60
Royal Naval Hospital 22, 65, 74
Royal Navy 21, 27, 29, 41, 42, 55, 56, 60, 62, 66, 108, 114, 135, 138, 175, 218, 236
Royal Netherlands Navy 30
Royal New Zealand Air Force 31
Royal Rifles of Canada 12, 16, 28, 29, 37, 46, 47, 66, 113, 116, 130, 131, 160, 216, 219, 236
Royal Scots Regiment, the 2nd Battalion 4, 15, 32, 36, 39, 55–57, 59, 60, 114, 141, 143, 170, 174, 201, 228, 231
Rozario, Private Cicero (HKVDC) 34, 134, 160, 161–3, 222, 228
Ruck, Sergeant Graham L. (Middlesex) 165
Rutherford, Lance Sergeant Archibald R. (Winnipeg Grenadiers) 139
Ryan, Major George (RA) 211

Saddington, Staff Sergeant Gordon E. (RAOC) 111
Sai On 177
Saigon 34
Saikung 35
Saipan 168
Sakurajima (Osaka #4 Dispatched Camp) 109, 113, 114, 123, 147, 154, 180, 187, 198, 238
Salesian Mission 15
Salmon family 136
Salter, Private Cedric (Royal Scots) 15, 39
San Francisco 112, 225, 226, 232, 233, 235
Sanderson, Musician 2nd Class Harvey (USN) 125
Sannomiya 224
Sauson, Sergeant Lester L. (Royal Rifles of Canada) 154

Sawyer, Lance Corporal Ken F. (RAVC) 42
Scott, Walter R. (HKPF, BAAG) 126, 138
Scriven, Captain Douglas (Indian Medical Service) 31–33
Seah, Private Tin Toon (HKVDC) 58
Seaman's Institute 15
Searle, ASP Lance A. (HKPF) 44
Selby, Dr John (Colonial Medical Service) 10
Selwyn-Clarke, Dr Selwyn (Director of Medical Services) 11, 21, 24, 46, 51, 52, 124, 125, 211
Sen Riiyama 220
Sendai 212
Senpaku 117
sepsis 73
septicaemia 72
Shackleton, Lieutenant Colonel Cedric O. (RAMC) 50
Shamshuipo POW Camp 16–18, 21, 22, 25–28, 30, 32–34, 36, 37, 40–44, 48, 49, 51, 52, 58, 59, 63, 64, 67, 69, 72–74, 107–9, 121–3, 126, 129, 130, 132–4, 137, 139–41, 144, 153, 155, 156, 158, 160, 165–7, 169–71, 174, 175, 178, 187–92, 198, 203, 205, 207, 211–4, 219, 221, 236
Shanghai 22, 43, 44, 47, 49, 61, 72, 98, 99, 108, 111, 136, 192, 195, 197, 203
Shatin Pass 118
Shau Kei Wan 5, 194
Shaw, Corporal Arthur (RASC) 12
Shayler, Private Henry A. (Winnipeg Grenadiers) 176
Shee, George 125
Shek O 143
Shenyang 129, 174
Sheppard, John O. (Civilian) 51
Sherry, Lieutenant (USN) 177
Shibaura 128, 210
Shields, Andrew (Civilian) 169

Shimonoseki 155, 212
Shinagawa (Tokyo Main Camp) 56, 57, 101, 108, 109, 127, 128, 147
Shinagawa Hospital 57, 109, 128, 132, 158, 159, 162, 175, 191, 217
Shing Mun Redoubt 4, 26, 69
Shinsei Maru (see *Washington Maru*)
Shintetsu 132
Shiodome 128
Shiogama 231
Shirakawa POW Camp 129
Shore, RSM Leslie W. (Royal Rifles of Canada) 116
Shouson Hill 13, 19
Showa Denki 116, 196
Shrigley, Lieutenant Ralph J. (HKVDC) 44, 166, 167
Silva, Private Ambrosio C. (HKVDC) 207
da Silva, M.A. 126
da Silva, Second Lieutenant Porphyric (HKVDC) 43, 44
Simson, Colonel John T. (RAMC) 50
Singapore 30, 47, 202
Singh, Gunner Atta 117
Singh, Basat (Civilian) 118
Singh, Naik Changahl (RA) 118
Singh, Lance Naik Dalip (RA) 70
Singh, Naik Jadat (RA) 118
Singh, Gunner Karkail 117
Singh, Kartar (Civilian) 171
Singh, Lance Naik Lashkar (RA) 69, 70
Singh, Gunner Madho (RA) 118
Singh, Rissaldar Major Mahinder (RIASC) 46
Singh, Havildar Mehnca (RA) 69
Singh, Naranjan (BAAG) 124
Singh, Policeman Narvant (HKPF) 70
Singh, Jemadar Sadara (RA) 118
Singh, Lance Naik Santokh (RA) 69
Siu Kwan 30
Skelton, Rifleman Sydney (Royal Rifles of Canada) 113, 137
Smart, Corporal Jack (RAPC) 35
Smith, Major James (HKVDC) 166

Smith, Private John S. (Winnipeg Grenadiers) 59
Smuggler's Reach 32
Soares, Private Alberto C. (HKVDC) 155
Socony 35, 134
Soden, CSM Edwin J. (Middlesex) 165
Solecki, Gunner Jan (HKVDC) 63
Sonley, Ship's Master Leslie (Merchant Service) 110
Soong Cheong 141, 142
South, Stoker Petty Officer James (RN) 177
Southampton 235
Speller, Signalman Lionel C. (RCCS) 116, 193
Spooner, Private William (Royal Scots) 203
Spoov, Nick (Civilian) 44,
Sprague, Private William (HKVDC) 42
Spry, Rose (Colonial Nursing Service) 214
St Albert's Convent 22, 36, 132
St John's Ambulance Brigade 18
St Margaret's School 40
St Paul's Hospital 51, 124, 125, 197
St Stephen's College 10, 24, 48
St Stephen's Prep School 27
St Teresa's Hospital 36, 37, 46, 51, 58
Standen, Lance Sergeant Charles W. (RAOC) 73, 139
Stanley 1, 9, 10, 12, 16, 21, 27, 28, 45, 48, 69, 70
Stanley Beach 138
Stanley Fort 8, 9
Stanley Gaol 21, 24, 40, 45, 46, 108, 126, 137, 205
Stanley Internment Camp 21, 24, 26, 29, 30, 38, 40, 43, 46–48, 50, 51, 55, 59, 65, 70, 73, 74, 104, 108–10, 121, 125, 126, 130, 136, 138, 151, 156, 158, 164, 166, 169, 172, 174, 175, 177, 178, 184, 187–9, 191, 197, 199, 208, 209, 213, 214, 219, 225, 226, 240, 243, 244

Stanton, John (Civilian)   136
Star Ferry   4, 16
Starbuck, Leonard (Civilian)   4
Stenning, Surgeon Lieutenant Commander Samuel (RAN)   157
Stericker, John (Civilian)   23, 24, 25, 49, 62, 189
Stevenson, Private Andy (RAPC)   26
Stewart, Douglas   64
Stewart, Lieutenant Colonel Henry (Middlesex)   3
Stimpson, Cornelius C. (HKVDC)   134
Stirling Lee, Lance Corporal John (HKVDC)   173, 176
Stodgell, Private Garnett J. (Winnipeg Grenadiers)   121
Stonecutters Island   52, 190
Stopforth, Private James (RAOC)   49, 59
Stott, Private Robert E. (HKVDC)   51, 52
Strachen, Captain Arthur W. (IMS)   212
Strong, Reverend Captain Charles (RNR)   65
Stubbs Road   132
Sumidagawa (Tokyo #10 Branch Camp)   128, 192, 238
Sumitomo   117
Sun Wah Hotel   29, 66, 108, 109, 125
Supreme Court   124, 139
Susa   203
Sutcliffe, Lieutenant Colonel John (Winnipeg Grenadiers)   39
Suter, Mr   199
Sutherland, Sergeant Alex (Royal Scots)   141
Sutton, Francis A. (Civilian)   175
Suwa (Tokyo #6 Branch Camp)   192, 193, 223, 238
Suzuki, Lieutenant   13-15
Sword, Staff Sergeant David L. (RCASC)   154
Swyer, Major James E. (RAMC)   212
Sydney, Australia   15, 231, 233-5

Tai Koon Hotel   16, 23
Taikoo   10
Tainan Maru   43
Taipei   131
Taipo Road   34
Taitam   6, 70
Taiwan   43, 109, 128, 129, 131, 142, 174, 226, 227
Takahama   155, 195
Takahashi, Sergeant   157
Takanaka   195
Takliwa   234, 235
Tamano (Hiroshima #3 Branch Camp)   203
Tandy, Gunner Edward J. (HKVDC)   176
Tarodati, Corporal   157
Tatayama Heavy Industry Co.   197
Tate, Private Arthur (HKVDC)   74
Tatsuta Maru   110, 112
Tatuta Maru (see *Tatsuta Maru*)
Taylor, Warrant Engineer Arthur W. (RN)   138, 158, 165, 170, 171, 177, 191, 207, 208
Taylor, Sergeant Henry (Royal Scots)   201, 231
Taylor, Mary (Civilian)   64
Taylor, Peggy (Civilian)   64
Techow Docks   142
Teia Maru   136
Telegraph Bay   13
Thomas, C.M.O. Osler (HKVDC)   15
Thomson, Lieutenant Basil (RNR)   30, 168
Thomson, Second Lieutenant John (Royal Scots)   26
Thompson, Captain Thomas (RAPC)   35
Thompson, Superintendent Walter (HKPF)   38, 70
Thorson, Hans (*see* Cedric Salter)
Thursby, Captain Eric N. (HKVDC)   121
Tien Ho   140

tiger 45
Tinian 168, 208
Tocher, Private James E. (HKVDC) 74
Tojo, Prime Minister Hideki 45
Tokunaga, Colonel Isao 42, 199
Tokyo 31, 56, 115, 128, 132, 165, 175, 192, 198, 204, 212, 217, 221-3, 225, 226, 232
Tokyo Sempaku 128
Toronto 244
Toya Steel 116
Toyama (Nagoya #8 Branch Camp) 197, 208, 210, 213, 216, 218, 222, 223, 237
Toyama (Nagoya #9 Branch Camp) 203, 223
Toyama Maru 142, 143, 155
Trapman, Second Lieutenant John A. (RA) 168
Tressider, Second Lieutenant Charles (RASC) 34
Trevor, Capt I.B. (HKVDC) 31, 32
Trick, Private Charles R. (Winnipeg Grenadiers) 8, 54, 193, 207
Trist, Major George (Winnipeg Grenadiers) 59
Tse Dickuan 49, 59
Tsumori 201
Tsuruga 212
Tsurumi (Tokyo #14 Branch Camp) 197, 239
Tsurumi Shipyard (Tokyo #3 Dispatched Camp) 109, 113, 115-7, 132, 148, 153, 158, 160, 169, 181, 187, 192-4
tuberculosis 143, 156, 174, 202, 203
Tugby, CSM Marcus C. (Winnipeg Grenadiers) 157
Tung Fong Hotel 23, 25
Tungshan Gaol 205
Tupper, Sergeant Sedley O. (RA) 42
Tweed Bay 214
Tweed Bay (Prison) Hospital 38, 51, 169, 191
Tyndall 126

Tyner, Staff Sergeant William T. (RAMC) 209

Umran, Driver Said (HKMC) 122
Union Building 69
US Marines 57, 72
USS *Admiral Hughes* 232, 234
USS *Benevolence* 217
USS *Chicago* 206
USS *Dickman* 235
USS *General R. L. Howze* 233, 235
USS *Goodhue* 229
USS *Gosselin* 224
USS *Grouper* 60
USS *Hyde* 232
USS *Indiana* 206,
USS *John Hancock* 220
USS *Joseph T. Dickman* 232
USS *Massachusetts* 206
USS *Mercy* 231, 232
USS *Monitor* 225
USS *Oconto* 226, 230
USS *Ozark* 224
USS *Rescue* 217, 224
USS *San Juan* 217
USS *South Dakota* 206
USS *Tryon* 225, 232
USS *Quincy* 206

Valentine, John (Civilian) 136
Valentine, Captain Robert K. (HKVDC) 74, 126
Valentine, Stuart (Civilian) 136
Vanbergen, G. 125
Vancouver 170, 233, 234
Victoria Barracks 11, 16, 18
Vimy Ridge 125, 159
Violet Hill 10

Wada, Lieutenant Hideo 110
Waichow 58, 117, 118, 140, 172, 173
Wakagawa (Sendai #10 Branch Camp) 201
Wakayama 196
Wakinohama 205

Walker, Sergeant Charles D. (HKVDC) 74
Walker, Captain Edward B. (Winnipeg Grenadiers) 110
Walker, Marine Engineer Guy (Merchant Service) 110
Waller, Private J.W. (Middlesex) 129
Wallis, Brigadier Cedric (Rajputs) 128
Wanchai 15
Wanstall, SPO David Y. (RN) 65
Washington Maru 61, 98
Watanabe 128
Watanabe, Reverend Kiyoshi 189, 199
Waterhouse, Rifleman William E. (Royal Rifles of Canada) 143
Waters, Lieutenant (Nursing Sister) Anna M. (RCAMC) 39, 136, 232
Way, Staff Sergeant Henry W. (RAOC) 111
Wedderburn, Lieutenant Jock (RA) 33
Weedon, Captain Martin P. (Middlesex) 117, 120, 127, 138, 165, 168, 171, 174, 195, 196, 211, 214, 221, 223, 224
Weill, Gunner Leo (HKVDC) 191
Weill, Maurice (Civilian) 192
West Point 203
Whillier, Lance Corporal Walter C. (Winnipeg Grenadiers) 59
White, Betty (Civilian) 156
White, Lieutenant Lynton (RA) 40
White, Peter (Civilian) 133, 156
White, Lieutenant Colonel Simon E. (Royal Scots) 211, 213
Whitehead, Bombardier John (RA) 17, 32, 35
Whiteley, Sister Joan (QAIMNS) 73, 214, 219, 221
Whitmore, Lance Corporal James W. (RAOC) 139
Willcocks, Lieutenant Wilfred J. (HKSRA) 69
Williams, Senior Sister Amy (Colonial Nursing Service) 10, 11

Williams, SSM Herbert J. (RAOC) 189, 190
Wilson, Sergeant John B. (HKSRA) 157
Wilson, Private Richard C. (Winnipeg Grenadiers) 41
Wilson, Stoker Robert G. (RN) 63, 64
Winnipeg Grenadiers 4, 5, 8, 10, 11, 25, 39, 41, 46, 47, 52, 55, 66, 107, 116, 130, 131, 157, 176, 202
Wiseman, Captain Eric P. (RASC) 46, 138, 175, 190, 203, 213, 226
Witchell, Nora (Civilian) 67
Wong, Yen Tou (SJA) 58
Wong, Private Yin Khoon (HKVDC) 58
Wong Nai Chung Gap 5, 7, 8, 10, 16, 17, 41
Wong Nei Chong Gap (*see* Wong Nai Chung Gap)
Woo, Dr Arthur 125
Wood, Sergeant Arthur F. (HKDDC) 132
Wood, Captain George 'Chippy' (HKVDC) 34
Woodward, Corporal John (RASC) 68
Woolley, Sergeant William J. (HKVDC) 158
Woosung 61, 99
Woosung POW Camp 35, 72
Wright, Frank (Civilian) 38
Wright, Private Robert J. (Middlesex) 62, 74, 201, 202, 205
Wright-Nooth, Assistant Superintendent George (HKPF) 23, 28, 41, 44, 158, 166, 174, 175

Yaholkovsky, Gunner George (HKVDC) 63
Yates, Stoker Petty Officer Thomas O. (RN) 177
Yeo, K.C. 125
Yokohama 47, 56, 60, 112, 115, 198, 200, 212, 220, 222–6, 229, 230
Yokohama Docks 56

Yokohama Firebrick (Tokyo #18 Dispatched Camp)   164, 166, 200, 201
Yokohama Stadium (Tokyo #3 Branch Camp)   56, 57, 102, 109, 148, 153, 158, 159, 164
Yokohama Stevedores (Tokyo #19 Dispatched Camp)   159, 164, 196, 201
Yoshihara Oil Refinery   117
Yoshima (Sendai #2 Branch Camp)   161–3, 181, 187, 194, 215, 222, 238

Young, Major Charles (Royal Rifles of Canada)   12, 29, 244
Young, Governor Sir Mark   3, 35, 129
Young, Lt. Commander Reginald S. (RN)   136, 143, 205
Yumoto (Sendai #1 Branch Camp)   192, 194

Zentsuji (Hiroshima #1 Branch Camp)   45, 127, 197
Zhoushan   60
Zindel, Rudolf (Red Cross)   126, 199

www.ingramcontent.com/pod-product-compliance
Ingram Content Group UK Ltd.
Pitfield, Milton Keynes, MK11 3LW, UK
UKHW021833210426
5322IPUK00012B/199/J